WordPress® Bible

WordPress® Bible

Aaron Brazell

WILEY

Wiley Publishing, Inc.

WordPress® Bible

Published by
Wiley Publishing, Inc.
10475 Crosspoint Boulevard
Indianapolis, IN 46256
www.wiley.com

To Devin, my only son, for giving me something to think about even when I don't realize I need to be thinking about it.

Credits

Senior Acquisitions Editor
Stephanie McComb

Executive Editor
Jody Lefevere

Project Editor
Katharine Dvorak

Technical Editor
Mark Jaquith

Copy Editor
Lauren Kennedy

Editorial Director
Robyn Siesky

Editorial Manager
Cricket Krengel

Business Manager
Amy Knies

Senior Marketing Manager
Sandy Smith

Vice President and Executive Group Publisher
Richard Swadley

Vice President and Executive Publisher
Barry Pruett

Project Coordinator
Lynsey Stanford

Graphics and Production Specialists
Andrea Hornberger
Melissa K. Jester
Ronald G. Terry

Quality Control Technicians
Rebecca Denoncour
John Greenough

Proofreading
Susan Hobbs

Indexing
BIM Indexing & Proofreading Services

Media Development Project Manager
Laura Moss

Media Development Assistant Project Manager
Jenny Swisher

Media Development Associate Producer
Shawn Patrick

About the Author

Aaron Brazell is the Lead Editor of Technosailor.com and the CEO of Emmense Technologies, LLC, a WordPress consultancy company located in the greater Washington, D.C. area. He has been an active member of the WordPress community since 2004 as a developer, user, and consultant. He advises small- and medium-sized businesses (and on occasion, an enterprise or non-profit organization) on innovative WordPress solutions and guides them in strategy and business decisions pertaining to their online endeavors.

He is a frequent public speaker, engaging with the WordPress community at WordCamps around the United States, as well as at marketing, social media, and other industry events. He is the lead organizer of WordCamp Mid-Atlantic, a WordPress community conference catering to the Greater Capital region, which includes Maryland, D.C., Delaware, and Northern Virginia. He believes in challenging conventional thinking and assumptions, and as a result, often takes actions that are provocative, strategic, and unconventional in an effort to move dialogue and popular opinion forward.

In addition to his work with WordPress and social media, Aaron is an avid photographer and sports fan (his favorite teams are the Boston Red Sox and Baltimore Ravens), and has one son, Devin Michael. He currently lives in Bethesda, Maryland.

About the Technical Editor

Mark Jaquith is a lead developer on the WordPress project and does full-time WordPress consulting and development through his company, Covered Web Services (`http://coveredweb services.com`). He specializes in custom plugins, performance, scaling, and security. Mark has been contributing to WordPress since 2004, and proudly dropped out of college in 2005 to do what he loves: enabling millions to easily publish their content on the Web. When he's not working on WordPress or Web publishing projects, he enjoys photography, philosophy, and films.

Contents

Contents

Contents

Contents

Contents

Contents

Contents

Contents

Contents

Foreword

When Aaron first mentioned he was writing the *WordPress Bible*, I immediately offered him a hand in editing. I figured it was a safe bet. After all, I'm a PHP guy with five years of Drupal experience and zero years of WordPress. In fact, my only involvement with WordPress was attending WordCamp Mid-Atlantic; I'd never even installed it before. I had to open my mouth....

Fast-forward a couple months and suddenly chapter after chapter fill my inbox. So I started digging into this alien environment from two different perspectives: first, from the community perspective and second, from a developer's perspective.

For open source projects, the community is important to understand. Not only do you need to know how to get involved, but also you also need to know how healthy it is. Is this project going to be active a month or year from now? Therefore, I started reading with the intent to learn about the WordPress community. I wanted to know its motivations, how it interacted, how decisions were made, and how information flows within, into, and out of the team. Delving into the community and help chapters, I learned quite a bit. I found myself dropping into IRC, exploring a mailing list or two, and hitting WordPress forums to see how new voices were welcomed. To be honest, I appreciated the perspective and guidance from someone who "gets it."

Secondly, one of the joys of open source is looking at things from a developer's perspective. Unfortunately, many open source projects are a pile of messy code with horrible documentation, and you'll find yourself huddled under a desk crying pitifully in under 15 minutes. With WordPress, I didn't have that experience. Sure, there were times when something didn't make sense at first pass, but I kept digging. I asked some harsh questions related to PHP 5 and object-oriented principles and coding standards and APIs and a variety of other things. Each response — even those which I disagreed with — was well-reasoned and internally consistent. More important, the documentation and explanations supporting the system were amazing and provided numerous great examples. In fact, the underlying concepts were useful enough that I've duplicated a few in one of my projects.

All that said, I enjoyed the book, I enjoyed exploring a new community and system, and I appreciated having Aaron as a guide.

And yes, I have installed WordPress now.

D. Keith Casey

CTO, Blue Parabola, LLC

http://blueparabola.com

Preface

WordPress, by most accounts, is the most popular self-hosted blogging platform in the world. WordPress.com is the second most popular hosted blogging platform in the world. The ecosystem built on openness and extensibility has helped the software thrive and overcome other rivals that, in some cases, have been around longer than WordPress has.

Developers now have the means to take a platform that was built for blogs and turn it into much more robust applications for content management, contact management, e-mail management, and more. I have yet to find something WordPress cannot be made to do with custom plugins and intuitive theming.

There are many books on WordPress available when you go to your local bookstore. Even if the books are not currently in stock, it's elementary to have them ordered or delivered directly to your home from Amazon.com. However, most of these books cover only a portion of WordPress or examine WordPress from a singular perspective. Until now, there has never been a book that covers the topic holistically and exhaustively and for all levels of expertise.

If you're a newbie just getting involved with WordPress, you should find value in these pages in the form of tutorials and tips. I cover the user interface and plugin management throughout this book and have endeavored to write in such a way that the least technical reader can still grab the concepts that are at work.

If you're a developer and have been hacking around with WordPress for years, you will also get value out of this book. With the extensive reference charts and appendixes, it will become the book that sits next to your computer and becomes a bit worn and dog-eared with torn pages from you picking it up over and over again.

Of course, designers have the opportunity to grasp the principles at work behind themes and templates, template hierarchy, and template tags. Design is much more than simply creating an elegant user interface in Adobe Photoshop and calling it a day. It's also using the tools that WordPress provides to create usable, smart themes that bring the power of WordPress to the reader.

WordPress Versioning

There is, of course, the question of versioning for this book. WordPress maintains a (rough) four-month release cycle for major releases. During the development of the next major release, there are typically security fixes that are released in the form of "dot releases." During the process of writing, I have been asked about what version of WordPress this book will cover.

Fortunately, 90 percent of WordPress stays the same. Part of the guiding principles of WordPress core development is maintaining backward compatibility unless it is absolutely mandatory that it be changed. To that end, it doesn't really matter for what version I wrote this book.

During the process of editing this book, WordPress 2.9 was released. That is the version this book is based upon. However, it is likely that WordPress 3.0 will be released around the time this book goes to print. Never fear. Though there will be new features in WordPress 3.0 that will not be covered in this book, the bulk of the software will remain intact and version neutral.

Getting the Most Out of This Book

The chapters in this book are organized into eight parts. Each part is a selection of chapters that all relate to each other in some way. You probably will not want, or need, to read the book from cover to cover, though I would be flattered if you did. Instead, you will find that different parts of the book address different levels and experiences with WordPress and you should feel free to flip back and forth to find the answers you need at different times.

For example, Part I, "Getting Started with WordPress," contains the initial introductory stuff that describes installing WordPress and basic steps to getting a WordPress blog off the ground, as well as background information to help you understand the philosophies that have guided the development of the software.

Part II, "Working with Plugins," gets more technical by examining plugins and describing the plugin application programming interfaces (APIs) in WordPress. This is the part that developers will likely use often to understand how to write new plugins for WordPress.

In Part III, "Working with Themes and Template Tags," I talk about the aspects of WordPress that have to do with themes and templates. If you have an Adobe Photoshop layout and need to hack it up into a WordPress theme, this is the series of chapters you'll want to get into. It is most suited for designers who need to understand how the WordPress theme system works.

Part IV, "Creating Content," is going to be the go-to series of chapters for the newbie who just wants to use WordPress to write or create content. This is not a super-technical part, and it doesn't assume that the reader is changing his theme. It does, however, describe the concepts and principles behind using the WordPress Admin and creating content.

No blogger wants to be caught with a hacked site because she did not keep up to date with upgrades and security fixes. To that end, Part V, "Keeping Up with the Joneses: Maintenance and Upgrades," is all about maintaining your WordPress blog, and provides suggestions, routines, and concepts behind the maintenance and upgrade routine. It also covers caching, an essential topic for anyone who owns a blog that receives, or will receive, a large amount of traffic.

In Part VI, "Alternate Uses for WordPress," I stretch the bounds of what WordPress can do. Hopefully by reading this part, you will be inspired to find alternate uses for WordPress and will see that WordPress is not just for blogging. I look forward to seeing how WordPress is used in new and creative ways.

In Part VII, "Looking at the WordPress Ecosystem," I bring everything full circle by talking about the surrounding community and ecosystem around WordPress. It seems that there is a new venture or product released around WordPress regularly. Many of these are associated with WordPress.com and Automattic, the owner of WordPress.com and patron of the WordPress project.

Part VIII, "Appendixes," includes all of the appendixes that are important corollary pieces to this book. In some cases, such as with Appendix A and Appendix B, they are reference guides that will be popular among developers who purchase this book. Other appendixes include articles that I have written for the *WordPress Bible* that describe an aspect or use of WordPress that is not necessarily relevant as "chapter material" but add to an understanding of the greater WordPress community. My favorite appendix? Appendix F, "WordPress in Government." Did you know that the United States intelligence community has more than 7,000 WordPress blogs across 14 different intelligence agencies? Exactly... who knew? And they aren't the only ones using WordPress in federal, state, and local governments around the world.

Using the Margin Icons

Throughout the book, you will find icons in the margin that address important things you should be aware of. Take note of these icons because they indicate important things that are relevant to the content you are reading.

Note
Notes highlight useful information that you should take into consideration. ■

Tip
Tips provide additional bits of advice that make particular features quicker or easier to use. ■

Caution
Caution warns you of potential problems before you make a mistake. ■

Cross-Reference
Watch for the Cross-Reference icon to learn where in another chapter you can go to find more information on a particular topic. ■

Web Resource
The Web Resource icon directs you to other material available online. ■

On the Web
This icon points you toward related files available on the book's Web site, `www.wiley.com/go/wordpressbible`. ■

Acknowledgments

Though I get the credit for this book, the load that is carried through the process is one that is shouldered by more than just me. In fact, if it wasn't for the incredible team of people behind it, it would only be vapor passing in the air. As a first-time author, I have come to lean and rely on these people, whether they were directly involved or pure mental and emotional support. These are my friends, colleagues, and the battle mates in getting this job done.

First of all, thank you, Stephanie McComb, my acquisitions editor, for reaching out to me. I was working in my local coffee shop, Murky Coffee (which has unfortunately since closed) in Arlington, Virginia, when her initial inquiry to write this book popped into my inbox in April of 2009. It was Stephanie indicating that she had heard of my work and extending that initial hand of opportunity for me to bring my knowledge to bear in this book. She has been a tremendous support through this process. Thank you for having the faith in me.

To Lynn Haller, my agent at StudioB, who took care of all the heavy lifting and even threw some blocks for me along the way. When I first started to consider this, I consulted with other authors. Some told me to get an agent and some said I should "go it alone." I'm glad you were there to take care of the business.

To Keith Casey, my friend, colleague, and fellow D.C. PHP rumbler. You had no idea about how WordPress worked as you come from a Drupal background. I asked you to be a safe valve for me since you didn't know WordPress but are an expert in PHP and could give an objective outside opinion. You agreed to bring your high level of expertise to bear to help me with sanity checks in this book before I submitted each chapter and caused me to think twice on more than one occasion.

To Mark Jaquith, the technical editor of this book, my friend, and WordPress colleague. Mark and I have worked together in one form or another since 2007. When Wiley asked me if I had recommendations for a technical editor, Mark was the only name that I wanted in that role. He is a rock star and could have written this book himself. There are only a few people on the face of the planet who know WordPress as well as Mark. I am not one of them.

To Erin Kotecki Vest, my best friend, who knows absolutely nothing about any of this stuff, but offered mental support all along the way. Often during the process of writing, I would hit a point of mental exhaustion at some point midday. It was at times like these that she was always available for a quick chat and encouraged me every step of the way. Thank you!

To the community on my blog, Twitter, Facebook, and all the other social networking outlets I participate in. You have been patient with me as I constantly talked about this book, the processes of writing, and the mental exhaustion I experienced at times. Your excitement has buoyed my efforts. Now go buy five of these books and give them to your families and friends as stocking stuffers during the holidays.

Part I

Getting Started with WordPress

Learning About WordPress

L ong before Johann Gutenberg invented the printing press and the first printed Holy Bible was mass-produced, humans were instinctually creating content. Civilizations scribed their experiences and histories on scrolls and in massive tomes by hand. In some cases, it was little more than pictures on the walls of caves.

Though these processes were tedious, they filled the human need to articulate thoughts and pass stories on to the next generation. The printing press has enabled humans to evolve scribing to another level. Content can be passed on in many forms, such as in personal or commercial literature, and is widely accessible.

Today, via the Internet, humanity has taken content production to yet another level with blogging platforms and content management systems. WordPress, a project of this evolution, has emerged as a preferred platform for content production and continues to evolve to meet our ever-changing content needs. It provides a vehicle to pass down stories, accounts, and histories to this, and future, generations.

WordPress is free and easy to install, so anyone can use it without much effort. It's also open source, so developers can take the code, re-use it, and improve upon it.

IN THIS CHAPTER

A brief history of WordPress

Leveraging the WordPress community

WordPress by the numbers

10 things you need to know about WordPress

Understanding open source and the General Public License

A Brief History of WordPress

Back in the old days of Web publishing (circa 1995–2000), if you wanted to have a Web site, you needed to have some degree of understanding of the code to put the site together. It was assumed that to have a Web site, you had to be a geek who could sit down, throw together some semblance of hypertext markup language (HTML), and then, if you were good enough, maybe have a Web site that attracted lots of people.

Of course, in those days, "lots of people" meant maybe 300 readers. The search engines were not designed to attract a lot of content. Unlike today, it was impossible to build a Web site that had millions of viewers, disseminated across the Internet. There was no such thing as RSS (Really Simple Syndication) feeds and every page was handcrafted for the content that existed on it.

The only *dynamic* content — that is, content controlled by a database and users and not prefabricated for a specialized Web site — that existed at that time was in the form of Bulletin Board Systems (BBS). Forums began evolving around Usenet, an early form of chat, and walled communities such as AOL.

In 1999, Evan Williams (known today as a persistent entrepreneur because of his involvement in major projects such as Blogger, Odeo, and Twitter) and Meg Hourihan launched a new service called Blogger. Blogger, which was eventually acquired by Google, became the great-grandfather of the modern day blog and set up an "arms race" between subsequent rivals SixApart (proprietor of the MovableType and TypePad platforms, to name a few) and a smattering of other smaller upstart competitors.

The rise to blogging had begun.

The creation of WordPress

In 2001, a new open source blogging platform, b2/cafelog, was released. Active development continued through 2003, when it was largely left abandoned. A young blogger, photographer, and freshman University of Houston student named Matt Mullenweg had been a user of b2/cafelog and decided in 2003, along with another active b2/cafelog user and developer, Mike Little, to take the b2/cafelog code and create a new project — a process called *forking* — and WordPress was born as WordPress 0.70.

A year later, in 2004, WordPress released its first game-changing release with version 1.2. This release brought about the fabled plugin architecture and application programming interface (API) that makes the WordPress platform so flexible. Figure 1.1 illustrates the evolution of WordPress from a simple administrative interface to its current version.

Cross-Reference
Plugins, plugin architecture, and the WordPress API are discussed in more detail in Part II. A full plugin hook reference is provided in Appendix A. ■

Rival platform, Movable Type, made a move in 2004 that ignited a massive exodus to WordPress. The creators of Movable Type took their wildly popular software and made it "pay per play," so to speak, charging all but the smallest blogs for access to the platform. Though they reversed this move in 2008, a large portion of the most influential bloggers at the time moved their sites to WordPress (and by move, I mean they moved the blog to the new platform and became very vocal advocates of "free," "open source," and WordPress).

FIGURE 1.1

The evolution of the WordPress administrative interface, from version 1.5 in 2004 to the current version (based on version 2.7 introduced in 2008)

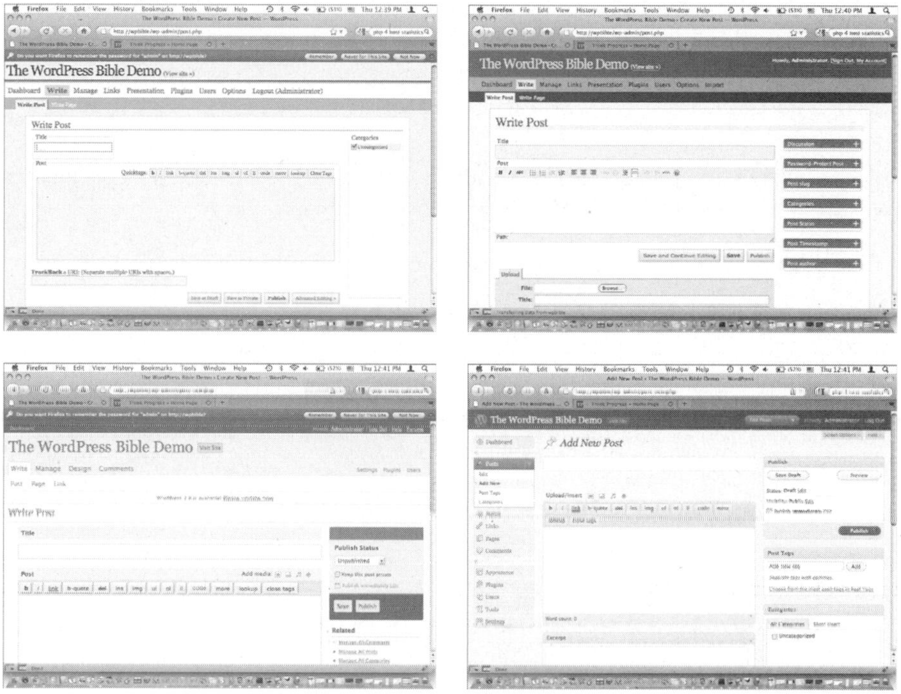

In 2005, the famed theme architecture and a page management feature debuted in WordPress 1.5. Pages and themes continue to be influencers that make WordPress versatile as a content management system, as well as a blog platform.

Note

WordPress releases take the name of jazz musicians due to the tradition started by founder Matt Mullenweg. As well as being a software developer, Mullenweg is an established jazz saxophone player. WordPress naming rights have been awarded to jazz legends such as Charles Mingus (v1.2), Billy Strayhorn (v1.5), Duke Ellington (v2.0), Michael Brecker (v2.5), John Coltrane (v2.7), and Chet Baker (v2.8). ■

Later that year, WordPress released version 2.0, which was included by Debian Linux, a popular distribution of Linux. As such, version 2.0 continued to be maintained alongside more current versions. Version 2.0 adopted a complete rewrite of major core components of the code and provided a new "visual text editor" that has continued to see massive improvements since its initial inception. Version 2.0 became the cornerstone for every release until version 2.7 was released in 2008.

The WordPress ecosystem emerges

Over the next three years, WordPress added more features to their offering, including widget support, taxonomies, and two new updates to the back-end administrative interface. In addition, WordPress MU, or WordPress Multi-User (a misnomer of sorts), came into play. WordPress MU enables bloggers to control multiple blogs from one installation. The most famous use of WordPress MU is WordPress.com.

Cross-Reference

At WordCamp San Francisco 2009, it was announced that WordPress and WordPress MU would merge their codebases. WordPress MU, and the ecosystem surrounding it, is discussed in Chapter 22. ∎

Beyond WordPress MU, other complementary software packages were produced to fill the holistic, and ever-growing, need for bloggers who were venturing into other aspects of Web 2.0. BuddyPress, a suite of WordPress MU plugins that adds social networking capabilities to a blog, became a wildly popular solution for WordPress-based social networks. bbPress provided a lightweight forum solution useful for building a community around a topic or site. The Akismet service was launched as a solution to fight the cancerous spam that existed around blogs. In addition, offline community events such as WordCamp (community-organized city and regional "unconferences" or loosely organized conference-like events) began to spring up, and WordPress user groups developed to support the extensive WordPress community.

The future of WordPress

For all intents and purposes, blogging and new media have become somewhat synonymous with WordPress and WordPress-based solutions. Active development continues as the roadmap for the platform expands to meet the need of a changing demographic of bloggers and developers. While blogs begin to evolve into social networks, WordPress and WordPress MU will merge, potentially bringing the power of BuddyPress to every WordPress blog on the planet. With the advent of new Web technologies, adoption of HTML 5-based themes may bring a whole new world of user interfaces to theme designers. As PHP developers build solutions for the greater Web, the choice of WordPress as a framework for development might continue to expand the reach of the platform beyond blogs. Regardless of what the future holds, WordPress continues to take the lead in providing solutions for publishing on the Web.

Leveraging the WordPress Community

Undoubtedly, the WordPress community consists of a wide variety of people of varying skill levels. In fact, it is this diversity that makes the WordPress community one of the strongest and most vibrant communities on the Web. With mailing lists, support forums, thousands of blog posts with "how tos" using WordPress, and dozens of WordCamp events organized around the world every year, it's clear that WordPress, unlike many other open source projects, has a self-sustaining community.

Though I talk more about the different venues of support that are part of the community later in this book, the mailing lists and forums tend to have the most WordPress activity.

Support

WordPress offers a number of different avenues of support for end users. Some are officially sanctioned and have the resources of the project behind them, while others serve as places where WordPress users gather "off the books."

Support forums

The official Web-based location for support in a snap is the WordPress support forums at `http://wordpress.org/support/`. The support forums are staffed by volunteers and provide a way for users to ask questions and receive answers. The forums also enable users to search for other incidents that may help them through a problem.

The WordPress Codex

The Codex, literally meaning "the ancient book of laws," is a wiki that any WordPress user can use to document and provide instruction on WordPress usage. It provides example usage of template tags, plugin compatibility guides, and other instructions on how to use the WordPress software.

Note

A wiki is a collaborative piece of software that allows easy editing and managing of Web sites. The most widely known wiki is Wikipedia (`www.wikipedia.org`). ∎

Caution

The WordPress Codex is community-driven and a continuous work-in-progress, so sometimes the organization of the Codex confuses users. ∎

IRC

Internet Relay Chat (IRC) is one of the oldest forms of chat rooms. It is also highly favored by many development shops and software development groups. WordPress has an IRC room (`irc:irc.freenode.net/#wordpress`) that you can tap into for real-time support, as shown in Figure 1.2.

Tip

IRC can be difficult to use and understand, but many resources are available on the Internet to help you with commands. In order to use IRC, you will need an IRC client such as mIRC for Windows or Colloquy for Mac. ∎

Development

There is a constant swirling of activity with WordPress development. As soon as one release is launched, work to develop a new release, as well as fix bugs and address any security issues, begins. For those of you who are eager to be part of the continual progress of the software, there are more than a few ways to be involved.

Hackers mailing list

The "hackers" mailing list, also known as wp-hackers, is a great place for conversation on the development of the software. Unlike the more widely understood definition of hacker, the members of the WordPress hackers mailing list are coders that tinker with WordPress code to make it better and often contribute back to the community with patches and code. Often ideas surface on this mailing list before they show up anywhere else.

FIGURE 1.2

Colloquy for Mac is an IRC client that you can use to get real-time support in the #wordpress IRC chat room. mIRC is a Windows IRC client.

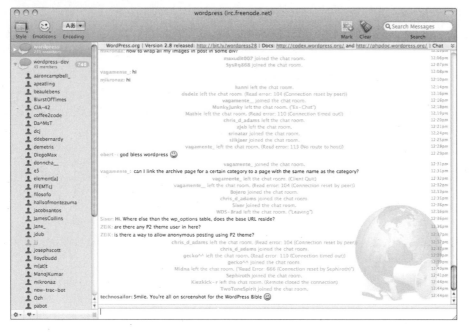

Testers mailing list

Similar to the hackers mailing list, the wp-testers list is where activity associated with development shifts leading up to a major release occurs. These individuals take WordPress and put it through extensive testing, including unit testing, to ensure it is ready for prime time.

Note

Unit testing is a type of testing that tries to isolate a function, class, or feature from the rest of the software and determine if it performs as it was designed and expected to do. Unit testing has been championed by several active WordPress users, but most vocally by Jacob Santos, a very active WordPress developer. ■

Trac

WordPress core developers and bug fixers rely on Trac, the WordPress bug-tracking system located at `http://core.trac.wordpress.org/` and shown in Figure 1.3, to keep track of bug reports and patches, consolidate decision-making conversations about features and bugs, and find out about changes made to the core software. Ultimately, any change to WordPress goes through Trac, making it an essential tool for anyone wanting to be involved in the development process.

FIGURE 1.3

Trac is where all bug reports, changes, or major decision-making discussion goes during the core development cycle.

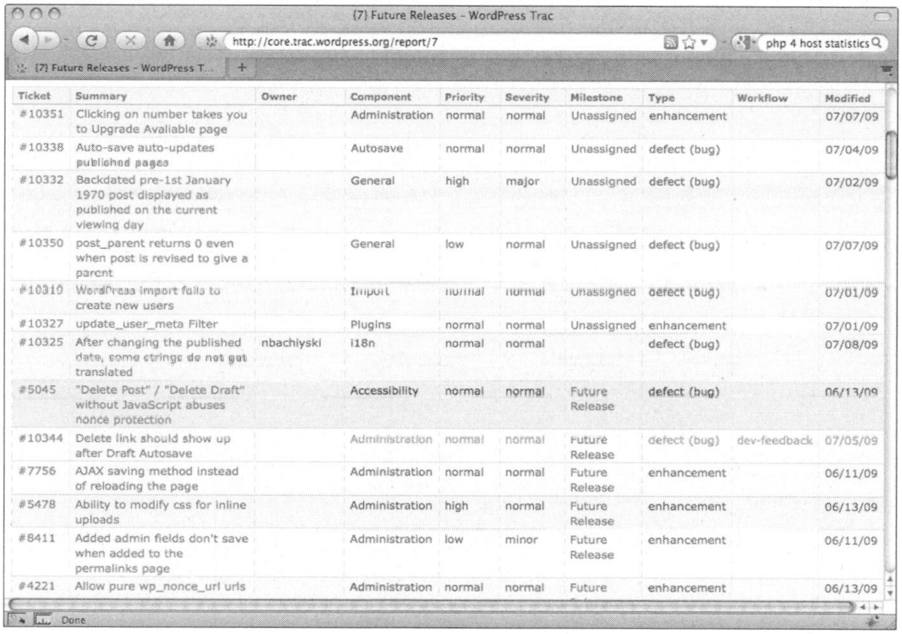

Ticket	Summary	Owner	Component	Priority	Severity	Milestone	Type	Workflow	Modified
#10351	Clicking on number takes you to Upgrade Avaliable page		Administration	normal	normal	Unassigned	enhancement		07/07/09
#10338	Auto-save auto-updates published pages		Autosave	normal	normal	Unassigned	defect (bug)		07/04/09
#10332	Backdated pre-1st January 1970 post displayed as published on the current viewing day		General	high	major	Unassigned	defect (bug)		07/02/09
#10350	post_parent returns 0 even when post is revised to give a parent		General	low	normal	Unassigned	defect (bug)		07/07/09
#10310	WordPress import fails to create new users		Import	normal	normal	Unassigned	defect (bug)		07/01/09
#10327	update_user_meta Filter		Plugins	normal	normal	Unassigned	enhancement		07/01/09
#10325	After changing the published date, some strings do not get translated	nbachiyski	i18n	normal	normal		defect (bug)		07/08/09
#5045	"Delete Post" / "Delete Draft" without JavaScript abuses nonce protection		Accessibility	normal	normal	Future Release	defect (bug)		06/13/09
#10344	Delete link should show up after Draft Autosave		Administration	normal	normal	Future Release	defect (bug)	dev-feedback	07/05/09
#7756	AJAX saving method instead of reloading the page		Administration	normal	normal	Future Release	enhancement		06/11/09
#5478	Ability to modify css for inline uploads		Administration	high	normal	Future Release	enhancement		06/13/09
#8411	Added admin fields don't save when added to the permalinks page		Administration	low	minor	Future Release	enhancement		06/11/09
#4221	Allow pure wp_nonce_url urls		Administration	normal	normal	Future	enhancement		06/13/09

WordPress by the Numbers

WordPress, as with any software, has competition. While it is superior in many ways, there is also a constant "war for the hearts and minds" of bloggers. At the end of the day, the philosophy behind the development of the software is to create a product that effectively disappears and enables bloggers to create the content. However, it would be remiss to not pay attention to the numbers behind this amazing software.

The top blogs, as listed by Technorati, one of the earliest and most well-known blog search and discovery sites, run a smattering of different platforms. Among these many blogs, almost one out of every three is WordPress-powered. WordPress.com powers more than 50 blogs for CNN and also runs blogs at Dow Jones, the *New York Times*, *People* magazine, Fox News, and the *Wall Street Journal*.

Even the United States federal government has gotten in on the game. With the newfound adoption of all forms of social media within the halls of the government, it's not surprising that many agencies have made WordPress their blog platform of choice. In 2008, the following agencies claimed to be using the software internally or externally:

- Central Intelligence Agency
- Defense Intelligence Agency
- Department of Education
- Department of Energy
- Department of Homeland Security
- Department of State
- Department of Treasury
- Drug Enforcement Administration
- Federal Bureau of Investigation
- National Geospatial-Intelligence Agency
- National Reconnaissance Office
- National Security Agency
- U.S. Air Force (shown in Figure 1.4)
- U.S. Army
- U.S. Coast Guard
- U.S. Marine Corps
- U.S. Navy

At WordCamp San Francisco 2009, Matt Mullenweg presented statistics on the ecosystem surrounding WordPress. The numbers, in some cases, are staggering and continue to grow:

- 3,500+ commits (changes) to the software since the last major release
- 11 million+ downloads
- 5.2 million+ downloads of WordPress 2.8
- 5.5 million+ WordPress.org self-hosted blogs
- 3.5 million+ WordPress.com blogs
- 60 million+ new WordPress.com posts
- 22 billion+ page views on WordPress.org and WordPress.com
- 850+ themes in the *WordPress Theme Directory*

- 5700+ plugins in the *WordPress Plugin Directory*
- 4.9 billion+ spam comments blocked by Akismet

In addition, 42 percent of all WordPress downloads are from non-English speaking countries.

FIGURE 1.4

The official blog of the U.S. Air Force (`http://airforcelive.dodlive.mil/`), powered by WordPress

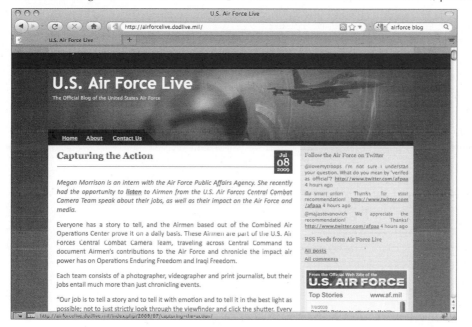

10 Things You Need to Know About WordPress

There are many benefits to using WordPress and I'll cover a significant amount in this book. Some will only be beneficial to plugin developers, while others exist purely as workflow enhancers for content producers.

Historically, on my own site, `http://technosailor.com`, I release a regular "10 Things You Need to Know About WordPress" article for every major new release. These articles serve as a snapshot of the new release and a quick reference of what is in it. While the following list is not release-specific, its purpose is the same — to provide a snapshot of what you should expect from WordPress, both from a user and a developer perspective.

Speed up the back-end with Google Gears

In WordPress 2.5, Google Gears was introduced. Gears is a product from Google that enables dynamic content to be cached locally (browser-side). Primarily, it was released to enable end users to use Google products like Gmail and Google Reader offline. However, WordPress is now able to use this add-on with supported browsers to speed up delivery of dynamic content in the WordPress administrative interface. Figure 1.5 demonstrates how to use Gears to speed up the WordPress experience.

Note

Google Gears is supported by Firefox and Internet Explorer browsers only. Firefox is available for all operating systems, while Internet Explorer is only available on Windows operating systems. ■

FIGURE 1.5

Speed up your WordPress administrative interface by using Google Gears to turbocharge the experience.

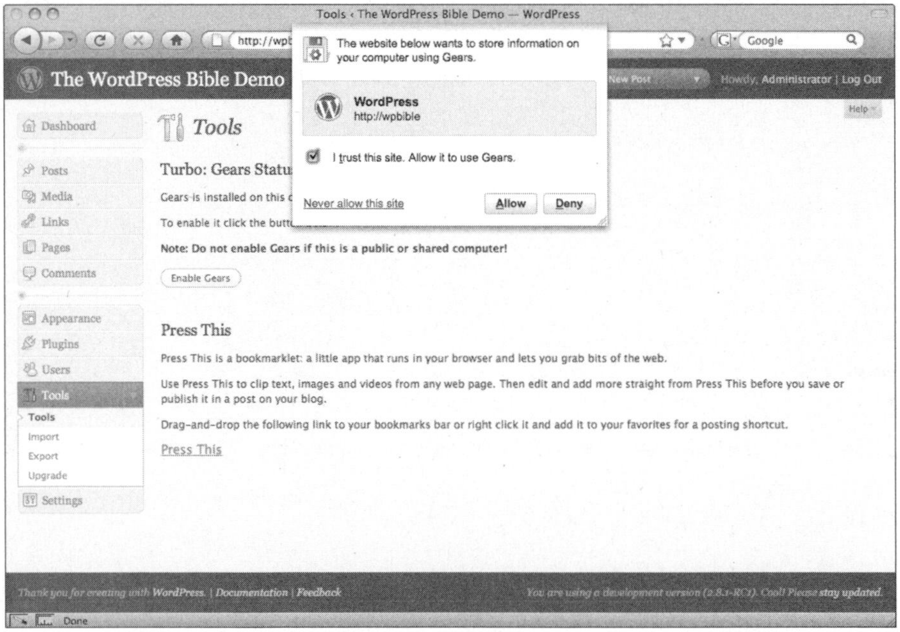

Generate content with an offline editor

Sometimes it's just easier, depending on your workflow and habits, to write blog posts in an environment that is more familiar to you. Notably, many people prefer to write blog posts offline and publish from those applications. By doing so, they are using one of two technologies: XML-RPC (XML Remote Procedure Call) or AtomPub (formerly known as APP, or Atom Publishing Protocol). Offline editors send content to WordPress using standardized protocols that WordPress supports.

Sometimes, particularly with older versions of WordPress, this feature becomes a security problem that hackers can exploit. Under the assumption that most people don't need to publish remotely, the option is not enabled. If you need to publish remotely, you can enable XML-RPC publishing in the Writing Options portion of the WordPress administrative interface, as shown in Figure 1.6.

Note

Many offline editors do not use the Atom Publishing Protocol at this time. The APP is a standardized format for data portability and has been adopted by major vendors such as Google. WordPress joined other publishing platform vendors in 2007 by incorporating APP in WordPress 2.3. ■

Cross-Ref

The XML-RPC and the Atom Publishing Protocol are discussed in more detail in Chapter 15. ■

FIGURE 1.6

In most cases, you only need to enable XML-RPC but sometimes you might need to enable the Atom Publishing Protocol as well.

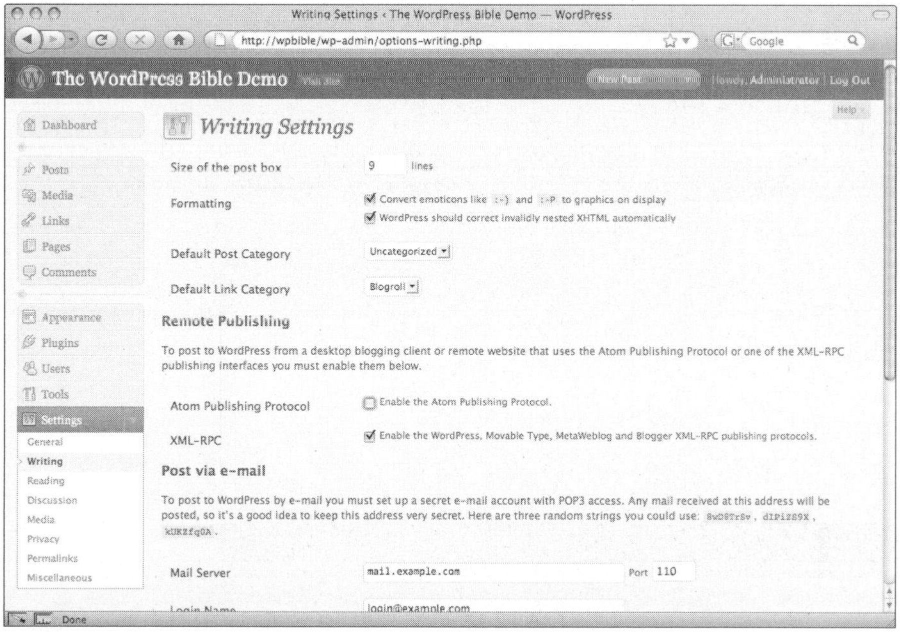

Benefit from built-in SEO features

Search engine optimization, or SEO, a multi-billion dollar industry in itself, is a primary concern for bloggers looking to create a presence beyond simple friends and family reach. For example, being listed in Google can make or break a company's chance of making money or going out of business online.

A key consideration in SEO is canonical URLs. *Canonical URLs* cause headaches for many administrators because Google, and other search engines, consider a domain starting with www as a different site than the same domain without www. Having a single site answer identically for both variants can easily be reflected the same way in the search engines. However, when search engines think there are two copies of the same page, they can penalize one as duplicate content, or at the very least, create a situation where two "versions" of your site are competing against each other in search engines. A canonical URL is the favored URL for accessing a certain Web page when multiple options exist.

Cross-Reference

SEO is an exhaustive topic of its own. The SEO ramifications and how WordPress helps in social media marketing is discussed in Chapter 3. ■

Fortunately, WordPress considers this and protects against duplicate content with canonical URL support. Based on what you set the blog address to in the site options, as illustrated in Figure 1.7, WordPress redirects content to the proper location.

FIGURE 1.7

WordPress provides canonical URL support based on how you set your site address, and helps you avoid duplicate content penalties from search engines.

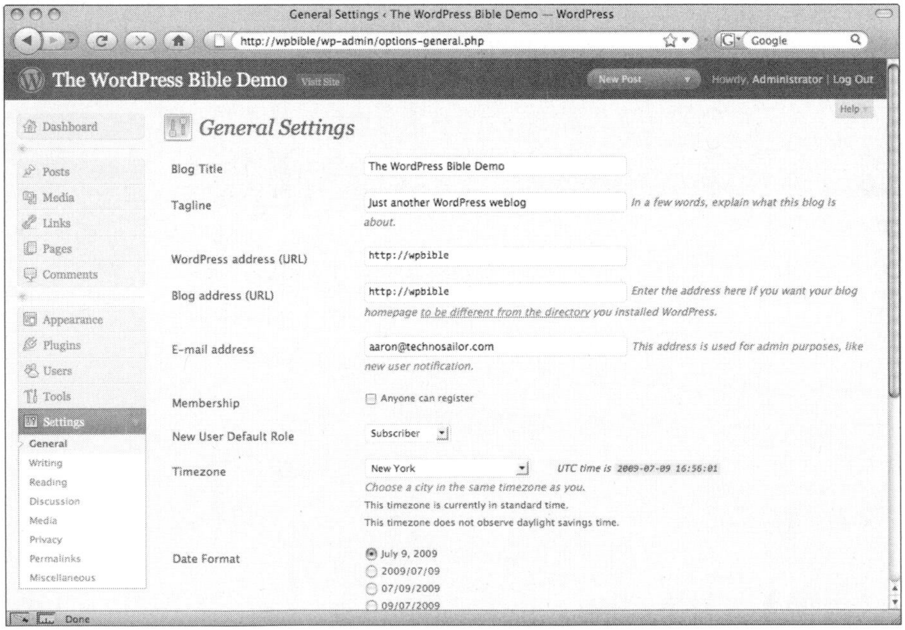

Widgetize your blog for a unique experience

It's too much work to have to manually hack code to reconfigure the way a blog sidebar appears. Fortunately, WordPress has an integrated *widget* system that enables you to reconfigure how portions of a blog (typically a sidebar, but potentially a footer or other portion of a theme layout) appear to readers. Simply drag and drop widgets into position on a blog, as shown in Figure 1.8, and instantly, you have a different look.

WordPress comes with a default set of widgets that include common features such as a Search form, recent comments from readers, recent posts, an RSS widget to parse out feeds from other places, and even a plain text box to deploy virtually anything else. Many plugins provide their own custom widgets, as well.

Cross-Reference
Widgets are discussed more in Chapter 6. ∎

Note
You can also use widgets on the WordPress Admin Dashboard. These widgets differ from sidebar widgets but are used much the same way. I talk about those in Chapter 5. ∎

FIGURE 1.8

Drag and drop available widgets to different locations in the sidebar boxes to render an entirely different look and feel to your blog.

Install themes, plugins, and core upgrades automatically

A few years ago, the only way to reliably add functionality and new themes, or upgrade WordPress was via file transfer protocol (FTP). Many users were frightened by FTP because they didn't understand how or why it should be used. They heard horror stories about files being accidentally overwritten or file permissions being changed.

In WordPress 2.6, functionality was added to upgrade plugins from within WordPress itself. In WordPress 2.7, that feature was extended to allow for one-click upgrades of the core WordPress software itself. Currently, you can add new plugins and themes and upgrade those as updates become available.

Cross-Reference
Auto-upgrades, security concerns, and system requirements are discussed in more detail in Chapters 16 and 18. ■

Turn your blog into a social network

When WordPress was initially created, it was all about blogging. There was very little you could do with it beyond that. When WordPress 1.5 was released, the introduction of Pages meant that you could now use WordPress not only for a blog, but also as a content management system. With the advent of Galleries in WordPress 2.5, you could take your site run on WordPress as a content management system and add photo galleries and features typically provided from a photo-sharing service such as Flickr.

Today, with the addition of BuddyPress to the WordPress universe, it is now possible to turn WordPress MU — which already has pages, galleries, and more — into a social network with private messaging, profiles, and journals.

Cross-Reference
BuddyPress was officially launched on April 30, 2009, as BuddyPress 1.0. BuddyPress solutions are discussed in more detail in Chapter 24. ■

Extend WordPress with plugins

WordPress was always built to be extremely extensible. This explains the almost 6,000 plugins being tracked in the WordPress plugin repository. Because of the open source nature of the software, developers love to build upon it and make it better.

The WordPress hook system is robust, and if there's one thing the WordPress core developers spared no expense on, it's hooks. WordPress 2.8 has more than 1,800 filter hooks and almost 900 action hooks. There's certainly some way to play around.

Cross-Reference
See Part II for more information about hooks and Appendix A for a full hook reference. ∎

Provide context with the WordPress taxonomy

With WordPress, metadata is everything. *Metadata* is best described as data that describes other data and it is essential for the growth of the organic Web. Discovery, exploration, and sharing are all principles that are important to end users. With it, users discover new content, explore blogs and social networks, and share that content with their friends and colleagues.

WordPress makes it easy to discover content with tags and categories. Bloggers can tag many things in WordPress (such as posts, images, and links), making them instantly discoverable. In addition to discoverability, this kind of metadata can also provide a helpful aid in providing structure to a blog. For example, many bloggers choose to use tags as metadata and utilize categories to provide site structure and navigation elements. Link tags and categories can provide a useful hierarchy for blogrolls — lists of blogs maintained by bloggers as blogs they read or recommend — or separate groups of links entirely.

Import your blog from any platform

With the popularity of WordPress, it is not uncommon for bloggers to want to switch to the platform. Often, new bloggers begin on another platform unaware of the benefits of WordPress. Other times, bloggers build entire communities around a site and feel locked into the platform, even though they want to use WordPress. Fortunately, WordPress bundles a large number of importers to assist in the migration of WordPress.

Importers exist for the following platforms:

- Blogger
- Blogware
- DotClear
- GreyMatter
- LiveJournal
- MovableType/TypePad
- RSS feeds
- Textpattern
- Other WordPress/WordPress.com blogs

Additionally, WordPress provides a number of import utilities for tags from a variety of WordPress tagging plugins, OPML/Blogroll importer and, if you're coming from an early version of WordPress (prior to WordPress 2.3), a category-to-tag importer.

Take advantage of multiple feeds

Most blogging platforms give you a single feed. You can't get comment feeds. Search feeds don't exist. Subscribing to a feed for only a single category is impossible. Fortunately for readers of WordPress blogs, feeds exist everywhere.

In addition to feeds being provided throughout the WordPress software, a variety of types of feeds are also available. Though the default is RSS 2.0, WordPress also supports Atom 1.0, RSS 0.92 and RDF feeds, making syndication possibilities endless.

Understanding Open Source and the General Public License

Open source is the cornerstone of WordPress and the WordPress community. Specifically, the General Public License (GPL) guides the principles surrounding WordPress development. The GPL has a couple variations. GPL version 2, which governs WordPress, provides an open source license that is generally considered more beneficial to developers, while GPL version 3 is seen by many to be more beneficial to end users.

The nice thing about the GPL is that it protects the freedom needed for open source software to grow and thrive. It protects the freedom to take, redistribute, reinvent, expand, or create derivative work and enables users to have the peace of mind that they can do anything they like with the software as long as they, too, protect those interests. Many people mistake that aspect of free with the monetary aspect of free and automatically assume that free software means no money has to exchange hands. On the contrary, GPL software can be sold but it cannot be sold with stipulations that the end user can't redistribute or reinvent it.

This concept of free enabled WordPress to be created in the first place, and it has allowed a few projects over the years to use the WordPress software to create commercial applications.

With the GPL's standard disclaimer that matters of legal weight should be referred to an attorney, it is important to understand the guiding principles behind WordPress. WordPress was created because the original blog software, b2/cafelog, was available as GPL'd software. If it had not been, it would be impossible to adopt the code base, improve it, and redistribute it.

Open source, and GPL specifically, does not necessarily mean *free*. Although WordPress is distributed for free, as are most GPL software products, the monetary definition of free is not applicable. GPL does require that the code used to build the software be included with the distribution of the software.

Cross-Reference

The entire GPL version 2 is included in Appendix H. ■

The common wisdom seems to be that any work that is a derivative of a GPL-protected work must also bear a license that is GPL compatible. A recent dustup within the WordPress community surrounded themes and licensing restrictions. Automattic, the proprietor of WordPress, asked for a legal interpretation of the GPL from lawyers at the Software Freedom Law Center, and received an opinion that interpreted that the GPL applies to any code, including the PHP portion of WordPress themes, that utilizes "derivative works of the WordPress Software":

> When WordPress is started, it executes various routines that prepare information for use by themes. In normal use, control is then transferred via PHP's include() function to HTML and PHP templates found in theme package files. The PHP code in those template files relies on the earlier-prepared information to fill the templates for serving to the client.
>
> In the WordPress themes, CSS [Cascading Style Sheet] files and images exist purely as data to be served by a Web server. WordPress itself ignores these files. The CSS and image files are simply read by the server as data and delivered verbatim to the user, avoiding the WordPress instance altogether. The CSS and images could easily be used with a range of HTML documents and read and displayed by a variety of software having no relation to WordPress. As such, these files are separate works from the WordPress code itself.
>
> The PHP elements, taken together, are clearly derivative of WordPress code. The template is loaded via the include() function. Its contents are combined with the WordPress code in memory to be processed by PHP along with (and completely indistinguishable from) the rest of WordPress. The PHP code consists largely of calls to WordPress functions and sparse, minimal logic to control which WordPress functions are accessed and how many times they will be called. They are derivative of WordPress because every part of them is determined by the content of the WordPress functions they call. As works of authorship, they are designed only to be combined with WordPress into a larger work.

However, there has never been a legal decision on GPL, so it continues to be a license that has not been tested in court. That said, it has been presumed to be a rock solid legal license for many years and will continue to be for many years to come.

The company culture of Automattic is that it will only support 100 percent GPL-compatible software. The core of all the software that is distributable (excluding service-oriented projects like PollDaddy) via WordPress.org is completely GPL. This includes WordPress, WordPress MU, bbPress, Intense Debate, BuddyPress, as well as the WordPress iPhone and BlackBerry applications.

Despite the quote from legal sources, Automattic has decided not to host anything on WordPress that is not 100 percent compatible. For theme authors, that means all CSS, image, and non-WordPress dependent inclusions must also be GPL.

How TiVo Changed Open Source

A few years ago, the first major non-judicial challenge came to the GPL (now called the GPLv2). TiVo, with its famous Digital Video Recorder (DVR) system, used an embedded version of Linux, an open source operating system licensed under GPL. For the sake of efficiency and cost reduction, this made the most sense.

The hardware used in TiVo boxes, however, was not open source and impeded the ability for users to compile and produce their own Linux software for use with the TiVo machines. The Free Software Foundation, proprietors of the GPL, found this utilization of GPL too restrictive on the users the GPL protected code was distributed to.

Advocates of the GPL suggested that developers should be able to distribute GPL code without giving away the keys to the kingdom, suggesting that distribution of GPL code that relied on non-GPL code, software, or hardware, was completely a legitimate use of the license.

The Free Software Foundation disagreed stating that in order for code to be protected under GPL, it must not rely or utilize derivative benefit from non GPL-compatible code. GPLv3 was born, with an emphasis on benefit to the end user.

Summary

- WordPress was created from a fork of b2/evolution in 2004.
- The WordPress ecosystem, including BuddyPress, WordPress MU, and bbPress, sprung up around WordPress.
- WordPress has had many iterations and improvements since it was launched in 2004.
- The WordPress support community includes mailing lists, forums, and online documentation.
- Developers of WordPress can tap into IRC, mailing lists, and the vast array of existing plugins to aid in their development.
- WordPress statistics are massive. Uptake by the U.S. government and major media puts the rubber stamp of approval on the WordPress project.

Installing and Configuring WordPress

WordPress is one of the simplest open source blog platforms to install. It has long bragged about its famous "five-minute install." In fact, installing WordPress can take much less than five minutes. The most time-consuming part is the creation of a database for WordPress to use. This process can be near instantaneous if you're a power user who can script the database creation, or a minute or two if a Web host control panel login is required.

Most Web servers are already set up out of the box to handle WordPress. If you have PHP 4.3 or better and MySQL 4.1.2 or better, then you are set to go. You can skip ahead to the part of this chapter that deals directly with handling the installation of WordPress.

If you are starting from scratch with your own server that doesn't have the required PHP scripting language and MySQL database build, or if you have to install the Apache or other Web server, then read on.

IN THIS CHAPTER

System requirements

Choosing a Web server

Installing WordPress

Tip
At this time, the most stable version of PHP is PHP 5.3.1. MySQL is stable at MySQL 5.1.36. ■

Note
PHP 4 reached its end of life on August 8, 2008, and is no longer supported by the PHP project. Quality hosts will not support it and though some still have it installed, I recommend avoiding hosts who do. ■

System Requirements

The developers of WordPress have gone to great lengths to make WordPress compatible with as many platforms as it can. To that end, it can run on Linux, Windows, and Mac OS X. The only requirement is the PHP scripting language and a Web server. The recommended system essentials are PHP 5, MySQL 5, and Apache 2 on a Unix-variant operating system such as the ones most hosting companies provide in their Linux packages.

Note
The minimum requirements for WordPress are PHP 4.3 and MySQL 4.1.2. However, PHP 5 will provide a richer experience as a developer. If your host does not support PHP 5, contact them and ask them to. ■

The foundational building blocks of WordPress are the PHP scripting language and the MySQL database. Though it is technically possible to run WordPress on a different database than MySQL, it is impossible to run WordPress without PHP.

With the assumption that the lowest common denominator and lowest barrier to technical entry translates into a larger, more broad-based market share, WordPress developers have strived to be compatible with the majority of hosts of the hosting market. To that end, the minimum requirements for WordPress 2.9 are PHP 4.3 and MySQL 4.1.2.

For optimal WordPress performance, edit your `php.ini` file (usually located at `/etc/php.ini` on Linux servers) and set (edit) the configurations to match those shown here:

```
memory_limit = 8M
upload_max_filesize = 8M
display_errors = Off
```

If you don't know where your `php.ini` configuration file is, you can create a small PHP configuration file on your site. Call it `phpinfo.php`, type **<?php phpinfo() ?>**, and save the file. Load it into your browser and you should see a descriptive configuration page describing your PHP setup, as shown in Figure 2.1. The location of the PHP configuration file is listed under Loaded Configuration File.

Perhaps the most important area for system optimization is the MySQL database, at large scale. Some of the most intensive activity in the WordPress system architecture occurs here. Out of the box, MySQL is unoptimized. It works well only when blogs are small. After that, it begins to bog down. For a blog with medium-sized traffic, consider adding (or editing if needed) the following directives:

```
key_buffer = 32M

max_allowed_packet = 16M

thread_stack = 128K

thread_cache_size = 8

tmp_table_size = 64M

max_heap_table_size = 64M

query_cache_limit = 1M

query_cache_size = 32M

log_slow_queries = /var/log/mysql/mysql-slow.log

long_query_time = 2
```

FIGURE 2.1

The PHP configuration file is useful for finding out where the php.ini file is located.

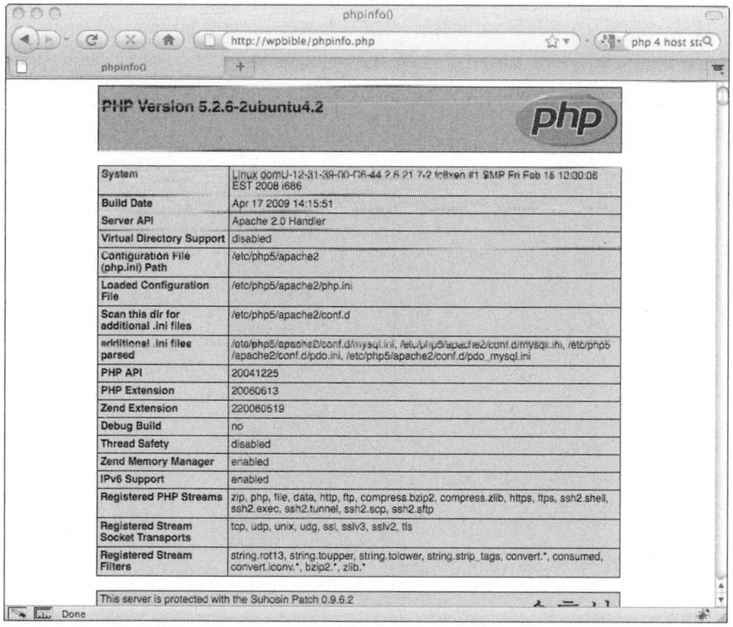

Note

This MySQL configuration is a suggestion for a blog with medium-sized traffic. You might need to modify your configuration based on hardware, traffic, or network bandwidth. ∎

Choosing a Web Server

In most cases, the choice of Web server is something that is pretty standard. Most Web hosts provide Linux hosting with Apache as the configured Web server. In most cases, the choice is automatic because it is the Web server that comes with virtually every distribution of Linux and is turned on, almost universally, by default.

With rare exception, these hosts are perfectly fine out of the box. Little additional configuration is needed to run a small blog. However, you should be a little cautious and ensure that the host has the minimum software requirements (PHP 4.3 and MySQL 4.1.2) and that they have the mod_ rewrite Apache module configured. Again, almost universally, it is.

Sometimes, however, circumstances such as scaling, business, or corporate requirements prevent the use of open source Web servers. For example, a corporation may have a strategic business alliance with Microsoft and be locked in to using Internet Information Services (IIS), the Microsoft Web server product. In these cases, the minimum requirement of PHP 4.3 and MySQL 4.1.2 still exists, but the means for configuring the Web server might be slightly different.

Caution

IIS causes problems with WordPress permalinks that require the Apache-only mod_rewrite module. Though there are some hackish solutions, these problems are an expected by-product of using this server platform. ■

Apache

Apache is an open source Web server that comes bundled with most Linux distributions. It is, by far, the most commonly used Web server on the Internet, and WordPress was designed perfectly for it. There is no minimum requirement for WordPress and Apache. The oldest still-used version of Apache is Apache 1.3 and it works functionally as well as Apache 2.2, which is the most stable.

Note

It is assumed, throughout this book, that you are using Apache on Linux as your Web server. Also, unless otherwise noted, it is assumed that you control your own server and are not on a shared host. Shared hosting users should consult with their hosting provider to implement any system-level changes suggested in this book. ■

Sean Walberg, a senior network engineer writing for IBM (www.ibm.com/developerworks/ linux/library/l-tune-lamp-2.html), suggests the following settings as an optimal configuration for Apache.

```
StartServers = 50

MinSpareServers = 15

MaxSpareServers = 30

MaxClients = 225

MaxRequestsPerChild = 4000
```

Lighttpd

Lighttpd (pronounced *lighty*) is a Web server that is popular among high-performance Web applications such as YouTube and Wikipedia. It was also used for some time by WordPress.com and Gravatar, another product owned by Automattic.

Lighttpd is an excellent, free, open source alternative to Apache and supports FastCGI, an open protocol that allows multiple persistent connections to the Web server. On high-capacity, or high-traffic, Web sites, the capability to remove the overhead that comes from starting and finishing a Web server process can buy tons of server CPU (central processing unit) cycles, energy, and load. Lighttpd runs on both Linux variants (including Mac OS X) as well as Windows.

However, this fast and efficient Web server does not come without limitations. Lighttpd poses some challenges when it comes to permalinks and the traditionally used mod_rewrite module for Apache. One suggested solution is to edit the Lighttpd configuration file (usually found on a Linux box in /etc/lightppd/lightppd.conf) by adding the code shown in Listing 2.1.

LISTING 2.1

Suggested configuration for Lighttpd to handle WordPress permalinks

```
server.modules += ("mod_rewrite")
$HTTP["host"] =~ "(www.)?example.com" (
url.rewrite-once = (
        "^/(.*)\.(.+)$"            => "$0",
        "^/(.+)/?$"               => "/index.php/$1",
)
)
```

The code in Listing 2.1 says in plain English that Lighttpd will enable its own mod_rewrite module, and if a request comes to the Web server for the domain example.com, it will try to fulfill rewrite rules in a way that WordPress expects it to.

Litespeed

Litespeed is a commercially available Web server that has both free and paid versions. In most cases, the free version should suffice for WordPress; however, the paid version provides a variety of other features, such as an enhanced number of unlimited connections (the free version allows up to 150).

It is a drop-in replacement for Apache and does virtually everything Apache does, including using .htaccess and mod_rewrite rules. It is currently used at WordPress.com.

Nginx

A small and highly undocumented Web server, Nginx is a hyper-fast Web server that is lightweight, supports virtual hosts, and contains a rewrite module. WordPress.com uses it in front of their Litespeed servers. To use Nginx to serve PHP-generated pages directly, you must have a FastCGI handler installed. Plenty of FastCGI libraries are available, and PHP provides one if it is compiled with that support.

A sample configuration for a WordPress site might look like the code shown in Listing 2.2.

LISTING 2.2

A sample virtual host configuration

```
server {
    listen      12.34.56.78:80;  # your server's public IP address
    server_name  example.com;        # your domain name
    location / {
        root    /home/example.com;  # absolute path to your WordPress install
        index  index.php index.html index.htm;
        # this serves static files that exist without running other rewrite
tests
        if (-f $request_filename) {
            expires 30d;
            break;
        }
        # this sends all non-existing file or directory requests to index.php
        if (!-e $request_filename) {
            rewrite ^(.+)$ /index.php?q=$1 last;
        }
    }
    location ~ \.php$ {
        fastcgi_pass    localhost:53217;  # port where FastCGI processes were
spawned
        fastcgi_index  index.php;
        fastcgi_param  SCRIPT_FILENAME    /home/example.com$fastcgi_script_
name;  # same path as above
        fastcgi_param  QUERY_STRING        $query_string;
        fastcgi_param  REQUEST_METHOD      $request_method;
        fastcgi_param  CONTENT_TYPE        $content_type;
        fastcgi_param  CONTENT_LENGTH      $content_length;
        fastcgi_param  SCRIPT_NAME        $fastcgi_script_name;
        fastcgi_param  REQUEST_URI        $request_uri;
        fastcgi_param  DOCUMENT_URI        $document_uri;
        fastcgi_param  DOCUMENT_ROOT      $document_root;
        fastcgi_param  SERVER_PROTOCOL    $server_protocol;
        fastcgi_param  GATEWAY_INTERFACE  CGI/1.1;
```

```
    fastcgi_param   SERVER_SOFTWARE     nginx/$nginx_version;
    fastcgi_param   REMOTE_ADDR         $remote_addr;
    fastcgi_param   REMOTE_PORT         $remote_port;
    fastcgi_param   SERVER_ADDR         $server_addr;
    fastcgi_param   SERVER_PORT         $server_port;
    fastcgi_param   SERVER_NAME         $server_name;
    # required if PHP was built with --enable-force-cgi-redirect
    fastcgi_param   REDIRECT_STATUS     200;
  }
}
```

Internet Information Services

Because PHP can be loaded into the Microsoft server product, Internet Information Services (IIS), WordPress can be run on it. IIS is not the optimal solution, but it works in scenarios where other server products are not available or permitted. IIS is bundled with Microsoft Server products as part of Active Directory.

The trickiest issues with WordPress on IIS are permalinks. There is no mod_rewrite module available for IIS, though there are a couple of options, including commercial modules. One built-in option requires a modification to your php.ini file and enables you to use user-friendly permalinks at the expense of requiring index.php in the permalink. To make this change, open php.ini in Notepad and add (or edit if it exists or is commented with a preceding semicolon) the following settings:

```
;cgi.fix_pathinfo = 0
cgi.fix_pathinfo = 1
```

Tip

Making the PATH_INFO fix shown here is helpful for allowing friendly permalinks. Unlike Apache solutions, which might show a friendly permalink as http://example.com/hello-world instead of http://example.com/?p=31, the IIS PATH_INFO fix only allows permalinks with index.php, such as http://example.com/index.php/hello-world. To implement Apache-like mod_rewrite effects, third-party modules like the ISAPI_Rewrite module are required. You can purchase ISAPI_Rewrite at www.helicon tech.com/order/#isapi_rewrite. ∎

Note

IIS 7.0, which ships with Windows 7 and can be installed on earlier versions of Microsoft Windows Server, supports a new URL Rewrite module, aptly named URLRewrite. WordPress supports rewriting with this module if available. For more information on URLRewrite, see http://blogs.iis.net/thomad/archive/2008/05/30/now-available-url-rewriter-tech-preview-1.aspx. ∎

Optional modules

You should consider a few optional modules when getting your Web server and PHP build ready for WordPress use. These will provide you and your readers with the best possible experience with WordPress and will ensure that you have an efficient blogging platform.

Apache mod_rewrite

In most standard Linux, Apache, MySQL, and PHP (LAMP) installs, Apache comes prebuilt with mod_rewrite. However, if you're unsure, you can verify it using the httpd command from the Linux command line (depending on the distribution of Linux, you might have to use apachectl or httpd instead). Type **apache2ctl −M** and press Enter to produce a listing of all shared and static modules that Apache is using. If you see rewrite_module in the list, as shown in Listing 2.3, then mod_rewrite is enabled.

LISTING 2.3

Verification that the rewrite_module is being used by Apache 2 on Ubuntu Linux 9

```
[root@wpbible ~]# apache2ctl -M
Loaded Modules:
 core_module (static)
 mpm_prefork_module (static)
 http_module (static)
 so_module (static)
 env_module (shared)
 ext_filter_module (shared)
 mime_magic_module (shared)
 expires_module (shared)
 deflate_module (shared)
 headers_module (shared)
 usertrack_module (shared)
 setenvif_module (shared)
 userdir_module (shared)
 alias_module (shared)
 rewrite_module (shared)
 php5_module (shared)
 proxy_ajp_module (shared)
 python_module (shared)
 Syntax OK
```

If your Apache release happens to not have mod_rewrite installed, you can add it by recompiling Apache with the −enable-mod-rewrite flag or by using your package manager, such as apt-get, to add the Apache development tools. For apt-get, type **apt-get install apache2-threaded-dev**.

Tip

Yum is a package manager provided by Red Hat Enterprise Linux, Fedora Core Linux, and CentOS Linux. apt-get is used by Debian-flavored Linux distributions, including Ubuntu. The instructions vary per Linux distribution and depend on which package manager is being used to control software installed on the box. Alternatives include the yum install, apache2-devel, or the apt-get install, apache-threaded-dev. Consult the documentation for your Linux distribution if you're unsure. ∎

On Ubuntu, the demonstration platform here, the previous command makes `mod_rewrite` available to Apache but it won't enable it. To do that, you need to make sure Apache knows how to load it. Follow these steps to create a symbolic link (better understood as a *shortcut* to Windows users) and restart the Web server:

1. **From the Linux command line, type** `ln -s /etc/apache2/mods-available/rewrite.load /etc/apache2/mods-enabled/rewrite.load`. If you're using Apache 1.3, simply replace `apache2` with `apache`.

2. **Type** `/etc/init.d/apache2 restart` **to make the changes take effect.**

3. **Type** `apache2ctl M` **to verify that rewrite_module is in the list of available Apache modules.**

The nice thing is that it is highly unlikely you will need to do this. On other variants of Linux, it is much easier to enable `mod_rewrite`. Ubuntu and Debian modularize the Apache configuration file (sometimes called `apache2.conf`, but typically called `httpd.conf`) and break the portions of the configuration into separate files. Usually, it's one big file that can be edited. The key bit that Apache needs is a line that says `LoadModule rewrite_module /usr/lib/apache2/modules/mod_rewrite.so` where `/usr/lib/apache2/modules/mod_rewrite.so` is actually the path to the compiled `mod_rewrite.so` file.

Tip

For any work on the command line that requires editing, I use Vim. You can use a text editor such as pico or nano and they may prove to be simpler. It's a personal choice. Vim is generally considered the most powerful of the Linux command line text editors but does come with a slight learning curve. The most basic (and common) commands are i (from "Command Mode") to enter "Insert Mode," which is the mode required to type. Esc returns the editor to "Command Mode." To save the changes made in a file, simply type :w from "Command Mode." You can type :q to quit Vim or can combine the save and quit routines by typing :wq. ∎

eAccelerator for PHP

eAccelerator is a PHP opcode cache software. Opcode cache software stores PHP scripts in their compiled state. When a request comes into Apache and it hands control of execution to PHP, the PHP processor compiles scripts into a faster binary form for execution. This is handled on the fly, but the overhead of compiling code on the fly and on every page load can cause significant load on the server. To offload this extra overhead, eAccelerator caches the WordPress PHP as compiled PHP and stores it for future use, eliminating the need for repeated compilations and reducing the load on the server.

To install eAccelerator, you must use the `phpize` command that is provided with the development version of PHP. As with `mod_rewrite`, you can install this package via apt-get by typing **apt-get install php5-dev**, as demonstrated in Listing 2.4. In order to use eAccelerator, PHP must be used as an Apache module (`mod_php`) or as a FastCGI module.

Web Resource

To find out more about configuring eAccelerator and to download the package, visit `http://eaccelerator.net.` ■

LISTING 2.4

Installing apt-get from the command line

```
[root@wpbible ~]# apt-get install php5-dev
Reading package lists... Done
Building dependency tree
Reading state information... Done
The following packages were automatically installed and are no longer required:
  libapparmor1 libapparmor-perl libterm-readkey-perl librpc-xml-perl
    libscrollkeeper0
Use 'apt-get autoremove' to remove them.
The following extra packages will be installed:
  autoconf automake automake1.4 autotools-dev libltdl7-dev libtool m4 shtool
Suggested packages:
  autoconf2.13 autobook autoconf-archive gnu-standards autoconf-doc libtool-
    doc automaken gfortran fortran95-compiler gcj
The following NEW packages will be installed:
  autoconf automake automake1.4 autotools-dev libltdl7-dev libtool m4 php5-
    dev shtool
0 upgraded, 9 newly installed, 0 to remove and 23 not upgraded.
Need to get 2700kB of archives.
After this operation, 10.8MB of additional disk space will be used.
Do you want to continue [Y/n]? y
Get:1 http://ec2-us-east-mirror.rightscale.com intrepid/main m4 1.4.11-1
    [218kB]
Get:2 http://ec2-us-east-mirror.rightscale.com intrepid/main autoconf
    2.61-7ubuntu1 [449kB]
Get:3 http://ec2-us-east-mirror.rightscale.com intrepid/main autotools-dev
    20080123.1 [62.6kB]
Get:4 http://ec2-us-east-mirror.rightscale.com intrepid/main automake
    1:1.10.1-3 [519kB]
Get:5 http://ec2-us-east-mirror.rightscale.com intrepid/main automake1.4
    1:1.4-p6-13 [233kB]
Get:6 http://ec2-us-east-mirror.rightscale.com intrepid/main libltdl7-dev
    2.2.4-0ubuntu4 [189kB]
```

```
Get:7 http://ec2-us-east-mirror.rightscale.com intrepid/main libtool
    2.2.4-0ubuntu4 [509kB]
Get:8 http://ec2-us-east-mirror.rightscale.com intrepid/main shtool 2.0.7-3
    [159kB]
Get:9 http://ec2-us-east-mirror.rightscale.com intrepid-updates/main php5-
    dev 5.2.6-2ubuntu4.2 [362kB]
Fetched 2700kB in 0s (5992kB/s)
Selecting previously deselected package m4.
(Reading database ... 122002 files and directories currently installed.)
Unpacking m4 (from .../archives/m4_1.4.11-1_i386.deb) ...
Selecting previously deselected package autoconf.
Unpacking autoconf (from .../autoconf_2.61-7ubuntu1_all.deb) ...
Selecting previously deselected package autotools-dev.
Unpacking autotools-dev (from .../autotools-dev_20080123.1_all.deb) ...
Selecting previously deselected package automake.
Unpacking automake (from .../automake_1%3a1.10.1-3_all.deb) ...
Selecting previously deselected package automake1.4.
Unpacking automake1.4 (from .../automake1.4_1%3a1.4-p6-13_all.deb) ...
Selecting previously deselected package libltdl7-dev.
Unpacking libltdl7-dev (from .../libltdl7-dev_2.2.4-0ubuntu4_i386.deb) ...
Selecting previously deselected package libtool.
Unpacking libtool (from .../libtool_2.2.4-0ubuntu4_i386.deb) ...
Selecting previously deselected package shtool.
Unpacking shtool (from .../shtool_2.0.7-3_all.deb) ...
Selecting previously deselected package php5-dev.
Unpacking php5-dev (from .../php5-dev_5.2.6-2ubuntu4.2_i386.deb) ...
Processing triggers for man-db ...
Processing triggers for doc base ...
Processing 2 added doc-base file(s)...
Registering documents with scrollkeeper...
Setting up m4 (1.4.11-1) ...
Setting up autoconf (2.61-7ubuntu1) ...
Setting up autotools-dev (20080123.1) ...
Setting up automake (1:1.10.1-3) ...
Setting up automake1.4 (1:1.4-p6-13) ...
Setting up libltdl7-dev (2.2.4-0ubuntu4) ...
Setting up libtool (2.2.4-0ubuntu4) ...
Setting up shtool (2.0.7-3) ...
Setting up php5-dev (5.2.6-2ubuntu4.2) ...
```

APC for PHP

APC, which stands for Alternative PHP Cache, is an alternative opcode cache to eAccelerator that doesn't have to be compiled to work. In fact, it's a PECL module. PECL, which stands for PHP Extension Community Library, is a sub-project of the PHP community, hosted at http://pecl. php.net, that provides a variety of community-supplied libraries for PHP. Generally, installing a PECL module is as simple as typing **pecl install apc.**

Tip

It's less likely you have PECL installed on your server than it is you would have mod_rewrite. **To install PECL on Ubuntu, type apt-get install php-pear. The PEAR (PHP Extension and Application Repository) library from PHP has the required software needed to use PECL.** ■

Once you have installed APC, you have to add one line to your PHP configuration file. On many systems, this file is located in /etc/php.ini. On Ubuntu, you can find it in /etc/php5/ apache2/php.ini. Open the file with Vim and add **extension=apc.so** to the end. Save and exit and restart Apache to make sure it gets loaded.

Caution

APC should not be used in conjunction with eAccelerator. Both modules are PHP opcode caches and will conflict with each other. ■

SSH2 module for PHP

As I discuss later in the book, security is not only a big deal for the developers of WordPress, but also it should be a big deal for the average user as well. Whenever possible, connect to your blog using Secure File Transfer Protocol (SFTP), which is part of Secure Shell (SSH), a network protocol that allows the exchange of data on a secure channel. SSH connections like SFTP encrypt the network connection between two computers. FTP, which is much more common, transmits data in plaintext and can be "sniffed" by people with network security software. It is possible for your password, or other private information being passed over the FTP connection, to be captured.

With the advent of WordPress' autoupgrade, plugin, and theme installations, I recommend installing the SSH2 PECL module for PHP. When WordPress connects to itself, it still has to do so using either FTP (the default) or SSH2/SFTP. The SSH2 module is considered beta, but works pretty reliably and can protect you from having private information captured while upgrading your site.

In order to install this module, the libssh2 module must be compiled and installed, as shown in the following steps:

1. **Type** wget http://downloads.sourceforge.net/sourceforge/libssh2/ libssh2-1.1.tar.gz?use_mirror=superb-west **to download the latest version of libssh2.** If this doesn't work, find the direct link from http://kevin. vanzonneveld.net/techblog/tag/libssh2/ and use it instead.

2. **Type** tar zxvf libssh2-1.1.tar.gz **to decompress the downloaded archive.** Replace the filename with the version you downloaded if there is a more recent library.

3. **Type** cd libssh2-1.1 **to change directories into the new folder.**

4. **Type** ./configure **to prepare the code for compiling.**

5. **Type** make **to begin compiling the library into a binary to install.** This may take a minute.

6. **Type** make install **to install libssh2 into the system.** After a moment, you should see a status line that says something similar to: `install ok: channel://pear.php.net/ ssh2-0.11.0`.

7. **Install the ssh2_sftp PECL module by typing** pecl install –f ssh2. The –f flag tells PECL to install the module even if there is no package in the "stable" tree. There isn't. (The module is still considered beta.)

8. **Ensure PHP knows about the new module by editing your php.ini file and adding** extension=ssh2.so **at the end.**

9. **Restart Apache by typing** /etc/init.d/apache2 restart.

Tip

You can check to see if the SSH2 module exists in PHP by performing a conditional `if( function_ exists('ssh2_connect') )` **check.** ■

FTP for PHP

If you are not able to install the SSH2 module for PHP, you should consider confirming the FTP module is installed. It is included by default with PHP 5 and with many of the prebuilt packages, including the packages from Ubuntu. If you are compiling PHP by hand, ensure that you include the –enable-ftp flag.

Installing WordPress

Now that you have all the elements in place to run WordPress efficiently — PHP 4.3 or better, MySQL 4.1.2 or better, Apache or another configured Web server, and perhaps some optional caching or communications modules — it's time to install WordPress itself.

The file size for a copy of WordPress is intentionally small. The total size of the ZIP file for WordPress 2.8 is 2.2MB. You can download the file at `http://wordpress.org/latest. zip`. Then unzip the file to find the `wordpress/` directory.

Configuring the database

When you installed MySQL earlier, you didn't create any databases. Most servers have some sort of Graphical User Interface (GUI) for doing this. Most of these GUIs use a Web-based software called phpMyAdmin for managing databases.

Tip

phpMyAdmin is useful for managing MySQL from a Web interface. You can download and find instructions for installing phpMyAdmin at `http://phpmyadmin.net` if your server provider hasn't already provided a means of interacting with MySQL from the Web. Be careful to ensure you have protected it, however. You don't want someone waltzing into your database and deleting your blog. ■

If you don't want to use phpMyAdmin, you can create a database from the command line as shown in Listing 2.5. The first command creates a new database called wordpress. The second command creates a new user called wpuser and sets the password to wppassword. It assigns the new wpuser to the wordpress database (and all tables in the wordpress database) and it gives it full access to that database, as long as the user is trying to access the server only from the same server (localhost). In some rare cases, your hostname will be different than localhost, but generally, for a single WordPress install on a single server, localhost will do.

LISTING 2.5

Creating a MySQL database, username, and password for WordPress

```
[root@wpbible ~]# mysql -uroot -p
Enter password: <enter root password>
Welcome to the MySQL monitor.  Commands end with ; or \g.
Your MySQL connection id is 1
Server version: 5.0.67-0ubuntu6 (Ubuntu)
Type 'help;' or '\h' for help. Type '\c' to clear the buffer.
mysql> CREATE DATABASE wordpress;
Query OK, 1 row affected (0.00 sec)
mysql> GRANT ALL PRIVILEGES ON wordpress.* TO wpuser@localhost IDENTIFIED BY
    'wppassword';
Query OK, 0 rows affected (0.00 sec)
<enter Ctrl-D to exit MySQL>
mysql> Bye
```

Now that you have created a new database to use, you have to tell WordPress about it. In the newly unzipped wordpress/ folder, you'll find a file called wp-config-sample.php. Copy this file and rename it to wp-config.php.

Tip

While any text editor should do the job in editing PHP files, I highly suggest (and recommend) that Mac users invest in Textmate from Macromates. You can download Textmate as a 30-day free trial at http://macromates.com. ■

Open the wp-config.php file in a text editor (Windows users can use Notepad; Mac users can use TextEdit) and make the following changes:

Note

Do not use a word processing application like Microsoft Word because the wp-config.php file is highly commented. ■

1. Replace `define('DB_NAME', 'putyourdbnamehere');` with `define('DB_NAME', 'wordpress');`.

2. Replace `define('DB_USER', 'usernamehere');` with `define('DB_USER', 'wpuser');`.

3. Replace `define('DB_PASSWORD', 'yourpasswordhere');` with `define('DB_PASSWORD', 'wppassword');`.

4. If your database host name is anything other than localhost, `define('DB_HOST', 'localhost');` with `define('DB_HOST', 'newdbhostname');` where newdbhostname is the name or IP address of the database server. This is optional and likely not required.

There are some additional optional settings in here as well. Notably, it is a good idea to change the table_prefix setting. It can be anything you want and defaults to wp_. Additionally, four other settings are defined — AUTH_KEY, SECURE_AUTH_KEY, LOGGED_IN_KEY, and NONCE_KEY — that should all be changed to unique strings or phrases. They can be anything you want, and you'll never have to see them again. They simply help WordPress operate securely. You can auto-generate random settings for these four secure keys by visiting https://api.wordpress.org/secret-key/1.1/ and copying and pasting the result on top of the exiting default settings. An example of randomly generated keys can be seen in Listing 2.6.

LISTING 2.6

An example of randomly generated secure keys from http://api.wordpress.org/secret-key/1.1/

```
define('AUTH_KEY',        '/~*:GN6QJE1,N^HayyNc@47?ug[)M|s)# 5(i{%W/
    VmvDlVhn[GU@yaN[X(uH|@x');
define('SECURE_AUTH_KEY', '5rXNA}tA#7DCm{=?EN-L/b2=3&7@4wPOfsJ<$]
    fIim=V=yIb(p]<t3k,8OA-!Uz!');
define('LOGGED_IN_KEY',   '3$+S?|mun`&GT2]|/,).I7X4s,&HR^V,%*nZ<j<Bg4|P-
    *I;+_!jn7>f@|];8`Pg');
define('NONCE_KEY',       'C-&mE>EmyLs^D_ZA,(Y+63W+GlUL)ZjS+,u-/@
    ubnu,z{j,/P#44gLW?Q+|$i(Y.');
```

Uploading your files

Once you have finished editing `wp-config.php`, it's time to upload your files to the server. FTP (or better yet, SFTP) the contents of the `wordpress/` folder to your new Web space. It will take a minute or two, but once that is complete, load your site in a browser. If everything is configured properly, you should see the first page of the installation wizard, as shown in Figure 2.2.

If you see a database error instead of the page shown in Figure 2.2, go back and double-check that the database credentials you supplied in `wp-config.php` are correct. Once you see this page, follow these steps to install WordPress:

1. **Type the name of your blog in the form field labeled Blog Title.** For this demonstration, I've used "The WordPress Bible."

2. **Enter your e-mail address.** This will become the general e-mail address that is used for administrative purposes on the site. It can be changed later.

FIGURE 2.2

Step 1 of the WordPress installation wizard

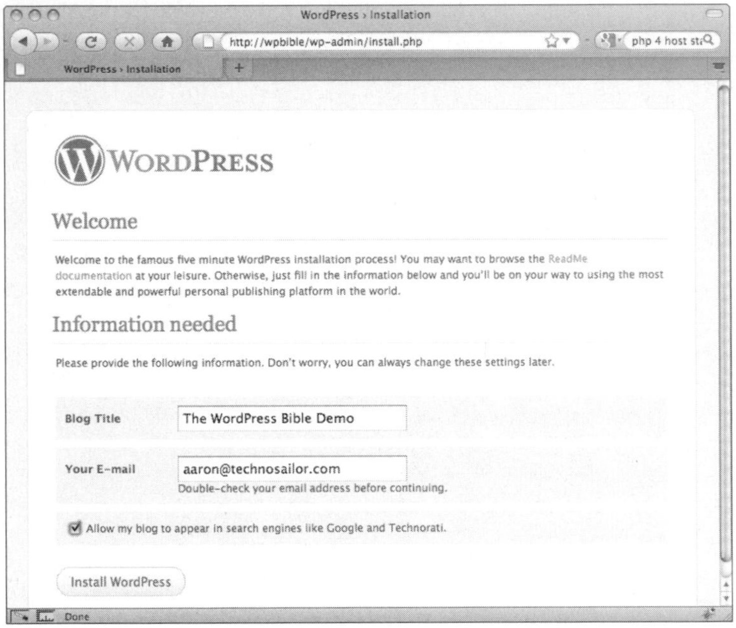

Note

If you are setting up a test blog or working on a development project, you probably do not want to select the Allow my blog to appear in search engines like Google and Technorati check box. When it is selected, the search engines are notified of new content as soon as it becomes published. For this demonstration, leave it unchecked. ■

3. Click the Install WordPress button.

There is only one step. The next page provides a randomly generated password for a new user called admin, as shown in Figure 2.3. This information will also be sent to the e-mail address you designated during installation.

FIGURE 2.3

After installation, WordPress generates a randomly generated password for the new user called admin.

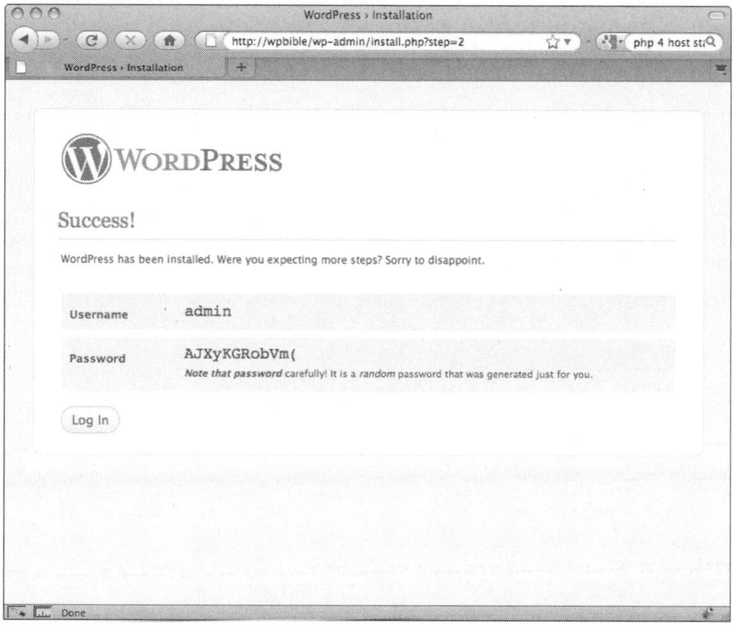

With the new username and password in hand, it's time to log in to WordPress for the first time.

Summary

- WordPress requires PHP 4.3+ and MySQL 4.1.2+. Most modern Web hosts provide a PHP 5+ build with at least MySQL 4.1. Many hosts provide PHP 5 as well.

- Apache 2 is the most common Web server in use today and is available in most Linux Web-hosting packages.

- PHP and MySQL should be optimized, particularly for blogs with more traffic.

- WordPress runs on a variety of Web server platforms, including Apache, Lighttpd, Litespeed, Nginx, and Internet Information Services (IIS).

- Beneficial system modules to include are mod_rewrite for Apache, eAccelerator, or APC for PHP, and the SSH2 and FTP libraries for PHP.

- You can interact with MySQL via phpMyAdmin or the command line.

- Use secure keys in WordPress to secure your database and cookie settings.

WordPress, SEO, and Social Media Marketing

I n today's super-connected world of the Internet, social media, blogs, Twitter, and Facebook, it's not surprising that the tools that are used online directly impact business. How you communicate on blogs and social networks can make or break your ability to find a job, get new business, or drive more traffic to your site.

Brian Solis, co-author of *Now is Gone* and *Putting the Public Back in Public Relations*, states in a blog post published on July 6, 2009 at www.brian solis.com/2009/07/pr does-not-stand-for-press-release-equalizing-spikes-and-valleys/:

> If you've studied the behavior and ensuing results associated with retweeting and linkbacks lately, you'd be surprised to learn just how few people actually click through to interact with the shared content, let alone using or referring the product or service contained in the link — no matter how influential you are. Of course, the more authority and trust you possess, the more retweets and shares you earn, but the follow-through never fails to dissipate without fuel and cultivation.

Brian is referring to the trend among marketers and publicists to focus on a broad push to win over constituents. He notes that, although this is the prevailing approach, building a community around ideas, companies, or start-ups is the only surefire way to create, and sustain, the drive needed to build the traffic and buzz.

In this chapter, I talk about some of the challenges facing bloggers when it comes to marketing their content. WordPress offers many possible solutions, including core features and plugins, to help bloggers successfully promote the content they produce.

IN THIS CHAPTER

Understanding the basics of search engine optimization

Leveraging social networks to extend your blog

Understanding the Basics of Search Engine Optimization

Search engine optimization (SEO) is the process of trying to get Web pages to rank higher in search engines. For example, when someone does a search on Google, she wants her Web page to be ranked higher than the competition. The holy grail of SEO is to get placement on the front page of a set of search results, preferably positioned as the first result. These results are known as Search Engine Results Page, or SERPs.

With massive firms working for clients and advertisers to improve their SERPs, SEO has become a multi-billion dollar industry worldwide. For example, a travel agency might want to rank well for the search phrase "cheap flights to Los Angeles" because it's a phrase consumers are likely to search for using Google or other search engine. Likewise, "Italian restaurant near Dupont Circle" could be a search phrase an Italian restaurant near Dupont Circle in Washington, D.C., uses in their quest to rank high.

Of course, for all the money and research that goes into the SEO industry, the best and most solid SEO practices are things any blogger can, and should, do anyway. WordPress assists in some ways while others practices are simply behavioral habits a blogger should strive for.

Canonical URLs

Canonical URLs are URLs that are considered to be authentic and authoritative for a given resource. The word derives from the word *canon*, which describes law and genuineness. The problem with many blog platforms is that the same content often appears in different places on a site, with exactly the same presentation but an entirely different URL.

An example of this problem would be if I set up a site with the domain `example.com`. When I type **http://example.com** into the browser address bar, it displays the same content as if I typed in **http://www.example.com**.

Web servers handle URLs as parts. The first part, `http://`, is the protocol that is going to be used. Everyone who surfs the Web on a regular basis is familiar with the `http://` protocol. It tells the server that the browser is requesting a page over the normal Hypertext Transfer Protocol (HTTP). While it's far less likely, you can also see URLs with an `ftp://` or even a `file://` protocol.

The second part of the URL is the domain and while, generally speaking, the domain by itself will be exactly the same as if you added www, it is not necessarily the same. Server configurations could point `www.example.com` to a completely different Web site than `example.com`. Because of this technicality, the search engines cannot assume that the two are the same.

Google and the other search engines have spent a tremendous amount of time and resources trying to ascertain authority of Web sites, Web pages, and content. To that end, content that is found in multiple places (for example, URLs with www as well as those without it) is treated as duplicate content and the version found to be non-authoritative is penalized. Site owners run the risk of being penalized by Google if their sites are considered spam (a verdict that is rare for most bloggers but exists nonetheless).

Canonical URLs redirects were added to WordPress in version 2.3 to help alleviate this problem. The added functionality has been hailed by Matt Cutts, the head of Web spam (the guy to shape the quality of search results and filtering spam from the Google index) as eliminating the problem of duplicate content as much as possible.

WordPress tries to eliminate all the potential duplicate content areas by consolidating content to a single URL. Using the WordPress Address and Blog Address settings defined in General Settings in conjunction with the settings defined in Permalink Settings, WordPress redirects traffic to any potentially legitimate location to the proper one.

Depending on your preference, you might want to set your Blog Address setting to use the www or the non-www version of the domain. Both are equally fine, so it is merely a personal choice. However, if you already have an existing site that has been indexed by the search engines, you can use some tactics to figure out which one is best for you.

Google searches

Google provides a neat search "hack" that enables you to find out how many pages have been indexed for a given site. By prepending `site:` to a search and adding the domain name, it gives you a peek into how many pages Google knows about.

For example, in Figure 3.1, you can see that my site, `www.technosailor.com`, has more than 13,000 results for the non-www version of my domain.

FIGURE 3.1

At the time of writing this book, my site, `www.technosailor.com`, had more than 13,000 results in Google when you search for site:technosailor.com.

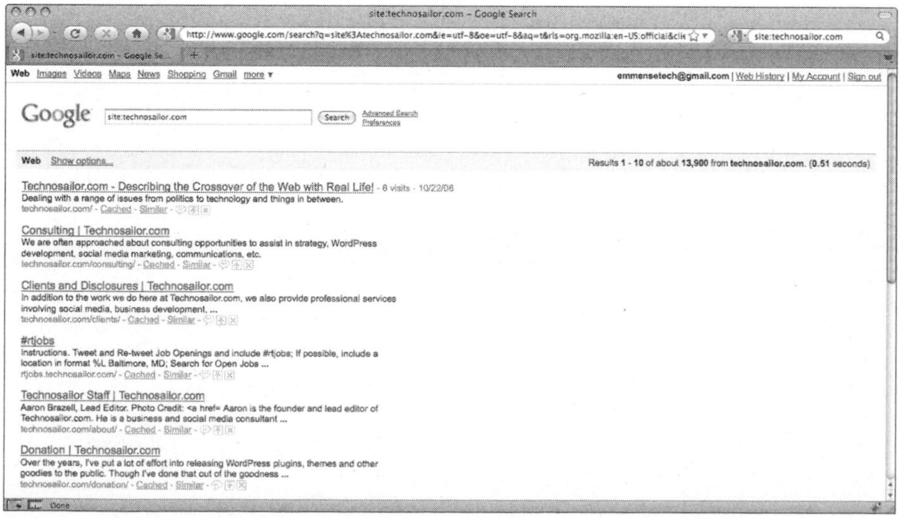

It is a well-indexed site and those numbers are right on track. Yahoo! shows more than 10,000 results while Bing shows nearly 12,500 results.

What happens, however, when the same search is done with the www version of my site? Instead of more than 13,000 results, it's a mere 2, as shown in Figure 3.2.

FIGURE 3.2

When www is added to the domain name, the results are startling. Only two pages show up in Google when searching this way.

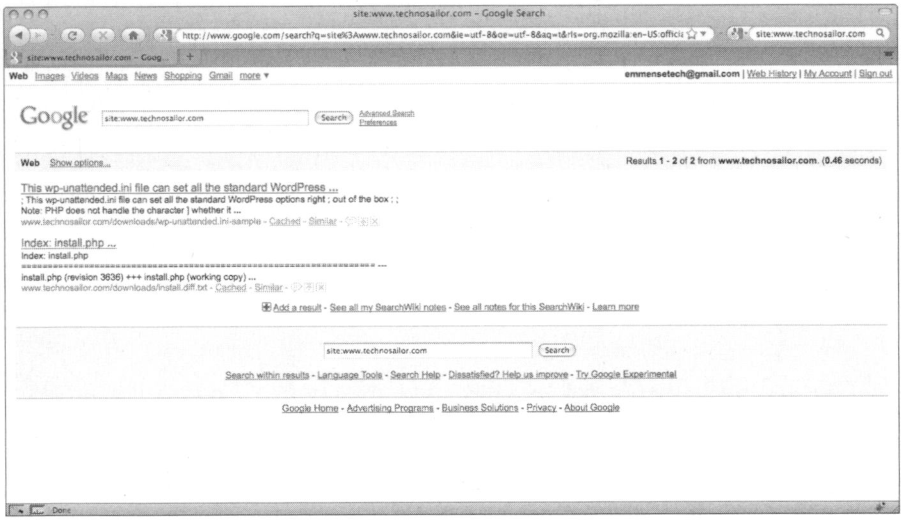

In the same search, Bing showed 388 results while Yahoo! showed 305.

Google Webmaster Tools

Google provides a suite of tools called the Google Webmaster Tools (`www.google.com/webmasters/tools/`). After some configuration and verification, you will be able to use the tools to get a high-level snapshot of how Google views your site as well as tell Google to specifically not index specific pages. Notably, however, you can also tell Google which version (www or non-www) of your site it should pay attention to, as shown in Figure 3.3.

Note

Be very careful that you ensure that the choice you make in Google Webmaster Tools is identical to the WordPress address setting you choose in General Settings. If you tell WordPress one thing and Google another, you will prevent your site from being indexed. ■

By using Google Webmaster Tools, you can extend the canonical URL functionality of WordPress by telling Google which version of the site to pay attention to and which part to ignore.

Steps for setting up proper canonical URL redirection

Now that you've decided which format of URL you want to be authoritative (say, the non-www version), you can get everything set up properly. To set up the proper URL redirection for your site, follow these steps:

1. Log in to the WordPress Admin.

2. Click on the Settings menu or Expand the Settings menu and choose General.

3. In the Blog Address field type your blog's URL in the format http://example.com.

4. Click Save Changes.

5. Log in to Google Webmaster Tools at **www.google.com/webmasters/tools/**.

6. Click the plus sign next to Site Configuration to expand the Site Configuration menu.

7. Click the Settings link.

8. Under preferred domain, select the Display URLs as www.example.com option.

9. Click Save to complete the process.

Using Keywords Effectively in Posts and Titles

Keywords are the lifeblood of SEO. Travel bloggers want to use keywords that are important to their blog and industry such as travel, flights, and low fares. Depending on the focus of the blog, they might want to include names of locations and tourist attractions, such as Piccadilly Circus or Times Square, as well. Likewise, science bloggers want to use words such as Newton, chemical, phosphorus, or Hodgkin's Disease in their content and post titles.

Using keywords that are relevant to the content is encouraged. It will not guarantee high rankings for those terms because the SEO market is highly competitive, but it is a move in the right direction. It is not recommended that you avoid "stuffing" keywords in an attempt to get highly ranked. Keyword stuffing is a *black-hat* (or unethical) approach to SEO, where a blogger tries to get a ranking based on high-conversion terms that are unrelated to the topics described in the content. While the technical term is keyword stuffing, most agree, including the search engines, that such practice is also spamming. If search engines realize you're doing this, they'll likely penalize your site.

Effective keyword usage is a behavioral habit, not a software habit. WordPress cannot force you to use effective titles or use great keywords in your post content. It cannot force you to categorize or use tags that describe your content. All it can do is provide the tools needed to do these things. And it does.

For example, on the WordPress Add New Post screen, you can choose previously used categories in an effort to keep relevant posts in the same vertical silo. Likewise, you can do the same thing with tags. With tags, WordPress provides auto-completion of tags as you are typing.

The Meta tag boost

An often overlooked, yet highly important, aspect of any blogger's SEO needs is *meta tags*. Meta tags are hypertext markup language (HTML) tags that sit in the header area of the page's source code. They are not viewed by readers unless they take a look at the source code, but search engines view all of them.

Meta keywords tag

The meta keywords tag is an all-important tag that provides over-arching descriptive keywords for the page itself. Listing 3.1 is an example of how an effective meta keyword tag would look. The content of the tag should not be more than 160 characters long because search engines tend to ignore everything after the first 160 characters.

LISTING 3.1

The meta keywords tag

```
<meta name="keywords" content="phones, cell phones, iPods, gadgets,
    electronics, consumer electronics, technology, reviews" />
```

Meta description tag

The meta description tag offers site owners the ability to describe the content of their site for search engines. Like the meta keywords tag, the meta description tag should not be longer than 160 characters. It should be a one-sentence description of what the site is about, as demonstrated in Listing 3.2.

LISTING 3.2

The meta description tag

```
<meta name="description" content="A technology and consumer electronics news
    and review site focusing on the mobile device market" />
```

Search engines will use this text in SERPs if they are unable to find any other descriptive text for the site, so it's important to get your message across. Likewise, you should try to use keywords that you defined in the meta keywords tag.

Title tag

Technically, the title tag is not a meta tag, but it ranks right up there in importance when it comes to SEO. Used in conjunction with the meta keywords and meta description tags, the title tag can provide additional bounce when it comes to search engine rankings. Many people assume that the title tag should be the title of the site and, therefore, many themes are coded with a title tag format similar to that shown in Listing 3.3.

LISTING 3.3

The title tag format

```
<!DOCTYPE html PUBLIC "-//W3C//DTD XHTML 1.0 Transitional//EN"
    "http://www.w3.org/TR/xhtml1/DTD/xhtml1-transitional.dtd">
<html>
    <head>
        <title><?php bloginfo('title') ?></title>
        ...
    </head>
...
</html>
```

Cross-Reference

The `bloginfo()` function is a WordPress template tag that is used to insert data about the WordPress blog directly in a theme. I talk more about template tags and themes in Part III. A complete reference to WordPress template tags can be found in Appendix B. ■

Instead, consider including your blog description in the title tag and prepending the description before the blog title. You can do this by editing the header of your blog (usually in `header.php`) as shown in Listing 3.4.

LISTING 3.4

Placing this description before the title of the blog will help it rank higher

```
<!DOCTYPE html PUBLIC "-//W3C//DTD XHTML 1.0 Transitional//EN"
    "http://www.w3.org/TR/xhtml1/DTD/xhtml1-transitional.dtd">
<html>
    <head>
        <title><?php bloginfo('description') ?> - <?php bloginfo('title')
?></title>
            ...
    </head>
...
</html>
```

This produces a title tag that reads along the lines of, "Your home for mobile gadgets on the Web – My Mobile Phone." In this case, both the blog title, "My Mobile Phone," and the blog description, "Your home for mobile phone gadgets on the Web" produce less than 160 combined characters, but some long titles and descriptions could end up cut off. By placing the description up-front, you ensure the chance for the search engine to get the most descriptive words indexed.

You can even get fancy and replace the blog description with the title of a post on individual blog posts, as shown in Listing 3.5.

LISTING 3.5

Using WordPress conditional tags, you can have WordPress format the title tag more effectively for different kinds of pages

```
<!DOCTYPE html PUBLIC "-//W3C//DTD XHTML 1.0 Transitional//EN"
    "http://www.w3.org/TR/xhtml1/DTD/xhtml1-transitional.dtd">
<html>
    <head>
        <title>
        <?php
        if( is_home() )
        {
        ?>
            <?php bloginfo('description') ?> - <?php bloginfo('title') ?>
        <?php
```

```
        }
        else
        {
        ?>
            <?php the_title() ?> - <?php bloginfo('title') ?>
        <?php
        }
        ?>
        </title>
        ...
    </head>
    ...
</html>
```

On the Web

The code in Listing 3.5 is available for download at `www.wiley.com/go/wordpressbible`. ■

Tip

The All in One SEO plugin, which I discuss in the next section, can handle the title tag manipulation and provides a large degree of customization. However, theme authors cannot rely on the installation of this plugin by end users. It is always a good idea to build the logic into the theme just in case. ■

The All in One SEO plugin

If you're serious about your SEO (and you should be), there is a single plugin that is virtually a requirement for any blog. The All in One SEO plugin automatically takes care of much of what I have already talked about in this chapter.

When you install and activate the plugin, from within WordPress or by downloading and installing it from the WordPress plugin repository at `http://wordpress.org/extend/plugins/all-in-one-seo-pack/`, you will find a new top-level navigation item, titled All in One SEO, in the WordPress Admin. Clicking it brings you to a new administrative menu where you can configure everything about the plugin, as shown in Figure 3.4.

Home Title

The first field you can fill in for the All in One SEO plugin is the Home Title. This value overrides the Blog Title field on the WordPress General Settings page. If you leave it blank, the normal Blog Title is used instead. This value pertains to the title tag.

Home Description

If you leave the Home Description field blank, it defaults to the Blog Tagline set under General Description. However, if you want more control over the text that is listed in the meta description tag, change this option.

FIGURE 3.4

The administrative options page for the All in One SEO plugin

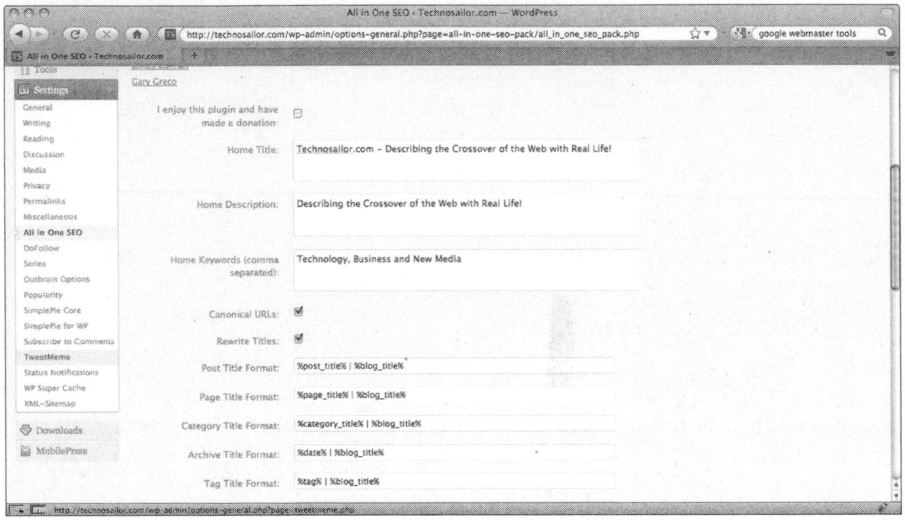

Home Keywords

Like Home Description, the Home Keywords field controls a meta tag. Namely, it populates your meta keywords tag with descriptive keywords for your site. Make sure you list all your keywords as comma-separated values (that is, phones, blackberry, mobile, wireless, iPhone).

Canonical URLs

Selecting the Canonical URLs check box ensures that All in One SEO will add the `rel=` `"canonical"` attribute to URLs. While this is supposed to help search engines understand how to handle canonical URLs, it has been found to be largely ineffective. For more on the potential risks for using this feature, see the excellent write up at `www.quickonlinetips.com/` `archives/2009/04/seo-wordpress-plugin-drops-google-pagerank/`.

Rewrite Titles

Selecting the Rewrite Titles check box ensures that no matter which page you find yourself on, the title tag will always be rewritten to make the most sense from an SEO standpoint. Post titles that are set when you create a new page or blog post will be used where applicable, and the home page title tag will be reoriented in a way that is most beneficial for search engine comprehension.

Title Formats

If you select the Canonical URLs check box to allow the All in One SEO plugin to rewrite title tags, the Format fields gives you the opportunity to set the order and preference for each type of page. Be especially careful in this area because "placeholder words" are used to represent key data points. By default, the following formats are used:

```
Post Title Format = %post_title% - %blog_title%

Page Title Format = %page_title% - %blog_title%

Category Title Format = %category_title% - %blog_title%

Archive Title Format = %date% - %blog_title%

Tag Title Format = %tag% - %blog_title%

Search Title Format = %search% - %blog_title%

Description Format = %description%

404 Title Format = Nothing Found for %request_words%

Paged Format = Part %page%
```

Use Categories for META Keywords

In addition to the keywords that you set, you have the opportunity to append the categories a single post is in. Presumably, if you use categories for your blog post (as opposed to as a structural element that many people have begun to use), these keywords can be appended into the meta keywords field as well. This can help further define the context and relevancy to the search engines.

Dynamically Generate Keywords for Posts Page

In most cases, the Dynamically Generate Keywords for Posts Page option is not required. For some setups, however, the normal flow of posts is on a separate page. This is often the case when a WordPress install is used as a content management system and the bulk of the layout more closely resembles a traditional site. The "blog" is often designated to a separate area of the site and uses a custom page template. For situations like this, the All in One SEO plugin provides the opportunity to dynamically populate the meta keywords tag on this page with the keywords you have chosen.

Noindex Options

The All in One SEO plugin also provides three options for to eliminating certain pages from being indexed by the search engine. These options are useful in avoiding duplicate content penalties but can also be overkill. Therefore, it is completely optional to designate archives, tag archives, and category archives as "noindex" links. When the search engine spiders encounter these links, the content behind them will not be indexed.

Autogenerate Descriptions

You have the option of having the All in One SEO plugin automatically generate meta description tags for all non-home pages. Usually, these meta description tags are generated with the post excerpt, something the author can predefine or WordPress can automatically generate. In the event that the plugin cannot find an excerpt, selecting this option enables it to automatically create a description that fits the blog post.

Additional Headers

Not necessarily relevant to SEO, but possibly helpful nonetheless, the three Additional Headers options enable you to insert extra text or tags into the header. An example of this might be JavaScript snippets from third-party sites.

Leveraging Social Networks to Extend Your Blog

The advent of blogging as a popular mainstream activity signified a new trend in communication. It is now possible for anyone to get her feet wet with self publishing, and free, open source solutions like WordPress have played a large role in that. Traditional journalism has eyed blogs suspiciously, considering them something only untrained, unvetted writers do. A cold war arose as the traditional means for disseminating news and information shifted from the front page of the newspaper to the home page of a Web site. Later, the same type of conflict developed between bloggers and communications professionals.

When social networks like Facebook and Twitter emerged, the role of the blog changed again. For some, blogging took a back burner to the means of instant communication, such as microblogs and aggregation tools. For others, social networks gained importance, complementing blogging and blogs.

Today, most blogs, traditional news sources, and public relations firms use social networks to extend their reach. Blogs that don't have some kind of feature to share content across social networks are perceived as isolationist and likely have seen a decrease in their traffic over the past few years. It is considered imperative to have integration with social networks to extend the blog's reach.

WordPress, for its part, has many plugins that integrate some aspect of social media. A quick search of the plugin repository shows almost 300 varieties of Twitter plugins and almost 100 varieties of Facebook plugins.

It is important to know the technical implementations of social network integration on the growth and sustainability of a blog, and equally important to have a good understanding of the marketing benefits of these tools. Realistically, there are plugins that automatically send a tweet of a Post title and URL every time you click Publish, but does this actually increase the blog's traffic and exposure? As it turns out, less than you might think.

Facebook

Facebook is an ever-evolving source of traffic. To many, it's nothing more than a network to keep friends and family involved in their lives. Others use it to share links from their blogs and provide additional places for friends to comment or voice their approval.

Fan Pages on Facebook centralize and inform readers of new content. It also can serve as a nifty replacement for e-mail marketing services, such as FeedBurner. Facebook simply enables people to join a group or leave a group and, in doing so, replaces the e-mail delivery and opt-in requirements needed to avoid spam.

WordPress provides many options for Facebook integration, all in the form of plugins. You can use some or all of them to extend the blog to one of the largest social networks.

Facebook Photos for WordPress

The Facebook Photos plugin is also known by a few other misleading names — Facebook Plugin for WordPress and TanTan Facebook, after the name of the company that created it, TanTanNoodles. It gives the blogger the ability to tie his blog to a specific Facebook account and use photos from the Facebook account in blog posts. You can download the Facebook Photos plugin from http://tantannoodles.com/toolkit/facebook-photos/.

WP-FacebookConnect

Facebook Connect is a relatively new offering based on Facebook opening up their application programming interface (API) to allow third-party developers to authenticate against Facebook and use user profile data in their applications. The WP-FacebookConnect plugin provides authentication against Facebook, so Facebook users can leave a comment using their Facebook account information. Additionally, it will publish the comment to Facebook as a newsfeed item, a feature that is critically important for the dissemination of viral content. Finally, the WP-FacebookConnect plugin uses the Facebook user photo as the avatar displayed in comments, if you have opted to use avatars.

The WP-FacebookConnect plugin is not trivial to install. It requires an API Key and a Secret Key from Facebook. The plugin does provide links to the Facebook application registration page, where you can find this information, as shown in Figure 3.5. Additionally, it does require some small template modifications.

FIGURE 3.5

The Facebook application registration page needs two pieces of information: the application name (use your blog name) and consent to the Facebook Terms of Service. You might add an "icon" that would be consistent to your brand as well. This icon will show up next to every post WP-FacebookConnect places on the Facebook service.

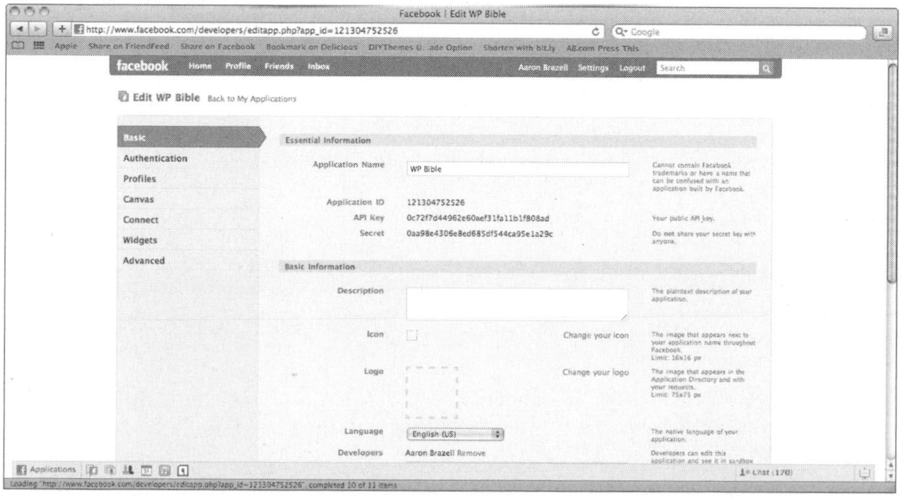

Twitter

Like Facebook, Twitter represents a critical network for content distribution. It may be the most widely used tool on the social web at this time, and it levels the playing field. At one time, bloggers had to rely on word of mouth, interlinking between blogs, and more organic forms of traffic growth; Twitter gives everyone with a cell phone or computer the ability to compete in the same arena as the world's biggest celebrities, brands, and other bloggers.

Twitter, for the uninitiated, is a short-form Web platform that provides for communication between users and their followers — the people who have opted to get notifications from the user. Likewise, the user receives notifications every time anyone that she chooses to follow updates his status. The paradigm is asynchronous, so there does not have to be a mutual friendship option for communication to work.

Many corporate WordPress users have adopted Twitter as a medium for content distribution; and groups of political bloggers and activists who tend to flock around political action use the viral nature of the service to organize and push conversations and agendas forward.

Of course, like Facebook, there are plenty of WordPress plugins to add Twitter integration and functionality to a blog. In fact, there are many thousand more Twitter integration options than there are Facebook plugins.

Twitter Tools

Twitter Tools is a plugin developed by Alex King and Crowd Favorite. It does a number of things that may or may not actually be useful for your particular type of use. Twitter Tools was one of the earliest tools to bring some order to the Twitter chaos.

Twitter Tools provides an administrative interface, as shown in Figure 3.6, that you can use to configure what behavior is used. You can download it from the WordPress plugin repository at `http://wordpress.org/extend/plugins/twitter-tools/`.

In addition, Twitter Tools can do the following:

- **Create weekly or daily digests of your tweets.** This creates a new post on your WordPress blog that only contains a bulleted list of tweets that you've sent out. It's benefit is questionable when it comes to providing a productive outcome. Nonetheless, the functionality exists.

- **Create a blog post each time you tweet.** This feature is probably most beneficial if you only use Twitter a handful of times each day. If a blog becomes overrun and too much for many readers by posting six or seven blog posts in a day, Twitter can, in essence, drown that community out. Depending on the volume, it can be a useful feature to extend conversation onto your WordPress blog.

- **Autopost new Posts to Twitter.** A frequent use for Twitter tools functionality is to allow WordPress to automatically post a headline and title with the post permalink to Twitter as soon as it is published. I recommend that you make sure your Twitter audience knows of new posts, however. I also recommend caution in using any automated method to do so.

- **Offer extra hooks.** For developers, Twitter Tools provides a number of useful hooks. Included is a filter, `tweet_blog_post_url`, which you can use to modify the default URL being sent to Twitter (for example, if you wanted use a URL shortening service like Bit.ly or TinyURL), and an action, `aktt_add_tweet` which you can use to do something with the tweet content, such as post to a different service in addition to Twitter.

FIGURE 3.6

The Twitter Tools Options admin interface provides a number of options for integrating Twitter into WordPress blogs.

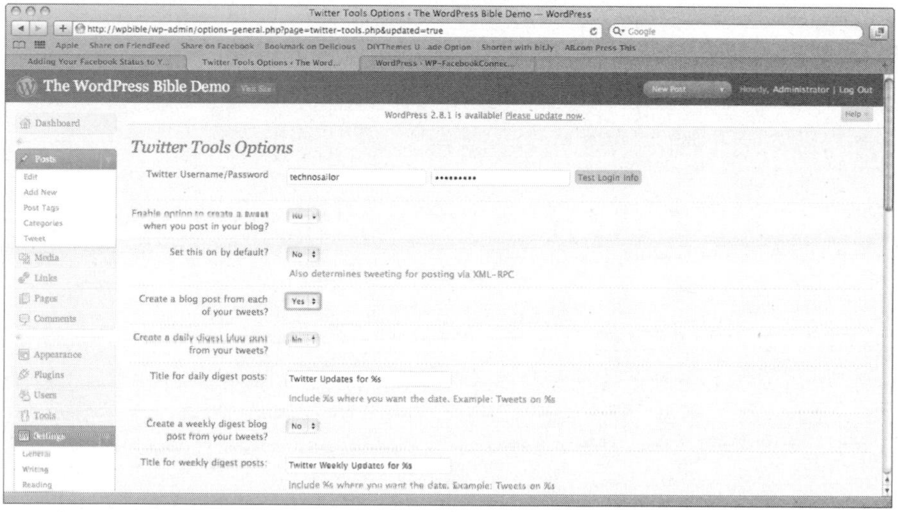

Cross-Reference

I'll get into the heart of hooks, actions, filters, and other aspect of plugin development in Chapter 4. If you're interested in seeing what hooks WordPress uses specifically, refer to Appendix A. ■

Note

As much as I would like to write about Twitter, Twitter marketing, and effective conversations in social media, the topic is beyond the scope of this book. In WordPress blogging, bloggers are intimately connected to the counterpart services on other blogging platforms as well as other parts of the social web. They develop strategies for building blogs and choosing platforms based on the holistic benefit gained from them.

The recommendations for Twitter Tools use provided in this chapter are subjective. Every blog and blogger is unique, and every blog has its own life flow. Consider your goals, means, and comfort level with engagement and make educated choices based on results and experimentation. A great book, especially for communicators and people looking to market their blog using Twitter, is 140 Characters: A Style Guide for the Short Form available at www.wiley.com/WileyCDA/WileyTitle/productCd-0470556137.html. ■

TweetMeme

The TweetMeme plugin is a simple WordPress plugin that provides a user interface, such as the interface shown in Figure 3.7. It is a popular plugin and appears on many different sites across the Internet. It provides a means for readers to share their stories on Twitter. Additionally, sites shared in this manner are aggregated on www.tweetmeme.com, giving users an opportunity to see the hottest stories shared on Twitter at any given moment.

FIGURE 3.7

The TweetMeme plugin administrative interface provides a place where you can configure how the TweetMeme button functions.

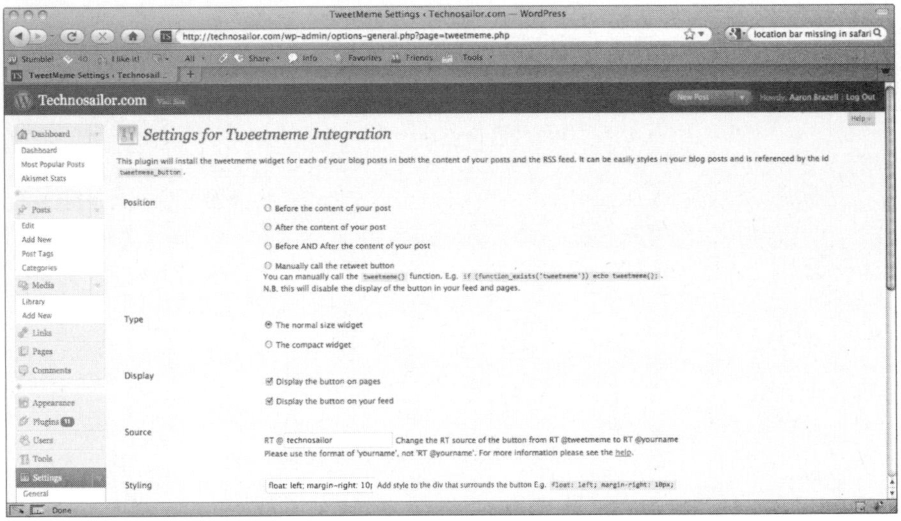

The TweetMeme plugin adds a small button to each post. This button is a one-click button that shares the story and displays a count of the number of times the story has already been shared, highlighting the popularity factor. The TweetMeme plugin allows the following customizations:

- **Position.** Depending on your preferences and, possibly, theme layout, you can choose to position the TweetMeme button automatically before your post, after your post, or both. Additionally, you can opt to manually code the button into your template.

- **Type.** You can choose to display your TweetMeme button as a square large button or a small rectangular button.

- **Display.** Depending on your preference and needs, you can choose to have the TweetMeme button added on pages, in addition to posts. You can also have it inserted into your feeds.

- **Source.** You should change this if you have any interest in developing name or brand recognition. By default, tweets are sent with a credit to the TweetMeme Twitter ID (@tweetmeme). Most bloggers change this to their own Twitter ID.

- **Styling.** If the button doesn't fit perfectly into your theme, you can add custom Cascading Style Sheets (CSS) to adjust the display behavior.

- **Ping TweetMeme.** You can to notify TweetMeme whenever a story is shared using this feature. In most cases, bloggers want to ensure this happens.

Summary

- SEO has become a multi-billion industry about getting keywords to rank highly in the search engines.

- WordPress handles canonical URLs automatically. Canonical URLs are the authoritative source that search engines should consider and are important for avoiding duplicate content penalties.

- SEO techniques in WordPress involve using effective keywords in post titles and meta tags without being spammy.

- Configuring the All in One SEO plugin will solve many of your SEO challenges.

- Social network and social media marketing are complementary to blogging with WordPress.

Finding Help in the WordPress Support System

When it comes to open source software, documentation and support are often the biggest make-or-break aspects in how much usage the software gets. Because there is no predefined rule or convention in how open source software is created, documented, or publicly released, well-documented software has a distinct advantage over relatively undocumented software.

The ultimate question for new user adoption is, "How easy is the software to understand out of the box?" Many users don't want to try installing something just to find that out. Call it a time issue or fear of the unknown. Whatever it is, if they can go to a Web site and find a wiki or support forum that spells out requirements, thorough documentation (including installation information), and an ample amount of tutorial material, the software stands to have a strong success rate. If this documentation and related tutorials are easy to find, then even better!

Note

Wikis **are extremely powerful pieces of software. They are collaborative, browser-based applications that enable anyone to add, delete, or modify an existing page. They are popular in open source documentation because it allows community contribution. The most famous wiki is Wikipedia (**www. wikipedia.org**).** ∎

Fortunately, WordPress has an enormous community providing assistance and documentation on official WordPress sites and mailing lists, or on independent blogs (that are most likely running on WordPress themselves). In this chapter, I look at some of these resources. Of course, this book in itself adds to the resources available for users and developers. It should never be too hard to find help with WordPress.

Using the WordPress Codex

The most thorough, organized online documentation for WordPress is the WordPress Codex. The WordPress Codex is actually a wiki and is maintained by the WordPress community. Significant effort has gone into making the Codex not only usable but also current. Prior to major releases that introduce new functionality, modified behavior of existing code, and other changes to WordPress, there is generally a large effort within the community to ensure that the Codex is up to date.

The Codex is comprehensive in most areas, providing examples of how template tags should be used and theme hierarchies are laid out, as well as plugin compatibility reports from different releases of WordPress. It strives to be the collective consciousness of the entire WordPress community and does a good job in most measurable ways.

However, the Codex, for all its wealth of knowledge (and many FAQ sections), can be somewhat disorienting for users trying to find out how to do something specific without knowing, for example, where to start looking or what to even call the problem.

The main page of the Codex is shown in Figure 4.1. When you first log on to the Codex (`http://codex.wordpress.org`), you'll immediately notice that you can also get it in other languages, such as German or Turkish. There is even a Vietnamese version of the Codex. Localization has become a big area of focus within the WordPress community and it is reflected in documentation, in the core development philosophy, and in many plugins.

Note

Localization, or internationalization, is a key effort of WordPress core development. Often, localization is referred to simply as i18n, a clever shortened version of "internationalization," with the "18" representing the eighteen letters in between the "i" and the "n." ∎

Cross-Reference

Information about how to localize plugins can be found in Chapter 5. You can use the same approach to localize themes. ∎

The Codex is divided into eight sections that provide some guidance for users trying to find documentation:

- Getting Started with WordPress
- Working with WordPress
- Design and Layout
- Advanced Topics
- Troubleshooting
- Developer Documentation
- About WordPress
- Announcements

FIGURE 4.1

The WordPresss Codex is the official online documentation of WordPress.org.

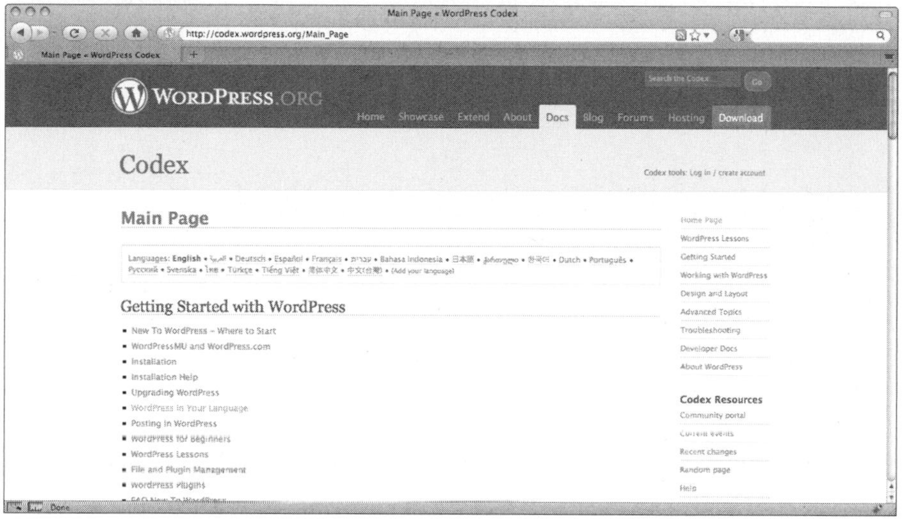

Plugin developers will most likely find the most help in the Developer Documentation section, which includes a lot of useful information about the Plugin application programming interface (API) and Option Reference. Other more critical information, such as a complete hook reference, is described in this section but is not well documented in the codex.

Cross-Reference

A complete hook reference is provided in this book. See Appendix A for information on the more than 800 actions and filters available to developers. ■

Theme developers may benefit most from the Design and Layout section, which documents template tags and template file hierarchies. In this section you can find information about child themes, WordPress Cascading Style Sheet (CSS) selectors, and more.

Cross-Reference

Theme developers can reference the chapters in Part III of this book for thorough documentation on all aspects of theming. ■

You will find information about leveraging WordPress' upgrade features, posting screen, widget interface, and much more in the Getting Started with WordPress section. Although WordPress is pretty intuitive for most users, sometimes having an overview of user functionality is helpful. User documentation in the Codex is generally identical on both self-hosted WordPress.org sites and the free-hosted WordPress.com sites.

Staying in the Loop with Mailing Lists

A popular format of support in open source software, and perhaps one of the oldest, is the mailing list. E-mail has existed for over 30 years and continues to be the most reliable form of communication for many people.

Fortunately, for people who do best with e-mail, WordPress provides many options and avenues for e-mail participation.

wp-hackers

One of the more popular mailing lists is for WordPress developers. Most of the people who subscribe to the wp-hackers mailing list are submitting patches and discussing the technical aspects of the software. It is not a support venue and shouldn't be used as such.

Note

When the term "hacker" is used in this context, it is used to describe someone who hacks on code in a productive way that makes the community better. Often, these "hackers" submit patches for inclusion in the WordPress core. They are typically the coders who take interest in moving the software forward. This is in stark contrast to the more malicious meaning of "hacker" that is indicative of "breaking and entering" on a site for the purpose of defacement or other nefarious ends. ∎

Much of the discussion about ideas for the WordPress roadmap happens on this mailing list with active participation from plugin developers, core developers, theme developers, and community members trying to get involved in the project. Competency with WordPress development is assumed, so it tends to be populated with intermediate to advanced technical users.

You can subscribe to the wp-hackers mailing list at `http://lists.automattic.com/mailman/listinfo/wp-hackers`.

wp-testers

The wp-testers mailing list is also a high-volume mailing list that increases in volume, on average, about a month before a major release. This is synchronous with the amount of testing and bug reporting that goes into a new release as it is prepped for shipping.

This mailing list is designed to cater to a portion of the community who love to see WordPress perfected before it's released. The members are people who take a lot of time going through the software to find the security problems, usability issues, and just plain old bugs. They look at Trac, the official buglist and repository of changes that have been made to the WordPress core, and test patches that have been applied to the core to try to find areas that break under actual use.

Many of the testers on this mailing list also run blogs with pre-release software, and this method has been effective in finding problems when the software is used in real time on a real blog. The testers recognize that using pre-release software is not something that can be supported, but that their helpful feedback aids the actual core developers in polishing their product in advance of a release.

You can subscribe to the wp-testers mailing list at `http://lists.automattic.com/mailman/listinfo/wp-testers`.

wp-docs

The documentation mailing list was specifically designed to aid community members in their maintenance and upkeep of the Codex. Members discuss strategies for documenting important areas of WordPress, and the strategies of how (and who) will cover these topics. They work together to try to make sure it is up to date with current and valid information.

The wp-docs mailing list members frequently participate in other mailing lists, particularly wp-testers, in advance of new releases. There tends to be a lot of overlap to ensure that end users have all the information they need about a WordPress release.

You can subscribe to the wp-docs mailing list at `http://lists.automattic.com/mailman/listinfo/wp-docs`.

wp-pro

The WordPress professional mailing list is specifically for finding and hiring consultants who do paid WordPress work. It is setup so that parties seeking professional WordPress services can advertise their projects and solicit direct responses from WordPress service providers.

The wp-pro mailing list is not designed to be a support forum or mailing list, and does not focus on WordPress development. Responses should be directed to the poster, not broadcast to the entire list. The wp-pro mailing list complements the list of providers of professional services listed at `http://codepoet.com/`.

You can subscribe to the wp-pro mailing list at `http://lists.automattic.com/mailman/listinfo/wp-pro`.

wp-xmlrpc

The wp-xmlrpc mailing list has fairly low traffic. It is a place to discuss the XML-RPC functionality of WordPress. It also serves as a point of discussion around the AtomPub module WordPress provides. XML-RPC, a remote procedure call that uses Extensible Markup Language, is the functionality that enables remote publishing to a blog. AtomPub provides uniform data portability and is a spec that is standardized by a third party. Though AtomPub is currently in WordPress, the spec has not been finalized, so it is subject to change. This mailing list is used most by technical subscribers who are involved with data portability and remote publishing.

You can subscribe to the wp-xmlrpc mailing list at `http://lists.automattic.com/mailman/listinfo/wp-xmlrpc`.

wp-polyglots

Like the wp-testers list, wp-polyglots is a mailing list that often gets busy in the month before a major release. It is designed for localization, and i18n community members who are translating WordPress into other languages.

You can subscribe to the wp-polyglots mailing list at `http://lists.automattic.com/mailman/listinfo/wp-polyglots`.

wp-svn

An announcement-only mailing list, the wp-svn mailing list sends e-mails tracking any new changes or patches applied to the development software. It is useful for technical users who are tracking the software or developing patches.

You can subscribe to the wp-svn mailing list at `http://lists.automattic.com/mailman/listinfo/wp-svn`.

wp-trac

Like the wp-svn mailing list, wp-trac is a read-only mailing list. You cannot send anything to it, but is useful for keeping close tabs on the development cycle. Any time a new ticket is submitted, edited, or new patches or comments are made, subscribers receive an e-mail detailing the transaction.

You can subscribe to the wp-trac mailing list at `http://lists.automattic.com/mailman/listinfo/wp-trac`.

Finding Help in the WordPress Support Forums

Some of you don't like having community content pushed directly into your e-mail in boxes, as is the case with the mailing lists. Sometimes, you just want to have the content you need, when you want it, on your terms. Other times, it's a matter of having access to support information that is searchable and has a great depth of archives. Forums do that for you.

Beyond the benefits of forums, however, is the fact they are the only official place you can go to get help for yourself, besides Internet Relay Chat (IRC). IRC tends to be a little more technical for some users, and it certainly isn't searchable. It's great for real-time support, but the WordPress support forums tend to offer the richest support experience for the most people. The support forums home page (`http://wordpress.org/support`) is shown in Figure 4.2.

Cross-Reference
More information about IRC and the #wordpress IRC chat room can be found in Chapter 1. ■

The WordPress support forum is built on bbPress and offers the most common method of getting help with WordPress.

Understanding the support forum layout

The support forums are divided up into sub-forums, as is common with most Internet forums. This gives you a useful visual breakdown of content types available and helps you locate the proper place to ask questions or search for answers. There are also tags, in the form of tag clouds, that provide a visual cue as to commonly discussed topics. The following sections outline the main sub-forums found on the main WordPress Forums page.

Installation

The questions that plague users when they begin using WordPress experience are often the same. For example, in the Installation forum, users might ask about how to get WordPress running on a different server and importing their content from a database backup. They might also want help getting a database set up.

How To and Troubleshooting

Once WordPress is up and running, people often encounter issues with things like themes. For example, they might want the date show up in the theme and when it doesn't by default, they can't figure out why. Other problems might have something to do with folder permissions that prevent them from uploading images.

Plugins and Hacks

Developers needing assistance with some aspect of plugin development tend to come to the Plugins and Hacks forum. They might have some conflict between two plugins and don't know how to find it. Or perhaps they need some assistance implementing a new shortcode. Whatever the reason, they might ask in this forum.

Note

Shortcodes are a relatively new feature of WordPress that enable plugin authors to provide a "placeholder" for use in WordPress posts and pages. When encountered, these shortcodes (which are generally designated with square brackets like this, [shortcode]) are replaced with dynamic content. Shortcodes are a way to include potentially dangerous content in a safe way. ■

WP-Advanced

As the name suggests, the WP-Advanced forum is a place for the serious and complex problem areas. Someone might be trying to do something that is so squirrelly and complicated that no one has tried it before. The person might stop by this forum to problem solve with members or to pick the brains of other developers.

Your WordPress

Everybody is proud of a job well done. Perhaps you've just designed a new theme or built a new plugin that implements some crazy new feature. The Your WordPress forum is not a place to ask for help but to show off your accomplishment and get a pat on the back, and maybe give someone else a pat on the back, as well. If you're smart, you can get ideas here that you can possibly mash-up into something else without wholesale stealing them.

Miscellaneous

As the title suggests, the Miscellaneous forum is for any type of request or thread that doesn't fit anywhere else. I've seen all kinds of things discussed here (mostly WordPress-related, but some not). It might be recommendations for a plugin to do something or solicitations for hosting recommendations. Whatever the request, if it fits nowhere else, it has a home in the Miscellaneous forum.

Requests and Feedback

In the WordPress world, there are many passionate users. They love WordPress but also have better ideas for it. At least, they think they are good ideas. Many good ideas end up making it into the core, while unpopular or unwise ideas do not. The Requests and Feedback forum is one of the locations designated for feature requests.

Alpha/Beta

With a three-four month development cycle on most major WordPress releases, an increasing number of testers and users use early stage (alpha, alpha-danger-danger, beta1, beta2, RC1, and so on) versions and nightly builds. While these pre-release versions are not officially supported, they can be discussed in this forum.

Posting in the support forums

Posting in the support forums is straightforward. If you have a WordPress.org username, you can log on immediately and start posting your questions or helping other people with theirs. If you don't, however, follow these steps to get up and running quickly:

1. In the upper-right corner of http://wordpress.org, click the Register link to the right of the Login form.

2. On the register page, as shown in Figure 4.3, enter a username and password for your new account.

3. Optionally, add information about your Web site, location, occupation, and interests.

4. If you want to hear important WordPress announcements (important when critical security problems arise, and so on), make sure you select the Subscribe to announcement list check box as well.

5. Check your e-mail for a randomly created password.

FIGURE 4.3

The registration form for the WordPress support forum

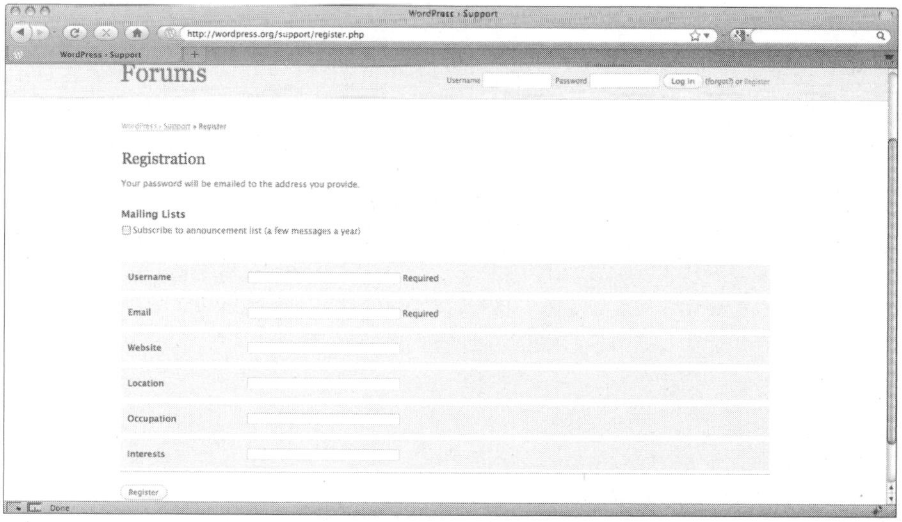

Of course, these steps are just for getting set up for an account. If you actually want to post a new topic, descend into one of the sub-forums and start a new topic. Here are the steps:

1. **Click Add New next to the sub-forum title.** A form appears at the bottom of the sub-forum, as shown in Figure 4.4.

2. **Enter a descriptive title.** Remember people won't click on the topic unless it catches their eye.

3. **Select the version of WordPress from the drop-down menu.** This is also very important as it will help support-forum volunteers advise you in a way that is consistent with your version of the software.

4. **Type your question.** Be helpful. Think about what someone might want to know concerning your particular question. If it's a theme issue, make sure you include information about your operating system and browser. If it's a permalink problem, it would be helpful to know information about your server.

5. **Tag your content with helpful and descriptive keywords designed to help people find your question.**

FIGURE 4.4

Posting a new topic is pretty easy. When you click Add New, this form appears at the bottom of the forum.

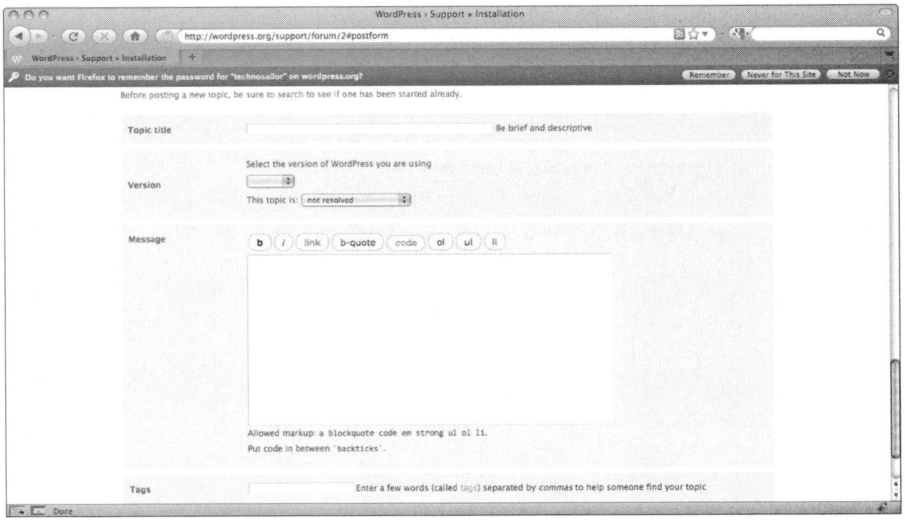

Summary

- The Codex is the official online documentation for WordPress.
- The Codex is also available in multiple languages as part of internationalization (i18n) and localization efforts.
- There are a number of WordPress mailing lists that community members can, and in some cases should, subscribe to. These mailing lists are for coders, testers, professional services consultants, and more.
- The support forums provide a rich depth of searchable content and archived assistance between users.
- Being descriptive when posting new forum topics can ensure your question gets answered quickly.

Part II

Working with Plugins

Extending WordPress with Plugins

T he beauty of WordPress is its extensibility. Some of the WordPress lead developers have said that the most exciting WordPress features are the ones that don't ship with the software.

It is possible to make WordPress do just about anything you can think of with plugins. The framework for this extensibility is made up of a very simple *hook* system. With hooks, plugin developers can change existing content and hypertext markup language (HTML) before it is actually rendered by the browser, or they can fire off actions when a certain event occurs.

Hooks are places in the WordPress code where plugins have the capability to "hook" into the core and add some bit of functionality. Hooks are an extensive part of the WordPress plugin architecture and are essential to the concept of modifying WordPress behavior without modifying any core code.

This event-driven architecture gives plugin developers extreme flexibility. In fact, many core WordPress features are implemented through the hooks system, which means that plugins are not second-class functionality, but are on par with the WordPress core. The WordPress core developers have not been hesitant to add more and more hooks to WordPress. It's really generally only a matter of asking.

Using this hook architecture, WordPress is able to remain small in size and lean in scope. It is not the intention to make WordPress everything to everybody by default. It is about creating a lightweight blogging platform that has all the necessary framework elements to enable users to extend and modify WordPress to fit their specific needs.

IN THIS CHAPTER

Understanding WordPress hooks

Writing your own plugin

Extending the WordPress Admin

Creating events with actions

Modifying content with filters

Using multi-argument hooks

Localizing plugins

Cross-Reference

There are more than 800 hooks in WordPress 2.8. It is not possible to cover them all in this chapter. However, I have created a complete core hook reference guide that you can refer to (see Appendix A). ∎

Understanding WordPress Hooks

The bulk of the WordPress plugin application programming interface (API) is made up of two core elements, or hooks: *actions* and *filters*. They are conceptually different, but very similar in practice.

Actions are event-driven. When specific events occur in WordPress, such as saving a post, loading an admin page, or sending HTML to a browser, plugins have the capability to "hook" into these events and create their own events. As an example, a plugin might ping a server when a post is saved. Or it might update a social network profile using their API when a WordPress user profile is updated.

Filters modify content. The content could be the text of a post, an author name, or an option pulled from the database. Filters always take data and returns data after processing it. An example of a plugin using a filter would be modifying a user avatar with a different third-party avatar solution. In this scenario, a filter might replace the WordPress default Gravatar-based avatar and replace it with a user's Twitter avatar. As the name suggests, filters are always Data in, Data out while actions are event-based and do not require any kind of data processing.

Note

At this point, it might be necessary to distinguish some terminology. On the Web, an avatar is an image or icon that represents a person. The term was made popular in recent years by virtual reality games like World of Warcraft and Second Life, but has become a commonly used word in social networks as well. Gravatar, short for Globally Recognized Avatar, is a specific brand associated with providing avatars. Gravatar.com was purchased by Automattic and is the default provider for WordPress avatars. ∎

The anatomy of a hook

Hooks are generally called using the `add_action()` or `add_filter()` function. They can also be removed by using the `remove_action()` or `remove_filter()` function. You might consider doing this if there are undesirable (or conflicting) events with another plugin, or if you want to disable a WordPress core feature that is implemented through the hooks system.

In their most basic form, these functions take two arguments. The first argument is the *hook name*, such as `save_post` or `the_content`. The second argument is the *callback* you want to pass to the hook, such as `insert_author_description` or `add_google_analytics`. Generally, the second argument is a custom function provided in a plugin or theme `functions.php` file, but it can also be a core WordPress function or a class and method name.

Tip

If the callback is a function, the second argument will be a string that is the name of the function (for instance `add_action('pre_post_save','function_name');`). If you are using object-oriented programming

(OOP) and need to refer to a class and method, do so by making the callback an array with the first member the name of the class and the second member the name of the method (for instance, `add_action('pre_post_save',array('className','methodName'));`). ■

Note

Though most custom functionality comes via plugin files, you can also have code included in a file called `functions.php` **inside a theme. Most themes will already have a** `functions.php`, **but if yours doesn't, you can simply add one. This file exists so that theme authors can provide custom functionality specific to their theme, and it behaves exactly the same way that plugins work. The only difference is that you don't have to manually activate this file in the same way that you do for a plugin. It is included automatically when the theme is active.** ■

While most of the time it is only necessary to provide the hook name and the callback as two arguments when calling a hook, there are two other arguments that you can optionally use. The first of these arguments (and the third overall) is *priority*. Priority is an integer that designates which order the hook reference is called. The lower the number, the higher its priority, and thus, the earlier it is called. This is particularly useful when you have a number of other plugins or functions hooking to the same hook. The higher priority hook reference will be executed first. The default priority is 10.

Note

WordPress hooks are scattered throughout the WordPress core. Before any HTML is returned to the browser on a page load, WordPress runs through a lot of code determining what the client (browser) needs to see. Throughout this process, hooks are "fired," or executed. Plugins and the theme `functions.php` file add all the necessary callbacks to each hook in a queue, based on priority order. When WordPress fires each hook, it iterates through every callback tied to that hook. All the resulting HTML and Cascading Style Sheets (CSS) in aggregate make up what is ultimately returned to the browser and seen by the reader. ■

The final argument is the number of accepted arguments you want to pass to the callback. In most cases, a hook only provides a single parameter and so this is not needed. However, some hooks can provide more than one parameter, and your callback might need that extra data. In this case, your hook reference would have an integer designating the number of additional arguments to pass.

Theme hooks

It is becoming standard for theme authors to include hooks in themes. Themes like the popular Thesis theme make it a point of loading many custom hooks into the themes. Not only does it benefit users to have a lot of different options in the theme they use, but also has a significant benefit of turning themes into extendable frameworks.

However, themes are not required to have any extra hooks. They can operate perfectly fine without them. Three hooks, however, are virtually required for inclusion in any theme because so many plugins use them. Two of these hooks — `wp_head()` and `wp_footer()` — actually look like function calls and not actual hooks, but buried beneath the function are action hooks. The third is a more standard-looking hook and is positioned in the comment form:

```php
<?php do_action('comment_form', $post->ID); ?>
```

Writing Your Own Plugin

With an understanding behind the concept of hooks (I'll talk more specifically about them in a bit), it's time to get your feet wet by writing your own plugin. Doing this is fun and can open up a whole new world of possibilities. There is a sizable plugin repository already at `http://wordpress.org/extend/plugins/`, but sometimes you may have to write your own to accomplish a task no one else has or to do it better. Whether you write the plugin for your own use or release it to the world, you are sure to begin to understand the plugin building process better the more you do it.

Every plugin requires a set of headers for use in the plugin. You should try to come up with a unique name for the plugin. WordPress reads these headers and uses them in a variety of ways, including displaying them inside the WordPress administration panel (referred to as the WordPress Admin) and determining whether there are upgrades available for the plugin.

In this chapter, I walk through the steps to build a plugin that adds copyright text throughout a blog. To do this, you must first create a new folder inside of WordPress' `wp-content/plugins/` folder that you'll call `copyright-notices` and then create a new file inside that folder called `copyright-notices.php`. The headers for this plugin might look like the code shown in Listing 5.1.

LISTING 5.1

The headers needed by WordPress to display (and make available) a plugin in the WordPress Admin

```
/*
Plugin Name: Copyright Notices
Plugin URI: http://emmense.com/copyright-notices/
Description: A plugin that allows the user to set Copyright text in the
    theme and control it from WordPress Admin.
Author: Aaron Brazell
Version: 1.0
Author URI: http://technosailor.com/
*/
```

The headers are self-descriptive but it is important to note that only a plugin name is absolutely required. WordPress parses this data out for use in the WordPress Admin, as shown in Figure 5.1.

Note

All plugin files are created with the PHP scripting language. Though PHP files can have HTML in them, unless otherwise specified, every file must begin with the PHP opening tag `<?php`. You can optionally add a closing `?>` at the end of the file, but if you do, ensure there is no extra whitespace or your blog will break. ∎

FIGURE 5.1

Using the header data provided in a plugin, WordPress is able to parse out the key information such as the name and description of the plugin.

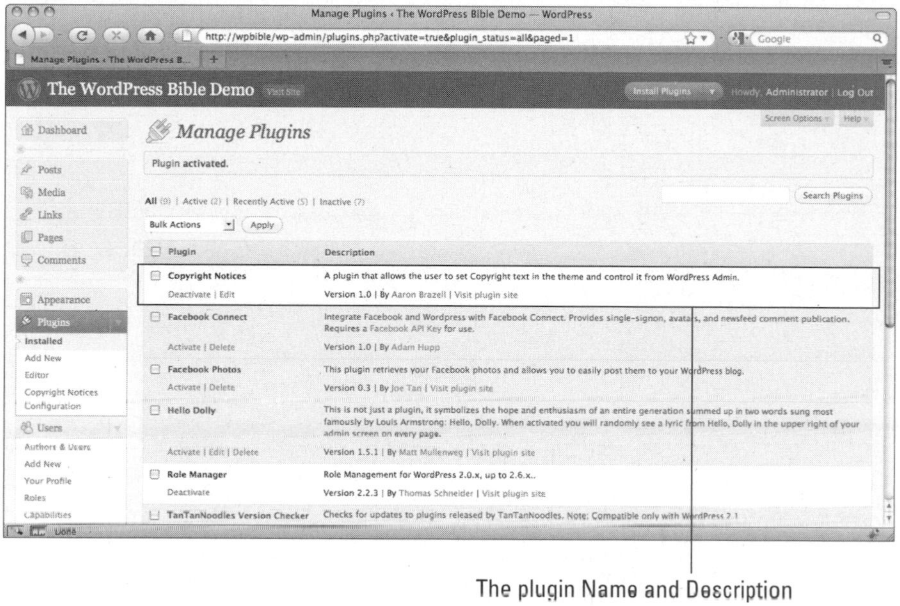

The plugin Name and Description

Extending the WordPress Admin

Development of administrative interfaces for a plugin is often where plugin development begins. Conscientious plugin developers provide some sort of interface for managing her plugin without having to resort to asking the end user to go in and edit a file. However, taking this kind of approach to plugin development ensures problems later on when the plugin is upgraded, because any modifications made to the plugin will be overwritten. It's much better practice to actually store setting data in the database and avoid hard coding it in the plugin itself.

Aside from the upgrade complications involved in not having a WordPress Admin page, there is also a usability question. Most WordPress users are non-technical users. They don't know what to do with PHP or object-oriented programming. They don't know what a curly brace means or why semicolons are important. Making them dive into code to configure the plugin is a recipe for making sure the plugin doesn't have a high adoption rate.

Fortunately, WordPress offers a large number of hooks and functions inside the WordPress Admin that assist in creating new administrative plugins. Next, I'll show you how to build a very simple plugin that adds a Copyright line in the footer of a blog and has an administrative interface to do this.

Creating an admin interface

The first step in creating a Copyright plugin is to create a function that generates the HTML that is going to be used inside the WordPress Admin. Most of the administrative duties will be done in this function, as shown in Listing 5.2.

LISTING 5.2

This function includes code to render an administrative interface

```
function copyright_notices_admin()
{
    ?>
    <div class="wrap">
        <?php screen_icon(); ?>
        <h2>Copyright Notices Configuration</h2>
        <p>On this page, you will configure all the aspects of this
plugins.</p>
        <form action="" method="post" id="copyright-notices-conf-form">
            <h3><label for="copyright_text">Copyright Text to be inserted
in the footer of your theme:</label></h3>
            <p><input type="text" name="copyright_text" id="copyright_
text" value="<?php echo esc_attr( get_option('copyright_notices_text') )
?> " /></p>
            <p class="submit"><input type="submit" name="submit"
value="Update options &raquo;" /></p>
        </form>
    </div>
    <?php
}
```

On the Web

The code in Listing 5.2 is available for download at www.wiley.com/go/wordpressbible.com. ∎

The first thing you might notice about the code in Listing 5.2 is that I have used very specific HTML markup to create the administrative panel. For consistency with the rest of the WordPress Admin, it is a good practice to fall into. The entirety of the panel should be wrapped in `<div class= "wrap"></div>` to inherit the default formatting for the page. Main titles of sections of the panel should be wrapped in `<h2>` tags. The `screen_icon()` function inserts an appropriate icon, associated with the section of the WordPress Admin that the page will be loaded under, next to the header. You'll use a lot of form fields, and so you'll want to wrap the `<label>` tags in `<h3>` tags.

Tip

To avoid the possibility of function names colliding, adopt a naming convention that is unique to you. It could be an abbreviation for the plugin followed by an underscore (like `mup_doit()`) or it could mean using a class to "namespace" your functions. If a user activates your plugin and it has the same function name as a core function or a function provided elsewhere in WordPress, they will get errors and not be able to use your plugin. ∎

Having observed standard formatting (which, of course, you can depart from with varying results), you'll notice that when you try to activate the plugin on the Plugins page, it will gladly activate, but nothing will happen.

Looking further at the code, the second thing you'll notice is the use of the get_option() function. Don't worry about this too much right now. Until you tie the plugin to the database, nothing will actually be displayed here. Later, it will show saved text and can be updated at will.

Adding an admin panel to the WordPress Admin navigation menu

Next you need to hook this function into WordPress itself by adding an Admin panel to the WordPress Admin navigation menu. Right now, this function is merely a standalone function. You need to tell WordPress about it and give it a menu position. To do this, you will create a new function and use the add_submenu_page() function to register the new panel.

The add_submenu_page() function exists to enable you to insert new WordPress Admin pages under top-level navigation items. It takes six parameters:

- **$parent.** The filename of the parent page. In this case, you are using plugins.php, which is the page that controls the Plugins top-level navigation item. Others might be dashboard.php, edit.php, and so on.
- **$page_title.** The name of the page you want to add.
- **$menu_title.** How the page will be displayed in the navigation.
- **$access_level** A capability synonymous with the permission level that should have access (such as edit_options for the blog admin).
- **$handle.** A unique text string ("handle") to identify your menu item.
- **$callback.** The function that is handling the initialization/execution of this page.

Finally, you'll want to plug that function into the menu using the admin_menu action, as shown in Listing 5.3.

LISTING 5.3

Integrating the code for the new administrative page

```
function copyright_notices_admin_page() {
    add_submenu_page( 'plugins.php','Copyright Notices Configuration',
  'Copyright Notices Configuration', 'manage_options', 'copyright-notices'
  'copyright_notices_admin');
}
add_action('admin_menu', 'copyright_notices_admin_page');
```

On the Web

The code in Listing 5.3 is available for download at www.wiley.com/go/wordpressbible.com. ■

Tip

This is not dictated anywhere within the WordPress universe, but I make it standard habit when developing plugins, to tie plugin admin pages under the plugins primary navigation item in the WordPress Admin. A good example of this is the Akismet anti-spam plugin that places its configuration under Plugins. As a best practice, I find it almost universally better and semantically correct to have these kinds of admin panels located there. However, WordPress gives you the capability to create a new navigation under any primary navigation area or to create an entirely new one. Many developers choose these other options because there is no right or wrong convention. ■

As an alternative to the `add_submenu_page()` function, you can use one of the wrapper functions that WordPress provides around this function. These alternative functions are listed in Table 5.1.

TABLE 5.1

Alternative Functions for Adding Submenu Pages

Function Name	Function Syntax	Function Description
`add_management_page()`	add_management_page('Name of Plugin', 'Menu Title', 'capability', 'handle', callback);	Adds a submenu page under the Tools primary navigation.
`add_options_page()`	add_options_page('Name of Plugin', 'Menu Title', 'capability', 'handle', callback);	Adds a submenu page under the Settings primary navigation.
`add_theme_page()`	add_theme_page('Name of Plugin', 'Menu Title', 'capability', 'handle', callback);	Adds a submenu page under the Appearance primary navigation.
`add_users_page()`	add_users_page('Name of Plugin', 'Menu Title', 'capability', 'handle', callback);	Adds a submenu page under the Users primary navigation.
`add_dashboard_page()`	add_dashboard_page('Name of Plugin', 'Menu Title', 'capability', 'handle', callback);	Adds a submenu page under the Dashboard primary navigation.
`add_posts_page()`	add_posts_page('Name of Plugin', 'Menu Title', 'capability', 'handle', callback);	Adds a submenu page under the Posts primary navigation.
`add_media_page()`	add_media_page('Name of Plugin', 'Menu Title', 'capability', 'handle', callback);	Adds a submenu page under the Media primary navigation.
`add_links_page()`	add_links_page('Name of Plugin', 'Menu Title', 'capability', 'handle', callback);	Adds a submenu page under the Links primary navigation.

Function Name	Function Syntax	Function Description
`add_pages_page()`	add_pages_page('Name of Plugin', 'Menu Title', 'capability', 'handle', callback);	Adds a submenu page under the Pages primary navigation.
`add_comments_ page()`	add_comments_page('Name of Plugin', 'Menu Title', 'capability', 'handle', callback);	Adds a submenu page under the Comments primary navigation.
`add_page_menu()`	add_page_menu('Name of Plugin', 'Menu Title', 'capability', 'handle', callback, 'Custom icon URL');	Adds a new primary navigation menu item with the added benefit of being able to specify an Icon for the menu. If no icon is specified, a default will be used.

With your submenu added under the plugins primary navigation, you should see a new submenu item called Copyright Notices Configuration. Clicking this should show you a page that looks like the page shown in Figure 5.2.

FIGURE 5.2

Using the `add_submenu_page()` within a function that hooks into `admin_menu` enables you to display your own custom Admin menu.

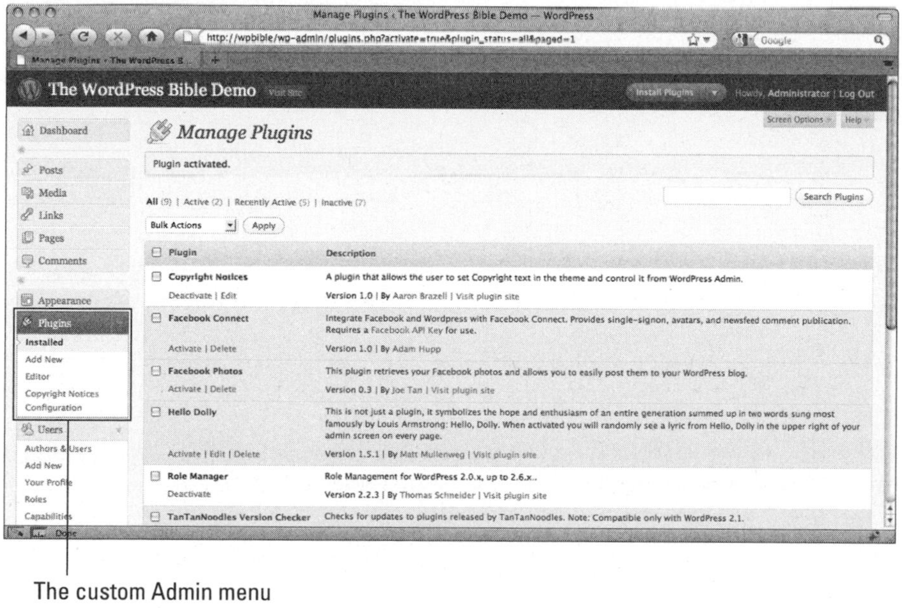

The custom Admin menu

Creating unique nonces for plugin form security

Nonces are an important part of plugin security for WordPress. They exist to ensure that a hacker or spammer does not forge data being sent by a form. Nonce is a computer science word meaning "a number used once" and is a unique identifier for a request. To secure your plugin from cross site request forgery, or more commonly known as CSRF, you need to ensure that you create a unique nonce in your form. You can do this by passing a distinct and unique string to the `wp_nonce_field()` function from inside your `<form>` tags. On the other end of the request, you will also verify that this randomly generated number is authentic. With the nonce included, the code for your form would look like Listing 5.4.

LISTING 5.4

Securing the form with a nonce

```
function copyright_notices_admin()
{
    ?>
    <div class="wrap">
        <h2>Copyright Notices Configuration</h2>
        <p>On this page, you will configure all the aspects of this
plugins.</p>
        <form action="" method="post" id="copyright-notices-conf-form">
            <h3><label for="copyright_text">Copyright Text to be inserted
in the footer of your theme:</label></h3>
            <p><input type="text" name="copyright_text" id="copyright_
text" value=" <?php echo esc_attr( get_option('copyright_notices_text') )
?> " /></p>
            <p class="submit"><input type="submit" name="submit"
value="Update options &raquo;" /></p>
            <?php wp_nonce_field('copyright_notices_admin_options-
update'); ?>
        </form>
    </div>
    <?php
}
```

On the Web

The code in Listing 5.4 is available for download at www.wiley.com/go/wordpressbible.com. ∎

Processing data and interacting with the database

Next, you need to add the form to the database. To do this you first need to verify that the request is authentic by checking the nonce created in Listing 5.4 using the `check_admin_referer()` function. After the request is verified, update the database with the plugin API provided by WordPress. The code to do this is shown in Listing 5.5.

LISTING 5.5

Code to update options and redirect to the same page if the update occurs successfully

```
function save_copyright_notices()
{
    if( check_admin_referer('copyright_notices_admin_options-update') )
    {
        if( update_option( 'copyright_notices_test', stripslashes( $_
POST['copyright_text'] ) ) )
            wp_redirect( __FILE__ . '?updated=1' );
    }
}
add_action( 'load-copyright-notices.php', 'save_copyright_notices' );
```

On the Web

The code in Listing 5.5 is available for download at www.wiley.com/go/wordpressbible.com. ∎

In this listing, you have specifically checked the nonce with `check_admin_referer()`. In the event of a *Cross Site Request Forgery* (CSRF) attack, this check would fail and nothing would happen. Because this works in the context of your plugin, the rest of the code in this listing will also work.

After the nonce check is verified, you can use the `update_option()` to change the value. You are simply using the form data and don't have to worry about doing a lot of data sanitization. WordPress already does the heavy lifting in this area.

Note

One of the many benefits of staying within the framework of the WordPress API is that you can count on data being sanitized while using `add_option()` **and** `update_option()`. **Likewise, these functions will serialize non-string data that you might pass to it, and** `get_option()` **will un-serialize data automatically. You get out what you put in.** ∎

The final portion of the code instructs WordPress to display a friendly "Options Saved" message if the transaction was successful. Congratulations. You have created your first WordPress plugin. With hooks, though, you can do even more to this plugin.

Loading JavaScript libraries

WordPress comes pre-packaged with a number of JavaScript libraries commonly used in user interface and Ajax development. The most common libraries — jQuery, Prototype, and Scriptaculous — are all bundled with WordPress, with jQuery being the preferred library for WordPress core development.

Cross-Reference

Details of all the JavaScript libraries that come bundled with WordPress are provided in Chapter 10. ∎

Note

Ajax is an abbreviation of Asynchronous JavaScript and XML. Ajax is a loose-fitting word that describes highly interactive and transactional programming. It is notable because a Web site using Ajax can load data and perform actions transparently without the need for a refresh of the browser page. WordPress uses Ajax for a number of things, including Quick Edit functionality, category and tag creation from the Write screen, and more. ∎

There are specific mechanisms in place to ensure that scripts are loaded with required dependencies and, of course, you as a plugin or theme developer, have the tools needed to allow your own JavaScript files and libraries to be loaded. WordPress does this using two functions: `wp_enqueue_script()` and `wp_register_script()`.

Preparing JavaScript with wp_enqueue_script()

The first function used to add a script to the WordPress page load is `wp_enqueue_script()`. It takes all the JavaScript that it has to load and orders the scripts according to dependency. Typically, this function takes one or two arguments, unless it requires another library. Add-ons or plugins for existing JavaScript frameworks fall into the latter category.

The first argument is a friendly name, or a handle, for the script. This handle might already exist if it comes preloaded with WordPress or if it has been registered (using `wp_register_script()`) somewhere else via the plugin. Otherwise, you can call a new piece of JavaScript anything as long as it is unique.

Note

Using a non-unique name will not break WordPress, but it will replace a previously named script. Likewise, if another `wp_enqueue_script()` is used in another plugin or later in your own plugin and it uses the same handle, then whichever script is declared last wins. ∎

The second argument is the URL or path to the JavaScript file. It is optional, but if provided, it will also register the script with WordPress (similar to `wp_register_script()`).

The third argument is a PHP array that lists each required library. Note that this list of libraries is by handle, not by URL. Optionally, you could add a fourth argument designating a version number of the library (such as 1.2 for jQuery 1.2), and a fifth argument that you would set to `true` if you want the JavaScript loaded in the footer or `false` if not. By default, the version is always the most recent and scripts are not loaded in the footer — they are loaded in the head. An example of loading the jQuery Cycle plugin is shown in Listing 5.6.

LISTING 5.6

Loading the jQuery Cycle plugin

```
wp_enqueue_script('jquery=cycle','scripts/jquery.cycle.all.js',
    array('jquery'));
```

Creating new Dashboard widgets

With the advent of WordPress 2.7, the project formerly known as "Crazyhorse," a major usability concern was addressed. One of the longest-standing requests in the WordPress community was to provide a way for users to customize the WordPress Admin Dashboard. This request was not only addressed on a global level; it was also addressed on an individual user level.

The Dashboard incorporates the "drag and drop" capability, enabling you to pull widgets around and place them in the Dashboard according to preference. You can also hide widgets. Even more importantly, plugin developers can now make new Dashboard widgets available. Creating new widgets for the Dashboard requires three things: a function that generates the HTML in a widget, a function that registers the widget for the Dashboard, and a line that hooks the second function into the proper hook. An example of this widget creation is shown in Listing 5.7.

LISTING 5.7

An example of how to add a Dashboard widget

```
function example_db_widget_html()
{
    ?>
    <p class="sub">A great (but useless) Dashboard Widget</p>
    <p>Hello World!</p>
    <?php
}
function example_db_widget_init()
{
    wp_add_dashboard_widget('example-dashboard-widget','Example Widget',
    'example_db_widget_html');
}
add_action('wp_dashboard_setup','example_db_widget_init');
```

On the Web

The code in Listing 5.7 is available for download at www.wiley.com/go/wordpressbible.com. ■

In this code, the first function, `example_db_widget_html()`, provides HTML for the widget. Its formatting matches existing WordPress Dashboard widgets for consistency. While the function in this example is fairly useless, it demonstrates exactly what this type of function should look like. You can, of course, use it for anything. Many plugin developers use data from third-party APIs such as Google Data APIs, Google Maps, or anything that fits their purposes.

The second function, `example_dv_widget_init()`, provides controller code that makes the widget available to WordPress. It only needs the `wp_add_dashboard_widget()` function. This function requires three arguments. The first argument is a unique handler for the widget. This name will also become part of the CSS class that wraps around the HTML, so you can apply a custom look and feel for the widget. The second argument is the display name for the widget. Finally, the third argument is the *callback*, or function name, that will provide the HTML. In this case, the callback is the name for the first function, `example_db_widget_html`.

Note

Callbacks are used in programming to refer to an external function, class, or method that handles the actual execution of code. ■

The third portion of this code hooks the `example_db_widget_init()` function into the `wp_dashboard_setup` hook. I talk about hooks next. However, it is essential for the code to get "hooked" into the WordPress runtime.

Creating Events with Actions

Now that you've created your administrative panel and have stored your copyright text in the database, you can use it within WordPress. The most obvious place for this is in the footer of your theme. Fortunately, most themes come with a `wp_footer` action that you can use to display the copyright text.

But first, you need to write a function that will display the copyright text. This might look like Listing 5.8.

Cross-Reference

It is recommended that every theme have the `wp_head` and `wp_footer` hooks built in. This and other best practices for themes are discussed in more detail in Chapter 11. ■

LISTING 5.8

A simple function to display copyright information

```
function display_copyright()
{
    if( $copyright_text = get_option('copyright_notices_text' ) )
```

```
    {
          echo '<p class="copyright_text">' . $copyright_text . '</p>';
    }
}
```

Because you are using an action hook to accomplish the task, there is no need to pass any arguments in the function. This is a distinct difference from filters that require an argument to be passed.

Now that you have created a semi-useful function for adding copyright text, you can add it to the theme via an action. For this, we use the action hook wp_footer like this:

```
add_action('wp_footer','display_copyright');
```

When you hook the display_copyright() function to the wp_footer hook, the function is added to the queue, to be executed when the wp_footer hook is fired in the header of the theme. In order for this to work, the wp_footer(); function (which is a wrapper around the wp_footer action hook) must be included in the theme.

The final code for this example looks like the code shown in Listing 5.9.

LISTING 5.9

The copyright code and appropriate hook Inclusion

```
function display_copyright()
{
    if( $copyright_text = get_option('copyright_notices_text' ) )
    {
        echo '<p class="copyright_text">' . $copyright_text . '</p>';
    }
}
add_action('wp_footer','display_copyright');
```

Modifying Content with Filters

The second kind of hook is called a *filter*. Filters, as their name suggests, take data, do something to it, and return modified data back. They are useful if you want to do something such as add an attribution notice to the end of every post or generate custom content for feeds. As an example, I'll show you how to add some copyright text to the end of every feed item to ensure that anyone using the feed cannot do so without some kind of enforced copyright notice (effective in combating spam blogs that scrape content and repurpose it as their own).

The function for adding this line might look something like the code shown in Listing 5.10.

Function that adds a copyright notice to the end of post content

```
function display_copyright_feed( $post_content )
{
    if( !$copyright_text = get_option('copyright_notices_text') )
        return $post_content;
    return $post_content . $copyright_text;
}
```

This function simply adds the attribution line to the end of the content and, for all intents and purposes, will work fine. Instead, though, you want to ensure that it only displays when the_ content() function (which includes the_content filter) is executed in a feed. You do that by using conditional logic with is_feed(), as shown in Listing 5.11.

Using conditional logic, you can determine to which post content you want to add the copyright notice

```
function display_copyright_feed( $post_content )
{
    if( !$copyright_text = get_option('copyright_notices_text') || !is_
feed() )
        return $post_content;
    return $post_content . $copyright_text;
}
```

Tip
WordPress has several expected coding conventions. They are enforced throughout the core and are often adopted by plugin and theme authors as well. The sample code shown earlier in Listing 5.2 demonstrates one of those coding conventions by checking if the conditional logic is not true. Checking for false (as in "this post is not in category 4") is often easier and cleaner than checking for true. ■

In this case, you performed a conditional check to ensure that the content was not in a feed. If it is in a feed, you return the content exactly as you got it. However, if it is not in a feed, then you proceed to return the post content with the attribution line appended to the end.

Finally, you need to hook this function to a hook like this:

```
add_filter('the_content','display_copyright_feed');
```

As with an action, hooking the `display_copyright_feed()` function to the `the_content` hook causes it to be fired every time `the_content` is fired in the Loop, the mechanism used by WordPress to generate and iterate over posts. Because this is a filter, the `content_attribution()` function expects the post content to be passed to it and it return modified content back into the Loop.

Cross-Reference

The Loop is an integral part of WordPress. It is where the magic involving printing blog posts and content into a theme happens. The mechanics of the Loop are discussed in Chapter 8. For now, just understand that it is where WordPress processes the requirements for the selection of posts, fetches them from the database, and returns the data to WordPress for processing. It is, notably, how WordPress is able to have a number of posts on one page, rendering the blog in expected reverse-chronological order. ■

The final code block for this section looks like the code shown in Listing 5.12.

LISTING 5.12

Using a filter to add a copyright notice to the end of every post

```
function display_copyright_feed( $post_content )
{
    if( !$copyright_text = get_option('copyright_notices_text') || !is_
  feed() )
        return $post_content;
    return $post_content . $copyright_text;
}
add_filter('the_content','display_copyright_feed');
```

On the Web

The code in Listing 5.12 is available for download at `www.wiley.com/go/wordpressbible.com`. ■

Using Multi-Argument Hooks

There are certain exceptions to the one-in, one-out nature of most hooks. In some cases, you need to be able to pass arguments to the functions being hooked and traditional hook usage won't cut it. The fourth parameter for a hook, which was discussed at the beginning of this chapter, specifies the number of arguments the function can take. If, for example, a filter requires three arguments, you have to hook in like this:

```
add_filter('author_link', $modified_link, 10, 3);
```

An action that requires multiple parameters would be hooked into in a similar fashion:

```
add_action('save_post', 'notify_google', 10, 2);
```

Multi-argument hooks can sometimes be a difficult concept to wrap your head around, particularly if you are familiar with PHP development outside of frameworks and software packages such as WordPress. In a traditional sense, if you invoke a function, you need to also be able to directly pass arguments to it. WordPress handles all this transparently, but you do need to ensure that the arguments the function is calling for are available in the scope that the hook is fired in.

For example, if you need to pass the $post variable to an action, you also need to ensure that the $post variable is available to be used in that scope. WordPress handles much of this with core hooks, but defining your own hooks in plugins and themes could prove tricky if you don't understand this concept.

Tip

You can add your own hooks with the `do_action()` and `apply_filters()` functions. Each function takes a single argument that designates the hook name, while actions take optional additional values to be passed to the function (multi-argument hooks), and filters require a second parameter with the value that is being filtered; for example, `do_action('below_post_1')` or `apply_filters('author_name','Aaron Brazell')`. ■

Note

Variable scope is an important subject with PHP. It is outside of the scope (pardon the pun) of this book, but it is essential to understand nonetheless. You can find out more about PHP variable scope at `http://us3.php.net/manual/en/language.variables.scope.php`. ■

Localizing Plugins

WordPress development efforts have put a major emphasis on *localization*. Also known as internationalization, or i18n, which means "i plus 18 more letters plus n," WordPress has been translated into more than 70 different languages, from Farsi to Spanish, and even into the obscure language, Esperanto.

Beyond the scope of the core, which many international developers rightly provide internationalization support and translation efforts for, many plugins also support multiple languages. In fact, sometimes efforts go into localizing themes as well.

Localization is not a difficult process but it is a bit of work. Functions exist throughout the WordPress core that you can use in plugins as well. The engine that does the hard work of translation is called gettext and is included in PHP by default. The gettext library offers developers an API for localization and is very robust.

Web Resource

Gettext is a system module that provides an API for translation. PHP comes, by default, with gettext and so it is assumed you have support for it. For more information on gettext, visit the official GNU gettext site (www. gnu.org/software/gettext/) or the PHP gettext documentation (http://us.php.net/gettext). ■

Enabling plugin code for translation

Throughout your plugin code, you should use one of two forms of notation to ensure the gettext API knows to translate the text. Listing 5.13 demonstrates how to use _e() to echo a localized string.

LISTING 5.13

To echo a localized string directly, use the _e() function

```
_e('Hi, my name is Aaron');
```

Likewise, Listing 5.14 shows how to use __() when the localized string is to be returned instead of echoed.

LISTING 5.14

To return the localized string, use the __() function

```
$intro = 'Hi, '. __('my name is') . ' Aaron';
echo $intro;
```

Both examples are valid examples of localizing a string. The _e() constructor is best used for individual terms or commonly used strings, not for sentences. The __() constructor is best used in the context of a longer string, sentence, or paragraph to isolate keywords for translation. However, you can use either interchangeably depending on your preference.

Returning to your copyright plugin, you probably want to localize the code, which is shown in Listing 5.15. In order for localization to occur, each localized string must have a textdomain (which will be covered later in this chapter) passed in as a second argument, and the textdomain must be loaded in the plugin (also covered later, but included in this code).

LISTING 5.15

Localizing the copyright plugin code

```php
<?php
/*
Plugin Name: Copyright Notices
Plugin URI: http://emmense.com/copyright-notices/
Description: A plugin that allows the user to set Copyright text in the
    theme and control it from WordPress Admin.
Author: Aaron Brazell
Version: 1.0
Author URI: http://technosailor.com/
*/
function i18n_copyright()
{
    $plugin_path = plugin_basename( dirname( __FILE__ ) .'/translations' );
    load_plugin_textdomain('copyright-notices', $plugin_path );
}
add_action('init','i18n_copyright');
function copyright_notices_admin_page() {
    add_submenu_page( 'plugins.php',__('Copyright Notices Configuration'),
    __('Copyright Notices Configuration','copyright-notices'), 0, 'manage_
    options', 'copyright-notices', 'copyright_notices_admin');
}
add_action('admin_menu', 'copyright_notices_admin_page');
function copyright_notices_admin()
{
    if( $_POST['submit'] )
        {
            if( check_admin_referer('copyright_notices_admin_options-
    update') )
            {
                $options_saved = false;
                if( $oldvalue = get_option('copyright_notices_text') )
                {
                    update_option( 'copyright_notices_text', $_
    POST['copyright_text'] );
                    if( $oldvalue == get_option('copyright_notices_
    text') )
                    {
                        $options_saved = true;
                    }
                }
                else
                {
                    if( add_option( 'copyright_notices_text', $_
    POST['copyright_text'] ) )
                        {
```

```php
                              $options_saved = true;
                         }
                    }
                }
           }
           if( $options_saved )
           {
                echo '<div id="message" class="updated fade"><p>' . __
   ('Options Saved','copyright-notices') . '.</p></div>';
           }
     ?>
     <div class="wrap">
           <h2><?php _e('Copyright Notices Configuration','copyright-
   notices') ?></h2>
           <p><?php _e('On this page, you will configure all the aspects of
   this plugins.','copyright-notices') ?></p>
           <form action="" method="post" id="copyright-notices-conf-form">
                <h3><label for="copyright_text"><?php _e('Copyright Text to
   be inserted in the footer of your theme','copyright-notices') ?>:</
   label></h3>
                <p><input type="text" name="copyright_text" id="copyright_
   text" value="<?php echo get_option('copyright_notices_text','copyright-
   notices') ?> " /></p>
                <p class="submit"><input type="submit" name="submit"
   value="<?php _e('Update options &raquo;','copyright-notices'); ?>" /></p>
                <?php wp_nonce_field('copyright_notices_admin_options-
   update'); ?>
           </form>
     </div>
     <?php
}
function display_copyright()
{
     if( $copyright_text = get_option('copyright_notices_text' ) )
     {
          echo '<p class="copyright_text">' . $copyright_text . '</p>';
     }
}
add_action('wp_footer','display_copyright');
function display_copyright_feed( $post_content )
{
     if( !$copyright_text = get_option('copyright_notices_text') || !is_
   feed() )
     {
          return $post_content;
     }
     return $post_content . $copyright_text;
}
add_filter('the_content','display_copyright_feed');
```

On the Web

The code in Listing 5.15 is available for download at www.wiley.com/go/wordpressbible.com. ∎

Notice throughout the entire plugin, I've wrapped text that was not inserted into the database because of the action of the user – specifically, form data – in localized functions. Later, I'll get into creating translations for these strings, but for now just note that content sent to the browser that is not the result of user input will be localized.

Sometimes you need to be able to use placeholder in a string because the number or text will change according to the context that the string is used. A simplistic, though not all that useful in the real world, example would be to create a function for use in the copyright plugin admin page that shows how many words have been used in the copyright text. You would use the PHP function printf to do replacements and the translation would occur afterwards, as shown in Listing 5.16.

Web Resource

For more information about the PHP function printf, go to http://us3.php.net/printf. ∎

LISTING 5.16

Using __() and printf() together, you can create dynamic translatable strings

```
function copyright_count_words()
{
    $words = explode(' ', get_option('copyright_notices_text'));
    $word_count = count( $words );
    printf( __('The current copyright text is %d words long.'), $word_count
    );
}
```

There are two other localization functions that are used less often, but you can use nonetheless:

- _c() is used when you want to include a comment for the translator. After the translatable string, a pipe (|) is used with the text of a comment afterwards; for example, _c('Configuration Panel|relates to wp-admin').

- __ngettext() is used with replacement text when there are the chances of singular or plural versions of the text. In the example code shown previously in Listing 5.16, you would instead use the code shown in Listing 5.17.

LISTING 5.17

Using __ngettext() allows you to have singular and plural versions of localized strings

```
function copyright_count_words()
{
    $words = explode(' ', get_option('copyright_notices_text'));
    $word_count = count( $words );
    printf( __ngettext('The current copyright text is only %d word long.',
  'The current copyright text is %d words long.' , $word_count ) );
}
```

Providing a textdomain for the plugin

Textdomains are essential for properly translating the plugin. Once you have marked up the plugin code with all the appropriate translator constructs, you need to load a unique textdomain. This can be any unique string, but it is advisable that you used a name that includes the plugin file name for distinction and clarity.

Because you have named your plugin filename copyright-notices.php, you can simply call the textdomain copyright-notices. You can load this textdomain by creating a function that uses the load_plugin_textdomain() function and hooks into the init action (the very first hook that is executed), as shown in Listing 5.18.

LISTING 5.18

Loading the textdomain

```
function i18n_copyright()
{
    $plugin_path = plugin_basename( dirname( __FILE__ ) .'/translations' );
    load_plugin_textdomain('copyright-notices', $plugin_path );
}
add_action('init','i18n_copyright');
```

The syntax here is pretty simple but important. The first argument passed to the load_plugin_ textdomain() function is the name of the textdomain you chose. The second and third arguments are the path to the plugin folder from ABSPATH and relative to the plugin directory itself (a redundancy that might seem odd but has its purposes in the translation process).

Note

ABSPATH is one of several constants defined in WordPress. You can set it manually, but in almost every case, it should not be. WordPress figures out what ABSPATH should be automatically by figuring out what the absolute path is on the server system. It will always be the absolute path to the document root where WordPress is located. ■

After making sure the plugin will load the proper textdomain and all the translation constructs added, you have to add the textdomain to all translation constructs. All of the constructs, `__()`, `_e()`, `_c()`, and `__ngettext()`, require a second argument for translation. This argument is the textdomain and looks like `__('A string','textdomain')`.

Fortunately, there is a PHP console script provided by WordPress as a separate download that will automatically convert all the translatable elements to the proper format. You can download it at `http://svn.automattic.com/wordpress-i18n/tools/trunk/add-textdomain.php`.

Once this file is downloaded (and uploaded to the server), follow these steps to convert your plugin to the proper format:

1. Type `chmod 755 add-textdomain.php` to ensure you can execute the file from the command line.

2. Type `php add-textdomain.php -i 'copyright-notices' *` to convert all files in the plugin directory (in this case only one) to the proper i18n format.

Tip

If your plugin is in the official WordPress repository (and it should be if you plan to release it to the public and it is General Public License (GPL) or GPL-compatible), you can do this automatically. Under the admin menu, you can click Add Domain to gettext Calls. ■

Generating a POT file for translators

The final step in making your plugin truly localized is to generate a specially formatted template file called a POT file. A portable object template (POT) file contains all the translatable strings in your plugin and it is what other developers and translators work off of when translating your plugin.

Web Resource

An extremely handy plugin for doing most of this directly in WordPress is the Codestyling Localization plugin available at `http://wordpress.org/extend/plugins/codestyling-localization/`. With this plugin, you can create, modify, and translate all from within the WordPress Admin. ■

Fortunately, there are scripts that can automatically generate these files for you. The `makepot.php` file, available with the i18n tools at `http://svn.automattic.com/wordpress-i18n/tools/trunk/`, is one of these files. Like the `add-textdomain.php` file, you should put it on your server or wherever your plugin files are.

To generate a POT file for your plugin, follow these steps:

1. Download all of the i18n files to a separate directory using Subversion.
2. Type chmod –R 755 * from within the i18n tools directory (you must have all the files) to ensure that all the scripts will be executable from the command line.
3. Run php makepot.php wp-plugin ../copyright-notices/ where ../copyright-notices/ is the path to the plugin directory.
4. Type cp copyright-notices.pot ../copyright-notices/ where ../copyright-notices is the directory the plugin is in.

Note

Subversion is the software used for version control of software. It is the tool of choice for WordPress core developers and patch contributors. Subversion, also known as SVN, is an exhaustive topic of its own and is out of scope for this book. However, you can download the official documentation at http://svnbook.red-bean.com/. ∎

If you open up the newly generated POT file in a text editor, you'll see a neatly parsed file that provides all instructions and translatable strings to the translators, as shown in Listing 5.19.

LISTING 5.19

The POT file used to provide string translations

```
# SOME DESCRIPTIVE TITLE.
# Copyright (C) YEAR Aaron Brazell
# This file is distributed under the same license as the PACKAGE package.
# FIRST AUTHOR <EMAIL@ADDRESS>, YEAR.
#
#, fuzzy
msgid ""
msgstr ""
"Project-Id-Version: Copyright Notices 1.0\n"
"Report-Msgid-Bugs-To: http://wordpress.org/tag/copyright-notices\n"
"POT-Creation-Date: 2009-07-19 19:59+0000\n"
"PO-Revision-Date: YEAR-MO-DA HO:MI+ZONE\n"
"Last-Translator: FULL NAME <EMAIL@ADDRESS>\n"
"Language-Team: LANGUAGE <LL@li.org>\n"
"MIME-Version: 1.0\n"
"Content-Type: text/plain; charset=CHARSET\n"
"Content-Transfer-Encoding: 8bit\n"
"Plural-Forms: nplurals=INTEGER; plural=EXPRESSION;\n"
```

continued

LISTING 5.19 *(continued)*

```
#: copyright-notices.php:12 copyright-notices.php:40
msgid "Copyright Notices Configuration"
msgstr ""
#: copyright-notices.php:36
msgid "Options Saved"
msgstr ""
#: copyright-notices.php:41
msgid "On this page, you will configure all the aspects of this plugins."
msgstr ""
#: copyright-notices.php:43
msgid "Copyright Text to be inserted in the footer of your theme"
msgstr ""
#: copyright-notices.php:45
msgid "Update options &raquo;"
msgstr ""
#: copyright-notices.php:74
#, php-format
msgid "The current copyright text is only %d word long."
msgid_plural "The current copyright text is %d words long."
msgstr[0] ""
msgstr[1] ""
#. Plugin Name of an extension
msgid "Copyright Notices"
msgstr ""
#. Plugin URI of an extension
msgid "http://emmense.com/copyright-notices/"
msgstr ""
#. Description of an extension
msgid ""
"A plugin that allows the user to set Copyright text in the theme and
    control "
"it from WordPress Admin."
msgstr ""
#. Author of an extension
msgid "Aaron Brazell"
msgstr ""
#. Author URI of an extension
msgid "http://technosailor.com/"
msgstr ""
```

Summary

- Hooks are what make WordPress so flexible and extensible. Actions are event-driven while filters take a piece of content, perform some sort of action on it, and return it to be used elsewhere.

- When writing your own plugin, make sure you include descriptive header data that will be used by WordPress.

- It's always a good idea to include an admin menu for plugins. It prevents non-technical users from having to figure out code. It also preserves personalization when the plugin is upgraded because settings are stored in the database and not a file.

- WordPress provides a number of functions that you can use to provide new administrative pages. You can hook administrative pages into any aspect of the navigation, but, semantically, they should be hooked under Plugins.

- You protect form data with nonces.

- WordPress includes a lot of JavaScript libraries. You can use any of these or register your own and WordPress will be sure that they are all used in the proper order.

- Allow users to personalize their WordPress Admin experience with Dashboard widgets. New widgets can be added with two functions and a hook.

- Some filters take multiple arguments. This is a tricky concept to understand, but important for anyone wanting to take full advantage of the hook system.

- When localizing plugins, make sure you wrap strings that require translation with `_e()`, `__()`, `_c()` or `__ngettext()`.

- Every localized plugin requires a unique textdomain, which provides translation context for the plugin.

- Use scripts to ensure that localized plugins use the proper textdomain throughout.

- Provide a POT file for translators. There are many people around the world trying to translate WordPress plugins and core into other languages and their workflow and tools require these POT files. There is a script that will generate this for you.

CHAPTER 6

Widgetizing WordPress

IN THIS CHAPTER

Using widgets in WordPress

Building widgets with the widget API

Widgetizing your theme

For many end users, plugin application programming interface (API) is something that doesn't make a whole lot of difference. They know WordPress is easy to use and easy to install. They know they can write posts quickly, get maximum search engine optimization (SEO) benefit, and build traffic. Customization is what they really want, though. They know they want to change the look of their blogs without having to know any code. Fortunately, WordPress' flexible widget system does just that.

Widgets are little pieces of hypertext markup language (HTML) or JavaScript that can be placed on a site to add new functionality. As you travel the Internet, you're likely to find popular widgets in sidebars that list recent posts, comments, popular posts, ads, or blogrolls. Widgets can be anything, and since their adoption in WordPress 2.2, they have become standard fare in WordPress themes and many plugins also provide them.

Widget support used to be provided by a plugin called Sidebar Widgets. While this plugin is still available for older WordPress installs (WordPress 2.1 and earlier), it is now part of the core offering.

Widgets are installed like any other plugin. Simply install widgets in the plugins folder (`/wp-content/plugins/`) and activate. Like plugins, widgets can also be included in a themes `functions.php` file and, in that case, are automatically included when the theme is active.

Using Widgets in WordPress

Widgets are configurable on the Appearance ➪ Widget panel of WordPress Admin and comes with a convenient drag-and-drop-interface. Available (but unused) widgets are in the left column while widgets in use are positioned in expandable sidebar boxes on the right side of the screen, as shown in Figure 6.1.

97

FIGURE 6.1

Widgets are available (and can be reused) on the left side of the Widgets screen. They can be dragged to and from sidebars on the right side.

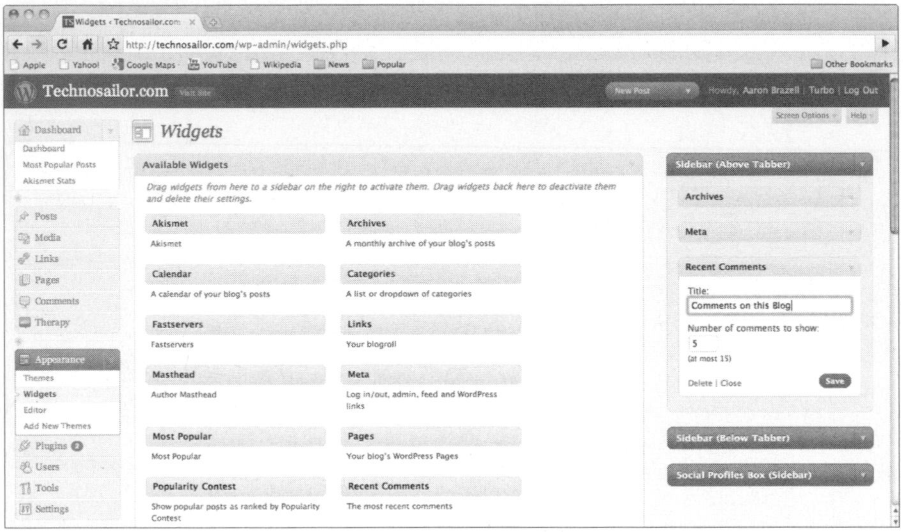

Below the Available Widgets section is a section called Inactive Widgets, which lists the widgets that you don't want to use in a sidebar, but that you want to keep for their settings (see Figure 6.2).

As an example, you'll implement a standard blogroll, something bloggers like putting on their blogs to list other blogs that the author finds interesting. In WordPress, the blogroll widget is called the Links widget. Links have categories, so you can have a group of links with a blogroll category (this exists by default in WordPress), and have a separate group of links for something else. You can manage these links and link categories under the Links menu in the WordPress Admin, as shown in Figure 6.3.

When you drag this widget to Sidebar 1, a dashed line outline appears where the widget will be positioned. These positions are automatically saved when you drop them in new locations. Once you have positioned the widget in the sidebar, you can configure it.

Many widgets have configuration options. The Links widget has five options: a drop-down menu where you choose which category to display links from, and four check boxes that you can select to display various pieces of metadata about each link. For this example, you're going to display all links in the "Blogroll" category with only the link name and description.

FIGURE 6.2

When you drag a widget from a sidebar and drop it back into Available Widgets, it loses all the settings you have configured for it. While this might be okay, sometimes you want to retain the configuration for later use. To do this, drop the widget in the Inactive Widgets section at the bottom of the Widget Admin page.

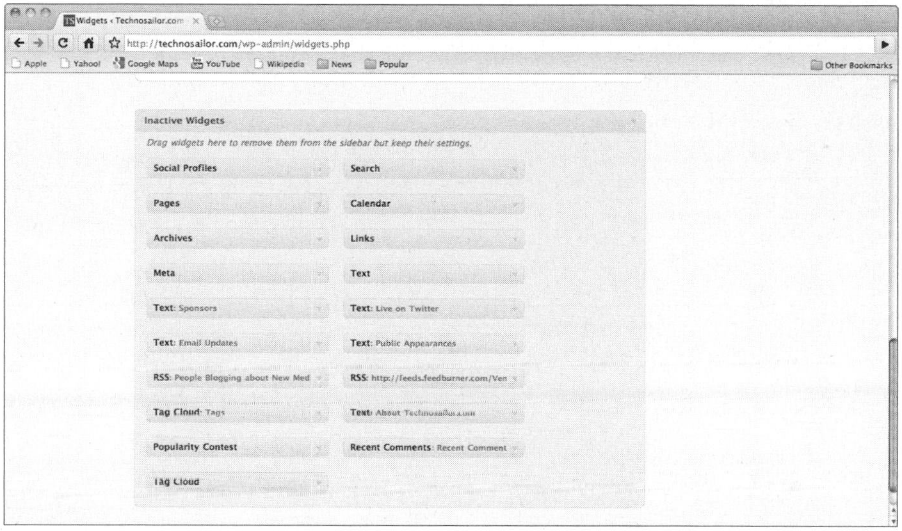

FIGURE 6.3

Each link, which you can configure under the Links category in the WordPress Admin, comes with a number of pieces of data. The ones you'll use most often are the Name of the link (the anchor text), the Web Address, and Categories. You can also add a Description of the link, specify if you want the link to open in a new window, open an image, or open an icon for the link, and other pieces of metadata.

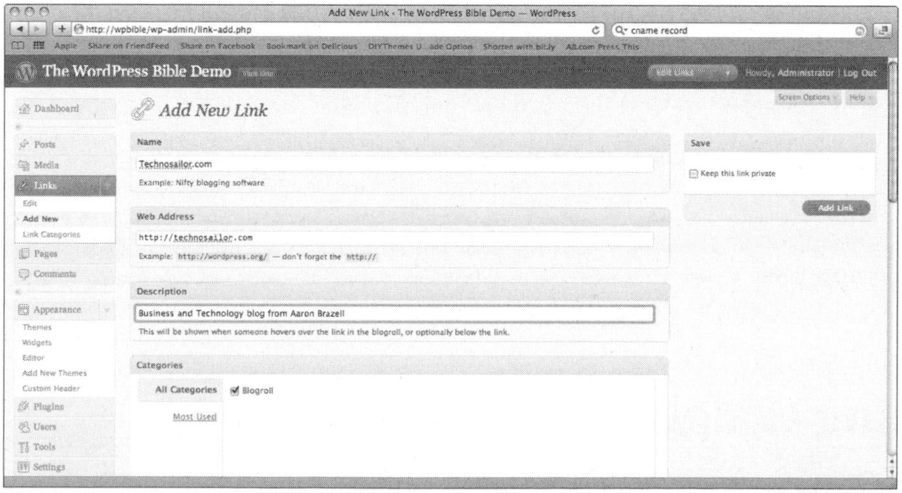

To implement the blogroll with this configuration, follow these steps:

1. **Select Blogroll from the drop-down menu.** By default, this is the only Link category available.

2. **Deselect Show Link Image.**

3. **Select Show Link Name.**

4. **Select Show Link Description.**

5. **Deselect Show Link Rating**

6. **Click Save at the bottom of the widget configuration dialog box, as shown in Figure 6.4.**

FIGURE 6.4

All configuration options are optional. Though you can customize many widgets, default settings will be applied if you choose not to customize.

After you have configured the Links widget, visit your blog. If all has gone well, you will see a new blogroll in your sidebar. Of course, you can add other widgets as well and position them in whichever order you'd like. If you are using a theme that provides more than one sidebar, you will see each of these sidebars as separate "drop zones" in the Widgets interface.

A secondary benefit of widgets, and a new feature since WordPress 2.8, is reusable widgets. You can use every widget in WordPress multiple times in multiple sidebars. Before, there was a restriction that would only allow a widget to be used once. Some older widgets from third-party plugin developers added their own support for more than one of a specific widget, but not all. Now, every widget can be used multiple times if it uses the new improved Widget API that I talk about later in this chapter.

Building Widgets with the Widget API

For plugin developers familiar with creating widgets, the game has recently changed. As of WordPress 2.8, you have an entirely new way of creating widgets. If you're familiar with the old style of creating widgets, you can rest assured that this still works; however, the new API provides an entirely new interface with much improved ease and simplicity. For those of you who are familiar with Object-Oriented Programming (OOP), the new method of adding widgets will not be foreign.

Note

Object-Oriented Programming is a way of programming that involves classes, among other things. Objects are a type of data structure that contains other functions (known as methods), variables (known as properties), and abstractions of data. The main point of OOP is to provide reusable code that separates processes and data, as well as isolating possible problems that can develop from procedural code. Procedural code, on the other hand, is code that is executed in a linear format and often creates messy code with minimal data separation. This effect, known as "spaghetti code," can be complex and difficult to debug. Much of WordPress is written in an object-oriented fashion. KillerPHP.com has a fantastic introduction to object oriented PHP with tutorials and videos at `www.killerphp.com/tutorials/object-oriented-php/.` ■

In order to build a new widget using the new Widget API, you must create a new class (again, in a plugin or the themes `functions.php`) that extends the WP_Widget class. This child class (called such because it is derived from the `WordPress_Widget` parent class) should have three methods (functions). The first method will handle the HTML output of the widget. The second method will handle the control (or configuration panel) of the widget. These two methods were needed in older widget routines, as well. The final method required to use the new Widget API is a save or update method.

Next, you'll build a simple widget that displays a few random trivia bits on every page load.

Building a new widget plugin

To start out, you'll create a new plugin for your widget called `widget_trivia.php`. This plugin will contain standard plugin headers and will include a new child class that extends the WP_Widget class, as shown in Listing 6.1.

Cross-Reference

See Chapter 5 for the basics of creating a new plugin including the metadata required as headers. ■

LISTING 6.1

The basic skeleton of a plugin for building a WordPress 2.8-style widget

```php
<?php
/*
Plugin Name: Random Trivia Bits
Plugin URI: #
Description: A widget that will display random pieces of trivia in a blog
    sidebar
Author: Aaron Brazell
Version: 1.0
```

continued

LISTING 6.1 *(continued)*

```
Author URI: http://technosailor.com/
*/
class Widget_Trivia extends WP_Widget {
    function Widget_Trivia()
    {
    }
    function widget()
    {
    }
    function form()
    {
    }
    function update()
    {
    }
}
```

This is only a framework for your plugin and has nothing in it that will benefit your cause or create widgets. The methods provided will override the methods provided in the WP_Widget parent class. While the constructor method (`Widget_Trivia`) is required as well, I will cover that one last. The first method needed will display the HTML in the sidebar of the blog. For your widget, you'll work on the `widget()` method (see Listing 6.2).

Note

The base WP_Widget class contains three methods which should be overridden by the child class. These three methods are `widget()`, `update()`, and `form()`. The `widget()` method generates HTML. The `update()` method saves the configuration data. The `form()` method provides a user interface for configuring the widget.

LISTING 6.2

The widget method performs all widget logic needed to display the widget HTML on the blog

```
function widget( $args, $instance )
{
    extract( $args, EXTR_SKIP );
    $title = ( $instance['title'] ) ? $instance['title'] : 'Random Trivia';
    $trivia_data = array(
        'The Code of Hammurabi is the oldest known surviving "set of
    laws".',
        'The Battle of Wavre was the last battle of the Napoleonic Wars.',
        'The Hundred Year war lasted 116 years and ended in 1453.'
    );
    echo $before_widget;
```

```
        echo $before_title;
            echo esc__html( $instance['title'] );
        echo $after_title;
        echo $trivia_data[array_rand($trivia_data)];
    echo $after_widget;
}
```

On the Web
The code in Listing 6.2 is available for download at www.wiley.com/go/wordpressbible. ∎

I'll step through this code because it has several important elements that you should understand. First of all, notice that this method (remember, a method is just a function inside a class) takes two arguments. The $args argument is an array containing the standard widget configuration as provided by the theme developer. This includes property values for $before_widget, $after_widget, $before_title, and $after title. You'll use these in this method, so it's important to note where exactly they come from. (I'll talk about widgetizing themes later in this chapter.)

Those of you who are familiar with the old method of developing widgets will note that the $instance argument is new. This is because the new WordPress API allows multiple instances of each plugin. The $instance described here is an array that contains all the configuration options for a particular instance of a widget.

The first event that happens inside this method is an extract() call on $args. You do this to make the theme-provided arguments available for use inside the method. The second parameter, EXTR_SKIP, won't overwrite existing variables, and is always a good safety measure. To ensure there is always a title for the widget, you set one if the instance doesn't have one.

Next, you have to make trivia data available to the widget. In this case, the data is fairly slim. In a real-world scenario, this data might be in the database or pulled from an RSS feed off another site. For the sake of simplicity, though, an array with three bits of trivia is populated.

Finally, the widget generates HTML output from the data passed in $args and your $trivia_data array. Notably, you make use of a WordPress function called esc_html(). This function handles data sanitization for outputted text between HTML tags — most notably taking care of potentially unsafe HTML and character encoding. You should try to maintain the structure shown here when creating output for the widget, but there might be cases where you don't want, or need, to. This is perfectly legitimate.

Creating a control interface for the plugin

An expected, but completely optional, feature for a widget is a control interface. It's in these control interfaces where bloggers can set custom titles for their widgets and configuration options around how data is displayed. The widget in this example is pretty simple so the only thing you want to do is allow the user to set a custom title. To do this, you use (and override) the existing form() method, as shown in Listing 6.3.

LISTING 6.3

The form method is used to provide a widget instance configuration panel

```php
function form( $instance )
{
    ?>
    <p>
        <label for="<?php echo $this->get_field_id( 'title' ); ?>">
        <?php _e( 'Title:' ); ?>
        <input id="<?php echo $this->get_field_id( 'title' ); ?>"
            name="<?php echo $this->get_field_name( 'title' ); ?>"
            type="text"
            value="<?php echo esc attr( $instance['title' ); ?>" />
        </label>
    </p>
    <?php
}
```

On the Web

The code in Listing 6.3 is available for download at www.wiley.com/go/wordpressbible. ∎

Unlike the `widget()` method, the `form()` method only takes a single argument: `$instance`. Like the previous method, however, `$instance` is an array that contains all the configuration data about the widget. Because you're only going to be allowing the user to set the widget title, this will be the only member of the `$instance` array.

With the adoption of the new Widget API, you gain new methods for generating Cascading Style Sheet (CSS) classes and registering widget options: `get_field_id()` and `get_field_name()`. Instead of supplying these attributes by hand, you have to use these new methods in your form. This automatically sets the correct values for this instance.

Tip

In object-oriented PHP, `$this` is a reserved property to describe the current class and is only used in the class. As child classes are derived from their parent classes, all non-private properties and methods declared in the parent class are accessible to the child class. ∎

Saving configuration data

The final method that is required for new widget is the `update()` method. The `update()` method takes two arguments: `$new_instance` and `$old_instance`. Both are arrays with configuration data for the widget. As the name suggests, one is new configuration data after the user clicks the Save button and the other is the previous data that is being changed. Technically, your widget does not need this as the inherited method should work. However, it's always a good idea to process the data and ensure any data sanitization is performed. WordPress provides a number of sanitizing function, including `sanitize_title()`, which is most commonly used for post titles and strips HTML and PHP code, as shown in Listing 6.4.

LISTING 6.4

The update() method is used for saving configuration information about a single instance

```
function update( $new_instance, $old_instance )
{
    $instance = $old_instance;
    $instance['title'] = sanitize_title( $new_instance['title'] );
    return $instance;
}
```

On the Web

The code in Listing 6.4 is available for download at www.wiley.com/go/wordpressbible. ■

Putting it all together

With these three methods, you have now created most of the code necessary to implement a new, re-usable widget. You are still missing two key elements, however. The first is a constructor. In object-oriented PHP 5, the constructor is a method called __construct(). PHP 4.3 compatibility suggests that you use a method that takes the same name as the class itself. This method is automatically called when the class is instantiated. If you are using the PHP 5 constructor, ensure that instead of using $this->WP_Widget(), you use `parent::WP_Widget()` to initiate the widget.

In the WordPress widget world, this is the method where you tell WordPress about the name of the widget, the size of the control form, and so on. These properties are defined in the WP_Widget parent class as $widget_options (values that are passed to the widget) and $control_options (values that are passed to the control form). The $widget_options only take classname and description as array members and the $control_options take height and width as array members. Once you set these, you can pass them to the $this->WP_Widget method for registration.

The WP_Widget method takes four arguments: a string representing a unique widget string, a string that represents the title of the widget as it will be displayed (make it localized), the $widget_options array, and the $control_options array (see Listing 6.5).

LISTING 6.5

Using a PHP 4–style constructor (method name with same name as the class), pass configuration options to the parent method to register the widget

```
function Widget_Trivia()
{
    $widget_options = array(
        'classname'         => 'widget-trivia',
        'description'       => __('Random tidbits of trivia')
        );
    $control_options = array(
        'height'         => 300,
    'width'          => 250
        );
    $this->WP_Widget( 'widget_trivia', __('Random Trivia'), $widget_
    options, $control_options );
}
```

On the Web

The code in Listing 6.5 is available for download at www.wiley.com/go/wordpressbible. ■

The final part is some glue to stick it into the WordPress widget system. For that, you need a function that calls a registration function, register_widget(), and will live outside of your class, and that you'll hook into the widgets_init action hook (see Listing 6.6). This ensures that when WordPress is loaded, it knows all about your widget and will allow the blogger to use it.

LISTING 6.6

A function outside of the class should be used to hook into the widgets_init hook and actually do the widget registration

```
function widget_trivia_init()
{
    register_widget('Widget_Trivia');
}
add_action('widgets_init','widget_trivia_init');
```

On the Web

The code in Listing 6.6 is available for download at www.wiley.com/go/wordpressbible. ■

When you activate this plugin and visit the Widgets Admin interface, you should see a new widget in the Available widgets box called Random Trivia. Dragging this into a sidebar automatically saves your widget layout and it is immediately viewable on your site, as shown in Figure 6.5.

FIGURE 6.5

The widget is immediately displayed on the site as soon as it is dropped into a sidebar on the Widgets Admin interface.

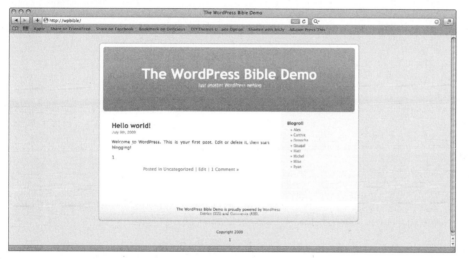

Replacing existing widgets

Replacing widgets is nearly as simple as creating new ones. Along with the `register_widget()` function provided, you have, naturally, an `unregister_widget()` function that works with the same parameter. If you wanted to unregister the default search widget, for example, you could do so in a similar way to how you registered the Widget_Trivia widget. Simply pass it the child class name of the widget class (see Listing 6.7).

Note

All the default widget classes are defined in `wp-includes/default-widgets.php`. **Refer to this file for their proper class names.** ■

LISTING 6.7

Unregistering the default WordPress search widget

```
function widgets_unregister()
{
    unregister_widget('WP_Widget_Search');
}
add_action('widgets_init','widget_trivia_init');
```

Replacing the widget is actually a misnomer. After unregistering the widget that you want to replace, simply register a new one in the same way you did earlier: create a new child class that extends the WP_Widget class; ensure that it has a `widget()`, `form()`, and `update()` method as well as a constructor; create or add to a function that registers widgets; and make sure it is hooked to the `widgets_init` action.

For transparency in your "replacement," make sure your constructor has the same name, description, and standard options as the original. Chances are, if all you want to do is change the HTML structure of the widget (the most common reason for doing a widget replacement), you can simply copy and paste the original widget, give it a new name, and only update the `widget()` method.

Caution

When unregistering a widget for the purpose of replacement, make sure the priority of the newly registered (replacement) widget is higher than the priority of the unregistered version of the widget. Otherwise, you will unregister your new widget and be left with none! ■

TextMate Widget Snippet

If you're a Mac OS X user and use TextMate to do your coding, then try this code snippet from Mark Jaquith (the technical editor of this book). When in TextMate, select Bundles ➪ Bundle Editor ➪ Edit Snippets. Add a new bundle by clicking the + button in the lower-left corner of TextMate and selecting New Bundle. Then, select that new bundle from the listing on the left side of the editor and choose New Snippet from the same button as before. Paste the following code, which is available for download from www.wiley.com/go/wordpressbible, into the editor panel on the right side of the window.

A TextMate snippet for quickly creating WordPress widgets

```
class ${1:PREFIX_Name}_Widget extends WP_Widget {
    function $1_Widget() {
        \$widget_ops = array( 'classname' => '${2:CSS class name}',
'description' => '${3:Description}' );
        \$this->WP_Widget( '$2', '${4:Title}', \$widget_ops );
```

```
    }
    function widget( \$args, \$instance ) {
        extract( \$args, EXTR_SKIP );
        echo \$before_widget;
        echo \$before_title;
        echo '$4'; // Can set this with a widget option, or omit
altogether
        echo \$after_title;
        //
        // Widget display logic goes here
        //
        echo \$after_widget;
    }
    function update( \$new_instance, \$old_instance ) {
        // update logic goes here
        \$updated_instance = \$new_instance;
        return \$updated_instance;
    }
    function form( \$instance ) {
        \$instance = wp_parse_args( (array) \$instance, array( ${5:array
of option_name => value pairs} ) );
        // display field names here using:
        // \$this->get_field_id('option_name') - the CSS ID
        // \$this->get_field_name('option_name') - the HTML name
        // \$instance['option_name'] - the option value
    }
}
add_action( 'widgets_init', create_function( '', "register_widget('$1_
    Widget');" ) );
```

Widgetizing Your Theme

From the perspective of a plugin developer, widgets are only good if the theme the blog has adopted supports widgets. While all themes available in the WordPress Themes Directory (http://wordpress.org/extend/themes/) are required to support widgets, some custom themes do not. So, how do you ensure that your WordPress theme is prepared for widgets?

First, it's important to note that a theme can support any number of sidebars. For each sidebar supported by the theme, the blogger will have a sidebar "drop zone" in the widget interface. If there is only one sidebar, there will only be one drop zone.

It's also important to note terminology. Though sidebars are most often used with traditional sidebars, they are really only "zones" on a page. These zones could be lists, specially formatted divisions, or any other HTML markup that makes sense for designating a "zone". It is not uncommon for a theme to have one sidebar that is really the footer or three sidebars that represent three zones of a single sidebar. Really, sidebars for the sake of widgets can be anything.

Declaring sidebars

Say you want to have two sidebars in a theme you are building. You can widgetize a theme with two simple steps: declare the sidebars, and modify your template files. Before you can modify your template files, you have to declare their existence. You do that in the theme `functions.php` file (see Listing 6.8).

LISTING 6.8

Using register_sidebar() to "declare" new widgetized sidebars for a theme

```
if ( function_exists('register_sidebar') ) {
    register_sidebar(array(
        'before_widget' => '<li id="%1$s" class="widget %2$s">',
        'after_widget' => '</li>',
        'before_title' => '<h2 class="widgettitle">',
        'after_title' => '</h2>',
    ));
}
```

In this example, which comes from the default WordPress theme (also known as Kubrick), a single sidebar is declared with the `register_sidebar()` function. You check for the existence of the function just in case the WordPress blog that is using it is WordPress 2.0 or less, a very rare occurrence but always a possibility when releasing a theme to the public.

If you recall from earlier in this chapter, the `$args` argument that is passed to a widget is an array with four members: `before_widget`, `after_widget`, `before_title`, and `after_title`. You can declare these, on the theme level, by passing an array with these members to the `register_sidebar()` function.

Note

In the example provided, you might notice the notation involved in the `before_widget` member. WordPress uses these placeholders to insert the ID and class of the widget based on the widget. This placeholder system is handled elsewhere in the WordPress code but follows the syntax outlined with the PHP function `printf()`. For more information, see `http://php.net/printf`. ■

You can use the example here out of the box to create a single widget; however, you want two widgets. A fifth array member that can be passed to the `register_sidebar()` function is name or ID. This array key can be a number, if the key name is *id* (an ID number will automatically be assigned if omitted), or a string, if the key name is *name*. This enables you to have two sidebars. Simply copy and paste the `register_sidebar()` code and pass both function calls a unique number or name (see Listing 6.9).

Tip

If you decide to use a name instead of an ID number, make sure you localize it. ■

LISTING 6.9

You can register more than one sidebar with different names

```
if ( function_exists('register_sidebar') ) {
    register_sidebar(array(
        'before_widget' => '<li id="%1$s" class="widget %2$s">',
        'after_widget' => '</li>',
        'before_title' => '<h2 class="widgettitle">',
        'after_title' => '</h2>',
        'name' => __('First Sidebar')
    ));
    register_sidebar(array(
        'before_widget' => '<li id="%1$s" class="widget %2$s">',
        'after_widget' => '</li>',
        'before_title' => '<h2 class="widgettitle">',
        'after_title' => '</h2>',
        'name' => __('Second Sidebar')
    ));
}
```

This gives you two sidebars that you can use in your theme but the nice thing is, you can make this cleaner and simpler. WordPress provides a second function for registering new sidebars in the case you want to register more than one. With the `register_sidebars()` (plural) function, you can't set unique names, but unique ID numbers will be created.

The `register_sidebars()` function takes two arguments. The first argument is an integer representing the number of sidebars you want created and the second argument is an array identical to what you would have passed to `register_sidebar()` but without the name key (having the name key would create colliding CSS selectors and potentially wreak havoc with your page). Instead of having two `register_sidebar()` calls, simplify it down to a single `register_sidebars()` call, as shown in Listing 6.10.

LISTING 6.10

If you need multiple sidebars but don't need custom names, use the register_sidebars() function

```
if ( function_exists('register_sidebars') ) {
    register_sidebars( 2, array(
        'before_widget' => '<li id="%1$s" class="widget %2$s">',
        'after_widget' => '</li>',
        'before_title' => '<h2 class="widgettitle">',
        'after_title' => '</h2>'
    ));
}
```

It's that easy. If you want to simplify even farther, you can skip passing an array of options at all. WordPress has defaults that, if you code your theme along the lines of the default, will work perfectly fine.

Cross-Reference
There are coding conventions (and expectations) throughout WordPress. Of course, with widgets, you can take your own route and inform WordPress what it is. WordPress will adeptly adapt to your workflow and structure for widgets, but if as a theme designer, you don't want to overly customize your theme structure, there are best practices you can follow. I talk about theming and these conventions in the chapters in Part III. ■

Integrating widgetized sidebars in themes

Once you have declared your widgetized sidebars, it's time to integrate them into your theme. As a designer, the most likely location for this is in the literal sidebar, most often found in `sidebar.php`.

Cross-Reference
Template file hierarchy and how best to use it can be found in Chapter 10. ■

For this example, assume that `sidebar.php` is a very simple set of divisions containing some markup, as shown in Listing 6.11.

LISTING 6.11

Example of markup for a standard sidebar in a WordPress theme

```
<div id="sidebars">
    <div id="sidebar-1">
        <ul>
            <li><?php echo get_search_form(); ?></li>
        </ul>
    </div>
    <div id="sidebar-2">
        <ul>
            <li><?php echo wp_list_pages(); ?></li>
        </ul>
    </div>
</div>
```

Without having to get too deep into the actual nuts and bolts, you will find some traditional markup for a two sidebar layout. Within this layout, each sidebar is composed of an unordered list and each portion of the sidebar is a list item. Of course, you can style this to make it look however you want if you don't want to use this style of markup. The missing ingredient in this markup, however, is the code required to make this sidebar widgetized. To do that, you need a function called `dynamic_sidebar()`. In the event of only a single sidebar, this function does not require arguments. If you have more than one sidebar, as you do in our ongoing example, you will have to pass it the ID of the sidebar or the name. Because you simplified your code to use `register_sidebars()` in Listing 6.10, you will have two sidebars with IDs 1 and 2.

In order to integrate the sidebars into WordPress, you need to do some conditional logic (see Listing 6.12). The logic exists to ensure that the `dynamic_sidebar()` function exists (it has automatically since WordPress 2.1) and to discover if there are any widgets actually configured for the sidebar. If the blogger hasn't actually put any widgets into the sidebar, then WordPress displays the default HTML coded into the template file.

Tip

If you can guarantee that a blogger will always use widgets, then you can omit sidebar code from your `sidebar.php` or template files. However, that is an assumption that is hard to make. Many times, bloggers install themes and never change the widget layout, in which case, it is extremely important to provide some default structure and code. ■

LISTING 6.12

Using the dynamic_sidebar() function to designate sidebar "zones" in your theme

```
<div id="sidebars">
    <div id="sidebar-1">
    <?php if ( !function_exists('dynamic_sidebar')
            || !dynamic_sidebar(1) ) { ?>
        <ul>
            <li><?php echo get_search_form(); ?></li>
        </ul>
        <?php } ?>
    </div>
    <div id="sidebar-2">
        <?php if ( !function_exists('dynamic_sidebar')
                || !dynamic_sidebar(2) ) { ?>
        <ul>
            <li><?php echo wp_list_pages(); ?></li>
        </ul>
        <?php } ?>
    </div>
</div>
```

With this last bit of code, your theme is now prepared for widgets. Users will have some default sidebar HTML in case they don't want to use widgets, and if they do want to use widgets, they will now see a Sidebar 1 and Sidebar 2 drop zone in their Widget Admin interface.

Summary

- Widgets are installed just like plugins: from the plugin installation interface inside the WordPress Admin, or by uploading to `/wp-content/plugins` and activating them.

- Widgets can also be provided by individual themes from within the theme `functions.php` file.

- A blogger can adjust which widgets are used and in which sidebar they are used in simply by dragging and dropping inside the Widget Admin interface (Appearance ➪ Widgets).

- Bloggers can adjust settings in many widgets simply by expanding the widget while it is in a sidebar. Clicking Save or navigating away from the page saves any changes.

- WordPress 2.8 provides a new widget API. The old procedural method still works but is not recommended. Using the new method makes your widgets automatically capable of having multiple instances.

- The Widget API is provided by the core class `WP_Widget`. New widgets should declare a new class that extends this parent class.

- Each new widget should include three methods that override the existing methods provided by the parent class. These three methods are `widget()`, which provides the HTML output for the widget; `form()`, which provides the configuration panel accessible on the Widget Admin interface; and `update()`, which saves configuration settings.

- Every widget should have a construct method that provides important operational information needed to register the widget in WordPress.

- Every widget should have a `register_widget()` call that takes the name of the new widget class. This function is usually called from within a function that is hooked into the `widgets_init` action.

- Theme designers can declare sidebars in their theme `functions.php`. You can register multiple sidebar by calling `register_sidebar()` more than once or simplifying and using `register_sidebars()`.

- Theme designers need to encapsulate portions of their theme structure (usually in `sidebar.php` or `footer.php`) with the `dynamic_sidebar()` function.

- The `dynamic_sidebar()` function replaces traditionally coded HTML with widget provided HTML when widgets have been assigned to the sidebar. If no widget has been assigned, the default HTML will be used.

Understanding the WordPress Database Class

I f you've been developing Web sites or applications with PHP for any length of time, you are probably familiar with PHP database functions such as `mysql_query()`, `mysql_fetch_array()`, and so on. You might also be familiar with database abstraction classes. Like other abstraction classes, the database class used by WordPress provides an abstraction layer between the developer and the raw MySQL functions in PHP.

Note

A *database abstraction layer* is a class or library that sits between your code and a series of databases. As every database has its own nuances, and the built-in database functions are messy and inconsistent, a database abstraction layer sorts out that messiness by providing a consistent interface to multiple databases. ■

The database class used by WordPress — ezSQL — is an extremely light-weight MySQL database abstraction class that, like much of WordPress' core, originated elsewhere. The original author, Justin Vincent, still maintains this class at www.woyano.com/jv/ezsql. It can be found in WordPress in /wp-includes/wp-db.php.

Before diving too far in, you should take note that ezSQL is not a database abstraction layer; it is a MySQL abstraction layer. It is possible, however, to take the `wp-db.php` file and manipulate it to talk to other database systems such as PostgreSQL or Microsoft's SQL Server. If you do this, simply save the file as `db.php` and drop it in the `wp-includes/` folder. WordPress looks to see if a `db.php` file exists first when *bootstrapping*, the process of getting WordPress connected to the database, and will use it instead of `wp-db.php` if it exists. You still need to know and understand MySQL or your underlying database. The class merely makes it easier to leverage.

ezSQL is not a full-featured abstraction engine like, for example, PHP 5's PHP Data Objects (PDO) library. It is a lightweight class that proves useful in many aspects of PHP development. It is perfectly suited to use within WordPress based on its licensing, size, and speed.

Examining the Schema and Properties of the Database Class

Because the database class is an object, it has quite a few properties and methods. Understanding these is critical for plugin developments because you will be using the database a lot.

The database object is assigned to the handler $wpdb throughout WordPress. Whenever you create a function that requires transactions with the database, excluding the use of core application programming interface (API) functions like get_option() or other similar functions, you need to ensure that you introduce $wpdb into the function or method using the global keyword, as demonstrated in Listing 7.1.

LISTING 7.1

Make the $wpdb object global whenever you write a function that needs to access the database

```
function my_function()
{
    global $wpdb;
    // Function code here
}
```

By making the $wpdb object available to your function, you expose all the properties and methods available to it.

The database properties

Every table and a variety of options are available as properties to be used with the database class. To access these properties, use $wpdb->{property} the same way you would use variables.

show_errors

The show_errors property is a true or false (also known as Boolean) property. By default it is set to false, but if you want to be able to debug SQL error messages in the process of development, set show_errors to true.

Note

$wpdb->show_errors **should always be set to** false **in production.** ∎

suppress_errors

The suppress_errors property is similar to show_errors in that it is a Boolean. In addition, it is similar because it is useful for debugging. However, this property pertains to suppressing database errors involved in bootstrapping.

last_error

The last_error property is a string that holds the last SQL or bootstrap error. It is useful for debugging, even if $wpdb->show_errors is false. By default, it is empty. This is not a log file and is reinitialized every time WordPress loads (page load).

num_queries

Like other properties already mentioned, the num_queries property is useful for debugging. It tracks the number of actual (not cached) queries that have been executed up to the moment it is called within WordPress. At initialization, this is 0 but it is incremented with every real SQL query.

last_query

The last_query property, despite its name, does not store the SQL of the most recent query at the time of execution. Instead, it stores the last dataset of the last query that was run.

col_info

If you want to retrieve specific information about a column in a database table, use $wpdb->col_info. The col_info property stores information such as column type, name, and so on.

queries

Sometimes there is a need to save queries. It's not common in the WordPress world given WordPress provides its own caching mechanism; however, the capability exists. The queries property is an array of saved queries that requires the constant SAVEDQUERIES to be defined as true. Because queries is a private property, you'll never actually use it directly but the database class itself will.

prefix

The prefix property is commonly used in WordPress and is set to the table prefix that you defined in your wp-config.php file. By default, this prefix is wp_, but it can be anything.

Note

Because prefix **is a private property, never set it using the object. Set it in** wp-config.php**.** ∎

Plugin authors should also take note that `prefix` is a very important property. When creating queries within your functions for custom tables, never assume that table prefixes are wp. Always use `$wpdb->prefix` instead. This ensures that your plugin is compatible with all possible WordPress installs, including WordPress MU blogs.

ready

Another internal (private) property, `ready`, will never be used outside of the database class itself. This property is set to false by default, and is internally set to true when queries are ready to be executed.

posts

The `posts` property holds the name of the posts table, including the table prefix. Most often, it is set to `wp_posts`. The `posts` table schema is shown in Table 7.1.

TABLE 7.1

Database Schema for the Posts Table

Field	Type	Null	Key	Default	Extra
ID	bigint(20) unsigned	No	Primary	Null	auto_increment
post_author	bigint(20) unsigned	No		0	
post_date	datetime	No		0000-00-00 00:00:00	
post_date_gmt	datetime	No		0000-00-00 00:00:00	
post_content	longtext	No		Null	
post_title	text	No	Multiple	Null	
post_category	int(4)	No		0	
post_excerpt	text	No		Null	
post_status	varchar(20)	No	Multiple	publish	
comment_status	varchar(20)	No		open	
ping_status	varchar(20)	No		open	
post_password	varchar(20)	No			
post_name	varchar(200)	No	Multiple		
to_ping	text	No		Null	
pinged	text	No		Null	
post_modified	datetime	No		0000-00-00 00:00:00	

Field	Type	Null	Key	Default	Extra
post_modified_gmt	datetime	No		0000-00-00 00:00:00	
post_content_filtered	text	No		Null	
post_parent	bigint(20) unsigned	No	Multiple	0	
guid	varchar(255)	No			
menu_order	int(11)	No		0	
post_type	varchar(20)	No	Multiple	post	
post_mime_type	varchar(100)	No			
comment_count	bigint(20)	No		0	

Tip

In a WordPress data context, it is important to note that several types of content are included in the post table. Posts in a data context could include blog posts (default), pages, attachments like image uploads, and so on. It is conceivable that plugin authors could provide their own new type of post. The type of post (post, page, revision, attachment) is determined by the `post_type` column. WordPress ignores post_types it doesn't know about, making this a good place to store data, as an alternative to creating your own tables. ■

postmeta

The `postmeta` property holds the name of the postmeta table, including the table prefix. Most often, it is set to `wp_postmeta`. The database schema for the postmeta table, which includes additional data related to individual posts, is shown in Table 7.2. Generally, these are custom fields but plugin authors could use the table for storing their own metadata relating to posts.

TABLE 7.2

Database Schema for the Postmeta Table

Field	Type	Null	Key	Default	Extra
meta_id	bigint(20) unsigned	No	Primary	Null	auto_increment
post_id	bigint(20) unsigned	No	Multiple	0	
meta_key	varchar(255)	Yes	Multiple	Null	
meta_value	longtext	Yes		Null	

Cross-Reference

Custom fields are a powerful ingredient when you're using WordPress as a content management system. This metadata will be discussed in greater detail in Chapter 21. ■

users

The users property holds the name of the user table in WordPress, including the table prefix. Most often, it is set to wp_users. It is one of two tables that include all the pertinent information about the users in your WordPress blog. The table schema for this table is listed in Table 7.3.

TABLE 7.3

Database Schema for the Users Table

Field	Type	Null	Key	Default	Extra
ID	bigint(20) unsigned	No	Primary	Null	auto_increment
user_login	varchar(60)	No	Unique		
user_pass	varchar(64)	No			
user_nicename	varchar(50)	No	Multiple		
user_email	varchar(100)	No			
user_url	varchar(100)	No			
user_registered	datetime	No		0000-00-00 00:00:00	
user_activation_key	varchar(60)	No			
user_status	int(11)	No		0	
display_name	varchar(250)	No			

usermeta

The usermeta property holds the name of the usermeta table in WordPress, including the table prefix. It holds all information that is required for user authentication, including the user's role, and works in conjunction with the user table to provide a personalized WordPress experience, including user preferences. Plugin authors can add ad hoc meta data regarding a user as well. The table schema for the usermeta table is listed in Table 7.4.

TABLE 7.4

Database Schema for the Usermeta Table

Field	Type	Null	Key	Default	Extra
meta_id	bigint(20) unsigned	No	Primary	Null	auto_increment
user_id	bigint(20) unsigned	No	Multiple	0	
meta_key	varchar(255)	Yes	Multiple	Null	
meta_value	longtext	Yes		Null	

comments

The `comments` property contains the name of the comments table in WordPress, including the table prefix. The table schema for the comments table is listed in Table 7.5.

TABLE 7.5

Database Schema for the Comments Table

Field	Type	Null	Key	Default	Extra
comment_ID	bigint(20) unsigned	No	Primary	Null	auto_increment
comment_post_ID	bigint(20) unsigned	No	Multiple	0	
comment_author	tinytext	No		Null	
comment_author_email	varchar(100)	No			
comment_author_url	varchar(200)	No			
comment_author_IP	varchar(100)	No			
comment_date	datetime	No		0000-00-00 00:00:00	
comment_date_gmt	datetime	No	Multiple	0000-00-00 00:00:00	
comment_content	text	No		Null	
comment_karma	int(11)	No		0	
comment_approved	varchar(20)	No	Multiple		
comment_agent	varchar(255)	No			
comment_type	varchar(20)	No			
comment_parent	bigint(20) unsigned	No		0	
user_id	bigint(20) unsigned	No		0	

commentmeta

The `commentmeta` property contains the name of the table containing metadata about individual comments. It can be used by plugin authors to add ad hoc data about comments to the database. The table schema for the commentmeta table was added in WordPress 2.9 and is listed here in Table 7.6.

TABLE 7.6

Database Schema for the Comment Meta Table

Field	Type	Null	Key	Default	Extra
meta_id	bigint(20) unsigned	No	Primary	Null	auto_increment
user_id	bigint(20) unsigned	No	Multiple	0	
meta_key	varchar(255)	Yes	Multiple	Null	
meta_value	longtext	Yes		Null	

links

The links table name is stored in the `links` property. This table contains all the data stored surrounding blogrolls, link lists, bookmarks, and so on, and is managed under the Links administrative panel. The table schema for this table is listed in Table 7.7.

TABLE 7.7

Database Schema for the Links Table

Field	Type	Null	Key	Default	Extra
link_id	bigint(20) unsigned	No	Primary	Null	auto_increment
link_url	varchar(255)	No			
link_name	varchar(255)	No			
link_image	varchar(255)	No			
link_target	varchar(25)	No			
link_category	bigint(20)	No	Multiple	0	
link_description	varchar(255)	No			
link_visible	varchar(20)	No	Multiple	Y	
link_owner	bigint(20) unsigned	No		1	
link_rating	int(11)	No		0	
link_updated	datetime	No		0000-00-00 00:00:00	
link_rel	varchar(255)	No			
link_notes	mediumtext	No		Null	
link_rss	varchar(255)	No			

options

The options table collects and stores all the settings for WordPress and many plugins. The name of this table, including the table prefix, is stored in the options property. Plugin authors should feel comfortable using this table for setting storage. It can be manipulated with add_option(), update_option(), and get_option(). The schema for this table is listed in Table 7.8.

TABLE 7.8

Database Schema for the Options Table

Field	Type	Null	Key	Default	Extra
option_id	bigint(20) unsigned	No	Primary	Null	auto_increment
blog_id	int(11)	No	Primary	0	
option_name	varchar(64)	No	Primary		
option_value	longtext	No		Null	
autoload	varchar(20)	No		yes	

terms

The terms property stores the name, including table prefix, of the terms table. The terms table stores metadata that are referred to generically as terms. Terms can be categories, tags, or link categories and can be extended to other areas by plugin developers. The schema for this table is listed in Table 7.9.

TABLE 7.9

Database Schema for the Terms Table

Field	Type	Null	Key	Default	Extra
term_id	bigint(20) unsigned	No	Primary	Null	auto_increment
name	varchar(200)	No	Multiple		
slug	varchar(200)	No	Unique		
term_group	bigint(10)	No		0	

term_taxonomy

The name of the term_taxonomy table is a table that stores types of terms and is stored in the term_taxonomy property. This is a table that relates a term to a specific taxonomy and can contain data specific to the term as it exists in that taxonomy (for example, categories can have a parent, but tags are flat). The schema for this table is listed in Table 7.10.

TABLE 7.10

Database Schema for the Term Taxonomy Table

Field	Type	Null	Key	Default	Extra
term_taxonomy_id	bigint(20) unsigned	No	Primary	Null	auto_increment
term_id	bigint(20) unsigned	No	Multiple	0	
taxonomy	varchar(32)	No	Multiple		
description	longtext	No		Null	
parent	bigint(20) unsigned	No		0	
count	bigint(20) unsigned	No		0	

term_relationships

The term_relationships table is a junction table that relates a term_taxonomy entry to some data object (like a post or a link). The schema for this table is listed in Table 7.11.

TABLE 7.11

Database Schema for the Term Relationships Table

Field	Type	Null	Key	Default	Extra
object_id	bigint(20) unsigned	No	Primary	0	
term_taxonomy_id	bigint(20) unsigned	No	Primary	0	
term_order	int(11)	No		0	

tables

The tables property is private and, thus, shouldn't be accessed directly, if at all. The property contains an array of the table names that are used by WordPress.

field_types

The field_types property is new in WordPress 2.8. It contains an array of field names where you can specify what character type (integer or string) to return field data as. This is set in wp-settings.php, but can be re-declared in a plugin function that hooks into the init action hook.

124

Deprecated Tables and Properties

For the sake of backward compatibility, WordPress waits a long time before removing functions, classes, methods and, in this case, table name properties from the core. This is because plugin authors, in many cases, try to build plugins that will work on any version that has been released. When WordPress 2.3 was released, it introduced the concept of tags when before, the only metadata available for posts was in the form of categories. During those days, there were a number of tables that existed, but were replaced with the "terms" tables instead.

categories

The categories table existed to hold category names, IDs, and descriptions. Even though categories still exist, they are now stored as terms. The database class maintains the $wpdb->categories property to hold the name of this deprecated table.

post2cat

The post2cat table existed as a join table to associate posts with the categories they were assigned to. This table was eliminated with the advent of the terms infrastructure. The database class maintains $wpdb->post2cat to hold the name of this deprecated table.

charset

Like the table properties, the charset property stores the character set of the database itself, which is generally UTF-8. The charset property is unlikely to be used often in WordPress plugin development.

collate

Similar to the charset property, the collate property holds the collation value for the database. It is unlikely to be used often in WordPress plugin development.

real_escape

The final property available in the database class, the real_escape property, instructs WordPress on whether to use the mysql_real_escape_string() function. The function is set to false by default because data sanitization is handled elsewhere in WordPress, making the need for this property unlikely.

Adding Data to MySQL with WordPress

Two main API methods are used to add data to MySQL: insert() and update(). These methods take care of sanitizing and preparing all data for insertion or updating MySQL from within WordPress.

Inserting new data into MySQL

To insert data into MySQL, you can safely use the insert() method. This method takes three arguments: the table name, an array of column/value pairs, and an optional format array (%s or %d) that will force the data to be either a string or number.

The data that is going to be inserted does not need to be sanitized, and in fact, should be "raw" — that is, *unescaped*. WordPress will handle all the heavy lifting on this.

Listing 7.2 illustrates an example of how a function might use the insert() method.

LISTING 7.2

Using the insert() method to insert a post with a possible custom post type, mp3

```
function add_music_post( $music_title, $music_description )
{
    global $wpdb;
    $wpdb->insert( $wpdb->posts, array('post_title' => $music_title, 'post_
content' => $music_description, 'post_type' => 'mp3'), array('%s', '%s',
    '%s') );
}
```

Updating data in MySQL safely

A second data insertion method is the update() method. This method, like the insert() method, is intended to make the process of changing data in MySQL a safe process free of SQL injection. It carries a similar format as the insert() method but adds a few additional arguments.

The first argument is the table name, the second argument is an array of data to be changed in field/value pairs, and the third argument is an array of field/value pairs used to provide "where" conditions for the update. All three of these arguments are required.

Note
The first two arguments are identical to the insert() method. ∎

The fourth and fifth arguments, respectively, behave similarly to the format argument in insert(). The fourth argument is an array of data formats (%s for string and %d for number) that forces the data that will be inserted into the database to be treated as the appropriate data type. The fifth argument is identical, except it pertains to the data used in the WHERE clause.

Listing 7.3 illustrates an example of how the update() method is used.

LISTING 7.3

Using the update() method to safely update data in MySQL

```
function edit_music_post( $post_id, $new_title, $new_description )
{
    global $wpdb;
    $wpdb->update( $wpdb->posts, array( 'post_title' => $new_title, 'post_
    content' => $new_content ), array( 'ID' => $post_id ), array( '%s',
    '%s'), array( '%d' ) );
}
```

Retrieving Data from MySQL with WordPress

It's great that the database class has so many properties but what good is a Web application if it can't read and write to a database? Of course, WordPress can and does. A number of methods exist that will retrieve data in an elegant, object-oriented way if necessary.

It is always good practice to avoid having to include raw SQL in a plugin when possible. The reality is that plugins that rely on raw SQL are often the ones that break later on. A good example of this is the myriad of plugins that used the categories table prior to WordPress 2.3. When the $wpdb->categories and $wpdb->post2cat tables disappeared and were replaced by the new terms paradigm, the plugins that were querying the categories tables directly broke.

In many cases, WordPress provides methods and functions to retrieve data from MySQL as part of its plugin API. Where this API exists, you should use it because it is generally forward compatible.

Retrieving a single value from a table

In the event that an API doesn't exist to retrieve the data needed, you can use the $wpdb->get_var() method to retrieve a single value from the database. Simply pass your SQL statement to the method. The SQL that is passed must return only a single field from a single row like this:

```
$post_id = $wpdb->get_var("SELECT ID FROM ' . $wpdb->posts . ' WHERE
    post_author = 1 LIMIT 1");
```

In plain English, this query will retrieve the ID of the most recent post written by the author with an ID of 1. You'll notice that this line of code uses the $wpdb->posts property as well. If you recall, this property held the name of the posts table. You'll also notice that the query itself is only retrieving a single field (ID) from a single row (in this case, you added LIMIT 1 to the query).

Retrieving a column of data

What if you wanted to get all the IDs of the posts by the author with an ID of 1? For this use case, you want to use the $wpdb->get_col() method, which is shown in Listing 7.4. When only one field will be retrieved, but there will be more than one row of data, you need to use this method. By default, the data that is returned will be in the form an object; however, you can pass the method a second argument of ARRAY_A or ARRAY_N to have data returned as an associative or numerical array.

LISTING 7.4

Using the get_col() method

```
$object = $wpdb->get_col("SELECT ID FROM ' . $wpdb->posts . ' WHERE post_
    author = 1");
$assoc_array = $wpdb=>get_col("SELECT ID FROM ' . $wpdb->posts . ' WHERE
    post_author = 1", ARRAY_A);
$num_array = $wpdb=>get_col("SELECT ID FROM ' . $wpdb->posts . ' WHERE post_
    author = 1", ARRAY_N);
```

Retrieving a row of data

Similar to $wpdb->get_col(), the database class also provides $wpdb->get_row(), a method for retrieving only a single row of data. Ignoring the fact that WordPress provides a get_userdata() function as an API function to retrieve information about a user, you might use this method to retrieve information about a user with ID 43, as shown in Listing 7.5.

LISTING 7.5

Using the get_row() method

```
$userdata = $wpdb->get_row("SELECT * FROM ' . $wpdb->users . ' WHERE ID =
    43");
$user_assocarray = $wpdb->get_row("SELECT * FROM ' . $wpdb->users . ' WHERE
    ID = 43", ARRAY_A);
$user_numarray = $wpdb->get_row("SELECT * FROM ' . $wpdb->users . ' WHERE ID
    = 43", ARRAY_N);
```

Retrieving a full data set

If you have to do raw SQL queries, try to limit the scope of what data you are actually retrieving from the database. If you can just retrieve a column of data, then use $wpdb->get_col(). If you only need a single value, consider the $wpdb->get_var() method.

However, sometimes you will need an entire dataset. Fortunately, you have the $wpdb->get_results() method. Like the $wpdb->get_col() and $wpdb->get_row() methods, you can pass ARRAY_A or ARRAY_N as a flag so the returned data comes back as an array.

The example in Listing 7.6 finds all users who were created after July 1, 2009.

LISTING 7.6

Using the get_results() method

```
$users = $wpdb->get_results("SELECT * FROM ' . $wpdb->users . ' WHERE user_
    registered > '2009-07-01'");
$users_assocarr = $wpdb->get_results("SELECT * FROM ' . $wpdb->users . '
    WHERE user_registered > '2009-07-01'", ARRAY_A);
$users_numarr = $wpdb->get_results("SELECT * FROM ' . $wpdb->users . ' WHERE
    user_registered > '2009-07-01'", ARRAY_N);
```

Performing other queries

The WordPress database class provides a $wpdb->query() method for other types of SQL queries. For example, you can use it to get a listing of all tables in the database (something that might be helpful because other plugins might supply their own tables):

```
$wpdb->query("INSERT INTO {$wpdb->prefix}my_plugin table SET field1 =
    '$safe_value', field2 = '$safe_value2' WHERE field3 - 'some
    value'");
```

You could also use this method for INSERT, DELETE, or UPDATE SQL queries if your plugin provides its own tables.

Preventing SQL Injection

If you've spent any serious time developing Web applications, you know of the risk of *SQL injection*. SQL injection is caused when data is inserted into the database that hasn't been properly sanitized. For example, a classic demonstration of SQL injection would be an exploit that gives a malicious person administrator access to your site.

Caution

It is hard to emphasize the importance of preventing SQL injection with your plugin. WordPress is only as secure as its weakest link. It provides many options to access data that do not require any SQL at all. If you can, it is imperative that you use these functions and API methods. You should only use SQL when it's absolutely essential. Using it without proper care can destroy someone's blog. I cannot emphasize this enough. ■

Say you have an HTML form that requires a username and password. Each of these form fields are named "user" and "pass," respectively. On the backend, the authentication mechanism checks the username and password against the database like this:

```
SELECT * FROM example_usertable WHERE username = '$input_user' AND
    password = '$input_pass';
```

If form data is unsanitized but the user actually inputs a proper username and password, then the SQL query works and authentication is granted. However, if someone enters a more malicious string, they can wreak havoc on your system. For example, if the user entered a username of `user' OR 1=1;--` and any password, then the SQL will also be valid and will give the user access to the protected system. The query that would actually be run is shown here:

```
SELECT * FROM example_usertable WHERE username = 'user' OR
    1=1;--random password
```

To understand the practical danger in this query, you have to understand that two dashes (`--`) is equivalent to a comment. In essence, everything after the `--` is ignored by MySQL so it doesn't matter if an invalid password is provided. It could be anything. Also, because you haven't "escaped" the single quote in the username, the single quote becomes the "end" of the value being checked against the username field. Though this is probably invalid as well, it doesn't matter because the attack adds an `OR 1=1` (which is always true) into the query. The query reads, "Retrieve the record from the usertable where the username is 'user' or where 1=1." Because 1 always equals 1, the SQL always evaluates as true and an attacker can access the protected resources, application or, possibly, a WordPress plugin.

To prevent against a possible SQL injection attack (which could be as simple, or far more complex, than this example), the WordPress database class provides the `$wpdb->prepare()` method. This method, added in WordPress 2.3, uses the PHP `printf()` syntax (`http://php.net/printf`) for field replacement. It handles data sanitization of SQL statements to prevent against SQL injection, as shown in Listing 7.7. Note that, like `printf()`, placeholders can use an "order" index. Instead of using `%d` to indicate a numerical replacement, you could use the `%1$d` syntax to indicate, "replace this placeholder with the first replacement value in the format of a number."

Note

The two placeholders the `prepare()` method supports are `%d` for integers and `%s` for strings. Note that in neither case do you quote the placeholder. WordPress will take care of proper quoting for you. ■

LISTING 7.7

Using the prepare() method to sanitize SQL against SQL Injection attacks

```
$sanitized_sql = $wpdb->prepare("'INSERT INTO my_plugin_table SET field1 =
    %1$d, field2 = %2$s, field3 = %3$s', 32, 'Aaron Brazell', 'Washington,
    D.C')";
$wpdb->query( $sanitized_sql );
```

Summary

- The WordPress database class is a modified version of ezSQL.

- ezSQL is not a database abstraction library; it is a MySQL abstraction library.

- Support for other databases exists by putting a modified version of the database class in the `wp-includes` folder. The file must be called `db.php` and must be of the same class structure as `wp-db.php`.

- Plugin developers should be careful if making `$wpdb` global inside any function or method that needs to access MySQL directly.

- The WordPress core provides many functions and methods for accessing the core tables. Avoid using raw SQL unless absolutely necessary.

- Use available properties to designate table names. This ensures maximum compatibility with various versions of WordPress.

- If you need to retrieve data, you can use `$wpdb->get_var()`, `$wpdb->get_col()`, `$wpdb->get_row()`, and `$wpdb->get results()` With the exception of `$wpdb->get_var()`, all these methods are returned as objects. They can be returned as associative or numerical arrays by adding the `ARRAY_A` or `ARRAY_N` flag.

- Use the `$wpdb->prepare()` method to protect your queries against SQL injection.

Dissecting the Loop and WP_Query

I f you've made it this far in this book, you understand how to build plugins, use the WordPress hook system to alter the way WordPress behaves, develop themes to present the content to the user, and leverage the widget system to modify the look and feel of a blog. In this chapter, I address the single most important piece of WordPress: *the Loop*.

The Loop is what makes a blog a blog. The Loop uses something called a *query* to grab the data from the database, organize the posts and comments, and display them. By default, the Loop is displayed in a reverse chronological order, with the most recent post appearing first on the page. However, bloggers have become very creative with how they display their content and WordPress provides some assistance.

Note

The *Loop* and the *query* are similar, yet two different things. The query retrieves data from the database according to parameters passed (or assumed based on default). The Loop iterates over this data and displays it on a blog. The Loop and the query are often referred to interchangeably but, in practice, they do two different things in conjunction with each other. One could say that they represent the perfect WordPress marriage. ■

Upon the Loop initialization, WordPress looks for "sticky" posts. *Sticky* posts are the posts that the user has requested be "stuck" at the top and will be displayed first. Sticky posts get their name because the posts "stick" to the top of the first page of posts, or more accurately, to the top of the Loop.

This is only one aspect of the Loop. I discuss the Loop and all the fine details later in this chapter, but in short, the Loop iterates over an object that is returned that includes all the posts that meet the query parameters and carries information about categories, tags, author information, and so on. After the object, called $wp_query, is returned, many theme developers will use conditional template tags such as is_author(), is_search(), is_single(), and so on, to further transform how the data is displayed.

Cross-Reference
See Chapter 12 for more information about how conditional template tags are used after the posts have been returned. ■

Defining the Loop

In practice, the Loop consists of three core components: the query, the post, and the bits that occur inside each post iteration. A typical Loop looks something like Listing 8.1.

LISTING 8.1

The basic structure of the Loop

```php
<?php
if (have_posts()) :
    while (have_posts()) :
        the_post();
    ?>
    <!-- Post content -->
    <?php
    endwhile;
endif;
?>
```

On the Web
The code in Listing 8.1 is available for download at www.wiley.com/go/wordpressbible.com. ■

Note
One of the many WordPress conventions for coding involves the code style for the Loop. Notably, instead of curly braces, WordPress conventions use the colon method. When a conditional, or Loop, is used with a colon, there must be an ending statement (for example, if/endif, while/endwhile, foreach/endforeach, and so on.) ■

By default, every page load in WordPress includes a population of the $wp_query object. This happens transparently and does not have to be explicitly done in a theme. By default, this query returns the ten most recent posts in reverse chronological order, with sticky posts at the top of the Loop.

Tip

WordPress displays ten posts at a time unless the `showposts` parameter is used in the query (more on that later). You can change the number of posts displayed from the WordPress Admin under Settings ⇨ Reading. You can also change the Blog pages show at most option to affect the blog itself. The Syndication feeds show the most recent option controls how many posts are shown in feeds. ■

A class called `WP_Query` handles the retrieval of post and page data. Though I will get deeper into customizing this data later in this chapter, Listing 8.2 demonstrates how the default home page query is put together behind the scenes.

LISTING 8.2

The default arguments supplied to the query

```
$posts = new WP_Query( array(
      'showposts'           => 10,
      'offset'              => 0,
      'category'            => 0,
      'orderby'             => 'post_date',
      'order'               => 'DESC',
      'include'             => '',
      'exclude'             => '',
      'meta_key'            => '',
      'meta_value'          => '',
      'post_type'           => 'post',
      'suppress_filters'    => true,
      'post_status'         => 'publish'
      )
);
```

This query is executed internally against MySQL and a number of properties are returned in the object. Depending on the values of these properties, the template loading process, which is determined by the Loop, could behave different ways. For example, if the `$wp_query->is_search` property is set to true as a result of the query, WordPress will use the `search.php` template, if available, to serve up data to the browser.

Cross-Reference

Template file hierarchies are discussed in Chapter 10. ■

The methods and properties available to the `$wp_query` object are listed in Table 8.1.

TABLE 8.1

Methods and Properties Available to $wp_query

Method/Property	Definition
$query	Holds the query string that was passed to the $wp_query.
$query_vars	An associative array containing the dissected $query: an array of the query variables and their respective values.
$queried_object	Applicable if the request is a category, author, permalink, or page. Holds information on the requested category, author, post, or page.
$queried_object_id	Simply holds the ID of the previously property.
$posts	Holds the requested posts from the database.
$post_count	The number of posts being displayed.
$current_post	An index of the post currently being displayed.
$post	The post currently being displayed.
$is_single, $is_page, $is_archive, $is preview, $is_date, $is_year, $is_month, $is_time, $is_author, $is_category, $is_tag, $is_tax, $is_search, $is_feed, $is_comment_feed, $is_trackback, $is_home, $is_404, $is_comments_popup, $is_admin, $is_attachment, $is_singular, $is_robots, $is_posts_page, $is_paged	Booleans (true or false) dictating what type of request the query is. The type of request, in conjunction with the template hierarchy system, can alter the way a WordPress blog is displayed.
init()	Initializes the object. Sets all properties to null, zero, or false.
parse_query()	Takes a query string defining the request, parses it, and populates all properties except $posts, $post_count, $post, and $current_post.
parse_query_vars()	Reparse the old query string.
get()	Get a named query variable.
set()	Sets a named query variable to a specific value.
get_posts()	Fetch and return the requested posts from the database. Also populates $posts and $post_count.
next_post()	Iterates to the next post in $posts. Increments $current_post and sets $post.
the_post()	Iterates to the next post, and sets the global $post variable.
have_posts()	Determines if there are posts remaining to be displayed.
rewind_posts()	Reset $current_post and $post.
query()	Calls parse_query() and get_posts().
get_queried_object()	Set $queried_object if it's not already set.
get_queried_object_id()	Sets $queried_object_id if it's not already set.
WP_Query()	Constructs the class and takes a query string as an optional value.

Source: The WordPress Codex (http://codex.wordpress.org/Function_Reference/WP_Query).

Wrangling the Loop with Plugins

Back in Chapter 5, I spent a significant amount of time explaining action hooks and filters. These are the cornerstone for plugin development and, depending on the goal and type of hook, can be used to initiate an event or replace specific content with new content.

Discovering query hooks

In order to adjust the default behavior of the query, you will need to use one of the hooks available. Certainly, if a plugin requires a custom Loop, you can instantiate a new instance of WP_Query and pass parameters that will possibly provide the data that you expect. In many cases, though, you cannot accomplish your goals simply by instantiating a new query object and carrying on. Sometimes you actually have to modify how the query is sent or how content is sorted.

Most of the work involving the query is in a file, aptly named, query.php (/wp-includes/query.php). In this file, you will find the WP_Query class with a number of helper functions to assist in managing and using the class. You will also find 7 action hooks and 26 filters, all of which are listed in Table 8.2. This portion of the WordPress provides the richest opportunity for modification due to the high number of hooks.

Cross-Reference

Appendix A contains a full reference to hooks and Chapter 5 explains how hooks are used. ∎

Note

When it comes to the query, I don't have enough space in this book to demonstrate how to use all these hooks effectively. A good rule of thumb when dealing with the query is to recognize that because most of the available hooks are filters, the content being filtered is going to MySQL in the form of SQL statements, and not to the browser as hypertext markup language (HTML). If you keep this concept in mind, you will find the modification of the query data easier to digest. ∎

TABLE 8.2

Filters and Actions Available for the Query

Hook	What It Does	Hook	What It Does
posts_where	Filter: Alters SQL WHERE clause	posts_orderby_requests	Filter: Used for caching only. Use posts_orderby for plugins.
posts_join	Filter: Alters SQL JOIN clause	posts_distinct_request	Filter: Used for caching only. Use posts_distinct for plugins.

continued

TABLE 8.2 *(continued)*

Hook	What It Does	Hook	What It Does
comment_feed_join	Filter: Alters comment SQL JOIN clause	posts_fields_request	Filter: Used for caching only. Use posts_fields for plugins.
comment_feed_where	Filter: Alters comment SQL WHERE clause	post_limits_request	Filter: Used for caching only. Use post_limits for plugins.
comment_feed_groupby	Filter: Alters comment SQL GROUP BY clause	posts_request	Filter: Can be used to replace the query entirely with raw SQL.
comment_feed_orderby	Filter: Alters comment SQL ORDER BY clause	posts_results	Filter: Can be used to supply a custom dataset, effectively overriding the entire SQL query.
comment_feed_limits	Filter: Alters comment SQL LIMIT clause	found_posts_query	Filter: Can be used to replace the FOUND_ROW() SQL query.*
posts_where_paged	Filter: Alters SQL paging for posts using WHERE clause	found_posts	Filter: Effectively identical to found_posts_query but is used to override the result of the FOUND_ROW() query.
posts_groupby	Filter: Alters SQL paging for posts using GROUP BY clause	the_preview	Filter: Can be used to adjust the "Preview Post" function on the Write Post or Page screens in WordPress Admin.
posts_join_paged	Filter: Alters SQL paging for posts using JOIN clause	the_posts	Filter: Can be used to supply a different dataset of posts than what is provided through the standard query.
posts_orderby	Filter: Alters SQL paging for posts using the ORDER BY clause	parse_query	Action: Specify your own handler for query arguments.
posts_distinct	Filter: Alters SQL paging for posts using the DISTINCT keyword	pre_get_posts	Action: Specify an event to occur before posts are retrieved.
post_limits	Filter: Alters SQL paging for posts using the LIMIT clause	posts_selection	Action: Intended for caching, this announces the current selection parameters.

Hook	What It Does	Hook	What It Does
posts_fields	Filter: Alters SQL for paging for posts by designating fields to be SELECTed	loop_start	Action: An event that occurs on the first post in the Loop.
posts_where_request	Filter: Used for Caching only. Use posts_where_paged for plugins	loop_end	Action: An event that occurs on the last post of the Loop.
posts_groupby_request	Filter: Used for caching only. Use posts_groupby for plugins	comment_loop_start	Action: An event that occurs on the first comment in the Loop.
posts_join_request	Filter: Used for caching only. Use posts_join_pages for plugins	the_post	Action: An event that occurs after the first post has sent post_content

* The FOUND_ROWS() function is documented at `http://dev.mysql.com/doc/refman/5.0/en/information-functions.html`.

Altering the query with hooks

Consider being practical for a moment. Say you want to create a Loop that only consists of posts that don't include a tag called 'Food'. In this hypothetical example, the tag 'Food' has an ID of 15. If you recall back in Chapter 7, the WordPress tables that handle categories, tags, and link categories are the terms tables: `term_relationship` and `term_taxonomy`. These tables work in conjunction with each other so that metadata can be assigned to different pieces of content.

In the next example, you'll run the SQL query that is shown in Listing 8.3.

LISTING 8.3

Example of the SQL query that will be run in this demonstration

```
SELECT * FROM wp_posts
    LEFT JOIN $wpdb->term_relationships
        ON ( $wpdb->term_relationships.object_id=$wpdb->posts.ID)
    LEFT JOIN $wpdb->term_taxonomy
        ON( $wpdb->term_taxonomy.term_taxonomy_id =
$wpdb->term_relationships.term_taxonomy_id )
    LEFT JOIN $wpdb->terms
        ON ( $wpdb->term_taxonomy.term_id = $wpdb->terms.term_id )
    WHERE $wpdb->term_taxonomy.taxonomy = 'post_tag'
        AND $wpdb->terms.term_id != 15;
```

To be fair, this is a complicated query and probably more excessive than will typically be used. Really, you can get most of your data with two LEFT JOIN clauses, eliminating the need to tap into the `term_taxonomy` table that defines types of taxonomy. In summary though, this query fetches all posts from WordPress that do not have a tag (`post_tag`) with ID 15. The query needs to be able to look at the `term_taxonomy` table to find only the tags on the post, and it needs to look at the terms table to get the ID of the tag itself.

By default, the WordPress query is not going to make any effort to eliminate the posts that have the Food tag. The query that is sent will be much simpler than this. Clearly, you need to modify this query but in such a way that won't introduce security problems or break the way WordPress functions. You'll do this with a number of the query hooks and functions.

First you'll create a new function in the plugin file for the JOIN clauses. Assume that WordPress or a plugin that is active is already supplying the query with a JOIN statement of some type and so you probably don't want to change that behavior. The function can use the `posts_join_paged` filter to add your own JOINs, as shown in Listing 8.4.

LISTING 8.4

A function that can be used to alter the JOIN portion of the query using the posts_join_paged filter

```
function plugin_custom_sql_join( $joins )
{
    global $wpdb;
    $new_joins = array(
        "LEFT JOIN $wpdb->term_relationships ON ( $wpdb->term_
    relationships.object_id = $wpdb->posts.ID)",
        "LEFT JOIN $wpdb->term_taxonomy ON( $wpdb->term_taxonomy.term_
    taxonomy_id = $wpdb->term_relationships.term_taxonomy_id )",
        "LEFT JOIN $wpdb->terms ON ( $wpdb->term_taxonomy.term_id = $wpdb-
    >terms.term_id )",
        $joins
        );
    return implode( ' ', $new_joins );
}
add_filter('posts_join_paged', 'plugin_custom_sql_join');
```

Tip

The function can be written in a variety of ways. In this case, you added each JOIN as an array member, including the JOIN that is passed into the function. The function then uses `implode()` on the array to glue all the pieces together. Remember that all filters must have at least one argument passed in and one value returned. ■

The next part of the query that you need to construct involves the SQL WHERE clause. It needs to ensure that WordPress is not looking at non-tags (categories, link categories) and that it is identifying the proper tag ID to avoid. You can do this using the `posts_where_paged` filter. It operates in a similar fashion as `posts_join_paged`, as shown in Listing 8.5.

LISTING 8.5

A function that can be used to alter the WHERE portion of the query using the posts_where_paged filter

```
function plugin_custom_sql_where( $wheres )
{
    global $wpdb
    $new_wheres = array(
        "$wpdb->term_taxonomy.taxonomy = 'post_tag'",
        "$wpdb->terms.term_id != 15",
        $wheres
        );
    return implode( ' AND ', $new_wheres );
}
add_filter('posts_where_paged','plugin_custom_sql_where');
```

Note

Astute readers might notice that there are four filters that can be used to modify JOINs and WHEREs. The `posts_where` and `posts_where_paged` functionally are nearly identical while `posts_join` and `posts_join_paged` are virtually identical. The "paged" filters are used when results are paged, or delivered in sets of data. Generally, WordPress delivers content in sets of ten posts or whatever you have set in Settings ⇨ Reading and therefore, most situations will call for the "paged" versions of the hooks. ∎

Tip

A better way to modify the query involves the use of the function `parse_query()`. More specifically, the `parse_query()` function includes an action hook `parse_query`. By feeding an array of query variables to this hook, you can adjust all the specifics of the query without having to deal with the SQL. ∎

Developing Custom and Multiple Loops

Fortunately for many developers (and particularly theme developers), most instances of a Loop do not require modification of the query. Many of the special cases for Loop generation can be handled simply by passing a query string to a new `WP_Query` instance or by using `query_posts()`.

Using query_posts() and rewind_posts()

If you only have a single Loop on a page (including sidebar Loops like the "Recent Posts" widget), query_posts() functions fine. It simply returns all resulting data to the $wp_query object and the Loop can be handled in a typical fashion. In order to reuse this object, you would call the function rewind_posts() afterwards, as shown in Listing 8.6.

LISTING 8.6

The Loop can be modified using query_posts() and rewind_posts() to reset the Loop counter to the beginning

```php
<?php
query_posts( array('cat => 15, 'order' => 'ASC') );
if( have_posts() ) :
    while( have_posts() ) :
        the_post();
        ...
    endwhile;
endif;
rewind_posts();
?>
```

On the Web

The code in Listing 8.6 is available for download at www.wiley.com/go/wordpressbible.com. ∎

You'll notice that I have passed query_posts() in an array. I could have also passed in a query string like 'cat=15&order=ASC'. However, using an array is more flexible, as some of the options only work in array mode, such as the parameter, which takes an array of values. I discuss all the available options in a bit, but it's important to note that this query string affects what data is retrieved by the query. In this case, the query is only going to get posts from the category with an ID of 15 and it will sort in ascending order (default is descending). At the end of the code, the rewind_posts() function "resets" the Loop back to the first post, enabling you to use the same set of data again in another place on the page (such as the "Recent Posts" widget).

Instantiating a new Loop with WP_Query

There is a second, and arguably preferred, option for creating a custom Loop. It involves the instantiation of a new WP_Query object. It also takes a query string or array just like query_posts() (see Listing 8.7).

LISTING 8.7

The Loop can be instantiated with the WP_Query class

```php
<?php
$custom = new WP_Query('cat=15&order=ASC');
if( $custom->have_posts() ) :
    while( $custom->have_posts() ) :
        $custom->the_post();
        ...
    endwhile;
endif;
?>
```

On the Web

The code in Listing 8.7 is available for download at www.wiley.com/go/wordpressbible.com. ■

The key difference here is that instead of reusing $wp_query we are creating a separate object: $custom. $wp_query still exists and, if writing code that requires it, will still be accessible. The instantiation of a new object, however, enables both objects to exist and be accessible. As a result, there is no need to rewind_posts() afterward. The only other change we need to make is to use the object reference notation (such as, $custom->have_posts()) to execute the Loop.

Using variables to alter the query

WordPress enables you to pass many query string variables to adjust the data request of the query. The variables can be in an array or in a query string, which is a set of key/value pairs separated by ampersands (&). You can pass in as many or as few of these as you wish.

The query string variables available include the following:

- **order.** This can be either ASC for ascending or DESC for descending. By default, the query will retrieve data in descending order (equivalent to reverse chronological or "newest first" order). (Example: 'order' => 'ASC')

- **orderby.** This designates the field to order the set of posts. (Example: 'orderby' => 'title')

  - **author.** Order by the ID of an author.

  - **date.** Order by the date.

  - **title.** Order by the title.

  - **modified.** Order by the timestamp when posts were last modified. This will be identical to the date if it has not been edited since publishing.

  - **menu_order.** Order by the order set when you designate a numerical value, Order, on the page edit screen. (Order can only be set for pages from the WordPress Admin, not posts.)

  - **parent.** WordPress posts don't have parents, but pages and attachments do.

- **ID.** Order by the autogenerated numerical ID of the post or page.

- **rand.** Random order.

- **meta_value – a custom field value.** This can only be used if the `meta_key` variable is used in the query.

  - **none.** Used if you don't want to set a specific order. Note that this will default to the ID of the post.

- **cat, tag.** This variable is an integer or comma-separated list of integers specifying category or tag IDs. If a negative number is passed, WordPress eliminates that category or tag ID from the dataset. If zero (0) is passed, all categories or tags are included. (Example: `'cat' => '1,3,6,-4'`)

- **category_name.** If you pass a category display name (not sanitized), you can use this variable to select data only from the specified category. (Example: `'category_name' => 'Featured Story'`)

- **category__and, tag__and.** With this variable, you can pass an array of category or tag IDs to select only posts that are fit the requirements. (Example: `'category__and' => array(3,7,2)`)

- **category__in, tag__in.** Similar to `category__and`, this variable selects content that is in any of the specified category or tag IDs. (Example: `'category__in' => array(3,7)`)

- **category__not_in.** Similar to `category__in`, this variable enables you to designate an array of category IDs, and WordPress ensures that none of the content selected is in any of those IDs. (Example: `'category__not_in' => array(10,2)`)

- **tag_slug__and.** This variable selects content that includes all the tag IDs in the passed array. (Example: `'tag_slug__and' => array(10,11,12)`)

- **tag_slug__in.** This variable selects content that is in one of the tag IDs in the passed array. (Example: `'tag_slug__in' => array(13,54,2)`)

- **showposts.** An integer that specifies how many posts should be queried from the database. This overrides the setting chosen for the default Loop in Settings ➪ Reading. (Example: `'showposts' => 5`)

- **p.** If all you want is to retrieve a specific post (not a page), you can use this variable to specify the ID. (Example: `'p' => 3`)

- **name.** The slug of a post (WordPress lowercases and replaces spaces with hyphens). (Example: `'name' => hello-world`)

- **page_id.** Similar to the p variable, this variable designates the content of a specific page (not a post). (Example: `'page_id' => 13`)

- **pagename.** This variable is a string that designates the slug of a page title. In the event that you are trying to retrieve a child page, the slug of the parent and child must be included, separated by a forward slash (/). (Example: `'page_name' => 'about-us/contact'`)

- **post__in.** This variable enables you to specify an array of post IDs for inclusion. (Example: `'post__in' => array(5,6,7,8)`)

- **post__not_in.** This variable enables you to specify an array of post IDs to exclude. (Example: `'post__not_in' => array(10,4,3)`)

- **post_type.** This variable enables you to specify a specific type of post to include in the query. WordPress uses `post`, `page`, and `attachment` as defaults but a plugin developer could provide his own `post_type` as well. (Example: `'post_type' => page`)

- **post_status.** This variable allows the designation other than publish (which is the default). You can use this if you want to find posts with a different status. (Example: `'post_status' => draft`)

- **author.** This variable enables you to specify the ID of an author. When the ID is designated, only posts from this author will be returned. If the number designated is negative, all posts from this author will be excluded. (Example: `'author' => 12`)

- **author_name.** With this variable you can pass the display name of an author. (Example: `'author_name' => 'Aaron Brazell'`)

- **hour.** With this variable you can select posts published in a certain hour (0–23). (Example: `'hour' => 13` [for 1:00pm])

- **minute.** With this variable you can select posts published on a certain minute (0–59). (Example: `'minute' => 23` [23rd minute in any hour])

- **second.** With this variable you can select posts published on a certain second (0–59). (Example: `'second' => 2` [2nd second in any minute])

- **day.** With this variable you can select posts published on a certain day of the month (1–31). (Example: `'day' => 24` [24th day of any month])

- **monthnum.** With this variable you can select the numerical designation of a month (1–12). (Example: `'monthnum' => 9` [September of any year])

- **year.** With this variable you can set the four-digit year number. (Example: `'year' => 2010`)

- **w.** With this variable you can set the numerical number of the week in a year (1–53). (Example: `'w' => 1` [The week of January 1 in any year])

- **paged.** This variable designates the selection of posts that would appear on a given page of results. If you have set 15 posts in Settings ⇨ Reading or via the showposts query variable, the second page of results would be results 15–29. (Example: `'paged' => 2`)

- **offset.** This variable specifies an arbitrary result to begin querying posts at. If the offset is 1, the query will begin data retrieval after the first post. (Example: `'offset' => 5`)

- **meta_key.** This variable retrieves posts that have the designated custom field name. (Example: `'meta_key' => 'Executive Summary'`)

- **meta_value.** This variable retrieves posts that have any custom field with the designated value. (Example: `'meta_value' => 'thumbnail'`)

- **meta_compare.** If this variable is set, the default comparison operator for `meta_value` (which by default is =) is replaced by !=, >, >=, <, or <=. (Example: `'meta_compare' => '<='`)

Examples of WP_Query in action

The WP_Query method of creating custom Loops (as well as query_posts() to a lesser extent) is extremely useful. Here are some ideas for using custom Loops in your themes.

Featured stories

Situation: You are asked to create a masthead for a site. The masthead will include three thumbnails for featured stories. All featured stories are in a category called Featured Stories and many, but not all, of the stories have a custom field called Feature Thumbnail. The site will look odd if all the stories don't have thumbnails, and it would take too much time to go through each one and attach an image. Instead, you decide to create a custom Loop that pulls the most recent three featured stories that also have the designated custom field (see Listing 8.8).

LISTING 8.8

Using WP_Query to show the three most recent posts in the Featured Stories category that have a custom field called Feature Thumbnail

```
$masthead = new WP_Query( array('showposts' => 3, 'category_name' =>
    'Featured Stories', 'meta_key' => 'Feature Thumbnail') );
```

Future posts

Situation: You want to provide teasers for stories that are going to be written on a very busy news blog. Inside a widget that will be displayed on the sidebar, you want to get the titles of the posts so that readers can know what's coming up (see Listing 8.9).

LISTING 8.9

Using WP_Query to show the five most recent posts that are scheduled for publishing

```
$future = new WP_Query( array('showposts' => 5, 'post_status' => 'future')
    );
```

Display only sticky posts

Situation: You want a section of your site to display the most recent four sticky posts except the first one. You know the first sticky post will be in your main Loop and you've already worked out the query to ensure that only the first sticky post will be included in that Loop. You will be sending readers to this other section of your site to read the rest of the sticky posts.

You know that there isn't a direct option in the query to find sticky posts but that an array of post IDs of sticky posts are included in the options table. You can use a combination of `include` and `showposts` to limit the Loop results to only the four most recent sticky posts after the first (see Listing 8.10).

LISTING 8.10

Using WP_Query to display only the four most recent Sticky posts

```
$loop = new WP_Query( array('showposts' => 4, 'post__in' => get_
   option('sticky_posts') ) );
```

Our Loop uses `'showposts' => 4` to restrict how many results are going to be returned and `post__in` to provide our array of stickies.

Alternative Means of Retrieving Sticky Posts

Another way to perform the same function as shown in Listing 8.10 is with the following code:

```
function get_stickies( $begin = 0, $count = 10 )
{
    $all_stickies = get_option('sticky_posts');
    rsort( $all_stickies );
    return array_slice( $all_stickies, $begin, $count+1 );
}
$stickies = get_stickies(1,4);
$loop = new WP_Query('showposts=4&posts__in=' . $stickies);
```

This example provides its own function, `get_stickies()`, which does a little bit of the muscle work. It retrieves an array of post IDs from the database. This array is continually appended whenever you designate a post as sticky and save it and, thus, it is not necessarily in order. As a result, the function uses the PHP function `rsort()` to order the array in reverse chronological order. The higher numbers (most recent posts because post IDs increment upward) are placed first in the array with the lower IDs of older posts placed at the end. Finally, the function slices up the array to grab the IDs that are needed.

The function takes two arguments. The first is the `$begin` argument. This argument represents the offset; keep in mind that arrays in PHP begin with a key of 0 instead of 1. (You'll notice I increment the `$count` argument by one to fudge some numbers.) By default, this function assumes that numbering starts at the beginning of the array of stickies (array key 0). The second argument represents the number of sticky IDs that are actually going to be retrieved. Here, it's set at 10 but as you'll see, you're not going to use either default.

To retrieve the most recent four sticky posts, offset by 1, simply use `get_stickies(1,4)`. This retrieves array keys 1–5 in the sorted stickies array and returns it to `$stickies`.

Using Loops Strategically

Throughout this chapter, I've presumed you will use `WP_Query` to instantiate a custom Loop. This is seen by many to be a best practice because it enables you to operate with more than one Loop.

As the cornerstone of WordPress, the Loop is very important and it is common to need to query the posts more than once to achieve different results. Some sites will use featured stories "sliders" like those seen on popular news sites. Others use layouts that segment the page according to categories and display the Loop specific to those needs.

Caution

Using more than one Loop, while useful, introduces a potential performance problem. Multiple queries to the database, especially as they become more expensive (or complex), can bog down a database. This can be exacerbated by an unoptimized database. ■

Cross-Reference

For discussions about database optimization, see Chapter 2. To gain some overhead and caching benefits, see Chapter 18. ■

Though `query_posts()` can take all the same query string variables as `WP_Query`, it limits you to a single Loop.

Smashing Magazine author Jean-Baptiste Jung provides a fantastic list of ideas (`www.smashing magazine.com/2009/06/10/10-useful-wordpress-loop-hacks/`) that you can use in one or more Loops. Combining these ideas, as well as your own, can really liven up a site and enhance discoverability and search engine optimization (SEO).

Cross-Reference

Discoverability and SEO are key marketing strategies that are discussed in Chapter 3. ■

Following are more ideas for enhancing your site:

- Get posts published between two dates.
- Use more than one Loop on a page without duplicating results.
- Insert ads after the first post.
- Get posts with a specific custom field or value.
- List upcoming posts (I discussed this earlier).
- Use the Loop to create an "Archive" page template.
- Create your own WordPress Loops using the `WP_Query` object (I discussed this earlier).
- Get only the latest sticky posts (I discussed this to an extent earlier).
- Create a Loop of images.

These are only some ideas. Some are more common than others. Between these ideas as well as filters provided for the query, you are only limited by your imagination.

Summary

- The Loop is an integral mechanism of WordPress that includes the query (or retrieval) of data from the database and the rendering of the data in a theme.

- There are 26 filters and 6 actions available for query modification.

- You can use `query_posts()` and `WP_Query` to develop custom Loops. Using the `WP_Query` class enables you to have more than one Loop.

- Both `WP_Query` and `query_posts()` use the same query string variables passed as a named array or a query string.

- Sticky posts are placed at the top of the Loop. An array of sticky posts IDs is stored in the options table.

- You might try some interesting variations on the Loop such as featured stories, future dated posts, and so on. Keep in mind potential performance hits when using multiple customized Loops.

Part III

Working with Themes and Template Tags

Using Free or Premium Themes

I n WordPress, themes are a major part of the user experience. As with any Web site, the user interface can make or break a site's capability to build traffic, expose content for discovery, and enhance user stickiness.

Finding the balance between these three areas is a somewhat fuzzy, experimental process. Many WordPress users change their themes often. Some do it to experiment to see what works best while others do it to showcase their own design abilities and to try new things. Still others change themes regularly for no other reason than that they are bored.

IN THIS CHAPTER

Understanding the user experience

Finding and implementing free themes

Finding and implementing premium themes

Note

Stickiness **refers to how long readers stay on a site. The longer they stay around and read articles, the higher the site's stickiness. If a blog contains many long-form articles (more than 300 words), the site will have an enhanced stickiness level. If readers click to many pages and read them, this also enhances stickiness.** ■

Understanding the User Experience

Much science (or in some cases, voodoo) goes into creating a good user experience. Experts agree on many principles, but the devil is usually in the details. Many of the practicalities of user experience are subjective or change based on the demographic of a site, or the messaging and branding involved.

Note

Cascading Style Sheets (CSS) and styling is outside the scope of this book; however, it is also an intimate part of designing (or modifying) themes for WordPress. For a jump-start on design and user experience development, I recommend picking up the *HTML, XHTML, and CSS Bible, 4th Edition* by Steven M. Schafer (Wiley, 2008). ∎

Typography

User experience experts strongly agree good typography is essential, but the opinions diverge from there. Some will say that using a serif font (like the popular Georgia font) sends a strong message of stoicism and tradition while arguments on behalf of sans-serif fonts (Arial, Helvetica, and so on) send messages of elegance and clarity. You can see the comparison in Figure 9.1.

FIGURE 9.1

A comparison of serif and sans-serif font faces

An example of a serif font

An example of a sans-serif font

Font discussion continues beyond font type to sizing, styling, words per line, line spacing, and so on. Every user-experience professional holds to basic principles of font selection, but many diverge on specifics because it tends to be a topic of personal taste.

White space

Another common consideration when selecting a theme is white space. White space tends to make a site more readable but, like fonts, does not guarantee the site will draw users. One technique is to add vertical spacing between lines of text. Additionally, you can enhance white space with ample padding and margins around images, pull quotes, or sidebar spacing. When white space is not used with care, a site can become "cluttered" and visually chaotic. Readers tend to have little patience for this kind of experience.

Note

Pull quotes are most often used in newspapers and magazines. They area layout element that sets apart a quote or some notable text to draw the reader into the article. They are usually eye catching, often in a larger font size, and can be a different color than the body text. Smashing Magazine provides a good overview on pull quotes and styling at `www.smashingmagazine.com/2008/06/12/block-quotes-and-pull-quotes-examples-and-good-practices.` **∎**

VentureBeat.com, a technology news site covering the business behind the venture capital and Web startup industries, provides a good example of the use of white space (see Figure 9.2). The navigation elements of the site maintain a vertical balance between elements at the top of the page and the start of content below. Because it uses many thumbnail images to represent articles, you can see margins and spacing in play to attract readers' eyes from the image and into the article itself. On the edges, there is an adequate amount of neutral space, providing a sense of space without conveying a sense of emptiness.

FIGURE 9.2

VentureBeat.com uses ample white space around the edges of the page and around key elements of the page.

Fixed or fluid width

A third element to consider when choosing a theme is whether the theme has a fixed-width or fluid-width layout. Fixed-width layouts have a specific width that never changes, regardless of the size of the browser window. Fixed-width layouts often are designed to accommodate a specific screen resolution and can have too much white space when viewed on monitors that are larger, or with resolution that is higher, than specified. However, they are usually easier to design because dimensions and expectations are determined before the design starts and there is much less room for unknowns.

A good example of a fixed-width Web site design is the BBC news site at http://bbc.co.uk. As the browser window is resized, the elements of the layout don't change, even when the browser window width is smaller than the overall width of the page.

On the other hand, fluid-width sites adapt to the browser window and scale accordingly. These layouts, while popular, can be difficult to achieve when imagery is part of the structure. Fluid-width sites are often good for content-rich sites but introduce a lot of nuances to the design process. Different browsers render differently and fluid-width layouts make it difficult to completely address all types of user choices and preferences.

Engadget (`http://engadget.com`), the popular gadget blog from AOL, employs a fluid-width layout. While certain elements are constricted to a minimum width, creating some fixed-width behavior at lower resolutions, when the browser is resized, many of the page elements are flexible.

Sidebars

Most WordPress themes (and blogs in general) have sidebars. Depending on your site, you might want a single sidebar or more than one. You can even go with no sidebars. (Often, sites without sidebars have "normal" sidebar elements as part of their footers.)

Sidebars are often used to display ads, recent posts, recent comments, popular posts, or information from other social networks such as Flickr or Twitter. Because most themes are built to be able to use widgets, it is easy to configure or reconfigure them.

Cross-Reference
WordPress themes that support widgets are easy to configure. I talk about configuring widgets, providing widgets in themes and plugins, and designing themes with widgets in mind in Chapter 6. ∎

Finding and Implementing Free Themes

WordPress themes are the other side of WordPress extensibility. In Part II of this book, I took a long, hard look at plugins, hooks, widgets, and other aspects of extending WordPress with plugins. The other side of that equation is themes.

As with plugins, WordPress has an entire theme infrastructure available for theme developers to use. The theme application programming interface (API) is comprised of an abundance of template tags and, as with plugins, themes can be installed with one click from inside the WordPress Admin.

Bloggers who want to install themes from within WordPress can do so by choosing Appearance ➪ Add New Themes. This interface provides a rich set of filters based on colors, columns, layout type (fixed or fluid), feature set, or subject (a gooey kind of filter based around "intent of the theme").

In addition, you can search for themes by keyword. The filter interface is simply an interface that inserts the commonly used keywords associated with the filter name, such as "two-columns."

Note
The WordPress theme installer uses the WordPress Themes Directory located at `http://wordpress.org/extend/themes/`, which I discuss later in this chapter. ∎

As an example, you'll find a dark-colored theme with a fluid (also known as *flexible*) layout and threaded comment support. To do this, follow these steps:

1. Choose the Appearance ⇨ Add New Theme page in WordPress Admin, select the Dark check box in the Colors group, select the Flexible check box in the Width group, and select the Threaded Comments check box in the Features group.

2. Click Find Themes to perform a search of the available themes with those options in the WordPress Themes Directory.

3. Review the available options and click Install next to your desired theme. You can click Preview to see a sampling of what the theme will look like and click Details to get version and rating information about the theme. For this example, click the Install link under the Charcoal theme.

4. Click the Install button in the preview box. You will need to have your FTP (or if available, SFTP) connection information to enable WordPress to perform the install.

5. To activate the theme after a successful installation, click the Activate link. You can also activate the theme from the Appearance ⇨ Themes page.

This interface is shown in Figure 9.3.

FIGURE 9.3

The WordPress Admin interface for installing themes

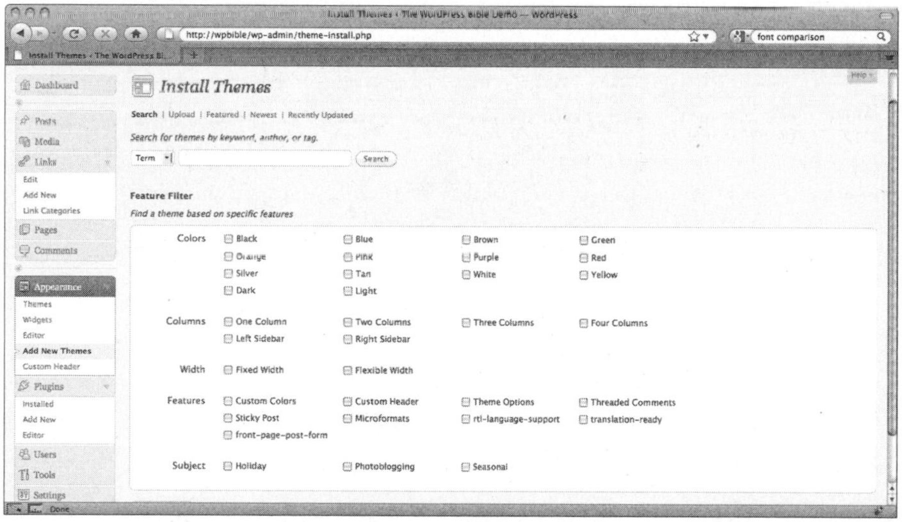

Once you have installed the theme (and optionally activated it), you can make theme modifications with CSS or adjust the code as needed. Once you activate it, you can customize it further with widgets. With no additional configuration, widgets, or code changes, your site should look similar to Figure 9.4.

FIGURE 9.4

WordPress with a theme that is configured to use widget, but with no widgets configured, has a default layout for the sidebar. This is coded according to the wishes of the theme designer but disappears once any widget is configured for use.

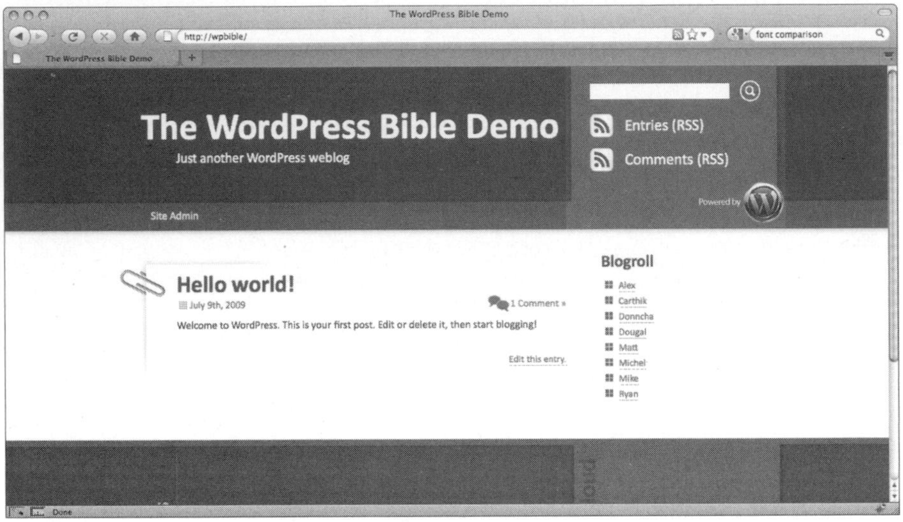

If you don't want to use the WordPress Admin to install a new theme, or if you want to use a theme not currently listed in the WordPress repository (there are still many themes that have not been added to the repository, are not necessarily under the General Public License (GPL), or are custom designed and made), you can manually upload your theme. To do this, follow these steps:

1. **Download the theme zip file from the WordPress Themes Directory or third-party download site.**

2. **Extract the zip file.** This creates a folder with all the theme files inside it.

3. **Upload the theme via FTP or SFTP to the /wp-content/themes folder.** For example, if the theme folder is called `cool-theme/`, you would upload the folder and end up with `/wp-content/themes/cool-theme/`.

4. **From the WordPress Admin, choose Appearance ⇨ Themes.**

5. **To Preview the theme before activating it, click the Preview link below your new theme.** To activate the theme without previewing it first, skip to Step 7.

6. **To activate the theme from the Preview window, click the Activate link in the upper right corner.**

7. **To activate the theme without previewing it first, click the Activate link under the theme listing.**

Finding and Implementing Premium Themes

Theme designers in the WordPress community are split down the GPL line. From the Automattic side of the house (the main proprietor of WordPress), there is no endorsement of premium themes (whether by explicit blessing or by implicit inclusion in the Themes Directory). In fact, this side of the argument has been historically hostile to the use of premium themes.

This position is based largely on some historical abuses by premium theme developers that carry licenses requiring inclusion of links back to the developer or sponsor site, or even by inclusion of hidden keyword stuffing routines intended to generate traffic for some other source. Fortunately, this is not as common as it used to be when premium themes first arrived on the scene.

However, despite this abuse by some premium theme developers, many popular premium themes out there don't carry the same burden. These themes, such as the very popular and extensible Thesis theme (shown in Figure 9.5) from DIYThemes, provide the blogger with a multitude of configuration options, theme hooks, and WordPress Admin configuration interfaces.

Premium themes are different than free themes in one key area — you pay for them. These premium themes can cost as little as $70 (U.S. dollars, or USD) or as much as several hundred dollars. Some premium themes, like the ones available from WooThemes (`http://woothemes.com`) have licenses that are compatible with WordPress' license and give you as much freedom as you have with WordPress itself. Others, such as the Thesis theme, have proprietary licenses that restrict your use of the theme and may also require that you keep a link to the creator of the theme displayed on your site.

FIGURE 9.5

The Thesis theme is one premium theme that has so many built-in hooks and functionality that it has turned into somewhat of a theme framework.

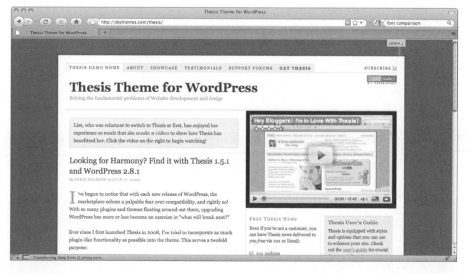

Premium themes are often a good compromise between using a common free theme available from the WordPress Themes Directory or other source, and having a completely unique custom-designed theme that could cost thousands of dollars. Table 9.1 provides a list of premium theme suppliers and price ranges.

TABLE 9.1

A Selection of Premium Theme Providers

Supplier Name	URL	Price Range (USD)*
DIYThemes (Thesis Theme)	http://diythemes.com	$87–$164
WooThemes	http://woothemes.com	$70–$200
StudioPress	http://studiopress.com	$59.95–$199.95
iThemes	http://ithemes.com	$79.95–$199.95
Colorlabs Project	http://colorlabsproject.com	$70–$240
Theme Galaxy	http://themegalaxy.net	$60–$120

* Prices as of July 2009.

An attractive feature of most premium themes is a built-in administrative interface that helps bloggers stand up new sites quickly and efficiently. Depending on the theme, design and configuration options driven from the WordPress Admin can change a theme entirely. The WooThemes administrative interface, shown in Figure 9.6, enables bloggers to choose prebuilt color schemes, upload logo files, create thumbnail sizes, and more.

FIGURE 9.6

The WordPress administrative interface for WooThemes

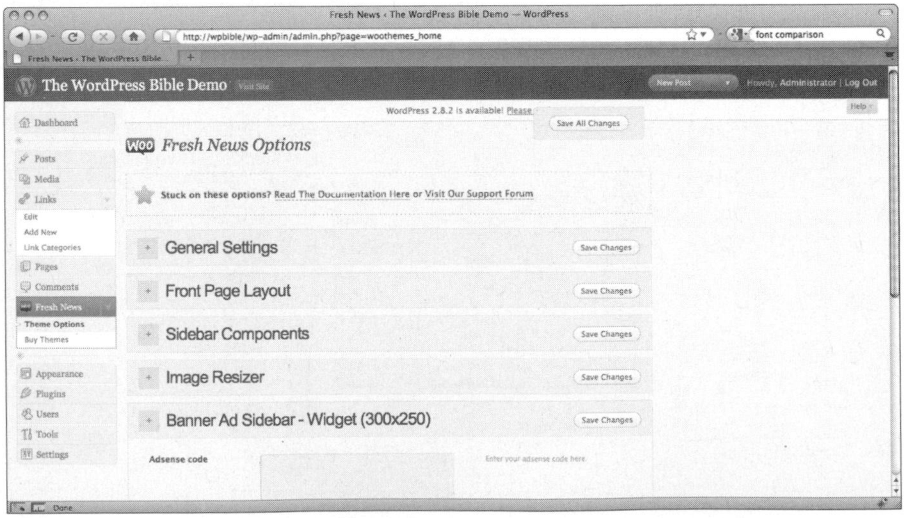

Regardless of whether you opt to use a premium theme, a free theme, or just design your own, the theme system for WordPress has many options to fit your taste and blogging goals. There are certainly many outstanding free themes you can use or modify, and you can radically configure premium themes with a click of a button.

Summary

- When looking for a theme, look for solutions that will build traffic, expose content, and enhance stickiness.

- Typography is an elegant way to enhance a user experience in a theme.

- Use white space to create context or pull a reader's eye to important information.

- Fixed-width themes are easier to build because fewer assumptions about the user's browser need to be made. Fluid- (or flexible-) width layouts expand and contract with a browser window size, but can create unexpected results if not tested thoroughly.

- Hundreds of free themes are available online. Many of them are in the WordPress Themes Directory and can be installed directly from WordPress Admin.

- Premium themes cost money, but they are usually well polished, easy to configure, and can quickly provide a distinct appearance from more common themes.

Understanding the Template File Hierarchy

WordPress provides a robust theme system. With its system of files and file hierarchy, it is possible to create very complex or very simplistic themes that render different content in different ways.

The first order of business, before describing the template file hierarchy, is to determine the different types of content WordPress can handle out of the box. As noted in the database schema for the posts table (see Table 7.1 in Chapter 7), WordPress comes with four different content types: posts, pages, attachments, and revision. Each of these data types can have a unique template.

Cross-Reference

See Chapter 7 for more information about the WordPress database schema and interacting with the database. ∎

With this data classified, it is also possible to recognize a few key groupings of content. These groupings can best be thought of as ways to organize content. *Archives* are the most common, but archives can be broken down further into category archives, tag archives, and date-based archives. And then each of these groupings can have individual templates.

Of course, there are basic template files as well. Every theme needs a stylesheet, for example, while most themes include a template file for the structural elements of a page such as the header, footer, and sidebar. I cover all the files and their hierarchies throughout this chapter.

Looking at the Minimum Necessary Template Files

The WordPress theme system needs a minimum of one file to operate: `style.css`. Most themes use more, but a minimalistic theme could use just this one file and rely on another theme as a parent theme.

Note

Throughout this chapter, remember that `index.php` is the catch-all file that handles all theming if a template doesn't exist for the request. For example, without a `search.php`, file, `index.php` handles the rendering of search data according to the markup you provide. ■

style.css

Every theme must have a `style.css` file and it must be named as such. Of course, you are free to include other Cascading Style Sheet (CSS) files, such as Internet Explorer-specific CSS if you'd like, but this file must exist for WordPress to recognize the theme.

The `style.css` file contains a set of headers, much like you would see in a plugin file. This set of headers is necessary for WordPress to read the theme and display information (including activation information) about it.

Cross-Reference

The theme headers are similar to the plugin headers. See Chapter 5 for more information. ■

A typical set of `style.css` headers might look like Listing 10.1. It is the CSS file from the default Kubrick theme that I reference throughout this chapter.

Note

WordPress purists tend to dislike the Kubrick theme for many reasons; they might not like its design, have other personal preferences, or feel is doesn't fit the need for different blog concepts. However, it forms the basis for many other themes that exist publicly and provides a solid foundation for theme concepts. Given it is included with WordPress, I will use it as a reference point. However, I tend to agree with the purists, and believe it should be replaced with a more semantic, simplified theme that designers can build upon, without having to channel the design tastes of another designer, and it should provide more flexibility in a world where blog design is emerging to fill new needs. ■

LISTING 10.1

The style.css headers in the default Kubrick theme

```
/*
Theme Name: WordPress Default
```

```
Theme URI: http://wordpress.org/
Description: The default WordPress theme based on the famous <a
    href="http://binarybonsai.com/kubrick/">Kubrick</a>.
Version: 1.6
Author: Michael Heilemann
Author URI: http://binarybonsai.com/
Tags: blue, custom header, fixed width, two columns, widgets
*/
```

As with plugin files, you are required to provide the Theme Name header, while other headers are optional. It is recommended that you supply all headers because it provides more metadata for WordPress to use to identify the theme in the WordPress Admin. The Tags header is especially useful if you wish to make your theme publicly available (and searchable) on the WordPress.org theme repository or hope to have it included as an available theme on WordPress.com. WordPress also will use a thumbnail image to display the theme. This image should be called screenshot. png and be included in the root of the theme directory.

WordPress Admin, as noted, will use this metadata to identify the theme for the user. Figure 10.1 illustrates how the Kubrick theme appears with its provided metadata.

The header data provided in style.css is parsed out by WordPress to provide useful information for the user in selection of the theme. The thumbnail used is called screenshot.png and should be included in the theme as a piece of helper data.

index.php

The `index.php` file is the second required file for a theme. It is the catchall file for a WordPress theme. As WordPress descends through the hierarchy of files it looks at to render data, the `index.php` file serves as the lowest common denominator for the blog. As such, it should be flexible enough to handle all types of data. Realistically, it could be as simple as a static hypertext markup language (HTML) file with no PHP, WordPress template tags, or logic, though this is not overly useful and defeats the purpose of WordPress.

In general, the `index.php` file should include a minimal Loop. The Loop will handle query data and render it accordingly. In most cases, `index.php` will be the home page of a blog, though increasingly, more complex themes are introducing cases where `index.php` is not the home page. This generally happens when WordPress is used as a content management system (CMS) primarily with a blog as secondary.

Cross-Reference

The Loop is an integral part of WordPress and can be used to make WordPress do very powerful things. The Loop is discussed in more detail in Chapter 8. ■

Note

It is important to note that a theme `index.php` is not the same as the WordPress `index.php`. When I discuss `index.php` in this context, I am referring to a file that is called far down the order of operations for WordPress. When WordPress begins its bootstrap, the WordPress `index.php` in the blog root is called first. Depending on a variety of circumstances, execution is passed to other files along the way, and eventually to the theme itself. When the theme rendering begins, the `index.php` is called if conditions for other template files can't be met. ■

A typical `index.php` file looks similar to the code shown in Listing 10.2.

LISTING 10.2

A minimal representation of a typical index.php file

```php
<?php
get_header();
if( have_posts() ) :
    while( have_posts() ) : the_post();
    ?>
    <h2><a href="<?php the_permalink(); ?>"><?php the_title(); ?></a></h2>
    <small>Published on <?php the_time(); ?> by <?php the_author(); ?></small>
    <?php the_content(); ?>
    <?php comments_template(); ?>
    <?php
    endwhile;
```

```
else :
    ?>
    <h2>Post Not Found</h2>
    <p>The post cannot be found.</p>
    <?php
endif;
get_sidebar();
get_footer();
?>
```

On the Web

The code in Listing 10.2 is available for download at `www.wiley.com/go/wordpressbible`. ∎

Ignoring the HTML involved (it will vary from theme to theme), there are a couple key things to take note of here. First of all, you'll notice a few template tags that call other template files. The `get_header()` function includes the template file `header.php` while `get_sidebar()` and `get_footer()` does the same for `sidebar.php` and `footer.php`, respectively. A fourth template tag, `comments_template()`, performs the comments query and includes the `comments.php` file inside the Loop.

Cross-Reference

Template tags are discussed in Chapter 12. ∎

Tip

If you've worked in PHP before, you know that variables that are declared inside a function are not available outside of this scope unless you intentionally make them global. The same principle holds true with the `get_header()`, `get_sidebar()`, and `get_footer()` functions. If you declare a variable inside the `header.php` file and then use the template tag to include that file, you will not be able to reliably use these variables in other parts of the theme without globalizing them — something that could cause security problems or conflicts with other parts of WordPress. Instead, use the PHP function `include()` to include template files that have variables that you intend to use in other parts of your theme. ∎

The key takeaway when building your `index.php` file is that you should keep it simple. It should be able to handle any data that is handed to it, even if you intend to include other template files in your theme. If you do not intend to include other template files in your theme, consider using conditional tags like `is_category()` or `is_search()`, or even `is_404()` to render your data appropriately. The downside of this approach is that it is very easy to turn your files into spaghetti code.

Note

WordPress has done a fantastic job in the past few versions of ensuring that every element that is dynamically rendered in a theme has semantic markup with semantic IDs and classes. This makes it all the more easy to render different pages with different appearance without altering markup. ∎

Understanding the Common Template Files

Most themes include a set of files that are, by most people, considered necessary for the proper functioning of a theme. As a best practice, you should probably include all the common template files in your theme even though you technically only need the `style.css` mentioned earlier.

Each of the files discussed in this section has a specific role and can help break up your theme into easily maintained and modified files. Certain files, such as `header.php`, `footer.php`, and `sidebar.php` make it easy to segregate key portions of your blog into a single location, making modification and upkeep that much simpler. Figure 10.2 demonstrates the complete order of operation with template files.

FIGURE 10.2

WordPress operates with this template file hierarchy, as described in this chapter. In general, `index.php` serves any request where WordPress does not offer a suitable template.

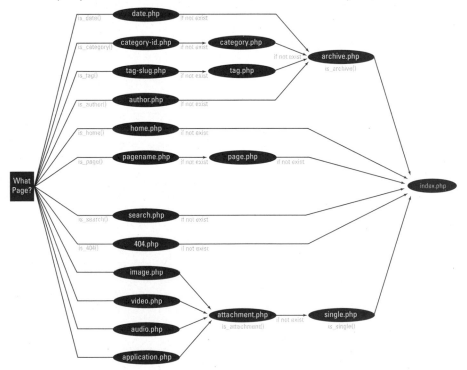

Credit: The WordPress Codex (`http://codex.wordpress.org`)

header.php

The top portion of the HTML source that is rendered with a theme is most likely consistent across all portions of the site. (See Figure 10.3 for an example of a header provided by the `header.php` file.) This is for branding as well as consistency. In a typical HTML page, there is a `<head>` tag that includes all relevant information about the page, such as location of the stylesheet, meta tags, title tags, and any JavaScript necessary to render the page. It also provides information to feed readers about the location of your RSS or Atom feed. This is all information that is likely to be consistent across your theme (or include logic that is self contained to render the included code appropriately).

FIGURE 10.3

The highlighted area shows the section of the default template provided by `header.php`.

The default portion rendered by the header.php file

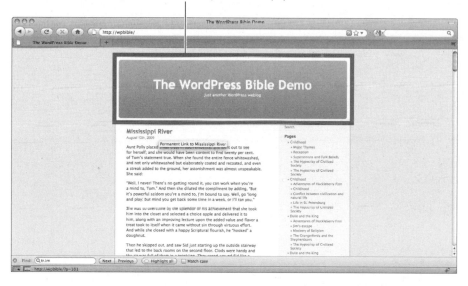

Many theme designers include upper portions of their site, such as the masthead or logo area, as part of `header.php`. The important thing is that all consistent data should be included in the `header.php` file. The default theme has a fairly standard `header.php` (shown in Listing 10.3) that many people rip off for their own themes. (It's under the General Public License [GPL], so you can legally rip it off!)

LISTING 10.3

The default theme header.php

```
<!DOCTYPE html PUBLIC "-//W3C//DTD XHTML 1.0 Transitional//EN" "http://www.
    w3.org/TR/xhtml1/DTD/xhtml1-transitional.dtd">
<html xmlns="http://www.w3.org/1999/xhtml" <?php language_attributes(); ?>>
<head profile="http://gmpg.org/xfn/11">
<meta http-equiv="Content-Type" content="<?php bloginfo('html_type'); ?>;
    charset=<?php bloginfo('charset'); ?>" />
<title><?php wp_title('&laquo;', true, 'right'); ?> <?php bloginfo('name');
    ?></title>
<link rel="stylesheet" href="<?php bloginfo('stylesheet_url'); ?>"
    type="text/css" media="screen" />
<link rel="pingback" href="<?php bloginfo('pingback_url'); ?>" />
<style type="text/css" media="screen">
<?php
// Checks to see whether it needs a sidebar or not
if ( empty($withcomments) && !is_single() ) {
?>
    #page { background: url("<?php bloginfo('stylesheet_directory'); ?>/
    images/kubrickbg-<?php bloginfo('text_direction'); ?>.jpg") repeat-y top;
    border: none; }
<?php } else { // No sidebar ?>
    #page { background: url("<?php bloginfo('stylesheet_directory'); ?>/
    images/kubrickbgwide.jpg") repeat-y top; border: none; }
<?php } ?>
</style>
<?php if ( is_singular() ) wp_enqueue_script( 'comment-reply' ); ?>
<?php wp_head(); ?>
</head>
<body <?php body_class(); ?>>
<div id="page">

<div id="header" role="banner">
    <div id="headerimg">
        <h1><a href="<?php echo get_option('home'); ?>/"><?php
    bloginfo('name'); ?></a></h1>
        <div class="description"><?php bloginfo('description'); ?></div>
    </div>
</div>
<hr />
```

This code should give you a fairly good idea of how to use many of the template tags. The function `bloginfo()` is a template tag that wraps around the `get_option()` function used in many plugins. It has a variety of different options that are used in templates, most notably `"name"`, "description", "home", "siteurl", "stylesheet_directory", and "stylesheet_ url". These are, of course, only a fraction of the options available to bloginfo().

In the case of the default theme, some of HTML that is generated after the <body> tag is also included. This varies from theme to theme and depends largely on how many commonalities are on each template. For example, if a theme is going to have a different header image on each page, the easiest way to do this would be to exclude that HTML from header.php and use it on the individual templates.

Another thing to note about header.php is the inclusion of a function called wp_head(). This function is a wrapper around the action hook wp_head and should be included in every theme to ensure complete compatibility with plugins that rely on this hook to inject JavaScript, CSS, or other tags into the header.

footer.php

Like header.php, the footer template in footer.php isn't mandatory. It is, however, highly recommended given a footer is a standard part of most sites. Like the header, the footer is generally consistent across all aspects of a site, so moving it to its own file is beneficial for maintenance and clean code (see Figure 10.4).

FIGURE 10.4

The highlighted area shows the section of the default template provided by footer.php.

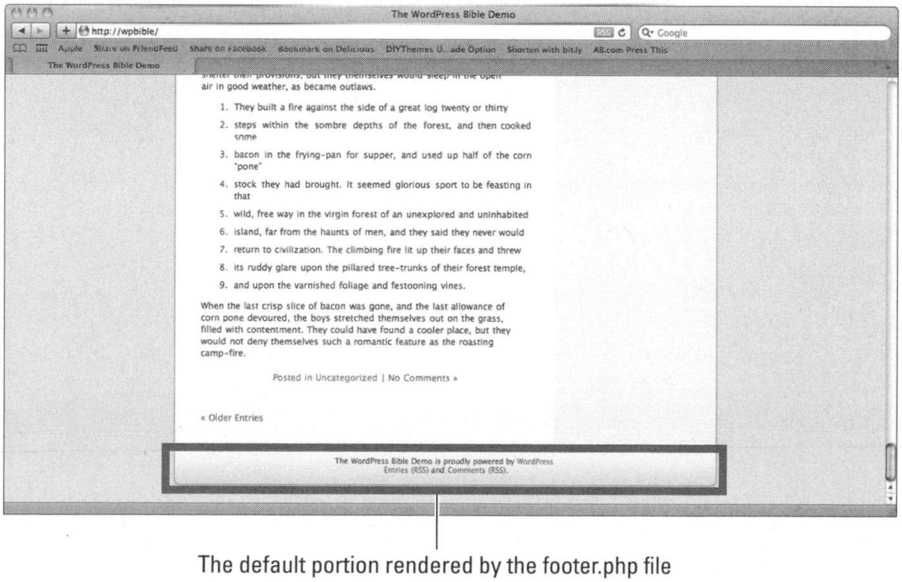

The default portion rendered by the footer.php file

The default theme uses a fairly standard style of footer that is emulated by many themes (see Listing 10.4.). You'll want to ensure that you use the `wp_footer()` function which, like `wp_head()` used in the header, is a wrapper around the action hook `wp_footer`. This hook is often used by plugins and should be included in every theme to ensure maximum plugin compatibility.

LISTING 10.4

The default theme footer.php

```
<hr />
<div id="footer" role="contentinfo">
<!-- If you'd like to support WordPress, having the "powered by" link
    somewhere on your blog is the best way; it's our only promotion or
    advertising. -->
    <p>
        <?php bloginfo('name'); ?> is proudly powered by
        <a href="http://wordpress.org/">WordPress</a>
        <br /><a href="<?php bloginfo('rss2_url'); ?>">Entries (RSS)</a>
        and <a href="<?php bloginfo('comments_rss2_url'); ?>">Comments
(RSS)</a>.
        <!-- <?php echo get_num_queries(); ?> queries. <?php timer_
stop(1); ?> seconds. -->
    </p>
</div>
</div>
<!-- Gorgeous design by Michael Heilemann - http://binarybonsai.com/kubrick/
    -->
<?php /* "Just what do you think you're doing Dave?" */ ?>
        <?php wp_footer(); ?>
</body>
</html>
```

sidebar.php

The third common element in any theme is the sidebar (see Figure 10.5.). Many themes have more than one sidebar (two- and three-column themes are extremely popular). Whenever the `get_sidebar()` template tag is called, WordPress looks for `sidebar.php`. While sidebars get their name from historically appearing in an "off to the side" portion of a Web site (and in most cases, still do), sidebars can be horizontally oriented and placed anywhere on a page.

Most theme sidebars today are widgetized and have become known as places where users can personalize their blogs from within the WordPress Admin. To that end, many sidebars might consist of different "sidebars" within sidebars, a language nuance that stems from the difference between the structural sidebars discussed here and widgetized sidebars discussed in Chapter 6.

The highlighted area shows the section of the default template provided by sidebar.php.

The default portion rendered by the sidebar.php file

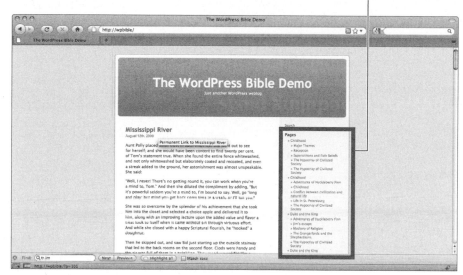

When you're using sidebar.php, there are a few things to remember. Always try to make your sidebars widgetized so bloggers can configure the theme to their tastes and needs. In addition to widgetizing the sidebar, always try to provide a default configuration. If a blogger chooses not to use widgets, WordPress looks to the HTML you provide in sidebar.php for markup.

Tip

For the best performance and SEO (search engine optimization) benefit, try to include the get_sidebar() **tag after your main content Loop. WordPress renders HTML in a straight-down fashion and, on slow network connections, you want the main content — the stuff people came to read, and probably the most important for your site — to render first. If the page load takes too long due to images or JavaScript widgets you might put in your sidebar, readers might not be patient enough to wait for the page to fully load to read the content. Putting your content first is also a good way to emphasize the "meat" of your page to search engines. ■**

comments.php

The comments_template() template tag prepares the comments query and includes the comments.php file. Alternatively, the comments_template() tag could invoke the comments-popup.php file, but this file is less commonly used as it forces a popup window — a practice that has become unpopular on the Web and might be blocked by browsers or third-party software.

The comments.php file commonly consists of a form for readers to leave comments, and includes WordPress core logic to determine if comments are open on a post or not. Typically, this template tag is only used on individual posts (rendered by `single.php` if available) or on individual pages (rendered by `page.php` or custom templates).

Most `comments.php` files include logic to ensure that comments are open on a post or a page, but also include logic to ensure that a user is logged in if the blogger requires it or enters a password if the post is password protected.

Tip

To set reading permission settings, choose Settings ⇨ Reading in the WordPress Admin. ■

As of WordPress 2.7, theme authors have access to a few new template tags that simplify the comment Loop. The first template tag, `wp_list_comments()`, handles all aspects of the comment Loop and can take an optional argument specifying type of comment. See Listing 10.5 for different variations.

LISTING 10.5

wp_list_comments() can display all comments, only pingbacks, or only real comments

```
// Displays all comments
wp_list_comments();
// Displays only pingbacks
wp_list_comments('type=pings');
// Displays only comments
wp_list_comments('type=comment');
```

Tip

The `wp_list_comments()` function takes more than just a single argument. It also can use `max_depth`, `style`, `callback`, `end-callback`, `page`, `per_page`, `avatar_size`, `reverse_top_level`, and `reverse_children`. Many of these query variables exist for the sake of threading comments and can be set by choosing Settings ⇨ Reading in the WordPress Admin. The most common template file usage, however, is to use `wp_list_comments()` to separate pingbacks from real comments. ■

Cross-Reference

I talk more about the `wp_list_comments()` template tag and others in Chapter 12. ■

A basic `comments.php` structure is shown in Listing 10.6. It includes logic to handle if comments are open and/or users are logged in, and separates pingbacks from comments. It also includes a form. Keep in mind that this example is a bare-bones example and overlooks semantic markup (such as the use of `<label>` tags in the form) and "paged comments" functionality. To see how this functionality is coded, refer to the `comments.php` file in the default theme (`/wp-content/themes/default/comments.php`).

LISTING 10.6

The comments.php file

```php
<?php
if (!empty($_SERVER['SCRIPT_FILENAME']) && 'comments.php' == basename($_
    SERVER['SCRIPT_FILENAME']))
     exit ('Please do not load this page directly. Thanks!');
if ( post_password_required() ) { ?>
     <p class="nocomments">This post is password protected. Enter the
    password to view comments.</p>
<?php
     return;
}
if( have_comments() ) :
     <h3>Pingbacks</h3>
     <ol><?php wp_list_comments('type=pings'); ?></ol>
     <h3>Comments</h3>
     <ol><?php wp_list_comments('type=comment'); ?></ol>
     if( comments_open() ) :
?>
<form action="<?php echo bloginfo('siteurl') ?>/wp-post-comment.php"
    method="post">
     <p>Name:</p>
     <input type="text" name="author" id="author" />
     <p>URL:</p>
     <input type="text" name="url" id="url" />
     <p>E-mail:</p>
     <input type="text" name="email" id="email" />
     <p>Comment:</p>
     <textarea name="comment" id="comment"></textarea>
     <input type="submit" id="submit" name="submit" value="Submit" />
</form>
<?php
     else :
          echo '<p>Comments are closed.</p>';
     endif;
endif;
?>
```

On the Web

The code in Listing 10.6 is available for download at www.wiley.com/go/wordpressbible. ■

single.php

When you go to a blog and click on a story, you are taken to a page that is most likely similar to other pages in the blog. However, it is likely to have a comment form and, if you take a closer look at the $wp_query object, you will note that the is_single property is set to true. Individual post pages are rendered by single.php. If this file doesn't exist, WordPress will use index.php instead.

Cross-Reference
For more on the Loop and $wp_query, **see Chapter 8.** ∎

If you're developing plugins that insert any code into individual pages, you'll want to use the is_single() conditional tag to limit the action to individual post pages.

Typically, single.php pages look almost identical to index.php in terms of code structure. The general difference (and again, I speak in generalities because individual theme designers might choose to change the way these pages render) is single.php includes the comments_template() template tag that inserts comments, pingbacks, and a comment form onto the page as shown in Figure 10.6.

On the back end, the Loop for the individual page only includes one post — the post that is being viewed at the time.

FIGURE 10.6

The single.php template renders an individual post along with the comments template.

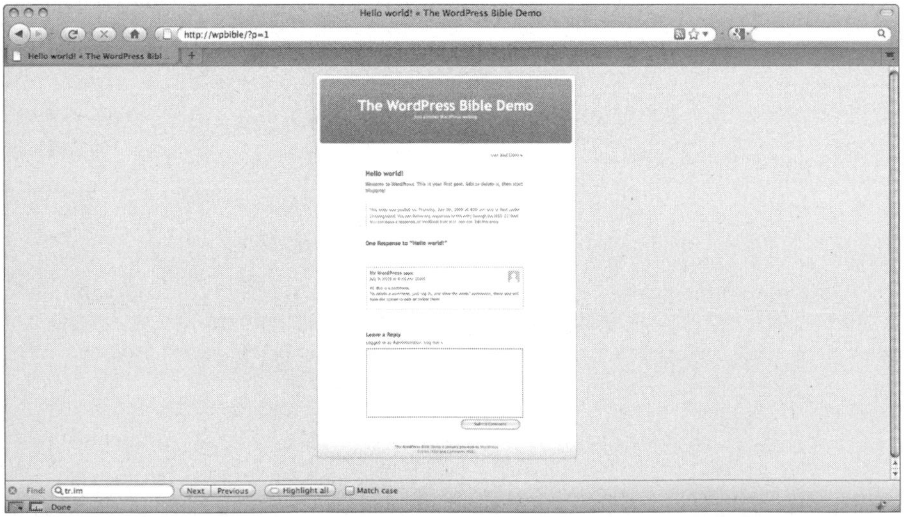

archive.php

The `archive.php` file provides a hierarchy for any kind of archive. In WordPress lingo, an *archive* can be anything from a tag-based archive (all posts with a given tag), a category-based archive, or a date-based archive. It can even be an author archive displaying all posts from a given author.

These types of archives provide a useful catch-all style template for most archive types, although, as I discuss later in the chapter, they can also be served up by other template files. If there is no `archive.php` file, `index.php` serves up the content.

When plugin developers examine the contents of the `$wp_query` object on this page, they'll find the `is_archive` property set to `true`. Depending on the type of archive it is, WordPress also sets one or more other properties (`is_month`, `is_year`, `is_day`, `is_tag`, `is_category`, or `is_author`). As a result, you can use the conditional template tags that relate to these types of archives to display custom content if you choose not to have individualized template files serve up content (`is_month()`, `is_year()`, `is_day()`, `is_tag()`, `is_category()`, or `is_author()`).

A typical `archive.php` file often looks very similar to `index.php` and generally includes the header, footer, and sidebar template tags.

page.php

WordPress pages are very similar to posts but represent a post type that most closely resembles static content. The `page.php` template is the generic template that serves this content and is similar to `single.php` Though pages are generically served by `page.php`, WordPress pages can be configured to be served from different files altogether. For example, it's entirely possible to create custom templates that are only available to WordPress pages (more on that later).

Pages are the one content type that is most likely to need specialized templates, and this is because they exist to extend WordPress beyond a "blog" and into a more traditional Web site model that you see when WordPress is used as a content management system.

On many sites that incorporate blogs into their offering, you will likely see traditional non-blog pages that inherit the look and feel of the Web site as a whole but might radically vary the structure of a site. For example, a corporate site might have a two-column blog that has a header, footer, sidebar, and content area while other areas of the site that are powered by WordPress pages might eliminate the sidebar altogether.

If there is one template file that deserves precise care, it is the `page.php` file. In the default WordPress theme, the `page.php` file looks very similar to the `single.php` file. It has a standard Loop and a comments template tag. It also includes a template tag, `wp_list_pages()`, that displays child pages. This is not a common practice, but it is worth noting that this template can be used differently than more traditional template files in the site. If there is no `page.php` in a theme, WordPress serves up the content of the page as `index.php`.

search.php

Whenever you do a search on WordPress, the results come up on a page called `search.php`. This page can take on the similar look and feel of the rest of the site or can be styled closer to the Google-style search results page. If you are using the WordPress search functionality (most themes do), this template, like the others, includes a standard Loop.

However, some plugins provide their own search results page, and some might offer their own application programming interface (API). At one point, I used a service that provided an API and my `search.php` file did not include a WordPress Loop. Instead, results were retrieved from the service and the PHP looped through those results.

Whenever a search is performed in WordPress (that is, a query string `s=searchterm` is passed in the URL), the `$wp_query` property `is_search` is set to true and WordPress looks to find `search.php` in the active theme. If no `search.php` is located, it uses `index.php` instead.

functions.php

It would be a straightforward process if themes only existed in a world of HTML, CSS, and template tags with minimal PHP requirements. Unfortunately, as the worlds between developer and designer intermingle, there is a need for custom PHP functionality. For this reason, `functions.php` exists.

The `functions.php` file provides a location for any ad-hoc PHP classes, functions, and logic that is needed for the theme specifically. It is used to make sidebars widget-ready (the original reason for its inclusion as a template file), and has come to be a place where theme configuration panels are created and added to the WordPress Admin, widgets are replaced, widgets are created, and other general plugin-like capabilities are created.

Cross-Reference
Widgets are discussed in Chapter 6 and plugins in Chapter 5. ■

The `functions.php` file can do anything that can be done in a plugin file. The difference is that it is self contained (meaning it does not require special activation to be included) and it is theme-specific. (If you choose a different theme, you no longer gain functionality or features provided by the original themes `functions.php` file.)

screenshot.png

Thumbnail images that provide a visual representation of a theme in the WordPress Admin are not necessary but they are certainly useful for bloggers. WordPress looks for the inclusion of `screenshot.png` and uses it as that visual representation. Though this image can be anything, it most often is a small (300×225 is a good average size) thumbnail of the site itself. Figure 10.7 is the `screenshot.png` for the default WordPress theme.

FIGURE 10.7

The screenshot.png image for the default WordPress theme

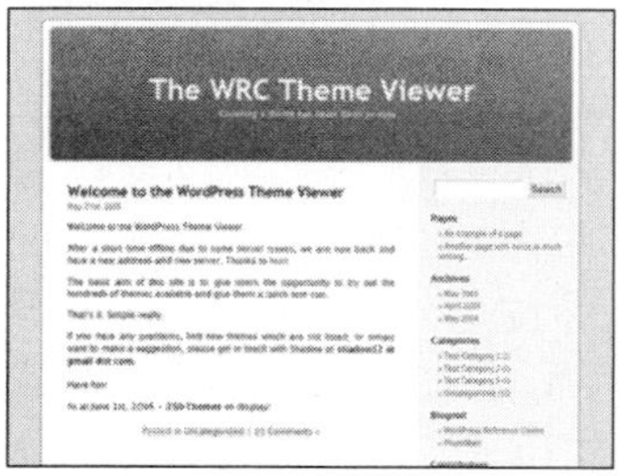

Enhancing the User Experience with Template Files

The Template hierarchy shown earlier in Figure 10.2 demonstrates that, though you will most often use the common template files described earlier in this chapter, they provide only a single layer in a theme. Realistically, you can get even more granular with your theme and offer more specific templates for different content types.

attachment.php

The `attachment.php` file is used in WordPress theming to display images and other extra-media types uploaded via the WordPress attachment uploading system. In theory, this template could be beneficial for bloggers who use WordPress as a photoblogging platform, but it can be used to display media of any sort.

When WordPress populates the `$wp_query` object on this page, the `is_attachment` property is set to true when the `post_type` is attachment. Keep in mind that posts, pages, and attachments are all stored in the posts table in the database and, as a content type, are all treated as "posts."

If `attachment.php` doesn't exist in the theme, WordPress uses `single.php` instead. ■

Cross-Reference
Using photoblogging as an alternative form of blogging is discussed in Chapter 20. ■

image.php, video.php, audio.php, and application.php

A more granular way to handle various media types is to use the `image.php`, `audio.php`, `video.php`, and `application.php` template files. Depending on the type of content being served, you could have a different template file for uploaded images or YouTube videos. These template files are not often used, but they are available to the creative theme developer.

If these files don't exist, the request is handled by `attachment.php`.

author.php

One of the varieties of archives I alluded to earlier in this chapter is an author archive. When `author.php` exists, it will be used to serve any archive request (the `$wp_query` property `is_author` is set to true) for authors. In its most simple form, `author.php` includes a standard Loop that displays posts from the author; however, many theme designers use this page to include information about the author as well (contact information, a picture, bio, and so on).

Figure 10.8 demonstrates how I have displayed an author archive on my site, Technosailor.com. In my version, I display the author photo and a bio. I also display subscription options so that readers can subscribe to the RSS or Atom feed of the specific author being viewed. Finally, I display some contact information before displaying a Loop providing recent posts that the author has written. Of course, a site owner can display author archives in other ways that suit the individual publication.

If no `author.php` file exists, a request for an author archive is served by `archive.php`.

FIGURE 10.8

On Technosailor.com, the author archive displays a number of profile-powered data items, including the contact information and bio, before displaying recent posts by the author.

tag.php

Another archive type you can use in a theme is `tag.php`. Like `author.php`, this file serves as an archive request for all posts (or page and attachment content if you so choose) that have a given tag. In typical form, this archive contains a standard Loop and the `$wp_query` property `is_tag` is set to true.

If no `tag.php` exists, tag archives are served by `archive.php`.

tag-{slug}.php

If you want to get even more granular with tag archives, you can do so by creating template files called `tag-{slug}.php` where `{slug}` is the sanitized version of the tag name. (My Tag becomes `my-tag`.) I cannot recall ever seeing this template tag used, and cannot think of many cases for it, but WordPress provides enough options that a creative theme developer could use this kind of template file to provide tag-based archives for individual tags.

If `tag-{slug}.php` does not exist, WordPress looks to `tag.php` for templating.

category.php

Similar to `tag.php` in almost every way, you can use the `category.php` template file to display category archives in a different way. Interestingly, the trend in theme development has revolved around categories as structural elements in a blog while tags have become synonymous with meta-data involving a post. Categories have become a way to structurally present different sections of a site, often in such a way that they appear to be entirely different blogs.

To that end, you can use the `category.php` file to provide some context to how data is presented in different ways. You can further drill down, as I'll talk about later in this chapter, by providing specific categories with different contexts to achieve an even richer result.

In its most common form, `category.php` includes a basic Loop and the `$wp_query` propery `is_category` is set to true.

If no `category.php` exists, `archive.php` serves all category archives.

category-{x}.php

On a more granular level, you can provide a specific template for specific categories. To do this, simply name the file `category-1.php` for category archives in category 1. This is an especially useful trick to use when developing themes with a category structural role. If you have a category called Business with a category ID of 10 and a separate category called Technology with an ID of 23 and these two categories serve to separate your blog into two entirely different verticals, you might want to have a `category-10.php` and a `category-23.php` file in your theme.

Generally these category archives are based off the more commonly used and provided `category.php`, but there are almost always distinct differences in markup to justify this type of extra granularity. (There's no reason to have category specific templates if they are all identical! Simply use `category.php`.)

As an example, there was a time on my blog where I had integrated another blog, Venture Files, into mine. To maintain the perception of two distinct content streams, I had one category with an ID of 1 for my general Technosailor.com content and assigned all the Venture Files content to a separate category, which had an ID of 58. I then created template files that matched different branding and had a slightly modified structure to the `category-58.php` file to serve a special Venture Files experience while all other content retained my standard `category.php` structure. This is only one example, but integrating blogs is common nonetheless.

If no `category-{x}.php` exists, `category.php` handles the request.

date.php

In the same way that `category.php` and `tag.php` serve up archive types, `date.php` does the same thing. It serves up any date-based archive type, including yearly archives, monthly archives, or day-specific archives. This template is used whenever any of the `$wp_query` properties `is_date`, `is_month`, `is_year`, or `is_day` is set to true.

If no `date.php` exists, `archive.php` handles the workload.

year.php, month.php, day.php

A more granular version of the generic date-based archive is the use of `year.php`, `month.php`, and `day.php`. All three of these template files, if they exist, serve up the appropriate date-based archived. These template files are rarely used, but could be for special rendering. Absent the appropriate template file, WordPress will use `date.php` instead.

home.php

One of the more interesting uses for WordPress is as a content management system (CMS). Even when it is not used as a CMS, often bloggers want their front pages to take on a different looks. Perhaps a magazine layout that presents excerpts of articles is useful. Maybe a page that not only shows posts, but also pulls recent photos from Flickr or Tweets from Twitter is an asset. The front page is often a key marketing strategy for any site.

When `home.php` exists, WordPress uses it to display the home page of your blog (not necessarily your site). Whenever WordPress is on the blog home page, the `$wp_query` property `is_home` is set to true.

If no `home.php` template exists, WordPress uses `index.php` to serve the front page.

404.php

If WordPress is not able to serve a request because it can't find any content fulfilling the query request, it looks to find a `404.php` file. Those familiar with HTTP status codes will recognize a 404 error as a "Page Not Found" error.

Developing Custom Template Files

Beyond all the flexibility afforded to bloggers and theme developers through the wide variety of template file types, yet another level of flexibility is available that's specific to Pages. In WordPress, you can create a custom template that can be selected on the Write Page or Edit Page screen in the Page Template drop-down form, as shown in Figure 10.9.

FIGURE 10.9

On the Write or Edit Page screens, WordPress provides a Page Template form. When custom templates are available to the page, you can select them with this drop-down menu.

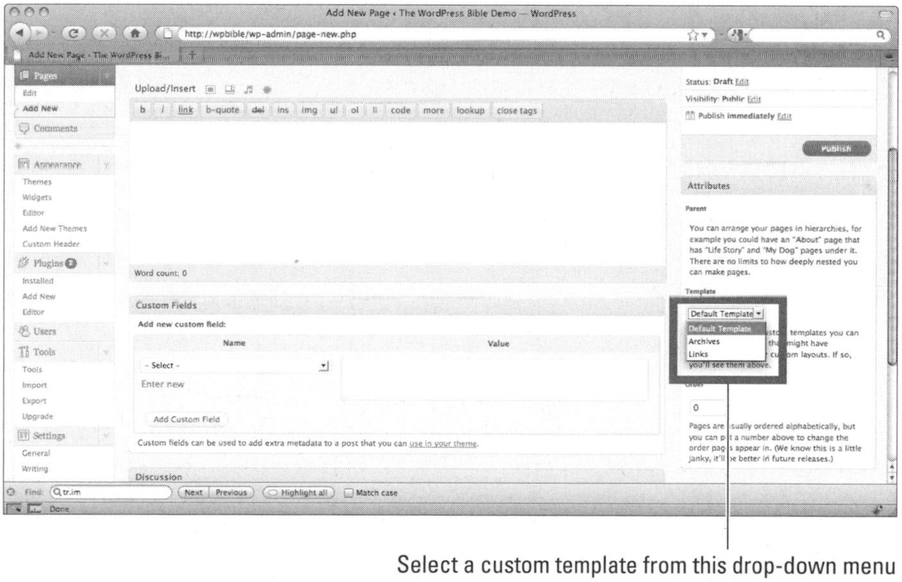

Select a custom template from this drop-down menu

Most of the time, custom page templates are modified versions of `page.php`; however, they can be entirely different structures, layouts, colors, and so on. To create a custom template, simply include a simple header, Template Name, at the top of the template file. This header is in the same format as the headers included in plugins and theme `style.css` files. The default theme includes a custom page called `archives.php` that lists a number of different archive types (see Listing 10.7).

LISTING 10.7

The archives.php file in the default theme

```php
<?php
/*
Template Name: Archives
*/
```

Note

The `archives.php` file included in the default theme should not be mistaken for the `archive.php` file. The `archive.php` file is a standard template file that handles the display of a variety of different archive types, as noted earlier in this chapter. On the other hand, `archives.php` is a file that uses an assortment of template tags to display monthly and category archive listings. Of course, this is an example of how custom templates can be used and is not a requirement for themes. ■

Summary

- At a bare minimum, a WordPress theme must have a `style.css` file. The `style.css` file must contain headers that will assist WordPress in identifying it. A theme using only a stylesheet is a child theme and inherits the file qualities of another designated theme.

- Common shared elements of a layout can be moved to `header.php`, `footer.php`, `sidebar.php`, and `comments.php`. WordPress provides `get_header()`, `get_footer()`, `get_sidebar()`, and `comments_template()` as wrapper functions for inclusion of these files.

- Common template files are `archive.php`, `search.php`, `single.php`, `page.php`, and `functions.php`.

- You can control a theme more granularly by including category archives pages, tag archives pages, and the author archives pages.

- If you include a `home.php` file, WordPress uses it to render the front page of your blog.

- Custom templates can be designed to provide WordPress pages with unique layouts. They must contain a Template Name header and can be chosen on a page-by-page basis in the WordPress Admin.

Adding JavaScript and CSS to Themes

A s the Internet evolves and more emphasis is placed on interactivity and user experience, the need for JavaScript increases. Using JavaScript has evolved from being painfully difficult, requiring browser detection and massive duplication of code to achieve a consistent user experience, to relatively simple, with implementations that work across all browsers. What once took developers 50 lines of code or more to achieve can now be done in just a few lines and is more reliable.

JavaScript is a client-side language, meaning it is not executed on a server as PHP is. Instead, it relies on Web browsers to interpret it and handle it accordingly. The benefit is a simplistic concept of distributed computing, where the weight of processing and execution is not handled in a central spot, but distributed across all the computers accessing the Web page or Web application. In recent years, JavaScript has also been a cornerstone of highly interactive Web applications.

With the advent of Ajax (Asynchronous JavaScript and XML), Web applications gained the capability to use a hybrid model, where most of the user experience happens on the front end while background communication with servers handles most of the processing. This hybrid model provides a much more robust way to gain all the distribution and user experience of JavaScript with all the security and dynamic database communication of a server side system, such as PHP and MySQL.

At the same time, user experience and themes require Cascading Style Sheets (CSS). CSS, like JavaScript, is a client-side technology. It is handled and parsed directly by the browser. There are a few versions of CSS, with varying levels of support from the various browsers and browser versions.

For example, CSS 1 is the most basic level of CSS and is supported by all modern browsers. CSS 2.1 is supported nearly universally by all browsers, but CSS 3, the most aggressive and feature-rich version, is currently supported in only varying degrees.

Note

The specifics of CSS are beyond the scope of this book; however, if you're not overly familiar with CSS, I recommend reading the HTML, XHTML and CSS Bible, 4th Edition by Steven M. Schafer (Wiley, 2008). ■

Both CSS and JavaScript enhance the user experience in WordPress and are worth considering for any theme. Throughout this chapter, I examine the JavaScript frameworks that are included in WordPress — jQuery and Prototype. I also show some examples of how they can be used in beneficial ways. In addition, the JavaScript libraries that are bundled in WordPress can enhance various portions of WordPress and the WordPress Admin. Though these libraries are included in the WordPress core for specific reasons, creative theme and plugin developers can use them for other purposes as well.

Note

For the sake of clarity, it's important to note how I'm differentiating between a JavaScript framework and a JavaScript library, given the two terms are frequently interchanged depending on context. In this book, a JavaScript framework is a bundle of JavaScript that makes it easy for developers to create cross-client JavaScript code, applications, and widgets.

A JavaScript library, however, describes a bundle of JavaScript that is developed to perform a single, specific function, such as uploading images or providing WYSIWYG (what you see is what you get) text editing. Many times, JavaScript libraries use JavaScript frameworks. ■

Examining the jQuery and Prototype Frameworks

WordPress makes it easy for developers to use the most common JavaScript frameworks available, jQuery and Prototype, and the Prototype-dependent framework, script.aculo.us. Most JavaScript in WordPress Admin is written in jQuery because it is a lightweight, but very powerful, library. However, script.aculo.us/Prototype provides richer animations and can be a more familiar development environment for some developers.

jQuery

jQuery, documented at `www.jquery.com`, powers most of the JavaScript in the WordPress Admin. However, you can also use it in themes by enqueuing (which means "adding a new item to the queue") the script in a function or plugins.

Cross-Reference

The `wp_register_script()`, `wp_enqueue_script()`, and `wp_print_scripts()` functions are described in Chapter 5. ■

In Listing 11.1, I used the `wp_enqueue_script()` function to give the theme access to the jQuery library. Because WordPress includes jQuery as a bundled framework, there is no need to instruct WordPress about where to find the script. Typically, when you use a non-bundled JavaScript file — maybe a different library or one that you have custom developed yourself — the second argument passed to `wp_enqueue_script()` is the URL of the JavaScript file. If your included library depends on another JavaScript file, library, or framework, the third argument (also not included in this example) would be an array of handles that are required.

LISTING 11.1

Using wp_enqueue_script() in a theme to make the jQuery Framework available to the rest of the theme

```
function my_theme_js()
{
    wp_enqueue_script('jquery');
    wp_print_scripts();
}
add_action( 'wp_enqueue_scripts', 'my_theme_js' );
```

On the Web

The code in Listing 11.1 is available for download at www.wiley.com/go/wordpressbible. ■

Note

WordPress handles each JavaScript file registration with a unique handle. These handles are simply unique identifiers that WordPress can use to locate the JavaScript file. You can use `wp_register_script()` to make new JavaScript frameworks or libraries available to WordPress on a global, plugin, or theme basis by hooking a function into WordPress at the `init` or `admin_init` action hooks. `wp_enqueue_script()` automatically registers a script if it is not already registered, so you might consider not using `wp_register_script()` at all, though using it is much more explicit and easier for others to maintain later. ■

The jQuery framework operates on the principle of *chaining*, or connecting expressions end to end. It usually uses a dollar sign ($) to begin an expression. jQuery developers will often replace the $ notation with the word "jQuery" because Prototype developers are used to the identical notation. In WordPress, for compatibility reasons, jQuery is used in this "no conflict" mode, which uses jQuery instead.

Note

Technically, the `jQuery()` function in jQuery literally means "an element designated by a CSS string." While jQuery often uses complex selectors, it always references a CSS selector. This differs from Prototype, which uses Document Object Model (DOM) IDs, discussed later in this chapter, where `$` indicates "element with ID of." The nuance between these two paradigms is slight, but is extremely important to understand in development. ■

To use jQuery in a theme, you must have a *ready event*. The ready event is a statement that ensures that the entire page, or DOM as it's known in JavaScript development, has been loaded. It is expressed as `jQuery(document).ready()` and wraps around all jQuery expressions, as shown in Listing 11.2.

LISTING 11.2

Wrapping all expressions in a ready event

```
<script type="text/javascript">
jQuery(document).ready(function() {
    // Insert all jQuery expressions here
});
</script>
```

In a practical sense, you can use jQuery for almost anything. For example, assume that you implement a search form in a hidden layer. The way this form is exposed is by clicking on a link. The basic HTML structure would look like Listing 11.3.

LISTING 11.3

Basic HTML structure for a div that contains a search form and a link

```
<a id="search_link" href="#">Search</a>
<div id="example_search_form">
    <?php get_search_form() ?>
</div>
```

On the Web

The code in Listing 11.3 is available for download at www.wiley.com/go/wordpressbible. ■

The next step is to ensure the form is hidden. Add the function shown in Listing 11.4 to your theme's `functions.php` file. Add any further CSS you would like to make the link integrate with your theme. Also, make sure the theme has the `wp_head` hook so the CSS can be added. Alternatively, you can hardcode CSS in `style.css`, but I recommend against doing so if you want to preserve changes when you upgrade your theme.

LISTING 11.4

Using a function to add CSS to the theme

```
function additional_css()
{
    ?>
    <style type="text/css">
    #example_search_form { display:none; }
    </style>
    <?php
}
add_action('wp_head','additional_css');
```

On the Web

The code in Listing 11.4 is available for download at www.wiley.com/go/wordpressbible. ■

> With the HTML and CSS structure set properly, it's time to implement the jQuery needed to make the form display when users click the link. To do this, I declare a new function in functions. php (or in a plugin) that will insert the jQuery, as shown in Listing 11.5. The effect can be seen before and after in Figure 11.1.

LISTING 11.5

Using jQuery to create a click event to display the form

```
function additional_js()
{
    wp_enqueue_script('jquery');
    wp_print_scripts();
    ?>
    <script type="text/javascript">
    jQuery(document).ready(function(){
        jQuery('a#search_link').click(function() {
            jQuery('#example_search_form').show("slow");
        });
    });
    </script>
    <?php
}
add_action('wp_head','additional_js');
```

On the Web

The code in Listing 11.5 is available for download at www.wiley.com/go/wordpressbible. ■

Clearly, this is a simplistic example. You can use jQuery to provide many different interactive possibilities to a Web site and, for the WordPress Admin, it is the preferred JavaScript framework to use because it is already in use throughout the backend.

FIGURE 11.1

Before and after screenshots demonstrating the "click-show" effect

Before the jQuery Show() event fires

After the jQuery Show() event fires

Prototype

The second JavaScript framework that is bundled and available to WordPress developers by default is Prototype (documented at www.prototypejs.org/). Like jQuery, Prototype uses the $ function throughout but unlike jQuery, it does not provide a way for a "no conflict" mode.

Prototype is used by the WordPress core in only three parts of the WordPress Admin. Primarily, it is used in conjunction with TinyMCE (the rich text editor provided by WordPress for writing posts), the flash-based media uploader (shown in Figure 11.2), and the Blogger import script.

FIGURE 11.2

The media uploader in WordPress is based on Flash and Prototype.

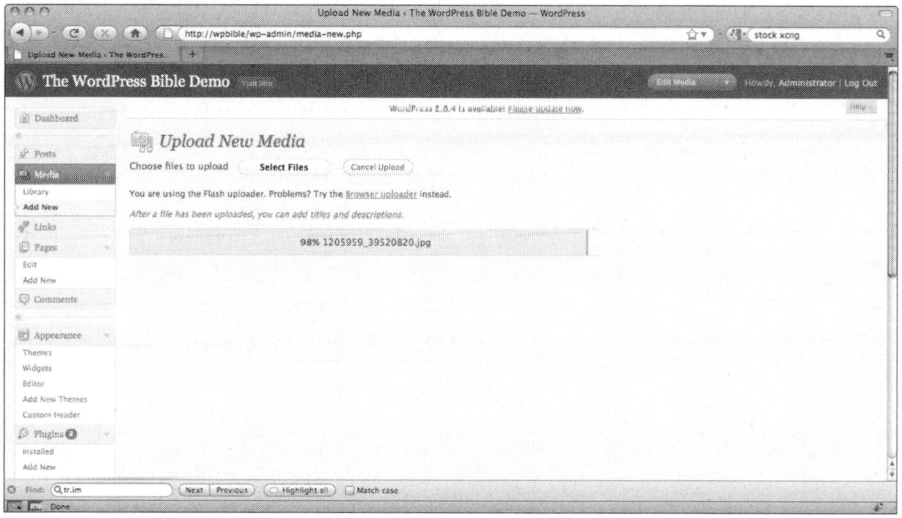

However, Prototype was used more in the past, but many plugins still rely on the framework, so it is still part of a bundled JavaScript framework, and some of the core features of WordPress make use of it.

You can also write the hidden search box code built earlier in Listing 11.3 with Prototype, as shown in Listing 11.6.

LISTING 11.6

Using Prototype, the hidden search box can be exposed by clicking the link with ID #search_link

```
function wpb_enqueue_prototype()
{
    wp_enqueue_script('prototype');

}
function wpb_additional_js()
{
    wp_enqueue_script('prototype');
    wp_print_scripts();
    ?>
    <script type="text/javascript">
    var HiddenSearchShower = Class.create({
        initialize: function(field) {
            Event.observe(document, 'click', this.showSearch );
        },
        showSearch: function(event) {
            $('example_search_form').setStyle({display:'block'});
        }
    });
    var SearchForm = new HiddenSearchShower("#search_link");
    </script>
    <?php
}
add_action('wp_head', 'wpb_additional_js');
add_action('wp_enqueue_scripts','wpb_enqueue_prototype');
```

On the Web

The code in Listing 11.6 is available for download at www.wiley.com/go/wordpressbible. ∎

While the beauty of jQuery is its capability to "chain" events end to end, the real beauty of Prototype is creating object oriented JavaScript. For developers familiar with the Ruby programming language (in particular, Ruby on Rails developers), the syntax of Prototype will be very familiar.

Comparing the frameworks

Both jQuery and Prototype are bundled in WordPress. Developers familiar with other JavaScript frameworks (such as Moo Tools, Dojo, or Spry) are free to add these libraries via a plugin (using wp_register_script() or wp_enqueue_script()), but developers who focus in WordPress tend to use the bundled packages.

Both frameworks offer benefits and drawbacks. For example, jQuery provides a light framework that mixes in some effects and has a robust plugin architecture to extends its core use, but it may not be as robust as a scripting language for user-interface/webapp-style blogs.

On the other hand, Prototype is a rich object-oriented JavaScript framework that will be familiar to developers from the Ruby on Rails world, but lacks the included effects that jQuery offers. For that, developers will need script.aculo.us, a library that is discussed later in this chapter.

Both frameworks have benefits, but the libraries of code built around them, in the form of plugins or extensions, is what really makes them useful in WordPress. The differences outlined in Table 11.1 can help you choose which one is right for you.

TABLE 11.1

Comparative Differences Between jQuery and Prototype

	jQuery	Prototype
Overall file size	56K	124K
Object oriented	No	Yes
Expression chaining	Yes	Yes, but not preferred
Extends DOM	No	Yes
Uses $ function	Represents CSS selector	Represents DOM ID
Ajax support	Yes: $.ajax(), $.get(), $.post()	Yes; Ajax object
Effects	Core	Third-party (script.aculo.us)

Leveraging WordPress' JavaScript Libraries

As I note earlier in this chapter, the JavaScript frameworks bundled in WordPress are powerful pieces of software that allow for quick and clean JavaScript development. With these libraries, developers can radically alter the way a theme behaves or how a user interacts with the WordPress Admin. The preferred library in WordPress development is jQuery, but some developers are just more familiar with Prototype, especially if they have come from a Ruby on Rails background. Both libraries can be used in conjunction with each other.

In the next section, I'll introduce you to the JavaScript libraries (extensions to the JavaScript frameworks) that are bundled with WordPress. This should not prevent developers from including other frameworks manually if they prefer to do so.

Prototype: script.aculo.us

Built on Prototype, script.aculo.us (http://script.aculo.us/) is a series of libraries that provides effects, animations, and other user interface enhancements. It is not used anywhere in the WordPress core, but is provided as a legacy library for plugins that need it.

The script.aculo.us library provides plenty of effects that can be useful in plugin development. Some include the capability to make page elements semi-transparent (opacity) in a cross-browser fashion, moving elements on the screen, and Ajax data retrieval.

The main downfall to script.aculo.us is its weight (it weighs in at a hefty 632K), so it is not recommended that plugins load the entire library. You can choose to load the entire suite or just the portions needed, but make sure you load all the dependent libraries as well. Table 11.2 shows the script.aculo.us libraries that WordPress has made available along with their dependencies.

TABLE 11.2

script.aculo.us Libraries and Dependencies

Library	Handle	Dependencies
script.aculo.us (Core)	script.aculo.us-root	Prototype
script.aculo.us Builder	script.aculo.us-builder	script.aculo.us (Core)
script.aculo.us Drag & Drop	script.aculo.us-dragdrop	script.aculo.us Builder
script.aculo.us Effects	script.aculo.us-effects	script.aculo.us (Core)
script.aculo.us Slider	script.aculo.us-slider	script.aculo.us Effects
script.aculo.us Sound	script.aculo.us-sound	script.aculo.us (Core)
script.aculo.us Controls	script.aculo.us-controls	script.aculo.us (Core)

Prototype: TinyMCE

Many rich text editors are available on the Web. TinyMCE was adopted into the WordPress core because it is lightweight, is entirely General Public License (GPL)–compatible, and the team behind TinyMCE was willing to work closely with WordPress to develop a product that could be distributed to millions of blogs.

TinyMCE, created by Moxiecode (`http://tinymce.moxiecode.com/`), can turn a form into a rich editing experience where bloggers can write stories in an interface that gives them formatting controls similar to what they are familiar with in a word processing program (see Figure 11.3).

Outside of the WordPress Admin, another common use for TinyMCE is with the comment box on a theme. This approach enables readers to leave rich comments without having to use HTML. The TinyMCEComments plugin (`http://wordpress.org/extend/plugins/tinymcecomments/`) does just that. If a theme has a `comment_form` hook in the comments template, this plugin hooks into the form, hijacks the `<textarea>` tag, and replaces it with the TinyMCE editor, as shown in Figure 11.4.

Tip

When developing themes, take extra care to ensure that your `comments.php` has the action hook `comments_form` in it. If you base your themes comments template after the default theme `comments.php` file, you will already have this hook. If not, insert this code inside the form code:

```php
<?php do_action('comments_form', $post->ID); ?>
```
■

TinyMCE provides the rich text editing experience in the WordPress Admin.

The plugin, TinyMCEComments, replaces the standard comment `<textarea>` with an instance of the TinyMCE editor.

jQuery: Autosave

Autosave is a WordPress-specific jQuery plugin that saves posts while the blogger writes. It uses the "autosave" handle and offers limited additional benefit outside of saving posts.

Note
Keep in mind that handles are unique identifiers that are used with `wp_register_script()` and `wp_enqueue_script()`.■

jQuery: hoverIntent

This plugin is available to WordPress with the handle "hoverIntent". The hoverIntent plugin works with mouse movement to determine if a user is intending to hover over an element. If it determines that mouse speed has slowed, for example, it might fire the mouseover DOM event.

Web Resource
You can find more information and documentation on the hoverIntent plugin at `http://cherne.net/brian/resources/jquery.hoverIntent.html`. ■

jQuery: Farbtastic

Farbtastic is a popular jQuery plugin that enables plugin developers to include an interactive color picker. It is referred to with the handle "farbtastic" and you can find documentation on it at `http://acko.net/dev/farbtastic`. Currently, it is only used in the WordPress core to allow bloggers to customize the color of the header in the default theme, shown in Figure 11.5; however, it is bundled to make the library available to other plugins.

FIGURE 11.5

The Farbtastic jQuery plugin provides a color picker that can be used in WordPress. The default theme uses it to enable bloggers to pick their header color.

jQuery: jQueryUI

The most important set of jQuery plugins to WordPress are the jQueryUI plugins. This suite of plugins provides the drag-and-drop widgets interface, and the capability to reorganize and order the WordPress Dashboard and Write Post/Page screens, as well as manage all the user interface effects in the WordPress Admin navigation.

Of course, the effects used here are only a fraction of the possibilities available to plugin developers. At a very minimum, jQueryUI can be loaded using the "jquery-ui-core" handle. Other plugins can be loaded using similar handles (see Table 11.3), but all must have both "jquery" and "jquery-ui-core" as dependencies when enqueued.

Web Resource
You can find more information and documentation on jQueryUI at `http://jqueryui.com/`. ∎

TABLE 11.3	
Bundled jQuery UI plugins	
Plugin Name	**Handle**
jQuery UI Core	jquery-ui-core
jQuery UI Tabs	jquery-ui-tabs
jQuery UI Sortable	jquery-ui-sortable
jQuery UI Draggable	jquery-ui-draggable
jQuery UI Droppable	jquery-ui-droppable
jQuery UI Selectable	jquery-ui-selectable
jQuery UI Resizable	jquery-ui-resizable
jQuery UI Dialog	jquery-ui-dialog

Examining WordPress Plugins that Use JavaScript Effects

As the Web world gets more interactive, creative plugin developers continue to add more interactivity to blogs. Much of this interactivity is as a result of the bundled JavaScript frameworks and libraries. These plugins are free to use and may provide inspiration for what is possible when the frameworks are used. They can give you a sense of how to develop JavaScript code for use in plugins if you are just learning.

jQuery Reply to Comment

With WordPress 2.7, the commenting application programming interface (API) was rewritten to support threaded and paged comments. When Threaded comments are enabled, Reply links are provided with each comment. Users can simply click the Reply link to create a threaded conversation around an existing conversation.

The jQuery Reply to Comment plugin (`http://wordpress.org/extend/plugins/jquery-reply-to-comment/`) takes this concept one step farther by allowing commenters to quote a comment with their replies.

Social Bookmarks

The Social Bookmarks plugin (`http://wordpress.org/extend/plugins/social bookmarks/`) is like the smattering of other social tools integration plugins. It adds a selection of social network icons to the end of posts, enabling readers to share your articles on those networks. It uses script.aculo.us for all JavaScript functionality.

Cross-Reference
Social network integration is a very important part of marketing and promoting a blog. In some cases, traffic generated through other social networks exceeds organic search from search engines themselves! Social media marketing strategy for a blog is discussed in Chapter 3. ■

WP Conditional Digg This Badge

The WP Conditional Digg This Badge plugin (`http://wordpress.org/extend/plugins/conditional-digg-this-badge/`) uses Prototype to access the Digg.com API to determine how many "Diggs" an article has. Using conditional logic based on blogger-defined parameters (such as how many Diggs are required), it displays an interactive Digg This badge in a post.

WPTouch iPhone Theme

Given the popularity of the iPhone these days, iPhone-specific versions of a blog are in demand. The WPhone iPhone Theme plugin (`http://wordpress.org/extend/plugins/wptouch/`) uses jQuery to render a version of a WordPress blog that is formatted for the iPhone. The results are shown in Figure 11.6.

FIGURE 11.6

The WPTouch iPhone Theme plugin renders a WordPress blog in an iPhone format. It uses jQuery.

Looking at Theme Styles

Through most of this chapter, I talked about JavaScript, but you don't want to forget about CSS. CSS order is not as important as JavaScript library order, but you do have to remember the "cascading" nature of Cascading Style Sheets. For example, with JavaScript, you encounter conflicts that have the potential of breaking a page if you load script.aculo.us before you load Prototype. This is why the `wp_enqueue_script()` function exists. Dependencies can be determined and scripts injected into the blog in the appropriate order, avoiding potentially site crippling side effects.

Queuing styles

While the `wp_enqueue_style()` function effectively does the same thing, CSS conflicts generally won't cripple a site. However, the nature of CSS is to "cascade." Styles cascade from a top-level hierarchy, and can be overridden later in a page execution. To this end, conflict is avoided using a similar syntax to `wp_enqueue_script()`. The first argument passed to `wp_enqueue_style()` must be a unique handler. The second argument should be the fully qualified URL to the stylesheet, while the third argument, which is completely optional, should be an array of dependencies (using the dependency handler name), as demonstrated in Listing 11.7.

LISTING 11.7

Using wp_enqueue_style() function to solve CSS cascading issues

```
function wpb_additional_css()
{
    wp_enqueue_style('my-styles', WP_CONTENT_DIR . '/themes/my-theme/style.
  css');
    wp_enqueue_style('ie-my-styles', WP_CONTENT_DIR . '/themes/my-theme/
  ie.css', array('my-styles'));
    wp_print_styles();
}
add_action('wp_enqueue_scripts','wpb_additional_css');
```

On the Web

The code in Listing 11.7 is available for download at www.wiley.com/go/wordpressbible. ∎

WordPress also provides some helper functions for the style queue. For example, the function `wp_style_is()` is useful when you need to determine if a style has been queued. You can register style with `wp_style_register()` or unregister them with `wp_style_deregister()`. You can do the latter if a different plugin conflicts with the styles that your plugin uses, but typically, if that is the case, it is more helpful to create and use unique CSS selectors.

Tip

You cannot deregister styles that have not been registered in the style cue. For example, it is impossible to deregister styles that have been supplied with a direct `<link>` tag in WordPress core, plugins, and so on. The number of plugins and themes that use the style queue currently is unknown because it is a relatively new feature (WordPress 2.7), so your mileage may vary.

Also, keep in mind that the traditional method of injecting a stylesheet URL into a theme is via the `bloginfo('stylesheet_url')` template tag. This does not queue the style. It merely injects a `<link>` tag. ∎

Using JavaScript to style elements

Sometimes it is necessary to use JavaScript to adjust styles on the fly. This is because some kind of event (hover, click, and so on) has occurred on a page after all the CSS files have been loaded and applied when the page initially loads.

Fortunately, both the jQuery and Prototype frameworks discussed earlier in this chapter have ways to apply styling to an element after the page loads.

For example, maybe you want to change the background color of a post when you hover over it. Using the default WordPress theme, you can write a function that adds some jQuery inside the <head> tag, as shown in Listing 11.8.

LISTING 11.8

Using jQuery to change the hover background CSS of a post

```
<script type="text/JavaScript">
jQuery.noConflict();
jQuery(document).ready(function(){
    jQuery('.entry').hover(
        function() {
            jQuery(this).css('background', '#eee');
        },
        function() {
            jQuery(this).css('background', '#fff');
        }
    );
});
</script>
```

On the Web

The code in Listing 11.8 is available for download at www.wiley.com/go/wordpressbible. ■

This simple jQuery function uses the hover event to change the background color of a post to #eee (light grey) when users hover over it, and reverts the background color to #fff (white) when users are not hovering over the element. Figure 11.7 shows the result.

If you're more familiar with the Prototype framework, it can do the same thing. The same code is replicated in Prototype format, though for this sort of functionality, jQuery is quicker and more compact.

Using jQuery, a plugin can alter the defined style of an element. In this case, the background color of a post changes to a light grey when you hover over it.

Summary

- WordPress provides a variety of JavaScript frameworks that assist JavaScript format and syntax, and libraries that provide specific functionality that aids JavaScript deployment.

- jQuery is the light framework used throughout most of the WordPress Admin. Its "chaining" syntax enables expressions to be connected together as a single expression.

- Prototype is used sparsely throughout the WordPress core; it has a much richer experience when you extend the DOM and uses object oriented, Ruby-like syntax.

- script.aculo.us extends Prototype, providing a large library of user interface extensions, animations, and effects.

- WordPress provides several jQuery plugins as part of the core. Though these plugins are used throughout the WordPress Admin, they can be used by plugins as well.

- TinyMCE provides a rich text editing interface and is used in the WordPress Admin to provide rich editing for post and page writing. Plugins can use the library as well.

- Styles can be queued in a similar fashion as JavaScript. Dependencies are loaded as specified and styles can be deregistered if they're implemented with the style queue.

- JavaScript can be used to alter CSS, creating a dynamic user experience.

Dissecting the Comment Loop, Template Tags, and Theme Best Practices

C reating themes for WordPress is still a somewhat subjective process. Perhaps this is because designers, as a demographic, tend to be free-thinking artists rather than straight-line developers. There is no real "right" or "wrong" way to create a theme. However, there are certainly best practices and elements that are useful.

As WordPress continues to evolve, there is a lot of discussion cropping up in the WordPress community about standardizing themes and coding practices. Whether anything truly takes hold depends largely on the community's capability to demand standards and hold designers feet to the fire on them, as the community did with plugins.

Already, WordPress.com requires certain elements for all themes that will be hosted on WordPress.com. The WordPress Themes Directory, located at `http://wordpress.org/extend/themes`, also enforces certain standards if designers want to have their themes hosted and gain the marketing advantages of being listed in the directory.

As the community has grown and WordPress has greater influence, the need for standardization has become forefront. Plugin developers must adhere to the WordPress application programming interface (API) standards; when they don't, their plugins might no longer work with future updates of WordPress.

Tip

Plugin developers should always use the WordPress API to perform tasks. Generally, plugins that don't use the API perform raw SQL queries instead — a problem that introduces security risks and the possibility of plugin incompatibility when the MySQL schema changes in future versions.

Throughout every version of WordPress, a guiding principle for core developers has been to enforce and ensure backward-compatibility. Plugin developers who use the provided APIs to perform tasks will have plugins that are likely to stand the test of time. ■

From the perspective of scaling the community, it only makes sense that standardization now applies to theme designers, as well. Though standards, or more accurately, conventions, can never truly be enforced since the prerogative lies with the theme designer, it only benefits the greater community, and provides some leverage in enforcing best practices across the greater community, when designers choose to adhere to these conventions.

Much of what is described in this chapter surrounding conventions and standards is discussed elsewhere in this book from a different perspective. Whether building plugins or themes, there are steps that should be taken to ensure compatibility and make for a good user experience. This chapter is specifically geared toward theme designers: more specifically toward user experience and plugin compatibility and extensibility, and less toward plugin developers.

In this chapter I'll talk about some of the standards that have come to the theming world and discuss the challenges going forward. The community as a whole benefits when all segments are based on a similar play book, with some room for expression and personal style.

Using Hooks in Themes

Hooks are the catalyst for extensibility. They were adopted to avoid core files being overwritten to produce customized effects.

The principle of hooks, or event-driven programming, is used in many software packages these days, including WordPress' competitor Drupal. However, theme-based hooks have not been widely adopted by plugin and theme developers. I've made a lot of noise in the community in an effort to get theme developers to add hooks to their themes. Creating any software package, plugin, theme, extension, or library that does not allow core functionality to be modified directly is short sighted.

The poster child theme for this kind of functionality is the proprietary WordPress Thesis theme from DIYthemes (available at `http://diythemes.com`). The Thesis theme adopts the theory that even themes should be extensible, and provides an extremely extensible theme with well over a dozen available hooks.

Cross-Reference

See Chapter 5 for more information about hooks. See Chapter 10 for more about template files, their hierarchy, and their purpose. ■

Common hooks

Three hooks should be made available in every theme to ensure compatibility with the most number of WordPress users:

- `wp_head()`
- `wp_footer()`
- `comment_form`

wp_head()

The `wp_head()` function is a wrapper function around the `wp_head` hook. The WordPress code is shown in Listing 12.1.

LISTING 12.1

wp_head() is a wrapper around the wp_head action hook

```
function wp_head() {
    do_action('wp_head');
}
```

Plugins that hook into `wp_head` can be anywhere inside the `<head>` tags; however, as a point of best practice, many plugins hook in their own Cascading Style Sheets (CSS). With its cascading nature, CSS provided via this hook should not be placed above CSS originally included in the theme. The CSS hook runs the risk of being blocked or overridden. As a point of best practice, and to avoid this kind of conflict, the `wp_head` hook should be placed just before the closing `</head>` tag, as shown in Listing 12.2.

LISTING 12.2

Place wp_head() just before the closing </head> tag

```
<html>
    <head>
        <title><?php bloginfo('name'); ?></title>
        <link rel="stylesheet" type="text/css" href="<?php echo
    bloginfo('stylesheet_url')" />
        <?php wp_head(); ?>
    </head>
    <body>
```

---

wp_footer()

Similar to the `wp_head()` function, the `wp_footer()` function is also a wrapper around the `wp_footer` action hook. It also should be included in every theme because many plugins, particularly analytics plugins, use this hook to include code in the blog footer. As a general rule, `wp_footer()` should be included before the closing `</body>` tag, as shown in Listing 12.3.

LISTING 12.3

Place wp_footer() just before the closing </body> tag

```
        <div id="footer">
            <p>Copyright <?php echo date('Y'); ?>. All Rights Reserved.</p>
        </div>
        <?php echo wp_footer(); ?>
    </body>
</html>
```

On the Web

The code in Listing 12.3 is available for download at www.wiley.com/go/wordpressbible. ∎

comment_form

The final basic hook that should be included in every theme to ensure maximum compatibility with plugins is the `comment_form`. It should be included inside the closing `</form>` tag of the comments template. This hook takes an additional argument, `$post->ID`, opposed to standard actions, which usually only require the hook name (see Listing 12.4).

LISTING 12.4

Include the comment_form hook before the closing </form> tag in the comments template

```
<form>
    <input type="text" name="author" id="author" />
    <input type="text" name="email" id="email" />
    <input type="text" name="url" id="url" />
    <textarea name="comment" id="comment" cols="100%" rows="10" /><textarea>
    <input name="submit" type="submit" id="submit" value="Submit Comment" />
    <?php do_action('comment_form', $post->ID); ?>
</form>
```

On the Web

The code in Listing 12.4 is available for download at www.wiley.com/go/wordpressbible. ∎

Additional hook suggestions

Outside of the basic hooks provided by the WordPress core — `wp_head`, `wp_footer`, and `comment_form` — theme developers can create their own hook system in their themes. There is no standard or convention for these hooks, but I recommend that developers create a system for naming hooks that is unique and won't collide with other parts of WordPress.

Tip

One idea for naming hooks is to prepend the name of the theme with an underscore (`mytheme_`) followed by the name of the hook. ∎

Suggestions for hooks to be included in themes are listed in Table 12.1. Note that in my effort to have a standard for the community, my suggestions eliminate theme specifics from the identifier. My hope is that the community will adopt these suggestions and add to them to make more themes compatible with more plugins. At the end of the day, bloggers shouldn't have to hack the core code of a theme to make it do what they need it to do.

TABLE 12.1

Suggested Hooks to Be Included in Themes

Hook Name	Hook Type	Example Usage
Header Area		
before_masthead	action	do_action('before_header');
after_masthead	action	do_action('after_header');
masthead_image	filter	apply_filters('masthead_image','<img src="default.jpg" />');
theme_logo	filter	apply_filters('theme_logo','<a href="<?php bloginfo('home')">' <img src="logo.png"></a>');
primary_navigation	filter	apply_filters('primary_navigation', $generated_ul);
secondary_navigation	filter	apply_filters('secondary_navigation', $generated_ul);
Content Area		
before_content	action	do_action('before_content');
after_content	action	do_action('after_content');
after_post_{x}	action	do_action('after_post_{x}');

continued

TABLE 12.1	*(continued)*	
Hook Name	**Hook Type**	**Example Usage**
after_the_content	action	do_action('after_the_content');
after_the_excerpt	action	do_action('after_the_excerpt');
before_comment_form	action	do_action('before_comment_form');
Sidebar Area		
before_sidebar	action	do_action('before_sidebar');
after_sidebar	action	do_action('after_sidebar');

The list in Table 12.1 is by no means exhaustive, but it does provide the framework for a nice standardized approach to theme development. Between providing multiple customization options to bloggers and widget capability, a theme could very well become one of the more powerful aspects of WordPress.

Implementing Scripts in Themes

Scripts are an important part of the user experience. In some cases, the limitations of CSS make the need for JavaScript effects necessary. For example, I'm a fan of rounded corners (when used moderately). Rounded corners, at this time, cannot be reliably implemented in all browsers without using images, an ugly hypertext markup language (HTML) structure or some other "hack." However, with the JavaScript framework, jQuery, the jQuery Rounded Corners plugin (`http://plugins.jquery.com/project/corners`) can be used to create elegant, cross-browser rounded corners that enhance the aesthetics of a site.

Regardless of what you use JavaScript for, you need to ensure that you use `wp_enqueue_script()` and `wp_print_scripts()` to do it. Besides solving dependency issues with required JavaScript libraries, the use of these functions from the WordPress API ensures forward compatibility and script compatibility.

Using the `wp_enqueue_script()` and `wp_print_scripts()` functions is a best practice that is lacking with many themes and should be standardized. Not using these functions to provide JavaScript to a theme inevitably means conflicts later on and represents one of those most telling loopholes in the non-standardization of themes.

Cross-Reference

Using `wp_enqueue_script()` and `wp_print_scripts()` is described in more detail in Chapter 5. ■

In addition, theme developers have access to a `functions.php` file. `functions.php` is a file that provides additional functionality to a theme via PHP — a format that will be familiar to plugin developers. It is a good idea to create a function in `functions.php` that handles all of the

JavaScript in a theme. For a more hook-friendly approach, consider adding an action hook inside a <script> tag in this function, as shown in Listing 12.5.

LISTING 12.5

Using an action hook to allow the addition of JavaScript to your theme-provided scripts

```
function theme_javascript()
{
    wp_enqueue_script('jquery-corners', 'http://example.com/path/to/jquery.
corners.js', array('jquery'));
}
function theme_print_scripts(){
    ?>
    <script type="text/javascript">
    jQuery.noConflict();
    jQuery(document).ready(function() {
        <?php do_action('jquery_add_scripts'); ?>
    });
    </script>
    <?php
}
add_action('wp_head', 'theme_print_scripts');
add_action('wp_enqueue_scripts','theme_javascript');
```

On the Web

The code in Listing 12.5 is available for download at www.wiley.com/go/wordpressbible. ■

Using Template Tags to Make Themes Dynamic

Template tags, which are simply PHP functions called by a different name and made very simple for templating purposes, are the bread and butter of theming. They are what enable a theme to operate on any WordPress install, on any server, and, in general, be portable.

Template tags form the API for themes. By using tags instead of specific data points you ensure that the theme is flexible enough and will be forward compatible for future versions of WordPress.

Cross-Reference

Though many of the template tags are covered in this chapter, it is impossible to cover all of them. For an exhaustive reference on template tags, see Appendix B. ■

Using bloginfo() to access blog metadata

One powerful template tag, `bloginfo()`, is a tag used for displaying (or retrieving) blog-level metadata such as the URL to the blog, the tagline, and the user's version of WordPress. The `bloginfo()` tag can retrieve data for 23 different data points, all of which are listed in Table 12.2.

TABLE 12.2

Blog Metadata Retrieved by the bloginfo() Template Tag

Argument — bloginfo('arg')	Sample Value
admin_email	admin@example.com
atom_url	www.example.com/feed/atom/
charset	UTF-8
comments_atom_url	www.example.com/post-slug/comments/feed/atom/
comments_rss2_url	www.example.com/post-slug/comments/feed/
description	An example blog in an example world
home	http://example.com/
html_type	text/html
language	en-US
name	The Example Blog
pingback_url	www.example.com/xmlrpc.php
rdf_url	www.example.com/feed/rdf
rss_url	www.example.com/feed/rss
rss2_url	www.example.com/feed
siteurl	www.example.com
stylesheet_directory	www.example.com/wp-content/themes/default
stylesheet_url	www.example.com/wp-content/themes/default/style.css
template_directory	www.example.com/wp-content/themes/default
template_url	www.example.com/wp-content/themes/default
text_direction	ltr
url	www.example.com
version	2.8.4
wpurl	www.example.com

The `bloginfo()` tag is used between `<head>` tags and, structurally speaking, in common template areas such as the header and footer (for example, in `header.php` and `footer.php`).

Cross-Reference
Template files and hierarchy is discussed in Chapter 10. ∎

As an example of how to take a standard HTML template and leverage template tags, particularly the `bloginfo()` tag, consider the following static HTML (see Listing 12.6). Listing 12.6 illustrates a skeleton framework for an HTML page. From this HTML, template tags can be added to make it more dynamic and compatible with WordPress.

LISTING 12.6

Leveraging template tags in a standard HTML template

```
<!DOCTYPE html PUBLIC "-//W3C//DTD XHTML 1.0 Transitional//EN"
    "http://www.w3.org/TR/xhtml1/DTD/xhtml1-transitional.dtd">
<html>
    <head>
        <title>Blog Name</title>
        <link rel="stylesheet" href="style.css" type="text/css"
   media="screen" />
    </head>
    <body>
        <!--body content-->
    </body>
</html>
```

Because not likely that all blogs will be named Blog Name, it is necessary to abstract that to the name that is stored in WordPress for the blog name. To do this, pass the argument `'name'` to `bloginfo()`, as shown in Listing 12.7.

Note
Remember that the blog name is designated at setup and modified in the WordPress Admin by choosing **Settings ⇨ General. ∎**

LISTING 12.7

Using bloginfo('name') to dynamically display the name of the blog

```
<!DOCTYPE html PUBLIC "-//W3C//DTD XHTML 1.0 Transitional//EN"
    "http://www.w3.org/TR/xhtml1/DTD/xhtml1-transitional.dtd">
<html>
    <head>
        <title><?php bloginfo('name'); ?></title>
```

continued

LISTING 12.7 *(continued)*

```
        <link rel="stylesheet" href="style.css" type="text/css"
    media="screen" />
      </head>
      <body>
        <!--body content-->
      </body>
</html>
```

Tip

The `bloginfo()` template tag always displays something. Whether it's the name of the blog, the RSS URL, or the language the blog is using, it is always displayed. If you need to return the data for further usage with PHP, use `get_bloginfo()` instead. The `get_bloginfo()` function takes all the same arguments as `bloginfo()` but returns the data instead of printing it. ■

In the skeleton HTML, the CSS `<link>` tag needs to be adjusted as well. WordPress looks to the theme directory for a `style.css` file (a required file), so simply referencing `style.css` is not enough. Fortunately, the `stylesheet_url` argument can be used with `bloginfo()` to generate the complete URL to the stylesheet based on blog address settings and the active theme (see Listing 12.8).

LISTING 12.8

Using bloginfo('stylesheet_url') to display the URL for the stylesheet as generated from blog address settings, the active theme, and style.css

```
<!DOCTYPE html PUBLIC "-//W3C//DTD XHTML 1.0 Transitional//EN"
    "http://www.w3.org/TR/xhtml1/DTD/xhtml1-transitional.dtd">
<html>
    <head>
        <title><?php bloginfo('name'); ?></title>
        <link rel="stylesheet" href="<?php bloginfo('stylesheet_url'); ?>"
    type="text/css" media="screen" />
      </head>
      <body>
        <!--body content-->
      </body>
</html>
```

The code shown in Listing 12.8 is clearly a barebones theme. The `<head>` tag only consists of a title tag and a CSS reference. Many other things should be in a theme. For example, there should probably be a meta "content type" tag to ensure browsers know how to handle odd characters. To do this, you can add two more `bloginfo()` references — this time, to `html_type` (typically text/html) and `charset` (generally UTF-8); see Listing 12.9.

Note

The `html_type` is almost universally text/html. Feeds and other document types not generally rendered as typical Web sites might use an alternative `html_type` such as text/xml, but mainly, the type will always be text/html.

The `charset`, or character set, will almost always be one of two character types: UTF-8 or iso-8859-1. The latter is an ASCII character set that is common among English and Romance languages and consists of 255 characters. UTF-8, also known as Unicode, is a character set that represents all computer-printable languages and character types in the world. UTF-8 is the best character set to use for a blog that might be accessed anywhere in the world. It also matches the character set used in the database by default. ■

LISTING 12.9

Using bloginfo('html_type') and bloginfo('charset') to print a meta content type tag

```
<!DOCTYPE html PUBLIC "-//W3C//DTD XHTML 1.0 Transitional//EN"
    "http://www.w3.org/TR/xhtml1/DTD/xhtml1-transitional.dtd">
<html>
    <head>
        <title><?php bloginfo('name'); ?></title>
        <meta http-equiv="Content-Type" content="<?php bloginfo('html_
type'); ?>; charset=<?php bloginfo('charset'); ?>" />
        <link rel="stylesheet" href="<?php bloginfo('stylesheet_url'); ?>"
type="text/css" media="screen" />
    </head>
    <body>
        <!--body content-->
    </body>
</html>
```

There are still a few more `bloginfo()` tags that you can add to this template. The `pingback_url` argument can be passed to output a specially formed URL for remote comment notification. Additionally, the `name` argument, representing the blog name, and the `description` argument, representing a tagline, can be injected into the theme itself with the `home` argument, which outputs the URL for the home page, as shown in Listing 12.10.

Note

The `pingback_url` generates a specially formed URL that is used only by other blogs. It is used to notify you when someone has linked to your blog from another site. ■

LISTING 12.10

Using the pingback_url, home, name, and description arguments with bloginfo()

```
<!DOCTYPE html PUBLIC "-//W3C//DTD XHTML 1.0 Transitional//EN"
     "http://www.w3.org/TR/xhtml1/DTD/xhtml1-transitional.dtd">
<html>
    <head>
         <title><?php bloginfo('name'); ?></title>
         <meta http-equiv="Content-Type" content="<?php bloginfo('html_
type'); ?>; charset=<?php bloginfo('charset'); ?>" /
         <link rel="stylesheet" href="<?php bloginfo('stylesheet_url'); ?>"
type="text/css" media="screen" />
         <link rel="pingback" href="<?php bloginfo('pingback_url'); ?>" />
    </head>
    <body>
         <div id="header">
              <h1><a href="<?php bloginfo('home'); ?>"><?php
bloginfo('name'); ?></a></h1>
              <h2><?php bloginfo('description'); ?></h2>
         </div>
         <!--body content-->
    </body>
</html>
```

Using template tags in the Loop

When you're ready to start coding up a Loop somewhere, you have a number of template tags at your beck and call. Typically, template tags in the Loop cannot be used outside of the Loop, but generally, you can use more abstract alternatives. (See the section later in this chapter on using Loop template tags outside the Loop.)

Cross-Reference

For more information about the Loop and how to produce custom Loops, see Chapter 8. ∎

In the Loop, the primary template tags used are:

- the_title()
- the_permalink()
- the_author()
- the_author_posts_link()
- the_date()
- the_time()

- the_excerpt()
- the_content()
- the_category()
- the_tags()

Many more template tags are available as are creative opportunities for useful behavior, but these are the core tags. Listing 12.11 demonstrates a Loop that uses all of these template tags.

LISTING 12.11

A Loop containing the most common Loop template tags

```php
<?php
if( have_posts() ) :
    while( have_posts() ) : the_post();
    ?>
    <div class="post">
        <h1><a href="<?php the_permalink(); ?>"><?php the_title(); ?></a></h1>
        <small>By <?php the_author(); ?> :: Written on <?php the_date() ?>
    at <?php the_time('g:i a'); ?> :: Read more by <?php the_author_posts_
    link(); ?></small>
        <?php
        if( is_single() )
        {
            the_content();
        }
        else
        {
            the_excerpt();
        }
        ?>
        <div class="post-meta">
            <p>Categorized: <?php the_category(',') ?></p>
            <?php the_tags( '<p>Tagged: ', ', ', '</p>'); ?>
        </div>
    </div>
    <?php
    endwhile;
endif;
```

On the Web

The code in Listing 12.11 is available for download at www.wiley.com/go/wordpressbible. ■

Note that most of the tags in Listing 12.11 do not take any arguments at all. However, some, such as the_tags(), the_category(), the_content(), the_date(), and the_time() accept optional arguments:

- the_tags() accepts:
  - Argument 1 — HTML to use before a list of tags
  - Argument 2 — Separator between each tag
  - Argument 3 — HTML to use after the list of tags
- the_category() typically accepts:
  - Argument 1 — Separator between each category
- the_content() typically accepts:
  - Argument 1 — Text for Read More link that is rendered when a bloggers use the <!--more--> tag in their content
- the_date() takes a PHP date() style format (see http://php.net/date)
- the_time() takes a PHP date() style format

Note

The two date-based template tags, the_date() and the_time(), are similar but differ in one key way: the_date() only outputs once a day and the_time() outputs every time it is invoked. Specifically, in a list of five posts from the same day, the formatted date produced by the_date() will only be printed once. ■

The Loop shown in Listing 12.11 can, and should, be extended a bit to provide error checking if no posts fit the criteria of the query (in this case, default criteria would only fail if there were no posts in WordPress at all) and to provide paging to browse to the next set of posts (see Listing 12.12).

LISTING 12.12

The Loop can be extended to provide error checking and results paging

```php
<?php
if( have_posts() ) :
    while( have_posts() ) : the_post();
    ?>
    <div class="post">
        <h1><a href="<?php the_permalink(); ?>"><?php the_title(); ?>
</a></h1>
        <small>By <?php the_author(); ?> :: Written on <?php the_time('F
jS, Y') ?> at <?php the_time('g:i a'); ?> :: Read more by <?php the_
author_posts_link(); ?></small>
        <?php
```

```php
            if( is_single() )
            {
                    the_content();
            }
            else
            {
                    the_excerpt();
            }
            ?>
            <div class="post-meta">
                    <p>Categorized: <?php the_category(',') ?></p>
                    <?php the_tags( '<p>Tagged: ', ', ', '</p>'); ?>
            </div>
    </div>
    <?php
    endwhile;
    ?>
    <p class="alignleft"><?php next_posts_link('&laquo; Older Entries')
?></p>
    <p class="alignright"><?php previous_posts_link('Newer Entries
&raquo;') ?></p>
    <?php
else :
?>
    <h2 class="center">Not Found</h2>
    <p class="center">Sorry, but you are looking for something that isn't
here.</p>
    <?php get_search_form(); ?>
<?php
endif;
```

On the Web

The code in Listing 12.12 is available for download at www.wiley.com/go/wordpressbible. ∎

The next_posts_link() and previous_posts_link() template tags can be used to take a single argument: the text to be displayed for the anchor text. If no posts are found matching the query criteria, the code in Listing 12.12 outputs a search form instead using the get_search_ form() template tag.

Tip

The get_search_form() template tag is hookable. You can use the get_search_form filter to modify the content of the search form. This is very useful if you want to provide alternative styling or structure to your search form. ∎

Using Loop template tags outside the Loop

Much of the data that is rendered by template tags inside the Loop can potentially be useful outside the Loop. Unfortunately, the Loop template tags rely on data populated in the $post object. This object is not created until the_post() function is executed at the beginning of the Loop. However, the the_post() function cannot be run outside the Loop; therefore, the data that is retrieved by Loop template tags cannot be accessed outside the Loop either.

Fortunately, there are some alternatives to accessing Loop data outside your standard Loop. You could create a custom Loop for one post and iterate as normal (for example, $newloop = new WP_Query(array('p' => 123);). The better method would be to use one of the alternative functions, which are similar to their Loop template tag cousins, but take the post ID as an argument. Table 12.3 lists the "out of Loop" alternatives to template tags.

TABLE 12.3

Out of Loop Alternatives to Loop Template Tags

Loop Template Tag	Out of Loop Alternative
the_title()	get_the_title($postid)
the_permalink()	get_permalink($postid)
the_author()	Retrieve user data with get_userdata($authorid) and use $author->display_name
the_author_posts_link()	get_author_posts_url($authorid, 'Display Name');
the_date()	Retrieve post with get_post($postid) and format $post->post_date with the PHP function date()
the_time()	Retrieve post with get_post($postid) and format $post->post_date with the PHP function date()
the_excerpt()	Retrieve post with get_post($postid) and use $post->post_excerpt
the_content()	Retrieve post with get_post($postid) and use $post->post_content
the_category()	get_the_category($postid)
the_tags()	get_the_tags($postid)

Creating Conversations with Threaded Comments and Paged Comments

Two relatively new features of WordPress, introduced in WordPress 2.7, are *threaded comments* and *paged comments*. For blogs with high comment counts, these two features are especially useful.

By default, WordPress uses a flat commenting system in which all comments are listed in the order in which they are made. Hierarchal changes to comments enable comments to have parents, similar to what has been around for a long time with nested Categories and Pages features.

The change to threaded comments doesn't change the way comments are displayed explicitly, but makes it possible for comments to be listed in a nested format. This is extremely useful when comments derive into multiple streams of conversation.

Likewise, blogs that have a lot of comments often employ paged commenting. After a designated number of comments are displayed on a page, navigation elements enable readers to browse to the next set of comments. This has a positive effect of reducing database load.

Along with the WordPress 2.7 enhancement to comments came a new paradigm in creating comments templates. The old style, which I mention only because it still represents many themes that are available, works in newer versions of WordPress. However, you cannot get the effects of comments or paging with these old style comment Loops.

Cross-Reference

The `comments.php` **format is discussed in Chapter 10.** ∎

WordPress commenting options for threaded comments, paged comments, and avatars can be set in WordPress Admin on the Discussion Settings page (Settings ➪ Discussion), which is shown in Figure 12.1.

FIGURE 12.1

Choose Settings ➪ Discussion to set comment options in the WordPress Admin.

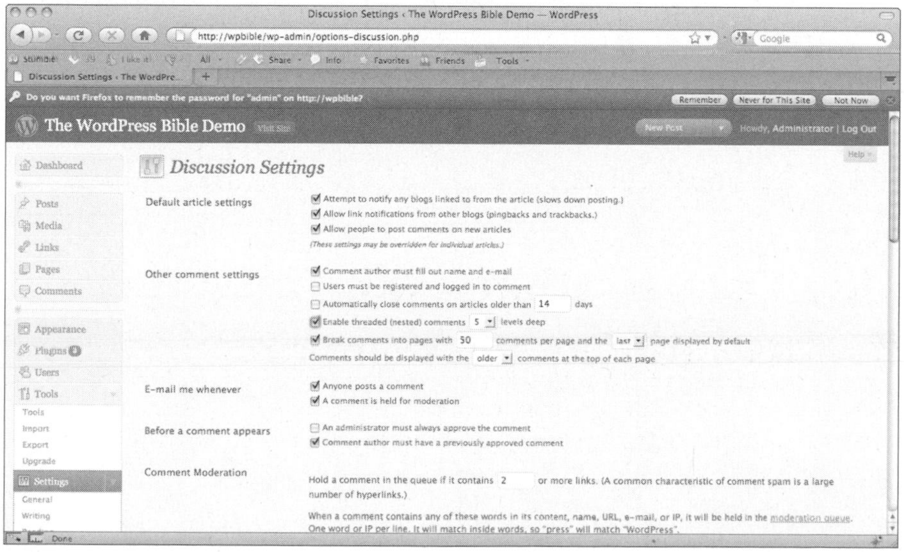

The important settings for a blogger to have enabled in WordPress to take advantage of threaded and paged comments are:

- Enable threaded (nested) comments *x* levels deep
- Break comments into pages with *x* comments per page and the *first/last* page displayed by default

Depending on the number you select in the Enable threaded comments drop-down menu, once a comment thread reaches a certain depth in the hierarchy, no more Reply links appear.

However, the actual theming process requires a few parts. First, the single pages need a bit of JavaScript to enable the comment links. You can do this by writing a function that is included in the themes functions.php file, in which you add the comment-reply JavaScript library via the wp_head hook, as shown in Listing 12.13.

LISTING 12.13

Include this function in the themes functions.php to enable the JavaScript needed for threaded replies

```
function enable_threaded_comments_js()
{
    if( is_singular() )
        wp_enqueue_script('comment-reply');
}
add_action('wp_enqueue_scripts','enable_threaded_comments_js');
```

On the Web

The code in Listing 12.13 is available for download at www.wiley.com/go/wordpressbible. ■

Your comments.php file should start with a simple check to make sure that it's not being accessed directly and that (if the post is password protected) the security checks are made. Add the code shown in Listing 12.14 verbatim to ensure that the file is not accessed directly and that the password-protected posts stay protected.

LISTING 12.14

Begin comments.php with this line to perform a simple security check

```
if (!empty($_SERVER['SCRIPT_FILENAME']) && 'comments.php' == basename($_
    SERVER['SCRIPT_FILENAME']))
    die ('Please do not load this page directly. Thanks!');
```

```
if ( post_password_required() )
{
    echo 'This post is password protected. Enter the password to view
comments.';
    return;
}
```

On the Web

The code in Listing 12.14 is available for download at www.wiley.com/go/wordpressbible. ∎

Tip

Though the default WordPress theme is a useful reference for seeing how template tags and files are implemented, it is generally okay to reuse the comments.php file included in the theme. You can then modify it for HTML structure. ∎

The next step is to find out if the post has any comments attached to it. You do this with a Comments Loop that is very similar to the posts Loop. Instead of using have_posts(), though, the Comments Loop is checked with have_comments(), as shown in Listing 12.15.

LISTING 12.15

Using have_comments to check the Comments Loop

```
if( have_comments() ) :

    // Comments
endif;
```

Inside the Comments Loop, comment listing is handled with a new template tag, wp_list_comments(), which outputs each comment as a list item and nests threaded comments if comment threading is enabled. Therefore, you'll want to make sure you wrap the template tag in an unordered or ordered (more typical) list, as shown in Listing 12.16.

LISTING 12.16

The wp_list_comments() template tag outputs all comments as list items

```
<ol>
    <?php wp_list_comments(); ?>
</ol>
```

Comment paging is handled with two template tags: `previous_comments_link()` and `next_comments_link()`. These two template tags output a Previous and Next link unless comment paging is turned off. When paging is turned off, nothing is printed to the screen. See Listing 12.17 for an example of how this is done.

LISTING 12.17

previous_comments_link() and next_comments_link()display paging links when comment paging is enabled

```
<p class="alignleft"><?php previous_comments_link(); ?></p>
<p class="alignright"><?php next_comments_link(); ?></p>
```

Finally, because JavaScript is used for much of the commenting experience now, there are a few requirements for your comment form:

- You must include `<?php comment_id_fields(); ?>` between your comment form `<form>` tags. This template tag provides two hidden form fields that contain the comment ID and the comment ID of the parent comment.

- Your comment `<textarea>` tag must have an ID of comment: `<textarea id="comment" name="comment"></textarea>`.

- The comment form must be wrapped in a div with an ID of respond: `<div id="respond"><form>...</form></div>`.

- You include the `comment_form_title()` template tag to create a dynamically changing title that changes from Leave a Reply to Leave Bill a Reply.

- You use the `cancel_comment_reply_link()` template tag to create a Cancel link in the form.

Personalizing the Reader Experience with Avatars

In October 2007, Automattic purchased a small company called Gravatar. Gravatar provides images, or *avatars*, for people by enabling them to sign up for free accounts and associating an image with their e-mail addresses. The concept was that when people commented on blogs using their registered e-mail addresses, the blogs that had Gravatar enabled, whether by plugin or otherwise, would display the avatar next to the readers comment.

With the acquisition of Gravatar by Automattic, that functionality got baked directly into the WordPress core. With the flick of a switch, WordPress bloggers can turn avatars on or off, set the rating, which is modeled after the Motion Picture Association of America rating system (G, PG, R, NC-17), or choose a default avatar to display when the user isn't registered with Gravatar. The avatar settings page in WordPress is shown in Figure 12.2.

The avatar magic happens with a function called `get_avatar()`. This function takes a minimum of one argument (the user ID from WordPress, which is associated with an e-mail address, or is the e-mail address itself). Additionally, it can take an optional second argument, which is an integer designating the size of the avatar. The default is 96, which means the avatar will be 96 × 96 in size. The third argument, typically provided internally by WordPress, is an optional URL to a default image when no avatar is available. The fourth optional argument is alt text for the image. Typically, `get_avatar()` is only called with the e-mail address and size, however.

WordPress loads a file called `pluggable.php` that includes a number of functions that are declared if they haven't been declared elsewhere or by plugin. Therefore, if you were to define your own `get_avatar()`,WordPress' version would not be loaded.

Tip

Whenever writing functions that override WordPress' functions, ensure that your function takes the exact same arguments as WordPress' version. This ensures compatibility with all other themes, plugins, or internal functions that use that function. ■

FIGURE 12.2

With WordPress, you can choose whether or not to use avatars on your blog and put limits on what avatars will display.

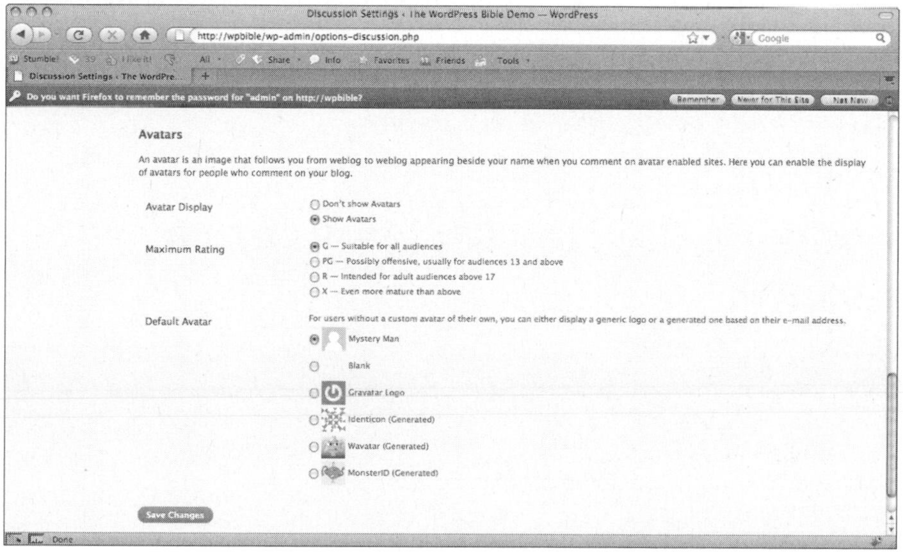

A second, alternative way of modifying get_avatar() is with the get_avatar filter. This is also a safer method, greatly reducing the possibility of introducing security holes. Functions using the get_avatar filter inherit the four arguments described earlier. You may not need them, depending on how you are getting different avatars, but you certainly have access to them.

Summary

- Every theme should include the wp_head() and wp_footer() functions. These functions are wrappers around hooks that are used by many plugins. Additionally, every theme should have the comment_form hook.

- Theme authors should consider standardizing around hooks in themes. Many more hooks should be included and are not strictly enforced, but could provide many options for bloggers.

- You need to ensure that JavaScript introduced in a theme uses wp_enqueue_script() and wp_print_scripts().

- The bloginfo() template tag is one of the more versatile template tags, providing metadata to a theme about the blog.

- WordPress provides a robust set of template tags for use inside the Loop.

- It's possible to create most of the functionality of Loop template tags outside the Loop.

- Threaded and paging comments provide a more interactive approach to a theme, enabling conversations and sub-conversations to develop.

- Avatars in comments are a nice touch to provide some insight into the identity of a commenter.

Part IV

Creating Content

Navigating the Content Production Experience

I n the earlier chapters in the book, I focus on technical procedures and implementations to a good extent. Though technical application programming interface (API) instructions and processes are important for developers, most WordPress users blog just because they want to write. They don't consider themselves hackers or coders. They just want to write or publish video.

The folks behind WordPress have put a lot of effort into streamlining the user experience and making the WordPress software a natural fit for anyone. Vast configuration options enable writers to tweak preferences, and they can easily modify layouts to fit their style.

In this chapter, I discuss some of the user interface elements of WordPress and provide some context around how you would get around using the software from that perspective.

Customizing Your Workspace

When it comes down to writing, having an intuitive layout is necessary for a productive writing experience. Every blogger has a specific need.

For example, in a newsroom-style environment with multiple writers and editors, the most important aspects of the Write Post and Write Page screens are the title, content area, and excerpt. Of secondary importance are categories and possibly custom fields for associated images or other related items.

A photoblogger probably has a much different set of requirements. Photobloggers might need the title and content areas, but probably need tags more than categories — a nuance I discuss later in this chapter.

On the other hand, a political blogger (a demographic of blogger that is generally text-focused and usually consists of a single person writing commentary) probably needs only the title and content areas, and categories or tags.

In addition, plugins or themes often add additional fields to the Write Post and Write Page screens that serve important purposes. (You probably didn't install a plugin that supplies additional post screen fields if you don't need it.)

Fortunately, WordPress enables a blogger to customize the Write Post and Write Page screens according to taste and need simply by dragging and dropping modules into new positions on the screen, as shown in Figure 13.1.

FIGURE 13.1

To rearrange the Write pages, simply drag modules to a new position on the screen.

Leveraging the Elements of Content Creation

The Write Post screen (also called the Write Post page) is where you do most of your content creation. It is the hub for filling out your blog with posts, videos, and images. Even though you will inevitably spend time in other areas of the WordPress Admin, the main command center is the Write Post screen.

The Write Post screen is a strategic page. You can configure and tweak it to match your workflow, and it is where you will make huge decisions that affect how your blog fairs in search engines and with readers. You will need to consider your community of readers, search engine options, and possibly your customers. Fortunately, WordPress provides ways to assist you.

Using the title strategically

The title of a post may be the most important strategic marketing portion of a post. When the Google search engine indexes content, for example, the title is what helps the search engine understand what the page is about. On individual post pages (permalinked posts), the title of the post is generally the title tag on the page itself, boosting the importance of this post title to the marketing and search engine optimization (SEO) of a site.

Cross-Reference
For more information about SEO and why it is an important consideration when creating your blog, see Chapter 3. ■

If you have a blog about making home improvements and write a post about hanging a door, you might feel inclined to write a human-friendly title. In other words, your title might be written with the assumption that people who regularly read will, in fact, be the ones to read a post. Your title in that situation might be, "The Door Broke." This title doesn't provide any context for anything or anyone (search engines or people) about the situation. Regular readers might take an interest, but statistically, search engine traffic, not "regular readers," dominates most blog traffic.

A better title would be, "Fixing a Broken Door in Three Easy Steps." This title provides context to new readers and longtime readers and provides keyword context for search engines.

You'll notice that after you enter a title on the Write screen and then move the cursor to a different field, WordPress generates and displays a permalink (the permanent URL to your individual post) under the title, as shown in Figure 13.2. When you type a title, this permalink reflects the title of the post.

Note
Though WordPress autosaves a post and creates a permalink, this permalink does not exist until the post is published. ■

FIGURE 13.2

WordPress initially generates and displays a permalink when a post is autosaved or published (whichever comes first).

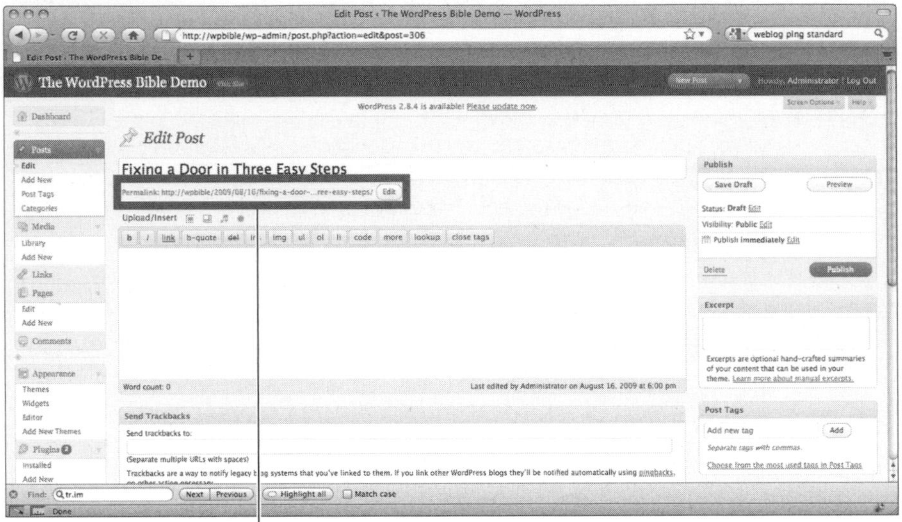

The WordPress-generated permalink

Designating an excerpt

An *excerpt* in WordPress is a short summary of a post. Depending on the style of theme, post excerpts may or may not be used. In WordPress, you have the option on the Write screen to manually designate text to be an excerpt.

Note

Excerpts, while often used, are not a mandatory aspect of theme development in WordPress. ■

If you use a theme that uses excerpts, you'll want to pay close attention to your post writing and always ensure that you designate one. If you don't specify an excerpt and WordPress looks for one, WordPress automatically tries to create one on the fly. This usually has mixed results and paragraphs are cut off prematurely.

Using excerpts is also an excellent opportunity to further refine the searchability of your content. While excerpts typically are taken directly from the post content itself, there is nothing that says an excerpt can't be something completely different (yet related!) to the post itself. Think of your excerpting possibilities as akin to writing an executive summary of an article.

Enhancing searchability of content

Content is only as useful as its capability to drive traffic to a site. As a general rule, most sites get between 60 percent and 80 percent of their traffic directly from search engines. Many new bloggers assume that if they only tell their friends and families about a blog, those people are the only ones who read it. This is not true at all. WordPress has a *ping* mechanism that alerts search engines immediately when a new post is published and Google has been known to index new posts within a minute or two of the content being online. Because of the nature of the Internet, you should take every step you can to enhance the capability of search engines to drive traffic to your WordPress blog.

Tip

Plugin developers can wrangle the ping data with a couple of hooks. Developers can filter a list of URLs to ping (all these URLs will be notified of a new post when it is published) with `get_to_ping`. A plugin can simply add a URL to the list of URLs that will be pinged for a specific post using the `add_ping` filter. ∎

Adjust the title slug

Strategically, you can adjust the permalink (or more accurately, the shortened, sanitized version of the title called the *slug*) to read in a different way than the actual title. Because search engines look at both the title text as well as the URL of the page, leveraging this feature can have a significant impact on your search engine marketing strategy.

Consider the situation in which you have the title, "Fixing a Broken Door in Three Easy Steps," and you want to make the slug more reflective of how someone might search. You could solve the problem by changing the slug to "how-to-fix-a-broken-door."

To change the slug, click the permalink below the title (or click on the Edit button) and type a new slug, as shown in Figure 13.3. WordPress sanitizes the slug, but you can as well by making all words lowercase, using no punctuation, and separating words with hyphens.

Note

In order to change the slug using the method described here, WordPress must be using friendly permalinks, which are much more readable URLs that are more readable and visually more appealing, instead of the default permalink style. The default permalink style is `http://www.example.com/?p=12345` for maximum compatibility with different server setups. ∎

FIGURE 13.3

To change the slug of a post, click the permalink or Edit button below the title and type the new slug.

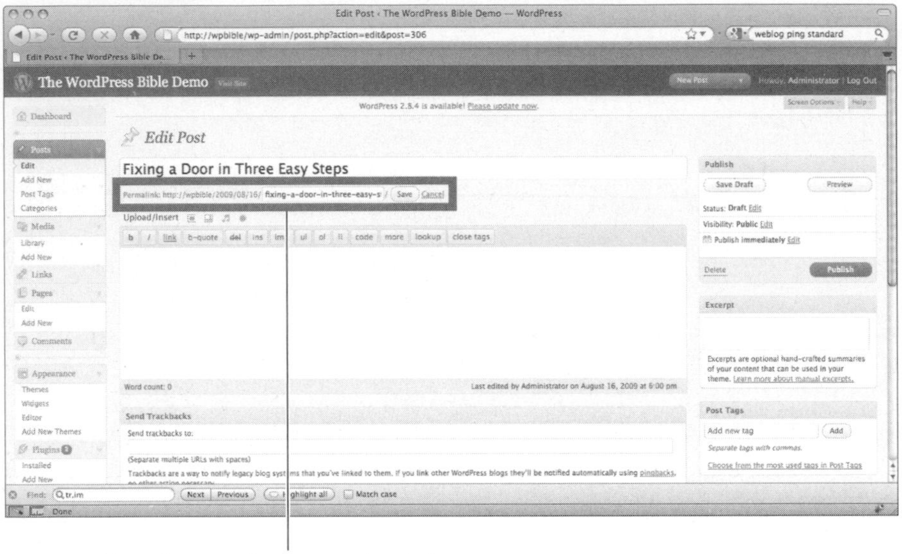

Type the new slug here and click Save

Use "bold" font to enhance importance

The bold tag, in hypertext markup language (HTML), comes in two forms. Visually, both the <b> tag and the <strong> tag are identical. However, there is some disagreement in the SEO community about which is a better tag to use for keyword emphasis. The <b> tag is a presentational element that displays text in bold while the <strong> tag represents a semantic understanding of a strong emphasis on a word or phrase. Visually, browsers all render both tags as "bold," though the semantic meaning changes.

Disagreement over semantics aside, making a keyword or phrase bold instructs the search engines to take special note of the words and factor them into how search results are put together. Using this technique while producing your content helps shape how search engines index the page.

Add descriptive text to videos and podcasts

As the Internet becomes more of a venue for "rich media" like video and audio, new problems arise with searchability. When search engines index a page, they read the generated HTML in its entirety, then process it through algorithms and parsing engines to decipher the page. If you embed a YouTube video, however, the search engines are not going to see it. The search engines are only going to see code like the example shown in Listing 13.1.

Search engines can only read text. They are smart and can process linguistic anomalies (such as British and American spellings of common words), misspellings, and even understand intent, in some cases. However, with video embeds, images, and audio files, the search engines have no real text to process and gain context around what the content is. You could post a funny video of your friend in a hotdog eating contest, but all Google is going to see is "Embed code."

For this reason, it's extremely important to put keyword rich context around video and audio, particularly, and ensure the use of "alt" tags in images (WordPress can do this automatically when you upload images).

LISTING 13.1

YouTube video content is virtually invisible to a search engine

```
<object width="425" height="344"><param name="movie" value="http://www.
    youtube.com/v/5oiQdTfMAmo&hl=en&fs=1&"></param><param
    name="allowFullScreen" value="true"></param><param
    name="allowscriptaccess" value="always"></param><embed src="http://www.
    youtube.com/v/5oiQdTfMAmo&hl=en&fs=1&"
    type="application/x-shockwave-flash" allowscriptaccess="always"
    allowfullscreen="true" width="425" height="344"></embed></object>
```

When generating content for your blog, always add descriptive text to videos. Likewise, if you are producing content around a podcast, always provide "show notes" or a transcript.

Adding descriptive text to videos and podcasts solves two problems:

- It provides search engines with context to understand what the podcast is about.
- It provides readers with the ability to scan notes for key information so they can determine if they want to listen.

Write well

As simply as I can put it, it is important to write good content. I have been involved in this industry for years now and can say, without a shadow of a doubt, that well-written, authoritative content always performs better with search engines than poorly written content with the maximum emphasis possible on SEO.

As a writer, spend less time worrying about all of the little nuances of SEO and focus on putting your mind into action, extracting the thoughts that wander around in your brain and conveying them in content. Clearly, this book isn't going to teach you how to write. Everyone has a unique style or approach. However, finding and leveraging this passion and authority into quality, original content will always help your blog perform better than simply optimizing keywords.

Cross-Reference

Later in this chapter, I'll talk about ways you can "hack your life" from a writing perspective. Hacking your life, despite its connotation, is a good thing to help focus on writing. You can address the technical details of SEO, including using titles, slugs, and keywords effectively, after you've finished writing. ∎

Looking at categories and tags: What's the difference?

WordPress supports two types of descriptor data that can be used synonymously or differently. The first type of descriptor data is *categories*. In the early days of WordPress, categories were the only type of "bucket" that bloggers could put blog entries into. It was simply associating a description with content: "This blog entry is about football so I'll put it in the Sports category."

Soon, a movement toward more granular description information came along. Much of the argument revolved around searchability and putting some organization around the world's data. The theory was that, even though a post could be assigned to multiple categories, it was easy to derive into a generic mold where posts were only vaguely relevant to the category.

WordPress adopted *tags* with an intention to provide bloggers with the ability to put much more granular, ad-hoc metadata around posts. As time has passed, tags have become somewhat standard among most bloggers while categories represent a more vertical, or single topic-based, kind of organization. Many bloggers, whether semantically correct or not, have adopted the concept of categories as infrastructure mechanisms, and tags to provide actual metadata for a post.

Note

From a technical perspective, there is no difference between categories and tags. They are both stored in the same database table and, though each have different APIs for accessing, they are identical in every technical way. The difference really is how the blogger decides to use categories and tags. Categories have a hierarchical nature to them and the user interfaces around categories promote this use case. Tags are generally perceived as "flat" and, as a result, the use cases where tags are most often used promote a flat taxonomy. ■

Search implications

Ironically, although the concept of tags came about because of the need to put more context around content to improve search and discoverability, the major search engines (Google, Yahoo!, and Bing) do not use categories or tags in any kind of discoverable way. Blog-oriented search tools (Technorati or Google Blog Search) do use this metadata but treat them identically.

WordPress' notifications of these services do not include any category or tag information. It is simply an XML Remote Procedure Call (XML-RPC) to search engines and services. A standardized weblogUpdate call is shown in Listing 13.2.

The weblogUpdate call demonstrates that very little specific information is given to the search engines regarding the post. All it does is alert the search engines that there is new content to look at. The search engines can then find the new post and use any information they can find about the post.

It is important at this point to provide category or tag data in the theme. If both categories and tags are used in your content creation, ensure that both are displayed in your theme using the `the_ category()` and `the_tags()` template tags.

LISTING 13.2

When a post is published, WordPress sends an XML-RPC notification to search engines

```xml
<?xml version="1.0"?>
<methodCall>
    <methodName>weblogUpdate.ping</methodName>
    <params>
        <param>
            <value>Home Improvement Blog</value>
        </param>
        <param>
            <value>http://example.com</value>
        </param>
    </params>
</methodCall>
```

Cross-Reference

Template tags, including `the_category()` and `the_tags()`, are discussed in more detail in Chapter 12. ■

Architectural implications

Many bloggers, including myself, have taken an approach that uses categories as an architectural element of a blog. The assigned categories, with this approach, are not used as metadata but as a way to place content in different buckets that are used to divide the blog into multiple parts.

In some cases, blogs need to appear to be multiple blogs, with multiple authors. With WordPress MU (WordPress Multi-User), true multi-blog capability can be achieved; however, sometimes WordPress MU can introduce incompatibilities with plugins, support issues, and other problems that keep bloggers from using it. Thus, using categories as an architectural element can provide the appearance of multiple blogs.

Cross-Reference

WordPress MU is discussed in more detail in Chapter 22. ■

Managing categories

WordPress category management can be done in two places. It can be done from the Write Post screen and from a separate Category management page in the WordPress Admin.

By default (keep in mind that the Write Post screen can be arranged according to preference and workflow), a multi-tab widget is positioned at the bottom of the right column (see Figure 13.4). The first tab lists all categories, and the second tab lists the most commonly used categories.

Adding new categories is as simple as clicking the Add New Category link and naming a new category. New categories can have parent categories, as well, so it's possible to create hierarchies for category display.

FIGURE 13.4

On the Write screen, you can use the Categories module to add new categories or select an existing category.

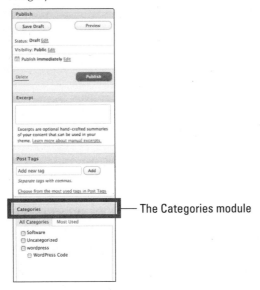 ——— The Categories module

A second, and more detailed, method of managing categories is via the Categories screen in the WordPress Admin. This screen can be accessed by choosing Posts ⇨ Categories and is shown in Figure 13.5.

In the left column of this screen, you can add new categories. The only field that is required is the Category Name. You can specify a slug for the category, but if you omit it, WordPress sanitizes the title and creates a slug in the same way that post slugs are generated. That means that a category called WordPress Code will have a slug called wordpress-code.

If you'd like to leverage the category hierarchy (parent/child categories), you can designate a parent category as well or write a short description of the category for use in templates and themes.

In the right column, you can edit pre-existing categories by clicking the Quick Edit link that appears when you hover over the category (see Figure 13.6) or by clicking the name of the category itself. While Quick Edit allows only category names and slugs to be renamed, the latter editing option reveals a screen with a form similar to the one that appears on the left side of the Add Category page (see Figure 13.7).

FIGURE 13.5

Categories can be fully managed from the Categories screen.

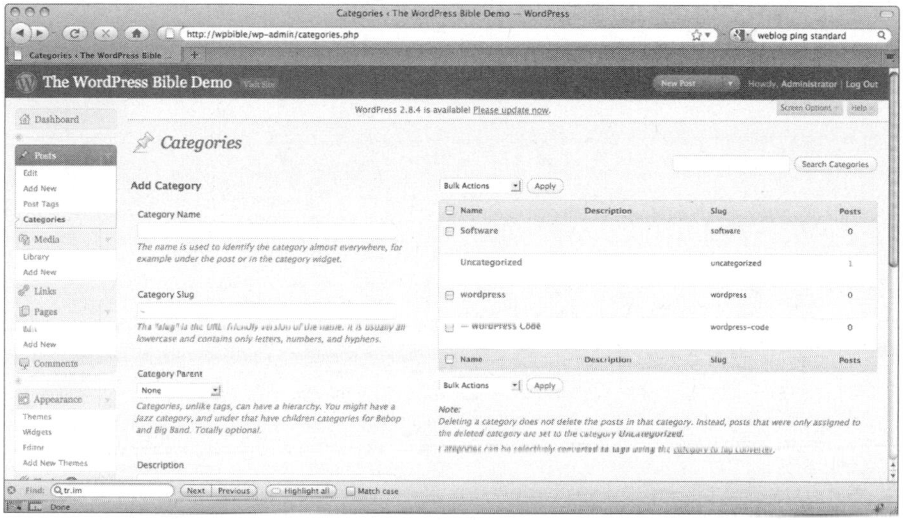

FIGURE 13.6

The Quick Edit form can be activated from the Quick Edit link that appears when you hover over a category name.

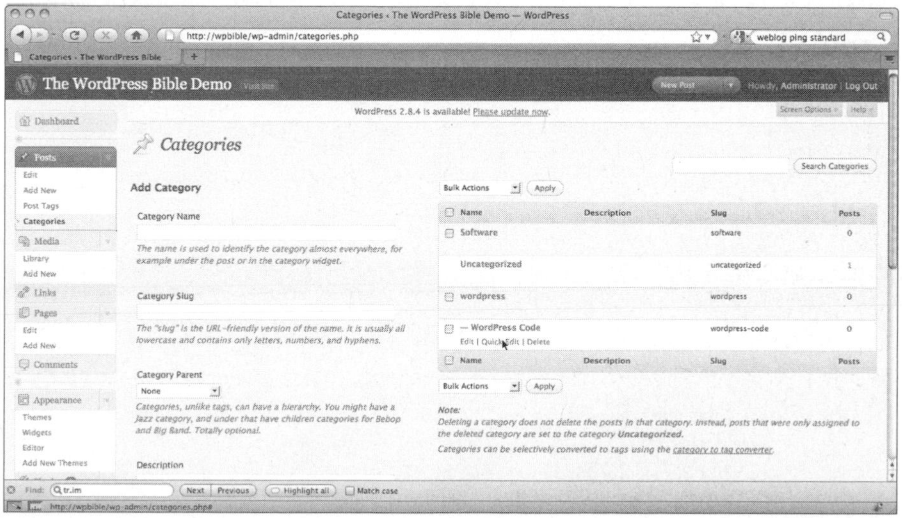

FIGURE 13.7

When you click the category name, you can edit the details of a category.

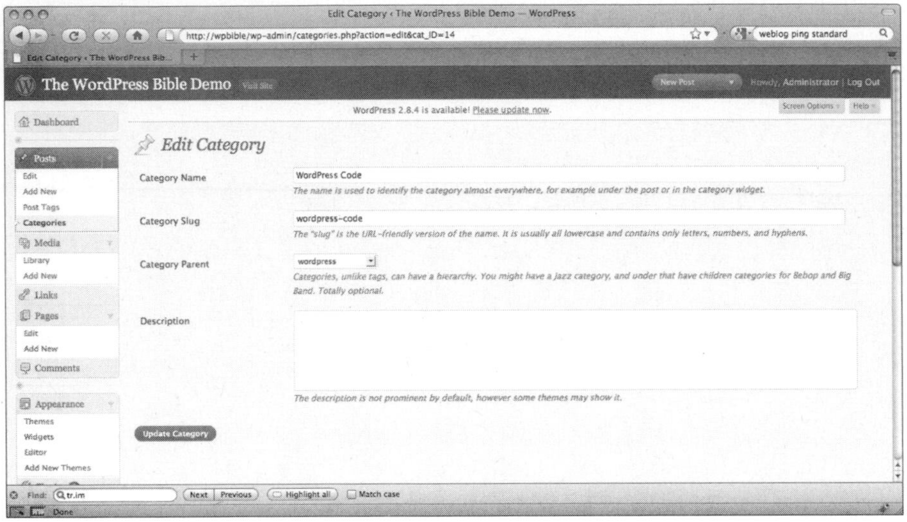

Managing tags

Functionally, tags work in a similar way to the categories. They both exist in the same table, and can both be used the same way. Yet, the principle behind tags is much more ad-hoc than structured. Where a story about a football game might be categorized as Sports, the same story could be tagged as "nfl," "football," "baltimore ravens," "pittsburgh steelers," "joe flacco," "pigskin," "week 16," "james farrior," "sack," and on and on. Each comma-separated word will be entered into the database as a separate tag. The concept behind tags is much more ad hoc; therefore, the interface on the Write Post screen that is used to enter them is also ad hoc. By default, the tag entry box is the second box in the right column, as shown in Figure 13.8.

A nice feature of tag entry on the Write Post screen is that WordPress auto-suggests tags from the tags that have already been created. You can choose an auto-suggested tag or simply keep typing keywords separated by commas.

Note

When WordPress first introduced tagging in WordPress 2.3, there was very little user interface around tagging. Intentionally, it was left as open concept to allow the community to create plugins and express opinions about how it wanted a tagging interface to be implemented. The current interface took inspiration from Flickr, whose elegance formed the cornerstone of WordPress' tagging interface. ■

FIGURE 13.8

Enter comma-separated tags in the Post Tags box on the Write Post screen. WordPress automatically suggests tags from tags that have already been already created.

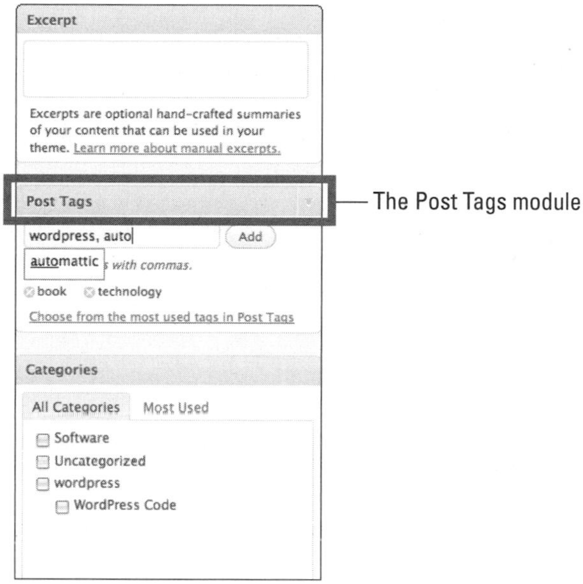

The Post Tags module

As with categories, you also can manage tags from a separate administrative panel. Like the Categories page, the Tags page (Posts ⇨ Post Tags) consists of a two-column interface (see Figure 13.9). On the left side, you can manually add individual tags; in the right column, you can use a "Quick Edit" interface to quickly edit a tag or click the tag to enter more information. You can bulk edit and delete tags as well by selecting more than one tag and choosing the appropriate option from the drop-down menu at the top or bottom of the interface.

Tip

On the Tags page and throughout the WordPress Admin, you can select multiple items from a list (check boxes) by selecting each box individually. You can also choose a series of items in a list by selecting the first check box, holding down the Shift key, and selecting the last check box. This is especially useful when performing mass edits on a large scale, such as deleting categories or reorganizing posts. ∎

FIGURE 13.9

Tags can be individually managed from the Tags page. It has a similar interface to the screen for managing Categories.

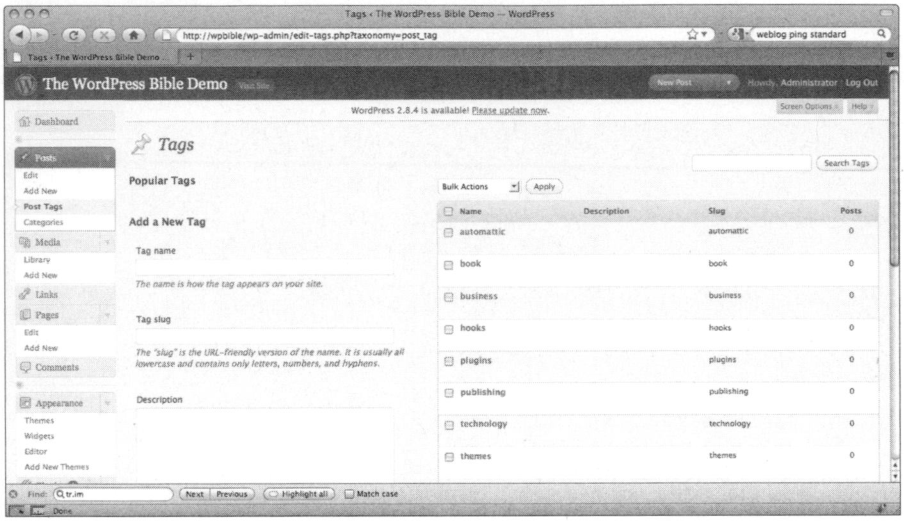

Publishing and scheduling posts

Another important aspect of producing content is letting WordPress know when the content should be made available to the world. Every post has a post time that is stored in the database. Unless a time is manually specified, posts are given the current timestamp when published. To WordPress and the mechanics of the Loop, this post becomes immediately viewable online. However, you can set the date manually as well.

Additionally, every post has a post *status*: draft, published, scheduled, or pending. A post in draft status can have a timestamp in the past, present, or future. A post in published status can only have a timestamp in the past or present. Scheduled posts are published posts that have not reached their specified timestamp yet. Pending posts are posts that are written by a user in the Author role or a lower role. These users don't have the `publish_post` capability, so instead of seeing the Publish box at the top-right corner of the Write screen (see Figure 13.10), they see "Submit for Review."

Using the Publish module, you can change the status of a post by clicking the Edit link next to Status. Likewise, you can click the Edit link next to Visibility to expose other post configuration options. Notably, the Publish panel is where you can set a post to Sticky and designate the post to the top of the Loop. The third Edit link exposes a panel for altering the publish date. If this date is in the future, the post will be published as Scheduled.

Cross-Reference
The technical implementation of Sticky posts is described in Chapter 8. ∎

FIGURE 13.10

The Publish module, with all three panels expanded, enables an author to set the date and time for publishing, along with other data, including making the post Sticky.

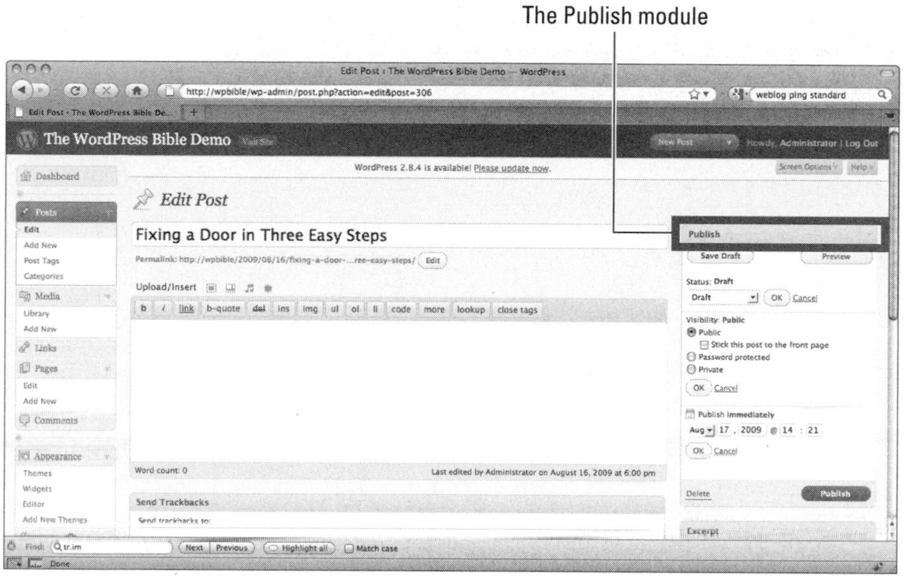

The Publish module

Using custom fields

The final aspect of WordPress content creation is *custom fields*. Custom fields are actually post metadata that is associated with the post. There is no expectation or structure to this data per se, but it can open up an avenue for custom theme display.

Custom fields are made up of key/value pairs. Keys that have been used in the blog in the past are available via a drop-down menu located in the Custom Fields module below the post editing box (see Figure 13.11). If you would like to create a new custom field, you can create a new one here.

Note

The most common use case for custom fields was associating an image URL with a custom field. These image URLs have historically been used to provide "magazine-style" layouts where a story or post would have a catchy image as well. In WordPress 2.9, a new template tag, the_post_thumbnail(), is used to retrieve the first post attachment (an image uploaded through the WordPress media uploader) and render it in the layout. ■

Tip

Theme and plugin developers who want to use custom fields can do so by using the get_post_meta() function described in Chapter 12. ■

In WordPress, custom fields can hold any key/value pair that you would like to associate with a post. Most commonly, custom fields are used to provide additional images for themes, but can be anything that might be of use.

Hacking Your Experience: Getting the Most Out of Writing

When bloggers are asked why they blog, the answers are wide and varied. Some think about making money from their blogging, while others do it to build a reputation. Some write for their companies and others do it for other personal reasons. It is clear, though, from talking to bloggers, that when they sit down to write a post, they want to do it as efficiently as possible.

Fortunately, WordPress has a number of features that will help you "hack your experience" and make it the most positive it can be.

Using the visual text editor

Many bloggers prefer to use an interface that is familiar to them. They don't want to write posts using HTML. They want to be able to select text, make it bold or italic, and so on. WordPress provides a visual text editor for just those kinds of users.

The WordPress visual text editor can be toggled at the top of the content editor. It is rendered with a tab aptly named Visual. Many power users prefer HTML mode, where they have greater control over the formatting of their post. The visual editor (based on a JavaScript library called TinyMCE) is not without its problems, but largely, it does the job well.

Tip

To use the visual text editor, the Disable the visual text editor option must be unselected in your user profile. If you cannot see the Visual and HTML tabs, make sure this option is unselected in your user profile. ■

Using the visual text editor exposes a number of shortcut keys. Readers coming from the Getting Things Done (GTD) management mentality, taught by training consultant David Allen, are probably already familiar with many of these shortcuts, which are listed in Table 13.1.

TABLE 13.1

Visual Text Editor Shortcuts

Action	Windows Shortcut	Mac Shortcut
Insert a link	Alt + Shift + A	Option + Shift + A
Apply a blockquote	Alt + Shift + Q	Option + Shift + Q
Unordered list item	Alt + Shift + U	Option + Shift + U
Ordered list item	Alt + Shift + O	Option + Shift + O
Left align	Alt + Shift + L	Option + Shift + L
Center align	Alt + Shift + C	Option + Shift + C
Right align	Alt + Shift + R	Option + Shift + R
Switch to HTML mode	Alt + Shift + E	Option + Shift + E
Insert <!--more-->	Alt + Shift + T	Option + Shift + T
Show full toolbar	Alt + Shift + Z	Option + Shift + Z
Full Screen mode	Alt + Shift + G	Option + Shift + G
New paragraph	Ctrl + P	Command + P
Copy	Ctrl + C	Command + C
Paste	Ctrl + P	Command + P
Bold	Ctrl + B	Command + B
Italic	Ctrl + I	Command + I
Underline	Ctrl + U	Command + U
New heading (h1–h6)	Ctrl + 1–6	Command + 1–6

Using Full Screen mode

Writers understand the need to block everything out and focus on their task at hand. That is why some bloggers like to use Full Screen mode to write (see Figure 13.12). Full Screen mode takes over the entire browser window, blocking out all other aspects of WordPress. This helps many bloggers take advantage of a blank canvas, so to speak, and concentrate on writing.

FIGURE 13.12

Full Screen mode takes over the entire browser and blocks everything else out — a useful tool for writers needing to focus only on their writing.

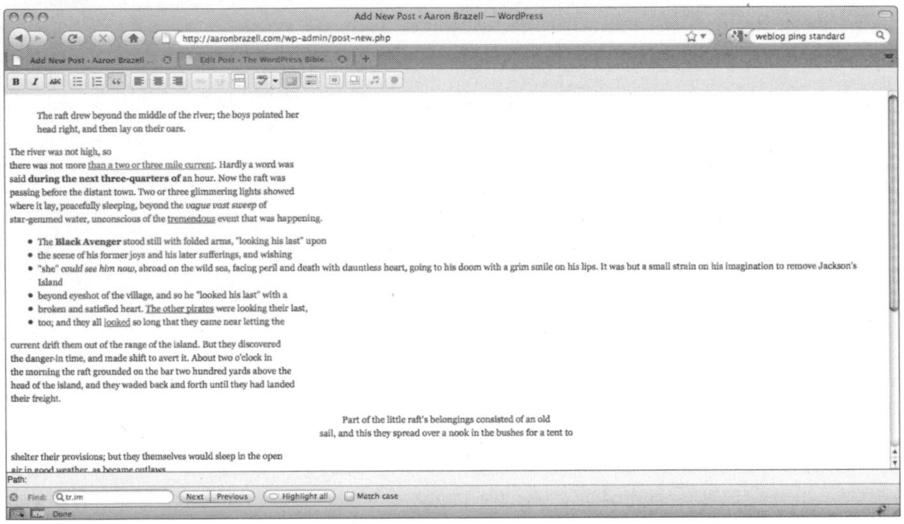

Using the Press This bookmarklet

WordPress users who tend to write quick, ad hoc entries (perhaps simply sharing links with their audience) may find value in Press This. Press This is a *bookmarklet* that is available from the Tools menu and can be dragged to your browser toolbar.

Bookmarklets represent a link, generally using JavaScript, that can be used in any context of Web browsing (any time or any site) to perform a task. For example, Delicious.com provides a bookmarklet for bookmarking pages. Tumblr provides a bookmarklet for quick posting. Similar to Tumblr, WordPress provides a bookmarklet for quick posting as well.

When you visit a Web site, clicking the Press This bookmark link in your browser toolbar launches a mini version of WordPress with a slimmed down interface for posting, as shown in Figure 13.13. This slimmed-down version provides a content editing interface (with full support for visual editing), a tag box, and a publish box.

Press This is intended for quick, ad-hoc posting. For more in depth, feature-style posting, bloggers tend to simply log in to WordPress and write as they usually would.

FIGURE 13.13

The Press This window resembles the Write Post screen; however, it is much slimmer and does not have as many features.

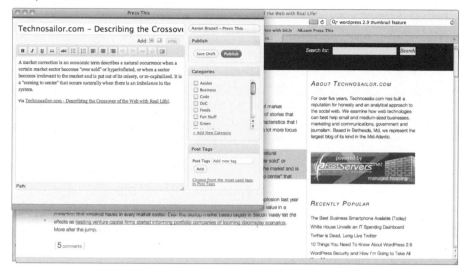

Summary

- You can customize the WordPress Write Post and Write Page screen by dragging individual modules to locations on the screen that suit your workflow and preference.

- On the Write Post and Write Page screen itself, WordPress provides a user interface for the title tag, the content editor, tags and categories, and custom fields.

- You can customize excerpts. If an excerpt is not specified, WordPress automatically generates one when needed.

- You can modify post slugs by clicking the generated link and entering a new slug.

- Categories provide a vertical structure to a blog while tags are more ad hoc. Both have interfaces on and off the Write Post screen to manage this metadata.

- If you use the visual text editor, you expose features like Full Screen mode and shortcut keys to make your WordPress writing experience better.

- Press This provides a mini version of the Write Post interface and is useful for quick, light posting.

Using Offline Editors

A s our world becomes incredibly interwoven, tied together via the Internet, it is becoming increasingly necessary to find simpler ways to do Internet-related jobs. iPhones make it easier to access the Web and rich media from mobile phones. Web services, like Mint.com, make it easier to manage personal finances. It seems natural that there would be an easier way to manage content creation as well.

As powerful as WordPress is and as intuitive as the interface has become since WordPress 2.7, many people simply want to write without having to log into a Web site. Likewise, bloggers who spend a lot of time on the road often find it easier to write offline and publish later. Internet access might be scarce or patchy, or not available at all.

Enter *offline editors*, more technically known as *XML-RPC editors*. These offline editors are typically desktop clients, but can take the form of a smart phone application as well. In this chapter, I introduce you to some of the offline options out there.

IN THIS CHAPTER

What is XML-RPC?

Understanding XML-RPC security risks

Looking at offline blog editors

What Is XML-RPC?

Fortunately, WordPress supports offline editing via an XML Remote Procedure Call (XML-RPC) application programming interface (API). The XML-RPC, protocol was designed in 1998 to handle remote Web service interaction. It quickly became a standard in the early blogging platform Radio Userland (http://radio.userland.com/), and became the basis of the MetaWeblog API that is supported by most blogging platforms, including WordPress.

XML-RPC, simply described, is a protocol in which data is sent in the format of XML to a server or Web application — in this case, WordPress — over standard Internet transfer protocols. When the service receives the data, it is able to process it according to predefined standards, perform an action, and return data back to the client. It is the same concept that enables server administrators to send a remote shutdown command to a server or remotely activate a process on another server, except in this case, the protocol allows WordPress to publish or edit a new post remotely.

WordPress-supported remote protocols

WordPress has taken remote procedure call APIs very seriously. Three supported remote publishing standards — the Blogger API, MetaWeblog API, and Movable Type API — are built into the standard WordPress package. WordPress has also extended the Movable Type API with specialized, WordPress-specific API methods that, as a whole, is referred to as the *WordPress API*. In addition to these similar but non-federated APIs, WordPress supports the Atom Publishing Protocol (APP), which is a federated API that is standardized by a third party and is strictly enforced by all platforms that support it.

In addition to publishing protocols, WordPress uses other XML-RPC services. Most notably, the pingback protocol is used in a similar client-server model as previously described, though instead of an offline editor and WordPress, the pingback protocol is used between blogs for notifications.

Note
Developers interested in understanding how the XML-RPC interfaces work from a technical perspective can find all the related classes and methods in the `xmlrpc.php` file. ∎

Blogger API

The Blogger API is one of the oldest XML-RPC APIs available, though it is very limited in functionality. It contains nine methods that are supported by WordPress; however, I do not recommend that you use it. These days, even the Blogger API uses the MetaWeblog API, which is discussed in the next section.

The Blogger methods supported by WordPress are listed in Table 14.1.

TABLE 14.1

Blogger API XML-RPC Methods Supported by WordPress

Method Name	Description
blogger.getUsersBlogs	Retrieves a listing of all Blogger blogs listed for the designated user.
blogger.getUserInfo	Retrieves information about the designated user.
blogger.getPost	Retrieves information about a single post containing post content, date, user ID, and post ID.

Method Name	Description
blogger.getRecentPosts	Retrieves a listing of recent posts by a given user. Default enumeration is 10.
blogger.getTemplate	Retrieves the content of a file.
blogger.setTemplate	Writes content to a file.
blogger.newPost	Publishes a new Post. Supports blog id (Multi-User WordPress [Word Press MU]), author id, post date, post content, post title, post category, and post status. For other fields, uses a different API.
blogger.editPost	Edits a given post with the same fields as blogger.newPost.
blogger.deletePost	Deletes a given post.

MetaWeblog API

The most common XML-RPC blogging standard by far, the MetaWeblog API was created in an effort to enhance the Blogger API, which was considered severely limited. The MetaWeblog API, also weak by today's standards, has ten methods, four of which are aliases to Blogger API methods.

Note

The WordPress XML-RPC API is based off of the MetaWeblog API. ∎

The MetaWeblog methods supported by WordPress are listed in Table 14.2.

TABLE 14.2

MetaWeblog API XML-RPC Methods Supported by WordPress

Method Name	Description
metaWeblog.newPost	Creates a new post or page with the following allowed data: publish status, slug, post password, page parent id, page order, author id, excerpt, tags, allow comments, allow pings, date, categories, and URLs to ping on publish. It can also make a post Sticky.
metaWeblog.editPost	Modifies a given post using the same fields supported by metaWeblog. newPost. It can also make a post Sticky.
metaWeblog.getPost	Retrieves all MetaWeblog-supported data given a specific post ID.
metaWeblog.getRecentPosts	Retrieves a listing of recent posts by a given user. Default enumeration is 10.
metaWeblog.getCategories	Retrieves a list of categories. Note that the MetaWeblog API does not implicitly support Tags (though it can set keywords, which is an archaic means of tagging) through metaWeblog.editPost and metaWeblog.addPost.
metaWeblog.newMediaObject	Performs image upload functions.

continued

TABLE 14.2 *(continued)*

Method Name	Description
Blogger API Aliases	
metaWeblog.deletePost	Aliases blogger.deletePost
metaWeblog.getTemplate	Aliases blogger.getTemplate
metaWeblog.setTemplate	Aliases blogger.setTemplate
metaWeblog.getUsersBlogs	Aliases blogger.getUsersBlogs

Movable Type API

The Movable Type API was one of the major APIs early on and has been widely supported by blogging software. It is not a robust API and was built specifically for Movable Type and Typepad applications. WordPress adopted it early on, prior to branching and extending the MetaWeblog API to create the WordPress API.

The Movable Type API supports eight methods, which are listed in Table 14.3.

TABLE 14.3

Movable Type API XML-RPC Methods Supported by WordPress

Method Name	Description
mt.getCategoryList	Retrieves a list of categories that can be assigned to posts.
mt.getRecentPostTitles	Retrieves a listing of the most recent posts. Enumeration defaults to 10.
mt.getPostCategories	Retrieves a list of categories that have been assigned to a given post.
mt.setPostCategories	Assigns a selection of categories to a post on creation/edit.
mt.supportedMethods	A sanity check method to determine which methods an XML-RPC client can call.
mt.supportedTextFilters	Does nothing in WordPress; exists for compatibility with clients.
mt.getTrackbackPings	Retrieves a list of URLs that have been pinged for a given post.
mt.publishPost	Updates a post with the post_status of "publish."

WordPress XML-RPC API

The WordPress XML-RPC API is an extension of the MetaWeblog API but provides a much richer set of tools because, naturally, it is created by WordPress for WordPress and considers exclusive WordPress features when exposing the API.

The methods for the WordPress API are listed in Table 14.4.

TABLE 14.4

WordPress XML-RPC API Methods

Method Name	Description
wp.getUsersBlogs	Retrieves a list of blogs that the user is assigned to. Returns a single blog for WordPress and all blogs assigned for WordPress MU.
wp.getPage	Retrieves a page given the page id.
wp.getPages	Retrieves all pages that the user can manage.
wp.newPage	Creates a new page
wp.deletePage	Deletes a page with a given page id.
wp.editPage	Modifies a page with a given page id.
wp.getPageList	Retrieves all pages for a given blog.
wp.getAuthors	Retrieves a listing of all users assigned to a blog.
wp.getCategories	Retrieves a list of all available categories.
wp.getTags	Retrieves a list of all available tags.
wp.newCategory	Creates a new post category.
wp.deleteCategory	Deletes a designated category.
wp.suggestCategories	Retrieves a list of category based on fuzzy search.
wp.uploadFile	Uses WordPress' uploader to send files to the file system.
wp.getCommentCount	Retrieves an integer representing the number of comments on a post.
wp.getPostStatusList	Retrieves a list of post statuses. The list will include default statuses plus any additional statuses provided by a plugin.
wp.getPageStatusList	Retrieves a list of page statuses. The list will include default statuses plus any additional statuses provided by a plugin.
wp.getPageTemplates	Retrieves a listing of page templates available to individual pages.
wp.getOptions	Retrieves a listing of all configuration options for WordPress. These options are storied in the wp_options table.
wp.getComment	Retrieves a comment given a specified comment id.
wp.getComments	Retrieves a listing of comments.
wp.deleteComment	Deletes a comment from the WordPress comment queue.
wp.editComment	Modifies a comment given a specific comment id.
wp.newComment	Creates a new comment.
wp.getCommentStatusList	Retrieves a list of comment statuses. The list will include default statuses plus any additional statuses provided via plugin.

The bundled XML-RPC library

WordPress includes a PHP 4–compatible XML-RPC library that plugin developers can use if they need to provide XML-RPC services (client or server). The library is a solid XML-RPC known as the *Incutio* library and is included in the `wp-includes/class-IXR.php` file.

WordPress itself is an XML-RPC server and it is through the Incutio library that it is able to provide the XML-RPC interface. You can review how this is done by examining the `xmlrpc.php` file that is included in the WordPress core. This is also the endpoint for any WordPress blog when setting up your offline editor. You do not have to include the URL to the XML-RPC file as it will be automatically discovered in most cases. You can simply use the URL to WordPress.

For plugin developers looking to add to or modify the provided methods, you can use the xmlrpc_ methods filter to modify the array of methods available.

Web Resource
For more information on the Incutio library and using it differently than how it can be used to extend WordPress core usage, visit `http://scripts.incutio.com/xmlrpc/.` ∎

AtomPub and the upcoming standard of remote management

AtomPub, formerly known as the Atom Publishing Protocol (APP), is a relatively recent protocol that was created to standardize XML-RPC via a third-party oversight board. As a result, it received the blessing of the Internet Engineering Task Force (IETF) in 2007 and has operated as a working group under their umbrella.

The AtomPub protocol exists because all the major content management systems and blog platforms were creating their own competing protocols. By bringing a single standard under the watchful eye of a third party, remote publishing could proceed in a uniform way.

WordPress began supporting AtomPub is WordPress 2.3, though few offline clients actually support it, mainly because the final spec for AtomPub has not been ratified and is still considered a moving target.

Understanding XML-RPC Security Risks

XML-RPC has always been vulnerable to attack by software. If a malicious attacker can convince an application or user to perform some action from outside the walls of a firewall, then theoretically he could take full control.

As of WordPress 2.6, both AtomPub and XML-RPC APIs are disabled for security reasons. (Existing blogs were grandfathered in during the upgrade and the APIs were not disabled.) However, in all new installs of WordPress, one or both of the APIs must be manually enabled in order to be used. You can do this by choosing Settings ➪ Writing menu in the WordPress Admin, as shown in Figure 14.1.

WordPress, while historically very secure, has suffered from security setbacks over the past few years. Several of these flaws were a result of XML-RPC and it is considered a good move that the AtomPub and XML-RPC interfaces have been disabled by default. Most users will choose to use the WordPress administrative interface for writing new posts or publishing. The small subset of power users who make it their job to write on blogs a lot tend to be the users who are more likely to use offline editors. Because of this disparity, it is a better idea to turn XML-RPC off and let users turn them on when needed.

FIGURE 14.1

You can manually enable AtomPub and XML-RPC in the Settings ➪ Writing window of the WordPress Admin.

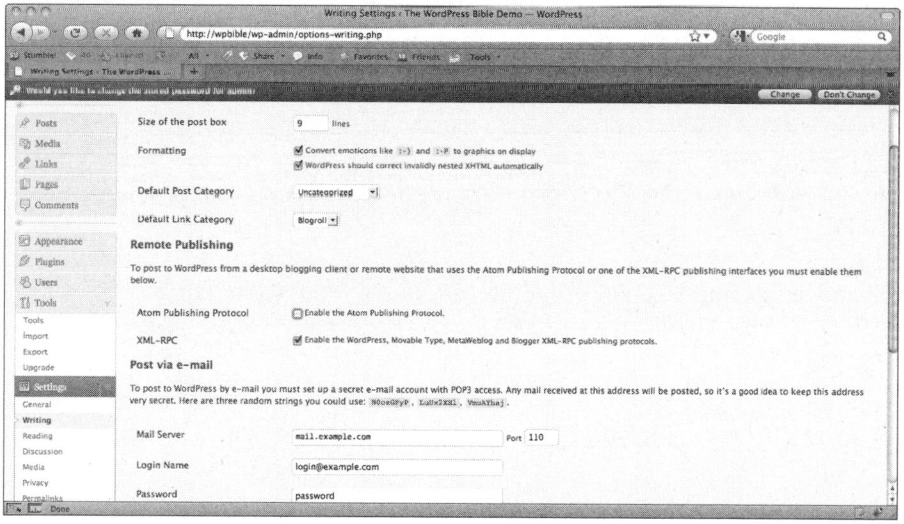

You can do a number of things to secure your XML-RPC interface if you don't plan to use it. Because many malicious users and automated scripts like to scan WordPress installations for open XML-RPC interfaces, the easiest way to "blind" them to your interface is to remove the links that are included in the head of your source code. If you look at the source code, you will likely see a couple of lines of code that look like the code shown in Listing 14.1.

Note

You may be curious about the `wlwmanifest.xml` file. This file exists as a requisite for using Windows Live Writer, Microsoft's desktop blog editor that is discussed later in this chapter. ∎

LISTING 14.1

Default code included to help XML-RPC clients auto-discover remote interfaces

```
<link rel="EditURI" type="application/rsd+xml" title="RSD" href="http://
    example.com/xmlrpc.php?rsd" />
<link rel="wlwmanifest" type="application/wlwmanifest+xml" href="http://
    example.com/wp-includes/wlwmanifest.xml" />
```

If you have no intention of using the remote interfaces, consider removing them altogether. The two lines of default code are not added by hardcoding the lines into theme templates, so it's not quite as simple as just deleting them. Instead, they are provided by two functions — `rsd_link()` and `wlwmanifest_link()` — that are hooked into WordPress in the `wp-includes/default-filter.php` file.

To remove these two functions, create a new function in your theme `functions.php` or as a standalone plugin (make sure it's active) and hook it into the `init` hook, which is fired after the initial hooking takes place (see Listing 14.2).

LISTING 14.2

Unhook rsd_link() and wlwmanifest_link() functions to remove them from a theme

```
function protect_xmlrpc()
{
    remove_action('wp_head','rsd_link');
    remove_action('wp_head','wlwmanifest_link');
}
add_action('init','protect_xmlrpc');
```

On the Web

The code in Listing 14.2 is available for download at `www.wiley.com/go/wordpressbible`. ∎

Web Resource

For great information on XML-RPC security and other XML-RPC suggestions, read WordPress developer Jeff Starr's write up at `http://digwp.com/2009/06/xmlrpc-php-security/`. ∎

Looking at Offline Blog Editors

Offline editors are the most common XML-RPC clients. Developers can certainly get creative with other application of XML-RPC; however, the most common use is via offline desktop editors that exist on all the major operating systems.

Windows Live Writer (Windows)

Windows Live Writer is possibly the most popular desktop client in existence. With Windows Live Writer, Microsoft has made it extremely easy to manage multiple blogs on multiple platforms and produce great, clean code in a WYSIWYG (what you see is what you get) format.

Web Resource

Windows Live Writer is available at `http://download.live.com/writer.` ∎

In order to get started with Microsoft's Windows Live Writer, fire up the application. If it is your first time setting up a blog in Windows Live Writer, follow these steps to get up and running:

1. **On the Configure Live Writer screen, click the Next button to begin the configuration process.**

2. **On the What blog service do you use screen, select Other blog service and click Next, as shown in Figure 14.2.**

FIGURE 14.2

Select Other blog service when prompted for the type of blog.

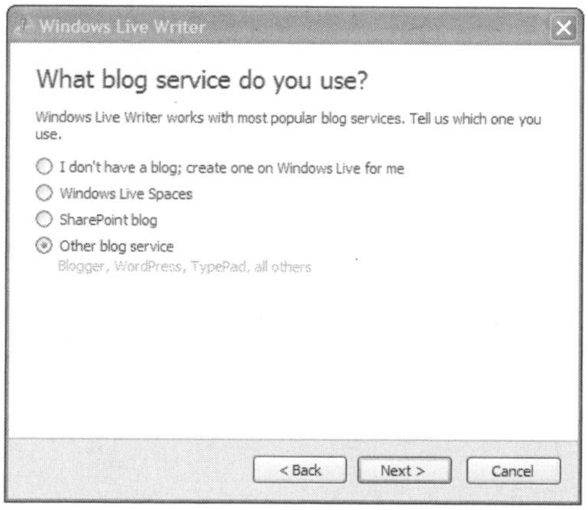

3. **Enter your WordPress URL in the Web Address of your blog field.**

4. **Enter your WordPress username and password and then click Next, as shown in Figure 14.3.** Windows Live Writer will configure itself and may take a minute the first time.

FIGURE 14.3

Enter your WordPress URL, username, and password when configuring your blog. If Windows Live Writer can't find your XML-RPC endpoint, add `/xmlrpc.php` on the end of the WordPress URL.

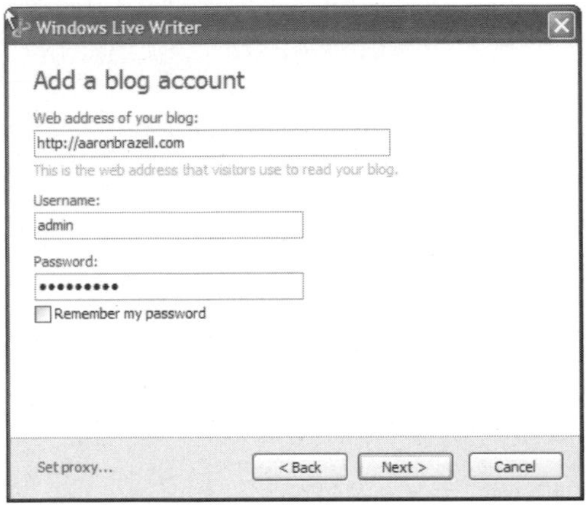

5. **Enter a nickname for your blog (call it anything) on the final screen.**
6. **Click Finish.**

During initial configuration, Windows Live Writer downloads your theme stylesheet so it can apply styling to your writing. It will never be an exact replica of how it will look on your site, but it will at least give you a sense of the formatting.

When the initial configuration is complete, an initial post screen appears, and you can use it to begin writing, as shown in Figure 14.4.

To edit your settings or add a new blog, select Accounts from the Tools menu.

In addition to a smart working interface, Windows Live Writer provides a basic photo editing and layout interface, YouTube integration, and many more features that provide much more flexibility when dealing with rich media than the standard WordPress interface.

If you plan to write your content offline and you're using Windows XP or Vista, Windows Live Writer is the best client to use.

The new post screen is a smartly laid out interface that uses your blog's existing stylesheet to apply formatting to your posts.

BlogDesk (Windows)

BlogDesk is a small piece of freeware you can download from `www.blogdesk.org/en/download.htm`. It comes from a developer in Germany who has taken a relatively simple approach to designing an offline editor.

Getting started with BlogDesk isn't quite as intuitive as Windows Live Writer. When you launch the application for the first time, it immediately takes you to the new post window. While that may be generally acceptable and optimal, a blogger cannot publish a new post without setting up BlogDesk to connect to a WordPress account.

To configure BlogDesk for the first time, follow these steps:

1. **Select Manage Blogs from the File menu, as shown in Figure 14.5.**

2. **Click New in the Manage Blogs dialog box.**

3. **Select a name for your blog and then click Next.** The name can be anything and is only needed for you to identify it.

4. **Enter your WordPress blog address, as shown in Figure 14.6.**

FIGURE 14.5

To add a new blog in BlogDesk, select Manage Blogs from the File menu.

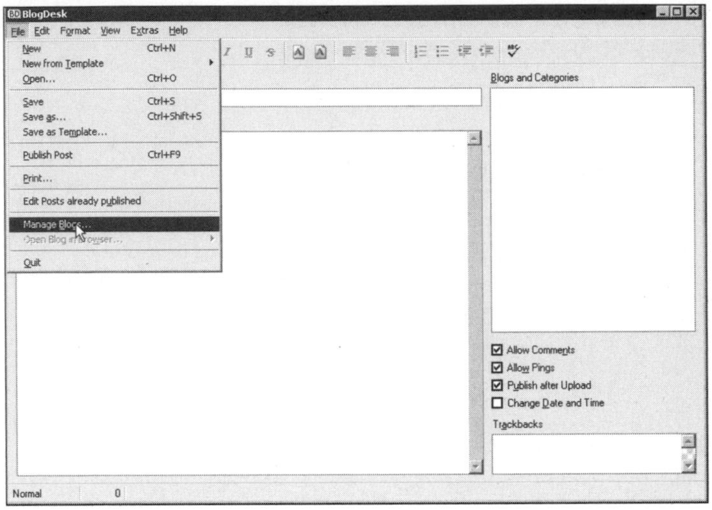

FIGURE 14.6

Enter your WordPress URL when prompted.

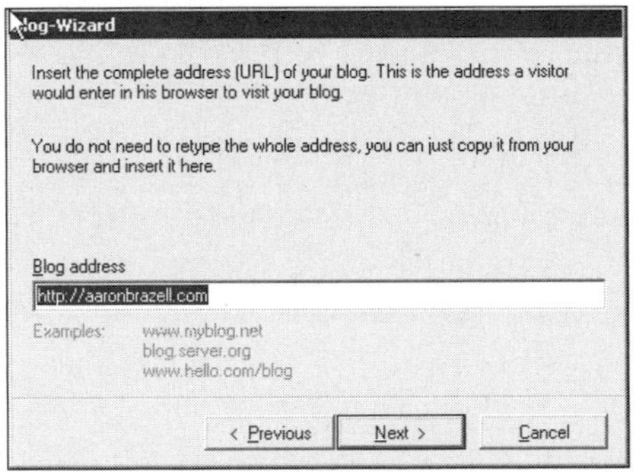

5. **Select WordPress from the Blog-Wizard dialog box and then click Next.** (Do not choose WordPress < 2.2.) BlogDesk will deduce what your XML-RPC endpoint is. If in doubt, this endpoint is your WordPress URL with `/xmlrpc.php` on the end.

6. **Enter your endpoint URL and click Next, as shown in Figure 14.7.**

7. **Enter your WordPress username and password when prompted and click Next.**

8. **Enter your Blog ID.** In a typical WordPress install, your Blog ID is 1. You can click the Get Blog ID button to have this automatically inserted. For WordPress MU, enter your Blog ID manually.

FIGURE 14.7

Enter your XML-RPC endpoint (also called the Entry Point) when prompted.

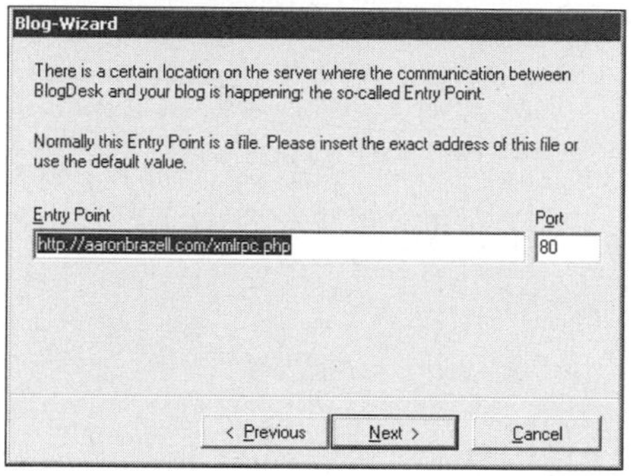

9. In the next dialog box, click the Get Categories button to download the categories from the blog and then click Next.

10. To ensure that images can be uploaded safely and no permission issues exist on the server, click the Test Upload button in the next dialog box.

11. When the test passes, click Next.

When all is said and done, you should see a new post interface that looks something like Figure 14.8. One of the key benefits BlogDesk users like is the image management tools. For bloggers using a lot of images, BlogDesk has a few nifty effects to make a blog look even more attractive.

FIGURE 14.8

The BlogDesk post writing interface is intuitively laid out.

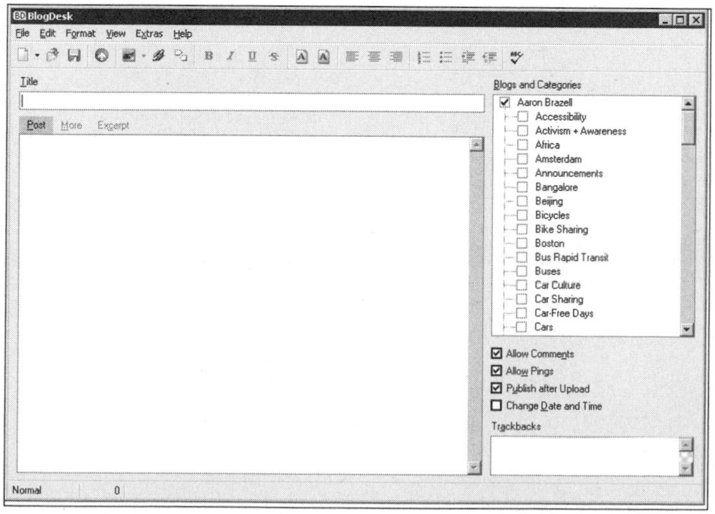

MarsEdit (Mac)

MarsEdit is a Mac XML-RPC application from Red Sweater Software. It has all the ease of use that is inherent in Mac-native applications, but offers no WYSIWYG interface. MarsEdit users only have HTML mode, which is fine if you're a power user.

Other handy features of MarsEdit include a media library, Flickr integration, and macro support so you don't have to write the same thing over and over again. Unlike the Windows applications, MarsEdit is not free. It costs $29.95 at the time of this writing and is compatible with OS 10.4–10.6.

Web Resource

You can download MarsEdit at www.red-sweater.com/marsedit/. ∎

If you have not set up a blog in MarsEdit before, follow these steps to install MarsEdit:

1. In theMarsEdit Quick Start dialog box that pops up if no blogs exist in the system, select I already have a weblog and click Continue.

2. Enter a name for your blog and your WordPress URL, as shown in Figure 14.9.

FIGURE 14.9

Enter the name of your blog and the WordPress URL when prompted.

3. Enter your WordPress username and password after MarsEdit completes communication with your blog.

Setting up MarsEdit is much more streamlined than the offline editors discussed previously and, unlike other pieces of software, the default screen makes a bit more sense to workflow: the opening page is a listing of posts for the blog (see Figure 14.10).

To select posts from the list to edit, double-click them or click the Edit Post button in the toolbar. Additionally, MarsEdit is loaded with shortcut keys such as ⌘+O for editing posts or ⌘+N to create a new post.

FIGURE 14.10

MarsEdit defaults to a listing of all recent posts.

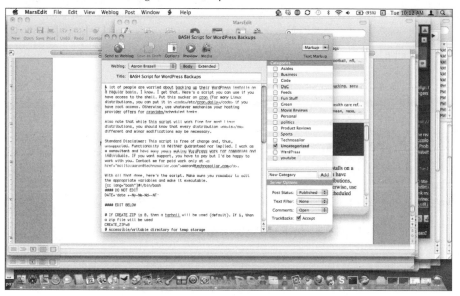

In the simple post-edit interface, MarsEdit hides some key functionality, such as tags or excerpts, by default. In order to modify the interface to add slug editing, excerpts, or tags, simply select what you want displayed in the View menu, as shown in Figure 14.11.

FIGURE 14.11

The MarsEdit screen hides some frequently used features, but you can enable them from the View menu.

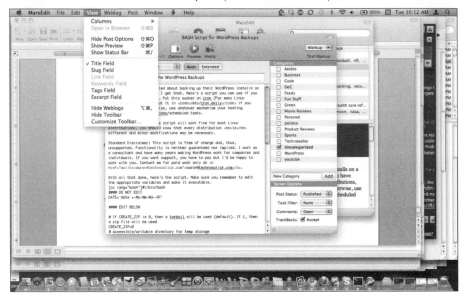

Ecto (Mac)

One of the longest standing offline editors in the history of blogging editors is Ecto. Ecto is available for Mac (it used to be Mac and Windows but no longer) for $19.95 (at the time of this writing) from `http://illuminex.com/ecto/`.

When you first load Ecto, it asks what blogging platform you're using and then takes you through the following configuration process:

1. **Select WordPress from the drop-down menu.**

2. **Enter the Blog URL in the Enter the address of your blog field, as shown in Figure 14.12.** Notice that it appears after you select WordPress from the drop-down menu.

3. **Enter your WordPress username and password when prompted.**

FIGURE 14.12

Select WordPress as your blogging platform and enter your WordPress URL when prompted.

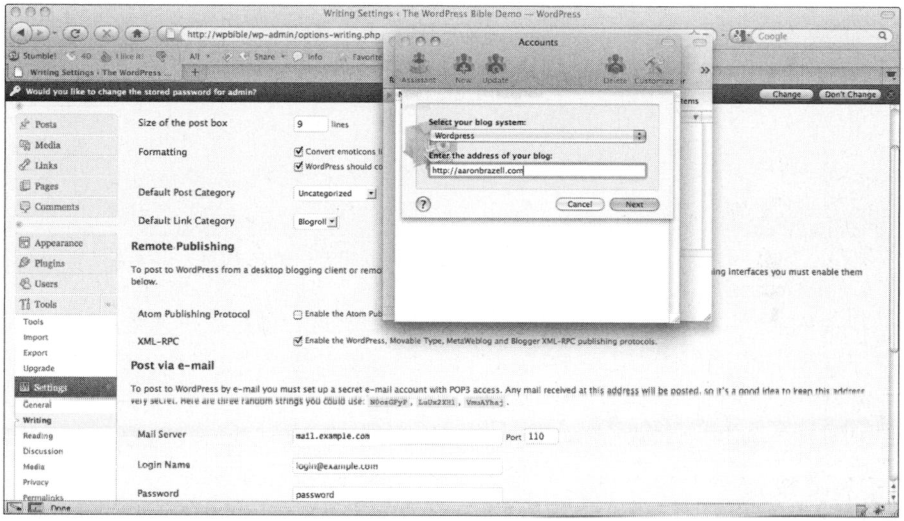

Drivel (Linux)

Drivel is an okay Linux blog editor. It is far from the best, but you'll often get half-baked software that is usable in this environment. It is only compatible with the GNOME windowing system so if you're a Linux user using KDE or another windowing system, you won't be able to use Drivel.

As with any Linux package, it is best to install using the distributions package manager because this solves any dependencies that occur. Alternatively, you can download the source (or an RPM) at http://dropline.net/past-projects/drivel-blog-editor/.

That said, Ubuntu is my Linux distribution of choice. The Ubuntu (and also Debian) package management system uses the apt-get function:

```
aaron@ubuntu:~$ sudo apt-get install drivel
```

The same kind of installation can be performed with the yum packaging system on most Red Hat Enterprise Linux flavors.

When you first load Drivel, you are greeted with a dialog box to create a new account, as shown in Figure 14.13. To continue the setup process, follow these steps:

1. **Enter your WordPress username and password.**

2. **Select Movable Type from the drop-down blog platform list.** Drivel does not support the WordPress XML-RPC API.

3. **Enter the URL for your xmlrpc.php file.** This is going to be your WordPress installation URL with a trailing /xmlrpc.php.

FIGURE 14.13

The Drivel blog client does not offer a lot of functionality, but it is useful for quick and dirty blogging from a Linux environment.

ScribeFire (All)

ScribeFire is cross-platform because it is a Firefox extension. If you can install Firefox (you can on all the major operating systems), then you can use ScribeFire. You can download the extension and install it at http://scribefire.com.

Once Firefox reboots after installation, you'll notice a small yellow icon in the lower right-hand side of your browser status bar. Clicking it opens up a pane in the lower portion of your browser window. This is ScribeFire. When you first open the pane, you are prompted to configure it for the first time. If you do not receive this notice, click the Blogs tab on the right side of the pane and click the Launch Account Wizard button, as shown in Figure 14.14.

ScribeFire is a Firefox extension for blogging. To activate it, click the yellow icon in the status bar and use the Blogs tab on the right side of the pane to configure blogs.

Click to launch ScribeFire

To configure ScribeFire, follow these steps:

1. **Enter your WordPress URL when prompted and then click Continue.**

2. **In the next dialog box, select WordPress from the drop-down menu that asks for your blogging software.** This may be auto-detected.

3. **For the API URL, enter the URL to your XML-RPC endpoint, as shown in Figure 14.15, and then click Continue.** This is your blog URL with a trailing /xmlrpc.php on the end.

FIGURE 14.15

Choose WordPress as your blogging platform and your XML-RPC URL for your API endpoint.

4. Enter your WordPress username and password when prompted and then click Continue.

5. After ScribeFire downloads account settings from your blog, click Continue to confirm that the connection was successfully made and then click Done.

Note

ScribeFire is a blog editor built by "make money online" bloggers for "make money online" bloggers. Therefore, it is bundled with tools to help this type of blogger make more money. The world has many types of bloggers and some do not wish to use their blogs for monetary gain. If you are a blogger who does, the extra tools built into ScribeFire will assist you. And if you don't wish to monetize, the blog editing tool is perfectly usable and functional. How you use ScribeFire is your decision. ■

Summary

- XML-RPC is a remote protocol for managing a software application.
- WordPress supports remote editing and administration by exposing the Blogger, MetaWeblog, Movable Type, and WordPress XML-RPC APIs.
- WordPress also provides the AtomPub interface, though it is not widely supported by clients.
- In order to use XML-RPC or AtomPub, they must be enabled from within WordPress Admin. This is a security precaution.
- All offline blog editors function in a similar manner. Windows Live Writer is the best editor available for Windows. MarsEdit is the best available for Mac OS X.
- ScribeFire is a Firefox extension that lets you blog anywhere that Firefox is installed.

Part V

Keeping Up with the Joneses: Maintenance and Upgrades

Performing Automatic Upgrades

As easy as WordPress installation has always been, upgrades have tended to create issues for some users. When upgrade time would come around, bloggers would bite their tongues and grit their teeth as they uploaded a new version of WordPress via a file transfer protocol (FTP) client. Less technical users sometimes found FTP a scary thing and did not understand how to connect to the server and perform the upgrade.

Likewise, whenever a theme or plugin needed to be installed or upgraded, bloggers had to rely on FTP to perform the installations or upgrades themselves. It was easy to recognize a solution, but took many cycles of upgrades before Automatic Upgrade was added to the WordPress core.

With Automatic Upgrade, bloggers can provide their server FTP login credentials and WordPress does the rest, downloading files transparently in the background, unpacking the files, and distributing them into place.

Note

Automatic upgrade is somewhat of a misnomer. It is often called *one-click* upgrading (which is also technically a misnomer, but much more accurate). There is actually nothing automatic about the upgrades. When a new version of WordPress or a plugin becomes available, the blogger has to manually provide credentials to WordPress that enables the process to happen.

For a truly automatic upgrade process to happen, you have to be willing to incur some risk of failure at the worst possible time or the introduction of a new security hole. The final decision on introducing new code into a production system should lie with the blogger. ∎

Meeting the Minimum Automatic Upgrade Requirements

WordPress uses one of three methods to perform an automatic upgrade — FTP; FTP over Secure Sockets Layer, or SSL (FTPS); or Secure Shell (SSH). The most commonly used method is FTP because it tends to meet the system requirements of most hosting providers. In many cases, hosting providers have the `safe_mode` option selected in their PHP build for security reasons. Because it is impossible to use more traditional means of writing files to a system with PHP, WordPress has to perform writes with the system user account to ensure ownership of files is set properly.

In order to use FTP, your PHP build must include the FTP module. Most hosting providers include this module by default, but if you are compiling PHP directly, ensure that `--enable-ftp` is included in your configuration.

The second method, FTPS, requires the OpenSSL module for PHP. This method enables WordPress to connect to the server over a secured connection. If you're compiling your own PHP, ensure that `--with-openssl` is included in the configuration.

The third method is the most secure, and also the least supported. WordPress can use an SSH (or Secure FTP) connection to perform writes in the upgrade process. The PHP library must include the ssh2 PECL (PHP Extension Community Library) module, which is available at `http://pecl.php.net/package/ssh2`. The ssh2 library is included, by default, with PHP 5.2+ but it can be loaded for earlier versions if you have root access to your server.

Cross-Reference
How to configure your server for WordPress is described in Chapter 2. ∎

Tip
If you're on a Windows server, you are most likely only able to use FTP and FTPS for connections. ssh2 is not a protocol that is used by Windows; therefore, even if PHP had ssh2 support, it would not work. ∎

If you don't have access to any of these protocols, you will have to use the traditional method of manual upgrades.

Disabling the "Upgrade Nag"

WordPress provides a system for notifying the blogger of available upgrades (see Figure 15.1). This "nag," in the form of a notification banner in WordPress Admin, is useful if you don't stay up to date with the latest WordPress release. However, there are many situations where the nag is unhelpful, unnecessary, or could just plain cause problems. For example:

- You run a network of blogs and take care of the technology. The writers don't need to see the nag and it turns into a distraction.

- You are the corporate IT administrator for your company and are responsible for the maintenance of the company blog. Disabling the nag helps streamline software maintenance policy.

- The new version has caused problems for other users and you want to upgrade on your own terms, instead of being reminded all the time.

FIGURE 15.1

When there are new upgrades available to the core, a "nag" message appears at the top of the WordPress Admin.

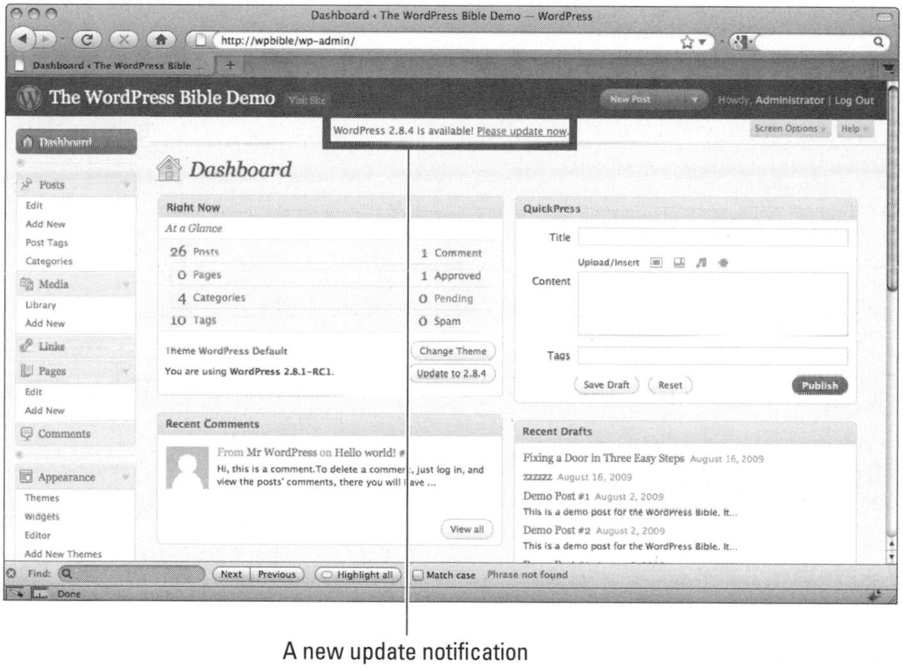

A new update notification

Technically, WordPress determines if there is an upgrade by comparing the available version at WordPress.org to the version installed. This is done through a request (hypertext transfer protocol, or HTTP) to WordPress.org and comparing version information in the database.

Similarly, plugins have a nag that comes in the form of a small red bubble that is superimposed on the Plugins navigation item (see Figure 15.2). The number in this bubble represents the number of plugins that are installed (active and inactive) that have upgrades available. This is based on information from the WordPress plugin repository, another valuable reason to include General Public

License (GPL)–compatible plugins in the repository. If the plugin is listed in a different repository or self hosted (via a blog, wiki, or other Web site), bloggers will not have the benefit of upgrade notifications.

The plugin upgrade notifier takes the form of a small red bubble superimposed on the Plugins navigation item in WordPress Admin. The number represents the number of upgrades that are available.

You can create a plugin that disables these messages. By looking into the core code, you will find that two functions handle upgrade notifications for the core. The first, `update_nag()`, notifies the blogger that there is an upgrade available. If the user (generally the admin) has the `manage_options` capability, it also provides a link to the upgrade page. The second function, `maintenance_nag()`, behaves essentially the same way except it alerts the blogger that an automatic upgrade has failed. Both of these functions are in `wp-includes/includes/update.php`.

As you explore these two functions, you'll notice that they are hooked into the `admin_notices` hook. When you search the rest of WordPress, you will see that other pieces throughout WordPress also use this hook for messaging and plugins can also use it. It doesn't make sense to disable those messages and, in fact, the hook is important in a multi-user environment where an admin might want to disseminate important information to the rest of the users.

The two functions are hooked into WordPress (again, in `wp-includes/includes/update.php`) with `add_action()`, as shown in Listing 15.1.

LISTING 15.1

WordPress hooks update_nag() and maintenance_nag() into admin_notices

```
add_action( 'admin_notices', 'update_nag', 3 );
add_action( 'admin_notices', 'maintenance_nag' );
```

Notably, the `update_nag()` function has been hooked in with a priority 3. In order to remove a hooked function, it must be removed with the same priority that it was added, as shown in Listing 15.2.

LISTING 15.2

Disabling the update_nag() and maintenance_nag() functions

```
remove_action('admin_notices','update_nag', 3);
remove_action('admin_notices', 'maintenance_nag';
```

If you add this code to a plugin, though, it fails to disable the nag. This is because plugins are loaded before this overhead code is loaded. Instead, you can hook on one of the last hooks fired before HTML is sent to the browser for the WordPress Admin, admin_head. Often times, this hook is used to add JavaScript or Cascading Style Sheets (CSS) needed in WordPress Admin, but in this case, it can also be used to remove the nag. To do so, wrap the remove_action() functions in a separate function and hook the separate function to admin_notices, as shown in Listing 15.3.

LISTING 15.3

Wrap all remove_action() calls in a single function and hook it into admin_head

```
function nag_removals()
{
    remove_action( 'admin_notices', 'update_nag', 3 );
    remove_action( 'admin_notices', 'maintenance_nag');
}
add_action('admin_head','nag_removals');
```

On the Web

The code in Listing 15.3 is available for download at www.wiley.com/go/wordpressbible. ■

Unfortunately, there is no hook to modify plugin upgrade notifications, but then only a single task is being performed and no hook is necessary. (There are many reasons to use the admin_notices hook, but there is no real use case for using the space in the navigation menu for Plugins for anything else.)

Because of this, disabling the bubble is as simple as using the CSS display property to hide it. As with the nag_removals() function, you can create a function to provide CSS hooked on admin_head , as shown in Listing 15.4.

LISTING 15.4

Using the admin_head hook, a plugin can provide CSS to hide the Plugin update nag

```
function remove_plugin_nag()
{
    ?>
    <style type="text/css">
    .update-plugins { display:none; }
    </style>
    <?php
}
add_action('admin_head','remove_plugin_nag');
```

Tip

In reality, you could combine the code shown in Listings 15.3 and 15.4 by adding the style declaration in Listing 15.4 with the `remove_nags()` function in Listing 15.3. ∎

Providing straight CSS is the simplest route in this case, but jQuery can also do the job if you're so inclined (see Listing 15.5). jQuery is automatically loaded in the WordPress Admin so there is no need to enqueue the script.

LISTING 15.5

The plugin update nag bubble can be hidden with jQuery

```
function remove_plugin_nag()
{
    ?>
    <script type="text/javascript">
        jQuery(document).ready( function(){
            jQuery('.update-plugins').css('display','none');
    });
    </script>
    <?php
}
add_action('admin_head','remove_plugin_nag');
```

On the Web

The code in Listing 15.5 is available for download at www.wiley.com/go/wordpressbible. ∎

Cross-Reference

The use of jQuery in WordPress is covered in Chapter 11. ∎

Performing Automatic Upgrades

The process of performing upgrades is straightforward. You can access the core upgrade page, shown in Figure 15.3, by choosing Tools ➪ Upgrade WordPress Admin. The core upgrade page is also the page that is linked to when an upgrade nag is provided. Similarly, upgrade nags for plugins lead to a similar page that installs or upgrades plugins. This screen also enables you to select the method of upgrade needed (FTP, FTPS, or SSH). When the ssh2 PHP library is not available, it is not listed as an option.

FIGURE 15.3

The WordPress Admin upgrade screen contains all the connection information necessary to perform upgrades.

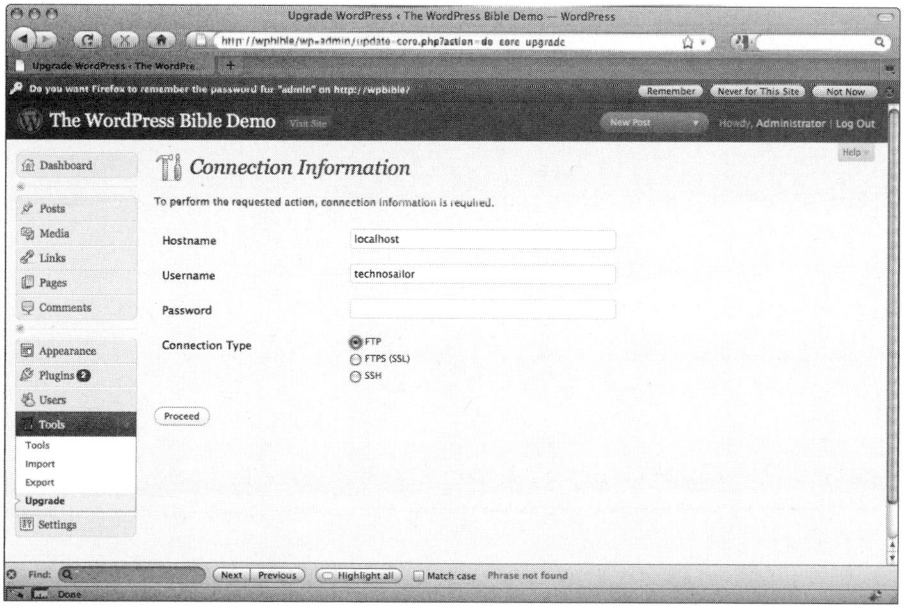

Tip

It's good practice to do backups of your data before an upgrade, though that takes a bit of the "automatic" out of automatic upgrades. It is encouraged that you take advantage of backup utilities provided by your host when possible, or develop your own backup routines. ∎

For both FTP and FTPS-style upgrades, you will need to provide WordPress with standard FTP connection information: host, username, and password. This information is not sent anywhere and only the hostname and the username are stored locally in the database. The password is never stored even though the presumption is that you control your own database and no one else will see that information.

Generally, unless you have a scale blog that has been *sharded*, or split up across multiple servers or a server cluster, the hostname will be localhost. If this doesn't work, you can use the IP address of the fully qualified domain name (FQDN) of the server. The username and password are the FTP connection username and password, not your WordPress username and password.

Tip

FTP has a significant security vulnerability recommend using it in general. That is, it is not an encrypted protocol so when you type in a username and password to access FTP resources, that data is sent in plaintext and could potentially be intercepted by anyone sniffing the data. I recommend FTPS, at minimum, or SSH, if possible, as an alternative.

That said, WordPress is conducting FTP operations on the server itself and, unless you're specifying a different server than the blog is stored on (fringe possibility), the username and password is never transmitted off the server and is unlikely to be intercepted. ∎

Using SSH for Automatic Upgrades

The most secure method of upgrading WordPress automatically is SSH. Despite the fact that sensitive data is not actually leaving the server, it's good practice and prevents malicious behavior that might come from a hacked server.

In addition to the standard hostname, username, and password needed to connect to the server over SSH, you can provide a private key as shown in Figure 15.4.

FIGURE 15.4

An added option for the Automatic Upgrades feature is that when you choose SSH as the protocol for upgrade, you can specify a public key and a private key.

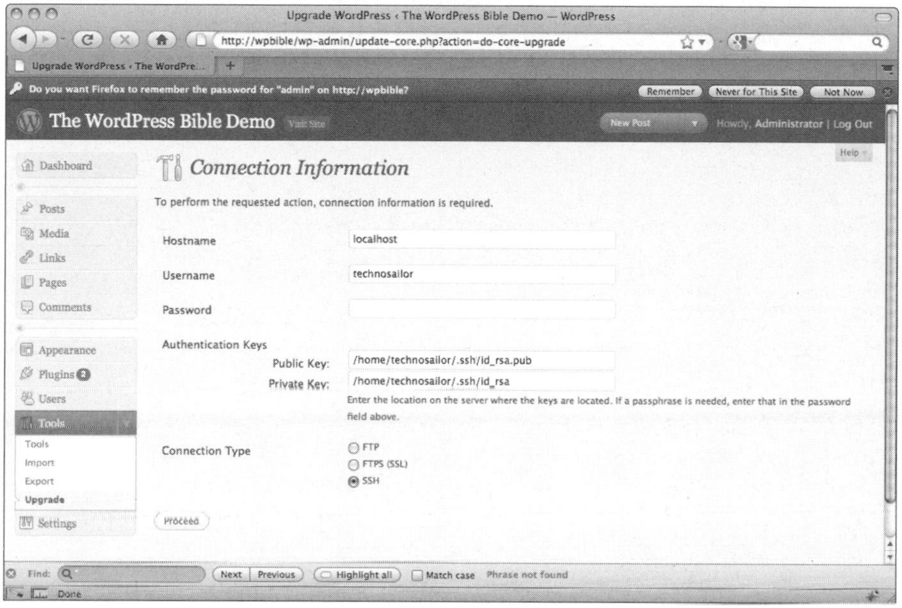

Using SSH with keys

In order to specify a public key and a private key, both need to be in a location on the server that is not in the document root. Generally, when using key entry to a server, there is a private key housed on a local machine (usually in `.ssh/id_dsa`) and a public key that can be shared by placing it on another server (generally the public key, usually found at `.ssh/id_dsa.pub`, is placed on the server in `.ssh/authorized_keys`). In the case of a local connection to a server, both the public and private keys should be in the same place. These keys will be listed with their full paths as shown in Figure 15.5.

Note

Password-less SSH is often used by systems administrators to ensure they can get into a server. It's easy to regulate who has access when using password-less entry because locking a rogue account is as simple as deleting the accounts public key from the `authorized_keys` **file. For more information on key generation and use, refer to any number of how-tos found online (search for ssh keygen). One such example can be found at** `www.puddingonline.com/~dave/publications/SSH-with-Keys-HOWTO/document/html/SSH-with-Keys-HOWTO-4.html.` ■

FIGURE 15.5

Enter the full path to the public and private keys if you wish to use password-less entry.

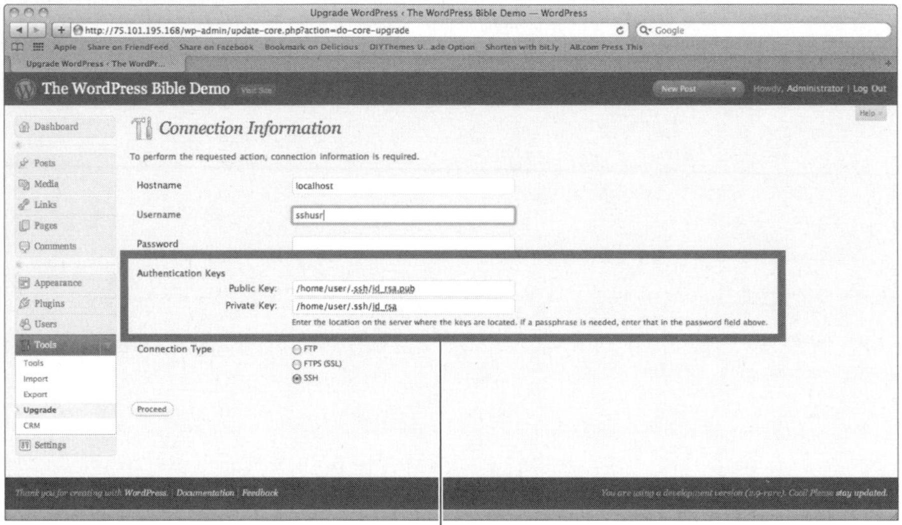

The public and private keys

Using constants to bypass credentials

When you have a large number of sites to maintain, or you just don't want to have to re-enter information every time you want to install a plugin or upgrade the core, WordPress enables you to hardcode this information as constants in wp-config.php and never have to enter it again. Table 15.1 lists the available constants you can set.

TABLE 15.1

Available Constants You Can Set in wp-config.php

Constant	Description
FTP_HOST	The hostname, IP or, likely, just 'localhost'.
FTP_USER	The FTP or SSH username.
FTP_PASS	The FTP or SSH Password. Leave this blank if using SSH key entry.
FTP_PUBKEY	Necessary only for SSH upgrades. Designates the absolute path to the public key file. (For example, /home/user/.ssh/id_dsa.pub)
FTP_PRIKEY	Necessary only for SSH upgrades. Designates the absolute path to the private keyfile. (For example, /home/user/.ssh/id_da)

To define these constants, use the code shown in Listing 15.6 in your configuration file (wp-config.php).

LISTING 15.6

Define these constants to skip the connection credentials dialog box

```
define('FTP_HOST','localhost');
define('FTP_USER','yourusername');
define('FTP_PASS','');
define('FTP_PUBKEY','/home/yourusername/.ssh/id_rsa.pub');
define('FTP_PRIKEY','/home/yourusername/.ssh/id_rsa');
```

Summary

- To use the WordPress Automatic Upgrade feature, you must have PHP installed with the FTP module at a minimum. FTPS, or FTP over SSL, requires the OpenSSL library while SSH requires the ssh2 PECL library.

- For a variety of business or personal reasons, you might choose to "hide" update nag messages alerting you, and all users with access to your blog (even subscribers who have an account), of available updates to the core.

- A WordPress administrator can use the Automatic Upgrades feature by simply providing their usernames, passwords, and hostnames. There is no need for intimidating interfaces for non-technical bloggers.

- Usernames and passwords can be defined as constants in the wp-config.php file. By doing this, you bypass any requests for connection credentials.

Moving to WordPress and Backing It Up

Because of the popularity of WordPress, many bloggers decide to move their blogs to WordPress. Depending on the blog publishing platform they are currently using, this can be a simple task or it can be extremely complex.

WordPress includes a number of bundled importers you can use to import a blog from a third-party blog host. Importers for all of the popular platforms are included, including importers for Blogger, Movable Type, and TypePad. The ideal off-the-shelf solution for importing a blog into WordPress, however, is to use the WordPress export file format (WXR), which is an extensible markup language (XML) file containing all of the data related to a WordPress blog.

In this chapter I discuss how to move a blog into WordPress from six blogging platforms: Blogger, Blogware, DotClear, LiveJournal, Moveable Type, and TypePad. I also discuss the importance of backing up your blog (and cannot stress enough the importance of this) and offer two reliable backup routines.

Moving a Blog to WordPress

For whatever reason, there may come a time when you want to move your non-WordPress blog to WordPress. All of the import processes for WordPress are in Tools ➪ Import menu, as shown in Figure 16.1.

On the WordPress Import screen, you will find several importers you can use to move your posts and comments from another platform into WordPress, including:

- Blogger
- Blogroll

- Blogware
- DotClear
- GreyMatter
- LiveJournal
- Moveable Type
- TypePad
- Textpattern

You use the WordPress Tools ⇨ Import menu for all imports.

Each of these importers is unique but the import process carries the same basic principle and workflow:

1. Connect to the originating blog.
2. Fetch all users.
3. Fetch all posts.
4. Fetch all comments and associate them with posts.
5. Fetch all categories and tags and associate them with posts.
6. Insert data into WordPress with the proper associations.

Each importer also carries the restrictions of the source platform. For example, to migrate from Blogger to WordPress, you will ultimately have to sacrifice retention of permalinks, which are very important for search engine optimization if you have not configured your Blogger blog to publish to a domain. In addition, Movable Type and TypePad URLs do not have a one-for-one equivalent on WordPress, so you need to use a plugin to alter WordPress permalinks to the appropriate Movable Type equivalent.

However, the most important aspect of a migration is the blog data itself, and you can migrate the data fairly reliably across all supported blogging platforms.

In the following sections, I discuss how to import data from six of the most popular blogging platforms into WordPress.

Tip

If you want to build an importer script for a platform that doesn't exist in the WordPress Core, you can build your importer and put it in the `wp-admin/import/` folder. The Textpattern importer is a good example of an importer to build off of. ■

Blogger

Blogger (`www.blogger.com`) is a free blogging platform from Google. The Blogger importer provides the most straightforward (and yet most likely to cause problems) import process. To use the Blogger importer, you must first set your Blogger blog to publish to a `*.blogspot.com` blog. You can publish your Blogger blog via file transfer protocol (FTP) or secure file transfer protocol (SFTP), but for the importer to work, your blog must be set to publish locally on Blogger. Ordinarily, this does not cause any real problems because switching from an FTP- or SFTP-published blog to a Blogger blog does not change or harm any content that has already been published to your own domain. You can make this change on a temporary basis and not publish new posts during the process.

Note

Be aware that Google makes no provision for disabling comments on a blog, so there is always a chance, especially on a busy blog, that you might lose comments in the process. It's always safe to redo the import afterwards if you are concerned about comment loss. ■

Once you have set the initial Blogger configuration to allow for importing, you can switch to the import screen in WordPress. In the Tools ➪ Import screen, select the Blogger importer. Once you have done this, you will need to click the Authorize button to get Google authentication, as shown in Figure 16.2. If you mess up and have to restart (or to do a re-import as mentioned earlier), click the Clear account information button to sever the connection between Blogger and WordPress. (You can do this as often as you need to without harming already imported content.)

Once you have authorized against your Google account, you will see the Blogger Blogs screen where all of the blogs associated with your account are listed (see Figure 16.3).

Note

You must be an admin on these Blogger accounts in order to have access to the posts to import them: otherwise, for example, any random blogger you give access to write a guest post could come in and take all of the content and republish it on his own. ■

FIGURE 16.2

Click the Authorize button on the Import Blogger screen to authorize against your Google account.

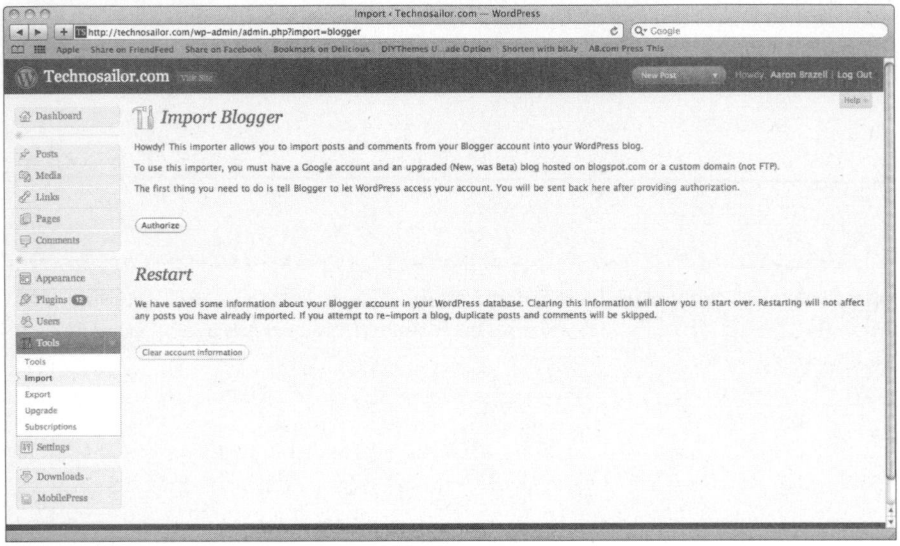

FIGURE 16.3

After authorizing against Google, you will be returned to a screen that displays all associated Blogger accounts.

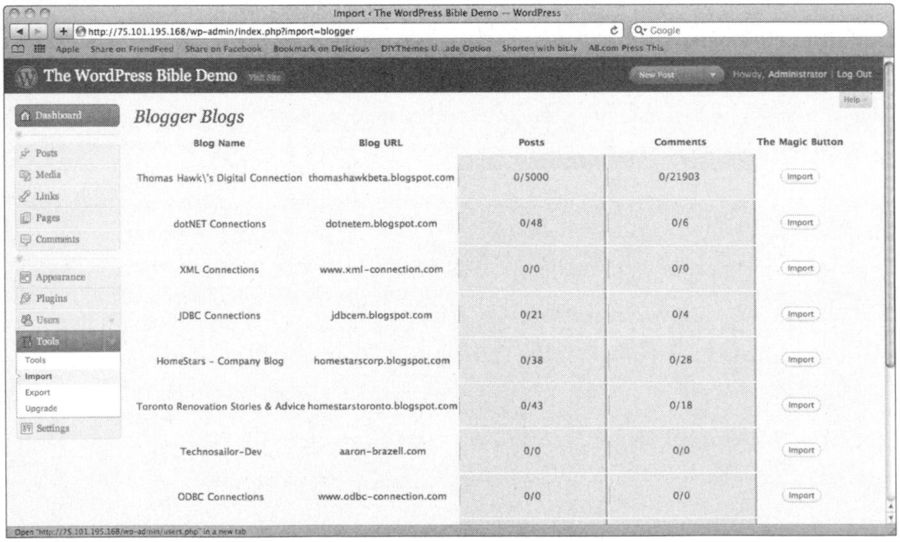

One thing you might notice on the Blogger Blogs screen is that blogs have Posts and Comments listed in the format *x/y*. This shows how many posts and comments WordPress has imported (x) and how many are available for import (y). If you have 0 posts listed for import, chances are Blogger is configured to post via FTP or SFTP, and not locally on Blogspot.

Note

Blogger has been largely "abandonware" from Google since it was purchased from Pyra Labs in 2003. Any major innovations have yet to occur. However, Google has focused on the service in recent months — for example, addressing the comment export limit — and I hope to be able to modify this note to include further improvements in future releases of this book.

Until recently, Blogger had a 5,000-comment export limit. WordPress' importer ties into Bloggers exporter so a Blogger blog with a large amount of comments (greater than 5,000) may still have some problems exporting all comments. If this is the case, contact the Blogger support team for assistance.

To Google's credit, they have been quite responsive to me when I have contacted them (on a case-by-case basis) to get this limitation corrected. This is due to their newfound adoption of data-portability and openness initiatives. ■

The final step of the import process is to click the Import button next to the blog you want to import, as shown in Figure 16.4. This initiates the import process automatically and displays a progress bar. The larger your Blogger blog, the longer it takes to perform an import.

FIGURE 16.4

Click the Import button next to the blogs you want to import to start the import process.

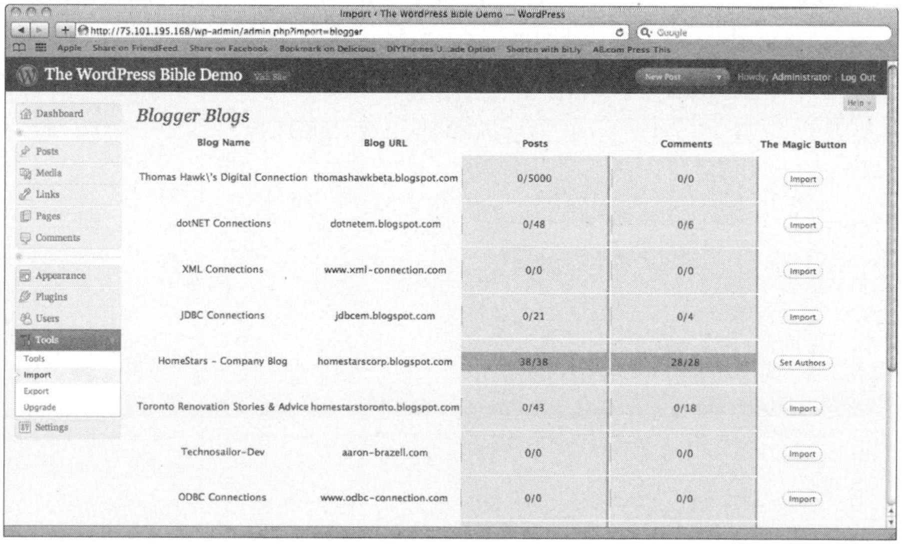

The process is fairly straightforward once you get into it. Blogger can experience moments of unavailability that might force you to begin the process all over again. You can do this without worrying about duplicating posts or comments.

Blogware

Blogware (http://blogware.com) is a little-used blogging platform that is fairly complex to use. It is only offered through retailers and some charge a fee for its use. To import posts from Blogware into WordPress, you have to export them in the XML export format shown in Listing 16.1. Because the Blogware XML format does not support the richness of post data that WordPress does, a lot of field matching occurs in the WordPress import. WordPress will also attempt to import any images and comments and associate them with the proper posts.

LISTING 16.1

The XML export format for Blogware

```
<?xml version="1.0" encoding="UTF-8"?>
<channel>
<blogTitle>wpbible</blogTitle>
<blogLink>http://wpbible.blogharbor.com/blog</blogLink>
<item type="article">
  <createDate>Tue, 29 Sep 2009 14:20:00 -0400</createDate>
  <pubDate>Tue, 29 Sep 2009 14:20:00 -0400</pubDate>
  <postStatus>publish</postStatus>
  <convertBreaks>0</convertBreaks>
  <formatType>html</formatType>
  <allowComments>1</allowComments>
  <allowTrackbacks>1</allowTrackbacks>
  <author>technosailor</author>
  <title>Test</title>
  <excerpt></excerpt>
  <body>Testing 123&lt;br&gt;</body>
<category>Main Page</category>
</item>
<item type="article">
  <createDate>Tue, 29 Sep 2009 14:20:00 -0400</createDate>
  <pubDate>Tue, 29 Sep 2009 14:20:00 -0400</pubDate>
  <postStatus>publish</postStatus>
  <convertBreaks>0</convertBreaks>
  <formatType>html</formatType>
  <allowComments>1</allowComments>
  <allowTrackbacks>1</allowTrackbacks>
  <author>technosailor</author>
  <title>Test 2</title>
  <excerpt></excerpt>
  <body>Lorem Ipsum&lt;br&gt;</body>
<category>Main Page</category>
</item>
</channel>
```

For developers who are interested in the nuts and bolts of this import, the field matching that occurs is listed in Table 16.1.

TABLE 16.1

Post Field Matches in a Blogware to WordPress Import

Blogware	WordPress
createDate	post_date
pubDate	post_modified
postStatus	post_status
allowComments	comment_status
allowTrackbacks	ping_status
Author	post_author
Title	post_title
Excerpt	post_excerpt
Body	post_content
Category	generates/associates categories

Tip

With the Blogware importer, and most importers that require uploading an export file to WordPress, you have to be cautious about file size. If an export file size exceeds the size allowed by PHP, you can change your PHP `upload_max_filesize` and `post_max_size` settings in `php.ini` to allow for larger file uploads. You cannot do this on shared hosts, though. In this case, break apart your file into smaller pieces. WordPress will not duplicate content. ■

DotClear

DotClear (`http://dotclear.org`) is a self-hosted blog platform that is popular in Europe. Unlike other previously mentioned platforms, the DotClear import process takes place by accessing a database.

When you click the DotClear importer from the WordPress Import screen, the Import DotClear screen appears, prompting you for database access credentials (see Figure 16.5). Enter your MySQL connection data as it is found in the `inc/config.php` file found in your DotClear installation path.

As you progress through the import process, the DotClear importer imports categories that have been created, any users that you had in DotClear, and all posts and related comments. The final step of the import process imports all of the links that constituted the DotClear blogroll.

FIGURE 16.5

The database connection information for DotClear can be found in `inc/config.php` and should be entered into the importer.

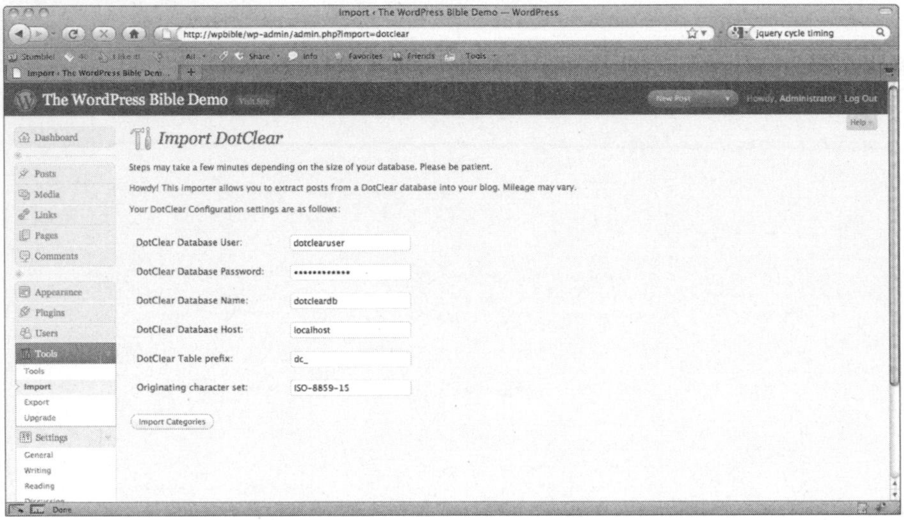

Caution

All users that are imported are assigned a password of password123. Please ensure that all user passwords are changed after they are brought into WordPress. Not doing so makes your blog vulnerable, and it can be severely compromised and hacked. ■

LiveJournal

WordPress offers import vehicles for LiveJournal (www.livejournal.com), one of three blog platforms from SixApart. LiveJournal is a free blog platform with some paid upgrades and is geared toward the non-professional blogger. In order to use it, you must have a LiveJournal username and password.

The import process is pretty simple. When you click LiveJournal on the WordPress Import screen, you are prompted for a LiveJournal username and password, as shown in Figure 16.6. When posts are pulled into WordPress from LiveJournal, they automatically are made public unless you add a post password as well. This is useful if you want to open up some posts but not others after the important.

Click Next to begin the import process. It is easy to timeout on LiveJournal imports because of a low limit on their API request allotment, so if this process ends up taking longer than usual, don't worry, it's normal.

Once the post import is done, the importer automatically begins importing comments. The final process will re-thread all of the comments in the proper order and associate them with the proper posts.

FIGURE 16.6

Enter your LiveJournal username and password to begin the import. If you don't want all posts to be public, add a post password as well.

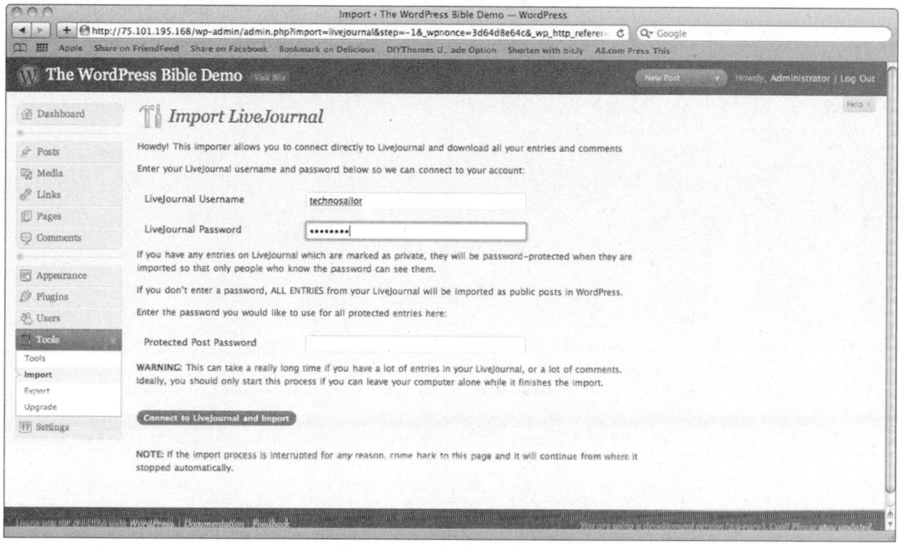

Movable Type and TypePad

SixApart's flagship blog platforms, Movable Type (www.movabletype.com) and TypePad (www.typepad.com) each provide an export format of their own. Their format, a flat text file with each field separated by five or eight dashes (-) to separate entries, is in plaintext and can be read as such. The format is shown in Listing 16.2.

LISTING 16.2

Movable Type and TypePad export format

```
AUTHOR: admin
TITLE: I just finished installing Movable Type 4!
BASENAME: i_just_finished_installing_movable_type_4
STATUS: Publish
ALLOW COMMENTS: 1
CONVERT BREAKS: 1
ALLOW PINGS: 0
DATE: 09/29/2009 08:27:35 PM
-----
```

continued

LISTING 16.2 *(continued)*

```
BODY:
Welcome to my new blog powered by Movable Type. This is the first post on my
    blog and was created for me automatically when I finished the
    installation process. But that is ok, because I will soon be creating
    posts of my own!
-----
EXTENDED BODY:
-----
EXCERPT:
-----
KEYWORDS:
-----
COMMENT:
AUTHOR: Aaron
EMAIL:
IP:
URL:
DATE: 09/29/2009 08:27:35 PM
Movable Type also created a comment for me as well so that I could see what
    a comment will look like on my blog once people start submitting comments
    on all the posts I will write.
-----

--------
AUTHOR: admin
TITLE: MT Test Post
BASENAME: mt_test_post
STATUS: Publish
ALLOW COMMENTS: 1
CONVERT BREAKS: richtext
ALLOW PINGS: 1
DATE: 09/29/2009 08:30:04 PM
-----
BODY:
This is a test post.
-----
EXTENDED BODY:
-----
EXCERPT:
-----
KEYWORDS:
```

Like the Blogware import, importing a Moveable Type or TypePad blog into WordPress is done via a file upload. In the WordPress Admin ➪ Import screen, click the Movable Type or TypePad import screen, find the `mt-export.txt` file that you exported from Movable Type or TypePad, and click the Upload file and import button, as shown in Figure 16.7.

FIGURE 16.7

The Import Movable Type and TypePad screen enables you to choose a Movable Type export file to upload or instruct WordPress to locate a file, titled `mt-static.txt`, in your `wp-content/` folder.

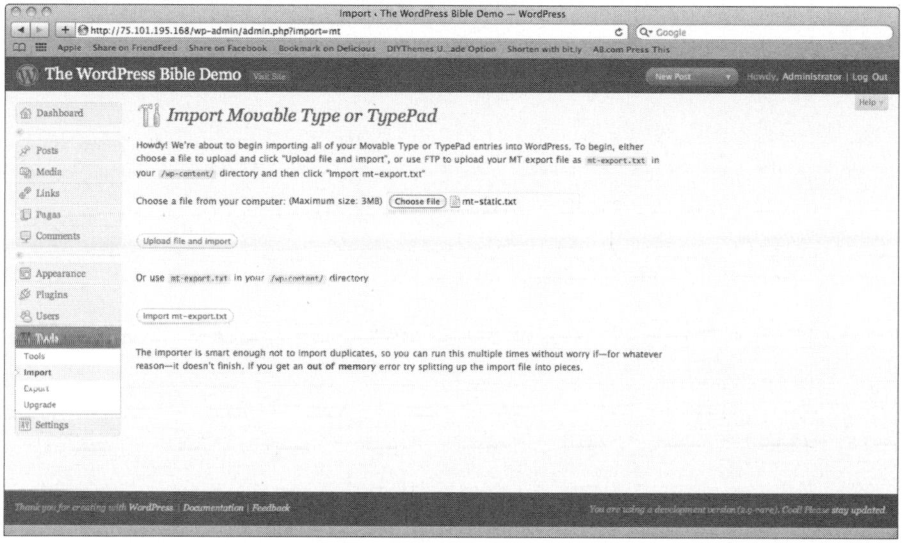

An alternative method to import your Moveable Type or TypePad file into WordPress (for example, if your file is too big for upload) is to upload it via FTP to your WordPress `wp-content/` folder. Make sure the name of the file is `mt-export.txt` and WordPress will automatically locate it.

Once the upload has been designated, the file will be parsed by WordPress for all unique authors. You have the option of creating new usernames (based on the Movable Type usernames) or mapping posts by specific authors to specific existing WordPress users. You can mix and match as needed (see Figure 16.8).

FIGURE 16.8

In the Assign Authors screen you can designate whether to map posts by specific Movable Type authors to WordPress users or create new users.

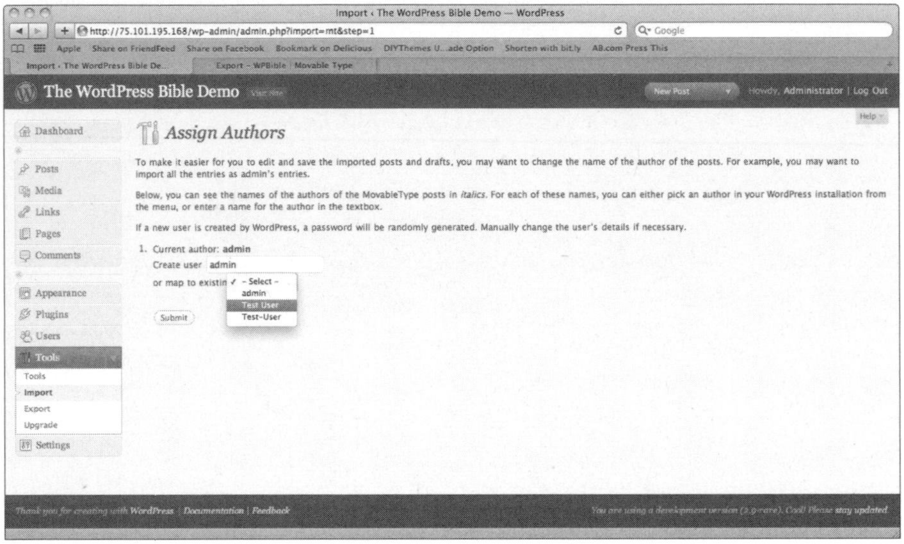

Click Finish and the Movable Type or TypePad posts, comments, and categories will be imported into WordPress. The Movable Type dataset is much slimmer than WordPress. Table 16.2 illustrates how the data that is imported from Movable Type is mapped to WordPress.

TABLE 16.2

Post Field Matches in a Movable Type to WordPress Import

Movable Type and TypePad	WordPress
AUTHOR	post_author
TITLE	post_title
BASENAME	guid
STATUS	post_status
ALLOW COMMENTS	comment_status
ALLOW PINGS	ping_status
DATE	post_date, post_modified
BODY	post_content
EXCERPT	post_excerpt
KEYWORDS	*inserted as categories*

WordPress

Naturally, the most seamless of all of the importers is the WordPress import. If you need to move a blog from WordPress.com to WordPress.org, WordPress.org to WordPress Multi-User (MU), or other combination in between, using the WordPress importer is the easiest (and sometimes the only) way to do it.

The WordPress export format (WXR) is an XML file that carries all of the post, link, tag, category, and comment data from one WordPress blog. An example of such a file is shown in Listing 16.3. It is the lengthiest of all the sample export files because the information included is highly detailed and geared specifically for WordPress.

LISTING 16.3

WordPress Export format (WXR)

```xml
<?xml version="1.0" encoding="UTF-8"?>
<!-- generator="WordPress.com" created="2009-09-27 13:12"-->
<rss version="2.0"
    xmlns:excerpt="http://wordpress.org/export/1.0/excerpt/"
    xmlns:content="http://purl.org/rss/1.0/modules/content/"
    xmlns:wfw="http://wellformedweb.org/CommentAPI/"
    xmlns:dc="http://purl.org/dc/elements/1.1/"
    xmlns:wp="http://wordpress.org/export/1.0/"
>
<channel>
    <title>Only in DC...</title>
    <link>http://onlyindc.wordpress.com</link>
    <description>For a good time, call your Congressman</description>
    <pubDate>Sat, 26 Sep 2009 20:57:36 +0000</pubDate>
    <generator>http://wordpress.org/?v=MU</generator>
    <language>en</language>
    <wp:wxr_version>1.0</wp:wxr_version>
    <wp:base_site_url>http://wordpress.com/</wp:base_site_url>
    <wp:base_blog_url>http://onlyindc.wordpress.com</wp:base_blog_url>
    <wp:category><wp:category_nicename>uncategorized</wp:category_
nicename><wp:category_parent></wp:category_parent><wp:cat_
name><![CDATA[Uncategorized]]></wp:cat_name></wp:category>
    <wp:tag><wp:tag_slug>ahmadinejad</wp:tag_slug><wp:tag_
name><![CDATA[ahmadinejad]]></wp:tag_name></wp:tag>
    <wp:tag><wp:tag_slug>capitol-hill</wp:tag_slug><wp:tag_
name><![CDATA[capitol hill]]></wp:tag_name></wp:tag>
    <wp:tag><wp:tag_slug>capitol-lounge</wp:tag_slug><wp:tag_
name><![CDATA[capitol lounge]]></wp:tag_name></wp:tag>
    <wp:tag><wp:tag_slug>cspan</wp:tag_slug><wp:tag_
name><![CDATA[cspan]]></wp:tag_name></wp:tag>
    <wp:tag><wp:tag_slug>graffiti</wp:tag_slug><wp:tag_
name><![CDATA[graffiti]]></wp:tag_name></wp:tag>
```

continued

| LISTING 16.3 | *(continued)* |

```
    <wp:tag><wp:tag_slug>henry-kissinger</wp:tag_slug><wp:tag_
  name><![CDATA[henry kissinger]]></wp:tag_name></wp:tag>
    <wp:tag><wp:tag_slug>tune-inn</wp:tag_slug><wp:tag_name><![CDATA[tune
  inn]]></wp:tag_name></wp:tag>
    <cloud domain='onlyindc.wordpress.com' port='80'
  path='/?rsscloud=notify' registerProcedure='' protocol='http-post' />
<image>
    <url>http://www.gravatar.com/blavatar/9ceaf79f07ac512e362cdd1868237732?
  s=96&#038;d=http://s.wordpress.com/i/buttonw-com.png</url>
        <title>Only in DC...</title>
        <link>http://onlyindc.wordpress.com</link>
    </image>
        <item>
<title>About</title>
<link>http://onlyindc.wordpress.com/about/</link>
<pubDate>Sat, 26 Sep 2009 20:00:50 +0000</pubDate>
<dc:creator><![CDATA[Aaron Brazell]]></dc:creator>
<guid isPermaLink="false"></guid>
<description></description>
<content:encoded><![CDATA[This is an example of a WordPress page, you could
  edit this to put information about yourself or your site so readers know
  where you are coming from. You can create as many pages like this one or
  subpages as you like and manage all of your content inside of
  WordPress.]]></content:encoded>
<excerpt:encoded><![CDATA[]]></excerpt:encoded>
<wp:post_id>2</wp:post_id>
<wp:post_date>2009-09-26 20:00:50</wp:post_date>
<wp:post_date_gmt>2009-09-26 20:00:50</wp:post_date_gmt>
<wp:comment_status>open</wp:comment_status>
<wp:ping_status>open</wp:ping_status>
<wp:post_name>about</wp:post_name>
<wp:status>publish</wp:status>
<wp:post_parent>0</wp:post_parent>
<wp:menu_order>0</wp:menu_order>
<wp:post_type>page</wp:post_type>
<wp:post_password></wp:post_password>
<wp:is_sticky>0</wp:is_sticky>
    </item>
<item>
<title>onlyindc.png</title>
<link>http://onlyindc.wordpress.com/?attachment_id=3</link>
<pubDate>Sat, 26 Sep 2009 20:06:53 +0000</pubDate>
<dc:creator><![CDATA[Aaron Brazell]]></dc:creator>
        <category><![CDATA[Uncategorized]]></category>
        <category domain="category" nicename="uncategorized"><![CDATA[Unca
  tegorized]]></category>
<guid isPermaLink="false">http://onlyindc.files.wordpress.com/2009/09/
  onlyindc.png</guid>
```

```
<description></description>
<content:encoded><![CDATA[http://onlyindc.files.wordpress.com/2009/09/
    onlyindc.png]]></content:encoded>
<excerpt:encoded><![CDATA[]]></excerpt:encoded>
<wp:post_id>3</wp:post_id>
<wp:post_date>2009-09-26 20:06:53</wp:post_date>
<wp:post_date_gmt>2009-09-26 20:06:53</wp:post_date_gmt>
<wp:comment_status>open</wp:comment_status>
<wp:ping_status>open</wp:ping_status>
<wp:post_name>onlyindc-png</wp:post_name>
<wp:status>inherit</wp:status>
<wp:post_parent>0</wp:post_parent>
<wp:menu_order>0</wp:menu_order>
<wp:post_type>attachment</wp:post_type>
<wp:post_password></wp:post_password>
<wp:is_sticky>0</wp:is_sticky>
<wp:attachment_url>http://onlyindc.wordpress.com/files/2009/09/onlyindc.
    png</wp:attachment_url>
<wp:postmeta>
<wp:meta_key>_wp_attached_file</wp:meta_key>
<wp:meta_value>/home/wpcom/public_html/wp-content/blogs.dir/761/9666475/
    files/2009/09/onlyindc.png</wp:meta_value>
</wp:postmeta>
<wp:postmeta>
<wp:meta_key>_wp_attachment_metadata</wp:meta_key>
<wp:meta_value>a:5:{s:5:"width";s:3:"527";s:6:"height";s:3:"273";s:14:"hwstr
    ing_small";s:23:"height='66' width='128'";s:4:"file";s:83:"/home/wpcom/
    public_html/wp-content/blogs.dir/761/9666475/files/2009/09/onlyindc.
    png";s:10:"image_meta";a:10:{s:8:"aperture";s:1:"0";s:6:"credit";s:0:"";s
    :6:"camera";s:0:"";s:7:"caption";s:0:"";s:17:"created_timestamp";s:1:"0";
    s:9:"copyright";s:0:"";s:12:"focal_length";s:1:"0";s:3:"iso";s:1:"0";s:13
    :"shutter_speed";s:1:"0";s:5:"title";s:0:"";}}</wp:meta_value>
</wp:postmeta>
    </item>
<item>
<title>32328196</title>
<link>/attachment/32328196/</link>
<pubDate>Sat, 26 Sep 2009 20:08:35 +0000</pubDate>
<dc:creator><![CDATA[Aaron Brazell]]></dc:creator>
        <category><![CDATA[Uncategorized]]></category>
        <category domain="category" nicename="uncategorized"><![CDATA[Unca
    tegorized]]></category>
<guid isPermaLink="false">http://onlyindc.files.wordpress.
    com/2009/09/32328196.jpg</guid>
<description></description>
<content:encoded><![CDATA[]]></content:encoded>
<excerpt:encoded><![CDATA[]]></excerpt:encoded>
<wp:post_id>5</wp:post_id>
<wp:post_date>2009-09-26 20:08:35</wp:post_date>
```

continued

LISTING 16.3   *(continued)*

```
<wp:post_date_gmt>2009-09-26 20:08:35</wp:post_date_gmt>
<wp:comment_status>open</wp:comment_status>
<wp:ping_status>open</wp:ping_status>
<wp:post_name>32328196</wp:post_name>
<wp:status>inherit</wp:status>
<wp:post_parent>9223372036854775807</wp:post_parent>
<wp:menu_order>0</wp:menu_order>
<wp:post_type>attachment</wp:post_type>
<wp:post_password></wp:post_password>
<wp:is_sticky>0</wp:is_sticky>
<wp:attachment_url>http://onlyindc.wordpress.com/files/2009/09/32328196.
   jpg</wp:attachment_url>
<wp:postmeta>
<wp:meta_key>_wp_attached_file</wp:meta_key>
<wp:meta_value>/home/wpcom/public_html/wp-content/blogs.dir/761/9666475/
   files/2009/09/32328196.jpg</wp:meta_value>
</wp:postmeta>
<wp:postmeta>
<wp:meta_key>_wp_attachment_metadata</wp:meta_key>
<wp:meta_value>a:5:{s:5:"width";s:3:"600";s:6:"height";s:3:"450";s:14:"hwstr
   ing_small";s:23:"height='96' width='128'";s:4:"file";s:83:"/home/wpcom/
   public_html/wp-content/blogs.dir/761/9666475/files/2009/09/32328196.
   jpg";s:10:"image_meta";a:10:{s:8:"aperture";s:1:"0";s:6:"credit";s:0:"";s
   :6:"camera";s:0:"";s:7:"caption";s:0:"";s:17:"created_timestamp";s:1:"0";
   s:9:"copyright";s:0:"";s:12:"focal_length";s:1:"0";s:3:"iso";s:1:"0";s:13
   :"shutter_speed";s:1:"0";s:5:"title";s:0:"";}}</wp:meta_value>
</wp:postmeta>
     </item>
<item>
<title>Review the Constitution, Fool</title>
<link>http://onlyindc.wordpress.com/2009/09/26/review-the-constitution-
   fool/</link>
<pubDate>Sat, 26 Sep 2009 20:09:08 +0000</pubDate>
<dc:creator><![CDATA[Aaron Brazell]]></dc:creator>
        <category><![CDATA[Uncategorized]]></category>
        <category domain="category" nicename="uncategorized"><![CDATA[Unca
   tegorized]]></category>
        <category domain="tag"><![CDATA[capitol hill]]></category>
        <category domain="tag" nicename="capitol-hill"><![CDATA[capitol
   hill]]></category>
        <category domain="tag"><![CDATA[graffiti]]></category>
        <category domain="tag" nicename="graffiti"><![CDATA[graffiti]]></
   category>
<guid isPermaLink="false">http://onlyindc.wordpress.com/?p=4</guid>
<description></description>
<content:encoded><![CDATA[Seen in a men's room on Capitol Hill.
```

```
<img class="alignnone size-full wp-image-5" title="32328196" src="http://
    onlyindc.files.wordpress.com/2009/09/32328196.jpg" alt="32328196"
    width="426" height="319" />]]></content:encoded>
<excerpt:encoded><![CDATA[]]></excerpt:encoded>
<wp:post_id>4</wp:post_id>
<wp:post_date>2009-09-26 20:09:08</wp:post_date>
<wp:post_date_gmt>2009-09-26 20:09:08</wp:post_date_gmt>
<wp:comment_status>open</wp:comment_status>
<wp:ping_status>open</wp:ping_status>
<wp:post_name>review-the-constitution-fool</wp:post_name>
<wp:status>publish</wp:status>
<wp:post_parent>0</wp:post_parent>
<wp:menu_order>0</wp:menu_order>
<wp:post_type>post</wp:post_type>
<wp:post_password></wp:post_password>
<wp:is_sticky>0</wp:is_sticky>
<wp:postmeta>
<wp:meta_key>_edit_lock</wp:meta_key>
<wp:meta_value>1254002889</wp:meta_value>
</wp:postmeta>
<wp:postmeta>
<wp:meta_key>_edit_last</wp:meta_key>
<wp:meta_value>674</wp:meta_value>
</wp:postmeta>
        </item>
<item>
<title>32334020-df4580afb3eef83a0bebbe423a0e2c7e.4abe77ad-full</title>
<link>http://onlyindc.wordpress.
    com/2009/09/26/a-capitol-hill-dive-bar/32334020-
    df4580afb3eef83a0bebbe423a0e2c7e-4abe77ad-full/</link>
<pubDate>Sat, 26 Sep 2009 20:22:55 +0000</pubDate>
<dc:creator><![CDATA[Aaron Brazell]]></dc:creator>
        <category><![CDATA[Uncategorized]]></category>
        <category domain="category" nicename="uncategorized"><![CDATA[Unca
    tegorized]]></category>
<guid isPermaLink="false">http://onlyindc.files.wordpress.
    com/2009/09/32334020-df4580afb3eef83a0bebbe423a0e2c7e-4abe77ad-full.jpg</
    guid>
<description></description>
<content:encoded><![CDATA[]]></content:encoded>
<excerpt:encoded><![CDATA[]]></excerpt:encoded>
<wp:post_id>9</wp:post_id>
<wp:post_date>2009-09-26 20:22:55</wp:post_date>
<wp:post_date_gmt>2009-09-26 20:22:55</wp:post_date_gmt>
<wp:comment_status>open</wp:comment_status>
<wp:ping_status>open</wp:ping_status>
<wp:post_name>32334020-df4580afb3eef83a0bebbe423a0e2c7e-4abe77ad-full</
    wp:post_name>
```

continued

LISTING 16.3   *(continued)*

```
<wp:status>inherit</wp:status>
<wp:post_parent>8</wp:post_parent>
<wp:menu_order>0</wp:menu_order>
<wp:post_type>attachment</wp:post_type>
<wp:post_password></wp:post_password>
<wp:is_sticky>0</wp:is_sticky>
<wp:attachment_url>http://onlyindc.wordpress.com/files/2009/09/32334020-
    df4580afb3eef83a0bebbe423a0e2c7e-4abe77ad-full.jpg</wp:attachment_url>
<wp:postmeta>
<wp:meta_key>_wp_attached_file</wp:meta_key>
<wp:meta_value>/home/wpcom/public_html/wp-content/blogs.dir/761/9666475/
    files/2009/09/32334020-df4580afb3eef83a0bebbe423a0e2c7e-4abe77ad-full.
    jpg</wp:meta_value>
</wp:postmeta>
<wp:postmeta>
<wp:meta_key>_wp_attachment_metadata</wp:meta_key>
<wp:meta_value>a:5:{s:5:"width";s:3:"480";s:6:"height";s:3:"640";s:14:"hwstr
    ing_small";s:22:"height='96' width='72'";s:4:"file";s:130:"/home/wpcom/
    public_html/wp-content/blogs.dir/761/9666475/files/2009/09/32334020-
    df4580afb3eef83a0bebbe423a0e2c7e-4abe77ad-full.jpg";s:10:"image_meta";a:1
    0:{s:8:"aperture";s:1:"0";s:6:"credit";s:0:"";s:6:"camera";s:0:"";s:7:"ca
    ption";s:0:"";s:17:"created_timestamp";s:1:"0";s:9:"copyright";s:0:"";s:1
    2:"focal_length";s:1:"0";s:3:"iso";s:1:"0";s:13:"shutter_speed";s:1:"0";s
    :5:"title";s:0:"";}}</wp:meta_value>
</wp:postmeta>
      </item>
</channel>
</rss>
```

Tip

If you are creating an exporter for a blog platform that does not have an importer, create it to export data into a WXR-style XML file. This enables you to import directly into any kind of WordPress blog. ■

The WordPress import process is similar to other file upload importers, such as the Movable Type and BlogWare importers. If your file is too big, you may need to break it up or adjust your php. ini settings for upload_max_filesize and post_max_size. This is usually only possible if you control your own server.

Like the Movable Type importer, the WordPress importer scours the uploaded WXR file for unique authors. You have the opportunity to map every author to a new WordPress username (the default is no password) or map an author to an already existing author.

Unlike other importers of its type, you also have an opportunity to download files. Remember that WordPress stores images as a post with a `post_type` of "attachment" in the database so there is a record of where they are stored. It's not simply something you can deduce based on the file system configuration and where images are uploaded to. This makes the WordPress image retrieval much more accurate, thorough, and reliable.

Tip

Here's an idea for a savvy developer to tackle. Instead of using XML imports and exports, it would be really neat to see an open source XML-RPC app that fetches all of the content via an XML-RPC (XML Remote Procedure Call) endpoint on one blog, WordPress or otherwise, and then uses XML-RPC to "push" content into WordPress. Bonus points to the developer who uses the AtomPub format, which is beginning to see more widespread adoption and is standardized, though incomplete, at this time. ■

Importing Tags into WordPress

Blog posts and comments are not the only type of content that can be imported into WordPress. In fact, a number of importers, such as the Simple Tag importer or the Ultimate Tag Warrior importer, were built for a variety of tagging systems when tags were first incorporated into WordPress in version 2.3. While some of the plugins that provided tagging no longer function (and are not even maintained), the importers exist for legacy blogs using older versions of WordPress, or for those WordPress installs that have not converted the older tags into current WordPress tags.

Converting categories to tags

The first tag importer is an internal importer that converts WordPress categories to WordPress tags. Categories are hierarchical metadata while tags are "flat," so sometimes it is necessary, depending on the strategy and needs of a blog, to convert categories to tags. This is also true when a blogger moves a blog from another platform that only uses categories but wants to begin to use WordPress tags after moving.

All categories can be converted as a batch. This is done from the WordPress Convert Categories to Tags page, shown in Figure 16.9, and found by choosing Tools ➪ Import. Simply select the categories you wish to convert into tags and click Import. All transactions will be done via the WordPress database layer so there is no need to do anything else.

FIGURE 16.9

Select the WordPress categories you wish to convert into tags and click the Import button to finish.

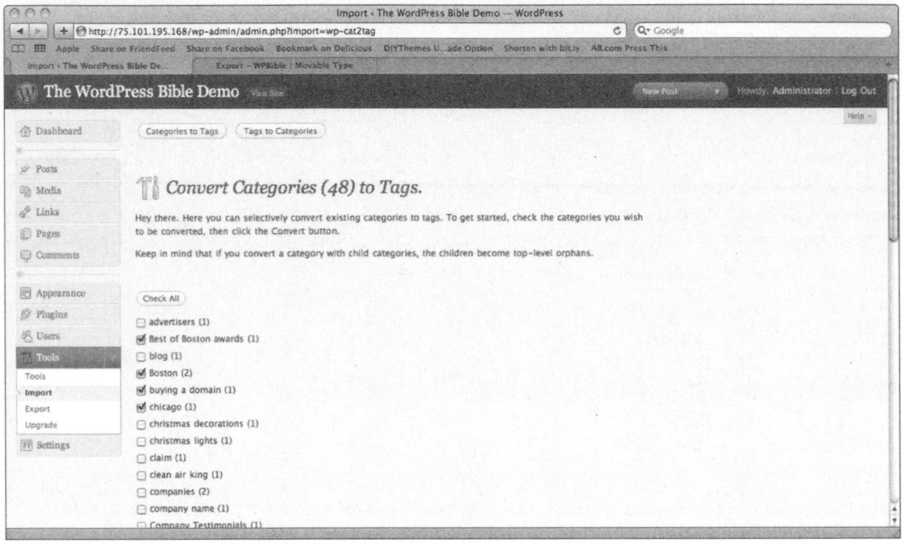

Importing Ultimate Tag Warrior tags

Prior to the inclusion of WordPress tags in WordPress 2.3, Ultimate Tag Warrior was the venerable champion plugin for tagging. It provided multitudes of ways to display tags in sidebars and at the end of posts, and provided an intuitive user interface on the Write Post and Page panels in the WordPress Admin.

However, due to the inclusion of tags in WordPress 2.3, the author of the Ultimate Tag Warrior plugin decided to cease development. Fortunately, for Ultimate Tag Warrior users, it is possible to import the tags from this system into WordPress. It is a short process that reads all the tags from the Ultimate Tag Warrior database table and transfers them into the WordPress tag system.

To import the tags from the Ultimate Tag Warrior plugin into WordPress, follow these steps:

1. **Click the Ultimate Tag Warrior link on the Tools ➪ Import screen.**

2. **Click the Step 1 button to start the import process.** Ultimate Tag Warrior tags are read from the database and displayed for confirmation.

3. **Click the Step 2 button to confirm that you want to import the listed tags.**

4. **Click the Step 3 button.** This step reads in the relationship of Ultimate Tag Warrior tags to posts.

5. **Click the Step 4 button to continue.** This step adds new WordPress tags to the posts based on the relationships read in Step 3.

6. **Close out of the import screen.** The import is complete.

Other Tagging Plugin Importers

Prior to WordPress 2.9, there were similar tagging importers are available for several other WordPress tagging plugins, including Bunny's Technorati Tags, Jerome's Keywords, and Simple Tagging. Many of these plugins were created early on as a response to WordPress' lack of tagging capability. Once tagging was added in WordPress 2.3, these other plugins became unnecessary. Chances are if you've adopted WordPress in the last two to three years, you will have not ever used or even needed these plugins. However, if you created your blog prior to 2008, you may have used these plugins at one point. In WordPress 2.9, the only importer of these three that still exists is the Simple Tagging plugin tag importer.

Looking at Backup Routines

Back up, back up, back up! It should be a process that is ingrained in every WordPress blogger's mind. Whenever you make an upgrade, back up. Develop routines around backing up on a regular basis.

The following section describes tools you can use to ensure quality backups. Use all or some of them or develop your own routines. The most solid routine you can use is a script that automatically does a database dump and archives all of your files on a daily basis. An upgrade to this process is to have the backup archives automatically copied to various places, including an offsite location (different server, different data center). If you work in information technology for a company, make sure your backup files are included in the company's offsite physical backup as well if this option is available (all but large enterprise companies may consider an offsite backup overkill and too expensive).

File backups

Using an FTP or SFTP client is the easiest way to back up files because it's a matter of dragging and dropping files from your server to your computer. The challenge for this method is that it is inconsistent. Unless you make an absolute habit out of doing these kinds of file transfers, you will probably fail in keeping regular backups. Use this method as a supplement to other backup routines.

MySQL backups

File backups are only one half of the equation. Arguably, the more important portion of your blog is your database. Because your MySQL database is not included in the files that would be backed up in a file system backup, you have to back it up with a MySQL utility such as mysqldump or via a user interface like phpMyAdmin.

Using mysqldump

The first, and most reliable, method of backing up a MySQL database is to use the mysqldump utility on the command line. In order to use it, you must be logged in to the server via SSH (Secure

Shell). The syntax for this command (which can vary slightly from server to server, but will likely be the same) looks like this:

```
mysqldump -h{hostname} -u{database username} -p {database name} >
    backup.sql
```

With this syntax, you can omit the hostname flag (-h) if the hostname is localhost. When you execute the command, you will be prompted to enter your database password. Optionally, you can add the password after the password flag (-p) but this is not considered best practice (or good security) because the database password will then be stored in the server history.

Using phpMyAdmin

There are many graphical user interfaces (GUIs) that can be used to manage a MySQL database. The most common, because it is Web-based, is phpMyAdmin. Your Web hosting provider probably uses this software for MySQL management via the control panel that they provide.

Backing up with phpMyAdmin is fairly simple, though your experience depends on your configuration and version. To start, go to the screen that lists the table names in your starting database, as shown in Figure 16.10.

FIGURE 16.10

The table listing screen in phpMyAdmin

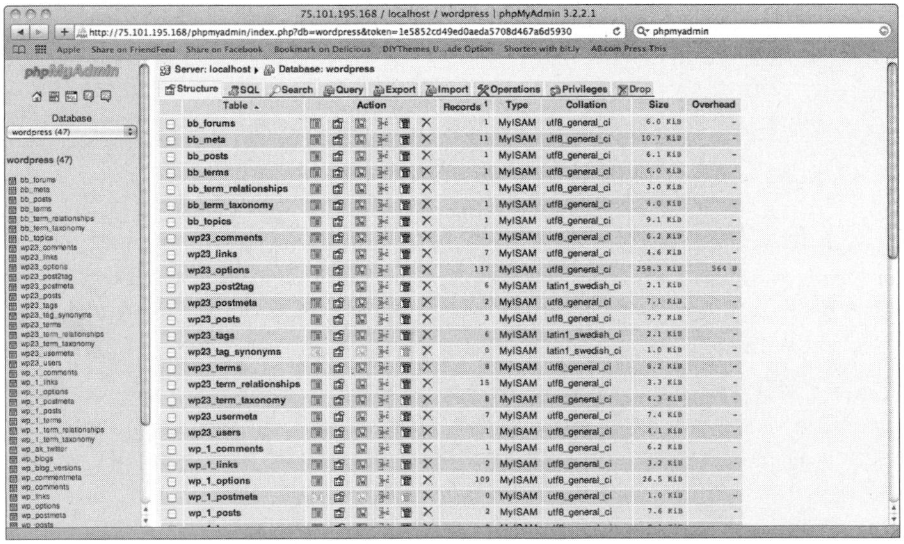

Next, click the Export tab at the top of the screen. This loads a screen similar to the one shown in Figure 16.11, which provides a variety of options for the export. In general, the defaults are perfectly fine options. Ensure that all of the WordPress tables are selected on the left side and that you are exporting the database to a file.

Finally, click Export to export the database to a file that can be stored for backup purposes.

Ensure that all tables are selected (default) and that you designate phpMyAdmin to export to a file (default).

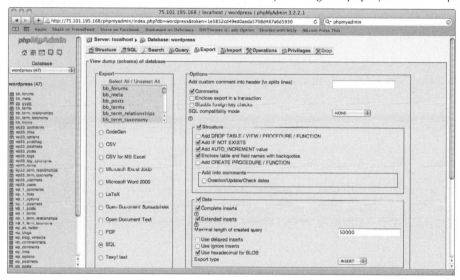

Backup scripting

The most thorough way to back up your system is to automate the backup process with a script that combines a database and file system backup. To do this, you'll need to be able to put your backup script on cron (scheduler for Unix-based systems) or in a Scheduled Task for Windows.

The script shown in Listing 16.4 offers a minimal example of how a backup routine can be done. It will only work on Unix-based systems as it is written in BASH, a Linux-based shell language. Make sure you edit the settings according to your needs, including your WordPress database credentials.

LISTING 16.4

A BASH script that shows how you can script the backup process

```bash
#!/bin/bash
#### DO NOT EDIT
DATE=`date +-%y-%m-%d--%T`
#### EDIT BELOW
# If CREATE_ZIP is 0, then a tarball will be used (default). If 1, then a
    zip file will be used
CREATE_ZIP=0
# Accessible/writable directory for temp storage
TMPDIR=/tmp
# Absolute path to WordPress backup storage location
WPBACKUP=/backups
# Absolute path to WordPress install.
WPDIR=/path/to/wordpress
# Enter Database connection details from your wp-config.php file
WP_DBUSER=user
WP_DBPASS=password
WP_DBHOST=localhost
WP_DBNAME=dbname
#### STOP EDITING
if [ ! -d $TMPDIR ]; then
        mkdir $TMPDIR/backup
fi
if [ ! -d $WPBACKUP ]; then
        mkdir $WPBACKUP
fi
# Dumps the database
mysqldump -h$WP_DBHOST -u$WP_DBUSER -p$WP_DBPASS $WP_DBNAME > $TMPDIR/
    backup/wordpress-db.sql

# Create Archive
if [[ CREATE_ZIP -eq 0 ]]; then
        # Tarballs the Database and WP files
        tar -cvf $TMPDIR/backup/backup$DATE.tar $WPDIR/.htaccess $WPDIR/
    wp-content $TMPDIR/backup/wordpress-db.sql 2>&1
        gzip $TMPDIR/backup/backup$DATE.tar
        # Move archive to backup location
        mv $TMPDIR/backup/backup$DATE.tar.gz $WPBACKUP/
else
        # Zips the database and WP files
        zip $TMPDIR/backup/backup$DATE.zip $WPDIR/.htaccess $WPDIR/*
    $TMPDIR/backup/wordpress-db.sql 2>&1
        # Move archive to backup location
        mv $TMPDIR/backup/backup$DATE.zip $WPBACKUP/
fi
```

On the Web

The code in Listing 16.4 is available for download at `www.wiley.com/go/wordpressbible`. ■

Summary

- You can import from a variety of blogging platforms, including Blogger and Movable Type.

- The Blogger importer requires authorization against Google, and provides an automated import process.

- The BlogWare importer requires an XML export from BlogWare. The field matching is minimal but provides the required data for a WordPress post.

- The DotClear importer connects to a DotClear database and imports posts and performs field matching directly, instead of via an uploaded XML file.

- The LiveJournal importer provides a similar type of import as Blogger, with the caveat that all posts are made public whether they were on LiveJournal or not.

- Movable Type and TypePad imports are based on a Movable Type export format that is uploaded to WordPress.

- WordPress.com, WordPress.org, or WordPress MU blogs can be exported and imported natively.

- The WordPress export format (WXR) is an XML format. When developing extensions or modules for platforms that don't have a native export or have a minimal export format, build the export functionality to put data into the WXR format.

- WordPress can import links and tags as well as post content from other platforms.

- Categories can be converted into Tags after a blog import or when a blogger decides to begin employing tags instead of categories.

- The Ultimate Tag Warrior importer brings in pre-WordPress 2.3 tags provided by the Ultimate Tag Warrior plugin. WordPress also supports imports from the Simple Tags plugin.

- Take backups very seriously. This chapter provides insight into how to do backups, including a helpful script you can use to automatically perform them.

WordPress Maintenance and Security

WordPress' upgrade cycle is pretty much set in stone. On average, a major release of the software is released three times a year (or about once every four months). These release cycles increase the version number by increments of .1 (WordPress 2.5, 2.6, 2.7, 2.8, and so on) and are referred to as "major" releases.

Security fixes are released as needed and append an additional digit to the version number (WordPress 2.8.1, 2.8.2, 2.8.3, and so on). These releases are called security releases or "point" releases.

Those in the WordPress community have often expressed frustration over the cycle and speed at which releases come. Many times, the fast-paced releases — particularly security releases — reflect the need to get flaws fixed quickly.

A main argument against open source software is that because the code is available to anyone, malicious hackers can roadmap their way to an exploit. Of course, this is also one of the strengths of open source software — security researchers can also find flaws, and inform others of them and address them, before a security problem becomes public knowledge.

WordPress takes an aggressive approach to security flaws, in some cases releasing security fixes quickly to address the issues. Of course, no software is ever perfect, WordPress included.

Upgrading WordPress

Keep an eye out for new releases of WordPress. WordPress displays a nag in your WordPress Admin when a new release of the software is available. With WordPress' auto-upgrade functionality, you can upgrade using a simple one-click process.

Cross-Reference

Using the auto-upgrade functionality for WordPress upgrades, plugin upgrades, and theme installs is discussed in Chapter 15. ■

Upgrading manually with FTP

Bloggers with installs of WordPress older than version 2.7 (shame on you!) don't have access to auto-upgrades. Also, depending on their server configuration, bloggers who have the most current version of WordPress may not be able to use the auto-upgrade functionality.

In these cases, the only way to upgrade WordPress is the old fashioned way — by hand. The process for upgrading manually is not difficult, but it does involve more steps.

There are two different approaches that bloggers take to upgrades involving file transfer protocol (FTP) or secure file transfer protocol (SFTP). The first involves overwriting existing files and is the quickest upgrade route.

Note

FTP upgrades are somewhat dangerous for two reasons. First, the FTP network protocol is inherently insecure because it transmits data unencrypted. This poses a significant risk in an era of public wireless networks. Anybody can be sitting in a café sniffing data packets being transmitted in plain text over the air, including your username and password!

The second inherent problem with FTP is lost connections. It is a stateless protocol, which means it carries no context or history of what it has done or is doing. In the event of a connection loss, data being transmitted over FTP is simply lost. There is no way to recover from a lost connection and files can be truncated mid-stream. Re-initiating an upload is the only way to recover from a lost FTP connection. ■

Tip

When possible, use SFTP for all data transfers, given it is an encrypted protocol and will avoid problems created by transfer losses. ■

To upgrade WordPress manually via FTP, follow these steps:

1. **Download WordPress from** `http://wordpress.org/download/` **or by choosing Tools ➪ Upgrade in the WordPress Admin.**
2. **Unzip the downloaded file.** The file is typically called `latest.zip`. If you use a Mac or Linux, you can seamlessly use the *tarball*, a different kind of archive that is typically called `latest.tar.gz`.
3. **Connect to a Web server using an FTP or SFTP client.**
4. **Browse to the WordPress directory.** Most often, this is in the document root (DOCROOT) system path. On cPanel-based hosts, the WordPress directory will be in the `public_html/` folder. Plesk users will find it in `{domainname}/httpdocs/`.

If WordPress is installed in a directory under DOCROOT, you'll have to browse to that folder (for example, `public_html/wordpress/`).

5. **Browse to the extracted wordpress/ directory that was created in Step 2.**

6. **Upload the contents of the wordpress/ directory into your DOCROOT.** The contents of the directory should include directories `wp-content`, `wp-admin`, and `wp-includes`, so you know you're on the right track if these folders are present.

7. **Once all files have been uploaded, point your browser to** `http://example.com/wp-admin/upgrade.php`, **where** `http://example.com` **is the location of your WordPress home directory.**

8. **Click the Upgrade WordPress Database button, as shown in Figure 17.1.**

FIGURE 17.1

The upgrade screen for WordPress contains a single button that performs all the database upgrade and preparation operations.

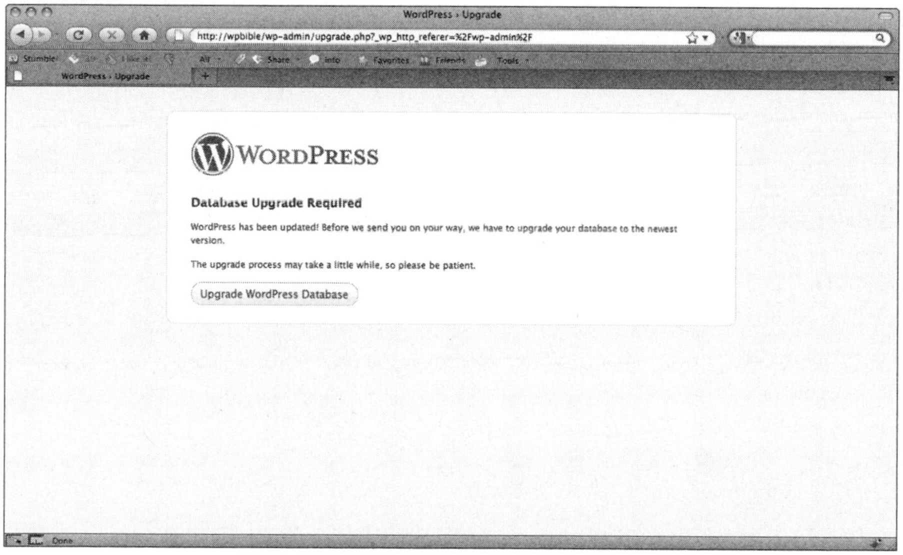

The previous steps describe a bare-bones manual upgrade process. While it should work, there are potential pitfalls here. Almost universally, major releases modify the database in some way. Depending on the database alterations, you may not be able to roll back a release. If you like to play loose and fast with your blog, you could end up with serious problems if there is a botched upgrade and no way to roll back. Always, always back up your blog before upgrading.

A better process for upgrading manually is one that includes backup routines.

Cross-Reference

For more information about backup routines and options, see Chapter 16. ∎

To upgrade WordPress manually while also backing up your database and files, follow these steps:

1. **Download WordPress from** `http://wordpress.org/download/` **or by choosing Tools** ⇨ **Upgrade in the WordPress Admin.**

2. **Unzip the downloaded file.** This is typically called `latest.zip`. If you use a Mac or Linux, you can seamlessly use the *tarball*, a different kind of archive that is typically called `latest.tar.gz`.

3. **Back up your database:**

   - From phpMyAdmin, select your database, click the export tab, and export the database to a file.
   - From SSH, type **mysqldump -u{dbuser} -p {dbname} > {dbname}.sql**. Refer to documentation for `mysqldump` to determine proper parameters.

Caution

Do not keep a backup in a Web-accessible location. ∎

4. **Back up your files (including your database dump):**

   - Download all files in the WordPress root directory.
   - From SSH, type **tar -cvf backup.tar path/to/wordpress/docroot/ /path/to/{dbname}.sql**, to create an archive of all your files. Then type **gzip backup.tar** to compress the archive.

5. **Connect to a Web server using an FTP or SFTP client.**

6. **Browse to the WordPress directory.** Most often, this is in the document root (DOCROOT) system path. On cPanel-based hosts, the WordPress directory will be in the `public_html/` folder. Plesk users will find it in `{domainname}/httpdocs/`. If WordPress is installed in a directory under DOCROOT, you'll have to browse to that folder (for example, `public_html/wordpress/`).

7. **Browse to the extracted wordpress/ directory that was created in Step 2.**

8. **Upload the contents of the wordpress/ directory into your DOCROOT.** The contents of the directory should include directories `wp-content`, `wp-admin`, and `wp-includes`, so you know you're on the right track if these folders are present.

9. **Once all files have been uploaded, point your browser to** `http://example.com/wp-admin/upgrade.php`, **where** `http://example.com` **is the location of your WordPress home directory.**

10. **Click the Upgrade WordPress Database button, shown earlier in Figure 17.1.**

Note

Because of the way WordPress has been built, there should never be a reason to alter core files. Therefore, an upgrade of the WordPress core should never overwrite any changes to your blog. User-modified files, such as `wp-config.php`, `.htaccess`, theme files, and plugins should never be touched by a WordPress upgrade. The only exception to this is when your theme is based on the default theme and is contained in the default directory. However, even if your theme is based on the default theme, it's good practice to duplicate that folder, name it something else, and activate it as a different theme. ■

Debugging problems with FTP upgrades

Many people end up having problems with WordPress upgrades, something that was a clear impetus for including the auto-upgrade feature in the WordPress core. It doesn't take much searching to find bloggers who have had a botched upgrade they don't know how to fix or debug. However, there are some things you can do to fix a failed upgrade.

Re-upload files

The first step to attempting to fix a botched upgrade is to try to upload all the WordPress files again. If you're using FTP, try to use SFTP if you can. If your FTP connection drops midstream, your files will not all be uploaded and, worse, some of the PHP files may be truncated mid-stream.

This is almost always a recipe for the "white screen of death" — a symptom that generally comes from a PHP error somewhere, and more specifically, from some kind of syntax error. If a PHP file is truncated mid-stream, you almost assuredly have a syntax error, even if the error was created by a dropped connection.

If your FTP connection is giving you problems and dropping regularly, try uploading WordPress in batches. Upload the `wp-admin` directory, followed by `wp-content/`, and `wp-includes/`. After uploading the three directories, upload all the root directory files (all of which begin with `wp-` except the `xmlrpc.php` file).

Check the error log

If you have access to server logs, you can often ascertain a problem with PHP by looking at the Web server error log. For Apache, this file is called `error_log` (or `error.log` on Ubuntu or Debian operating systems). The location of this file depends on your server configuration. Common locations for this file include:

- `/etc/httpd/log/error_log`
- `/home/vhosts/{username}/{domain}/statistics/logs/error_log`
- `/var/log/httpd/error_log`

Using the Unix tail command enables you to see the end (most recent portion) of the `error_log` and perhaps determine if there are PHP errors. Add a `-f` flag to the tail command to keep the log running and see new errors as they enter the log. Listing 17.1 shows what an error_log looks like. It does not show errors relating to WordPress; however, it does show interesting errors that could represent other problems.

LISTING 17.1

Use the Unix tail command on the Apache Web server error log to find hidden PHP errors

```
root@wpbible:/var/log/apache2# tail -f /var/log/apache2/error.log[Wed Aug 19
    19:45:07 2009] [error] [client 69.243.11.229] File does not exist: /var/www/
    favicon.ico
[Wed Aug 19 22:13:53 2009] [error] [client 211.95.78.112] script '/var/www/abc.
    php' not found or unable to stat
[Thu Aug 20 18:38:41 2009] [error] [client 66.167.186.106] File does not exist:
    /var/www/phpmyadmin
[Fri Aug 21 02:53:53 2009] [error] [client 190.196.23.170] Invalid URI in
    request GET HTTP/1.1 HTTP/1.1
[Fri Aug 21 02:53:54 2009] [error] [client 190.196.23.170] File does not exist:
    /var/www/install.txt
[Fri Aug 21 02:53:55 2009] [error] [client 190.196.23.170] File does not exist:
    /var/www/cart
[Fri Aug 21 02:53:56 2009] [error] [client 190.196.23.170] File does not exist:
    /var/www/zencart
[Fri Aug 21 02:53:56 2009] [error] [client 190.196.23.170] File does not exist:
    /var/www/zen-cart
[Fri Aug 21 02:53:56 2009] [error] [client 190.196.23.170] File does not exist:
    /var/www/zen
[Fri Aug 21 02:53:57 2009] [error] [client 190.196.23.170] File does not exist:
    /var/www/shop
```

The error_log method is an extremely important step to take in debugging WordPress after an upgrade. Generally speaking, you are not going to have PHP errors from a core upgrade if the connection never dropped and the complete transfer of files was performed.

The real problem occurs if there is a plugin incompatibility. With major releases of WordPress come major enhancements, and sometimes functions are removed from the core. Functions are never removed from the core without being deprecated in several versions first; however, plugin authors who are not aware of deprecated functions (refer to the wp-includes/deprecated.php file) and variables run the risk of including those functions, classes, and variables in a plugin, and then getting errors when WordPress eventually removes them. Using non-existent functions, classes, or variables may cause WordPress to break for what seems to be no apparent reason. These errors will be reported in the error_log.

Roll back to a previous version

In a worst-case scenario, there is no way to ascertain the problems resulting from a bad upgrade. There is no built-in "roll back" functionality in WordPress. The only way to actually roll back is with a manual intervention and with a database backup. (You did back up your database, right?)

To roll back to a previous version of WordPress, follow these steps:

1. Download the last version of WordPress that you need from `http://wordpress.org/download/release-archive/`.

2. Extract the archive to create a wordpress/ folder.

3. With phpMyAdmin or via the MySQL commandline (over SSH), drop all of the WordPress tables in the database. These usually start with wp_ but could be different based on the value of your `$table_prefix` variable in `wp-config.php`.

Caution

Dropping all of the WordPress tables in the database is a destructive action and should only be taken if you know you need to roll back and have a current backup. It is irreversible. ■

4. Delete all files via FTP or SFTP.

Caution

This too is irreversible. Make sure you have a current backup of your `wp content/` folder (where your theme and plugins are) and `wp-config.php` file. You can also back up `.htaccess` if it has more than WordPress rewrite rules, or just let WordPress regenerate it after the fact. ■

5. Import your MySQL backup via phpMyAdmin or from SSH.

6. Upload the older version of WordPress to the server.

7. Upload your backed-up wp-content/, wp-config.php and .htaccess files.

8. Regenerate your permalinks if you did not back up your .htaccess file by choosing Settings ⇨ Permalinks for WordPress 2.7 and later or Options ⇨ Permalinks for versions prior to WordPress 2.7.

Choosing an FTP Client

FTP processes cannot be performed without an FTP client. With the WordPress auto-upgrade routine, the blog itself acts as a client that speaks to the FTP server. However, when performing FTP transactions, you will need your own FTP client. In the following sections, I outline some of the basic FTP clients for both Windows and Mac users.

Note

Based on the security concerns surrounding FTP, my recommendations will be based not on popularity or price point, but rather on whether a particular client can handle SFTP transactions as well. ■

Windows FTP clients

Windows is the most common operating system for bloggers. It has a market share in every industry. There are plenty of FTP clients available for Windows, many of which are free. They all work on the same basic premise and so the differences are in the user interface and ease of use.

WS_FTP Professional

The WS_FTP Professional FTP client, shown in Figure 17.2, is one of the oldest and most notable of all FTP client solutions. Ipswitch, the company that provides this solution, provides a number of other solutions as well, including a free trial of the software, available at www.ipswitchft.com/products/ws_ftp_professional/try/.

FIGURE 17.2

WS_FTP is one of the oldest and best known FTP clients for Windows.

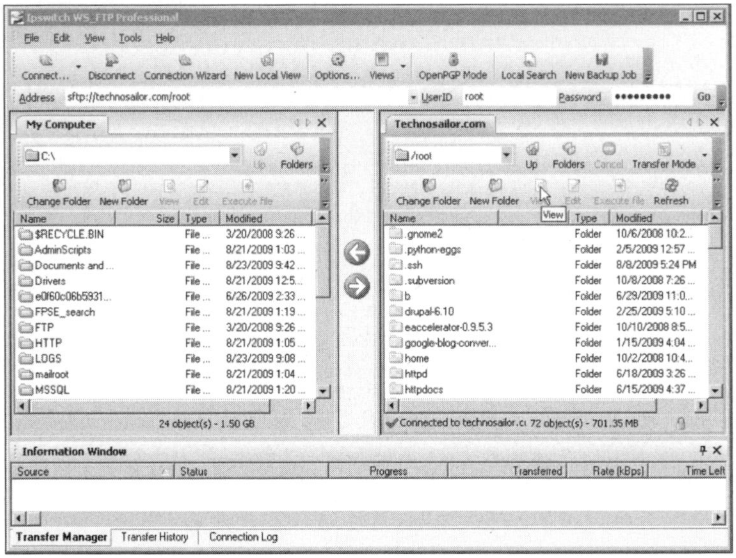

FileZilla

The FileZilla project is an open source project that supports FTP and SFTP. You can download it at http://filezilla-project.org. It provides clients for all operating systems — Windows, Mac, and Linux. The connection details are standard for FTP clients. Enter your username, password, host, and server type (FTP or SFTP). The FileZilla connection screen is shown in Figure 17.3.

The interface itself is set up in a somewhat visually confusing manner (see Figure 17.3). The panel across the top of the interface scrolls FTP log information regarding the activity and communications between FileZilla and the server.

The series of panels in the center of the screen describes the file system of the user's machine and enables the user to browse his file tree. The file system of the server is shown on the right side. Simply dragging and dropping files or directories from one side to the other performs transfers. Uploads occur by moving data from the local side to the remote side and downloads occur in reverse.

The transfer statuses of queued up files appear in the bottom panel. FTP can only perform a limited number of simultaneous transfers (designated by the server itself).

The FileZilla connection screen takes typical connection details.

Mac OS X FTP clients

Serious developers tend to use Macs and, to a lesser extent, Linux machines. The nice thing about Macs is their legendary ease of use. When applications are created with the "Apple-blessed" Cocoa framework, much of the usability is built right into the client. As with Windows clients, the premise behind FTP is standard, so the difference between a Windows and Mac or Linux FTP client is in execution. Unlike Windows, Mac and Linux operating systems have built-in support for SSH, making the file transfer experience smoother and more secure.

Note

Apple provides a few different programming environments for Mac software developers. Carbon is a procedural code application development. The preferred environment for Mac application developers is Cocoa, which is object-oriented. ■

Transmit

My favorite FTP client for Mac OS X (and my choice in clients) is Transmit for its ease of use. (Transmit is released by Panic Software and is available at www.panic.com/transmit). The Transmit interface, shown in Figure 17.4, consists of a left panel with the local file system and a right panel showing the remote file system. Progress indicators are minimized to a progress bar in the lower-right corner of the window.

Tip

For developers who use TextMate (http://macromates.com/**) as a code editor, as I do, you may find that the integration between the two applications is brilliant. TextMate provides extensibility via "bundles," which add extra functionality to the application, similar to the way plugins add functionality to WordPress. Developers using both Transmit and TextMate may want to consider the Transmit bundle for TextMate that provides solid integration between the two. Download it at** http://svn.textmate.org/trunk/ Bundles/Transmit.tmbundle/. ∎

FIGURE 17.4

Transmit provides a minimalistic interface for file transfers over FTP or SFTP.

Fetch

Another easy-to-use Mac FTP client is Fetch by Fetch Softworks. Represented by an iconic dog, Fetch is only slightly more difficult to use than Transmit. In an effort to keep the interface clean, the main interface is the remote file listing, shown in Figure 17.5. Local file listings are handled through the Finder. Fetch is available from http://fetchsoftworks.com/ and supports all the major transfer protocols.

The Fetch interface is clean and minimalistic, but hides key panels in expandable form.

Practicing Sound WordPress Security

The idea that there is no such thing as a completely secure software system is the guiding principle of hackers, whether they are *white hat* hackers who are involved in software security for the sake of helping software providers improve software from a standpoint of respect for the law and ethics guidelines or *black hat* hackers who find no problem with exercising their trade outside of the rules of ethics and legal restraints.

Many of the software flaws that have been fixed in WordPress over the years are may be directly attributed to hackers who have provided details of their research to the WordPress core developers. Throughout the WordPress core, you will find data sanitization, SQL injection prevention, and more. These principles should be applied whenever a plugin or code is supplied to WordPress.

Because WordPress offers vast extensibility options via hooks and APIs, plugin and theme developers run the risk of introducing massive security problems to the WordPress environment that are not caused by WordPress itself. For instance, any time a plugin provides functionality that includes a form, the developer runs the risk of malicious user input (*never, ever* trust user input) if that data is then not processed in a way that makes it safe for the rest of the system. This process is called *sanitization*, as it sanitizes the data for use in a safe manner. This, of course, is just one example.

Other potential problems involve inadvertently introducing unsafe SQL queries or, a classic user-facing problem, having files with permissions set that would allow an unauthorized user to modify the file, thus modifying the behavior of the file.

Data sanitization

By using the WordPress APIs, you can ensure that any data going into the database is sanitized. By *sanitized*, I mean that data that comes from an unknown source — another human being, another Web site, and so on — is turned into "safe" content to be inserted into the database.

Data sanitization can come in a number of forms. It could be as simple as stripping harmful characters out of the data, or it could involve ensuring that a number is truly being treated as a number and not as a string, an important factor as data types can, in some cases, alter the behavior of the script.

Casting variables

Casting variables is the practice of ensuring that the variable type expected by the system is the same variable type passed into it. Integers should always be integers. Strings should always be strings. Arrays should always be arrays.

You can ensure the variable type remains the same by enclosing the data type in parentheses as follows:

```
$variable = (int) $variable;
```

When passing data that can be a string or an array, you can cast the variable to an array and proceed from there by extracting the array or performing other actions on it, like this:

```
$array = (array) $possible_array;
```

Sanitizing HTML entities for XML

Whenever your plugin needs to output text to an XML file, you need to sanitize commonly used HTML entities, like   or ", into extensible markup language (XML)-safe entities. To do this, use the WordPress function ent2ncr().

In Listing 17.2, the ent2ncr() function replaces ".

The ent2ncr() function is used to make strings safe for use with XML

```
$kennedy = "Now the trumpet summons us again - not as a call to bear arms,
    though arms we need; not as a call to battle, though embattled we are -
    but a call to bear the burden of a long twilight struggle, year in and
    year out, &quot;rejoicing in hope, patient in tribulation&quot; - a
    struggle against the common enemies of man: tyranny, poverty, disease,
    and war itself."
$sanitized_kennedy = ent2ncr( $kennedy );
echo $sanitized_kennedy;
/*
Displays:
```

```
Now the trumpet summons us again - not as a call to bear arms, though arms
    we need; not as a call to battle, though embattled we are - but a call to
    bear the burden of a long twilight struggle, year in and year out,
    &#34;rejoicing in hope, patient in tribulation&#34; - a struggle against
    the common enemies of man: tyranny, poverty, disease, and war itself.
*/
?>
```

Using KSES to filter unsafe content

Whenever you have content that is posted in comments or as a post, the content is filtered through the KSES filter provided by the KSES library, a suite of functions that are used for sanitizing data. The function that does this, wp_kses(), takes two arguments. The first argument is the string to be sanitized and the second is an array of HTML tags that are allowed to remain in the string. The wp_kses() function is an important function for ensuring that no one can hijack your site via a Cross-site scripting (XSS) attack.

Typically, XSS occurs because someone inserts a malicious piece of JavaScript into a Web site that forces the browser to do something malicious, such as sending data to an attacker or redirecting it to a different Web site. Because the most useful vector for an XSS attack is user input from forms, the KSES filter is important to ensure such malicious code never makes it into your site.

Escaping and encoding HTML

Prior to WordPress 2.8, a single function, wp_specialchars(), was used to turn special characters such as <, >, and & (to name a few) into encoded entities (<, >, &, respectively). This function has been deprecated, but as with many deprecated functions, it remains in the core for now. You should use the newer, consolidated security API functions.

Note

At some point wp_specialchars() **will be removed from the WordPress core, so you should not rely on it.** ■

Since WordPress 2.8, wp_specialchars() has been replaced by three new functions: esc_html(), esc_html__(), and esc_html_e(). All three of these functions are similar but do slightly different things.

The esc_html() function returns a sanitized string of HTML to a variable. It takes a string of text to be encoded as a single argument.

For those performing localizations, the esc_html_() and esc_html_e() functions perform similar functions to the __() and _e() localization functions, in that the first returns a translated string and the second echoes it. Strings of text passed to these functions not only encode the text, but also makes it translatable.

Cross-Reference

Localization is discussed in more detail in Chapter 5. ■

Escaping and encoding HTML attributes

The need to escape HTML attributes is as important as encoding and escaping HTML itself. Prior to WordPress 2.8, the `escape_attribute()` function existed to do just that. It is now deprecated in favor of `esc_attr()`, `esc_attr__()`, and `esc_attr_e()`. Usage is identical to the `esc_html()`, `esc_html__()`, and `esc_html_e()` functions.

Escaping and encoding JavaScript

Similar to other escaping and encoding functions, the `esc_js()` function makes JavaScript code safe for the browser and database if you need to insert JavaScript into the database.

Sanitizing URLs

There are a number of ways to sanitize a URL. The primary way is with the `esc_url()` function. This function takes one or two arguments. The first argument is the URL that needs to be sanitized.

The second argument is an optional array of protocols such as `ftp`, `http`, or `mailto`. By default, and the most common usage, is to just set this argument to `null`. By doing so, it is assumed that all of the major protocols should be accepted: `http`, `https`, `ftp`, `ftps`, `mailto`, `news`, `irc`, `gopher`, `nntp`, `feed`, and `telnet`.

If you aren't creating a URL for use in an HTML context, you will want to use `esc_url_raw()`. This avoids encoding ampersands as `&amp;` for HTML validity. Use this function when you want to sanitize a URL for use in a redirect or for saving to a database (see Listing 17.3).

LISTING 17.3

URLs can be sanitized with the esc_url() and esc_url_raw() functions

```
$url = 'http://www.amazon.com/gp/product/0470568135?ie=UTF8&tag=emmensetec
   hno-20&linkCode=as2&camp=1789&creative=390957&creativeASIN=0470568135';
echo esc_url( $url );      # HTML display context
/* Displays: http://www.amazon.com/gp/product/0470568135?ie=UTF8&#038;tag=em
   mensetechno-20&#038;linkCode=as2&#038;camp=1789&#038;creative=390957&#038
   ;creativeASIN=0470568135
*/
echo esc_url_raw( $url );
/* Displays:
http://www.amazon.com/gp/product/0470568135?ie=UTF8&tag=emmensetechno-20&lin
   kCode=as2&camp=1789&creative=390957&creativeASIN=0470568135
*/
echo clean_url( $url, null, 'db' );
/* Displays:
```

```
http://www.amazon.com/gp/product/0470568135?ie=UTF8&tag=emmensetechno-20&lin
    kCode=as2&camp=1789&creative=390957&creativeASIN=0470568135
*/
```

Preventing SQL injection

The WordPress database class has a `prepare()` method that is useful for ensuring that data going into MySQL is properly escaped and will prevent unauthorized access to your site. The `prepare()` method uses a syntax that is familiar to PHP developers who have used `sprintf()`, `printf()`, and similar PHP functions.

Cross-Reference
Refer to Chapter 7 for discussion about how SQL injection works and documentation on how, specifically, to use the `prepare()` method. ∎

The concept is that of placeholders. SQL queries that are written use placeholders, such as `%d` or `%s`, for integers and strings, respectively. Developers then supply the data that replace the placeholders according to type. In this way, arbitrary content is prevented from being inserted in the database.

The WordPress API provided in the database class handles the heavy lifting of ensuring that SQL queries sent directly to the database are protected against SQL injections. Always use the `prepare()` method when performing raw SQL and, if possible, use the WordPress API that has other layers of protection, including SQL injection protection, built in.

File permissions

Perhaps one of the more common mistakes users make when installing WordPress is not ensuring that file permissions are set properly. The following sections outline file permissions for both Unix and WordPress and how to set them up properly when installing WordPress.

Unix file permissions

In a Linux world, file permissions are handled in a 10-byte manner. When you do a directory listing from a terminal, you'll see a listing that looks something like Listing 17.4.

LISTING 17.4

A directory listing of the document root for WordPress

```
root@wpbible:/var/www# ls -la
total 321
drwxr-xr-x  6 technosailor technosailor  4096 2009-08-19 17:00 .
drwxr-xr-x 18 root         root          4096 2009-07-07 13:15 ..
```

continued

LISTING 17.4   *(continued)*

```
-rw-rw-rw-  1 technosailor technosailor   205 2009-08-16 18:10 .htaccess
-rw-r--r--  1 technosailor technosailor   397 2008-05-25 20:33 index.php
-rw-r--r--  1 technosailor technosailor 15410 2008-12-06 07:47 license.txt
-rw-r--r--  1 technosailor technosailor  7642 2009-08-12 00:41 readme.html
drwxr-xr-x  6 technosailor technosailor  4096 2009-07-09 16:41 .svn
drwxr-xr-x  8 technosailor technosailor  4096 2009-08-19 17:00 wp-admin
-rw-r--r--  1 technosailor technosailor 40773 2009-08-13 20:47 wp-app.php
-rw-r--r--  1 technosailor technosailor   220 2008-10-14 06:22 wp-atom.php
-rw-r--r--  1 technosailor technosailor   274 2008-05-25 15:50 wp-blog-header.
     php
-rw-r--r--  1 technosailor technosailor  3649 2009-05-18 16:00 wp-comments-post.
     php
-rw-r--r--  1 technosailor technosailor   238 2008-10-14 06:22 wp-commentsrss2.
     php
-rw-r--r--  1 technosailor technosailor  1101 2009-08-18 15:20 wp-config.php
-rw-r--r--  1 technosailor technosailor  2626 2009-02-28 09:55 wp-config-sample.
     php
drwxrwxrwx  9 technosailor technosailor  4096 2009-08-19 17:00 wp-content
-rw-r--r--  1 technosailor technosailor  1254 2009-02-07 13:32 wp-cron.php
-rw-r--r--  1 technosailor technosailor   220 2008-10-14 06:22 wp-feed.php
drwxr-xr-x  7 technosailor technosailor  4096 2009-08-19 17:00 wp-includes
-rw-r--r--  1 technosailor technosailor  1946 2009-05-05 19:43 wp-links-opml.php
-rw-r--r--  1 technosailor technosailor  2341 2009-05-20 16:32 wp-load.php
-rw-r--r--  1 technosailor technosailor 21230 2009-08-11 06:03 wp-login.php
-rw-r--r--  1 technosailor technosailor  7113 2009-05-18 15:11 wp-mail.php
-rw-r--r--  1 technosailor technosailor   487 2009-04-20 21:50 wp-pass.php
-rw-r--r--  1 technosailor technosailor   218 2008-10-14 06:22 wp-rdf.php
-rw-r--r--  1 technosailor technosailor   316 2008-05-25 15:50 wp-register.php
-rw-r--r--  1 technosailor technosailor   220 2008-10-14 06:22 wp-rss2.php
-rw-r--r--  1 technosailor technosailor   218 2008-10-14 06:22 wp-rss.php
-rw-r--r--  1 technosailor technosailor 21520 2009-06-28 00:44 wp-settings.php
-rw-r--r--  1 technosailor technosailor  3434 2008-05-25 15:50 wp-trackback.php
-rw-r--r--  1 technosailor technosailor 92522 2009-07-04 02:49 xmlrpc.php
```

In the left column, each directory listing has a 10-byte listing. Most of them look like
-rw-r--r--. In order to understand what this means, you need to understand Unix file
permissions.

Each bit is set to on or off. If it is off, it is represented by a -. If it is on, it is represented by an r
(for read), w (for write), or x (for execute). The first byte is set to d (for directory) when it is on.
After the first byte, the rest is divided into three grouping of three bytes each.

Each grouping represents a type of user on the system. The first one is the owner of the file. The
second one is the group that owns the file. The group usually consists of just the owner of the file,
but could be different depending on configuration. The third grouping is the world, or anyone
who has access to the system.

Each of the three bits represent (in order): read, write, and execute. For most of the files in Listing 17.4, the permissions are set to the following:

- **Owner:** Read, Write
- **Group:** Read
- **World:** Read

Another way of looking at Unix permissions is numerically. Each grouping can be represented with an octal number (0–7). Each read byte is represented by the number 4, each write byte is represented by the number 2, and each execute byte is represented by the number 1. The sum of these bytes becomes a three-digit number representing the permission level for that file, as shown in Table 17.1.

TABLE 17.1

The Octal Number Permission System for Unix

	Owner	Group	World
Read	4	4	4
Write	2	2	2
Execute	1	1	1
Total	7	7	7

Web Resource

You can learn more about Unix file permissions at www.tech-faq.com/unix-file-permissions.shtml. ■

WordPress file permissions

With a basic understanding of file permissions in hand, you need to make some basic assumptions to understand a good WordPress file permission configuration.

- The .htaccess file does not ever need to be executable, but it does need to be writable by the Web server (for generating permalinks).
- The wp-content folder is where you keep your theme and plugins. It should be protected because someone with malicious intent could fool the Web server into injecting bad code and hacking your site. However, the wp-content folder does need some access because it needs to be able to upload images as well as perform auto-upgrades.

With these requirements in mind, follow these steps, whether via an FTP client or directly over SSH, to secure your WordPress installation:

1. **Set the permissions for every file and directory in WordPress to 644**. You can generally do this with one click or by using the –R flag, which means literally, "perform the operation recursively on all directories and files under here," with chmod on the command line.

Note
Files with 644 are readable and writable by you or any process using your system username. They are only readable for the group assigned to the file and to the world. ■

2. **Set the permission for wp-content/, wp-admin/, and wp-includes to 755**. These three directories need to be executable or the Web server can't traverse, or read, them.

3. **Set the permissions for all files in your active theme to 666**. This disables the capability to edit themes from within WordPress Admin but also means no one can hack your files from the outside in.

Summary

- WordPress maintains a fast release cycle between major updates (WordPress 2.7, 2.8, and so on) and security updates (2.8.1, 2.8.2, and so on).

- Upgrading WordPress with FTP is an older, sometimes more reliable, way of upgrading a blog. If the auto-upgrade feature doesn't work, or system configurations prevent it, you can upload WordPress manually and run the upgrade script.

- Recovering from a botched upgrade can take time, but I offer some possible debugging options.

- Data sanitization is a process that makes unknown, potentially harmful data safe. WordPress core already does this. Plugin developers and theme designers need to make sure they perform data sanitization as well.

- SQL injection can be avoided by using the database API. SQL injection is prevented by using core API functions when available and ensuring that the prepare() method from the database class is used when making raw SQL queries.

Caching Strategy to Ensure WordPress Scales

O ne big complaint from bloggers who have highly trafficked blogs is that WordPress doesn't *scale*. In fact, if you visit social networking sites like Digg.com, you will undoubtedly find people who talk about WordPress as being poorly written software that won't last online.

Out of the box, WordPress is effective for probably 99 percent of blogs with no additional work required. However, with a good, sound caching strategy, you can ensure that WordPress can scale to handle increasingly large amounts of traffic.

Typically, when looking at WordPress scaling requirements for clients, I consider three primary levels of caching: the software layer (WordPress), the core software layer (PHP and MySQL), and the infrastructure level (server hardware and network layout).

Implementing solutions in some or all of these caching "zones" may be enough to keep everything ticking along smoothly. But if you fail to put effective caching mechanisms into place before trying to sustain a major influx in traffic, you could encounter significant headaches down the road.

Understanding Caching

Caching is one of those things that is clear to most people on a conceptual level, but the actual nuts and bolts tend to be a bit evasive. In its simplest form, *caching* is a mechanism by which data of some sort is stored in some way so that the processes used to generate that data don't need to be repeated unless necessary.

A cache sits between a dynamic, generative process (for example, creating HTML [hypertext markup language] code, a MySQL query, and so on) and the requesting mechanism (for example, a browser, PHP, or processes in WordPress itself).

When data is dynamically generated and stored in a cache, it is given a "serial number" of sorts. This number is a key that is unique to a single stored bit of data. When that data *expires*, whether because a scheduled time has elapsed or because there is new data that replaces the old stale data, the cache *invalidates* the data and replaces it with a new set. This process is shown in Figure 18.1.

FIGURE 18.1

Caching involves requesting data and receiving data from a separate "storage" facility, if it is cached, or directly accessed from the dynamic data source, if cached data doesn't exist or has expired.

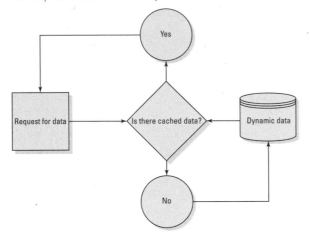

Depending on the cache, entire Web pages can be cached as a whole, or portions of a page can be cached and expired independently. In the WordPress model, however, it is not only front-end caching that takes place. Why should WordPress retrieve the same group of configuration options from the database every time a page loads if the data rarely changes? Why not just expire the cache when an option is changed and save all the additional queries that are unnecessary?

These are the theories behind caching in WordPress and what I examine in this chapter.

Using WordPress Caching Mechanisms

On the application level, WordPress has several options that can be used for caching. By default, WordPress has a built-in object cache that stores individual sets of data that are used throughout WordPress. For example, WordPress stores all the tags and categories that rarely change in a cache that is automatically expired when a new tag or category is added.

There are also a number of plugins, such as the WP Super Cache and Batcache plugins that are useful for implementing caching of a different variety directly from WordPress.

WordPress object cache

WordPress comes with an object cache built in. An *object cache* is an application level cache that stores sets of data, or "objects" of data such as a list of posts or links. There is no need to install or do anything specific to make this cache work. Plugin authors can utilize this object cache when developing plugins that retrieve data often from the database.

The key components of any cache is a mechanism to add a new set of data, delete the data, flush the whole cache (immediately expiring all cached data so it has to be re-generated), and retrieve the data. Some caching mechanisms, including the WordPress object cache, have a mechanism to replace an existing set of data, while other caching mechanisms replace data by expiring an old set and creating a new set with a new serial number.

The WordPress object cache has five functions (and a class if you so choose, but the functions just wrap around the related class methods) for all of these actions. Plugin developers should use these caching functions to ensure that the plugin "plays nice" with the rest of the system. Many of WordPress' own API functions have this object caching built in, and you don't need to do anything special to take advantage of it.

wp_cache_add()

If you want to cache data, you should use the function wp_cache_add(). This function takes two required arguments (an ID number and the data that is to be stored), a third that is entirely optional ($flag, which denotes a group of cached objects), and a fourth that is optional and unused, so it is unnecessary to include ($expire).

The first required argument of the wp_cache_add() function is an ID number. You can set this to whatever you want but make it unique. If the cache key (referred to in some caching systems as the *serial number*) is not unique, then using this function will replace the existing data. Please be very careful with how you use cache keys so as not to invalidate perfectly valid cached data.

If you wish to group sets of data, you can assign a group identifier, or $flag, as an optional third argument. Together, the $flag and the ID denotes a unique "address" from which to access cached data. The fourth argument, also optional, is not used in WordPress yet, but presumably will be at some point.

Tip
Just like plugins, cache keys should have their own namespace — that is, a naming convention that is unique and will never duplicate core WordPress naming conventions or the naming conventions of other cache keys. Cache keys should also have their own naming conventions. Consider something like an abbreviation for the plugin plus your initials, or something similar. Appending a Unix timestamp (generated with PHP's time() function) is a good way to ensure a cache key is entirely unique given the current Unix timestamp increments every second. ■

The second required argument is the data that is going to be stored. This data can be an integer, string, array, object, or any data type you wish.

If you want to provide your data with its own namespace — say, "myplugin" — you can also provide a unique group name. This will ensure that, even if there is another cache dataset with an identical cache key, it will not conflict with your data unless both have the same group name.

Listing 18.1 illustrates the use of the `wp_cache_add()` function. The example retrieves a list of authors (each one is an object) and stores the author data in an array, then adds it to a group called `aaronbrazell` with the key `all_contributing_authors`.

LISTING 18.1

The wp_cache_add() function

```
$main_authors = array( get_userdata(1), get_userdata(10), get_userdata(7) );
wp_cache_add( 'all_contributing_authors', $main_authors, 'aaronbrazell' );
```

wp_cache_delete()

Like adding new data to the object cache, you can delete the data from the cache. This is, essentially, the same process of expiring, or invalidating, the data. To remove data, you must use `wp_cache_delete()` and provide a cache key. If you are using cache groups, you should provide the name of the group as the second argument. Omitting a group name makes WordPress assume the cache key is located in a group called default. Listing 18.2 demonstrates how you would remove a cache key from the WordPress object cache.

LISTING 18.2

The wp_cache_delete() function

```
$main_authors = array( get_userdata(1), get_userdata(10), get_userdata(7) );
wp_cache_add( 'all_contributing_authors', $main_authors, 'aaronbrazell' );
wp_cache_delete( 'all_contributing_authors', 'aaronbrazell' );
```

wp_cache_get()

Retrieving cache data is also straightforward. When retrieving data, if the function misses (there is no data cached with the given cache key and group), you will need to retrieve the data directly from the database. In this case, you should probably add the dynamically retrieved data as a newly cached data set. To retrieve data from cache, use the `wp_cache_get()` function, which takes a required cache key ID and an optional cache group name. Listing 18.3 demonstrates the use of the `wp_cache_get()` function to retrieve data from the cache.

LISTING 18.3

The wp_cache_get() function

```
if( !$authors = wp_cache_get( 'all_contributing_authors', 'aaronbrazell' ) )
{
     $authors = get_contributing_authors();
}
```

wp_cache_replace()

The fourth cache mechanism in WordPress is the wp_cache_replace() function. It is almost identical to the wp_cache_add() function except that, if the data doesn't exist, it will return false. If you wish to add data to the cache even if it doesn't exist, use the wp_cache_add() function. If, however, the cached data already exists, then wp_cache_replace() will replace the existing data with your new data. The function takes the exact same arguments as the wp_cache_add() function. Listing 18.4 demonstrates the use of the wp_cache_replace() function.

LISTING 18.4

The wp_cache_replace() function

```
$main_authors = array( get_userdata(1), get_userdata(10), get_userdata(7) );
if( !wp_cache_replace( 'all_contributing_authors', $main_authors,
    'aaronbrazell' ) )
{
     echo 'I cannot replace a cache item that doesn't already exist.';
}
else
{
     echo 'Okay, the data has been replaced.';
}
```

wp_cache_flush()

The fifth and final mechanism for dealing with the WordPress object cache is wp_cache_flush(). In caching lingo, *flushing a cache* means that you erase (invalidate or expire) all data currently cached. This has the effect of forcing WordPress to do a "hard" reset on all data and reload it all dynamically. Though the flush happens immediately, the repopulation of cached data occurs at the time the dataset is re-requested. Little used data sets can take awhile to be re-generated.

The wp_cache_flush() function does not take any arguments, and is the equivalent of a reset button. It should be used with care on database-intensive sites (sites with a lot of traffic, multiple loops, and so on). See Listing 18.5 for an example.

LISTING 18.5

The wp_cache_flush() function

```
$main_authors = array( get_userdata(1), get_userdata(10), get_userdata(7) );
wp_cache_add( 'all_contributing_authors', $main_authors, 'aaronbrazell' );
if( wp_cache_flush() )
{
    echo 'The cache has been expired. There is nothing left to retrieve
  until data has been re-populated. Cache data will be repopulated object
  by object as it is requested.';
}
```

The WP Super Cache plugin

The WP Super Cache plugin is high on the list of plugins I recommend. The plugin performs full page caching. It is the successor to the popular WP Cache plugin and can operate in legacy WP Cache mode, or in the new WP Super Cache mode. The difference between the WP Cache mode and WP Super Cache mode, besides the fact that WP Cache mode is called Half On mode, is that WP Cache contains code that allows authors to designate dynamic portions of the page while WP Super Cache mode will invoke a special caching method for anonymous users that is completely static, without even loading PHP for a cache hit.

Web Resource

The WP Super Cache plugin is available for free at `http://wordpress.org/extend/plugins/` `wp-super-cache/`. ■

Whenever a blog goes through a spike in traffic, the best remedy is to simply load static HTML instead of dynamically generated content. Whenever dynamic content is loaded, Apache has to load the entire overhead of PHP to generate a page. In addition to the overhead of loading PHP on a pageload, there are likely multiple requests to MySQL.

Add all of this together, in addition to the computational aspects of generating a dynamic page, and it becomes clear that, while dynamically generated content is fast, a significant footprint is required to make a page. However, static HTML can simply be served back to the browser; the "cost" of rendering that page is isolated, mainly, to the browser and does not affect the server.

I'll talk about this aspect of caching when I discuss PHP caching later in this chapter, but the principle of static versus dynamic and server impact is important to understand for file caching.

The WP Super Cache plugin has a variety of different options. If you've never configured it before, you will need to perform some manual steps to get it to work properly:

1. **Edit your wp-config.php file and add define('WP_CACHE', true); below the WPLANG definition.** This should look similar to:

   ```
   define ('WPLANG', '');
   ```

2. **Make your wp-content/ folder writable.** You can do this by running `chmod 755 wp-content` via SSH (Secure Shell) from your WordPress document root. You can also do this using your FTP client.

3. **Ensure that a wp-cache-config.php exists in your wp-content/ folder.** The Super Cache plugin will try to automatically create this. If something goes wrong, copy `wp-cache-config-sample.php` from the plugin archive into the `wp-content/` folder.

4. **Ensure that an advanced-cache.php exists in your wp-content/ folder.** If it doesn't, copy it from the plugin archive into the `wp-content/` folder.

The first time you load the Super Cache Admin page (see Figure 18.2), if any of these configuration settings have not been done, it will alert you and prompt you with instructions on how to remedy the situation. Once the system configuration is set up properly, you will be able to enter the Admin panel and a new folder will be created on your filesystem that is located at `/wp-content/cache/supercache/`.

Note

If you already have a cache folder because of a different plugin or because you have used this plugin before, make sure it is writable as well. If it is not writable, the WP Super Cache plugin won't be able to create the requisite `supercache/` folder. ■

FIGURE 18.2

The WP Super Cache plugin Admin panel

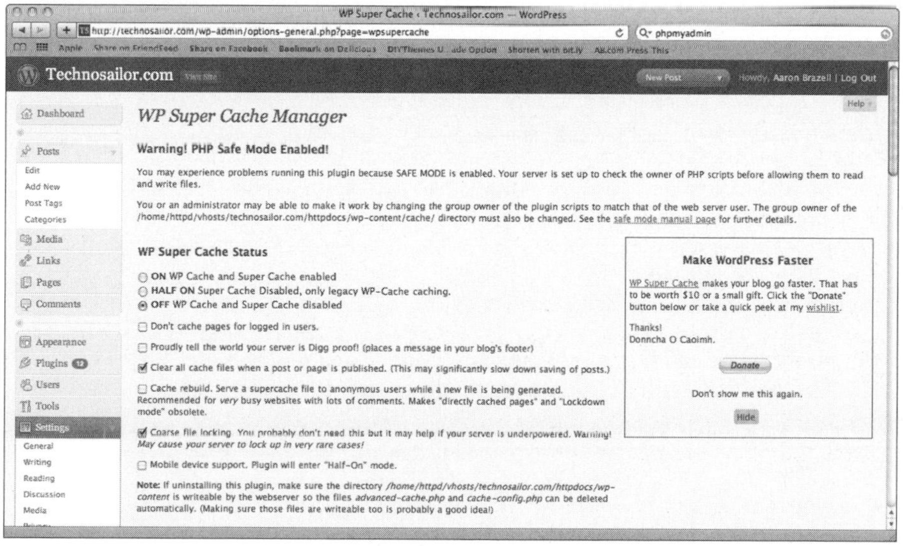

The configuration options for the WP Super Cache plugin vary. The first option designates whether the cache is Off, Half On (WP Cache and related dynamic content loading code), or On

(WP Cache and WP Super Cache functionality). Additionally, you can choose whether to disable caching for logged in users (if you have open registration, you might consider this), whether to flush the cache when a post or page is published, and whether to enable mobile support (Half On caching for mobile devices).

From the Admin panel, you can manually flush the contents of the cache (you can also do this from the dark grey drop-down menu at the top right of the WordPress Admin) by clicking the Delete Expired button. As noted below this button, the cache default expiry time is 3,600 seconds, or 1 hour.

You can also "whitelist" or "blacklist" strings; this way, if the string appears in a URL, it doesn't get cached or explicitly gets cached. This gives you the possibility to have granular control over the caching routines and possibly save some server processing time in the long run.

Finally, for really high traffic blogs, particularly ones that get huge surges of traffic from time to time, you may consider Lockdown mode. Lockdown mode ensures that a page is cached and is not flushed until it expires.

When the cache is not in Lockdown mode, certain activity (like approved comments on a cached post) will flush the cache and regenerate the page. While this is a good way to use the plugin for the most part, you don't want to have a situation where comments flood into a busy post and every comment flushes the cache and forces a regeneration of the cached page. This scenario might defeat the purpose of the plugin and the onslaught of traffic could bring your site down.

Memcached and the Batcache plugin

Another type of caching that is extremely useful in setups where more than one server is involved is Memcached. Unlike many systems, Memcached doesn't use file or database-style caching. Instead, it uses transient in-memory storage. Though it is entirely possible to use Memcached on a single server, it is most useful when shared among multiple web servers.

The Batcache plugin operates similarly to the WP Super Cache plugin but relies on an auto-expiring object cache backend (the Memcached backend being the obvious choice) and doesn't have quite the same performance boost (but does have benefits in some situations). Though the scope of Memcached installation is limited in this book, it is not hard to get up and running.

To enable Memcached object caching in WordPress, follow these steps:

1. **Install Memcached on all servers you wish to use.** You can download it from `http://danga.com:80/memcached/`.

2. **Install the memcache PECL module from** `http://pecl.php.net/package/memcache`.

3. **Install Ryan's Memcached Backend available from** `http://svn.wp-plugins.org/memcached/trunk/`.

Once the system prerequisites are set, install the Batcache plugin via the plugin installer in WordPress Admin or by downloading and uploading via FTP/SFTP (file transfer protocol/secure file transfer protocol).

Web Resource

The Batcache plugin can be downloaded from the WordPress Plugin Directory at `http://wordpress.org/extend/plugins/batcache/.` ■

Regardless of how you install the plugin, you will still need to log in to the filesystem via FTP/SFTP or over SSH and move the advanced-cache.php file to your `wp-content/` folder.

Batcache operates differently that WP Super Cache in that it doesn't cache every load. It only caches anonymous traffic, and only for URLs that have received three or more hits within 2 minutes. URLs that achieve those three hits within 2 minutes will have their output "frozen" and served from Memcached for 5 minutes. In this way, it focuses caching on URLs that are likely to be served up multiple times to anonymous viewers, and doesn't waste time caching pages that will never be served again. These "trigger" numbers are all configurable within the plugin's source code.

Note

Astute readers will notice that `advanced-cache.php` **is used by both WP Super Cache and Batcache. Unfortunately, you can only have one plugin or the other as they serve the same purpose.** ■

Optimizing PHP with Opcode Caching

Beyond the caching mechanisms that you can implement from the WordPress side, you also have a couple options for optimizing and caching PHP. Opcode caches reduces the PHP overhead that is required to run PHP scripts. Sometimes PHP opcode caches are referred to as *PHP accelerators*.

PHP is different than other languages like C++ or Java because it is a scripting language and is not precompiled. The system requires compiled code (otherwise known as opcode) to execute, and while other languages are compiled by the developer and are executable at any times, PHP is compiled on the fly. In other words, PHP is written and when it is requested, all of the required libraries and code are pulled into the page and compiled at run time.

Opcode caches reduce the load and overhead on a server by caching this compiled code for future use.

eAccelerator

I think the eAccelerator is the best PHP opcode cache currently available because, among other things, it is PHP 5–compatible. Because WordPress doesn't require PHP 5, you can use other opcode caches as well; however, eAccelerator has had the best results in my experience.

eAccelerator is going to increase the performance of your server by various amounts. For example, a test against my server without eAccelerator shows an almost 220 percent performance difference. Using Apache's tool, `ab`, to benchmark performance, I've run a test that hits the server with 1,000 requests. Without eAccelerator, these requests took 142 seconds (or nearly 2.5 minutes) to complete (see Listing 18.6).

LISTING 18.6

An Apache benchmark of a server without eAccelerator

```
[root@server1 ~]# ab -n1000 -c10 http://technosailor.com/
This is ApacheBench, Version 2.0.40-dev <$Revision: 1.146 $> apache-2.0
Copyright 1996 Adam Twiss, Zeus Technology Ltd, http://www.zeustech.net/
Copyright 2006 The Apache Software Foundation, http://www.apache.org/
Benchmarking technosailor.com (be patient)
Completed 100 requests
Completed 200 requests
Completed 300 requests
Completed 400 requests
Completed 500 requests
Completed 600 requests
Completed 700 requests
Completed 800 requests
Completed 900 requests
Finished 1000 requests


Server Software:        Apache/2.2.3
Server Hostname:        technosailor.com
Server Port:            80
Document Path:          /
Document Length:        39462 bytes
Concurrency Level:      10
Time taken for tests:   142.621772 seconds
Complete requests:      1000
Failed requests:        0
Write errors:           0
Total transferred:      39910000 bytes
HTML transferred:       39462000 bytes
Requests per second:    7.01 [#/sec] (mean)
Time per request:       1426.218 [ms] (mean)
Time per request:       142.622 [ms] (mean, across all concurrent requests)
Transfer rate:          273.27 [Kbytes/sec] received
Connection Times (ms)
              min  mean[+/-sd] median   max
Connect:        0    0   0.1      0       1
Processing:   534 1421 496.2   1345    4539
Waiting:      362  893 318.6    863    4373
Total:        534 1421 496.2   1345    4539
Percentage of the requests served within a certain time (ms)
   50%    1345
   66%    1538
   75%    1661
   80%    1762
   90%    2037
   95%    2324
```

```
 98%    2686
 99%    3042
100%    4539 (longest request)
```

By contrast, the same server with eAccelerator enabled reduces that test time, as demonstrated in Listing 18.7, to 63 seconds, or just over one minute.

LISTING 18.7

The same server as in Listing 18.6 shows a more than 200 percent bonus increase with eAccelerator

```
[root@server1 ~]# ab -n1000 -c10 http://technosailor.com/
This is ApacheBench, Version 2.0.40-dev <$Revision: 1.146 $> apache-2.0
Copyright 1996 Adam Twiss, Zeus Technology Ltd, http://www.zeustech.net/
Copyright 2006 The Apache Software Foundation, http://www.apache.org/
Benchmarking technosailor.com (be patient)
Completed 100 requests
Completed 200 requests
Completed 300 requests
Completed 400 requests
Completed 500 requests
Completed 600 requests
Completed 700 requests
Completed 800 requests
Completed 900 requests
Finished 1000 requests


Server Software:        Apache/2.2.3
Server Hostname:        technosailor.com
Server Port:            80
Document Path:          /
Document Length:        39462 bytes
Concurrency Level:      10
Time taken for tests:   63.256933 seconds
Complete requests:      1000
Failed requests:        0
Write errors:           0
Total transferred:      39910000 bytes
HTML transferred:       39462000 bytes
Requests per second:    15.81 [#/sec] (mean)
Time per request:       632.569 [ms] (mean)
Time per request:       63.257 [ms] (mean, across all concurrent requests)
Transfer rate:          616.12 [Kbytes/sec] received
Connection Times (ms)
```

continued

LISTING 18.7   *(continued)*

```
               min   mean[+/-sd] median    max
Connect:         0     0   0.0       0        0
Processing:    233   630 355.4     587     6817
Waiting:        88   284 208.4     269     5334
Total:         233   630 355.4     587     6817
Percentage of the requests served within a certain time (ms)
   50%    587
   66%    676
   75%    735
   80%    767
   90%    905
   95%   1055
   98%   1242
   99%   1575
  100%   6817 (longest request)
```

APC

A second popular opcode cache that is used in the WordPress community is APC. APC, which stands for Alternative PHP Cache, is available as a PECL (PHP Extension Community Library) install.

Cross-Reference

Installation of APC and eAccelerator is described in Chapter 2. ∎

APC is a close second to eAccelerator because its performance isn't quite as good. Still, with a 68-second request time, the performance boost is competitive (see Listing 18.8).

LISTING 18.8

APC gains PHP a nearly 200 percent boost in performance

```
[root@server 1 ~]# ab -n1000 -c10 http://technosailor.com/
This is ApacheBench, Version 2.0.40-dev <$Revision: 1.146 $> apache-2.0
Copyright 1996 Adam Twiss, Zeus Technology Ltd, http://www.zeustech.net/
Copyright 2006 The Apache Software Foundation, http://www.apache.org/
Benchmarking technosailor.com (be patient)
Completed 100 requests
Completed 200 requests
Completed 300 requests
Completed 400 requests
Completed 500 requests
Completed 600 requests
```

```
Completed 700 requests
Completed 800 requests
Completed 900 requests
Finished 1000 requests

Server Software:        Apache/2.2.3
Server Hostname:        technosailor.com
Server Port:            80
Document Path:          /
Document Length:        39462 bytes
Concurrency Level:      10
Time taken for tests:   68.421200 seconds
Complete requests:      1000
Failed requests:        0
Write errors:           0
Total transferred:      39910000 bytes
HTML transferred:       39462000 bytes
Requests per second:    14.62 [#/sec] (mean)
Time per request:       684.212 [ms] (mean)
Time per request:       68.421 [ms] (mean, across all concurrent requests)
Transfer rate:          569.62 [Kbytes/sec] received
Connection Times (ms)
             min   mean[+/-sd] median   max
Connect:       0     0    2.2       0      26
Processing:  238   681  509.5     583    8080
Waiting:      92   336  351.5     282    4465
Total:       238   681  509.6     583    8080
Percentage of the requests served within a certain time (ms)
  50%    583
  66%    693
  75%    772
  80%    827
  90%   1039
  95%   1227
  98%   1672
  99%   3282
 100%   8080 (longest request)
```

Tip

WordPress core developer and the technical editor of this book, Mark Jaquith, experienced some problems using WP Super Cache with APC. The solution he ultimately arrived at involves editing the APC configuration settings to set `apc.filters = wp-cache-config`. Doing this eliminates the `wp-cache-config.php` and `wp-cache-config-sample.php` from being cached by APC, and prevents system white screens. For more information, see Mark's blog post at `http://markjaquith.wordpress.com/2006/02/13/adventures-with-wp-cache2-apc/`. ■

Caching MySQL with HyperDB and the Query Cache

Now that you've addressed static pages and file system caching with WP Super Cache and the WordPress object cache, as well as optimizing PHP with opcode caching tools like eAccelerator and APC, there is another area where performance can be improved: MySQL.

MySQL, of course, is the database that runs WordPress. Most of the data stored in MySQL does not change all that often. The terms tables rarely change unless you add, edit, or delete a category or tag. The users table might change if you have open registration on your blog, but it is still fairly static and only updated when a user changes her password or other user settings. Posts and pages are updated frequently, but unless you're posting once a minute, it's likely this data can be cached as well. Still, finding ways to cache MySQL data can increase performance, particularly on high-traffic sites.

Cross-Reference
The WordPress database class is described in detail in Chapter 7. ■

MySQL query cache

Fortunately, MySQL comes with a built-in query cache that saves queries and their resulting datasets for use later. Though the query cache is disabled by default, enabling it is elementary if you have root access to your server.

You enable the query cache simply by editing or adding the lines shown in Listing 18.9 to your MySQL configuration file (usually stored in /etc/my.cnf).

LISTING 18.9

Enable the Query cache by adding these lines to your MySQL configuration

```
query_cache_type   = 1
query_cache_limit  = 1M
query_cache_size   = 32M
```

The query_cache_type designates whether the query cache is on (1), off (0), or "on demand" (2) — a designation that triggers the cache from within SQL statements.

The query_cache_limit sets a limit on what the maximum cached result can be. In this case, MySQL will not cache any result set greater than 1M.

The `query_cache_size` tells MySQL how much data can be included in the cache. WordPress should operate perfectly fine with the designated cache settings.

HyperDB

A second level of MySQL caching, though not truly a cache, is HyperDB. HyperDB allows WordPress to be *sharded*, or split across multiple MySQL databases and even across multiple data centers and networks. It is not so much of a cache as it is an extreme scaling tactic. It is the kind of tool that is used only for very large networks.

HyperDB is an open source database class that is modified from the default WordPress database class to allow sharding. By default, WordPress will use the `wp-includes/wp-db.php` file for instantiating the database object. However, WordPress is also built so that if a `db.php` file were added to the `wp-includes/` folder, this alternative database class would be used instead. Therefore, you could build a database class (modeled after the WordPress database class) to interact with other database systems like Oracle or PostgreSQL. The same methodology could be employed to use a variety of MySQL servers, all optimized to do different things.

Note

When it comes to sharding MySQL, you can certainly optimize tables to perform better for different types of queries. You can shard reads across multiple databases. However, you can't shard writes. Some kind of replication process still needs to happen to keep all of the database instances that will be read from in sync. ■

HyperDB, which can be downloaded via SVN from `http://svn.wp-plugins.org/hyperdb/trunk/`, is configured in two phases. The first phase is simply uploading `db.php` to the `wp-includes/` folder. This is necessary but does not change the behavior of WordPress yet.

To configure HyperDB, which is the second phase, follow these three steps:

1. Upload `db-settings.php` to the WordPress root.
2. Edit `db-settings.php` and configure for your environment. There is no hard-and-fast way to do this because your infrastructure will be unique to you. If you have a network large enough to need HyperDB, you probably also have a competent systems administrator who can understand the requirements outlined in the comments of this file.
3. Add require('db-settings.php'); near the top of your `wp-config.php` file.

Harnessing the "Cloud"

Media storage is the final area where you can make performance enhancements. As you dive into file types, you'll discover that PHP files are different than HTML files, which are different than binary files, such as images. Each binary file can be compressed or decompressed, but each one has its own overhead. In addition, images that are compressed gain far less "boost" than text files like HTML. Therefore, it makes sense that certain types of files can be optimized certain ways. Or rather, servers and storage facilities can be optimized to specifically serve particular content types such as images, video, or strictly HTML.

One option to consider is cloud-based computing. I'm not a fan of using cloud-based computing for everything. There is a movement to take everything, including applications, into "the cloud" but often redundancy and latency cause other problems.

Nonetheless, the cloud can be very effective for content types that don't need the computing power and immediacy that WordPress does. For this, solutions such as Amazon S3 (Simple Storage Service) cloud storage provides ample image storage. Installing the Amazon S3 for WordPress plugin (available at `http://wordpress.org/extend/plugins/tantan-s3/`) effectively replaces local media storage with S3 media storage.

Another option is to store content on a system level. You could create a "virtual directory" out of your standard WordPress `wp-content/uploads/` directory that maps to the Amazon S3 service. There will be latency, and it won't be speedy, but then you are serving images, not executing and compiling PHP. There's room to wiggle here.

Cloud Computing Does Not Spell the End for Common Sense IT Management

In 2008, during an Internet-wide debacle stemming from a prolonged Amazon S3 outage, I wrote this extremely snarky post on my blog. The post was the result of my experience in enterprise IT and as the Director of Technology for a WordPress-powered blog network. I share it here to emphasize the importance of redundancy and to make the point that no single one of these solutions, by themselves, will save you. Reliance on any third party for any mission-critical functionality is a recipe for disaster.

Sometimes I think I might be the only one who retains common sense. Really. At least in the area of IT Management. Though we had our share of growing pains at b5media, the knowledge gained from working in an enterprise environment at Northrop Grumman was only accentuated by my tenure as the Director of Technology at b5media.

Unfortunately, some common best-use practices in developing infrastructure are often put aside by those with shiny object syndrome surrounding "cloud computing."

Let me explain.

You may have noticed a severe hampering of many Internet services over the weekend. The culprit was a rare, but yet heavy-duty, outage of Amazon S3 (Simple Storage Service) cloud storage. S3 is used by many companies, including Twitter, WordPress.com, FriendFeed, and SmugMug, to name a few. Even more individuals are using S3 for online data backup or for small projects requiring always-on virtual disk space. Startups often use S3 due to the "always on" storage, defacto CDN, and the inexpensive nature of the service ... it really is cheap!

And that's good. I'm a fan of using the cheapest, most reliable service for anything. Whatever gets you to the next level quickest and with as little output of dollars is good in my book, for the same reason I'm a fan of prototyping ideas in Ruby on Rails (but to be clear, after the prototype, build on something more reliable and capable of handling multi-threaded processes, kthxbai.)

However, sound IT management practice says that there should never be a single point of failure. Ever. Take a step back and map out the infrastructure. If you see any place where there's only one of those connecting lines between major resource A and major resource B, start looking there for bottlenecks and potential company-sinking aggravation.

Thus was the case for many companies using S3. Depending on the use of S3, and if the companies had failover to other caches, some companies were affected more than others. Twitter, for instance, uses S3 for avatar storage but had no other "cold cache" for that data rendering a service without user images — bad, but not deadly.

SmugMug shrugged the whole thing off (which is a far cry from the disastrous admission that "hot cache" was used very little when Amazon went down back in February), which I thought was a bit odd. Their entire company revolves around hosted photos on Amazon S3 and they simply shrugged off an 8-hour outage as okay "because everyone goes down once in awhile." Yeah, and occasionally people get mugged in dark city streets, but as long as it's not me, it's okay! Maybe it was the fact that the outage occurred on a Sunday. Who knows? To me, this sort of outage rages as a 9.5/10 on the critical scale. Their entire business is wrapped up in S3 storage with no failover. For perspective, one 8-hour outage in July constitutes 98.9 percent uptime — a far cry from five 9's (99.999 percent) which is minimal mitigation of risk in enterprise mission-critical services.

WordPress.com, as always, comes through as a shining example of a company who economically benefits from the use of S3 as a cold cache and not primary access or "warm cache."

Let me stop and provide some definition. Warm (or hot) cache is always preferable to cold cache. It is data that has been loaded into memory or a more reasonably accessible location — but typically memory. Cold cache is filebased storage of cached data. It is less frequently accessed because access only occurs if warm cache data has expired or doesn't exist.

WordPress.com has multiple levels of caching because they are smart and understand the basic premise of eliminating single point of failure. Image data is primarily accessed over their server cluster via a CDN; however, S3 is used as a cold cache. With the collapse of S3 over the weekend, WordPress.com, from my checking, remained unaffected.

This is the basic principle of IT enterprise computing that is lost on so much of the "web world." If companies have built and scaled (particularly if they have scaled!) and rely on S3 with no failover, shame on them. Does it give Amazon a black eye? Absolutely. However, at the end of the day, SmugMug, WordPress.com, Friendfeed, Twitter, and all the other companies utilizing S3 answer to their customers and do not have the luxury of pointing the finger at Amazon. If their business is negatively affected, they have no one to blame but themselves. The companies who understood this planned accordingly and were not negatively affected by the S3 outage. Those who didn't were left, well, holding the bag.

A third option for high capacity sites is to use a third-party content delivery network (CDN). CDNs tend to be very reliable, but it's also recommended that you keep a cold cache locally that you can fall back on in the case of a failure or outage. CDNs are cloud-based storage solutions most often used with high-bandwidth video. Think of them like a dedicated private Internet because they are global, extremely fast, and do not suffer from the same bandwidth problems you might experience when dealing with the regular Internet everyone uses.

Many CDN companies exist, and the most common include Limelight, Akamai, and Level3 Communications. With a plugin like MyCDN (`http://wordpress.org/extend/plugins/my-cdn/`), you can "seed" the CDN once with all of your existing images, stylesheets, and so on, and then point WordPress in the right direction to retrieve data that is now hosted in the cloud. The plugin will handle redirecting all internal links so images won't be broken.

Summary

- The concept of caching is simple: If WordPress doesn't have to make additional requests for information, because it has made these requests previously and the data is stored elsewhere for re-use, it can reduce the load on the system.

- WordPress caching can be done with the internal object cache or with a plugin like WP Super Cache (file-based caching) or Batcache (Memory/Memcached-based caching).

- Opcode caches stored runtime-compiled PHP for future use, saving PHP the need to recompile on every page load.

- Opcode caches like eAccelerator and APC gain PHP a 200 percent boost in performance.

- MySQL caching with query cache prevents MySQL from having to retrieve the same data more than once. It can be enabled with only three lines in the configuration file.

- HyperDB enables large, distributed networks based on WordPress to distribute or share across multiple server or data centers.

- Using Amazon S3 (Simple Storage Service) cloud storage provides an ample way to serve data from the cloud, but it should be done with redundancy and failover in mind.

- Content delivery networks provide an opportunity for large content networks to offload rich media to a cloud-based, high-speed, low-latency dedicated network not unlike the Internet itself.

Understanding WordPress Roles and Capabilities

WordPress has its own authentication system. It is organized in a series of permissions, called *Capabilities*, which are subsequently bundled into groups that are called *Roles*.

This chapter assesses the out-of-the-box Capabilities and Roles that WordPress provides, and presents an overview of how you might use or modify these Roles in an editorial or development workflow.

Note
The WordPress Role and Capability system is due for an overhaul — something that seems to be on track for a WordPress 3.0 release. ■

Looking at WordPress Roles and Capabilities

The core of the WordPress permission and authentication system is Capabilities. The WordPress application programming interface (API) and internal permission structure that allows or disallows access to portions of the system uses Capabilities. For example, the `delete_page` capability is, as expected, used to determine whether an authenticated user has the permission to delete a page.

By default, the main user of a WordPress blog (usually with the username *admin*) is the Administrator. If you have other users, you can set their respective roles when you create their logins (see Figure 19.1), or on their user profile (see Figure 19.2). If you allow anyone to sign up for an account, you can set the default role on the General Settings page.

FIGURE 19.1

When creating users manually, you can designate the roles they are to be assigned.

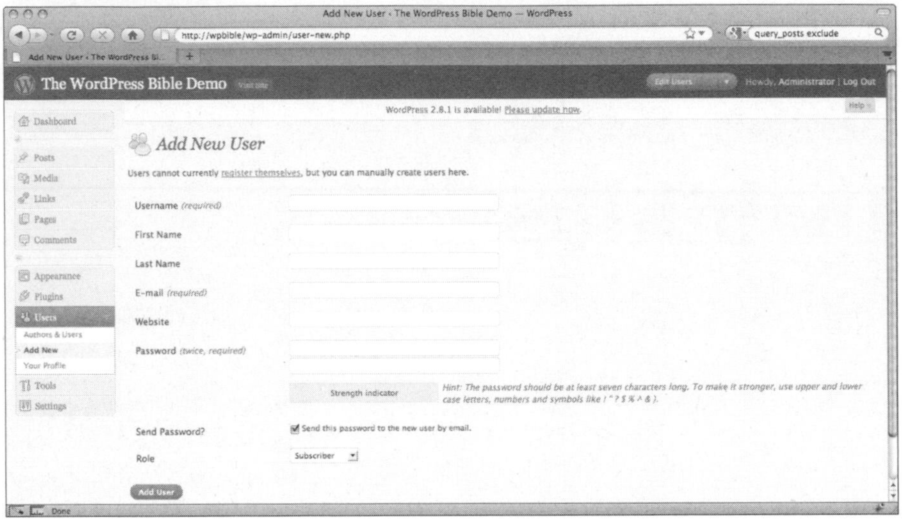

Tip

If you allow open registration on your blog, I recommend keeping the default user role set to Subscriber. If you solicit articles openly but don't want to worry about micromanaging the content solicitation process, consider Contributor as the default role. A user with the Subscriber role does not have access to the Write Post screen, and a user with the Contributor role cannot publish — Contributors can only publish to a Pending Review state. ∎

FIGURE 19.2

The User profile screen enables you to update a WordPress user's profile and manually set her assigned role.

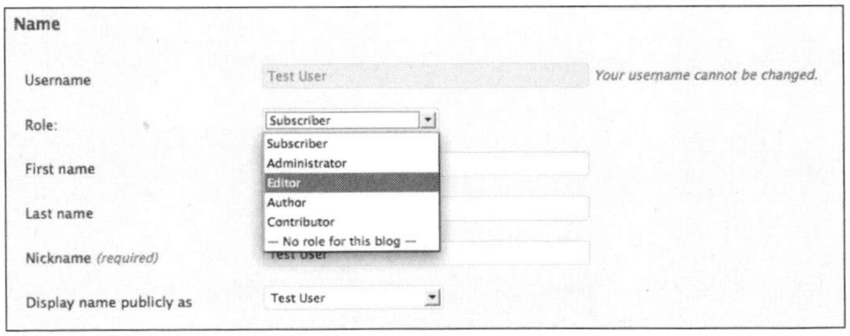

Plugin developers often use these Capability checks to allow access to administrative pages inside the WordPress Admin. The logic, for example, may look something like this:

- If a user can activate plugins (`activate_plugin`), give the user access to the plugin configuration page.

- If a user can edit someone else's post (`edit_others_post`), change the Cascading Style Sheet (CSS) background color of other user's posts on the edit posts page to provide a visual cue.

- If a user can post all hypertext markup language (HTML) safely (`unfiltered_html`), create an iframe button in the TinyMCE rich text editor toolbox.

Table 19.1 lists the WordPress default Capabilities for Subscribers, Contributors, Authors, Editors, and Administrators.

In general, single-user blogs will have a single username that is an Admin; however, in multi-user blogs, including those powered by WordPress MU, a greater degree of control and authority should be granted to other Contributors.

For example, a large news blog might have a typical "newsroom" type editorial flow. The owner of the blog might be an Admin and responsible for the business decisions around a blog. As a result, this person is able to control the theme that the blog uses as well as plugins and options that determine the configuration of the site. The Content Editor is responsible for all the authors, the editorial calendar, and the content deadlines on the site. As a result, this person would have the Editor role.

TABLE 19.1

Default Roles and Capabilities

Role Name	Definition	Capabilities
Subscriber	Subscribers are members only. They have no administrative Capabilities and are only able to keep and maintain a profile. Subscriber is a good role to provide if, for example, you want to make "premium" content available.	Read level_0
Contributor	Contributors also have a minimal amount of permission within the blog. Contributor is a good default role when community contribution of articles is desired.	edit_posts level_1 All Subscriber Capabilities
Author	The Author role is for autonomous content publishers. Authors have the Capabilities to contribute new content, review, and edit their own content and submit to an Editor for review. The Author role is akin to the level of authority provided to a newspaper beat writer.	upload_files edit_posts edit_published_posts publish_posts level_2 All Subscriber and Contributor Capabilities

continued

TABLE 19.1	*(continued)*	
Role Name	**Definition**	**Capabilities**
Editor	As the senior role in a typical content publication workflow, the Editor is the role that manages and oversees all the content production of a site. As such, the Editor has Capabilities suited to all content production workflows, including editing content that others have created.	moderate_comments manage_categories manage_links unfiltered_html edit_others_posts edit_pages level_3 level_4 level_5 level_6 level_7 All Subscriber, Contributor, and Author Capabilities
Administrator	Administrators control all aspects of a site. Not only does the editorial workflow fall under their wings, but also all aspects of management and configuration, including themes and plugins, as well.	switch_themes edit_themes activate_plugins edit_users edit_files manage_options import level_8 level_9 level_10 All Subscriber, Contributor, Author, and Editor Capabilities

Authors can publish and edit their own posts, but cannot do anything to any content other than their own.

Contributors might be utilized in a stricter editorial workflow, when all posts must go through an Editor or Admin before being published.

Tip

Authors and Contributors who plan to use popular content that is presented as embeddable code or JavaScript will need to be given the `unfiltered_html` **capability with a plugin like the Role Manager plugin. WordPress strips HTML that can be used for malicious content out of content published by untrusted users. Only Editor and Admin Roles have the** `unfiltered_html` **capability out of the box.**

An even better solution is to use a plugin that uses "shortcodes" to allow untrusted users to insert a string of text that serves as a placeholder and expands into trusted code that might be malicious if posted directly. ■

Web Resource

Smashing Magazine has a fantastic resource on how plugin developers can make "shortcodes" that are available for users to utilize when creating content. Go to `www.smashingmagazine.com/2009/02/02/` `mastering-wordpress-shortcodes.` ∎

Note

WordPress 2.9 now supports oEmbed, a technology that allows Web sites to "auto-discover" settings for embed code from sites that provide rich content like video or other embeds. In order for oEmbed to work, the provisioning site must be an oEmbed provider. More information on this new feature can be found at `www.` `viper007bond.com/2009/10/13/easy-embeds-for-wordpress-2-point-9/.` ∎

User levels

A legacy item from previous versions of WordPress, *user levels* are still used often with plugins and permission configuration. User levels, signified by the numbers zero through ten, have a rough breakdown similar to the user roles model adopted in more recent versions of WordPress (2.0 and later). User levels are now stored in the wp_usermeta table as metadata. They are mainly kept active for backwards compatibility and should not be used when creating a new plugin. Table 19.2 lists the user role/user level correspondence.

TABLE 19.2

User Role to User Level Mapping

User Role	User Level
Subscriber	0
Contributor	1
Author	2
	3
	4
Editor	5
	6
	7
Administrator	8
	9
	10

Caution

Approach plugins that use anything related to user levels cautiously because they might be potentially incompatible with future versions of WordPress. Because user levels were deprecated in WordPress 2.0, plugins falling into this category should constitute a red flag pertaining to plugin security, compatibility, or maintenance from the plugin author. It is recommended you avoid using these plugins at all cost. ■

Adding and removing custom capabilities

It is entirely possible to add or remove custom capabilities to the WordPress system. In fact, this method is employed by the Custom Role Manager plugin. However, for alternative implementations, plugin authors can use the add_cap() and remove_cap() methods provided by the WP_Roles class. WordPress provides a global object, $wp_roles, that can be used for this. This method takes two required arguments: $role, which consists of a role name like "administrator" or "author", and $capability, which is a unique handle identifying the capability (see Listing 19.1).

The third optional argument is $grant and is True by default. This third argument essentially lets WordPress know that this is a positive capability and not a denial of the capability. The ability to deny a user a specific capability is likely to go away in a future version of WordPress, and should not be used.

LISTING 19.1

Using add_cap() and remove_cap() as a function or method

```
// Add a new capability "wpb_plugin-x_manage" for editors
$wp_roles->add_cap( 'editor', 'wpb_plugin-x_manage' );
// Removes a capability "wpb_plugin-x_manage" for editors
$wp_roles->remove_cap( 'editor', 'wpb_plugin-x_manage' );
```

Checking capabilities in plugins

WordPress provides a robust API for plugin developers to use in determining permissions. This API can be used to determine whether a user should be able to see a plugin management page, render an alternate piece of code for logged-in users with specific permissions, among an assortment of other use cases.

The most commonly used API is the current_user_can() function. This function should be used with logic syntax, such as a conditional check using if/then. The function, in most cases, takes a single capability as an argument. An example is shown in Listing 19.2.

LISTING 19.2

Using current_user_can() to determine permission level

```
function plugin_admin_page()
{
    global $current_user;
    if( current_user_can('activate_plugins') )
    {
        add_dashboard_page( __('My Plugin'), __('My Plugin Config'),
    'activate_plugins', 'my-plugin-handle', 'plugin_admin_html' );
    }
}
```

Note

In most cases, the current_user_can() function takes a single argument — the capability. In some cases, however, the check takes an additional argument. The read_post, edit_post, delete_post, edit_page, and delete_page all take an ID of a post, page, attachment, or a comment as well. Additionally, the edit_user and delete_user function similarly and take a user ID as a second argument. ∎

The code shown in Listing 19.2 is a simplistic example of how current_user_can() might be used in a plugin. Without going too deeply into the specific details of the management page addition, the plugin might call this function that checks to see if the user currently logged on has the permission to manage and activate plugins. If so, you are also going to show the user a new admin panel for plugin configuration.

Cross-Reference

More detail about working with plugins is available in the chapters in Part II of this book. ∎

Tip

Sometimes it is necessary just to find out if someone has admin-like capabilities. The manage_options capability is a useful capability to check against to discover this information, given this capability, unless modified by a plugin, is only assigned to users with the Admin role. ∎

Another capability checking tool is the has_cap() method, which is part of the WP_Roles class and can be accessed using the global $wp_roles object. The has_cap() method typically is used when you know that a user is logged in, as the function will access the currently logged-in user's ID. Performing a check when a user is logged out will result in the function returning False (the current user does not have this capability).

Unlike the add_cap() and remove_cap() methods, the has_cap() method takes a single argument: the name of a capability. Expanding on the custom capability used in Listing 19.2, you can use the has_cap() method to check to see if the current user can use that capability (see Listing 19.3).

LISTING 19.3

Using the $wp_roles->has_cap() method to check for assigned capabilities

```
if( $wp_roles->has_cap( 'wpb_plugin-x_manage' ) )
{
    echo "This user can perform this action";
}
else
{
    echo "Sorry, you can't do this.";
}
```

Using the Role Manager Plugin

While the WordPress Role and Capability system is robust, it is not without its problems. In fact, during the early days of development of the system, it was thought of as too complex and criticized for not addressing fundamental problems in any Access Control List (ACL). While WordPress does provide "Roles," it is fundamentally inaccurate to consider "Roles" as anything more than "groups of capabilities" or a "wrapper around capabilities." At its core, the WordPress permission system is only about Capabilities and nothing more.

As such, it did not take long for the Role Manager plugin to make its debut. The Role Manager plugin provides an interface for a blog Admin to manage (and even create) Capabilities. It is possible to modify the Capabilities assigned to a Role (such as granting modify_options to an Editor), or even create entirely new Roles with any configuration of out of the box or custom Capabilities (see Figure 19.3).

Suddenly, WordPress as a content management system is a reality that can be appropriately pursued by any large multi-user blog, content network, or major media publication. These types of organizations are much more complex, in most cases, than an organization with only an Admin, an Editor, and Authors.

FIGURE 19.3

The Role Manager plugin enables you to create new Capabilites and assign those Capabilities to existing or entirely new Roles.

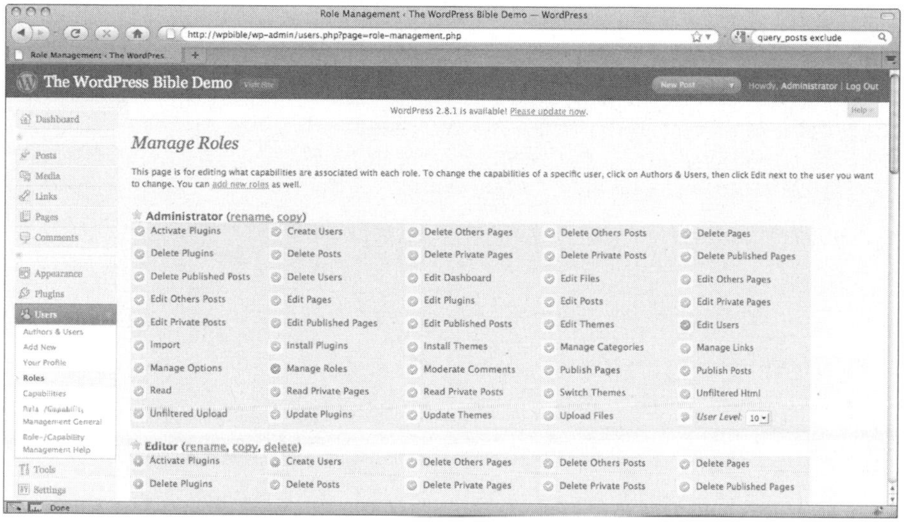

Cross-Reference

WordPress as a content management system is discussed in more detail in Chapter 22. ∎

For example, if you run a multi-author technology news blog where all contributors are autonomous, you might want to have an Admin and three Editors. In the case where you own a blog that anchors a larger community around celebrity gossip, you might want to configure WordPress to have an Admin, two Editors, and a Community Editor, which might be a custom role built to cater to community tip submissions; and allow anyone to sign up as an author.

Regardless of how you choose to pursue multi-role, multi-author sites, the Role Manager plugin can make life easy. As with most other rules of thumb in the security world, though, less is more. You can always loosen restrictions but it's harder to impose them later.

Web Resource

You can download the Role Manager plugin at `http://sourceforge.net/projects/role-manager`, and you can find more information about WordPress Roles and Capabilities `http://codex.wordpress.org/Roles_and_Capabilities`. ∎

Summary

- WordPress Roles are wrappers around Capabilities.

- Capabilities are assigned to users and enable them access to different portions of the software (for example, `activate_plugins`).

- When writing plugins, use `current_user_can()` to verify permissions and prevent a security bug from creeping into your code.

- User levels still exist, but have been deprecated. Be sure to try to steer clear of plugins that use user levels because it is a sign of potential security, compatibility, or upgrade problems.

- If you need more flexibility in permissions, consider using the Role Manager plugin, an excellent tool for fine-tuning and customizing your user security rules.

Part VI

Alternate Uses for WordPress

Using WordPress for Alternative Blogging

By far, the most traditional way of blogging is the article/comment model. It is not only the most established model, as it has been around the longest, but also it is the most typical one. WordPress is built out of the box to be used in a text format and the themes bundled with it are designed in such a way to present content in this manner.

However, blogging does not have to be this simple. It has evolved into a multi-media format, which includes videos and photographs. Further, the wide adoption of micro-blogging services such as Twitter challenges the traditional model of blogging.

Fortunately, the WordPress software is versatile. I have seen it power large sites like the 2007 Detroit Auto Show Web site as well as used to behave like a digital rolodex by organizing contact information. WordPress founder Matt Mullenweg even uses it to filter his e-mail!

One innovative developer built a virtual rolodex with WordPress (the WP Contact Manager) using WordPress custom fields, a custom design, and a few essential plugins to make access to the information private and to enhance searchability of the data. You can find the WP Contact Manager theme at http://artisanthemes.com/themes/wp-contact-manager/.

WordPress is only limited by the imagination of developers and designers. This why you see many alternative uses for the software beyond straightforward, traditional blogging. Photoblogging is one example.

Photoblogging with WordPress

It is undeniable that, in recent years, photography has become a full contact sport in our digital culture. Digital single lens reflex (SLR) cameras have reached a price point where average consumers can buy decent entry-level cameras and start learning the art of photography.

Photo sharing services like Flickr (`www.flickr.com`) encourage users to share their photos with their friends, family, and the world. To some photographers, including myself, sharing the best of the best is a great creative outlet.

Fortunately, there is nothing to prevent photographers from using WordPress to show off their photos in the form of a photoblog.

What is a Photoblog?

Photoblogs are blogs that features photography in regularly updated intervals. They are usually sites that exist to showcase a blogger's photography, but might include articles as well.

Because photoblogs tend to be about visual impact, photobloggers tend to take a more free-spirited, artistic approach to theme design, often with stunning results. As with traditional themes, those photoblog themes that direct viewers to the heart of the content are the most compelling.

Photoblogging began gaining in popularity a few years ago as sharing other rich media, such as videos and audio, became more prevalent. Photographers began taking advantage of the low barrier to entry with blogging and including it in their trade. Photoblogging was a natural extension of this crossover.

Some of the best photoblogs in WordPress use themes that showcase photos one at a time. Many also have a visual "browser" that enables people to scan other recent photos as well. Photos might be grouped together in a thematic way (black and white photography, events, architecture) using WordPress categories. Most photographers who photoblog also include Exchangeable Image Format (EXIF) information, which provides camera settings and insight into how various pictures were taken.

At their core, photobloggers want to display their photography and relevant information about a photo with the EXIF data, or tags. In this way, photobloggers are really no different than other bloggers.

Examples of notable photoblogs

As the world's most popular blogging platform, WordPress also provides a popular blogging platform for photoblogs. Some of the best photobloggers use it to showcase their work, as you see in this section.

ThomasHawk.com

Thomas Hawk is a well-known San Francisco-based photographer. His goal in life is to publish a million photos online before he dies. In 2009, he published his 20,000th photograph on Flickr. Many of these photos are republished directly on his blog (`http://thomashawk.com`), as shown in Figure 20.1.

FIGURE 20.1

ThomasHawk.com is the blog of San Francisco photographer Thomas Hawk. He uses his blog to showcase his photography and offer commentary related to the photography industry.

The Fine Arts Photoblog

The Fine Arts Photoblog (www.fineartphotoblog.com/) is a group site dedicated to fine art style photography. It is marketed as one part photoblog, where photos are posted each day from one of the artists; one part gallery, where every piece posted is sold as a high quality print; and one part search engine. Using rich EXIF data, tagging, and detailed descriptions, the site makes great photography easily accessible to readers.

Lens

The New York Times photoblog, Lens (http://lens.blogs.nytimes.com/), is a wonderful WordPress-powered photoblog. It is not exclusively a photo site. It also features high-definition video. The Lens blogs features six different photos or videos on a single page.

Clicking most of the images takes you to another site, making the photoblog a "link blog" of sorts. Most of the content is not original content, and links directly to rich media on other sites.

Cross-Reference

The New York Times has a major investment in WordPress. They are not only financial backers of Automattic but they also use WordPress on all of their blogs. For more on the New York Times WordPress usage, see Appendix G. ∎

Great WordPress photoblog themes

While there are a great many themes for standard WordPress blogs, there are very few for WordPress photoblogs. In fact, a quick search of the WordPress Themes Directory (`http://wordpress.org/extend/themes/`) turns up only four photoblog themes at the time of this writing.

However, a number of great themes are available beyond the Themes Directory. Generally, photobloggers have a flair for the aesthetic and may want to code up their own themes. Whatever works for your particular need, however, is perfectly fine. Thomas Hawk's blog, mentioned earlier in this chapter, uses a standard, modified blog template as opposed to a dedicated photoblog theme.

Monotone

Monotone (`http://wordpress.org/extend/themes/monotone`) is one of the smartest free WordPress photoblog themes. It uses the "rule of thirds" concept that is so important to photographers. The rule of thirds divides a field of view (or a photo) into nine equal "zones" created by two imaginary equally-spaced horizontal axes and two imaginary equally-spaced vertical axes (see Figure 20.2).

FIGURE 20.2

With the rule of thirds in photography, an image should be aligned with nine equal zones, created by two vertical imaginary lines and two horizontal imaginary lines.

Using the rule of thirds, Monotone identifies the pixel colors from the four intersecting axis points on a photo and dynamically creates a palette of colors based on these sampled colors. It uses this color palette to dynamically create a unique presentation for that particular photo.

Additionally, Monotone automatically determines the orientation and size of the original photo, and resizes it accordingly for consistent display.

StudioPress Black Canvas

StudioPress, best known for the release of the Revolution theme, originally a premium theme that was later released under the General Public License (GPL), has been working on a new generation of premium themes. Black Canvas is one of them and is a very polished photoblogging theme (see Figure 20.3).

The Black Canvas theme features a "ribbon" that displays other recently published photos along the bottom. This ribbon concept is common in many themes and is a visual representation of the typical "recent posts" feature used on most blogs.

Unlike Monotone, Black Canvas is not free. However, it is a fairly inexpensive theme at $59.95 (as of this writing). You can purchase and download it, along with other StudioPress premium themes, at www.studiopress.com/themes/blackcanvas.

FIGURE 20.3

The StudioPress Black Canvas theme provides a slick interface, framed in black.

Nautilus

The Nautilus theme takes advantage of the very popular K2 Theme for WordPress (`http://getk2.com`). K2, by itself, is an early approach to premium themes (though it is free and open source) that offers plenty of configuration options from inside the WordPress Admin without your having to edit code. It became known early on for revolutionizing the way themes were made and used. Blogger and theme designer Rebecca Weeks leveraged K2 and created a photoblog theme to take advantage of that framework.

Nautilus, available at `http://geek.marinegirl.co.uk/nautilus` for free, was built to leverage both K2 and the Flickr Blog This feature (see Figure 20.4). Images on Flickr can be manually designated as well and Weeks even suggests that manually uploading 740px (pixel) wide photos to Flickr might be the way to go. The reason for this is that Flickr only publishes 500px wide version of images using Blog This.

Cross-Reference

The Flickr Blog This feature uses XML-RPC (Extensible Markup Language-Remote Procedure Call) to publish to your blog. The difference between a typical offline editor and the Flickr feature is minimal technically. Both represent a client (the desktop client or Flickr) and a server (WordPress), but the delivery and execution is different. For more information on XML-RPC clients and functionality, see Chapter 14. ∎

The Nautilus theme requires two different versions of an image to function. It needs a 75px-wide image to serve as a thumbnail image, and a 740px-wide image for on the page that displays it full size image. Cascading Style Sheet (CSS) resizing occurs but it doesn't reduce file size, so make sure you're optimizing your image for best quality and smallest file size.

FIGURE 20.4

Use Flickr's Blog This feature to publish photos remotely to your WordPress blog.

Image Quality and Concerns

Images are the quintessential part of a photoblog. However, there can be significant limitations with images. Namely, file size is the Achilles' heel of any image. As a rule, you want the best quality image you can get, but at the same time, you want to keep the file size small enough to keep the page loading quickly, even on Internet connections that are sluggish.

As a rule, pages in general should not "weigh" more than 300K to 350K in file size. That is, the total sum of all the sizes of files used on the page plus the page (HTML and CSS) itself should not be more than 350K for optimal load times. In a mainly text medium, a server can perform some compression routines, such as gzip, that reduce the size of the data being passed back and forth; however, images don't compress well. This is why in large scale environments, images are often served from a separate, high-bandwidth server system or content delivery network — a configuration that is probably overkill for most average bloggers.

You can, however, pay attention to your file size. On a photoblog, you are most likely to use PNG or JPEG image formats. Both have their strengths. PNGs tend to provide better quality and are effective for screenshots and illustrations while JPEG format files are preferred for photographs. The PNG format, besides supporting transparency, is *lossless*, which means it can be compressed and decompressed without losing quality. But PNGs also tend to be bigger files than JPEGs. While JPEGs have the advantage of being smaller files, they lose quality as they are compressed and decompressed and do not support any kind of transparency.

The easiest way to check on the page weight of a site is to use the Net panel in the Firebug extension for Firefox, available at `http://getfirebug.com/`. This extension is an invaluable resource for anyone working on themes; and it will produce an analysis of load time as well, as shown in the following figure, which is an analysis of my photoblog.

Firebug provides an analysis of a pages weight and where the bottlenecks are on a page load.

You can see that the total weight of one of my photo pages is 145K. As a side note, you can also see the effect of third-party JavaScript services (in this case IntenseDebate, but ads can do the same thing) on load time.

Using EXIF data in a photoblog

The WordPress gallery feature was added in WordPress 2.5. Images can be uploaded en masse with the flash uploader that has become part of the WordPress core, and images can be added as a whole to a post as a gallery. Part of this attention to photo details is the extraction of EXIF (Exchangeable Image Format) data from the photos. Unfortunately, WordPress' implementation of EXIF leaves something to be desired.

First, you need to have an understanding of EXIF, at least on a basic level. Assume you have the photo that is shown in Figure 20.5. This is a photo that I took near the Upper Falls in Rochester, New York, during one of the notorious Western New York winters. If you were to open the image in a text editor, you'd see mostly a lot of gibberish machine language. However, plaintext descriptions are embedded throughout the photo: how the photo was taken in terms of aperture, shutter speed, ISO (International Organization of Standardization) settings, and other relevant information that means more to photographers than the average person. This is the EXIF data.

FIGURE 20.5

A photo in PNG or JPG format will have embedded data in the image itself. This data is called EXIF data.

Using an EXIF viewer (I use EXIF Viewer for Mac but there are many other viewers available), it's possible to find all the pertinent embedded EXIF data for this image. Listing 20.1 illustrates the EXIF data as it relates to Figure 20.5.

LISTING 20.1

EXIF data from Figure 20.5

```
File name:       IMG_9837.jpg
    File size:       3662139 bytes (3456x2298, 3.7bpp, 7x)
    EXIF Summary:    1/80s f/1.4 ISO1600 24mm
Camera-Specific Properties:
    Equipment Make:    Canon
    Camera Model:      Canon EOS DIGITAL REBEL XT
Image-Specific Properties:
    Image Orientation:    Top, Left-Hand
    Horizontal Resolution:    72 dpi
    Vertical Resolution:    72 dpi
    Image Created:    2009:01:08 20:52:14
    Exposure Time:    1/80 sec
    F-Number:    /1.4
    Exposure Program:    Aperture Priority
    ISO Speed Rating:    1600
    Lens Aperture:    f/1.4
    Exposure Bias:    0 EV
    Metering Mode:    Partial
    Flash:    No Flash, Compulsory
    Focal Length:    24.00 mm
    Color Space Information:    sRGB
    Image Width:    3456
    Image Height:    2298
    Rendering:    Normal
    Exposure Mode:    Auto
    White Balance:    Auto
    Scene Capture Type:    Standard
Other Properties:
    Resolution Unit:    i
    Exif IFD Pointer:    179
    Exif Version:    2.21
    Image Generated:    2009:01:08 20:52:14
    Image Digitized:    2009:01:08 20:52:14
    Shutter Speed:    1/80 sec
    Focal Plane Horiz Resolution:    3954 dpi
    Focal Plane Vert Resolution:    3958 dpi
    Focal Plane Res Unit:    i
```

Again, most of this data means nothing to the average user, but to the photographer, it is essential. EXIF data on photoblogs enables other photographers to learn how the photo was taken.

As a photographer, I am most interested in knowing these settings: shutter (how fast the shutter opened and closed), aperture (a number representing how wide the lens is open; it also affects depth of field: the smaller the aperture, the wider the lens is open but the less clarity you get farther out), and ISO (a number representing light sensitivity).

In this case, I know that this photo was taken with a 1/80 of a second shutter speed; the aperture was 1.4, a very low number that is great for low light; and it was taken at a 1600 ISO, a number that makes the camera less sensitive to light and colors (the higher the ISO, the greater the "noise" factor).

WordPress EXIF parsing is fairly weak because, though the numbers shown are formatted, the raw data is not and has to be calculated mathematically to display numbers that make sense to a reader.

The WordPress method for extracting EXIF information uses the function `wp_get_attachment_metadata()`. This function takes a single ID, which is the ID of the attachment. You can extract this ID two ways, neither of which is pretty. The first method involves going into the database and retrieving the attachment ID (recall that attachment is a `post_type` and attachment data is stored in the posts table). The second method involves inserting the image into a post (this does not have to be saved). Using the second method creates a shortcode in your post from which you can extrapolate the attachment ID.

Once you have the attachment ID, you can pass it to `wp_get_attachment_metadata()`, which in turn returns an array of limited EXIF data. An easy way to test this is with a function that you can use somewhere within WordPress, as illustrated in Listing 20.2.

LISTING 20.2

A function for testing EXIF extraction with WordPress

```
function wpb_format_image_exif( $post_id = '' )
{
    if( '' == $post_id )
        return false;
    $exif = wp_get_attachment_metadata( $post_id );
    echo '<pre>';
    print_r( $exif );
    echo '</pre>';
}
format_image_exif( 7911 );
```

On the Web

The code in Listing 20.2 is available for download at www.wiley.com/go/wordpressbible. ■

The resulting array will look like Listing 20.3.

LISTING 20.3

The array output of EXIF extraction data in WordPress

```
Array
(
    [width] => 3456
    [height] => 2298
    [hwstring_small] => height='85' width='128'
    [file] => 2009/10/IMG_9837.jpg
    [sizes] => Array
        (
            [thumbnail] => Array
                (
                    [file] => IMG_9837-80x53.jpg
                    [width] => 80
                    [height] => 53
                )
            [medium] => Array
                (
                    [file] => IMG_9837-250x166.jpg
                    [width] => 250
                    [height] => 166
                )
            [large] => Array
                (
                    [file] -> IMG_9837-690x458.jpg
                    [width] => 690
                    [height] => 458
                )
        )
    [image_meta] => Array
        (
            [aperture] => 1.4
            [credit] =>
            [camera] => Canon EOS DIGITAL REBEL XT
            [caption] =>
            [created_timestamp] => 1231465934
            [copyright] =>
            [focal_length] => 24
            [iso] => 1600
            [shutter_speed] => 0.0125
            [title] =>
        )
)
```

The data extracted from an image in WordPress is extremely limited. Much of the information extracted is not EXIF information at all, but dimensions of the image, including WordPress-generated data. However, the `$exif['image_meta']` nested array does contain some valuable unformatted information.

Notably, ISO is exactly what it should be and aperture, also known as *f-stop*, is almost what it should be (add an f/ in front of the number and you have the formatted string). The `created_timestamp` key displays the timestamp in Unix style but can be converted to a readable format with the PHP `date()` function. The `focal_length` key is a number in millimeters and represents the focal length of the lens. You can add mm to the end and have a formatted focal length number. Finally, shutter speed is usually formatted as a fraction, but is represented by a decimal in WordPress' metadata. Converting this decimal to a fraction is mainly a matter of logic and math.

A better way of doing this is to use PHP's built-in `exif_read_data()` function. This function takes a filename (it cannot be a URL). Using this function might look like the code in Listing 20.4 and has the added benefit of your not having to figure out what the attachment ID is. You just need the path to the file.

LISTING 20.4

A function for testing EXIF extraction with PHP functions instead of WordPress

```
function wpb_format_image_exif( $image_path = '' )
{
    if( '' == $image_path )
        return false;
    $exif = exif_read_data( $image_path );
    echo '<pre>';
    print_r( $exif );
    echo '</pre>';
}
format_image_exif( ABSPATH . '/wp-content/uploads/2009/10/IMG_9837.jpg' );
```

On the Web

The code in Listing 20.4 is available for download at www.wiley.com/go/wordpressbible. ∎

The result of using this function means you have much more data at your fingertips, but it takes much more math and logic to build. The result is shown in Listing 20.5.

LISTING 20.5

The result of PHP in-built EXIF parsing

```
Array
(
    [FileName] => IMG_9837.jpg
    [FileDateTime] => 1255106122
    [FileSize] => 3662139
    [FileType] => 2
    [MimeType] => image/jpeg
    [SectionsFound] => ANY_TAG, IFD0, EXIF
    [COMPUTED] => Array
        (
            [html] => width="3456" height="2298"
            [Height] => 2298
            [Width] => 3456
            [IsColor] => 1
            [ByteOrderMotorola] => 1
            [CCDWidth] => 22mm
            [ApertureFNumber] => f/1.4
        )
    [Make] => Canon
    [Model] => Canon EOS DIGITAL REBEL XT
    [Orientation] => 1
    [XResolution] => 72/1
    [YResolution] => 72/1
    [ResolutionUnit] => 2
    [DateTime] => 2009:01:08 20:52:14
    [Exif_IFD_Pointer] => 179
    [ExposureTime] => 1/80
    [FNumber] => 7/5
    [ExposureProgram] => 3
    [ISOSpeedRatings] => 1600
    [ExifVersion] => 0221
    [DateTimeOriginal] => 2009:01:08 20:52:14
    [DateTimeDigitized] => 2009:01:08 20:52:14
    [ShutterSpeedValue] => 7207/1140
    [ApertureValue] => 4164/4289
    [ExposureBiasValue] => 0/1
    [MeteringMode] => 6
    [Flash] => 16
    [FocalLength] => 24/1
    [FlashPixVersion] => 0100
    [ColorSpace] => 1
    [ExifImageWidth] => 3456
    [ExifImageLength] => 2298
    [FocalPlaneXResolution] => 118627/30
```

continued

LISTING 20.5 *(continued)*

```
    [FocalPlaneYResolution] => 150433/38
    [FocalPlaneResolutionUnit] => 2
    [CustomRendered] => 0
    [ExposureMode] => 0
    [WhiteBalance] => 0
    [SceneCaptureType] => 0
)
```

The PHP generated EXIF data is much more cryptic than WordPress' but it provides much more granular information, such as if the flash went off, image orientation, and so on. In this comparison to WordPress' built-in functionality, the data points of most concern here are FNumber (aperture), ISOSpeedRatings (ISO), ExposureTime (shutter speed), and FocalLength. Each of these numbers needs to be converted to a readable format. The plugin — provided only in this book — that will do this conversion for you is shown in Listing 20.6.

LISTING 20.6

A WordPress plugin to extract and convert EXIF data

```php
<?php
/*
Plugin Name: WP Bible Exif
Plugin URI: #
Description: A special plugin for photobloggers reading the WordPress Bible
    from Wiley Publishing
Version: 1.0
Author: Aaron Brazell
Author URI: http://technosailor.com
*/
    /**
     *
     * Released under the GPL license
     * http://www.opensource.org/licenses/gpl-2.0.php
     *
     * ****************************************************************
    **
     * This program is distributed in the hope that it will be useful, but
     * WITHOUT ANY WARRANTY; without even the implied warranty of
     * MERCHANTABILITY or FITNESS FOR A PARTICULAR PURPOSE.
     * ****************************************************************
    **
     */
class WP_Bible_Exif {
    var $attachment_id;
```

```
    var $fstop;
    var $timestamp;
    var $focal_length;
    var $shutter;
    var $iso;
    function __construct( $path_to_image )
    {
        $this->attachment_path = $path_to_image;
        $exif = $this->extract_exif();
        $this->fstop = $exif['FNumber'];
        $this->timestamp = $exif['FileDateTime'];
        $this->focal_length = $exif['FocalLength'];
        $this->shutter = $exif['ExposureTime'];
        $this->iso = $exif['ISOSpeedRatings'];
    }
    function extract_exif()
    {
        return exif_read_data( $this->attachment_path );
    }
    function img_aperture()
    {
        return 'f/' . $this->frac2dec( $this->fstop );
    }
    function img_iso()
    {
        return (int) $this->iso;
    }
    function img_timestamp( $format = '' )
    {
        if( $format == '' )
            $format = get_option('date_format');
        return date( $format, (int) $this->timestamp );
    }
    function img_focal()
    {
        return $this->frac2dec( $this->focal_length ) . 'mm';
    }
    function img_shutter()
    {
        $shutterbits = explode('/', $this->shutter);
        $speed = ( (int) $shutterbits[1] == '1' ) ? (int) $shutterbits[0]
: $this->shutter;
        return $speed . ' sec';
    }
    function frac2dec( $fraction )
{
        $bits = explode( '/', $fraction );
        $numerator = (int) $bits[0];
```

continued

LISTING 20.6 *(continued)*

```
        $denominator = (int) $bits[1];
        return $numerator / $denominator;
    }
    function __destruct() {}
}
function display_exif( $attachment_path )
{
    $exif = new WP_Bible_Exif( $attachment_path );
    echo '<ul>';
    echo '<li>' . sprintf( 'Aperture: %s', $exif->img_aperture() ) . '</
li>';
    echo '<li>' . sprintf( 'ISO: %d', $exif->img_iso() ) . '</li>';
    echo '<li>' . sprintf( 'Focal Length: %s', $exif->img_focal() ) . '</
li>';
    echo '<li>' . sprintf( 'Shutter Speed: %s', $exif->img_shutter() ) .
'</li>';
    echo '<li>' . sprintf( 'Time Taken: %s', $exif->img_timestamp() ) . '</
li>';
    echo '</ul>';
}
```

This plugin provides its own template tag, `display_exif()` but that doesn't prevent you from creating your own template tags (follow the format I used in the `display_exif()` function as a guideline). It is only PHP 5-compatible and is entirely object oriented. The class can also be extended if you wish to pull additional information out of the EXIF data parsed by PHP. (I've only used the most commonly used EXIF datapoints.) The relevant methods are listed in Table 20.1.

TABLE 20.1

The Relevant Methods Extended from the Class in Listing 20.6

Method	Description
img_aperture()	Returns a formatted Aperture/F-stop number. 7/5 becomes f/1.4
img_iso()	Does nothing particularly exciting except return the ISO number. It is already formatted properly and this method exists for the sake of continuity.
img_focal()	Returns a formatted focal length. 24/1 becomes 24mm.
img_shutter()	Returns a formatted shutter speed. 1/80 becomes 1/80 sec.
img_timestamp()	Returns a formatted timestamp. This method can take a PHP time format but if none is provided, then the default setting for WordPress is used. 1255106122 becomes Jan. 8, 2009, for example.

On the Web

The code in Listing 20.6 is available for download at www.wiley.com/go/wordpressbible. ∎

Implementing a Twitter-style Blog

WordPress can also be used as a microblogging platform. *Microblogging* is a loose term describing the posting content to the Web in tiny bite-sized pieces, generally in 140 characters or less (although there is no strict rule on this).

Twitter made microblogging popular and a number of other similar platforms, such as Identi.ca (http://identi.ca) and Yammer (http://yammer.com), have emerged as alternatives. But what if you like WordPress so much that you'd rather implement a WordPress blog that allows team collaboration and internal file sharing as those other microblogging platforms do?

By precedent, microblog posts are 140 characters or less, but they don't have to be. This became the norm because Twitter, the original microblogging service, needed to keep messaging under the character limit of 160 that is associated with text messaging, since the intent was for the service to be used with mobile devices. However, with WordPress, a microblog post is no different than a regular post. The difference is in how it is presented visually and used as a communications mechanism.

The WordPress.com folks created a theme internally for WordPress.com users and WordPress development called Prologue. They released it as a GPL theme for WordPress.org users. Later, they updated Prologue with the release of WordPress 2.7 and threaded commenting, and re-released the updated version as P2.

Web Resource

P2 can be downloaded from the WordPress Themes Directory at http://wordpress.org/extend/themes/p2. ∎

The P2 theme, shown in Figure 20.6, is a theme that enables user posts to be entered directly from the front page of the site. It does require WordPress user registration so you can choose to register users manually (in the case of a public, yet private, installation) or allow open registration.

The beauty of the P2 theme is that it doesn't create any new functionality. Every feature is an integrated part of WordPress. Posting? You can do that right from the front page. Adding insight or feedback on postings? Threaded comments to the rescue. Organizing metadata around threads of conversation? There's a tagging interface right in the P2 theme.

FIGURE 20.6

The P2 theme bears a resemblance to other microblogging services like Twitter and provides posting, tagging, and other post-writing functionality in the front page.

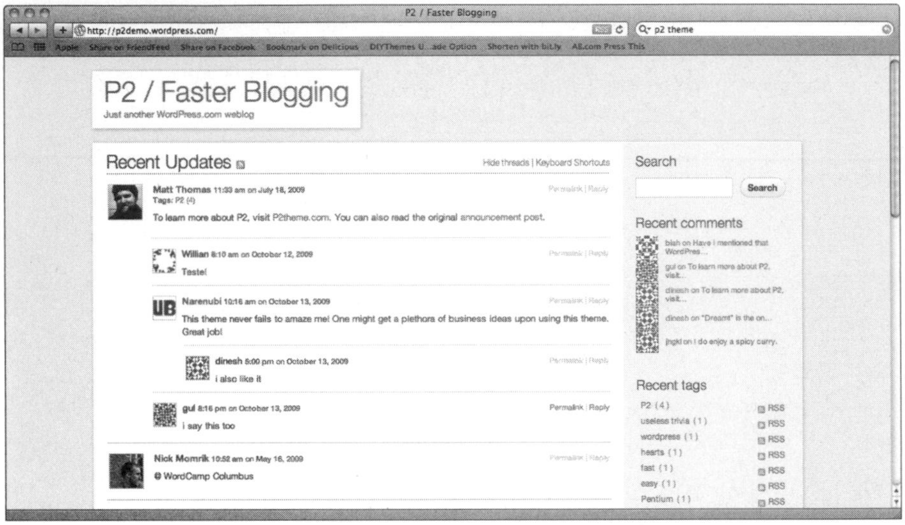

Using Press This for a Tumble Blog

A third use for WordPress, among many possibilities, is to use it in a similar way to Tumblr (http://tumblr.com). Tumblr set a precedent as a "quick blog," also known as a *Tumble blog*. Tumble blogs generally have a quick access point, whether via a browser extension or a link known as a *bookmarklet*, that enables users to submit content to their blogs without having to load up an entire blog platform.

Note
A bookmarklet is a link populated with JavaScript that can be dragged into a browser link bar or bookmarks. ■

The benefit of a Tumble-style blog is that it fits into the workflow of bloggers who don't really have time to blog. These bloggers don't want to have to sit down and get their brains in gear to write or produce "traditional" blogging content.

For a very long time, WordPress has provided a bookmarklet — which has now evolved into a full fledge quick posting system called Press This.

You can find the Press This bookmarklet under the Tools menu in WordPress Admin, as shown in Figure 20.7. The link, aptly named Press This, can be dragged into your browser link bar and dropped for future use. You can also right-click (control-click for Mac users) and add it directly into your bookmarks folder.

FIGURE 20.7

You can drag the Press This bookmarklet into your browser link bar, or add it directly to bookmarks by right-clicking and adding.

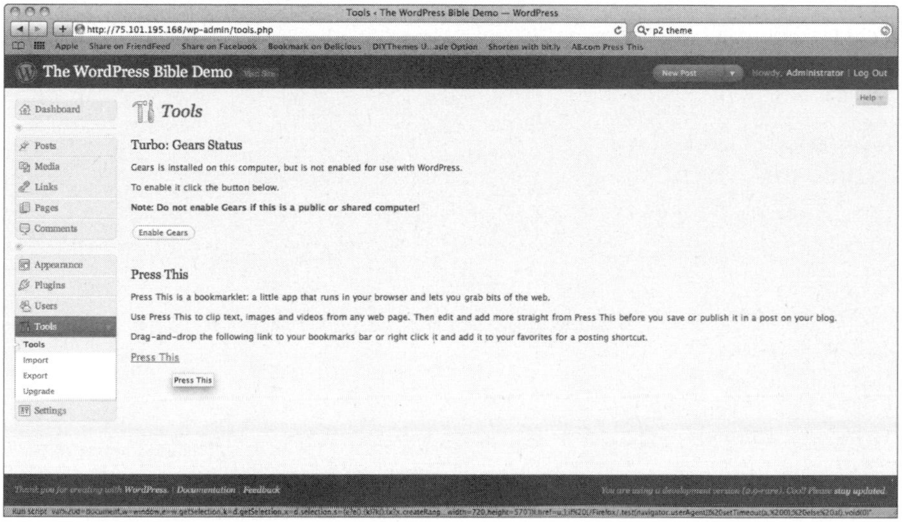

Once it is there, you can continue browsing the Web, doing your work, and so on. When you come across content that you want to add to your Tumble blog, select it and click the Press This bookmarklet. A miniaturized version of the WordPress quickpost user interface appears, as shown in Figure 20.8.

A second use of Press This is to create a "link blog" within WordPress. A link blog is simply a way to share links with your readers and commonly goes by the name *Asides*. Asides are meant to be complementary to your regular content. Depending on your theme, you might want to publish your Asides in the sidebar to keep the content outside of the normal flow of content. Or you might want to include Asides directly inline and style them differently.

When you implement Asides using Press This, make sure you have a special category that you only use for Asides. Using Press This, ensure that you choose the proper category before clicking the Publish button (though you can certainly log in to the WordPress Admin as you typically do and edit a post after the fact).

You'll probably want to style the Asides differently that the rest of your blog. Fortunately, WordPress provides theme designers with the ability to give every post a category CSS class. So if your category name is "Asides" (a typical name), then, as long as your theme supports it, you can style all posts that are wrapped in the category-asides CSS class.

On my personal blog, I keep Asides inline with normal content. I've done a number of things, such as writing a function to grab the *favicon* (a small image that Web sites can provide to browsers and other Web sites to represent the site in a visual form), from whatever site I'm linking to. I've also styled the Asides so they don't include post titles or metadata. The font size is smaller and generally does not resemble a typical post (see Figure 20.9).

FIGURE 20.8

Select the content you want to publish and click the Press This bookmarklet. The content will be populated into a miniaturized version of the WordPress Admin.

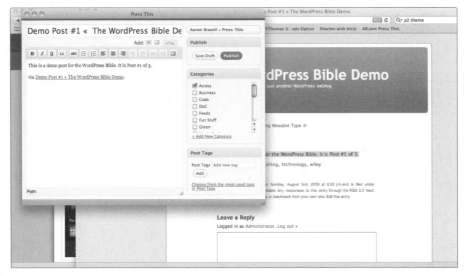

FIGURE 20.9

On my personal blog, Asides are displayed inline with regular posts but are styled quite differently.

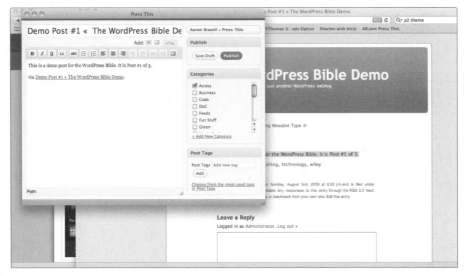

Summary

- Photoblogging is a major alternate use of WordPress.

- Themes developed as photoblogging themes include StudioPress' Black Canvas, Nautilus (a K2-based theme), and Monotone.

- EXIF data can be extracted from WordPress image attachments, but the PHP EXIF functions provide more information. I've included a plugin for extracting and presenting EXIF data on your photoblog.

- Using P2 fosters a collaborative, microblogging theme built for WordPress.

- WordPress can be used as a Tumblr-style blog using Press This.

- Press This can also be used to curate a link blog, also called Asides. With custom CSS options, Asides posts can be styled differently than regular posts.

WordPress as a Content Management System

A *content management system* (CMS) is a piece of software used to manage a Web site from a single administrative interface. The most well-known content management systems are Drupal (`http://drupal.org`), Joomla (`www.joomla.org`), and ExpressionEngine (`http://expressionengine.com`).

WordPress has had trappings of a CMS for years now. Since WordPress 1.5, pages — the main aspect of a CMS — have been available to WordPress users wishing to use the software to power largely static sites.

In fact, between pages, custom fields, and the media library, WordPress has everything that is needed to take a corporate site or a non-profit organization's Web site from a smattering of hand-coded static HTML (hypertext markup language) pages into a centrally managed, consistently themed site that can operate seamlessly and with little maintenance required.

IN THIS CHAPTER

Using WordPress as a content management system

Understanding Enterprise WordPress needs

Conveying a consistent message and brand

Understanding when a blog is not a blog

Using WordPress as a Content Management System

WordPress does a great job of providing the basics of a CMS out of the box. It is entirely possible to run a corporate, church, school, or any other kind of Web site using WordPress "pages" alone. Whether you include a blog ("posts") as well is completely optional.

The core of WordPress is the page system. *Pages* in WordPress behave similarly to posts, except pages do not have a category hierarchy. Further, unlike posts, pages offer a parent-child hierarchy, so it is possible to have pages describing the general service a company offers with child pages detailing each of these services individually.

Additionally, pages, unlike posts, can have special templates assigned to them. Therefore, it is possible to create different sections of your site that look and behave differently than others.

You can also use custom fields, which I talk about later in this chapter, to customize individual posts and pages. For example, you could create special "callout" text that attracts viewer's eyes to key phrases (a technique made popular by magazines where special text appears in the margins). You could also use custom fields to provide thumbnail images, location data, or anything you want to enhance the content of the post or the page.

In corporate environments particularly, you may need to modify the screens bloggers use to write posts to include additional options specific for your organization or limit confusion from unrelated functionality. (For example, you might not want the average corporate blogger to have access to categories reserved for the person editing the blog.) I discuss several plugins later in this chapter that tweak the way the edit screen appears to bloggers.

Before you can get too far down the road using WordPress as a CMS, however, you need to figure out the needs of your organization. Smaller companies have the luxury of being more nimble; there's a degree of flexibility and they can sometimes figure out what they need on the fly. Many enterprises, however, need to be a bit more strategic when it comes to how they deploy their software and Web sites.

Understanding Enterprise WordPress Needs

The needs of a large corporation are often very different than those of a small business, non-profit organization, or individual; and posting content onto the company Web site is often much more involved. Often within a large corporation, legal and public relations professionals need to vet the content before it can be posted.

Single sign-on authentication

Large corporations tend to have a centralized authentication system that is often based on Microsoft Server offerings and Active Directory. Often these corporations also already have authentication systems that include e-mail, Blackberries, group policies, and administrators who can remotely manage their systems, users, and devices via virtual private networks (VPNs). The last thing the information technology group needs is to throw a completely new system into place that alters their homogenous infrastructure.

Out of the box, WordPress can function perfectly fine as enterprise software, but it won't integrate with an Active Directory/LDAP (Lightweight Directory Access Protocol) style authentication system without some help. Fortunately, WordPress is so extensible that its entire authentication system can be replaced to authenticate against an external, LDAP-compatible directory system.

Note

When referring to the IT needs and requirements of large organizations, the term enterprise is often used. Enterprise describes not only the environment that software is used, but also the business and strategic needs, concerns, and requisites for software. In many cases, when WordPress is used by these organizations, it is also used as a CMS to support their business needs, and the blog is just a portion of the requisite need. ■

The Simple LDAP Login plugin (available from the WordPress Plugin Directory at `http://wordpress.org/extend/plugins/simple-ldap-login/`) integrates with any LDAP-compatible directory system, including Active Directory.

The authentication process that is followed using this plugin is shown in Figure 21.1.

FIGURE 21.1

The authentication process using the Simple LDAP Login plugin

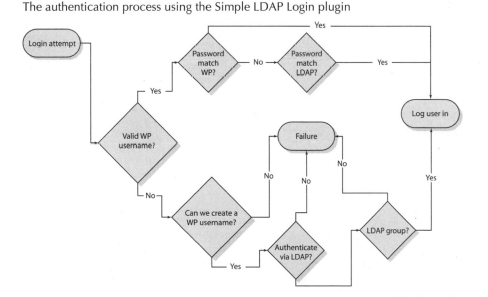

Of course, the authentication functions in WordPress are all pluggable — that is, they exist in the `wp-includes/pluggable.php` file. Every function in this file is only declared if it is not declared elsewhere via a plugin. Therefore, if you need to build authentication against some other system, including homegrown, single sign-on solutions, you can write your own functions to do so.

The key functions to think about and replicate in your own way include:

- `is_user_logged_in()`
- `wp_hash_password()`
- `wp_check_password()`
- `wp_generate_password()`
- `wp_set_password()`
- `wp_login()`
- `wp_logout()`
- `wp_authenticate()`
- `get_user_by_email()`
- `get_userdatabylogin()`
- `get_user_by()`
- `get_userdata()`

Depending on your single sign-on system, you may need all or only some of these functions.

Lead generation and CRM integration

Many enterprise companies, particularly sales organizations, want their Web sites to be "lead generators." In other words, any time a prospective customer ("lead") contacts the company, they want that customer lead inserted into their Customer Relationship Management (CRM) software.

The largest and most popular CRM software is Salesforce (`www.salesforce.com`). Fortunately, Salesforce offers a RESTful (Representational State Transfer) API for lead generation. RESTful APIs allow data to be transferred over standard Web protocols to a Web service (in this case, Salesforce) that processes the data. The SF Contact Form plugin for WordPress does just this, creating leads in Salesforce out of prospects who contact you through a Web form. The SF Contact Form plugin is available at `www.cuplaweb.com/software/wordpress-plugins/sf-contact-form/`.

Another CRM integration plugin for WordPress is Tactile CRM Contact Form, which behaves in a similar fashion to the Salesforce plugin. Prospective customers contact a company through a Web form, generating leads in the Tactile CRM. This plugin can be downloaded from the WordPress Plugin Directory at `http://wordpress.org/extend/plugins/tactile-crm-contact-form/`.

There is even a plugin that turns WordPress itself into a CRM platform: the CRM plugin available at `http://wordpress.org/extend/plugins/crm/`. With this plugin, all leads and opportunities are maintained directly in WordPress and can be managed from within WordPress (see Figure 21.2).

FIGURE 21.2

The CRM plugin for WordPress enables companies to manage leads and opportunities directly in WordPress.

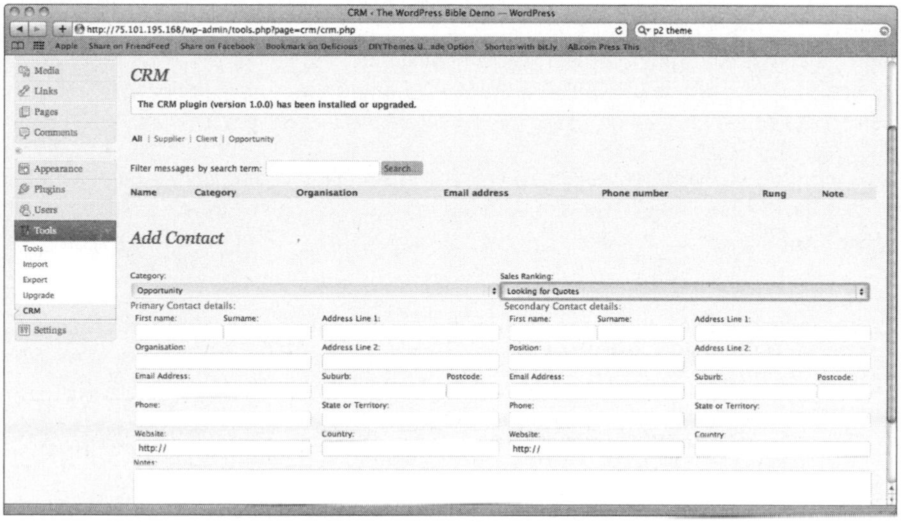

WordPress support

In any business, the goal is to make money. In an enterprise corporation, it's often better to have a Web site supplement efforts to make money than be a primary source because this can be an employee time-drain. In these cases, enterprises want to know that they can get support for their product in a hurry.

While Automattic guides WordPress development and innovation, it only offers professional services for WordPress.com VIP customers. Fortunately, there is a rich ecosystem of professionals and companies can contract them, or even employ then full time, to provide the same type of services.

Cross-Reference
WordPress.com VIP hosting is discussed in Chapter 26. ■

Cross-Reference
A list of WordPress consultants can be found in Appendix E. ■

Conveying a Consistent Message and Brand

Branding is a major concern among companies, particularly large corporate entities. Often the concept of the brand is conveyed through logos, marketing materials, and colors, and millions of dollars are poured into brand research and design every year. A brand, however, goes beyond the corporate identity, extending to customers and, in the case of a Web site, readers.

For me, a *brand* represents a trusting relationship between customer and company, though many still see a brand as having more tangible effects. A brand in many companies' eyes is not only about colors, fonts, logos, and taglines, but also about tone, perception, and the ultimate diplomatic dance.

With WordPress, companies can manage their brand and customer relationships through their blog's posting and comment features (talking to their customers, and letting them interact through comments), as well as through layouts, designs, templating, and logos. All of this is handled via the theme.

Cross-Reference
Chapter 3 offers more information about social media marketing and how to leverage social networks to extend your message. ∎

Who Are You Designing For... You or Your Customers?

This article was written on June 26, 2008, on my blog, Technosailor.com, by friend and colleague Mike Dougherty. I've included here as a guiding principle when you're developing and designing themes and identities for WordPress.

I called this entry "Who Are You Designing For...You or Your Customers" because most business owners can't see that what they are asking a designer, marketing firm, or neighbor down the street to do is create the image of how people who have different tastes and interests will perceive their over all brand. They say that first impressions are very hard to change, but triple that when a person picks up your business card or brochure, sees your ad in the paper, or looks at your Web site before she even talk to you — unless you've invested the time in your Brand Identity to ensure that it is reflective, and supported, in all of your marketing materials.

Let's understand the difference between Brand Identity and Brand Image before we go any further. Your Brand Identity is how you want people outside of your company to perceive your company. Your Brand Image is how people outside of your company are currently viewing your company. The two are separate, but the same. Your Brand Image should constantly be reinforced and supported by your Brand Identity. One can weaken the other.

Let's face it, when it comes to how effective your marketing materials are…the initial perception people get is reality to them. You could be the best schmoozer in the world, but hand someone something that looks like you put very little effort into the presentation and all your schmoozing is for nothing. Convincing, begging, and bribing may not drive the message home that your first round of marketing materials was done to be "cost effective"; instead they may came out making you, and your company, look less than stellar.

First and foremost your marketing materials should be created with your customers, current and future, in mind. When you sit down to have someone create your marketing materials, the building blocks of your Brand Identity, my best advice is to remove yourself from process as much as possible.

I don't mean that you should not be involved, but you should remember…you aren't trying to use these marketing materials to get you to invest into your company, product, or what have you. Sometimes that means you need to leave the confines of your office, ask your best customer some good questions on how she perceives your business and start looking at your company, product, or widget from the customer's side of the fence.

Your design is an impression, not a true test to your companies' capabilities, but like I said before, sometimes all you get is a first impression. Make it the best one you can.

How accurately do you think your companies marketing materials reflect the overall view of your company as a whole? Do your marketing materials work with or against the way your want your company to be perceived? How strongly do your marketing materials communicate the personality and ethics of your company?

In WordPress, when you're designing themes, you have all kinds of opportunities to maintain consistency across your blog. The first, and likely most obvious thing to do, is ensure you're leveraging the templating system to its best. Unless there is a need to have slightly different headers, footers, and sidebars on every page (there are legitimate reasons to do so, but they aren't common), try not to. If you must modify sidebars, or have completely different layouts on every page, pay close attention to how these layouts convey meaning, authority, and message.

It is entirely legitimate to have different sidebars placed different ways on different pages. A page displaying contact information might not need a sidebar at all. A simple Google map, contact form, and some copy will do the trick.

On a sales page, images of products, or representing services, in a sidebar might just be the perfect recipe. But an enterprise software company displaying code samples might need a different layout. Traditional blog formats typically have a sidebar on the right side of a page. However, traditional service companies typically use a left-side navigation bar.

Including advertising opens up an entirely new world when it comes to layouts. Though most enterprise companies consider having ads unprofessional, and a potential legal problem, many smaller companies, startups, and individuals advertise quite a bit.

Note

Google released a study a few years ago demonstrating the most effective placement of ad units. The study suggested that because the eye moved from left to right and top to bottom, the most effective ad placement was inline with content, and the second most effective ad placement was on the left side of the page, above the fold, in a sidebar. You can find the results of this study and related help topics at `www.google.com/adsense/support/bin/answer.py?hl=en&answer=17954`. ■

Consistency and layout have a tremendous effect on brand and site perception. Work closely with the marketing people in your organization or your client's organization to strike the right tone for the message they want to have.

Understanding When a Blog Is Not a Blog

First and foremost, WordPress is a blog platform. It is geared toward the user who posts regularly updated content to his site. However, as many other online industries are evolving, the blog is evolving as well. It is becoming more and more about content portals. Even the blog themes that are coming out are increasingly geared toward magazine-style formats and converging blogs and corporate Web sites.

Custom fields play a huge part in the WordPress platform. Using custom fields on posts and pages allows you to add metadata to every post and use conditional logic to determine the existence of metadata. The most common use for this kind of metadata is thumbnail images. Though WordPress includes an image resizing capability, sometimes custom sizes or different images are needed to convey a message. I use a custom field on the home page of my blog to add a "feature" image, as shown in Figure 21.3.

Note

As of WordPress 2.9, the common use of custom fields to display thumbnail representations in a theme layout has been made simpler. There is a new template tag, `the_post_image()`, which retrieves the first image attachment for a post, resizes it to an appropriate size, and displays it in a theme. Many themes still use the custom field method, however, as theme designers have not had the new template tag for very long. ■

Another way custom fields can be used is to provide one-line executive summaries or "teaser phrases" for posts. This technique is often used in newspapers, where a story is laid out with a title, a subtitle, and then post content. You might consider doing this with the excerpt of the post as well, since this can be manually designated, but you might want to have an excerpt and an executive summary for use on different kinds of pages.

This code shown in Listing 21.1 can be hooked into a theme hook if one is included, or it can be used directly as a template tag inside the Loop. Personally I use the template tag directly after the title of the post and only on individual posts and pages.

Using a custom field to choose a "feature" image enables me to create an aesthetically pleasing post flow. In the case of my theme, I use a custom field named `specialfeature-470x175`.

Add a custom field to personalize your posts and pages

Using the custom field byline_summary

```
function byline_tag()
{
    global $post;
    if (!is_single())
        return false;
    if( !get_post_meta( $post->ID, 'byline_summary', true ) )
        return false;
    echo '<h3 class="byline-summary">' . get_post_meta( $post->ID, 'byline_
summary', true ) . '</h3>';
}
```

On the Web

The code in Listing 21.1 is available for download at www.wiley.com/go/wordpressbible. ∎

The key part of this template tag is the `get_post_meta()` function. This function takes three arguments and returns the content of the designated custom field. The first argument is the post ID. If you're using the custom field inside the Loop, you can declare the `$post` variable as global; this gives you access to `$post->ID`, which you can then use with the function. The second argument is the name of the custom field. In the case of the template tag function shown in Listing 21.1, the custom field name is `byline_summary`.

The third and completely optional argument is a `true` or `false` value that designates whether the custom field value should be returned as a single string (`true`) or as an array (`false`). The default is `false`. Generally, you'll want to set this to `true` but if you have more than one custom field of the same name attached to a post, a single value will return the first value and an array will return all of them.

The result of this template tag in action can be seen in Figure 21.4.

FIGURE 21.4

Using a custom field, I am able to attach a tagline to a post that displays underneath the post title. This stylistically replicates layouts used by many major media organizations.

Custom content types

Notably, an area where I haven't seen too much effort put forth, but that offers very interesting scenarios, is post types. WordPress comes built in with four varieties of post types: post, page, revision, and attachment. It is entirely possible for completely different post types to be included in the database. Some possible ideas for these post types, which don't have any user interface associated and would require a plugin to provide context, might be "job_req", "podcast", or "press_release".

Note

It is likely that in WordPress 3.0, which has not been released in time for the writing of this book, there will be a new "post type" user interface and management system. I mention it because it is relevant to this discussion, though I can offer no specifics as to how this system will function. ■

However, as I noted, no user interface is yet provided for custom content types. Posts submitted through the Add Post page get a post_type of post and pages added through the Add Page interface get a post_type of page. Images uploaded always get an attachment type.

So how is it possible to really use new post types? As of WordPress 2.9, WordPress is shipping with abstracted functions that used to be limited to the core WordPress content management screens. With these functions in hand, you can create a plugin that supplies its own content editing screen, similar to Add Page or Add Post, and use the same meta boxes that exist on those pages if you need to. Then, it's only a matter on inserting a new post with the proper post type.

Web Resource

For a simple example of how this can be done, see Rick Mann's post, "Don't Mess with My Toot Toot" at http://wp-fun.co.uk/2008/10/09/dont-mess-with-my-toot-toot/. ■

There are also a few plugins that help create administrative interfaces for custom post types. One example of this that takes a slightly different approach to custom content types (it was released before WordPress 2.9) is the Custom Field Template plugin available at www.kevinleary.net/advanced-content-management-wordpress-custom-field-templates/.

The idea behind this plugin is that you can have fine-grained control over custom fields that are available to bloggers and control how they are presented in the WordPress Admin. It's more of a presentation change than a functionality change, but I've used it with clients before to help them not be confused by the layout of WordPress and the use of the simple-yet-confusing term "custom fields." See Figure 21.5 for how this plugin alters the Write screens.

FIGURE 21.5

The Custom Field template alters the way custom fields are presented in the WordPress Admin.

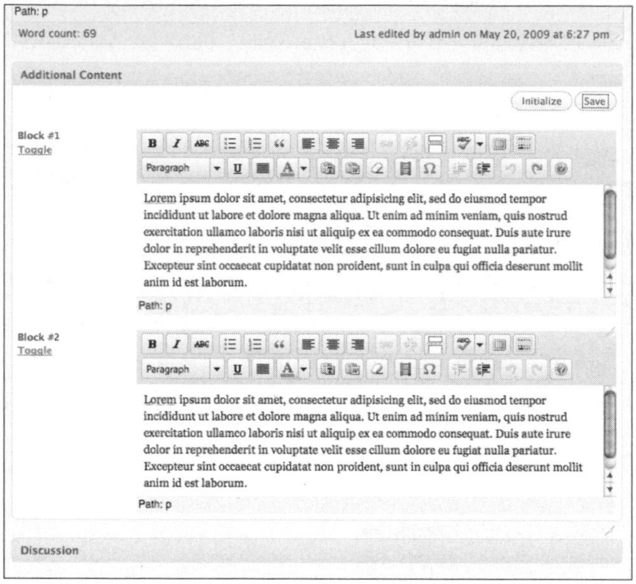

A second plugin that is extremely powerful is Flutter (`http://flutter.freshout.us/`). Flutter enables you to create new content creation panels on the fly. As with the Custom Field Template plugin, it does not actually create new content types, but it does create a perception of content types.

Summary

- With enterprise use of WordPress come considerations such as how to integrate with Active Directory and how to leverage WordPress to gain more sales.

- Use consistent theme templates and layouts to convey a unified message with your WordPress theme.

- Custom fields provide a tremendous customization opportunity.

- With WordPress 2.9, developers have more granular control over content types. It's possible to create entirely new content types and use common user interface elements to manage them.

Part VII

Looking at the WordPress Ecosystem

Leveraging WordPress MU and Multi-Blog Functionality

WordPress Multi-User, or WordPress MU, is the multi-blog variant of WordPress. It is built entirely on the same code base as WordPress but has additional features added to enable it to operate in a multi-blog environment.

Holistically, WordPress MU is a completely different approach to blogging. Whereas WordPress is fairly straight-line blogging — it's meant for individuals who want to have a blog to write or produce content on the Web — WordPress MU is meant for networks or hosting WordPress for other bloggers. To that end, though many of the management options for blogs using WordPress MU are similar to a single WordPress installation, the principles behind security, user management, and blog management are entirely different.

In addition, WordPress MU introduces an entirely new role called the *Site Administrator*, or Site Admin, who has Admin capabilities across the entire network of WordPress MU blogs. Regular administrators also exist, as they do in WordPress, but like in WordPress, administrators in WordPress MU are only Admins on their individual blogs and do not have global authority across the entire network of WordPress MU blogs.

Cross-Reference
User roles and capabilities in WordPress are discussed in Chapter 19. ∎

WordPress MU has gained significant appeal because of a suite of WordPress MU plugins called BuddyPress. BuddyPress adds social networking features to a WordPress MU install, which, in an era of social networks, is an important value add.

Cross-Reference

BuddyPress is discussed in more detail in Chapter 23. ■

Note

WordPress MU is going away as a separate software package. At WordCamp in San Francisco in May 2009, it was announced that the WordPress and WordPress MU codebases will be merged. At the time of this writing this merge is not yet on the timeline, but it is important to note it will likely occur with WordPress 3.0 and, while most of the WordPress MU functionality will be included, it is unclear how the final merged package will be delivered or what the upgrade path will be: if it's available from WordPress to WordPress MU or in reverse. ■

Installing and Configuring WordPress MU

WordPress MU is installed in a similar fashion to WordPress, though the steps are a bit more in-depth. For example, with the regular WordPress installation, the user is expected to edit her `wp-config.php` file, but with WordPress MU, the software automatically creates this file and generates the appropriate files as part of the installation.

Cross-Reference

For more information about system configuration recommendations and installing WordPress, refer to Chapter 2. ■

Installing WordPress MU

You can download WordPress MU from `http://mu.wordpress.org/download/`. As with WordPress, you will need to extract the archive and upload it to your Web space.

When you have uploaded your files, browse to the Web URL where the blog will be hosted. Because WordPress MU is not yet installed, you will see the installation screen that notes the system requirements needed for WordPress MU.

Note

While WordPress will install and work normally in almost any server environment without needing a special configuration or special access, WordPress MU is more advanced and requires some systems modification for best results. ■

For best results, make sure you have all of the following before continuing with your installation of WordPress MU:

- Access to the server to change file and directory permissions with FTP or Secure Shell (SSH).
- A valid e-mail address for administrative purposes.
- An empty MySQL database. (Avoid databases that have other WordPress installs that use `wp_` as the table prefix, as this will cause conflicts.)

- Wildcard DNS (Domain Name System) records for the domain if you're using WordPress MU in subdomain mode. You can add the following as a Canonical Name (CNAME) record in your DNS zone file: `*.example.com CNAME example.com.` (Consult with a systems administrator if you are not sure how to do this.)

On the initial installation screen shown in Figure 22.1, WordPress MU alerts you if the `wp-content/` folder is not writable by the server. It is imperative that this folder be writable for the configuration and initial setup of WordPress MU and it should be changed back so it's not writable later. (WordPress MU tells you how to do this.)

FIGURE 22.1

The initial installation screen in WordPress MU alerts you to file permission problems and instructs you how to change them.

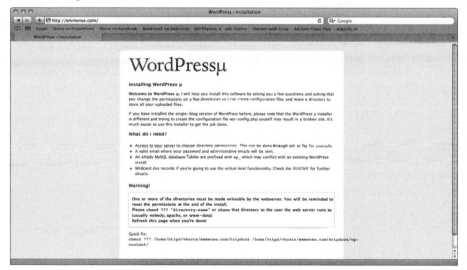

After all file or directory permissions have been resolved, refresh the page to continue the installation. You will be presented with a form that is needed to configure the site (see Figure 22.2). In the first portion of the form, enter your database configuration information: Database Name, User Name, Password, Database Host. Remember that, unless otherwise specified by your host or in your cluster configuration, the Database Host is almost always `localhost`.

The Server Address portion of the form is an important element of the WordPress MU installation because it will be used later throughout the installation. The Server Address should be the top-level domain, or the shortest possible subdomain where the installation will be hosted. WordPress MU provides examples: If your site is at `http://example.com`, you should enter `example.com` *not* `www.example.com` in the field. However, if your WordPress MU install is hosted at `http://blogs.example.com`, you should enter `blogs.example.com` instead.

FIGURE 22.2

When file permissions are correct, you need to provide the initial installation screen for WordPress MU with a few pieces of information to set the site up.

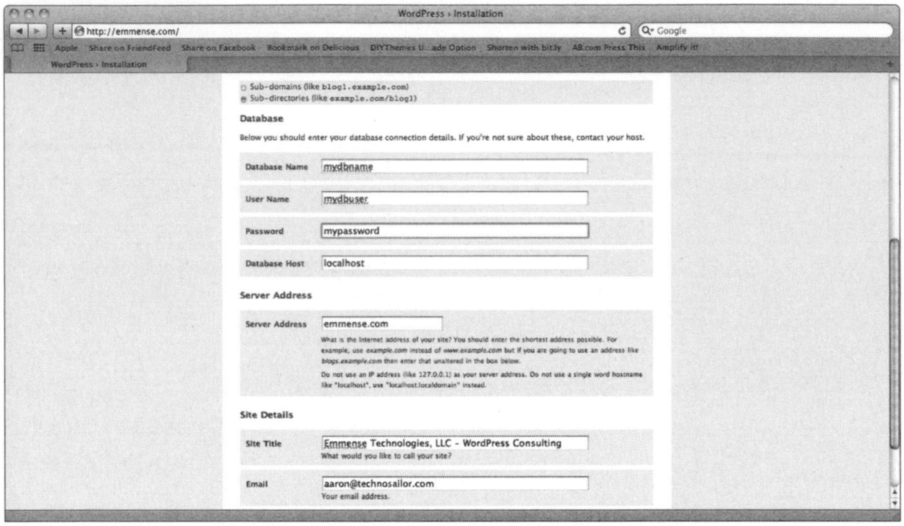

The final step in the installation process is to provide a site name (title) and an e-mail address for the Site Admin. You can't change these details later, so don't spend a lot of time here if you're not sure of the exact site name or administrator.

Caution

If you enter invalid information or incorrect database connection information during the initial installation and click the Save button, WordPress creates the `wp-config.php` **file necessary to run the site. However, if it can't connect to the database as a result, clicking the browser's Back button to correct and resubmit information will not modify the file. The only thing to do in this case is click the Back button, manually delete the** `wp-config.php` **file, make the necessary corrections on the installation screen, and resubmit.** ■

After completing the initial install, WordPress MU provides an administrative username and password that you can use to access the site and provide other essential information for a smooth operating site.

Configuring WordPress MU

WordPress MU can be organized into two configurations: subdomain-based or folder-based. A subdomain configuration enables blogs to take the form `blog1.example.com`, while a folder-based configuration puts a blog in the format `example.com/blog1`.

WordPress MU installs that cater to individual users, such as WordPress.com, tend to use subdomain installs (`blog1.example.com`). This is as much for branding as it is to provide the sense of individual ownership of a blog.

Folder-based installs are effective for internal organizations but provide no sense of inherent ownership of the blog. Folder-based installs are effective for corporations and organizations desiring the benefit of unified search engine optimization (SEO) across all blogs.

Note

Keep in mind that canonical URL theory treats subdomains as entirely different hosts than the domain itself. ■

Cross-Reference

For more information about canonical URLs, see Chapter 3. ■

Wildcard DNS configuration

The Domain Name System (DNS) is a hierarchical network of servers around the world that pass domain location information between each other. The system starts with a group of 13 DNS root servers that hold authoritative information about which domains are on what servers. Networks of DNS servers around the world sync up to each other and to these root servers so that the networks all have a record of where to route Internet traffic.

The DNS record for an individual domain is hosted where the domain is hosted and it notifies the DNS root servers of any changes to the domain that could affect routing (such as moving mail servers to different servers or providing new subdomains and routing information).

The easiest way for WordPress MU — which operates on an application level and not a network level — to handle subdomains is via *Wildcard DNS*. Wildcard DNS can best be thought of as a catchall. Any request coming to this domain that doesn't match any other criteria is routed to the main domain. Therefore, if the DNS zone is configured to have Wildcard DNS for the domain, any subdomain resolves to the same server.

Note

To truly understand the nuances in how Internet data is transferred for applications and for DNS , you have to understand the Open System Interconnection (OSI) model for networking. Though a discussion of the OSI model is beyond the scope of this book, the summary is that networking consists of seven layers of data modeling and handling: Physical (cables), Data (Mac addresses), Network (IP [Internet Protocol] addresses), Transport (TCP/UDP [Transmission Control Protocol/Universal Data Protocol] protocols), Session (a software layer for data transport quality), Presentation (encrypts/decrypts data to be sent across the wire), and Application (software for human interaction with data). ■

Web Resource

For more information about the OSI model, see `http://computer.howstuffworks.com/osi.htm`. ■

WordPress MU provides an application layer solution for site resolution. (Routing occurs inside the WordPress code and not prior to WordPress serving data.) To gain the same effect without Wildcard DNS, you would have to manually create entries for each subdomain in the domain zone or as individual zones, and then configure the Web server to point traffic to a specific location or directory.

Apache Wildcard Vhost configuration

As with DNS, it is necessary to ensure your Web server, in this case Apache, understands that when DNS passes requests to your server for a subdomain, it knows where to serve data from. To do this, you have to edit your Apache configuration and add a ServerAlias to the Virtual Host (Vhost) configuration for your domain.

To add a ServerAlias to the Vhost configuration for your domain, follow these steps:

1. **Edit your configuration file (or have a systems administrator do it for you), and add ServerAlias *.example.com to the configuration.**

2. **Restart Apache and test by entering any random subdomain like http://somerandom subdomain.example.com.** If all goes well, your random subdomain will resolve to WordPress MU, even though it has never been set up.

Converting a WordPress Blog to WordPress MU

Many bloggers interested in using WordPress MU already have a WordPress blog. Unfortunately, it is not possible to seamlessly turn WordPress installs into WordPress MU installs by simply uploading new files and upgrading. The only way to convert a WordPress blog to WordPress MU is to export your WordPress blog (choose Tools ➪ Export in the WordPress Admin), and then import it into a different WordPress MU installation.

Tip
Because of concerns with keeping data live and in production while making the migration, it is recommended that you import your blog into a separate install of WordPress MU (outside of your domain) and then, when everything is prepared and imported, delete your old WordPress install with all of your files and install WordPress MU (complete with your new database) into your domain space. ■

To convert a WordPress blog to WordPress MU, follow these steps:

1. **Disable comments on your WordPress install.** This ensures that no new data arrives in the database during the migration process.

2. **Perform a WordPress Export by choosing Tools ➪ Export.**

3. **Install WPMU in a separate folder, directory, or on a different blog.** For best results, perform the install on the same server that hosts your domain. This ensures a seamless cutover for the database and make moving files quick.

4. **Perform a WordPress Import by choosing Tools ⇨ Import ⇨ WordPress.** Make sure you select the check box to import attachments as well. If the process times out, try again. If the file is too large, break it into smaller pieces or adjust your PHP settings to allow the upload.

5. **Verify that your data has been migrated, including photos.** Photos will be stored in folders under `wp-content/blogs.dir/`. The numbers in this directory represent the blog ID so the first blog installed, the main blog, will have an ID of 1.

6. **Verify your permalink structure by choosing Settings ⇨ Permalinks.** You'll need this in WordPress MU.

7. **Download the wp-content/ folder that contains your theme and plugins.**

8. **Back up your WordPress blog, including files and the database.** This ensures that you can "roll back" to your current WordPress install in the event of catastrophe.

9. **Delete all files from your current WordPress location.**

10. **Move (or copy) all WordPress MU files and folders from their temporary location to your domain space.**

11. **Upload your theme to wp-content/themes.**

12. **Upload your plugins to wp-content/plugins.**

13. **Update MySQL to contain current proper URLs for WordPress MU.** Do this via the MySQL command line over SSH or via phpMyAdmin:

    a. Execute query: UPDATE wp_site SET domain='example.com' WHERE id=1;

    b. Execute query: UPDATE wp_blogs SET domain='example.com' WHERE blog_id=1;

    c. Execute query: UPDATE wp_1_options SET option_value='http://example.com' WHERE option_name in('siteurl','home');

14. **Open wp-config.php and update the defined constant DOMAIN_CURRENT_SITE if this is not set for your current domain.**

15. **Log in to WordPress MU using the same login page as you did in WordPress (http://example.com/wp-login.php).**

16. **Regenerate Permalinks for WordPress MU.** Do this by choosing Settings ⇨ Permalinks and using the same structure noted in Step 6.

17. **Make your theme Available to the WordPress MU blogs.** To do this, enable it by choosing Site Admin ⇨ Themes.

18. **Activate the theme for your blog by choosing Presentation ⇨ Themes as you would normally do to activate themes in WordPress.**

19. **Activate all required plugins under Plugins ➪ Installed.** Only Site Administrators will be able to access the plugins menu unless they activate them for other users by choosing Site Admin ➪ Options. Plugins can be activated for a single blog, as is typical for WordPress plugins, or activated site wide for all blogs.

20. **Update all options throughout WordPress MU to reflect your preferences.** Typically, these are a mirror image of what you had on your WordPress blog.

When you initially log in to WordPress MU, you'll notice a striking resemblance to the WordPress Admin you were familiar with before. WordPress MU is based on the same code as the single version of WordPress, but has key differences. One of the main differences in WordPress Admin is it includes a Site Admin panel in the navigation pane on the left side of the screen, as shown in Figure 22.3.

FIGURE 22.3

The WordPress MU Admin panel is similar to that of the single WordPress install but includes a Site Admin navigation panel.

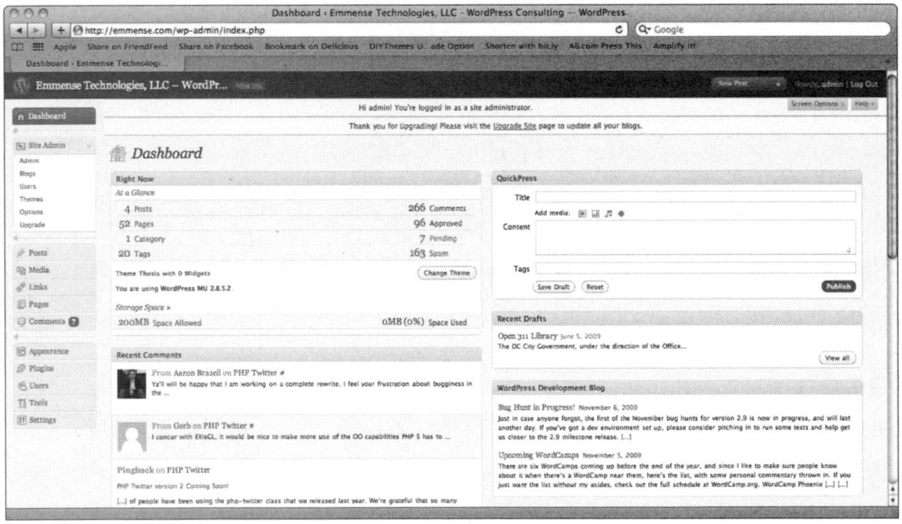

The Site Admin panel contains six additional Admin panels when expanded. Some of these are sparsely populated while others have a lot of WordPress MU options.

Admin panel

The WordPress MU Admin panel, shown in Figure 22.4, is a simplistic page that contains two search fields. You can search by users or by blogs as well as create a new blog or a new user. (Note that when you create users in WordPress MU in this manner, they are not automatically assigned to a specific blog.)

FIGURE 22.4

You can create or search for users and blogs from the Site Admin ➪ Admin panel.

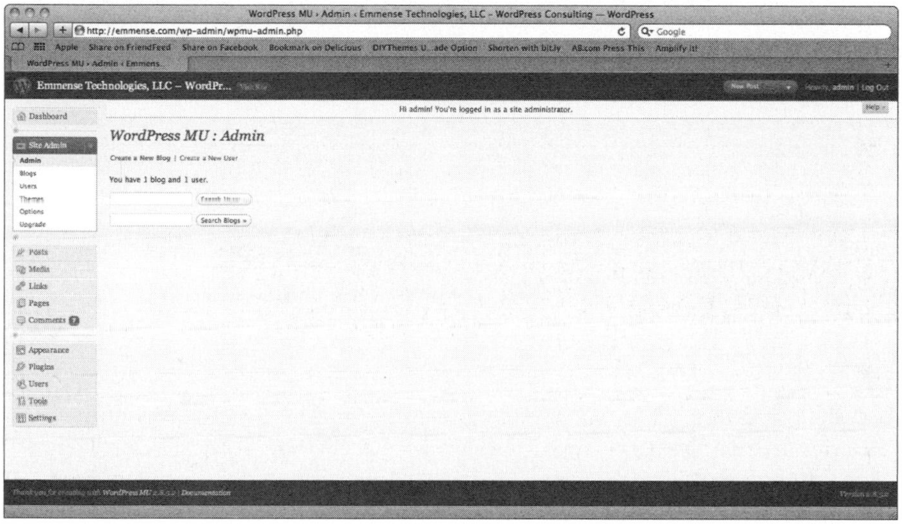

Blogs panel

The Blogs panel, shown in Figure 22.5, contains a listing of all blogs in WordPress MU. It also enables a Site Administrator to create a new blog.

The Blogs panel shows useful information about existing blogs, such as the blog ID, assigned users, and when a blog was last updated. By hovering over a blog, a menu is displayed that enables a Site Administrator to access the WordPress Admin for the particular blog, or edit details about the blog, delete it, and so on.

FIGURE 22.5

The Blogs panel enables a Site Administrator to create a new blog or modify or delete an old one.

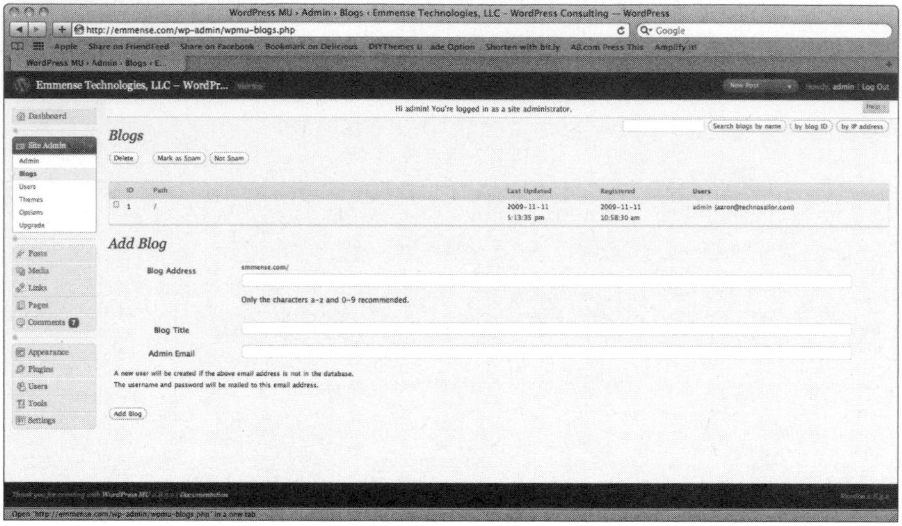

Users panel

The WordPress MU Users panel under Site Admin is similar to the Users panel in WordPress (see Figure 22.6). However, it is important to note that this Users panel is not the same as the Users panel under Users ➪ Authors & Users, which is used for specific blog user administration and not global user administration.

The Site Admin Users panel in WordPress MU is used for modifying and assigning users in the entire WordPress MU system to specific blogs. In addition, you can add new users from this panel but they are not added to any specific blog by default.

Note

Unlike WordPress, WordPress MU does not allow usernames that have spaces. Imported usernames that are made up of more than one word will be created with spaces, but Site Administrators specifically need to have usernames with no spaces. Ensure that any import is manually updated to ensure spaces are removed. ■

Themes panel

The Themes panel under Site Admin, shown in Figure 22.7, is used for making WordPress themes available to individual blogs. You can turn every theme that is in the wp-content/themes folder on or off across the board. Themes that are not enabled in this panel are not available, even to administrators, on the individual blogs.

FIGURE 22.6

The Site Admin Users panel is used to manage users and blog assignments for all of WordPress MU.

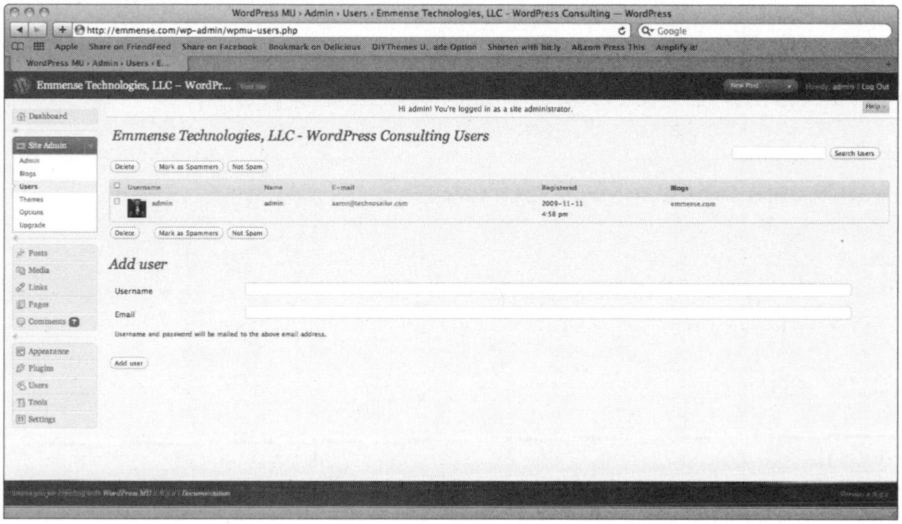

FIGURE 22.7

Themes must be activated in the Site Admin ➪ Themes menu before blog administrators can select the theme for use on their blogs.

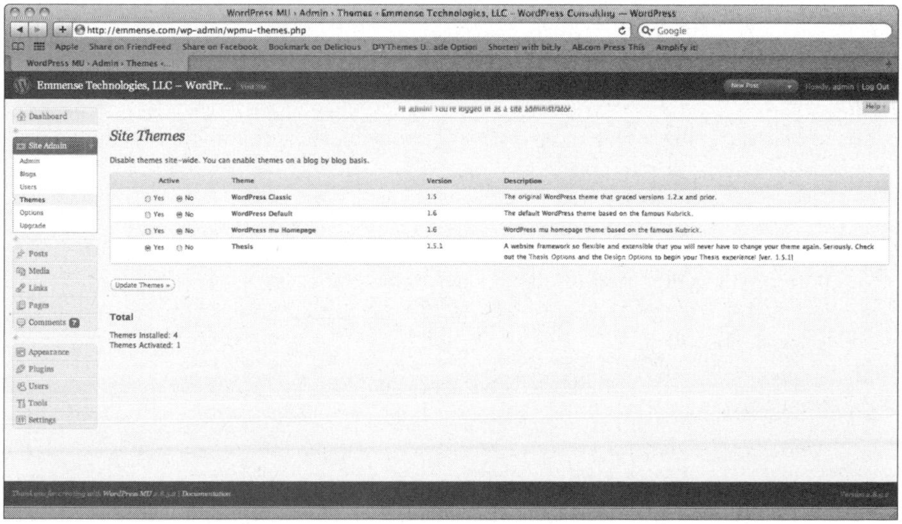

Options panel

The Options panel is probably the most important site configuration panel in all of WordPress MU. Almost all of the tweaking and configuration for the entire install is performed on this screen. The configuration options are described in Table 22.1.

TABLE 22.1

WordPress MU Configuration Options

Option	Description
Site Name	The name initially designated during the setup phase.
Site Admin E-mail	A valid e-mail address where all administrative e-mail messages will be set to and from.
Allow New Registrations	Specifies whether a WordPress MU installation allows new users to register blogs, just usernames, and so on.
	Note: If you allow this option to be enabled, please be vigilant about disabling spam accounts that will inevitably sign up.
Registration Notification	If enabled, the Site Admin E-mail will be notified of new registrations.
Add New Users	Allows blog administrators to create new user accounts for their blogs.
Dashboard Blog	The blog name (subdomain or folder) or blog ID that will be the default blog for new user registrations. If left blank, the main blog is used.
Dashboard User Default Role	The default user is generally Subscriber.
Banned Names	A space-separated list of words that can never be used for usernames.
Limited E-mail Registration	Allows blog creation from users with e-mail addresses from specific domains.
Banned E-mail Domains	Disallows blog creation from users with e-mail addresses from specific domains.
Welcome E-mail	An e-mail template that is sent to new users when they sign up.
First Post	A template for the default post that is added to a blog upon creation.
Upload Media Button	By selecting some, none, or all of the Images, Video, or Music check boxes, you enable bloggers to upload rich content to their blogs.
Blog upload Space	Enforce a maximum amount of data to be uploaded cumulatively. (By default, this is 10MB.)
Upload file Types	A space-separated list of extensions that WordPress MU will allow to be uploaded.
Admin Notices Feed	Provides the URL for a feed, and an excerpt from the most recent post is displayed on all blog dashboards.
Site Admins	A space-separated list of users (blog administrators) that you wish to grant Site Admin rights.

Option	Description
Default Language	Choose your default language to be used in WordPress MU. (Individual users can override this.)
Menus	Places check marks next to the menu items you want blog administrators to have access to.

Upgrade panel

WordPress MU's upgrade panel is an automated script that goes through all of the blogs on WordPress MU and runs the WordPress upgrade script from each one. You still have to upgrade the blogs files manually or with the inbuilt Auto Upgrade feature that is from WordPress.

Understanding WordPress MU Plugin Nuances

WordPress plugins that operate off of the standard WordPress plugin application programming interface (API) generally work as expected in WordPress MU because WordPress MU is built on the same codebase as WordPress. Therefore, on principle, plugins that work with WordPress also work with WordPress MU. The same cannot be said of WordPress MU plugins working on standard WordPress installs, however.

There are three main differences between WordPress MU and WordPress when it comes to plugin development: the concept of blog IDs, the use of different database schemas (which should not generally matter if you're using the plugin API), and the concept of multiple blogs as it pertains to plugins that use data from other blogs.

Blog ID

Both WordPress and WordPress MU use the $blog_id global variable. In WordPress, the $blog_id is always 1. In WordPress MU, however, the $blog_id is used throughout the codebase. Each blog has a $blog_id incrementing from 1, which is the main blog.

A unique function combo WordPress MU plugin developers can use to change the blog context that WordPress MU is operating in is the switch_to_blog() function combined with the restore_current_blog() function. Using these two functions enables plugin developers to switch a blog's context to a different blog to perform some action and then return to the original context. A good example of this is code that I wrote recently for WordPress MU (see Listing 22.1). This code can be turned into a WordPress MU plugin and activated. It grabs the first post from every WordPress MU blog except the current one. It is meant to be used in a theme sidebar so it can easily be incorporated into a widget using the Widget API as well.

LISTING 22.1

Using switch_to_blog() and restore_current_blog() functions to alter the WordPress MU context

```php
function wpb_mu_blog_agg()
{
    global $wpdb;
    $blogs = get_site_option( 'blog_list' );
    foreach( $blogs as $blog ) :
        $blog = (object) $blog;
        if( $wpdb->blogid == $blog->blog_id )
            continue;
        switch_to_blog($blog->blog_id);
        ?>
        <div class="mu_blog_side">
            <h3><a href="<?php echo bloginfo('home') ?>"><?php echo
bloginfo('name') ?></a></h3>
            <?php
            $this_query = new WP_Query('showposts=1&post_
status=publish');
            echo '<div>';
            if( $this_query->have_posts() ) :
                while( $this_query->have_posts() ) : $this_query->the_
post();
            ?>
                <h4 class="title"><a rel="bookmark" href="<?php
the_permalink() ?>"><?php the_title() ?></a></h4>
                <p><?php the_excerpt() ?></p>
            </div>
            <div class="right">
                <a href="<?php echo bloginfo('home') ?>">More
Articles &raquo;</a>
            </div>
            <?php endwhile;
            else :
                echo '<p>There are no posts from this blog.</p>';
            endif;
            echo '</div>';
        restore_current_blog();
    endforeach;
}
```

Cross-Reference

The WordPress 2.8 Widget API is the same Widget API used in WordPress MU. This API is discussed in Chapter 6. ∎

WordPress MU database schema

The WordPress MU database schema is very different than that of WordPress. Portions of WordPress that are blog-specific have been abstracted to different tables in WordPress MU. In fact, every blog in WordPress MU has its own set of tables that are blog specific. Installation-wide configuration data is stored in a series of other tables.

Site configuration tables

Tables having to do with larger, global settings are stored in centralized tables. Every blog accesses these for settings, and global settings that have been made in the Site Admin menus are also generally stored in the site configuration tables.

Blogs table

The Blogs table lists basic information about each blog registered with WordPress MU. The name of this table is stored in $wpdb->blogs. The schema for this table is listed in Table 22.2.

TABLE 22.2

Database Schema for WordPress MU Blogs Table

Field	Type	Null	Key	Default	Extra
blog_id	bigint(20)	No	Primary		Auto increment
site_id	bigint(20)	No		0	
domain	varchar(200)	No	Multiple		
path	varchar(100)	No	Multiple		
registered	datetime	No		0000-00-00 00:00:00	
last_updated	datetime	No		0000-00-00 00:00:00	
public	tinyint(2)	No		1	
archived	enum('0','1')	No		0	
mature	tinyint(2)	No		0	
spam	tinyint(2)	No		0	
deleted	tinyint(2)	No		0	
lang_id	int(11)	No	Multiple	0	

Blog Versions table

The Blog Versions table, stored with the name $wpdb->blog_versions, keeps a record of which database schema each blog is using. Keep in mind that an upgrade requires each blog to be kept up to date with the proper version of the WordPress database schema. The database schema for the Blogs Versions table is shown in Table 22.3.

TABLE 22.3

Database Schema for WordPress MU Blog Versions Table

Field	Type	Null	Key	Default	Extra
blog_id	bigint(20)	No	Primary	0	Auto increment
db_version	varchar(20)	No	Multiple		
last_updated	datetime	No		0000-00-00 00:00:00	

Registration Log table

Because the assumption behind WordPress MU is that many users will use it, WordPress MU developers provide a registration log table. The name of this table is stored in $wpdb->registration_log and its schema is listed in Table 22.4.

TABLE 22.4

Database Schema for WordPress MU Registration Log Table

Field	Type	Null	Key	Default	Extra
ID	bigint(20)	No	Primary		Auto increment
email	varchar(255)	No			
IP	varchar(30)	No	Multiple	0	
date_registered	datetime	No		0000-00-00 00:00:00	

Site table

The Site table is a sparsely populated site with generally a single record describing global configuration options for the entire site. The name of this table is held in $wpdb->site and its schema is listed in Table 22.5.

TABLE 22.5

Database Schema for WordPress MU Site table

Field	Type	Null	Key	Default	Extra
id	bigint(20)	No	Primary		Auto increment
domain	varchar(200)	No	Multiple		
path	varchar(100)	No	Multiple		

Site Meta table

The Site Meta table, whose name is stored in $wpdb->sitemeta, stores most of the information designated in the Site Admin ➪ Options table. The schema for this table is listed in Table 22.6.

TABLE 22.6

Database Schema for WordPress MU Site Meta Table

Field	Type	Null	Key	Default	Extra
meta_id	bigint(20)	No	Primary		Auto increment
site_id	bigint(20)	No	Multiple	0	
meta_key	varchar(255)	Yes	Multiple	Null	
meta_value	longtext				

Site Categories table

One of the more puzzling aspects of WordPress MU is the existence of the Site Categories table, whose name is stored in $wpdb->sitecategories. This table stores a unique list of all categories created by all users on all blogs. However, it is not actually used anywhere in WordPress MU. The schema for this table is listed in Table 22.7.

TABLE 22.7

Database Schema for WordPress MU Site Categories Table

Field	Type	Null	Key	Default	Extra
cat_ID	bigint(20)	No	Primary		Auto increment
cat_name	varchar(55)	No			
category_nicename	varchar(200)	No	Multiple		
last_updated	timestamp	No	Multiple		

Signups table

The Signups table exists to track new user registrations. Because new user registration might also mean the creation of a new blog, this table stores that information as well. The table name is stored in $wpdb->signups and its schema is listed in Table 22.8.

TABLE 22.8

Database Schema for WordPress MU Signups Table

Field	Type	Null	Key	Default	Extra
domain	varchar(200)	No			
path	varchar(100)	No			
title	longtext	No			
user_login	varchar(60)	No			
user_email	varchar(100)	No			
registered	datetime	No		0000-00-00 00:00:00	
activated	datetime	No		0000-00-00 00:00:00	
active	tinyint(1)	No		0	
activation_key	varchar(50)	No			

Blog-specific tables

Most of the tables plugin developers recognize from the WordPress world are carried over as blog-specific tables in WordPress MU. Blog-specific tables are named with the $table_prefix defined in wp-config.php, followed by the $blog_id and then the table name. In WordPress, if the table name were wp_posts, it might be wp_1_posts in WordPress MU.

The schemas for these tables are exactly what they are in WordPress. The tables that become blog-specific tables in WordPress MU include:

- Comments
- Commentmeta
- Links
- Options
- Postmeta
- Posts
- Term_relationships
- Term_taxonomy
- Terms

Adapting to WordPress MU

WordPress MU is slightly more difficult to adapt to if you've always been a WordPress user. From a user experience standpoint, the two are relatively the same. The WordPress Admin has one key navigation change I discussed already: the Site Admin. More differences lie below the surface, though.

By and large, users and developers that are used to WordPress will adapt easily to WordPress MU. However, there are "gotchas" along the way and, in some cases, a completely different way of thinking about WordPress.

Activating plugins site wide

Longtime WordPress MU users will note that there was a recent adoption of site-wide activation of plugins. Until recently, the only way to have a site-wide plugin — a global plugin for lack of a better word — was to include it in the `wp-content/mu-plugins` folder. All code, plugins or not, that are included in this directory are automatically included with no activation required.

However, with WordPress 2.7 and the adoption of the plugin Auto Upgrade feature and notifications, WordPress MU developers added the ability to activate plugins from the plugins page in WordPress Admin as well as the option to activate it on all blogs (see Figure 22.8).

FIGURE 22.8

With WordPress MU 2.7, the ability to activate plugins site wide from the plugins screen in WordPress Admin was added.

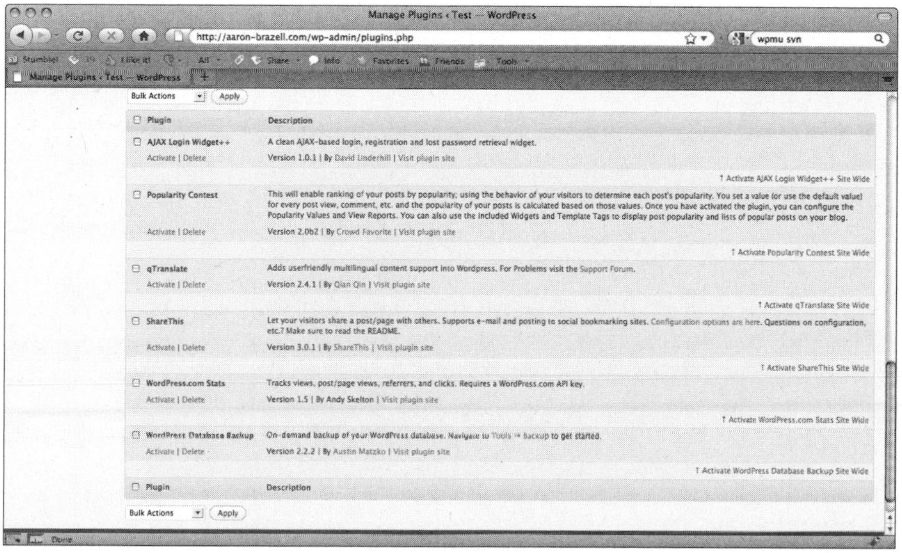

Constructing image permalinks

The method for constructing image permalinks in WordPress MU is slightly different than in WordPress. In WordPress, images are typically uploaded to `wp-content/uploads/` and then, depending on settings, images might be organized into year- and month-based folders.

In WordPress MU, however, images are uploaded to `wp-content/blogs.dir/{blog_id}/files/` and then organized into year- and month-based directories. Permalinks for files look like `http://example.com/files/2009/06/sample.jpg`, which is a major change from how WordPress generates image permalinks.

Using WordPress MU with different domains

A frequent request from WordPress MU users is to be able to use different top-level domains for each blog. This is a difficult problem to solve without server-level tweaks, but it is solvable. Donncha O. Caoimh, the lead developer of WordPress MU, released the WordPress MU Domain Mapping plugin, available at `http://wordpress.org/extend/plugins/wordpress-mu-domain-mapping/`.

This plugin is basic and solves some problems though not all of them. For example:

- If you log in on one domain, you will have to log in separately for another domain, even on the same WordPress MU install. This stems from cookies being domain-limited.

- It only works for WordPress MU installs using subdomains. It will not work with folder-based installs.

- Users have to point their domains to your installation via their domain registrar. You must provide them with an IP address for them to do that.

Summary

- Configuring WordPress MU is more involved that WordPress. Ensure that you have Wildcard DNS and a wildcard `ServerAlias` in your Apache configuration.

- WordPress standard installs can be exported and then imported into a separate WordPress MU install. Backup, backup, backup!

- WordPress MU is similar to standard WordPress but has nuances like `$blog_id` and a different database schema.

- Other nuances of WordPress MU include WordPress MU site-wide plugins, image uploading, and permalinks, and using different domains for a WordPress MU blog.

Adding User Forums with bbPress

O n December 28, 2004, Matt Mullenweg, the founder of WordPress, announced on a new blog that he had spent a weekend over the holidays hacking together a lightweight forum software that he dubbed bbPress.

He wrote it because all of the forum software that existed at the time had restrictive licensing and too many features. He wanted to develop forum software that could be used in a similar fashion as WordPress.

Five years later, bbPress has come a long way. In fact, as of BuddyPress 1.1 (a suite of WordPress plugins and themes), bbPress is included as a one-click install add-on.

Cross-Reference
BuddyPress and bbPress integration are discussed in Chapter 24. ■

Installing bbPress

bbPress is a lightweight forum software. Most notably, it serves as the official support forum software for the WordPress support forums (`http://word press.org/support/`), as shown in Figure 23.1. It is also often used by bloggers who have released popular software and wish to offer support venues.

IN THIS CHAPTER

Installing bbPress

Finding bbPress plugins

Understanding the bbPress theme system

The WordPress support forums are powered by bbPress.

bbPress is extremely easy to install. Just like WordPress, it can be set up in mere minutes. To get started, grab the latest version of bbPress at `http://bbpress.org/download/` and then follow these steps:

1. **Connect to your server using FTP or SFTP.**

2. **If you are adding bbPress to an existing site, create a new folder (such as forum/) in your Web-accessible Web directory.**

3. **Extract the downloaded bbPress archive and upload the contents of the bbPress folder to the location on your server where you want to install it (such as forum/).**

4. **Take note of the permission settings of the folder in which you are installing bbPress (generally 755) and make sure it is set to 777.** This is temporary and will ensure that the configuration file can be generated. If you don't want to do this step, you will be provided with the contents of the configuration file later and you will have to copy and paste those contents into a new `bb-config.php` file.

5. **Load the bbPress URL into your Web browser.** Because this is the first time you are installing bbPress, it will redirect you to an install URL similar to `http://example.com/forum/bb-admin/install.php`, as shown in Figure 23.2.

6. **Click the Go to step 1 button to begin the install process.** You will be prompted to enter your database information, as shown in Figure 23.3. If you plan on sharing information with WordPress, I highly suggest you use the same database and connection information as WordPress does. You won't hurt anything as long as you specify a different table prefix. (The default is bb_.)

7. **Select the Show Advanced Settings check box to reveal more information to fill in.** Generally, the defaults are fine, but if you have a reason to change these settings, due to hosting support or something else, this is where you would do it.

FIGURE 23.2

The install screen for bbPress takes you through a few short steps to configure bbPress.

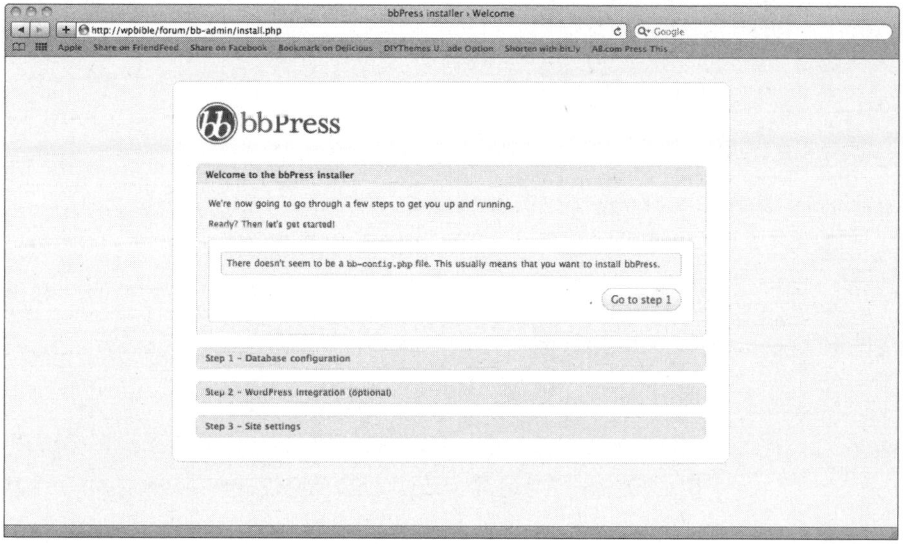

8. **Press the Save database configuration file button to save the database configuration.** If you changed the permission of the bbPress folder, change it back to what it was originally using your FTP client or SSH (probably 755).

9. **Click the Go to Step 2 button.** If you plan to integrate with WordPress, Step 2 is extremely important.

10. **Select the Add integration settings check box.** This will reveal two more check boxes, as shown in Figure 23.4.

FIGURE 23.3

Fill in all database connection information (use the same information as you did for WordPress if you plan to share settings) and select the Show advanced settings check box to reveal more optional configuration options.

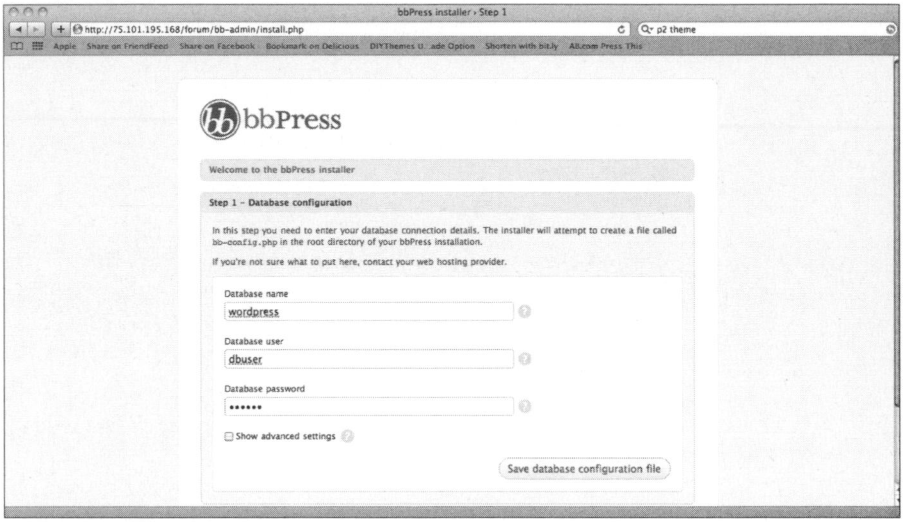

FIGURE 23.4

If you plan to integrate with WordPress, select all the integration settings check boxes and fill in the appropriate details.

11. Select the **Add cookie integration settings** checkbox to reveal another set of form fields:

   a. **Add your WordPress URL.** This must be exactly as it is in your WordPress install under Settings ➪ General.

   b. **Add your Blog address URL.** This must be exactly as it is in your WordPress install under Settings ➪ General.

   c. **Add your WordPress "auth" cookie key.** This must be exactly the same as the AUTH_KEY constant in your `wp-config.php` file. Leave the WordPress "auth" cookie salt field blank because bbPress will discover it from the WordPress database.

   d. **Add your WordPress "secure auth" cookie key.** This must be exactly the same as SECURE_AUTH_KEY constant from your `wp-config.php` file. Leave the WordPress "secure auth" cookie salt field blank because bbPress will discover it from the WordPress database.

   e. **Add your "logged in" cookie key.** This must be exactly the same as the LOGGED_IN_KEY constant in your `wp-config.php` file. Leave the WordPress "logged in" cookie salt field blank because bbPress will discover it from the WordPress database.

12. **Select the Add user database integration settings check box to reveal another set of form fields, as shown in Figure 23.5.**

Adding user database integration is the final step of the WordPress integration process.

13. **Add your WordPress table prefix.** If you are integrating with WordPress MU (Multi-User WordPress), add your primary blog ID (generally 1). In rare cases, if you chose to install bbPress in a different database than WordPress, you will also have to add your WordPress database settings.

14. **Select the Show Advanced Database settings check box and fill in the database connection details for WordPress.** Then, click the Save WordPress Integration Settings button to advance to the third step of the setup wizard. If you chose not to integrate WordPress, Step 3 prompts you to enter admin user information.

Note
Regardless of whether you decided to integrate with WordPress, Step 3 will ask you to enter some final information about your forums: the name of the forum, the site address (URL), and the name of your first forum (which you can change later). If you integrated with WordPress, you also have to choose which WordPress user you wish to make the Keymaster (admin) of the forum. ■

15. **After saving the information entered in Step 3, click the Complete Installation button to finalize the installation.** Your bbPress forum is installed at the URL you chose for your site address.

Finding bbPress Plugins

Just like WordPress, bbPress is extensible and was built on the same concepts as WordPress: lightweight and easily expanded. In fact, much of the code is the same thanks to the integration of the BackPress WordPress framework.

Cross-Reference
BackPress is discussed in Chapter 25. ■

There is not the rich ecosystem around bbPress that there is around WordPress. It has taken a much longer time to develop and had not seen significant uptake until BuddyPress became stable and people started using it. bbPress powers the discussions inside the BuddyPress paradigm so it has become an essential point of integration for many of the BuddyPress installs out there.

There are a variety of plugins, however, that extend bbPress. Most are hosted on the bbPress plugin repository at `http://bbpress.org/plugins/`, which itself is powered by bbPress.

The most popular plugins, by Automattic metrics, are listed in Table 23.1.

TABLE 23.1

Popular bbPress Plugins in the bbPress Plugin Repository

Plugin Name	Description	Download URL
Allow Images	Allows forum members to include images in their forum signatures	http://bbpress.org/plugins/topic/allow-images/
bbPress Signatures	Extends forum users' bios and enables them to have a signature on their posts	http://bbpress.org/plugins/topic/bbpress-signatures/
bbPress Attachments	Allows members to upload attachments to their forum posts	http://bbpress.org/plugins/topic/bb-attachments/
BBcode Lite	Adds bulletin board (BB) text formatting commonly used on other forum systems	http://bbpress.org/plugins/topic/bbcode-lite/
BBcode Buttons	Adds buttons to the forum post entry screen to allow quick access to BBcode	http://bbpress.org/plugins/topic/bbcode-buttons/

Understanding the bbPress Theme System

The theme system for bbPress is very similar to the theme system in WordPress. Unfortunately, you can't simply take a WordPress theme and drop it into bbPress because there are elements of a forum (such as forums, subforums, and topics) that are not consistent with the WordPress concept of pages, posts, and comments. Figure 23.6 illustrates what the default bbPress theme looks like.

FIGURE 23.6

The bbPress default theme, Kakumei

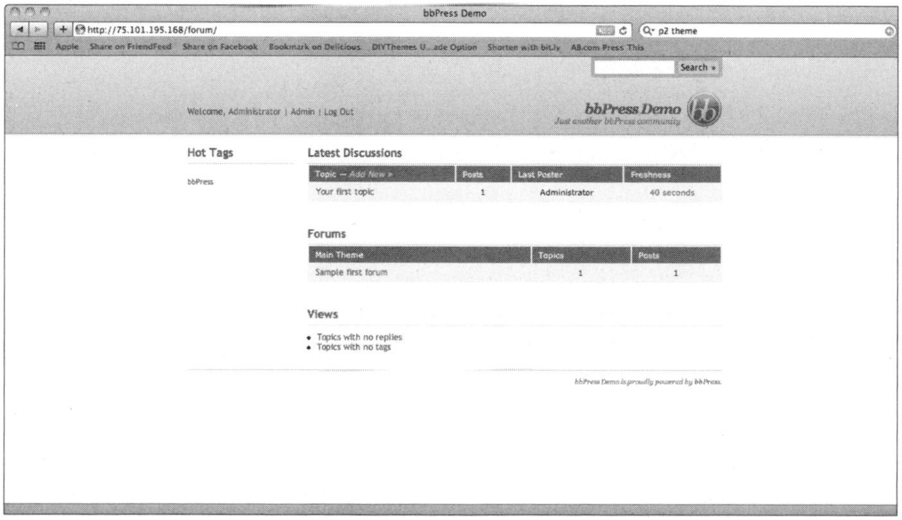

First, all bbPress themes go into the bb-templates/ directory. bbPress does not support child themes directly, but if you wish to use the stylesheet from your WordPress install, you can do so with the import keyword in CSS (Cascading Style Sheets). You can read up on how to use this rule at http://webdesign.about.com/cs/css/qt/tipcssatimport.htm. Using the @import rule, you can simply add the relevant CSS to your master stylesheet.

Because much of bbPress is not documented, there is some learning curve. Table 23.2 lists key template files and their purpose.

Note
bbPress hasn't seen a lot of development over the years. Much of this comes from the massive push to build out WordPress over the last five years (adoption drives innovation) and BuddyPress in the last year. ∎

bbPress is a great tool but is highly undocumented and can even be frustrating for developers to work with. Add to this that "forums" are of diminishing importance in a world dominated by social networks, and it is hard to see bbPress surviving as anything more than a side project on its own.

TABLE 23.2

Core bbPress Theme Files

Filename	Description
front-page.php	The main page that is loaded when the forum is visited.
404.php	The template that is used when there is no content at the address.
edit-form.php	The template used for editing comments on a posting.
edit-post.php	The template used for editing new posts in a forum.
favorites.php	A template used to allow users to create customized RSS feeds of topics based on specified criteria (for example, searches).
footer.php	Identical to the behavior of a WordPress footer.php.
forum.php	The template used to display a listing of topics in a specified forum.
header.php	Identical to the behavior of a WordPress header.php.
login-form.php	The template used to display a login form on a site.
login.php	A template used to provide a standalone login page.
post-form.php	The template used for adding a new post.
post.php	The template used to display the HTML for one poster's post.
profile.php	The template used to display a user's public profile.
profile-edit.php	The template used to allow a user to edit her profile.
search.php	A template used to render search results. Identical to WordPress' search.php.
tags.php	A template that reders a tag archive in a similar way to the WordPress template file with the same name.

Filename	Description
style.css	Identical to how WordPress works, the style.css file has descriptive theme headers and is required for a theme to function.
topic.php	The template used to display a single posting on a forum. Similar to WordPress' single.php.

The integration of bbPress into BuddyPress (discussed more in the next chapter) is a huge boon and might be the saving grace for the software. There is hope for this lightweight forum software as it won't have to find a way to survive on its own and is a key part of the social networking experience offered by BuddyPress.

(All of this, however, is only this author's opinion.)

Summary

- bbPress is a forum software built with the same basic premise as WordPress: to be lightweight and extensible.

- bbPress is simple to install, but you must enter information for integration exactly as specified. If you do not copy information directly and exactly, integration won't work.

- bbPress can share the same user table as WordPress or stand alone.

- A rich ecosystem for plugin development around bbPress doesn't exist. Much of this has to do with lack of documentation and lack of market share. However, as an extensible platform, plugins can be built in the same way as WordPress and hooks exist to make plugin development easier.

- Themes follow similar, yet very different, hierarchies than WordPress. Common template names like `header.php` and `footer.php` exist, but many more forum-specific template files can also be used. If a template file is omitted, bbPress looks to the default Kakumei theme for the file.

Creating Your Own Social Network with BuddyPress

For as long as WordPress has existed, it has been built as a blogging platform. Despite this, savvy developers have used the extensibility of the software to create new concept software around it.

In 2008, one such developer, Andy Peatling, used WordPress to create a social network for a client. The extensibility of the plugin architecture enabled him to create a concept that combined many of the features enjoyed on services like Facebook (www.facebook.com) into a single WordPress MU (Multi-User WordPress) install.

Soon, Automattic would acquire BuddyPress, and Andy would become their primary developer on the project. Since those early days, BuddyPress has seen a couple of releases and is starting to be adopted as a popular social networking platform.

What Is BuddyPress?

BuddyPress is a WordPress MU plugin with several components that can be enabled individually or altogether. Each component provides social network-like functionality to users. These features include private messaging, groups, and activity feeds.

By producing a different experience, Automattic implicitly endorses WordPress being used in alternative formats besides blogs. The BuddyPress experience (see Figure 24.1) essentially recognizes that social networking is as vitally important to users today as blogging was in 2006.

FIGURE 24.1

BuddyPress brings a whole new experience to WordPress, enabling readers to make friends, share stories, and personalize their experiences.

In WordPress (or WordPress MU), the main focus for the user is the blog. BuddyPress reverses this, placing the user's attention on his or her own profile, friends, groups, and activity. It is entirely possible with some installs of BuddyPress that the blog will never be viewed. Likewise, a site could be very much focused on the blog content, with a few social features layered on.

Note

All configuration of modules can be done from within WordPress MU in the Site Admin and BuddyPress menus. ■

Activity Stream

In essence, the Activity Stream module is the equivalent of the Facebook "Wall" (see Figure 24.2). It aggregates all activities from friends, groups, blog posts, and so on into one place. Naturally, it only includes activity from modules that have been configured and are active.

The Activity Stream has an application programming interface (API) associated with it so that developers who want to extend BuddyPress can do so and inject their own Activity notices into the stream.

FIGURE 24.2

The Activity Stream uses the same concept of the Facebook news feed. It aggregates all activities from configured modules in one place.

Blog tracking

Depending on how you configure BuddyPress, you can allow users to have their own blogs. If you choose to do this, you will probably want to enable the blog tracking module. This way, whenever your users post new content to their blogs, or comment on other blogs in your network, the activity will be tracked.

This can be especially useful for BuddyPress installations using groups because then conversations and users can be siloed into topics and around common interests.

bbPress integration

One of the key areas of any social network is communication among friends, groups, and connections. In the BuddyPress paradigm, this occurs through bbPress. Forums can be handled as standalone sites that integrate all the conversations, or the discussions can be connected and synced internally in BuddyPress itself (see Figure 24.3). As of BuddyPress 1.1, bbPress is bundled and does not have to be installed separately. It can be done from within WordPress MU as a one-click install.

Cross-Reference

For information on installing and configuring bbPress, see Chapter 23. ∎

When installing bbPress from within BuddyPress, the user experience will be different than what is expected out of typical forum software. In the context of BuddyPress, bbPress doesn't become a destination so much as it becomes the tool that powers conversations in a variety of contexts within the social network experience. Instead of visiting a forum, users interact with other users within the context of the BuddyPress social network and bbPress enables those conversations to happen in a supporting role.

FIGURE 24.3

BuddyPress can integrate with bbPress, drawing the forum discussions that would normally happen in bbPress into the user's BuddyPress profile, groups, and so on.

Friends

The Friends module is absolutely critical for a BuddyPress social network. Of course, it is not technically required; however, a social network without friends is like a boat without water. Enabling the Friends module enables your users to connect with each other in a standard reciprocal "friends" relationship. It is more along the lines of Facebook friendships in which there is a mutual approval process and it is not one-sided, as is the case with Twitter "following."

Groups

The Groups module, like the Friends module, is an important aspect of any sizable social community. Unlike the Friends module, it is easier to get away with omitting the Groups module.

However, the larger a community grows, the more important groups become because community members can fragment into areas of interest or common cause.

Enabling the Groups module places a new Groups icon in the users BuddyPress profile.

Private Messaging

An often-expected feature of a social network is private messaging. Though it is termed "Private Messaging," the functionality is no different than sending a message to a user through a standard inbox feature set containing an Inbox, Sent Messages, and so on (see Figure 24.4).

Private Messaging provides BuddyPress users with messaging capabilities.

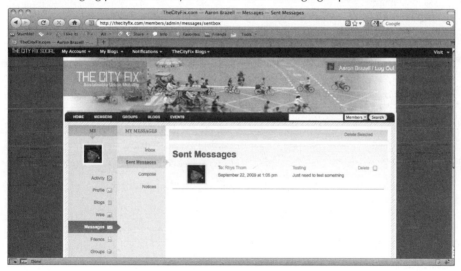

Comment Wire

The Comment Wire is analogous to Facebook's "Wall" feature. It enables BuddyPress users to interact with other members, groups, and custom modules by commenting directly on activity items. If a user creates a new blog post, commenting can happen directly on the blog post or within BuddyPress itself in the Activity feed or wherever else the blog post (or link to the blog post) is displayed.

This functionality is important in encouraging users to interact and engage with each other, especially when a community is new and sparsely populated. A challenge, often, in the blogging world is that the interaction with readers is largely driven by how much the blogger is able to engage his readers in comments. With this feature, that burden is removed from a single blogger and distributed across the network.

Extended Profile

The Extended Profile module is a major WordPress profile enhancement that enables users to have their own unique experience (see Figure 24.5). This module enables users to upload and provide their own user pictures, or *avatars*, and the administrator can create a set of profile fields that relate to the community and designate which ones are required. A science fiction community, as an example, may have an opportunity to designate their favorite sci-fi book or movie and a community of guitar players might have a field that can be populated with their guitar type.

FIGURE 24.5

The Extended Profile provides a unique experience to users by enabling them to fill in profile data or upload an avatar.

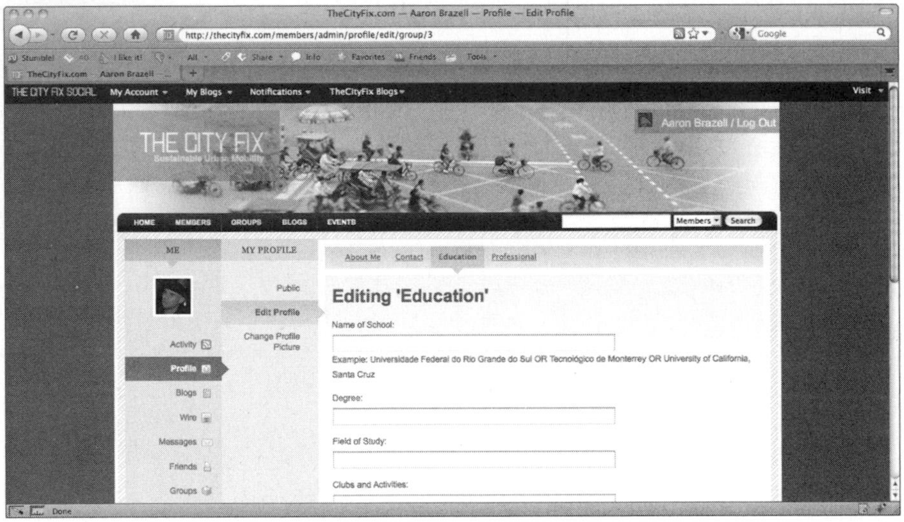

Configuring BuddyPress

BuddyPress is essentially a WordPress plugin. It can be downloaded at www.buddypress.org, extracted, uploaded, and activated just like any other plugin for WordPress. It can also be installed via the built-in plugin installer included in WordPress.

BuddyPress is compatible only with WordPress MU. Therefore, you cannot use it on single WordPress installations and, as of yet, it is not available on WordPress.com (though I believe it is only a matter of time before the BuddyPress option is made available to WordPress.com users).

BuddyPress is still undergoing active development and, though it is stable, it is probably for WordPress.com to consider offering it as an add-on to their bloggers because a lot of configuration options and tweaks might still be made. It is still a very young product, despite its seemingly viral adoption rate.

The first thing you'll notice when you activate BuddyPress is that there is a new BuddyPress top-level navigation item in your WordPress Admin. It is only available to site administrators, so individual blog administrators will not notice it.

Under the BuddyPress navigation, four menu items appear: General Settings, Component Setup, Forums Setup, and Profile Field Setup. If you add other BuddyPress plugins in the future, it's possible additional menu items may be added. If you're a plugin developer, you should add additional menus here using `add_submenu_page()`.

Cross-Reference

Plugin development, including the use of `add_submenu_page()`, is covered in Chapter 5. ■

General Settings

The General Settings menu, shown in Figure 24.6, as you may have gathered from the text at the top of the page, is where you make global setting changes for BuddyPress. You can modify settings related to the admin bar (the dark gray bar at the top of all BuddyPress pages and blogs), modify settings related to avatars, and so on.

FIGURE 24.6

You use the General Settings admin panel for WordPress to configure global settings for BuddyPress.

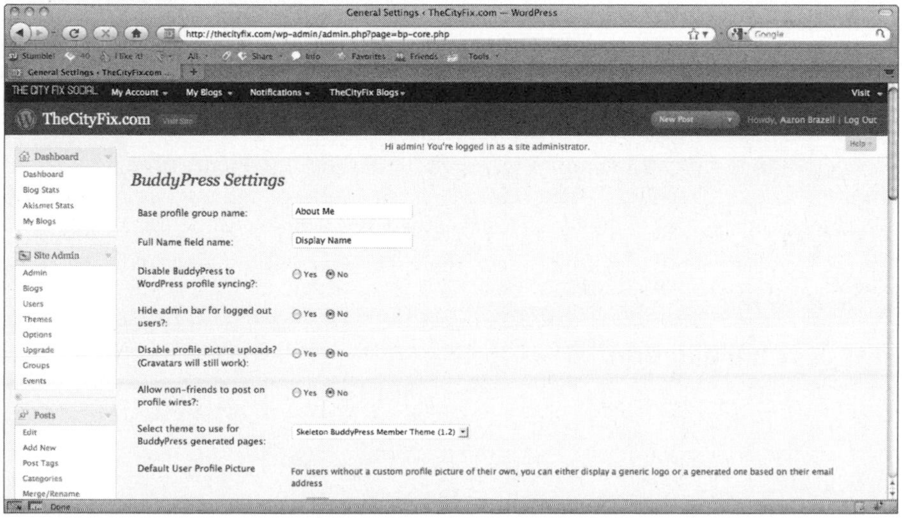

Base profile group name

When you set up profile fields, you can divide them into groups. There always must be one group, and that is what the form field named "Base profile group name" is for. You can name it "Base Profile" or "About Me" or whatever you want. It will become the label for the primary grouping of profile fields. (Setting up profile fields will be discussed in more detail later in this chapter.)

Full Name field name

The only required field for a profile (which is discussed in more detail later in this chapter) is the Full Name field name. Like the Base Profile group name, you can change the wording for this default field here.

Disable BuddyPress to WordPress profile syncing

In most cases, it is not necessary to disable this feature. However, if you want WordPress accounts to be kept up to date with BuddyPress accounts (generally ideal), leave the No radio button selected.

Hide admin bar for logged out users

The option to hide the admin bar is a subjective one and plays to your intentions for your site. Generally, I find it good practice to disable the admin bar for logged out users; this way the site will not draw undue attention to a new feature for the casual user. However, some BuddyPress admins prefer to have the admin bar present at all times to encourage signups.

Disable profile picture uploads

If you prefer to have users use the built-in WordPress Gravatar system, provide a different means of rendering avatars, or simply not support them at all, you can disable picture uploads by deselecting this radio button. One possible reason to disable this is server disk space limitations. However, if your community becomes large, it is likely that users will want to have photo uploads enabled.

Allow non-friends to post on profile wires

This configuration setting is a privacy feature, so to speak. It prevents non-friends from interacting with profiles and may be a configuration option to disable. Depending on the community, allowing non-friends to engage with your users could cause harassment or trolling issues. On the other hand, it opens your community up to a greater audience for participation. Weigh your options carefully and remember that it's easy to provide more features later than it is to take them away.

Disable user account deletion

In a social networking context, it becomes much more likely that you will not want to delete accounts as you might have done in other contexts. For a variety of reasons keeping users around (even if they are banned or inactive via other parts of BuddyPress) might be more ideal than simply deleting them wholesale.

Disable global forum directory

As described earlier in this chapter, bbPress has been integrated with BuddyPress. As such, it has become the framework for discussion as opposed to the point of discussion itself. However, if you would like to have a destination URL where the bbPress integration can be engaged with in a direct forum-like way, check the Yes checkbox on this option.

Default user profile picture

Similar to the Default Avatar option in WordPress' admin panel (Settings ➪ Discussion), this section enables you to designate a default user profile picture to be used if one is not specified.

Component Setup

As of version 1.1, BuddyPress comes with nine components. More components are expected in the future as well. The Component Setup panel shown in Figure 24.7 allows you to enable and disable the various modules. In most of the BuddyPress installs I have done, I have kept all nine modules enabled. This is, of course, a personal choice and is subject to the type of community you want to run. Designing and setting up a community is as much a series of business decisions, as it is technical, so choose according to your strategic needs.

FIGURE 24.7

The Component Setup admin panel enables the site administrator to designate which of the built-in BuddyPress modules are enabled and which ones are not.

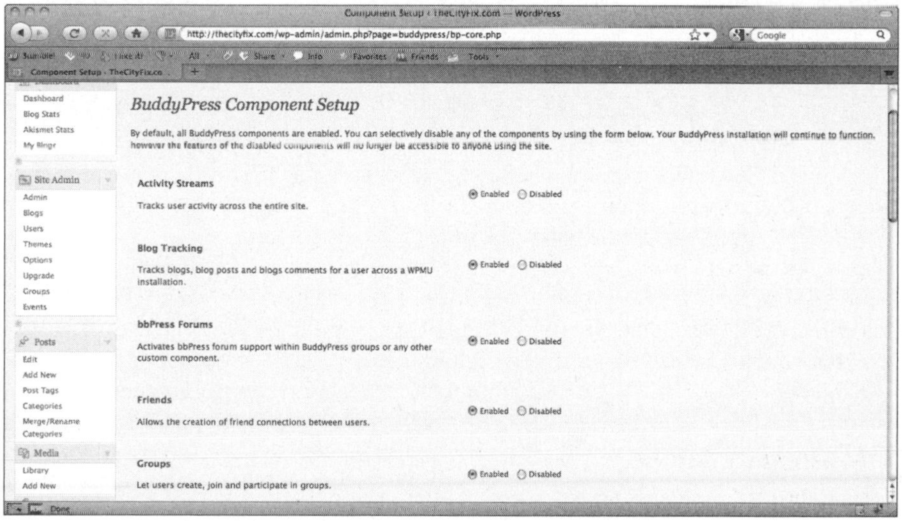

Forums Setup

The forum integration in BuddyPress, as mentioned earlier in this chapter, is done via bbPress. bbPress can be installed with one click from this panel. Additionally, if you have an older install of bbPress already set up, you can perform a one-click integration with your old, standalone bbPress forum installation.

Cross-Reference

If you would like to install bbPress separately and integrate it into BuddyPress, see Chapter 23. BuddyPress must have a working installation of bbPress. Most of the time, this can be done with internal BuddyPress controls. ■

BuddyPress integration of bbPress forums is great; however, bbPress can also operate on its own. When given a URL for the forum, users can browse and participate the same way they would do on any forum. Whether integrated with an external forum or with the built-in bbPress provided by BuddyPress, group administrators can enable discussions for the group (which uses bbPress). These forums can be set to public, private, or hidden.

Profile Field Setup

Earlier in this chapter, I mentioned profile fields, base group names, and the Full Name field name. Users can set up their profiles on the Profile Field Setup page, shown in Figure 24.8.

Whenever you have users, you want to give them the opportunity to personalize their experience. One of the ways to do that in BuddyPress is to give them a full profile to fill out. Every community will be different in terms of needs, so taking time to map this out in advance will pay off in the end.

For example, say you run a BuddyPress-based social network for a non-profit working with community members in developing countries. Providing profile fields such as "Country" or "Mode of Transport" might be helpful in this scenario. A video game network might provide a profile field with a drop-down menu that enables users to choose their favorite gaming console. Take your time to make sound strategic decisions when configuring your profile data points.

Profile fields can be grouped together according to similar fields. Each of these groups becomes a tab that a user can click through to enter extraneous information about them.

The Profile Field Setup page is a strategic point where BuddyPress admins can design their user experience. Fields can be of a variety of formats and grouped together according to similar data points.

Comparing BuddyPress and WordPress Development

BuddyPress and WordPress are built with the same philosophical basis. Both software packages provide APIs for plugin development and extension, though WordPress is far more mature in this way. WordPress also has many more developers looking at the code, providing patches, and dreaming up new features and approaches to problem; it has five core developers opposed to BuddyPress' one. And WordPress has existed longer: it's been around since 2004 whereas BuddyPress hit its first stable milestone in 2009.

Still, the philosophy for extensibility and development is similar.

In WordPress, every page has a $wp_query global object that carries most of the data regarding a page load. In BuddyPress, the global object is called $bp. WordPress has global objects like $post, which is automatically created inside the Loop and has data about each iteration of posts in the Loop. BuddyPress contains objects like $group or $member for similar interaction.

Cross-Reference
The WordPress Loop is discussed in Chapter 8. ■

WordPress themes contain hierarchal template files like `single.php`, `archive.php`, `category.php`, and `search.php`. BuddyPress adds additional template files to WordPress themes like `optionsbar.php`, `userbar.php` and directories like `wire/`, `messages/`, or `groups/`, all containing their own hierarchy of template files. In this way BuddyPress theme development is much more complex than WordPress.

Cross-Reference
WordPress template hierarchy is discussed in Chapter 10. ■

BuddyPress introduces all new template tags. In general, these template tags can be found in each of the folders in the `buddypress/` directory. For example, template tags having to do with the activity feed are found in `buddypress/bp-activity/bp-activity-templatetags.php`; template tags pertaining to friends can be found in `buddypress/bp-friends/bp-friends-templatetags.php`; and so on.

Note
BuddyPress template tags are to be used in BuddyPress member themes, not WordPress themes. ■

When developing for BuddyPress, remember that the philosophy for BuddyPress development is similar to WordPress but it is not identical. There are key differences and developers should expect to spend some time re-learning some aspects of development. Documentation is not overly thorough at this time, but it is my hope that it will become better over time, just as WordPress documentation has. (Of course, you can contribute to the documentation and, thus, the greater community if you're inclined.)

Looking at BuddyPress Theme Concepts

BuddyPress adopts much of the same principles of development, API, and extensibility as WordPress. It also adopts the same concept of theme hierarchy as WordPress. As of BuddyPress 1.1, BuddyPress themes are integrated with WordPress themes. BuddyPress and WordPress can use the same themes because they use different files in different contexts and never step on each other.

Cross-Reference
The basics of WordPress theme and template hierarchy are discussed further in Chapter 10. ■

BuddyPress ships with two themes: the default theme and a skeleton theme. The default theme demonstrates how to implement a child theme (discussed later ion this chapter), using only a `style.css` file. In this manner, a theme acts as a child theme to another. This same concept applies to all themeing in the WordPress world and, just as BuddyPress can piggyback on another theme, WordPress can as well.

Note

Parent-child theme relationships can be thought of as a front-end developer's object-oriented programming. The parent theme acts as a class/object and the child theme behaves as an extending or derivative class. The child theme inherits all of the resources and benefits of the parent theme and can override parent theme behavior. The comparison falls apart here, but it can help you wrap your head around the idea. ■

BuddyPress shares some of the same files as WordPress, such as `style.css`. However, each component of BuddyPress — groups, profiles, wire, and so on — has its own self-contained hierarchy generally comprised in a directory with a name such as `group/`, `profile/`, or `wire/`. Each of these directories contains other files that are used to generate the BuddyPress social experience. Table 24.1 lists the BuddyPress template file hierarchy.

TABLE 24.1

BuddyPress Template File Hierarchy

Template File	Description
`activity/just-me.php`	Provides layout for users' own activity feeds.
`activity/my-friends.php`	Provides layout for users' friends aggregated activity.
`blogs/create.php`	Provides layout for the blog creation interface.
`blogs/my-blogs.php`	Provides layout for listing users' blogs.
`blogs/recent-comments.php`	Provides layout for rendering recent comments.
`blogs/recent-posts.php`	Provides layout for displaying recent posts on subscribed blogs.
`friends/friends-loop.php`	Provides a new Loop used only for iterating through users' friends.
`friends/index.php`	Provides layout for displaying selected (all) users' friends.
`friends/requests.php`	Provides layout for displaying all pending friend requests.
`groups/create.php`	Provides layout for creating new groups.
`groups/group-loop.php`	Provides a new Loop used only for iterating through listed groups.
`groups/index.php`	Provides layout for displaying selected (all) groups.
`groups/invites.php`	Provides layout for allowing invitations to groups.
`groups/single/*`	Provides layout for all aspects of individual group rendering. The skeleton theme contains eight files and special forum rendering and should be examined closer for example usage.
`messages/compose.php`	Provides layout for composing new private messages.
`messages/index.php`	Provides layout for rendering the messaging system in BuddyPress.
`messages/notices.php`	Provides layout for alerts/error messaging related to private messaging.

continued

TABLE 24.1 (continued)

Template File	Description
messages/sentbox.php	Provides layout for an account outbox.
messages/view.php	Provides layout for an account inbox.
userbar.php	Provides the layout for the BuddyPress main navigation. In most child themes with the skeleton theme as the parent theme, this is the first column.
optionsbar.php	Provides layout for the BuddyPress sub-navigation. In most derivative themes with the skeleton theme as a parent theme, this is the second column.
profile/change-avatar.php	Provides layout for uploading a new avatar/user profile picture.
profile/edit.php	Provides layout for modifying a profile.
profile/index.php	Provides layout for rendering a profile.
profile/profile-header.php	Provides layout for content displayed before a profile.
profile/profile-loop.php	Provides layout for all the content of a profile.
profile/profile-menu.php	Provides layout for action items related to a profile.
registration/activate.php	Provides layout for user activation. Overrides WordPress' default.
registration/register.php	Provides layout for user registration. Overrides WordPress' default.

The beautiful thing about developing themes from a child theme perspective is that all of these files exist in the skeleton theme. Therefore, any templates that are omitted from your child theme are inherited from the parent theme.

To designate a theme as a child theme in BuddyPress, make sure you include a `Template:` header in the `style.css`. You can see this in how the headers are constructed in the `bp-default` theme (see Listing 24.1).

LISTING 24.1

Designating the child theme by adding a Template: header in the style.css

```
/*
Theme Name: BuddyPress Default
Theme URI: http://buddypress.org/extend/themes/
Description: The default theme for BuddyPress.
Version: 1.1-beta
Author: BuddyPress.org
Author URI: http://buddypress.org
Template: bp-sn-parent
*/
```

Extending BuddyPress

Extending BuddyPress is no different than extending WordPress. Because BuddyPress is a plugin for WordPress MU, extending it is the same as creating a new WordPress MU plugin. However, because any extension of BuddyPress requires that the proper BuddyPress modules be available, you should definitely test for the existence (or better, the absence) of key classes or functions using `if( !function_exists() )` or `if( !class_exists() )` for logic.

For example, if you want to extend the activity feed functionality, you might check for the existence of the `BP_Activity_Activity` class listed in `bp-activity/bp-activity-classes.php` (see Listing 24.2).

Testing for the absence of the BP_Activity_Activity class if your plugin extends the Activity module

```
function my_bp_extension()
{
    if( !class_exists('BP_Activity_Activity') )
        return false;
    /*
    Since we're this far, the Activity class must exist, so proceed
    with extension functionality.
    */
}
```

BuddyPress developer Andy Peatling and contributor Jeff Sayre have released a plugin that can be used as a guideline for BuddyPress plugin development. It is not intended to be used by itself, but provides the entire "roughed in" framework to get your plugin talking to all the various modules of BuddyPress. You can download this dummy plugin, called BuddyPress Skeleton Component, at `http://wordpress.org/extend/plugins/buddypress-skeleton-component/`.

The module is well documented and contains helpful tips for creating your own module from the code. Remember to rename the plugin as something else (`bp-example.php` is not a good name for a plugin!) and, though it is not required, consider releasing your code to the community as open source. The BuddyPress community and code is still very young and is a moving target in many ways. Any help that you, as a developer, can do to provide some assistance in shaping the community will be appreciated.

Summary

- BuddyPress is a WordPress MU plugin that turns WordPress into a social network.

- BuddyPress comes with nine default modules and more are in the pipeline. These modules can be extended or additional modules can be supplied via plugin.

- Configuration options in BuddyPress can be found in the Site Admin menu of WordPress MU or in the newly created BuddyPress navigation group.

- BuddyPress takes its cues from WordPress in terms of extensibility and APIs, theme construction, and coding standards.

- BuddyPress provides entirely new template files for customizing BuddyPress themes.

- Include the Template header in a BuddyPress theme style.css to make it a child theme.

- Use the BuddyPress Skeleton Component plugin to include all the necessary hooks into the BuddyPress modules.

# CHAPTER 25

Using BackPress as a Development Framework

In the world of development, it is rare when developers can completely develop with only one piece of software. Developers who do much of their work with WordPress still have a need to write code in other contexts and for other software packages.

As WordPress developers built out their own suite of services and tools, they realized they were re-engineering much of the same code that was already written in WordPress and that, instead of taking the time to rewrite code every time one of them would worked on a new tool, they should abstract most of the useful code in the WordPress codebase out to a separate library. This library could then be used elsewhere by other WordPress developers as a cornerstone of their development.

This endeavor became known as *BackPress* because it consists of the code that makes up the backbone of WordPress without being overly WordPress specific.

Web Resource

If you'd like to refer to or use BackPress as you read through this chapter, you can download it via SVN at `http://svn.automattic.com/ backpress/.` ∎

Defining BackPress

In the world of PHP, a number of good development frameworks exist, many of which use a Model-View-Controller (MVC) approach to development. One popular framework is Zend Framework, which is a PHP 5-only framework. CakePHP is another PHP framework that was inspired by the

Ruby on Rails system. Symfony provides a completely different development experience with dependence on YAML (ironically meaning YAML Ain't Markup Language), a data serialization standard.

Note

A Model-View-Controller (MVC) framework is a type of framework that separates application logic from presentation. In an MVC system, the Model is the portion of the application that contains data that will be used in the application; the View is the portion of the application that places a visual layer, usually hypertext markup language (HTML) or extensible HTML (XHTML), on top of the application; and the Controller constitutes the logic that ties the Model and View together. Most PHP frameworks operate on the MVC concept but WordPress technically does not (though it does have some MVC-ish characteristics with themes, database logic, and plugin application programming interfaces [APIs]). ∎

For many developers who operate in a world dominated by WordPress, familiarity offers the best framework of all. Depending on how much functionality is needed from WordPress, developers have historically included all of WordPress in their code (by including the `wp-load.php` file) and then proceeded from there, as shown in Listing 25.1.

LISTING 25.1

WordPress loaded in its entirety for the sake of using it as a backbone for development

```php
<?php
require_once('wordpress/wp-load.php');
// Perform application development using WordPress functions
```

The problem with this solution is code weight and size. Some functions simply can't, and shouldn't, be used outside of WordPress. Why include all of this extra code when it's not necessary? It adds too much overhead given only a fraction of the WordPress code can be used in a non-WordPress context.

In steps BackPress. With BackPress, most of the familiar (and useful!) classes and functions are abstracted to a series of files that can be included in any application so that WordPress becomes the framework for code development.

Developing with BackPress

With BackPress, there is no single file that makes all of the BackPress code loadable into an application. With the assumption that application developers only need to load what is actually required for their application, you can create a "loader" script that can be included to load the BackPress files. An example of such a file (`backpress-load.php`) can be seen in Listing 25.2.

<interim_title>Chapter 25: Using BackPress as a Development Framework</interim_title>

LISTING 25.2

This backpress-load.php file can be used to load up all BackPress files at once

```php
<?php
// Load all BackPress files
require_once('backpress/class.bp-log.php');
require_once('backpress/class.bp-roles.php');
require_once('backpress/class.bp-sql-schema-parser.php');
require_once('backpress/class.bp-user.php');
require_once('backpress/class.bpdb-multi.php');
require_once('backpress/class.bpdb.php');
require_once('backpress/class.ixr.php');
require_once('backpress/class.mailer-smtp.php');
require_once('backpress/class.mailer.php');
require_once('backpress/class.passwordhash.php');
require_once('backpress/class.wp-ajax-response.php');
require_once('backpress/class.wp-auth.php');
require_once('backpress/class.wp-dependencies.php');
require_once('backpress/class.wp-error.php');
require_oncc('backpress/class.wp-http.php');
/*
    You cannot include BOTH wp-object-cache-memcached.php
    AND wp-object-cache.php. Comment whichever one you
    Don't plan to use.
*/
#require_once('backpress/class.wp-object-cache-memcached.php');
require_once('backpress/class.wp-object-cache.php');
require_once('backpress/class.wp-pass.php');
require_once('backpress/class.wp-scripts.php');
require_once('backpress/class.wp-styles.php');
require_once('backpress/class.wp-taxonomy.php');
require_once('backpress/class.wp-users.php');
require_once('backpress/functions.bp-options.php');
require_once('backpress/functions.compat.php');
require_once('backpress/functions.core.php');
require_once('backpress/functions.formatting.php');
require_once('backpress/functions.kses.php');
require_once('backpress/functions.plugin-api.php');
require_once('backpress/functions.shortcodes.php');
require_once('backpress/functions.wp-cron.php');
require_once('backpress/functions.wp-object-cache.php');
require_once('backpress/functions.wp-scripts.php');
require_once('backpress/functions.wp-styles.php');
require_once('backpress/functions.wp-taxonomy.php');
require_once('backpress/interface.bp-options.php');
require_once('backpress/loader.wp-object-cache-memcached.php');
require_once('backpress/loader.wp-object-cache.php');
```

On the Web

The code in Listing 25.2 is available for download at www.wiley.com/go/wordpressbible. ∎

Including BackPress in your PHP project

To keep things simple and easily manageable, add all of the BackPress files to a directory called backpress. (You can call it anything you'd like, but for the sake of example, I'll assume it's in a backpress/ directory.)

Of course, a simpler way to do this would be to get a listing of the backpress/ directory, and include all of the BackPress files, as shown in Listing 25.3. However, from a security standpoint I consider it bad form to let any file load all the files in a directory sight unseen.

LISTING 25.3

A cleaner way of including all the BackPress files

```php
<?php
// Read all files and directories in the backpress/ directory
$backpress_dir = 'backpress/';
$backpress = scandir($backpress_dir);
// Bypass directory listings . and .. and include files.
// Also, don't include wp-object-cache-memcached.php
foreach( $backpress as $ikey => $inode ) :
    if( !in_array( $inode, array( '.', '..', 'wp-object-cache-memcached.
  php' ) )
    {
        require_once( $backpress_dir . $inode );
    }
endforeach;
```

On the Web

The code in Listing 25.3 is available for download at www.wiley.com/go/wordpressbible. ∎

Understanding the BackPress facilities

There is not enough room in this book to describe everything that is in BackPress. Chances are great that if you are using BackPress, you also are a PHP developer and feel comfortable looking through the various files and classes. If you're a WordPress developer, chances are you already know what is available to you simply by looking at the file names because most of the files are derivatives of the filenames used in WordPress itself. However, for the uninitiated, the general purpose of each file is described in the following sections.

class.bp-log.php

This class provides a generalized and abstracted logging facility. Logging can be sent to PHP (returned as a variable), written to a file, echoed to the display, or printed to the console. It can also be configured to catch specific types of errors such as warnings.

class.bp-roles.php

This class abstracts the WordPress Role and Capability system. It can easily be used within a WordPress authentication system (also included in BackPress) to develop against application-specific custom roles and capabilities.

class.bp-sql-schema-parser.php

This handy class can be used when comparing MySQL schema SQL statements with actual table structures. This is most often used as a sanity-checking mechanism to ensure SQL will actually work in the context of an actual database.

class.bp-user.php

One of the most commonly abstracted mechanisms of WordPress is the user and authentication system. This class ports the WP_User class to BP_User and carries most of that same system with it. It applies to a specific user object. The class.wp-users.php file contains methods that will work with the user system as a whole.

class.bpdb.php

The bpdb class is identical to the wpdb class in WordPress. It is the class that handles MySQL database abstraction and queries and has all the identical methods available to the $wpdb object in WordPress.

class.bpdb-multi.php

This class extends the bpdb class and is a modified version of HyperDB. It allows applications to *shard* the database across multiple servers or data centers.

Cross-Reference

For information about HyperDB, see Chapter 18. ■

class.ixr.php

The IXR class included in WordPress handles all XML-RPC (XML Remote Procedure Calls) requests to and from WordPress. In other words, it serves as both an XML-RPC server and client. This functionality is bundled up in this class for use by other applications.

class.mailer-smtp.php

This class provides Simple Mail Transfer Protocol (SMTP; outgoing mail) facilities for applications. It provides much more granular control over sent messages than PHP's built-in mail function because it connects directly to an SMTP server.

class.mailer.php

Related to the `class.mailer-smtp.php` class, this PHP class provides better control over the formatting and construction of e-mail messages to be sent.

class.passwordhash.php

With WordPress 2.5, passwords were no longer simply hashed with MD5 (an often used cryptographic hash function) and inserted into the database. The `phpass` class in WordPress provides a much more secure mechanism for password generation and security. This class in BackPress provides the same facilities for custom applications.

class.wp-ajax-response.php

For interactive applications, this class provides a mechanism for queuing responses to be sent to the client in a unified XML format.

class.wp-auth.php

The authentication class goes hand in hand with the user class. It is provided as a mechanism for authenticating users in the same way WordPress authenticates users.

class.wp-dependencies.php

This class is a derivative of the WordPress script enqueue API and provides similar functionality to applications.

class.wp-error.php

The `WP_Error` class is a mechanism for catching errors and debugging. It is used throughout WordPress. Methods exist to check if the class has been instantiated (indicating an error). Using this class is similar to using the PHP 5 `try()`/`catch()` functions.

class.wp-http.php

The `WP_Http` class in WordPress is available for making HTTP requests. The class does not include the more commonly used Client URL Library (cURL) functions because all hosts do not support it. This class is a good class to use in third-party applications that send requests to other Web services.

class.wp-object-cache.php and class.wp-object-cache-memcached.php

These two classes are nearly identical to each other. Both cannot be used at the same time because they have an identical class name, `WP_Object_Cache`. They both make the built-in WordPress object cache available to developers; however, one also includes Memcached as an option.

Cross-Reference
WordPress object caching is covered in more detail in Chapter 18. ■

class.wp-pass.php

This class contains methods for checking passwords as well as automatically generating random passwords in compatibility with the phpass class included in `class.passwordhash.php`.

class.wp-scripts.php

This class extends the `WP_Dependencies` class included in `class.wp-dependencies.php`. It is an abstraction of the script enqueue API.

class.wp-styles.php

Similar to the `WP_Scripts` class included in `class.wp-scripts.php`, this class extends `WP_Dependencies`. It is an abstraction of the style enqueue API.

class.wp-taxonomy.php

The `WP_Taxonomy` class is used to interact with the WordPress taxonomy tables (terms, term_ relationships, and so on).

class.wp-users.php

This class is one half of the `BP_User` class. `class.wp-users.php` handles the user system as a whole, while the other half handles activity for a specific user.

Solving BackPress Dependencies

Along with the numerous classes included with BackPress, WordPress developers will be familiar with plenty of functions in it. The more famous libraries include the KSES library, which is used to sanitize HTML and prevent users from posting harmful content. Additionally, the shortcode API is included to allow developers to write callback functions that allow users to use "safe" forms of HTML and scripts.

All in all, BackPress provides a solid framework for PHP development for developers familiar with WordPress. BackPress is not used in WordPress yet specifically, but is used in some of the other WordPress-related projects like bbPress and BuddyPress, which I discussed in previous chapters, and is often synced up with WordPress. As a fairly undocumented technology, developers should take necessary time to understand the layout of the BackPress libraries.

Class dependency is one of the big gotchas of BackPress. Because this trouble area is not documented explicitly, Table 25.1 provides an overview of which classes need to be included in your WordPress code.

TABLE 25.1

BackPress Class Dependencies

Class	Filename	Depends on	Filename
BP_Log	class.bp-log.php		
BP_Roles, BP_Role	class.bp-roles.php		
BP_SQL_Schema_Parser	class.bp-sql.schema.parser.php	BPDB or BPDB_Multi	class.bpdb.php or class.bpdb-multi.php
BP_User	class.bp-user.php		
BPDB	class.bpdb.php		
BPDB_Multi	class.bpdb-multi.php		
IXR_Value, IXR_Message, IXR_Server, IXR_Request, IXR_Client, IXR_Error, IXR_Date, IXR_Base64, IXR_ClientMultiCall	class.ixr.php		
SMTP	class.mailer-smtp.php		
PHPMailer	class.mailer.php	SMTP	class.mailer-smtp.php
PasswordHash	class.passwordhash.php		
WP_Ajax_Response	class.wp-ajax-response.php		
WP_Auth	class.wp-auth.php	BPDB or BPDB_Multi and WP_Users	class.bpdb.php, class.bpdb-multi.php, class.wp-users.php
WP_Dependencies	class.wp-dependencies.php		
WP_Error	class.wp-error.php		
WP_Http	class.wp-http.php		
WP_Object_Cache	class.wp-object-cache.php or class.wp-object-cache-memcached.php		
WP_Pass	class.wp-pass.php	WP_Users and PasswordHash	class.wp-users.php, class.passwordhash.php
WP_Scripts	class.wp-scripts.php	WP_Dependencies	class.wp-dependencies.php
WP_Styles	class.wp-styles.php	WP_Dependencies	class.wp-dependencies.php
WP_Taxonomy	class.wp-taxonomy.php		
WP_Users	class.wp-users.php	BPDB or BPDB_Multi	class.bpdb.php, class.bpdb-multi.php

Summary

- BackPress is the abstraction of core WordPress functionality into a reusable form.

- BackPress serves as a lightweight WordPress-oriented PHP framework.

- There is no file that includes all BackPress files. I've provided scripts to do this. Otherwise, include each file as needed.

- The most commonly used classes and functions included in WordPress are bundled into BackPress.

- Ensure that class dependencies are solved by including the necessary files in your code scripts.

# CHAPTER 26

WordPress.com and the Automattic Products

WordPress.org is the home of the open source, self-hosted WordPress software. Everything on http://wordpress.org is owned by the community, even though Automattic is the sponsor. Automattic has even gone out of its way to ensure that all of the core developers of WordPress are not Automattic employees.

WordPress.com, however, is a commercial venture of Automattic. It is one of the largest hosted blog platforms in the world using WordPress MU. Having a blog on WordPress.com is a free and easy way to get started blogging without having to install the blogging software yourself or wrestle with hosting.

Through this chapter, I'll discuss not only the WordPress.com offering, but also other products that Automattic provides to their own customers and the greater community.

About Automattic

Automattic was started by Matt Mullenweg, the co-founder of WordPress, several years into the WordPress project. Matt has become the public face of WordPress and is frequently on the speaking circuit, travelling to WordCamps around the globe, representing both WordPress and Automattic.

Cross-Reference
For more information about the beginnings of WordPress, see Chapter 1. ■

The company is currently made up of approximately 40 employees around the world. Many work in San Francisco, but even the employees in San Francisco work from home, most of the time.

Automattic is best known for WordPress.com but has other products as well, some homegrown and some as a result of acquisition:

- After the Deadline
- Akismet
- Gravatar
- IntenseDebate
- P2 Theme
- PollDaddy
- VideoPress
- VIP

In addition, Automattic is involved in several open source projects, funding much of their development. They are open source and include:

- WordPress.org
- BuddyPress
- bbPress
- BackPress
- WordPress app for iPhone
- WordPress app for BlackBerry

After the Deadline

After the Deadline is an open-source service from Automattic that checks grammar, writing style, and spelling. You install it as a WordPress plugin but developers are encouraged to build client pieces for other platforms as well. After the Deadline works in a client-server model: a client Web application, such as WordPress, sends data to After the Deadline servers and the results are sent back to the application. After the Deadline requires a free application programming interface (API) key, but other than that, there is no cost.

Web Resource
The WordPress plugin and more information on After the Deadline can be found at `http://afterthe deadline.com`. ■

Akismet

Akismet is Automattic's anti-spam service. It is open source in that the plugin and the APIs for interacting with Akismet over the Web are open; however, the server software and its spam recognition engine itself is not. This may not make a lot of sense for those who understand that Automattic's philosophy and commitment to open source is part of their DNA, but it makes complete sense in the context of fighting spam.

If the server side of Akismet were open source, spammers could easily reverse engineer their spam to evade the algorithms that flag it as spam. With spam prevention, obscurity is a powerful weapon.

Cross-Reference

Akismet is discussed further in Chapter 27. ■

Gravatar

Gravatar, short for Globally Recognized Avatar, is the second most popular Automattic product to WordPress.com. It began as an independent service years ago but suffered from scaling issues and lack of resources to develop it. The basis is users can sign up for an account and register an avatar to be used on any avatar-enabled blog. Having an account ensures that the user's image will appear next to comments across the Web.

When Automattic acquired Gravatar in 2007, it promptly placed the service on better servers with more scaling potential. WordPress incorporated avatar support (powered by Gravatar) into WordPress 2.5 and it continues to be a completely free service to this day.

Gravatar integration can be done on WordPress, WordPress MU (Multi-User WordPress), and WordPress.com blogs via the Settings ➪ Reading screen, shown in Figure 26.1; and many Automattic services, including IntenseDebate, incorporate Gravatar into their offering.

FIGURE 26.1

Gravatars can be configured inside WordPress, WordPress MU, or WordPress.com in the Settings ➪ Reading screen.

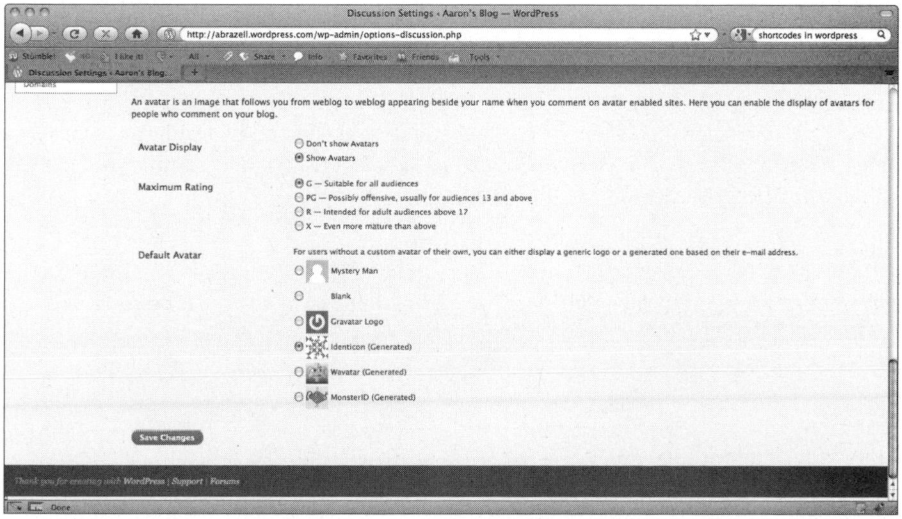

IntenseDebate

IntenseDebate, a hosted comment system that serves as a direct replacement to blog comments, was acquired by Automattic in late 2008. Though it is now owned by Automattic, IntenseDebate works on any blog platform.

Cross-Reference

IntenseDebate is discussed further in Chapter 27. ∎

P2 Theme

The P2 Theme is the successor of another Automattic-provided theme, Prologue. Both themes were inspired by Twitter and real-time microblogging updates. The P2 theme, shown in Figure 26.2, is probably best used in a collaborative environment such as a corporate or software development environment. It can be downloaded for free at `http://p2theme.com`.

FIGURE 26.2

The P2 theme, modeled after Twitter, has microblogging at its heart. It is effective for collaborative team blogs.

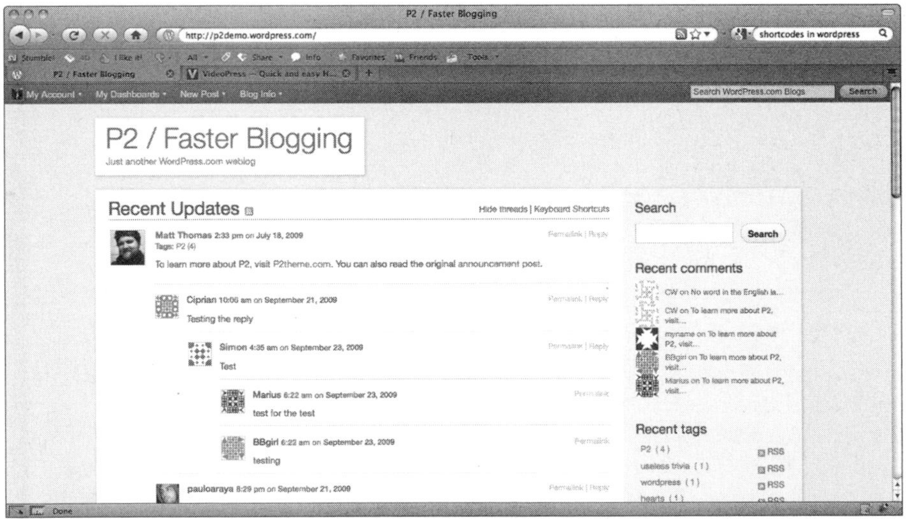

PollDaddy

PollDaddy was acquired by Automattic in 2009. It gives users with the ability to include polls on any site, including non-WordPress sites. It is a "freemium" cloud-based product, meaning a limited version is available for free and paid upgrades are available.

Cross-Reference

PollDaddy is discussed further in Chapter 27. ■

VideoPress

VideoPress is a video hosting service and a video player offering rich, high definition (HD) video (see Figure 26.3). Users of WordPress.com have had access to VideoPress for some time, but now WordPress.org users can use it as well. The way VideoPress works is that, after purchasing the VideoPress upgrade from WordPress.com, users can upload videos in WordPress.com. WordPress.org users install a plugin (`http://wordpress.org/extend/plugins/video/`) that ties into WordPress.com and enables a user to embed videos directly.

Web Resource

For more information on VideoPress, visit `http://videopress.com`. ■

FIGURE 26.3

VideoPress is a paid WordPress.com upgrade that provides a video player with HD video support.

VIP

WordPress.com VIP is reserved for the clients that spend hundreds or thousands of dollars on hosting annually. Though it is an advertised service, the vast majority of people looking to host their blogs on WordPress.com with VIP service will not qualify for the service. This decision as to who qualifies for VIP service lies exclusively with Automattic and there is no real formula. Generally speaking, a VIP candidate has tons of traffic and is high profile.

VIP customers have some of the access to their blogs that they would have on other servers. They can modify their themes, include JavaScript, and do more of the things that are generally not allowed with standard WordPress.com users. The key benefit to using WordPress.com VIP hosting is that Automattic is already doing the heavy lifting of providing a robust and secure WordPress infrastructure, including servers and network.

Some VIP customers include CNN.com, the GigaOM Network, the *Wall Street Journal*'s All Things Digital, Fox News, and more.

Taking a Look at Automattic's Propriety Products

Besides the Automattic-owned properties mentioned previously, Automattic is also the sponsor of a variety of other products, including the WordPress software itself. These open source software packages are not really "owned" by any one person or company, but certainly they would not have leadership or guidance without Automattic shepherding the projects forward.

WordPress

The topic of this book, and the most common self-hosted blogging software on the planet, Word Press is the flagship of the WordPress ecosystem. About half of the core developers of WordPress are directly employed by Automattic. As WordPress goes, so goes WordPress MU, WordPress.com, and all the other aspects of the WordPress ecosystem. WordPress can be downloaded for free at www.wordpress.org.

BuddyPress

If WordPress presents the blogging platform in such a way that the entire workflow revolves around a blogger and her audience, BuddyPress alters the paradigm, making the workflow and concepts revolve more around the users and less around the blogger. BuddyPress can be downloaded for free at http://buddypress.org.

Cross-Reference
For more information about BuddyPress, see Chapter 24. ■

bbPress

bbPress introduces the old concept of forums to the WordPress ecosystem. bbPress is an integral part of BuddyPress but can also exist as a standalone forum. It is the same software that powers the WordPress support forums found at http://wordpress.org/support. bbPress can be downloaded for free at http://bbpress.org.

Cross-Reference
For more information about bbPress, see Chapter 23. ■

BackPress

BackPress evolved out of the need to stop duplicating code in every WordPress-compatible package. As the WordPress ecosystem grew and more products were being built, it became necessary to think about abstracting some of the more common classes, methods, and functions out of WordPress and into a separate library. In essence, BackPress represents the official WordPress PHP framework because it caters to the developer familiar enough with WordPress development to have habits, workflows, and routines around WordPress code.

BackPress is only available as a Subversion (SVN) download and there is little documentation. Download it over SVN at `http://svn.automattic.com/backpress/`.

Cross-Reference
For more information about BackPress, see Chapter 25. ■

WordPress app for iPhone

The WordPress application for the iPhone (called WordPress 2 in the iTunes App Store) was one of the first apps launched in the iTunes app store when the iPhone was originally opened to third-party applications. It provides a slick interface (see Figure 26.4) that uses most of the WordPress XML-RPC (Extensible Markup Language Remote Procedure Call) API, including comment management directly from your iPhone or iPod touch.

It can be downloaded for free via the iTunes app store in iTunes or directly on your iPhone or iPod touch.

Cross-Reference
The WordPress XML-RPC API is discussed in Chapter 14. ■

FIGURE 26.4

The WordPress iPhone app enables users to publish or modify posts and pages as well as moderate comments.

WordPress app for BlackBerry

Those of you who use a BlackBerry as your smartphone, are not left out in the cold. Automattic recently commissioned a WordPress application for BlackBerry (see Figure 26.5), which is also open source.

The WordPress app for BlackBerry can be downloaded over the air or to your desktop (and loaded via Desktop Manager) at `http://blackberry.wordpress.org/install`.

FIGURE 26.5

The WordPress app for BlackBerry enables a blogger to write or edit posts and pages as well as moderate comments.

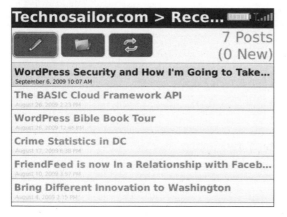

Using WordPress.com Themes

WordPress.com is a free blogging service. You can sign up for an account and be blogging within minutes. As part of this offering, Automattic provides tons of themes for users to select from. Some have configuration options that enable the blogger to customize some of the blog; however, full control of the Cascading Style Sheet (CSS) (and thus, most of the presentation of the blog) is reserved for those who pay for the Custom CSS upgrade.

The themes available to WordPress.com represent the philosophy of the company. The themes are completely free and compliant with the General Public License (GPL).

Cross-Reference
Building themes and understanding theme hierarchy is discussed in Chapter 11. ■

The folks at WordPress.com look at a few things when deciding on whether a theme should be included in the WordPress.com offering, some of which are fairly subjective:

- The theme must be GPL-compliant.
- The code must be clean.
- Inclusion of the theme must be driven by requests in the WordPress.com forum.

Additionally, you should follow other good practices if you hope to have your theme included in the WordPress.com offering:

- A good theme will be widget-ready.
- A good theme will not rely on plugins for support. (Required plugins should be included as part of the theme `functions.php`.)
- A good theme will not include any kind of attribution link (for example, Theme Design by Acme Corp.).
- A good theme will be hosted in the WordPress Theme Repository (`http://word press.org/extend/themes/`).

Cross-Reference

Widgets and widgetizing themes are discussed in Chapter 6. ■

WordPress.com users are limited to around 80 themes that are organized in alphabetical order by most popular and random, as shown in Figure 26.6. This is a required limitation for a hosted service that wants to control the quality of their product offering and protect the security of their users, something that I discuss later in this chapter.

FIGURE 26.6

WordPress.com users have access to nearly 80 themes and can purchase the Custom CSS upgrade, which gives them even more control over the look and feel of their blogs.

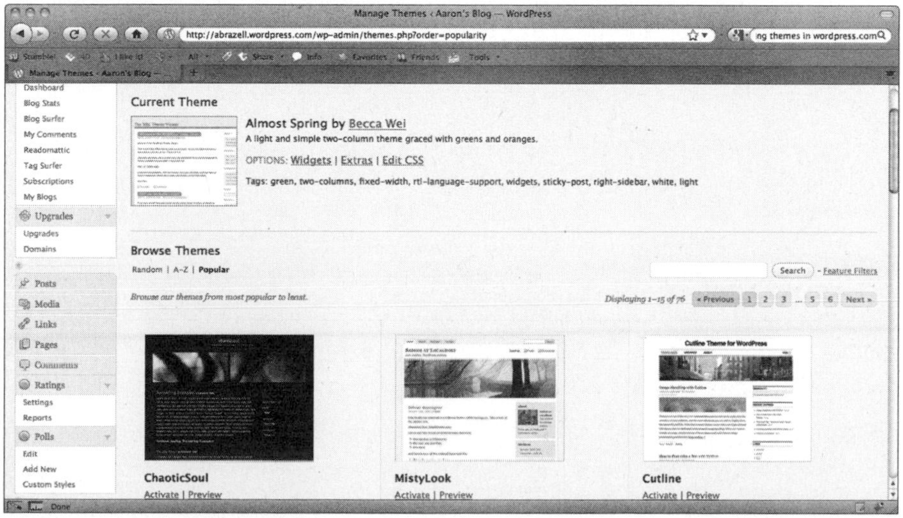

Getting Your Plugin Included in WordPress.com

WordPress.com users cannot install plugins. Because WordPress.com is a WordPress MU installation, the plugins available in the platform are reserved for only the Site Admins (Automattic) to install and configure. There is no publicly available information on how to get your plugin included in WordPress.com — but it is likely that user feedback drives some of these inclusion decisions.

Nonetheless, WordPress.com has noted that certain elements of a plugin should be included to have it considered for inclusion:

- The plugin must be GPL-compliant.
- The plugin must not allow users to insert JavaScript into posts or pages for security reasons. One way around this is to use "shortcodes" to allow users to embed safe content in a post. However, even with shortcodes, WordPress.com must support them (they must be approved).
- The plugin should have a significant demand, whether on the WordPress.com forums or in terms of numbers of downloads in the Plugin Repository. (The theory being that if WordPress.org users find it popular enough, it's probably worth offering to WordPress.com users as well.)

Note

Shortcodes are a relatively new feature in WordPress and serve to sanitize content that is entered into a post and protect the blog from XSS (cross-site scripting) attacks. ■

Cross-Reference

XSS attacks happen when unsafe JavaScript is inserted into a Web site. The primary vector of attack is through user-generated input (usually via forms). For more on WordPress security, see Chapter 17. ■

Shortcodes function in much the same way that hooks do. They use the function `do_shortcode ()`, which takes two arguments. The first argument is the name of the shortcode. This name will be inserted into a post, so if the shortcode name is *dosomething*, a blogger could use `[dosomething]` in a post. The second argument is a callback, or the name of a function that will be invoked when that shortcode is encountered.

Note

Shortcodes can take additional arguments as well, so that `[dosomething]` shortcode could also look like `[dosomething time=now urgency=high]`. They can also enclose other content, which will also be passed in, like `[dosomething]some content[/dosomething]`. ■

Your callback parses these attributes out and assigns defaults using the `shortcode_atts ()` function for attributes that haven't been specified by the blogger. The `shortcode_atts ()` function behaves similar to the PHP (Hypertext Preprocessor) function `array_merge ()`. It takes two arrays of attributes. The first array should contain all of the default attributes and the second array is generated automatically by the attributes the user specifies when using the shortcode.

An example of this concept is shown in Listing 26.1. The code inserts a safe YouTube embed and takes at least one attribute (`src`), which is the URL for a YouTube video. Other optional attributes are height and width and can be used to generate a custom size YouTube embed.

LISTING 26.1

Using shortcodes to include YouTube videos in posts

```
function youtube_in_post( $atts )
{
    $src_url = parse_url( $atts['src'] );
    $querystring = explode( '&', $src_url['query'] );
    foreach( $querystring as $qs )
    {
        $qsb = explode( '=', $qs );
        if( $qsb[0] == 'v' )
            $src_id = $qsb[1];
    }
    $atts['src'] = sprintf( "http://www.youtube.com/v/%s&hl=en&fs=1", $src_
id );
    extract( shortcode_atts( array(
                    'height'      => 344,
                    'width'          425,
                    'src'         => ''
                ), $atts
        )
    );
    return sprintf( '<object width="%1$d" height="%2$d"><param name="movie"
value="%3$s"></param><param name="allowFullScreen" value="true"></
param><param name="allowscriptaccess" value="always"></param><embed
src="%3$s" type="application/x-shockwave-flash"
allowscriptaccess="always" allowfullscreen="true" width="%1$d"
height="%2$d"></embed></object> ', esc_attr($width), esc_attr($height),
    esc_attr($src) );
}
add_shortcode('youtube','youtube_in_post');
```

Note

The code listed in Listing 26.1 may or may not ever make inclusion in WordPress.com. In fact, WordPress.com has its own YouTube inclusion feature that uses a shortcode. The use of shortcodes is an extremely important aspect of getting a plugin included, but it is not the only requirement. High demand, popularity, clean code, and security are also considered. The code in Listing 26.1 merely demonstrates one (simple) example of how shortcodes could be used. ∎

On the Web

The code in Listing 26.1 is available for download at `www.wiley.com/go/wordpressbible`. ∎

Buying Premium WordPress.com Features

The feature set in WordPress.com is pretty extensive for the average blogger. However, sometimes you might want to add additional features. For this, WordPress.com offers premium upgrades a la carte. You can purchase these upgrades in the Upgrades menu (see Figure 26.7).

The Upgrades menu in WordPress.com gives users the ability to purchase value-added options for their WordPress.com blogs.

Custom CSS

Sometimes you may want to add your own flair to one of the WordPress.com themes. Though you can't upload your own theme (unless you're a WordPress.com VIP customer), you can purchase the Custom CSS option, which as of this writing is $14.97/year. This option enables you to tweak your CSS to your heart's content. Anything that you can do with CSS, you can do via the Custom CSS add-on.

Disk space upgrades

WordPress.com has a finite amount of resources, even though their server cluster is vast and expansive. With millions of users, the allotment of space for each user is 3GB of storage in your upload directory (where images, specifically) are hosted. You can upgrade your available disk space to 5GB for $19.97/year, 15GB for $49.97/year, or 25GB for $89.97/year (as of this writing).

Domain mapping

I highly recommend using your own domain for your blog. WordPress.com users who do not purchase this upgrade will have their blogs hosted under the WordPress.com top-level domain (for example, `http://example.wordpress.com`).

For marketing, content ownership, and search engine optimization (SEO) strategy purposes, I always recommend that, when possible, people use their own domains. This is extremely important if you ever want to move your blog to a self-hosted WordPress.org blog or another blogging platform altogether. As of this writing, the upgrade is available for $14.97/year.

You can perform domain mapping through the Upgrades ➪ Domains menu in WordPress.com by entering the domain you want to use and assigning it to a blog, as shown in Figure 26.8.

You can map a domain to WordPress.com so that your blog will have its own marketable domain name instead of a subdomain of WordPress.com.

There is another step in the process, however, because domain mapping is not the same as using a competing product to "publish" to another domain. You will be required to update the Domain Name System (DNS) for the domain through your domain registrar.

Make sure you point your domain to the following nameservers and wait for DNS to propagate:

- ns1.wordpress.com
- ns2.wordpress.com
- ns3.wordpress.com

No-ads

Occasionally, WordPress.com serves ads on blogs. This is explained as a way to cover costs and pay for the service. However, if you never want to have ads from WordPress.com displayed on your blog, you can purchase the No-ads feature for $29.97/year (as of this writing).

Unlimited Private Users

If you have set up your WordPress.com as a private blog, you have a cap of 35 users that you can give blog access to. By purchasing the Unlimited Private Users add-on for $29.97/year (as of this writing), you can remove this cap.

VideoPress

Whether you are on WordPress.com or on WordPress.org, you may want to take advantage of the superb new video player and hosting available through WordPress.com. VideoPress was discussed earlier in this chapter, and it offers a high-quality way to display videos in standard or high definition. As of this writing, this add-on can be purchased for $59.97/year.

Summary

- Automattic is the sponsor of WordPress, but also runs WordPress.com, its flagship offering.
- Automattic offers a variety of products that can, in many cases, be used on WordPress and non-WordPress blogs. Akismet, IntenseDebate, and PollDaddy are a few examples.
- Automattic also contributes and shepherds a number of open source projects, including WordPress. Some of these are BuddyPress, bbPress, and the WordPress app for iPhone.
- WordPress.com themes and plugins must be GPL-compliant.
- Themes included for WordPress.com must have clean code, should be widgetized, and should not rely on other plugins that might not exist on WordPress.com.
- Plugins should not allow users to include JavaScript and should use shortcodes for insertion of potentially dangerous material.
- Plugins and theme inclusion is driven in large part by demand from the WordPress.com user community.
- You can tweak and enhance your WordPress.com blog by buying premium upgrades like VideoPress, domain mapping, and Custom CSS.

Leveraging Automattic Products

I n the blogging world, there are debates and wars over platforms and products. Historically, the WordPress world has been no different, as it has gone toe to toe with advocates and evangelists representing other blogging communities like Drupal and Movable Type. In the end, however, the blogging world is the blogging world and what is good for one platform is good for everyone.

Such is the case with many of the WordPress.com products released by Automattic. While most of these products are designed to integrate with WordPress directly, they are also Web services that can be used from any platform or cloud-based products that are integrated via JavaScript widgets.

In this final chapter, I look at some of these products and services and how they can be beneficial for any blogger on any platform.

Cross-Reference
See Chapter 26 for more information about Automattic and a full listing of its product offerings. ∎

IN THIS CHAPTER

Obtaining a WordPress.com API key

Using Akismet to kill spam

Making use of WordPress.com stats

Engaging readers with IntenseDebate

Crowdsourcing with PollDaddy

Obtaining a WordPress.com API Key

The WordPress.com API (application programming interface) key is essential for almost all of the WordPress.com distributed services. It is a randomly generated string that is unique to a single user account. You can obtain a WordPress.com API key by signing up for free at WordPress.com. During the signup process, you can request a user account or a blog. Either one is fine because both provide a WordPress.com API key.

Once you have your free WordPress.com account, you can obtain your WordPress.com API key by logging into WordPress.com (if you didn't sign up for a blog, your Dashboard will have a minimal amount of things that you can do) and opening up your profile. You can access your profile by clicking your username in the upper-right corner of the WordPress Admin or by clicking the Profile navigation item on the left side of the screen.

Your unique WordPress.com API key appears at the very top of your profile, above Personal Options, as shown in Figure 27.1.

FIGURE 27.1

Your WordPress.com API key is at the top of your profile.

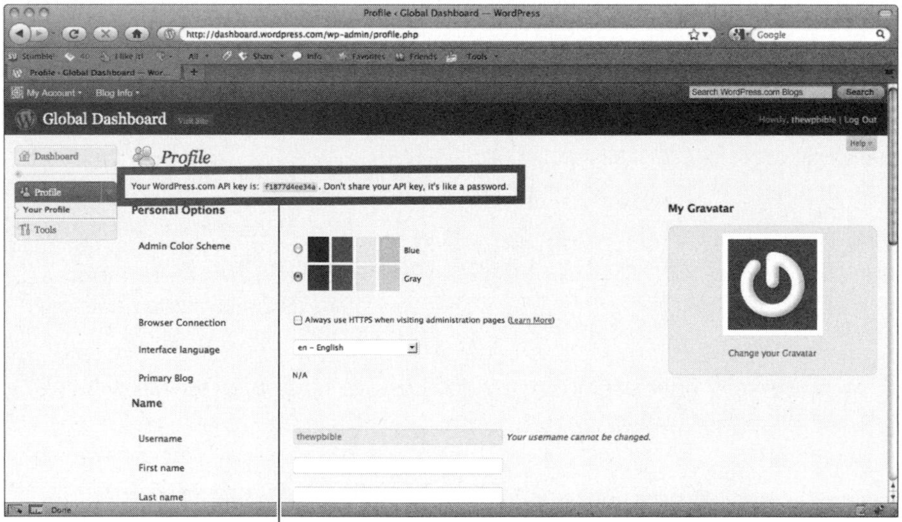

The WordPress.com API key

Using Akismet to Kill Spam

Spam is a problem on any blogging platform, but can be a major concern for WordPress blogs. Blog spam occurs when spammers try to slip links or other content onto a blog. With WordPress, most of the time, bloggers configure their blogs so only commenters who have been approved previously are unmoderated.

Therefore, if a spammer gets a blogger to approve a spam comment, the spammer might be able to put anything he wants onto his blog in the future. While the spammer might gain short-term benefits from having links, especially on popular sites, back to nefarious Web sites he wants to move up in search engine rankings, he quickly loses that benefit when the search engines de-list the nefarious Web site for spamming. It is a constant war that anyone who has been in the blog world long enough is well aware of.

A few years ago, Akismet was released to the WordPress community. Akismet is a Web application with a WordPress plugin by the same name that identifies and blocks comment spam on blogs. The WordPress plugin, which is under the General Public License, is bundled with WordPress and only has to be activated. It is free for personal use, and has a minimal fee for commercial use.

Tip

The Askimet plugin can also be downloaded from the WordPress plugin repository at `http://wordpress.org/extend/plugins/akismet/`. **It is also bundled with WordPress.** ■

The server side of Akismet is not open source and is a hosted service run by Automattic. It handles all the processing of comments and determines if a comment is spam or not.

The process of determining spam on the client side is straightforward. A comment is submitted to a blog (client). Before adding the comment to the database, it is sent to Akismet for processing. After determining if a comment is spam or not, Akismet sends a response of ham or spam back to the client. *Ham* comments are comments that seem to be okay, while *spam* comments, naturally, are those deemed to be spam.

Based on the response, the client either marks the comment as spam and, in the case of WordPress, assigns a comment status of "spam" or moves the comment to the approved list (if the commenter has commented before and WordPress recognizes it) or the moderation queue (if the commenter is a first-time commenter).

The Akismet API is a Representational State Transfer (RESTful) API. REST calls are made over standard Web protocols, also known as HTTP (hypertext transfer protocol). Almost all HTTP calls with the Akismet API are made to a subdomain generated from your WordPress API key. For example, if you have API key abcde12345, Akismet API calls will be made to `http://abcde12345.rest.akismet.com`. Only the verify-key method does not require an API key subdomain.

Note

All requests from Askimet are made using the POST method. ■

Verify Key

The Verify Key method is the method used to ensure the WordPress.com API key being used for Akismet is legitimate. The arguments required to verify an API key are listed in Table 27.1.

If the API key is verified, it returns as valid. If it is unverified, it returns as invalid with additional information.

TABLE 27.1

The Akismet API Call to Verify a WordPress API Key

Request URL	
http://rest.akismet.com/1.1/verify-key	
Argument	**Description**
key (required)	The WordPress.com API key to be verified
blog (required)	The front page of the blog making the request

Comment Checking

The Comment Checking API call is the core of Akismet. After a key has been verified, the Comment Checking method is used to verify that a comment is not spam. The arguments required are listed in Table 27.2.

If Akismet identifies the comment as spam, the call returns `true`. If it identifies the comment as ham, the call returns `false`.

TABLE 27.2

The Comment Checking API Call to Determine Spam or Ham

Request URL	
http://api-key.rest.akismet.com/1.1/comment-check	
Argument	**Description**
blog (required)	The front page of the blog making the request.
user_ip (required)	The IP address of the commenter.
user_agent (required)	A unique User Agent for your application. Should be in the format Application Name/Version | Plugin Name/Version.
referrer	The content of the HTTP_REFERER header.
permalink	The location of the place where the comment was submitted.
comment_type	An arbitrary comment type. WordPress default comment types are comment, trackback, or pingback.
comment_author	The name submitted with the comment.
comment_author_email	The e-mail address submitted with the comment.
comment_author_url	The URL, if any, submitted with the comment.
comment_content	The comment that is being checked.

Submit Spam

Sometimes Akismet servers go down for a period of time, or Askimet falsely identifies a comment as ham (not spam). In this case, it is necessary to notify Akismet of the error and submit the comment as spam. By doing so, Akismet learns what is spam and what is not. Table 27.3 lists the arguments for making a Submit Spam call.

TABLE 27.3

The Submit Spam API Call to Alert Askimet of Known Spam

Request URL	
http://api-key.rest.akismet.com/1.1/submit-spam	
Argument	**Description**
blog (required)	The front page of the blog making the request.
user_ip (required)	The IP address of the commenter.
user_agent (required)	A unique User Agent for your application. Should be in the format Application Name/Version | Plugin Name/Version.
referrer	The content of the HTTP_REFERER header.
permalink	The location of the place where the comment was submitted.
comment_type	An arbitrary comment type. WordPress default comment types are comment, trackback, or pingback.
comment_author	The name submitted with the comment.
comment_author_email	The e-mail address submitted with the comment.
comment_author_url	The URL, if any, submitted with the comment.
comment_content	The comment that is being checked.

Submit Ham

Similar to the Submit Spam API, whenever Akismet falsely identifies a comment as spam, you may need to correct it and set the record straight. When you know that a comment is actually ham, you would use the Submit Ham API call listed in Table 27.4.

TABLE 27.4

The Submit Ham API Call to Alert Askimet of Known Ham

Request URL
http://api-key.rest.akismet.com/1.1/submit-ham

Argument	Description
blog (required)	The front page of the blog making the request.
user_ip (required)	The IP address of the commenter.
user_agent (required)	A unique User Agent for your application. Should be in the format Application Name/Version | Plugin Name/Version.
referrer	The content of the HTTP_REFERER header.
permalink	The location of the place where the comment was submitted.
comment_type	Arbitrary comment type. WordPress default comment types are comment, trackback, or pingback.
comment_author	The name submitted with the comment.
comment_author_email	The e-mail address submitted with the comment.
comment_author_url	The URL, if any, submitted with the comment.
comment_content	The comment that is being checked.

Akismet on Other Platforms

Akismet is most often used on WordPress blogs; however, because it is an open API, anyone can build a plugin for any platform or build Akismet support directly into a Web application. Akismet is also very popular on other platforms, such as Movable Type. A selection of other platforms that support Akismet (there are more than what is listed, but just to give you an idea) is listed here:

- MT-Akismet (Movable Type version)
- Drupal
- phpBB
- blojsom
- Serendipty (s9y)
- Nucleus CMS
- b2evolution
- ExpressionEngine
- Coppermine
- Joomla

For developers, the following open source libraries for a variety of languages have been built to support Akismet:

- Python (David Lynch's Python Library)
- PHP 5 (PHP 5 Class by Alex)
- ColdFusion (CFAkismet for ColdFusion)
- Net::Akismet (Perl module)
- Ruby on Rails plugin
- .NET (1.1 and 2.0) bindings
- mod_akismet for Apache

Making Use of WordPress.com Stats

WordPress.com Stats is a service available to WordPress.com and WordPress.org users. One of the biggest draws to WordPress.com Stats is the charts and graphics available to it. Using the Stats plugin provides an interactive chart for measuring traffic and traffic sources (see Figure 27.2.).

FIGURE 27.2

You can access WordPress.com Stats from your WordPress Dashboard menu. From here, you can examine interactive charts and traffic data.

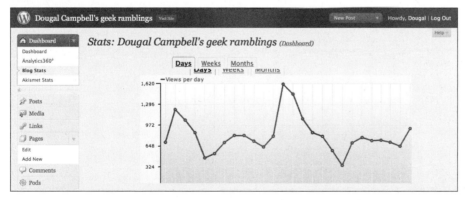

In addition to the interactive charts, WordPress.com will show you referring Web sites, the most popular posts or pages, search engine search terms that draw readers to your blog, and links that people click on your blog (see Figure 27.3).

FIGURE 27.3

WordPress.com Stats displays referring Web sites, the number of clicks on links on your site, popular posts, and search terms that bring readers to the blog.

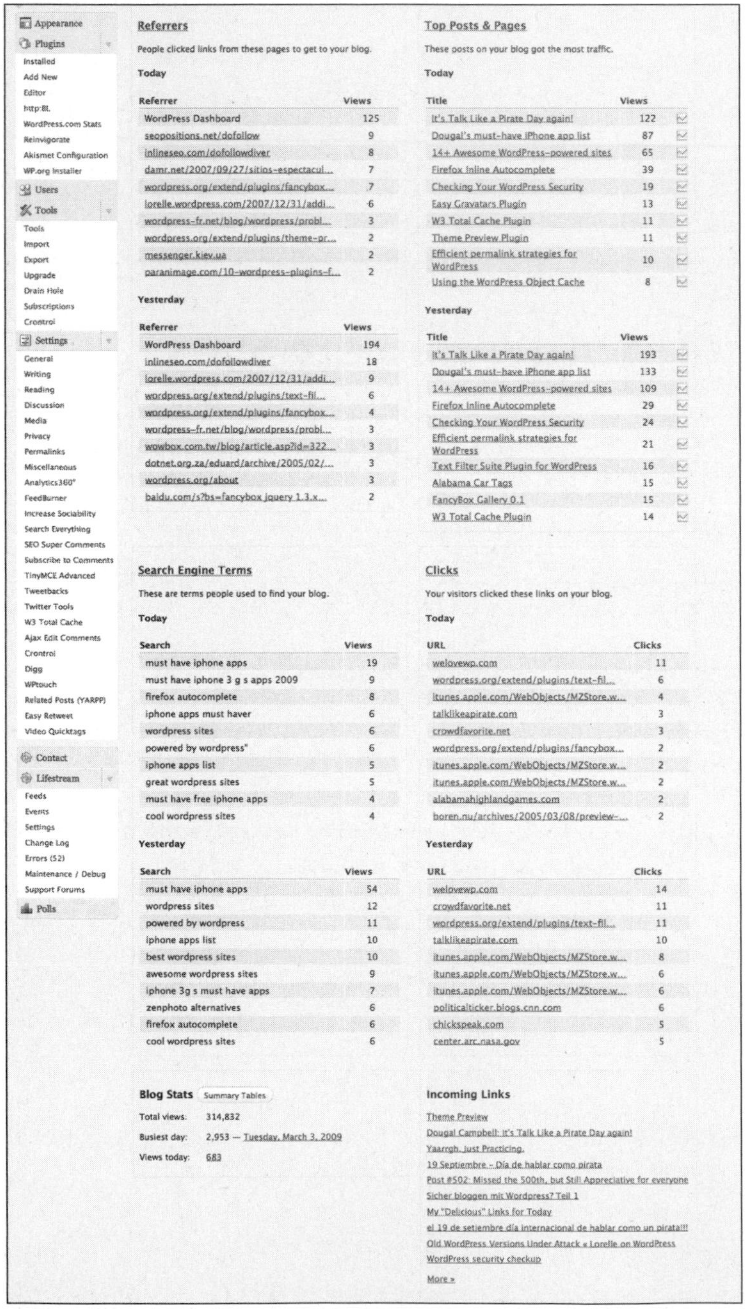

To use WordPress.com stats on your WordPress.org self-hosted blog, you will need to install the WordPress.com Stats plugin available at `http://wordpress.org/extend/plugins/stats/`. You will also need a WordPress.com API key, available on your WordPress.com profile page. WordPress.com Stats is free to use.

Engaging Readers with IntenseDebate

IntenseDebate is a plugin for WordPress that can be used on any blog, regardless of platform. It is a drop-in replacement for the standard WordPress comments and is rendered using JavaScript. In this way, the IntenseDebate plugin is more of a widget, in the generic sense of the word, than a Web service.

Note

Bloggers often like to use these kinds of comment replacement systems for data portability reasons. Additionally, unlike standard WordPress comments, IntenseDebate offers features such as "reply by e-mail." ■

To use IntenseDebate, go to `http://intensedebate.com` to sign up for a free IntenseDebate account. After going through the process of signing up, it's time to add a new blog to the service.

To add your blog to the IntenseDebate service, follow these steps:

1. **Click the Profile tab on the left side of the IntenseDebate administrative screen, as shown in Figure 27.4.**

FIGURE 27.4

Open the Profile tab on the left side of the IntenseDebate.com administrative screen to add a new blog.

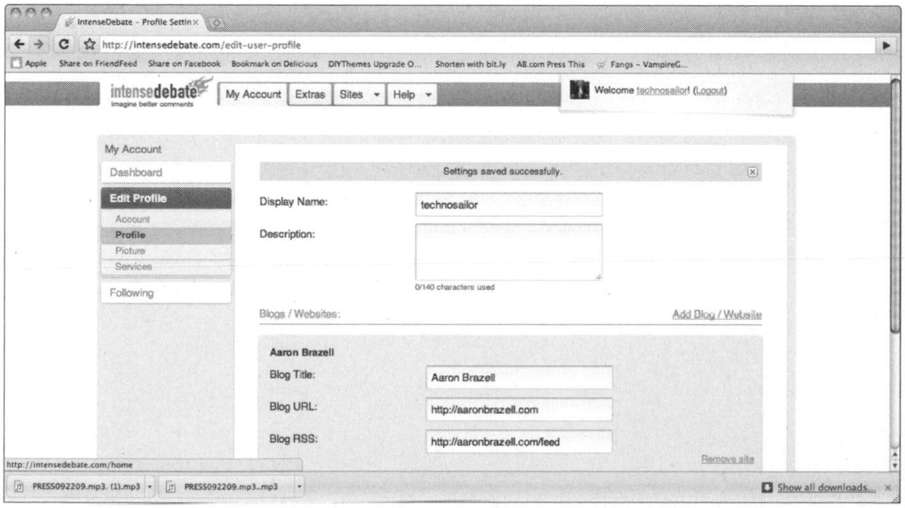

2. **Click the Add Blog/Website link and enter your blog name, WordPress URL, and RSS/Feed URL.** In WordPress, the RSS/Feed URL is generally your WordPress URL with `/feed` appended to the end.

3. **Click the Save Settings button when finished.**

Once you have added your blog to IntenseDebate, be sure to head to the Account tab and copy down your User Key. The User Key is an extremely important piece of information that enables IntenseDebate to work on your blog and behaves in a similar fashion to the WordPress.com API key. (I predict this will ultimately end up as a WordPress.com API key as the two companies further integrate, but I can't predict this for sure.)

While inside IntenseDebate, you may want to fill out your administration panel to customize your experience. Other things you can do from within IntenseDebate include:

- Adding an OpenID account.
- Signing up for a Gravatar account.
- Adding social network integration to sites such as:
  - Facebook
  - Twitter
  - FriendFeed
  - Flickr
  - LinkedIn
  - Last.fm
  - Digg
  - MySpace
  - Delicious
  - MyBlogLog
  - Orkut
- Configuring your comment widget behavior, including how many links in a comment before it is held for moderation, e-mail notifications, and so on.

After you finish making the adjustments needed for your IntenseDebate widget, you must log in to WordPress and install the IntenseDebate Comments plugin for WordPress available at `http://wordpress.org/extend/plugins/intensedebate/`. Once it's activated, you can configure the plugin on the IntenseDebate page located in the Settings menu, as shown in Figure 27.5. This page requires your IntenseDebate username and User Key.

FIGURE 27.5

On the IntenseDebate admin panel in WordPress, enter your IntenseDebate username and User Key.

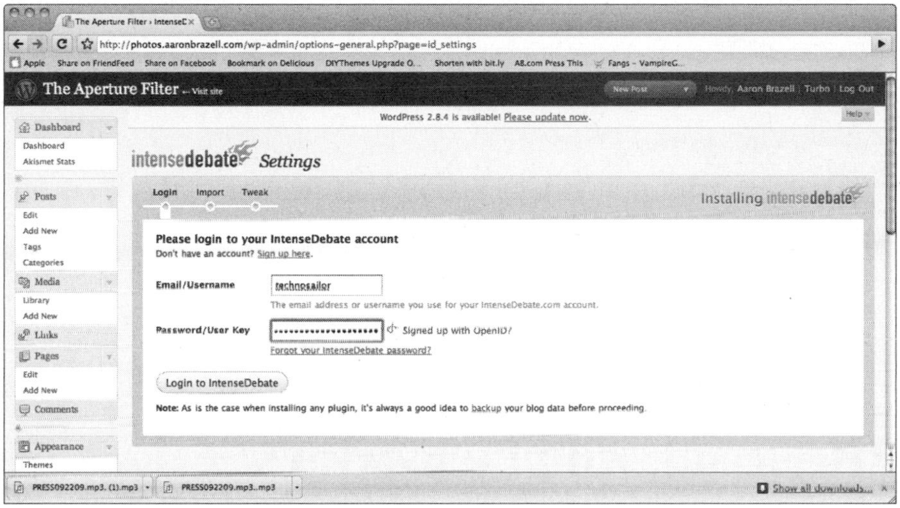

After activating the plugin, the next step in WordPress integration with IntenseDebate is comment synchronization. IntenseDebate, like other services like it, is a cloud-based service. Comments are stored in the cloud, but they are also stored locally in WordPress. Therefore, if you ever decide to stop using IntenseDebate or switch to another service, you retain a copy of all comments made on the blog. However, it's important to note that comments rendered by IntenseDebate are comment content stored in the cloud and not locally.

To synchronize your blog with IntenseDebate, click the Start Importing Comments button. The process may take awhile, depending on the size of your blog (see Figure 27.6).

FIGURE 27.6

Once you begin the comment synchronization phase, the process may take a little while depending on the number of comments. If you only have a few comments, the process will only take a minute or so. Large blogs may take hours.

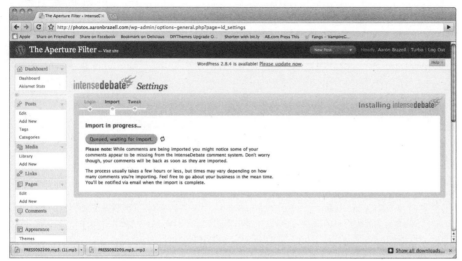

Crowdsourcing with PollDaddy

PollDaddy, one of the newest acquisitions of Automattic, is a hosted poll service that enables bloggers on any blog platform, not just WordPress, to create online surveys and polls and to *crowdsource* (a word describing the solicitation of community input around an idea or topic). Like IntenseDebate, it is a JavaScript-based widget (not in the sense of sidebar widgets that are built into WordPress, but as a separate module that can be used on a Web page).

PollDaddy is a "freemium" service. There is a limited free model that allows unlimited polls and unlimited surveys (though the surveys are limited to 100 responses each month). The Pro accounts, designed for heavy users, start at $200/year (as of this writing) and provide rich analytical reports of data, as shown in Figure 27.7.

PollDaddy allows any blogger on any platform with a PollDaddy account to create a poll and incorporate it in a post, sidebar, and other possibilities. For WordPress.com users, there is an Insert Poll icon on the write post screen above the title field, and alongside other icons for uploading images. For WordPress.org users, you can obtain the same thing via the PollDaddy Polls plugin for WordPress available at `http://wordpress.org/extend/plugins/polldaddy/`.

The permission system for polls created in WordPress are the same as the inherent WordPress permissions. Though users must have their own PollDaddy account, polls created with that account in WordPress are editable by Administrators. Editors can edit other Editor's polls as well as Author polls. Authors can only edit their own polls. Any polls created directly in PollDaddy, and not WordPress, do not gain the same permissions.

The PollDaddy Polls plugin also adds a new Polls menu item in the WordPress Admin for creating polls from directly in WordPress (see Figure 27.8).

FIGURE 27.7

For organizations trying to plot strategic direction with Pro accounts, the rich analytic reports on surveys and polls in PollDaddy are immensely important.

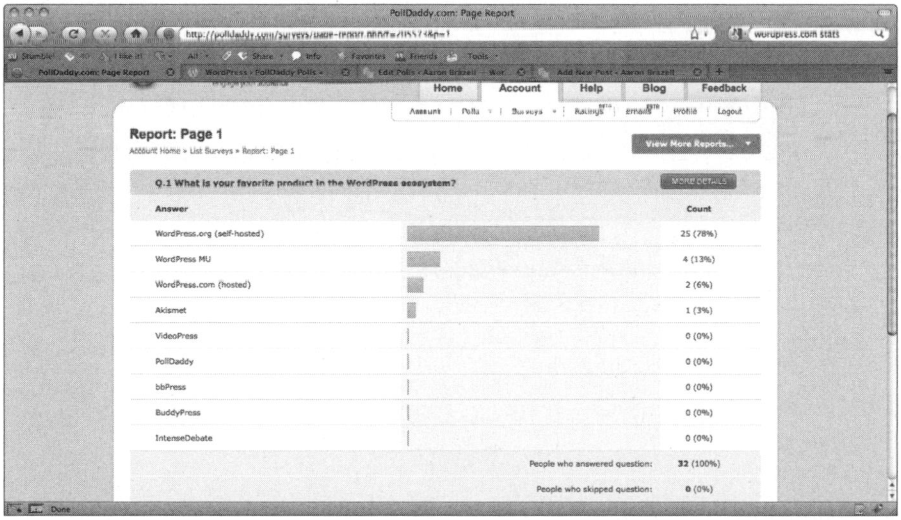

The PollDaddy Polls plugin provides a WordPress interface for creating new polls. Every blogger that blogs on a blog must have his own PollDaddy account.

Summary

- Many WordPress.com services require a WordPress.com API key that can be obtained on your WordPress.com user profile.

- Akismet is a WordPress plugin that identifies and blocks comment spam on blogs.

- WordPress.com Stats provide useful information about the traffic to and from a WordPress.com blog. Stats are also available as a plugin, and with a WordPress.com API key, for self-hosted WordPress installs.

- IntenseDebate is a JavaScript-based service that replaces (by synchronizing) the default WordPress comments for a blog with a richer experience. You can use IntenseDebate on any blogging platform.

- PollDaddy provides a free and pro model that enables bloggers to crowdsource their readers. Detailed analytics in the Pro accounts provide insight into reader and consumer engagement.

Part VIII

Appendixes

WordPress Hook Reference

W ordPress hooks are the lifeblood of WordPress and the developer ecosystem around it. They are what make WordPress truly extendable.

This appendix is a cheat sheet for developers to reference the 800+ hooks that are included in WordPress. You will find an alphabetical list of all hooks in WordPress 2.8 (Table A.1) and a breakdown of rough contexts that the hooks live in (Table A.2). Make sure you refer to the WordPress source code for exact usage.

Note

There is not enough room to cover how all these hooks work and it is expected that you are a developer who is familiar with the hook system and can find the usage in the WordPress code. ■

Cross-Reference

Hooks, including multi-argument hooks, are discussed in greater detail in Chapter 5. ■

Using Actions

Actions are a type of hook that are fired when an event happens. With actions, developers can tie into an action hook with the `add_action()` function. Likewise, they can remove an already hooked function with `remove_action()`. The first argument in both of these cases is the hook name and the second is the name of the function being added to or removed from the hook.

In Listing A.1, I demonstrate how to use the `add_action()` function to attach a function to a hook. This function uses the Bit.ly URL shortener service (`http://bit.ly`) to create a shortened URL for a post when it is saved and adds it as a custom field called `shorturl`. You could use it for Twitter or any other service you wish to use a shortened URL form for.

LISTING A.1

This function uses the Bit.ly service to produce short URLs when a post is saved

```
function shorten_bitly( $post_id )
{
    if ( get_post_meta( $post_id, 'shorturl', true ) )
        return $post_id;
    $post_permalink = get_permalink( $post_id );
    $b_api = 'Z_jkdsfahf98asdfhasd98DSA990n';
    $b_user = 'testuser';
    $qs = 'login=' . $b_user . '&apiKey=' . $b_api . '&version=2.0.1&format
=json&longUrl=' . $post_permalink;
    $request = 'http://api.bit.ly/shorten?' . $qs;
    $data = json_decode( file_get_contents( $request ) );

    foreach( $data->results as $bitly)
    {
        $shorturl = $bitly->shortUrl;
        if( !get_post_meta( $post->ID, 'shorturl' ) )
        {
            update_post_meta( $post_id, 'shorturl', $shorturl );
        }
    }
}
add_action('save_post','shorten_bitly');
```

Using Filters

Filters are similar to actions, except they take input, do something to that input, and return output in the same form as the input. They are, as the name suggests, a means to filter data according to whatever criteria you set in place.

You can hook into filters using the `add_filter()` and `remove_filter()` functions and, like actions, you can do this by supplying the hook name first and the function you're hooking second. This is demonstrated in Listing A.2, which illustrates a function that is "hardcoding" values for the Archives widget that is provided with WordPress.

Note

A function that is hooked into a filter must have at least one argument passed to it, and it must return that first argument (modified as needed). It cannot simply return a Boolean value of true or false. ■

Note

It is possible to have a hook that accepts multiple arguments. Anytime this happens, however, your function must still only return a single value. ■

LISTING A.2

A filter takes two arguments: the hook name and the name of the function being hooked

```
function archives_widget_args( $args )
{
    $new_args = array(
        'limit'            => 6,
        'type' => 'monthly',
        'show_post_count' => false
        );
    return $new_args;
}
add_filter('widget_archives_args','archives_widget_args');
```

Hook Reference: Alphabetical Listing

Table A.1 lists all of the hooks in WordPress 2.8 in alphabetical order.

TABLE A.1

Hooks in WordPress 2.8: Alphabetical Listing

Hook	Type
_admin_menu	action
_get_page_link	filter
_wp_post_revision_fields	filter
_wp_put_post_revision	action
activate_	action
activity_box_end	action

TABLE A.1   *(continued)*

Hook	Type
add_attachment	action
add_category_form_pre	action
add_link	action
add_link_category_form_pre	action
add_menu_classes	filter
add_ping	filter
add_tag_form	action
add_tag_form_pre	action
additional_capabilities_display	filter
admin_action_	action
admin_body_class	filter
admin_comment_types_dropdown	filter
admin_enqueue_scripts	action
admin_footer	action
admin_footer_text	filter
admin_head	action
admin_init	action
admin_menu	action
admin_notices	action
admin_page_access_denied	action
admin_print_footer_scripts	action
admin_print_scripts	action
admin_print_styles	action
admin_url	filter
admin_xml_ns	action
adminmenu	action
after_db_upgrade	action
after_plugin_row	action
akismet_spam_caught	action
akismet_tabs	action
all_options	filter
allow_password_reset	filter
allowed_redirect_hosts	filter
app_publish_post	action

Hook	Type
apply_filters	filter
args	action
atom_enclosure	filter
atom_entry	action
atom_head	action
atom_ns	action
atom_service_url	filter
atompub_create_post	action
atompub_put_post	action
attachment_fields_to_edit	filter
attachment_fields_to_save	filter
attachment_icon	filter
attachment_innerHTML	filter
attachment_link	filter
attachment_max_dims	filter
attribute_escape	filter
audio_send_to_editor_url	filter
audio_upload_iframe_src	filter
auth_cookie	filter
auth_cookie_bad_hash	action
auth_cookie_bad_username	action
auth_cookie_expiration	filter
auth_cookie_expired	action
auth_cookie_malformed	action
auth_cookie_valid	action
auth_redirect	action
authenticate	filter
author_email	filter
author_feed_link	filter
author_link	filter
author_rewrite_rules	filter
avatar_defaults	filter
block_local_requests	filter
blog_privacy_selector	action

continued

TABLE A.1	(continued)
Hook	**Type**
bloginfo	filter
bloginfo_rss	filter
bloginfo_url	filter
body_class	filter
bulk_edit_custom_box	action
cancel_comment_reply_link	filter
cat_row_actions	filter
category-$category->term_id	filter
category_feed_link	filter
category_link	filter
category_rewrite_rules	filter
category_template	filter
check_admin_referer	action
check_ajax_referer	action
check_comment_flood	action
check_password	filter
check_passwords	action
clean_object_term_cache	action
clean_page_cache	action
clean_post_cache	action
clean_term_cache	action
clean_url	filter
clear_auth_cookie	action
codepress_supported_langs	filter
comment_agent	filter
comment_atom_entry	action
comment_author	filter
comment_author_IP	filter
comment_author_email	filter
comment_author_rss	filter
comment_author_url	filter
comment_class	filter
comment_closed	action
comment_content	filter

Hook	Type
comment_cookie_lifetime	filter
comment_edit_pre	filter
comment_edit_redirect	filter
comment_email	filter
comment_excerpt	filter
comment_feed_groupby	filter
comment_feed_join	filter
comment_feed_limits	filter
comment_feed_orderby	filter
comment_feed_where	filter
comment_flood_filter	filter
comment_flood_trigger	action
comment_form	action
comment_id_not_found	action
comment_loop_start	action
comment_max_links	filter
comment_moderation_headers	filter
comment_moderation_subject	filter
comment_moderation_text	filter
comment_notification_headers	filter
comment_notification_subject	filter
comment_notification_text	filter
comment_on_draft	action
comment_post	action
comment_post_redirect	filter
comment_reply_link	filter
comment_row_actions	filter
comment_save_pre	filter
comment_status_links	filter
comment_text	filter
comment_text_rss	filter
comment_url	filter
commentrss2_item	action
comments_array	filter

continued

TABLE A.1 *(continued)*

Hook	Type
comments_atom_head	action
comments_number	filter
comments_open	filter
comments_per_page	filter
comments_popup_link_attributes	filter
comments_popup_template	filter
comments_rewrite_rules	filter
comments_template	filter
commentsrss2_head	action
content_save_pre	filter
content_url	filter
contextual_help	filter
contextual_help_list	filter
core_version_check_locale	filter
create_$taxonomy	action
create_term	action
created_$taxonomy	action
created_term	action
cron_schedules	filter
custom_menu_order	filter
date_formats	filter
date_i18n	filter
date_rewrite_rules	filter
day_link	filter
dbx_post_advanced	action
dbx_post_sidebar	action
deactivate_	action
default_avatar_select	filter
default_content	filter
default_contextual_help	filter
default_excerpt	filter
default_feed	filter
default_title	filter
delete_attachment	action

Hook	Type
delete_comment	action
delete_link	action
delete_post	action
delete_term	action
delete_user	action
deleted_link	action
deleted_post	action
deleted_user	action
deprecated_file_included	action
deprecated_file_trigger_error	filter
deprecated_function_run	action
deprecated_function_trigger_error	filter
disable_captions	filter
display_post_states	filter
do_feed_$feed	action
do_meta_boxes	action
do_robots	action
do_robotstxt	action
document.location.href=this.options[this.selected Index].value;	filter
documentation_ignore_functions	filter
dynamic_sidebar_params	filter
edit_$field	filter
edit_attachment	action
edit_bookmark_link	filter
edit_categories_per_page	filter
edit_category_form	action
edit_category_form_fields	action
edit_category_form_pre	action
edit_comment	action
edit_comment_link	filter
edit_form_advanced	action
edit_link	action
edit_link_category_form	action

continued

TABLE A.1   *(continued)*

Hook	Type
edit_link_category_form_fields	action
edit_link_category_form_pre	action
edit_page_form	action
edit_post	action
edit_post_$field	filter
edit_post_link	filter
edit_posts	action
edit_posts_per_page	filter
edit_tag_form	action
edit_tag_form_fields	action
edit_tag_form_pre	action
edit_tag_link	filter
edit_tags_per_page	filter
edit_term	action
edit_user_profile	action
edit_user_profile_update	action
editable_extensions	filter
editable_roles	filter
editable_slug	filter
editor_max_image_size	filter
esc_html	filter
example_filter	filter
excerpt_length	filter
exclude	filter
exif_read_data	filter
explain_nonce_	filter
export_wp	action
ext2type	filter
favorite_actions	filter
feed_content_type	filter
feed_link	filter
file_is_displayable_image	filter
file_send_to_editor_url	filter
filesystem_method	filter

Hook	Type
filesystem_method_file	filter
flash_uploader	filter
format_to_edit	filter
format_to_post	filter
found_posts	filter
found_posts_query	filter
gallery_style	filter
generate_rewrite_rules	action
get_attached_file	filter
get_avatar	filter
get_bloginfo_rss	filter
get_bookmarks	filter
get_categories_taxonomy	filter
get_comment	filter
get_comment_author	filter
get_comment_author_email	filter
get_comment_author_IP	filter
get_comment_author_link	filter
get_comment_author_url	filter
get_comment_author_url_link	filter
get_comment_date	filter
get_comment_excerpt	filter
get_comment_ID	filter
get_comment_link	filter
get_comment_text	filter
get_comment_time	filter
get_comment_type	filter
get_comments_number	filter
get_comments_pagenum_link	filter
get_edit_bookmark_link	filter
get_edit_comment_link	filter
get_edit_post_link	filter
get_edit_tag_link	filter
get_editable_authors	filter

continued

TABLE A.1 *(continued)*

Hook	Type
get_enclosed	filter
get_footer	action
get_header	action
get_image_tag	filter
get_image_tag_class	filter
get_lastpostdate	filter
get_lastpostmodified	filter
get_others_drafts	filter
get_pagenum_link	filter
get_pages	filter
get_post_modified_time	filter
get_post_time	filter
get_pung	filter
get_search_form	action
get_search_form	filter
get_search_query	filter
get_sidebar	action
get_tags	filter
get_term	filter
get_terms	filter
get_terms_orderby	filter
get_the_author_	filter
get_the_excerpt	filter
get_the_generator_$type	filter
get_the_guid	filter
get_the_modified_date	filter
get_the_modified_time	filter
get_the_tags	filter
get_the_time	filter
get_to_ping	filter
get_user_option_$option	filter
get_usernumposts	filter
get_users_drafts	filter
get_wp_title_rss	filter

Hook	Type
getarchives_join	filter
getarchives_where	filter
gettext	filter
gettext_with_context	filter
got_rewrite	filter
hierarchical_post_types	filter
home_template	filter
htmledit_pre	filter
http_api_curl	action
http_api_debug	action
http_request_args	filter
http_transport_get_debug	action
http_transport_post_debug	action
https_local_ssl_verify	filter
https_ssl_verify	filter
httpversion	filter
icon_dir	filter
icon_dir_uri	filter
icon_dirs	filter
iis7_supports_permalinks	filter
iis7_url_rewrite_rules	filter
image_add_caption_shortcode	filter
image_downsize	filter
image_make_intermediate_size	filter
image_send_to_editor	filter
image_send_to_editor_url	filter
image_upload_iframe_src	filter
img_caption_shortcode	filter
import_allow_create_users	filter
import_allow_fetch_attachments	filter
import_attachment_size_limit	filter
import_done	action
import_end	action
import_post_added	action

continued

TABLE A.1 *(continued)*

Hook	Type
import_post_meta	action
import_post_meta_key	filter
import_start	action
import_upload_size_limit	filter
in_admin_footer	action
in_widget_form	action
includes_url	filter
init	action
install_plugin_complete_actions	filter
install_plugins_	action
install_plugins_nonmenu_tabs	filter
install_plugins_pre_	action
install_plugins_table_header	action
install_plugins_tabs	filter
install_theme_complete_actions	filter
install_themes_	action
install_themes_nonmenu_tabs	filter
install_themes_pre_	action
install_themes_table_header	action
install_themes_tabs	filter
intermediate_image_sizes	filter
is_email	filter
jpeg_quality	filter
js_escape	filter
kubrick_header_color	filter
kubrick_header_display	filter
kubrick_header_image	filter
language_attributes	filter
link	filter
link_cat_row_actions	filter
link_category	filter
link_title	filter
list_cats	filter
list_terms_exclusions	filter

Hook	Type
load-{$hook}	action
load-widgets.php	action
load_default_widgets	filter
load_feed_engine	action
locale	filter
locale_stylesheet_uri	filter
login_form	action
login_form_	action
login_head	action
login_headertitle	filter
login_headerurl	filter
login_message	filter
login_redirect	filter
login_url	filter
loginout	filter
logout_url	filter
loop_end	action
loop_start	action
lost_password	action
lostpassword_form	action
lostpassword_post	action
lostpassword_url	filter
manage_	filter
manage_categories_custom_column	filter
manage_comments_custom_column	action
manage_comments_nav	action
manage_link_categories_custom_column	filter
manage_link_custom_column	action
manage_media_columns	filter
manage_media_custom_column	action
manage_pages_columns	filter
manage_pages_custom_column	action
manage_pages_query	filter
manage_posts_columns	filter

continued

TABLE A.1   (continued)

Hook	Type
manage_posts_custom_column	action
manage_users_custom_column	filter
map_meta_cap	filter
mce_buttons	filter
mce_buttons_2	filter
mce_buttons_3	filter
mce_buttons_4	filter
mce_css	filter
mce_external_languages	filter
mce_external_plugins	filter
mce_spellchecker_languages	filter
media_buttons	action
media_buttons_context	filter
media_meta	filter
media_row_actions	filter
media_send_to_editor	filter
media_upload_default_tab	filter
media_upload_default_type	filter
media_upload_form_url	filter
media_upload_tabs	filter
menu_order	filter
mod_rewrite_rules	filter
month_link	filter
muplugins_loaded	action
next_posts_link_attributes	filter
ngettext	filter
ngettext_with_context	filter
no_texturize_shortcodes	filter
no_texturize_tags	filter
nocache_headers	filter
nonce_life	filter
number_format_i18n	filter
option_	filter
option_$optionname	filter

Hook	Type
page_link	filter
page_rewrite_rules	filter
page_row_actions	filter
page_stati	filter
page_template	filter
parse_query	action
parse_request	action
password_reset	action
password_reset_message	filter
password_reset_title	filter
permalink_structure_changed	action
personal_options	action
personal_options_update	action
phone_content	filter
phpmailer_init	action
pingback_post	action
pings_open	filter
plugin_action_links	filter
plugin_install_action_links	filter
plugin_row_meta	filter
plugins_api	filter
plugins_api_args	filter
plugins_api_result	filter
plugins_loaded	action
plugins_per_page	filter
plugins_url	filter
populate_options	action
post	filter
post-flash-upload-ui	action
post-html-upload-ui	action
post-upload-ui	action
post_$field	filter
post_class	filter
post_comments_feed_link	filter

continued

TABLE A.1 *(continued)*

Hook	Type
post_comments_feed_link_html	filter
post_comments_link	filter
post_date_column_time	filter
post_gallery	filter
post_limits	filter
post_limits_request	filter
post_link	filter
post_mime_types	filter
post_rewrite_rules	filter
post_row_actions	filter
post_stati	filter
post_submitbox_start	action
postmeta_form_limit	filter
posts_distinct	filter
posts_distinct_request	filter
posts_fields	filter
posts_fields_request	filter
posts_groupby	filter
posts_groupby_request	filter
posts_join	filter
posts_join_paged	filter
posts_join_request	filter
posts_orderby	filter
posts_orderby_request	filter
posts_request	filter
posts_results	filter
posts_selection	action
posts_where	filter
posts_where_paged	filter
posts_where_request	filter
pre-flash-upload-ui	action
pre-html-upload-ui	action
pre-upload-ui	action
pre_$field	filter

Hook	Type
pre_category_nicename	filter
pre_comment_approved	filter
pre_comment_author_email	filter
pre_comment_author_name	filter
pre_comment_author_url	filter
pre_comment_content	filter
pre_comment_on_post	action
pre_comment_user_agent	filter
pre_comment_user_ip	filter
pre_get_posts	action
pre_kses	filter
pre_option_	filter
pre_option_$optionname	filter
pre_ping	action
pre_post_update	action
pre_remote_source	filter
pre_transient_	filter
pre_update_option_	filter
pre_user	filter
pre_user_description	filter
pre_user_display_name	filter
pre_user_email	filter
pre_user_first_name	filter
pre_user_id	filter
pre_user_last_name	filter
pre_user_login	filter
pre_user_nicename	filter
pre_user_nickname	filter
pre_user_url	filter
prepend_attachment	filter
preprocess_comment	filter
Preview_post_link	filter
previous_posts_link_attributes	filter
print_admin_styles	filter

continued

TABLE A.1 *(continued)*

Hook	Type
print_footer_scripts	filter
print_head_scripts	filter
print_scripts_array	filter
print_styles_array	filter
private_title_format	filter
private_to_published	action
profile_personal_options	action
profile_update	action
protected_title_format	filter
pub_priv_sql_capability	filter
publish_phone	action
query	filter
query_string	filter
query_vars	filter
quick_edit_custom_box	action
quick_edit_dropdown_pages_args	filter
rdf_header	action
rdf_item	action
rdf_ns	action
redirect_canonical	filter
redirection	filter
register	filter
register_form	action
register_post	action
registration_errors	filter
request	filter
request_filesystem_credentials	filter
restrict_manage_posts	action
retrieve_password	filter
retrieve_password	action
retrieve_password_key	action
retrieve_password_message	filter
retrieve_password_title	filter
rewrite_rules	filter

Hook	Type
rewrite_rules_array	filter
richedit_pre	filter
right_now_table_end	action
rightnow_end	action
role_has_cap	filter
root_rewrite_rules	filter
rss2_head	action
rss2_item	action
rss2_ns	action
rss_enclosure	filter
rss_head	action
rss_item	action
rss_update_frequency	filter
rss_update_period	filter
safe_style_css	filter
salt	filter
sanitize_comment_cookies	action
sanitize_email	filter
sanitize_file_name	filter
sanitize_file_name_chars	filter
sanitize_html_class	filter
sanitize_title	filter
sanitize_user	filter
save_post	action
screen_layout_columns	filter
screen_meta_screen	filter
script_loader_src	filter
search_feed_link	filter
search_rewrite_rules	filter
send_headers	action
set-screen-option	filter
set_auth_cookie	action
set_current_user	action
set_logged_in_cookie	action

continued

TABLE A.1 *(continued)*

Hook	Type
set_object_terms	action
setup_theme	action
shortcut_link	filter
show_password_fields	filter
show_user_profile	action
shutdown	action
sidebar_admin_page	action
sidebar_admin_setup	action
sidebars_widgets	filter
single_cat_title	filter
single_post_title	filter
single_tag_title	filter
site_url	filter
status_header	filter
style_loader_src	filter
style_loader_tag	filter
stylesheet	filter
stylesheet_directory	filter
stylesheet_directory_uri	filter
stylesheet_uri	filter
submitlink_box	action
submitpage_box	action
submitpost_box	action
switch_theme	action
tag_cloud_sort	filter
tag_escape	filter
tag_feed_link	filter
tag_link	filter
tag_rewrite_rules	filter
tag_row_actions	filter
tag_template	filter
tagsperpage	filter
taxonomy_template	filter
teeny_mce_before_init	filter

Hook	Type
teeny_mce_buttons	filter
teeny_mce_plugins	filter
template	filter
template_directory	filter
template_directory_uri	filter
template_redirect	action
term_id_filter	filter
term_link	filter
term_name	filter
terms_to_edit	filter
the_author	filter
the_author_{field}	filter
the_category	filter
the_category_rss	filter
the_content	filter
the_content_export	filter
the_content_more_link	filter
the_content_rss	filter
the_date	filter
the_editor	filter
the_editor_content	filter
the_excerpt	filter
the_excerpt_export	filter
the_excerpt_rss	filter
the_generator	filter
the_meta_key	filter
the_modified_author	filter
the_modified_date	filter
the_modified_time	filter
the_password_form	filter
the_permalink	filter
the_permalink_rss	filter
the_post	action
the_posts	filter

continued

TABLE A.1 (continued)	
Hook	**Type**
the_preview	filter
the_search_query	filter
the_tags	filter
the_time	filter
the_title	filter
the_title_rss	filter
the_weekday	filter
the_weekday_date	filter
theme_action_links	filter
theme_install_action_links	filter
theme_mod_$name	filter
theme_root	filter
theme_root_uri	filter
themes_api	filter
themes_api_args	filter
themes_api_result	filter
thread_comments_depth_max	filter
time_formats	filter
timeout	filter
timezone_support	filter
tiny_mce_before_init	filter
tiny_mce_version	filter
title	filter
tool_box	action
trackback_post	action
trackback_url	filter
transient_	filter
transition_comment_status	action
transition_post_status	action
uninstall_	action
update-custom_	action
update_attached_file	filter
update_feedback	filter
update_footer	filter

Hook	Type
update_plugin_complete_actions	filter
update_theme_complete_actions	filter
upgrader_clear_destination	filter
upgrader_post_install	filter
upgrader_pre_install	filter
upgrader_source_selection	filter
upload_dir	filter
upload_file_glob	filter
upload_mimes	filter
upload_size_limit	filter
url	filter
url_to_postid	filter
use_curl_transport	filter
use_fopen_transport	filter
use_fsockopen_transport	filter
use_http_extension_transport	filter
use_streams_transport	filter
user-agent	filter
user_alm_label	filter
user_can_richedit	filter
user_has_cap	filter
user_id	filter
user_jabber_label	filter
user_profile_update_errors	action
user_register	action
user_registration_email	filter
user_row_actions	filter
user_trailingslashit	filter
user_yim_label	filter
validate_username	filter
video_send_to_editor_url	filter
video_upload_iframe_src	filter
whitelist_options	filter
widget_archives_args	filter

continued

TABLE A.1 *(continued)*

Hook	Type
widget_categories_args	filter
widget_categories_dropdown_args	filter
widget_display_callback	filter
widget_form_callback	filter
widget_links_args	filter
widget_pages_args	filter
widget_tag_cloud_args	filter
widget_text	filter
widget_title	filter
widget_update_callback	filter
widgets.php	action
widgets_init	action
wp	action
wp_admin_css	filter
wp_admin_css_uri	filter
wp_ajax_	action
wp_ajax_nopriv_	action
wp_authenticate	action
wp_authenticate_user	filter
wp_blacklist_check	action
wp_check_post_lock_window	filter
wp_comment_reply	filter
wp_count_comments	filter
wp_create_file_in_uploads	action
wp_create_file_in_uploads	filter
wp_create_thumbnail	filter
wp_dashboard_setup	action
wp_dashboard_widgets	filter
wp_default_editor	filter
wp_default_scripts	action
wp_default_styles	action
wp_delete_file	action
wp_delete_file	filter
wp_delete_post_revision	action

Hook	Type
wp_dropdown_cats	filter
wp_dropdown_pages	filter
wp_dropdown_users	filter
wp_enqueue_scripts	action
wp_feed_cache_transient_lifetime	filter
wp_footer	action
wp_generate_attachment_metadata	filter
wp_generate_tag_cloud	filter
wp_generator_type	filter
wp_get_attachment_image_attributes	filter
wp_get_attachment_link	filter
wp_get_attachment_metadata	filter
wp_get_attachment_thumb_file	filter
wp_get_attachment_thumb_url	filter
wp_get_attachment_url	filter
wp_get_object_terms	filter
wp_handle_upload	filter
wp_head	action
wp_headers	filter
wp_insert_comment	action
wp_insert_post	action
wp_insert_post_data	filter
wp_list_bookmarks	filter
wp_list_categories	filter
wp_list_pages	filter
wp_login	action
wp_login_failed	action
wp_logout	action
wp_mail	filter
wp_mail_charset	filter
wp_mail_content_type	filter
wp_mail_from	filter
wp_mail_from_name	filter
wp_mail_original_content	filter

continued

TABLE A.1 *(continued)*

Hook	Type
wp_meta	action
wp_mime_type_icon	filter
wp_page_menu	filter
wp_page_menu_args	filter
wp_parse_str	filter
wp_print_footer_scripts	action
wp_print_scripts	action
wp_print_styles	action
wp_read_image_metadata	filter
wp_redirect	filter
wp_redirect_status	filter
wp_restore_post_revision	action
wp_set_comment_status	action
wp_sprintf	filter
wp_sprintf_l	filter
wp_tag_cloud	filter
wp_title	filter
wp_title_rss	filter
wp_trim_excerpt	filter
wp_update_attachment_metadata	filter
wp_update_comment_count	action
xmlprc_publish_post	action
xmlrpc_allow_anonymous_comments	filter
xmlrpc_blog_options	filter
xmlrpc_call	action
xmlrpc_methods	filter
xmlrpc_publish_post	action
xmlrpc_text_filters	filter
year_link	filter

Note

There is a lot of raw information in this appendix. Every release, WordPress adds more and more hooks with new features and new levels of control for the developer. Because WordPress has more than 800 hooks, it's difficult to know the best way to organize all the information. My hope is that this will be a jumping-off point for you to dive into the code and understand what is being used where, and why and how it is being used. ■

Hook Reference: General Uses

Table A.2 breaks down the hooks in WordPress 2.8 according to where and how they are used.

TABLE A.2

Hooks in WordPress 2.8: Generalized Contexts

Hook Name	Hook Type
Posts and Pages	
_wp_post_revision_fields	filter
_wp_put_post_revision	action
add_ping	filter
content_save_pre	filter
content_url	filter
default_content	filter
default_contextual_help	filter
default_excerpt	filter
default_feed	filter
default_title	filter
delete_post	action
deleted_post	action
display_post_states	filter
edit_$field	filter
edit_form_advanced	action
edit_page_form	action
edit_post	action
edit_post_$field	filter
edit_post_link	filter
edit_posts	action
edit_posts_per_page	filter
editable_slug	filter
esc_html	filter
example_filter	filter
excerpt_length	filter
exclude	filter
format_to_edit	filter

continued

TABLE A.2 *(continued)*

Hook Name	Hook Type
format_to_post	filter
found_posts	filter
found_posts_query	filter
get_categories_taxonomy	filter
get_edit_post_link	filter
get_enclosed	filter
get_lastpostdate	filter
get_lastpostmodified	filter
get_others_drafts	filter
get_pagenum_link	filter
get_pages	filter
get_post_modified_time	filter
get_post_time	filter
get_the_excerpt	filter
get_the_generator_$type	filter
get_the_guid	filter
get_the_modified_date	filter
get_the_modified_time	filter
get_the_time	filter
get_to_ping	filter
getarchives_join	filter
getarchives_where	filter
hierarchical_post_types	filter
htmledit_pre	filter
no_texturize_shortcodes	filter
page_stati	filter
post_$field	filter
post_class	filter
post_date_column_time	filter
post_gallery	filter
post_limits	filter
post_limits_request	filter
post_link	filter
post_stati	filter

Hook Name	Hook Type
post_submitbox_start	action
postmeta_form_limit	filter
pre_kses	filter
pre_post_update	action
pre_remote_source	filter
pre_transient_	filter
private_title_format	filter
quick_edit_custom_box	action
quick_edit_dropdown_pages_args	filter
safe_style_css	filter
save_post	action
set_logged_in_cookie	action
single_post_title	filter
submitpage_box	action
submitpost_box	action
transition_post_status	action
url_to_postid	filter
wp_delete_post_revision	action
wp_dropdown_pages	filter
wp_insert_post	action
wp_insert_post_data	filter
wp_list_pages	filter
wp_page_menu	filter
wp_page_menu_args	filter
wp_restore_post_revision	action
year_link	filter
Comments	
admin_comment_types_dropdown	filter
cancel_comment_reply_link	filter
check_comment_flood	action
comment_agent	filter
comment_author	filter
comment_author_IP	filter
comment_author_email	filter

continued

TABLE A.2 *(continued)*

Hook Name	Hook Type
comment_author_url	filter
comment_class	filter
comment_closed	action
comment_content	filter
comment_cookie_lifetime	filter
comment_edit_pre	filter
comment_edit_redirect	filter
comment_email	filter
comment_excerpt	filter
comment_feed_groupby	filter
comment_feed_join	filter
comment_feed_limits	filter
comment_feed_orderby	filter
comment_feed_where	filter
comment_flood_filter	filter
comment_flood_trigger	action
comment_form	action
comment_id_not_found	action
comment_loop_start	action
comment_max_links	filter
comment_moderation_headers	filter
comment_moderation_subject	filter
comment_moderation_text	filter
comment_notification_headers	filter
comment_notification_subject	filter
comment_notification_text	filter
comment_on_draft	action
comment_post	action
comment_post_redirect	filter
comment_reply_link	filter
comment_row_actions	filter
comment_save_pre	filter
comment_status_links	filter
comment_text	filter

Hook Name	Hook Type
comment_url	filter
comments_array	filter
comments_number	filter
comments_open	filter
comments_per_page	filter
comments_popup_link_attributes	filter
comments_popup_template	filter
comments_rewrite_rules	filter
comments_template	filter
delete_comment	action
edit_comment	action
edit_comment_link	filter
get_comment	filter
get_comment_author	filter
get_comment_author_IP	filter
get_comment_author_email	filter
get_comment_author_link	filter
get_comment_author_url	filter
get_comment_author_url_link	filter
get_comment_date	filter
get_comment_excerpt	filter
get_comment_ID	filter
get_comment_link	filter
get_comment_text	filter
get_comment_time	filter
get_comment_type	filter
get_comments_number	filter
get_comments_pagenum_link	filter
get_edit_comment_link	filter
post_comments_feed_link	filter
post_comments_feed_link_html	filter
post_comments_link	filter
pre_comment_approved	filter
pre_comment_author_email	filter

continued

TABLE A.2 (continued)

Hook Name	Hook Type
pre_comment_author_name	filter
pre_comment_author_url	filter
pre_comment_content	filter
pre_comment_on_post	action
preprocess_comment	filter
thread_comments_depth_max	filter
transition_comment_status	action
wp_comment_reply	filter
wp_count_comments	filter
wp_insert_comment	action
wp_set_comment_status	action
wp_update_comment_count	action
Admin	
_admin_menu	action
activity_box_end	action
add_menu_classes	filter
additional_capabilities_display	filter
admin_action_	action
admin_body_class	filter
admin_enqueue_scripts	action
admin_footer	action
admin_footer_text	filter
admin_head	action
admin_init	action
admin_menu	action
admin_notices	action
admin_page_access_denied	action
admin_print_footer_scripts	action
admin_print_scripts	action
admin_print_styles	action
admin_url	filter
admin_xml_ns	action
adminmenu	action
bulk_edit_custom_box	action

Hook Name	Hook Type
contextual_help	filter
contextual_help_list	filter
custom_menu_order	filter
day_link	filter
dbx_post_advanced	action
dbx_post_sidebar	action
do_meta_boxes	action
documentation_ignore_functions	filter
edit_link	action
favorite_actions	filter
icon_dir	filter
icon_dir_uri	filter
icon_dirs	filter
in_admin_footer	action
in_widget_form	action
manage_categories_custom_column	filter
manage_comments_custom_column	action
manage_comments_nav	action
manage_link_categories_custom_column	filter
manage_link_custom_column	action
manage_media_columns	filter
manage_media_custom_column	action
manage_pages_columns	filter
manage_pages_custom_column	action
manage_pages_query	filter
manage_posts_columns	filter
manage_posts_custom_column	action
manage_users_custom_column	filter
menu_order	filter
page_row_actions	filter
post_row_actions	filter
right_now_table_end	action
rightnow_end	action
screen_layout_columns	filter

continued

TABLE A.2 (continued)

Hook Name	Hook Type
screen_meta_screen	filter
shortcut_link	filter
show_password_fields	filter
tool_box	action
wp_admin_css	filter
wp_admin_css_uri	filter
wp_dashboard_setup	action
wp_dashboard_widgets	filter
wp_default_editor	filter
wp_default_scripts	action
wp_default_styles	action
wp_enqueue_scripts	action
wp_print_footer_scripts	action
Database	
all_options	filter
attribute_escape	filter
bloginfo	filter
bloginfo_url	filter
option_$optionname	filter
populate_options	action
pre_$field	filter
pre_option_$optionname	filter
pre_update_option_	filter
sanitize_comment_cookies	action
sanitize_email	filter
sanitize_file_name	filter
sanitize_file_name_chars	filter
sanitize_html_class	filter
sanitize_title	filter
sanitize_user	filter
site_url	filter
Query	
get_search_query	filter
parse_query	action

Hook Name	Hook Type
parse_request	action
posts_distinct	filter
posts_distinct_request	filter
posts_fields	filter
posts_fields_request	filter
posts_groupby	filter
posts_groupby_request	filter
posts_join	filter
posts_join_paged	filter
posts_join_request	filter
posts_orderby	filter
posts_orderby_request	filter
posts_request	filter
posts_results	filter
posts_selection	action
posts_where	filter
posts_where_paged	filter
posts_where_request	filter
pre_get_posts	action
query	filter
query_string	filter
query_vars	filter
request	filter
request_filesystem_credentials	filter
Feeds	
atom_enclosure	filter
atom_entry	action
atom_head	action
atom_ns	action
atom_service_url	filter
atompub_create_post	action
atompub_put_post	action
bloginfo_rss	filter
comment_atom_entry	action

continued

TABLE A.2 (continued)

Hook Name	Hook Type
comment_author_rss	filter
comment_text_rss	filter
commentrss2_item	action
comments_atom_head	action
commentsrss2_head	action
do_feed_$feed	action
feed_content_type	filter
feed_link	filter
get_bloginfo_rss	filter
get_wp_title_rss	filter
load_feed_engine	action
rss2_head	action
rss2_item	action
rss2_ns	action
rss_enclosure	filter
rss_head	action
rss_item	action
rss_update_frequency	filter
rss_update_period	filter
the_content_rss	filter
the_excerpt_rss	filter
the_permalink_rss	filter
the_title_rss	filter
Templates	
_get_page_link	filter
author_feed_link	filter
author_link	filter
body_class	filter
category_feed_link	filter
category_link	filter
category_template	filter
date_formats	filter
dynamic_sidebar_params	filter
get_footer	action

Hook Name	Hook Type
get_header	action
get_search_form	action
get_search_form	filter
get_sidebar	action
home_template	filter
loop_end	action
loop_start	action
month_link	filter
next_posts_link_attributes	filter
page_link	filter
page_template	filter
preview_post_link	filter
previous_posts_link_attributes	filter
print_admin_styles	filter
print_footer_scripts	filter
print_head_scripts	filter
print_scripts_array	filter
print_styles_array	filter
script_loader_src	filter
search_feed_link	filter
style_loader_src	filter
style_loader_tag	filter
stylesheet	filter
the_author	filter
the_author_	filter
the_content	filter
the_content_more_link	filter
the_date	filter
the_editor	filter
the_excerpt	filter
the_generator	filter
the_meta_key	filter
the_modified_author	filter
the_modified_date	filter

continued

TABLE A.2 *(continued)*

Hook Name	Hook Type
the_modified_time	filter
the_password_form	filter
the_permalink	filter
the_post	action
the_posts	filter
the_preview	filter
the_search_query	filter
the_time	filter
the_title	filter
the_weekday	filter
the_weekday_date	filter
wp_footer	action
wp_head	action
wp_meta	action
wp_title	filter
wp_title_rss	filter
Rewrite Rules	
author_rewrite_rules	filter
category_rewrite_rules	filter
date_rewrite_rules	filter
generate_rewrite_rules	action
got_rewrite	filter
mod_rewrite_rules	filter
page_rewrite_rules	filter
post_rewrite_rules	filter
rewrite_rules	filter
rewrite_rules_array	filter
root_rewrite_rules	filter
search_rewrite_rules	filter
Cron	
cron_schedules	filter
Media	
add_attachment	action
attachment_fields_to_edit	filter

Hook Name	Hook Type
attachment_fields_to_save	filter
attachment_icon	filter
attachment_innerHTML	filter
attachment_link	filter
attachment_max_dims	filter
audio_send_to_editor_url	filter
audio_upload_iframe_src	filter
delete_attachment	action
disable_captions	filter
edit_attachment	action
editable_extensions	filter
editor_max_image_size	filter
exif_read_data	filter
ext2type	filter
file_is_displayable_image	filter
flash_uploader	filter
gallery_style	filter
get_attached_file	filter
image_add_caption_shortcode	filter
image_downsize	filter
image_make_intermediate_size	filter
image_upload_iframe_src	filter
img_caption_shortcode	filter
jpeg_quality	filter
media_buttons	action
media_buttons_context	filter
media_meta	filter
media_row_actions	filter
media_send_to_editor	filter
media_upload_default_tab	filter
media_upload_default_type	filter
media_upload_form_url	filter
media_upload_tabs	filter
post-flash-upload-ui	action

continued

TABLE A.2 *(continued)*

Hook Name	Hook Type
post-html-upload-ui	action
post-upload-ui	action
post_mime_types	filter
pre-flash-upload-ui	action
pre-html-upload-ui	action
pre-upload-ui	action
prepend_attachment	filter
update_attached_file	filter
video_upload_iframe_src	filter
wp_create_file_in_uploads	action
wp_create_file_in_uploads	filter
wp_create_thumbnail	filter
wp_delete_file	action
wp_delete_file	filter
wp_generate_attachment_metadata	filter
wp_get_attachment_image_attributes	filter
wp_get_attachment_link	filter
wp_get_attachment_metadata	filter
wp_get_attachment_thumb_file	filter
wp_get_attachment_thumb_url	filter
wp_get_attachment_url	filter
wp_mime_type_icon	filter
wp_read_image_metadata	filter
wp_update_attachment_metadata	filter
Localization/Internationalization	
codepress_supported_langs	filter
date_i18n	filter
gettext	filter
gettext_with_context	filter
language_attributes	filter
locale	filter
locale_stylesheet_uri	filter
ngettext	filter
ngettext_with_context	filter

Hook Name	Hook Type
number_format_i18n	filter
Import/Export	
export_wp	action
import_allow_create_users	filter
import_allow_fetch_attachments	filter
import_attachment_size_limit	filter
import_done	action
import_end	action
import_post_added	action
import_post_meta	action
import_post_meta_key	filter
import_start	action
import_upload_size_limit	filter
the_content_export	filter
the_excerpt_export	filter
Plugins	
activate_	action
after_plugin_row	action
akismet_spam_caught	action
akismet_tabs	action
install_plugin_complete_actions	filter
install_plugins_	action
install_plugins_nonmenu_tabs	filter
install_plugins_pre_	action
install_plugins_table_header	action
install_plugins_tabs	filter
muplugins_loaded	action
plugin_action_links	filter
plugin_install_action_links	filter
plugin_row_meta	filter
plugins_api	filter
plugins_api_args	filter
plugins_api_result	filter
plugins_loaded	action

continued

TABLE A.2 *(continued)*	
Hook Name	**Hook Type**
plugins_per_page	filter
plugins_url	filter
update_plugin_complete_actions	filter
Login/Authentication/Roles	
allow_password_reset	filter
auth_cookie	filter
auth_cookie_bad_hash	action
auth_cookie_expiration	filter
auth_cookie_expired	action
auth_cookie_malformed	action
auth_cookie_valid	action
auth_redirect	action
authenticate	filter
author_email	filter
check_password	filter
check_passwords	action
clear_auth_cookie	action
get_editable_authors	filter
login_form	action
login_form_	action
login_head	action
login_headertitle	filter
login_headerurl	filter
login_message	filter
login_redirect	filter
login_url	filter
loginout	filter
logout_url	filter
lost_password	action
lostpassword_form	action
lostpassword_post	action
lostpassword_url	filter
password_reset	action
password_reset_message	filter

Hook Name	Hook Type
password_reset_title	filter
register	filter
register_form	action
register_post	action
registration_errors	filter
set_auth_cookie	action
wp_authenticate	action
wp_login	action
wp_login_failed	action
wp_logout	action
TinyMCE	
file_send_to_editor_url	filter
image_send_to_editor	filter
image_send_to_editor_url	filter
mce_buttons	filter
mce_buttons_2	filter
mce_buttons_3	filter
mce_buttons_4	filter
mce_css	filter
mce_external_languages	filter
mce_external_plugins	filter
mce_spellchecker_languages	filter
richedit_pre	filter
teeny_mce_before_init	filter
teeny_mce_buttons	filter
teeny_mce_plugins	filter
the_editor_content	filter
tiny_mce_before_init	filter
tiny_mce_version	filter
video_send_to_editor_url	filter
Upgrades/File System	
after_db_upgrade	action
filesystem_method	filter
filesystem_method_file	filter

continued

TABLE A.2 *(continued)*	
Hook Name	**Hook Type**
update_feedback	filter
update_footer	filter
upgrader_clear_destination	filter
upgrader_post_install	filter
upgrader_pre_install	filter
upgrader_source_selection	filter
use_curl_transport	filter
use_fopen_transport	filter
use_fsockopen_transport	filter
use_http_extension_transport	filter
use_streams_transport	filter
user-agent	filter
WordPress Runtime/System	
allowed_redirect_hosts	filter
block_local_requests	filter
blog_privacy_selector	action
check_admin_referer	action
check_ajax_referer	action
clean_url	filter
core_version_check_locale	filter
deactivate_	action
deprecated_file_included	action
deprecated_file_trigger_error	filter
deprecated_function_run	action
deprecated_function_trigger_error	filter
do_robots	action
do_robotstxt	action
explain_nonce_	filter
http_api_curl	action
http_api_debug	action
http_request_args	filter
http_transport_get_debug	action
http_transport_post_debug	action
https_local_ssl_verify	filter

Hook Name	Hook Type
https_ssl_verify	filter
httpversion	filter
iis7_supports_permalinks	filter
iis7_url_rewrite_rules	filter
includes_url	filter
init	action
is_email	filter
js_escape	filter
nonce_life	filter
permalink_structure_changed	action
phpmailer_init	action
private_to_published	action
protected_title_format	filter
pub_priv_sql_capability	filter
redirect_canonical	filter
redirection	filter
salt	filter
send_headers	action
set-screen-option	filter
shutdown	action
status_header	filter
time_formats	filter
timeout	filter
timezone_support	filter
upload_dir	filter
upload_file_glob	filter
upload_mimes	filter
upload_size_limit	filter
whitelist_options	filter
wp_ajax_	action
wp_ajax_nopriv_	action
wp_blacklist_check	action
wp_check_post_lock_window	filter
wp_generator_type	filter

continued

TABLE A.2 *(continued)*

Hook Name	Hook Type
wp_handle_upload	filter
wp_headers	filter
wp_mail	filter
wp_mail_charset	filter
wp_mail_content_type	filter
wp_mail_from	filter
wp_mail_from_name	filter
wp_mail_original_content	filter
wp_parse_str	filter
wp_redirect	filter
wp_redirect_status	filter
wp_sprintf	filter
wp_sprintf_l	filter
wp_trim_excerpt	filter
Widgets	
load_default_widgets	filter
sidebar_admin_page	action
sidebar_admin_setup	action
sidebars_widgets	filter
widget_archives_args	filter
widget_categories_args	filter
widget_categories_dropdown_args	filter
widget_display_callback	filter
widget_form_callback	filter
widget_links_args	filter
widget_pages_args	filter
widget_tag_cloud_args	filter
widget_text	filter
widget_title	filter
widget_update_callback	filter
widgets_init	action
XML-RPC/AtomPub	
app_publish_post	action
get_pung	filter

Hook Name	Hook Type
pingback_post	action
pings_open	filter
pre_ping	action
rdf_header	action
rdf_item	action
rdf_ns	action
trackback_post	action
trackback_url	filter
xmlprc_publish_post	action
xmlrpc_allow_anonymous_comments	filter
xmlrpc_blog_options	filter
xmlrpc_call	action
xmlrpc_methods	filter
xmlrpc_publish_post	action
xmlrpc_text_filters	filter

Summary

- Hooks are an integral part of WordPress that enable plugin authors to modify the behavior of WordPress.
- Actions are hooks that are fired when an event occurs.
- Filters are used to, as expected, filter content and possibly modify it along the way.
- Enclosed are two tables showing a listing of all hooks by alphabetical order and by context. Hooks are generally given names that make sense to the context they are used.

Template Tags

emplating systems have existed for a long time and have become a major part of most content management systems. The concept behind templating systems is that raw code is abstracted for the sake of ease of design and clean code for designers.

Understanding the Template Tag Concept

One of these templating systems include the Smarty template system (`www. smarty.net/`), which uses curly braces to designate a template tag (for example, `{include file-'header.php'}`). Additionally, many would consider PHP itself a templating system of sorts.

Each of the blog platforms that compete with WordPress also include template systems that assist in maintaining clean and easily understood themes. For example, Blogger uses tags similar to `<$BlogOwnerProfileURL$>` and Movable Type uses tags like `<$mt:AuthorDisplayName$>`.

Breaking Down the WordPress Templating System

WordPress has its own set of template tags. This appendix has been created as a reference to all of the template tags available to theme developers along with all Arguments that can be used.

Cross-Reference

For more on template tags, see Chapter 12. ∎

Many of the template tags listed here can take either an array of Arguments or a query string. An array of Arguments might look like this:

```
template_function( array( 'arg1' => 'val1', 'arg2' => 'val2' ) );
```

The same set of Arguments in a query string would look like this:

```
template_function( 'arg1=val1&arg2=val2' );
```

The following sections break down the WordPress template tags according to type. For instance, the tags that are all related to authors are included in that context. All the tags relating to pages are grouped in that way, and so on.

Include tags

Header

- **Tag:** `get_header()`
- **Description:** This template tag is used to include `header.php` in a theme.
- **Returns:** HTML (hypertext markup language) rendered with the active theme's `header.php`.
- **Arguments:** None

Sidebar

- **Tag:** `get_sidebar()`
- **Description:** This template tag is used to include `sidebar.php` in a theme.
- **Returns:** HTML rendered with the active theme's `sidebar.php`.
- **Arguments:** None

Search Form

- **Tag:** `get_search_form()`
- **Description:** This template tag is used to render a search form in a theme.
- **Returns:** HTML search form rendered dynamically. If `searchform.php` exists in a theme, it will be used instead.
- **Arguments:** None

Comments

- **Tag:** `comments_template()`
- **Description:** This template tag is used to make the comments query and include `comments.php` in a theme.

- **Returns:** HTML rendered with the active theme's `comments.php`.
- **Arguments:** None

Footer

- **Tag:** `get_footer()`
- **Description:** This template tag is used to include `footer.php` in a theme.
- **Returns:** HTML rendered with the active theme's `footer.php`.
- **Arguments:** None

Blog Info tags

Blog Info (Echoed)

- **Tag:** `bloginfo()`
- **Description:** This template tag is used to echo global descriptor and settings data to a blog.
- **Returns:** Echoes retrieved blog data. To return the same data to be used by PHP, use `get_bloginfo()`.
- **Arguments:** 1

Parameter	Returned Type	Description
admin_email	String	Prints the e-mail address for the admin set in Settings ➪ General.
atom_url	String	Prints the Atom 1.0 feed URL for the blog.
charset	String	Prints the character set encoding designated in Settings ➪ Reading.
comments_atom_url	String	Prints the Atom feed URI for an individual post/entry.
comments_rss2_url	String	Prints the RSS feed URL for an individual post/entry.
description	String	Prints the tagline set for a blog in General ➪ Settings.
html_type	String	Prints the HTML header information. Will always be text/html unless modified by plugin.
language	String	Prints the language code designated for the blog. Defaults to en-US. To localize a blog, see the procedures outlined in Chapter 5.
name	String	Prints the name of the blog as defined in Settings ➪ General.
pingback_url	String	Prints the XML-RPC (XML Remote Procedure Call) URL used to assist remote sources in auto-discovery of where to send pingbacks.
rdf_url	String	Prints the XML-RPC information needed for auto-discovery of XML-RPC server capabilities.
rss2_url	String	Prints the RSS 2.0 URL for the blog.
rss_url	String	Prints the RSS 0.92 URL for the blog.

continued

Parameter	Returned Type	Description
siteurl	String	Deprecated. Identical to 'url'.
stylesheet_directory	String	Prints the URL to the directory containing the active theme.
stylesheet_url	String	Prints the URL to the style.css file of the active theme.
template_directory	String	Identical to the 'stylesheet_url', but semantically means "point to the folder for the theme" instead of "point to the folder that contains the stylesheet," even though they are the same thing.
template_url	String	Identical to 'template_directory'.
text_direction	String	Prints the direction of how text is read on a blog. Defaults to ltr (left to right) unless the blog uses a language (such as Arabic) that is printed rtl (right to left).
url	String	Prints the URL for the WordPress install. Preferred over 'home' and 'siteurl' but functions identically.
version	String	Prints the current version of WordPress.
wpurl	String	Identical to 'url'

Blog Info (Returned)

- **Tag:** get_bloginfo()
- **Description:** This template tag is used to return global descriptor and settings data to a blog.
- **Returns:** Returns retrieved blog data. To simply echo the same data without need for further manipulation or use by PHP, use bloginfo().
- **Arguments:** 1

Parameter	Returned Type	Description
admin_email	String	Returns the e-mail address for the admin set in Settings ⇨ General.
atom_url	String	Returns the Atom 1.0 feed URL for the blog.
charset	String	Returns the character set encoding designated in Settings ⇨ Reading.
comments_atom_url	String	Returns the Atom feed URL for an individual post/entry.
comments_rss2_url	String	Returns the RSS feed URL for an individual post/entry.
description	String	Returns the tagline set for a blog in General ⇨ Settings.
html_type	String	Returns the HTML header information. Will always be text/html unless modified by plugin.
language	String	Returns the language code designated for the blog. Defaults to en-US. To localize a blog, see the procedures outlined in Chapter 5.
name	String	Returns the name of the blog as defined in Settings ⇨ General.

Parameter	Returned Type	Description
pingback_url	String	Returns the XML-RPC URL used to assist remote sources in auto-discovery of where to send pingbacks.
rdf_url	String	Returns the XML-RPC information needed for auto-discovery of XML-RPC server capabilities.
rss2_url	String	Returns the RSS 2.0 URL for the blog.
rss_url	String	Returns the RSS 0.92 URL for the blog.
siteurl	String	Deprecated. Identical to 'url'.
stylesheet_directory	String	Returns the URL to the directory containing the active theme.
stylesheet_url	String	Returns the URL to the style.css file of the active theme.
template_directory	String	Identical to the 'stylesheet_url', but semantically means "point to the folder for the theme" instead of "point to the folder that contains the stylesheet," even though they are the same thing.
template_url	String	Identical to 'template_directory'.
text_direction	String	Returns the direction of how text is read on a blog. Defaults to ltr (left to right) unless the blog uses a language (such as Arabic) that is printed rtl (right to left).
url	String	Returns the URL for the blog. Preferred over the deprecated 'home' and 'siteurl' but functions identically.
version	String	Returns the current version of WordPress.
wpurl	String	Returns the URL for the WordPress root directory.

Blog Info for RSS (Echoed)

- **Tag:** `bloginfo_rss()`
- **Description:** This template tag is used to echo global descriptor and settings data to an RSS feed.
- **Returns:** Echoes retrieved blog data to an RSS feed. This data is encoded properly for use by XML. To return the same data to be used by PHP, use `get_bloginfo_rss()`.
- **Arguments:** 1

Parameter	Returned Type	Description
admin_email	String	Prints the e-mail address for the admin set in Settings ⇨ General.
atom_url	String	Prints the Atom 1.0 feed URL for the blog.
charset	String	Prints the character set encoding designated in Settings ⇨ Reading.
comments_atom_url	String	Prints the Atom feed URL for an individual post/entry.

continued

Parameter	Returned Type	Description
comments_rss2_url	String	Prints the RSS feed URL for an individual post/entry.
description	String	Prints the tagline set for a blog in General ⇨ Settings.
html_type	String	Prints the HTML header information. Will always be text/html unless modified by plugin.
language	String	Prints the language code designated for the blog. Defaults to en-US. To localize a blog, see the procedures outlined in Chapter 5.
name	String	Prints the name of the blog as defined in Settings ⇨ General.
pingback_url	String	Prints the XML-RPC URL used to assist remote sources in auto-discovery of where to send pingbacks.
rdf_url	String	Prints the XML-RPC information needed for auto-discovery of XML-RPC server capabilities.
rss2_url	String	Prints the RSS 2.0 URL for the blog.
rss_url	String	Prints the RSS 0.92 URL for the blog.
siteurl	String	Deprecated. Identical to 'url'.
stylesheet_directory	String	Prints the URL to the directory containing the active theme.
stylesheet_url	String	Prints the URL to the style.css file of the active theme.
template_directory	String	Identical to the 'stylesheet_url', but semantically means "point to the folder for the theme" instead of "point to the folder that contains the stylesheet" even though they are the same thing.
template_url	String	Identical to 'template_directory'.
text_direction	String	Prints the direction of how text is read on a blog. Defaults to ltr (left to right) unless the blog uses a language (such as Arabic) that is printed rtl (right to left).
url	String	Returns the URL for the blog. Preferred over the deprecated 'home' and 'siteurl' but functions identically.
version	String	Prints the current version of WordPress.
wpurl	String	Returns the URL for the WordPress root directory.

Blog Info for RSS (Returned)

- **Tag:** `get_bloginfo_rss()`
- **Description:** This template tag is used to return global descriptor and settings data to an RSS feed.
- **Returns:** Returns retrieved blog data for use in an RSS feed. This data is encoded properly for use by XML. To simply echo the same data without need for further manipulation or use by PHP, use `bloginfo()`.
- **Arguments:** 1

Parameter	Returned Type	Description
admin_email	String	Returns the e-mail address for the admin set in Settings ⇨ General.
atom_url	String	Returns the Atom 1.0 feed URL for the blog.
charset	String	Returns the character set encoding designated in Settings ⇨ Reading.
comments_atom_url	String	Returns the Atom feed URL for an individual post/entry.
comments_rss2_url	String	Returns the RSS feed URL for an individual post/entry.
description	String	Returns the tagline set for a blog in General ⇨ Settings.
html_type	String	Returns the HTML header information. Will always be text/html unless modified by plugin.
language	String	Returns the language code designated for the blog. Defaults to en-US. To localize a blog, see the procedures outlined in Chapter 5.
name	String	Returns the name of the blog as defined in Settings ⇨ General.
pingback_url	String	Returns the XML-RPC URL used to assist remote sources in auto-discovery of where to send pingbacks.
rdf_url	String	Returns the XML-RPC information needed for auto-discovery of XML-RPC server capabilities.
rss2_url	String	Returns the RSS 2.0 URL for the blog.
rss_url	String	Returns the RSS 0.92 URL for the blog.
siteurl	String	Deprecated. Identical to 'url'.
stylesheet_directory	String	Returns the URL to the directory containing the active theme.
stylesheet_url	String	Returns the URL to the style.css file of the active theme.
template_directory	String	Identical to the 'stylesheet_url', but semantically means "point to the folder for the theme" instead of "point to the folder that contains the stylesheet," even though they are the same thing.
template_url	String	Identical to 'template_directory'.
text_direction	String	Returns the direction of how text is read on a blog. Defaults to ltr (left to right) unless the blog uses a language (such as Arabic) that is printed rtl (right to left).
url	String	Returns the URL for the blog. Preferred over the deprecated 'home' and 'siteurl' but functions identically.
version	String	Returns the current version of WordPress.
wpurl	String	Returns the URL for the WordPress root directory.

Lists and dropdowns

Authors List

- **Tag:** wp_list_authors()
- **Description:** Creates an unordered list of authors with a link to their author page (generally an author archive). It can also include post counts and an RSS feed.

- **Returns:** Returns or echoes a list of authors with requested data.
- **Arguments:** Array or query string

Parameter	Value	Description
echo	Boolean	Specifies whether to send output to display or return to PHP.
exclude_admin	Boolean	Specifies whether the admin should be included in the list.
feed	String	Specifies anchor text for authors RSS feed. Default is empty.
feed_image	URL to image	Specifies an image to be used in place of anchor text to display an author's feed. If provided, it overrides the feed parameter.
hide_empty	Boolean	Specifies whether to exclude authors with no posts.
html	Boolean	Specifies whether to display HTML for output. If false, the style parameter is overridden. Defaults to true.
optioncount	Boolean	Specifies whether to include author post counts.
show_fullname	Boolean	Specifies whether usernames should be displayed as first and last name.
style	list/none	Specifies whether to display output as an unordered list or a comma-separated list. Defaults to list.

Categories List

- **Tag:** `wp_list_categories()`
- **Description:** Creates a list of category links according to criteria specified.
- **Returns:** Returns or echoes a list of category links.
- **Arguments:** Array or query string

Parameter	Value	Description
child_of	Integer	Specifies a single category for which to show children categories for.
current_category	integer	Specifies the current category ID (fudging numbers) in case the list and current category needs to "think" it's under a different category.
depth	0, −1, 1, n	Specifies the depth of hierarchy for the request to descend to. If 0, all categories and child categories are displayed. If 1, only the top-level categories are displayed. If −1, all categories are displayed in a single non-hierarchical list (overrides hierarchical). If n (any number), the list descends n levels.

Parameter	Value	Description
echo	Boolean	Specifies whether to print the list or return it to PHP. Default is true.
exclude	Comma-separated list of category IDs	Specifies a comma-separated list of category IDs to be excluded from the list. If set, it automatically eliminates child_of.
feed	String	If included, specifies the anchor text for a category feed. Defaults to no anchor text or feed display.
feed_image	URL to image	Specifies a feed image to use. If present, will override feed.
feed_type	atom/rss2/rss	Specifies the type of feed to be displayed. If feed is not set, then feed_type is not needed.
hide_empty	Boolean	Specifies whether to display categories with no posts. Defaults to true.
hierarchical	Boolean	Specifies whether to nest child categories or display them as part of the same top-level list as parent categories. Defaults to true.
include	Comma-separated list of category IDs	Specifies a comma-separated list of category IDs to be included from the list.
number	Integer	Specified the maximum number of results to be displayed.
order	ASC, DESC	Specifies whether to sort the list in ascending or descending order. Default is ASC.
orderby	ID, name, slug, count, term_group	Specifies the sort order. Default is name.
show_count	Boolean	Specifies whether to display post counts for each category. Defaults to false.
show_last_updated	Boolean	Specifies whether to include the last updated timestamp. Default is false.
show_option_all	String	Specifies whether to include a link to all categories. Default is empty. A non-blank value will cause the link to display.
style	list/none	Specifies whether to display the list as an unordered list or as a list separated by HTML breaks ( ). Defaults to unordered list.
title_li	String	Specifies the title and style for a list. If set to false, will not wrap the list in a top level li.
use_desc_for_title	Boolean	Specifies whether to use the category description (if set) as the title attribute for the links created. Defaults to true.

Pages List

- **Tag:** `wp_list_pages()`
- **Description:** Creates a list of page links according to criteria specified.

- **Returns:** Returns or echoes a list of page links.
- **Arguments:** Array or query string

Parameter	Value	Description
authors	Comma-separated list of IDs	Specifies a comma-separated list of author IDs. Only pages written by the authors specified will be included.
child_of	Integer	Specifies a single page ID. Only child pages of this ID will be displayed
date_format	String	Specifies a date format to be used if show_date is not empty. Defaults to the blog date format as set in Settings ⇨ General
depth	0, 1, -1, n	Specifies the depth of hierarchy for the request to descend to. If 0, all pages and child pages will be displayed. If 1, only the top level pages will be displayed. If -1, all pages will be displayed in a single non-hierarchical list. If n (any number), the list will display up to n levels.
echo	Boolean	Specifies whether to display the list or return it to PHP. Defaults to true.
exclude	Comma-separated list of IDs	Specifies a list of IDs to be excluded from the list.
exclude_tree	Comma-separated list of IDs	Specifies a list of IDs to be excluded from the list. All child pages will also be excluded from under the specified IDs
include	Comma-separated list of IDs	Specifies a list of IDs to be included. Only the IDs specified will be included in the list.
link_after	String	Sets text or HTML to be appended to the link as part of the link.
link_before	String	Sets text or HTML to be prepended to the link as part of the link.
meta_key	String	Specifies a custom field key. Only pages with this custom field set will be included.
meta_value	String	Specifies a custom field value. Only pages with this custom field value will be included.
number	Integer	Specifies a maximum number of pages to include.
offset	Integer	Specifies a number of pages to be passed over before page inclusion begins.
show_date	modified, x, empty	Specifies whether to show the date modified, the original publish date (x) or no date at all. Default is empty ('')
sort_column	Any post column	Specifies the post column to sort on. Default is post_title. The WordPress Codex suggests most-often used columns as post_title, menu_order, post_date, post_modified, ID, post_author, and post_name.
sort_order	asc, desc	Specifies whether to sort the list in ascending or descending order. Default is ASC.
title_li	String	Specifies the title and formatting of the list heading. Defaults to __ ('Pages'). If set to false, will not wrap the list in a top level li.

Bookmarks/Links List

- **Tag:** wp_list_bookmarks()
- **Description:** Creates a list of bookmark links according to criteria specified.
- **Returns:** Returns or echoes a list of bookmark links.
- **Arguments:** Array or query string

Parameter	Value	Description
after	String	Specifies text or HTML to display after each bookmark. Defaults to </li>.
before	String	Specifies text or HTML to display before each bookmark. Defaults to <li>.
between	String	Specifies text or HTML to be placed between a bookmark and its description. Defaults to a newline character, \n.
categorize	Boolean	Specifies whether to display bookmarks in their categories or not. Defaults to true. If set to false, overrides title_li, title_before, and title_after.
category	Comma-separated list of IDs	Specifies a comma separated list of category IDs to be included in the list.
category_after	String	Specifies text or HTML to be appended to each category. Defaults to </li>.
category_after	Text or HTML	Specifies content to be included after each category. Defaults to </li>.
category_before	String	Specifies text or HTML to be prepended to each category. Defaults to <li
category_before	Text or HTML	Specifies content to be included before each category. Defaults to <li id="[category_name]" class="linkcat">.
category_name	Category name	Specifies a category by Name. Only links associated with this category will be included in the list.
category_orderby	ASC, DESC	Specifies whether the list categories should be ordered in ascending or descending order. Defaults to ASC.
class	String	Specifies the CSS (Cascading Style Sheet) class to be assigned to each category list item.
echo	Boolean	Specifies whether to display the list or return it to PHP. Defaults to true.
exclude	Comma-separated list of IDs	Specifies a list of category IDs to be excluded from the list.
exclude_category	Comma-separated list of IDs	Specifies a comma separated list of category IDs to be excluded from the list.

continued

Parameter	Value	Description
hide_invisible	Boolean	Specifies whether bookmarks set to not visible should be hidden. Defaults to true.
include	Comma-separated list of IDs	Specifies a list of category IDs to be included in the list. Overrides category, category_name, and exclude.
limit	Integer	Specifies a maximum number of bookmarks to display.
link_after	String	Specifies text or HTML to be appended to each bookmark link.
link_before	String	Specifies text or HTML to be prepended to each bookmark link.
order	ASC, DESC	Specifies how links should be sorted. Defaults to ASC.
orderby	Comma-separated list of these values: id, url, name, target, description, owner, rating, updated, rel, notes, rss, length, or rand	Specifies the values for which to sort the links. Generally this is a single value designation, but you can specify a hierarchical order of sorting with a comma-separated list. Defaults to name.
show_description	Boolean	Specifies whether to display a description associated with each bookmark. Defaults to false.
show_images	Boolean	Specifies whether to display images associated with each bookmark. Defaults to false.
show_name	Boolean	Specifies whether to show the name of the link as anchor text. Defaults to false.
show_private	Boolean	Specifies whether to show links that are marked as private. Defaults to false.
show_rating	Boolean	Specifies whether to include rating information with each bookmark. Defaults to false.
show_updates	Boolean	Specifies whether to display the last updated timestamp. Defaults to false.
title_after	String	Specifies content to be placed after the title. Defaults to </h2>.
title_before	String	Specifies content to be placed before the title. Defaults to <h2>.
title_li	String	Specifies the title and formatting of the list heading. Defaults to __('Bookmarks').

Comments List

- **Tag:** `wp_list_comments()`
- **Description:** List comments in `comments.php`.
- **Returns:** Echoes a list of comments for a post or page.
- **Arguments:** Array or query string

Parameter	Value	Description
avatar_size	Integer	Specifies the height/width of a commenter's avatar. The number can be between 1 and 512 and defaults to 32.
callback	String	The name of a function to be used in place of WordPress internal HTML structure. Defaults to Null.
login_text	String	Specifies text to be used to prompt for login if users must be registered and logged in to comment. Defaults to Log in to Reply.
reply_text	String	Specifies anchor text for the Reply link. Defaults to Reply.
style	div, ol, ul	Specifies the type of list to output comments as. Defaults to ul. Depending on style chosen, there must be a containing ul, ol, or div that corresponds to your selection and uses the class "commentlist". Example: <ul class="commentlist">.
type	all, comment, trackback, pingback, or pings	Specifies the type of comment to display. The pings selection is a combination of trackbacks and pingbacks. Defaults to All.

Archives List

- **Tag:** wp_list_archives()
- **Description:** Produces a list of archives based on criteria specified.
- **Returns:** Echoes or returns a list of archives.
- **Arguments:** Array or query string

Parameter	Value	Description
after	String	Specifies text or HTML to place after each link. Only works with format specified as HTML or custom.
before	String	Specifies text or HTML to place before each link. Only works with format specified as HTML or custom.
echo	Boolean	Specifies whether to print the list or return it to PHP. Defaults to true.
format	html, option, link, custom	Specifies a format for the generated list. HTML listings place the generated list in <li> tags. The option value makes the list a drop-down menu. The link option populates a series of <link> tags. The custom option enables you to specify your own values using before and after.
limit	Integer	Specifies a maximum number of archives to retrieve.
show_post_count	Boolean	Specifies whether to include post counts for an archive. Does not work with type postbypost.
type	yearly, monthly, daily, weekly, postbypost, alpha	Specifies the type of listing to return. postbypost is an archive listed by post date and alpha is the same, except also ordered alphabetically. Defaults to Monthly.

Page Menu/Navigation

- **Tag:** wp_page_menu()
- **Description:** Produces a navigation-style listing of pages.
- **Returns:** Echoes or returns a navigation-style list of pages, including a Home link.
- **Arguments:** array or query string

Parameter	Value	Description
echo	Boolean	Specifies whether to print the list or return it to PHP. Defaults to true.
exclude	Comma-separated list of IDs	Specifies a comma-separated list of IDs to be excluded in the menu.
exclude_tree	Comma-separated list of IDs	Specifies a comma-separated list of IDs to be excluded in the menu. All child pages for the specified IDs will also be excluded.
include	Comma-separated list of IDs	Specifies a comma-separated list of IDs to be included in the menu.
link_after	String	Specifies text or HTML to be appended to the links.
link_before	String	Specifies text or HTML to be preprended to the links.
menu_class	String	Specifies the CSS class assigned to the list.
show_home	Boolean/String	Specifies whether to include a Home link as the first list item in the menu. Default is false. If any other value other than true or false is provided, the value is set to true and the provided value is used as anchor text for the Home link.
sort_column	Any post column	Specifies the post column to sort on. Default is menu_order. The WordPress Codex suggests most-often used columns as post_title, menu_order, post_date, post_modified, ID, post_author and post_name.

Pages Dropdown

- **Tag:** wp_dropdown_pages()
- **Description:** Produces a drop-down menu containing pages meeting selection criteria.
- **Returns:** Echoes or returns a drop-down menu containing pages. There is no submit button needed.
- **Arguments:** Array or query string

Parameter	Value	Description
child_of	Integer	Specifies a page ID. Only child pages of this page ID will be included.
depth	0, 1, −1, n	Specifies a hierarchy depth to descend to. 0 designates all pages and subpages. 1 designates only top-level pages. −1 specifies all subpages with no special hierarchy. n specifies the number of levels of hierarchy to descend.
echo	Boolean	Specifies whether to print the list or return it to PHP. Defaults to true.
exclude	Comma-separated list of IDs	Specifies a list of page IDs to be excluded from the drop-down form.
exclude_tree	Comma-separated list of IDs	Specifies a list of page IDs to be excluded from the dropdown form. All child pages of these IDs will also be excluded.
name	String	Specifies the HTML attribute name to be assigned to the drop-down form.
selected	Integer	Specifies a page ID. This page will be the "selected" page in the HTML form.
show_option_none	String	Specifies text to be added as a "None" option in the drop-down form.

Categories Dropdown

- **Tag**: wp_dropdown_categories()
- **Description**: Produces a drop-down menu containing pages meeting selection criteria.
- **Returns**: Echoes or returns a drop-down menu containing pages. No submit button is needed.
- **Arguments**: Array or query string

Parameter	Value	Description
child_of	Integer	Specifies a category ID. Only child categories of this category ID will be included.
class	String	Specifies the CSS class selector to be assigned to the drop-down form.
depth	0, 1, −1, n	Specifies a hierarchy depth to descend to. 0 designates all categories and child categories. 1 designates only top-level categories. −1 specifies all categories and child categories with no special hierarchy. n specifies the number of levels of hierarchy to descend.

continued

Parameter	Value	Description
exclude	Comma-separated list of IDs	Specifies a list of category IDs to be excluded from the drop-down form.
exclude_tree	Comma-separated list of IDs	Specifies a list of category IDs to be excluded from the drop-down form. All child categories of these IDs will also be excluded.
hide_empty	Boolean	Specifies whether to include categories that have no posts with the publish status. Defaults to false.
hierarchical	Boolean	Specifies whether the list should be shown in hierarchical format, with child categories indented. Defaults to false.
name	String	Specifies the HTML attribute name to be assigned to the drop-down form.
order	ASC, DESC	Specifies whether the list of categories should be ordered in ascending or descending order. Defaults to ASC.
orderby	ID, name	Specifies how to order the categories. Defaults to ID.
selected	Integer	Specifies a category ID. This page will be the "selected" category in the HTML form.
show_count	Boolean	Specifies whether to include the post count in each category. Defaults to false.
show_last_update	Boolean	Specifies whether to include the post date of the last post in the category. Defaults to false.
show_option_all	String	Specifies text to be added as a "All" option in the drop-down form.
show_option_none	String	Specifies text to be added as a "None" option in the drop-down form.

Users Dropdown

- **Tag:** wp_dropdown_users()
- **Description:** Produces a drop-down menu containing users meeting selection criteria.
- **Returns:** Echoes or returns a drop-down menu containing users. No submit button is needed.
- **Arguments:** Array or query string

Parameter	Value	Description
class	String	Specifies the CSS class selector to be assigned to the drop-down form.
exclude	Comma-separated list of IDs	Specifies a list of category IDs to be excluded from the drop-down form.

Parameter	Value	Description
include	Comma-separated list of IDs	Specifies a list of category IDs to be included from the drop-down form.
multi	Boolean	Specifies whether to skip the ID attribute on the <select> tag. Defaults to false
name	String	Specifies the HTML attribute name to be assigned to the drop-down form.
order	ASC, DESC	Specifies whether the list of users should be ordered in ascending or descending order. Defaults to ASC-.
orderby	ID, user_nicename, display_name	Specifies how the user list is ordered. Defaults to display_name.
selected	Integer	Specifies a user ID. This user will be the "selected" user in the HTML form.
show	ID, user_login, /'display_name	Specifies how to display a user's name. Defaults to display_name.
show_option_all	String	Specifies text to be added as an "All" option in the drop-down form.
show_option_none	String	Specifies text to be added as a "None" option in the drop-down form.

Login/Logout tags

Logged in or Logged out?

- **Tag:** `is_user_logged_in()`
- **Description:** Conditional template tag to determine if the user is logged in or not.
- **Returns:** True or False
- **Arguments:** None

Login URL

- **Tag:** `wp_login_url()`
- **Description:** Returns a URL for the user to use to login to WordPress.
- **Returns:** URL
- **Arguments:** 1

Parameter	Value	Description
redirect	URL	Specifies a URL to redirect to on successful login. Optional.

Logout URL

- **Tag:** wp_logout_url()
- **Description:** Returns a URL for the user to use to log out of WordPress.
- **Returns:** URL
- **Arguments:** 1

Parameter	Value	Description
redirect	URL	Specifies a URL to redirect to on successful logout. Optional.

Lost Password URL

- **Tag:** wp_lostpassword_url()
- **Description:** Returns a URL for the user to use to retrieve a lost password.
- **Returns:** URL
- **Arguments:** 1

Parameter	Value	Description
redirect	URL	Specifies a URL to redirect to after retrieving a lost password. Optional.

Logout

- **Tag:** wp_logout()
- **Description:** Logs a user out and destroys session and cookie information.
- **Returns:** True or False
- **Arguments:** None

Login and Out URL

- **Tag:** wp_loginout()
- **Description:** If the user is logged in, this retrieves a link for logout. If the user is logged out, it retrieves a link for login.
- **Returns:** URL
- **Arguments:** 1

Parameter	Value	Description
redirect	URL	Specifies a URL to redirect to on login or logout. Optional.

Register URL

- **Tag:** `wp_register()`
- **Description:** Returns a URL for users to register with.
- **Returns:** URL
- **Arguments:** 2

Parameter	Value	Description
after	String	Specified text or HTML to append to the Register link. Optional.
before	String	Specifies text or HTML to prepend to the Register link. Optional.

Post tags

Most of these tags must be used inside the Loop.

Post ID

- **Tag:** `the_ID()`
- **Description:** Displays the ID of the current post. Use `get_the_ID()` to return the value.
- **Returns:** True or False
- **Arguments:** None

Post Title

- **Tag:** `the_title()`
- **Description:** Displays the title of the post.
- **Returns:** True, False, or String
- **Arguments:** 3

Parameter	Value	Description
after	String	Specified text or HTML to append to the title. Optional.
before	String	Specifies text or HTML to prepend to the title. Optional.
display	Boolean	Specifies whether to display the title or return it to PHP. Optional. Defaults to true.

Post Title (RSS)

- **Tag:** `the_title_rss()`
- **Description:** Displays the title of the post encoded for XML.
- **Returns:** True or False
- **Arguments:** None

Post Title Attribute

- **Tag:** `the_title_attribute()`
- **Description:** Displays the title of the post in a cleaner format than `the_title()`.
- **Returns:** True, False, or String
- **Arguments:** 3, query string

Parameter	Value	Description
after	String	Specified text or HTML to append to the title. Optional.
before	String	Specifies text or HTML to prepend to the title. Optional.
echo	Boolean	Specifies whether to display the title or return it to PHP. Optional. Defaults to true.

Post Title (Single)

- **Tag:** `single_post_title()`
- **Description:** Displays the title of the on a single post page and can be used outside of the Loop.
- **Returns:** True, False, or String
- **Arguments:** 2, array

Parameter	Value	Description
display	Boolean	Specifies whether to display the title or return it to PHP. Optional. Defaults to true.
prefix	String	Specified text or HTML to prepend to the title. Optional.

Post Content

- **Tag:** `the_content()`
- **Description:** Displays the content of a post.
- **Returns:** True or False
- **Arguments:** 3

Parameter	Value	Description
more_file	String	Specifies a custom file for a "more" link to point to. Optional. Defaults to current page.
more_link_text	String	Specifies anchor text for "Read More" if it exists in the post. Optional. Defaults to (more...).
strip_teaser	Boolean	Specifies whether content preceding a more tag (<!--more-->) be hidden or displayed. Optional. Defaults to false.

Post Content (RSS)

- **Tag**: the_content_rss()
- **Description**: Displays the content of a post encoded for XML.
- **Returns**: True or False
- **Arguments**: 5

Parameter	Value	Description
cut	Integer	Specifies the number of words to display before ending the content. Default is 0 (display all).
encode_html	0, 1, 2	Specifies the level of encoding required for the feed. 0 parses out links for numbered "url footnotes". 1 overrides the cut parameter and filters content through htmlspecialchars(). 2 strips HTML and character and entity codes all the content.?
more_file	String	Specifies a custom file for a "more" link to point to. Optional. Defaults to current page.
more_link_text	String	Specifies anchor text for "Read More" if it exists in the post. Optional. Defaults to (more...).
strip_teaser	Boolean	Specifies whether content preceding a more tag (<!--more-->) be hidden or displayed. Optional. Defaults to false.

Post Excerpt

- **Tag**: the_excerpt()
- **Description**: Displays the excerpt of a post. If you have designated an excerpt manually, this will be used instead of being autogenerated.
- **Returns**: True or False
- **Arguments**: None

Post Excerpt (RSS)

- **Tag:** `the_excerpt_rss()`
- **Description:** Displays the excerpt of a post formatted for XML. If you have designated an excerpt manually, this will be used instead of being autogenerated.
- **Returns:** True or False
- **Arguments:** None

Post Pagination Links

- **Tag:** `wp_link_pages()`
- **Description:** Produces links for posts with pagination using the `<--nextpage-->` tags in posts.
- **Returns:** True or False
- **Arguments:** Array or query string

Parameter	Value	Description
after	String	Specifies text or HTML to be appended to the end of the link list. Defaults to </p>.
before	String	Specifies text or HTML to be prepended to the front of the link list. Defaults to <p>Pages:
echo	Boolean	Specifies whether the page list should be displayed or returned to PHP. Defaults to true.
link_after	String	Specifies text or HTML to be appended to each link.
link_before	String	Specifies text or HTML to be prepended to each link.
more_file	String	Specifies a custom file to serve up pages.
next_or_number	number, next	Specifies whether page numbers or "next" should be used.
nextpagelink	String	Specifies the anchor text for the "Next page" link. Defaults to Next page.
pagelink	String	Specifies the format for the page numbers. Uses % to designate the page number.
previouspagelink	String	Specifies the anchor text for the "Previous page" link. Defaults to Previous page.

Next Post Link

- **Tag:** `next_post_link()`
- **Description:** Displays a link to the next post in an archive or category, or from a single page.
- **Returns:** True or False
- **Arguments:** 4

Parameter	Value	Description
excluded_categories	Comma-separated list of IDs	Specifies a list of category IDs from which the next post should not be retrieved from.
format	String	Specifies the format for the anchor text. Use %link as a placeholder to represent the link to the next post. Defaults to %link »
in_same_cat	Boolean	Specifies whether the link should go to the next post in the category or the next post incrementally. Defaults to false.
link	String	Specifies the anchor text to be used for the link. Use %title as a placeholder for the title of the next post. Defaults to ('%title').

Next Posts Link

- **Tag:** `next_posts_link()`
- **Description:** Displays a link to the earlier posts and generally used on the front page.
- **Returns:** True or False
- **Arguments:** 2

Parameter	Value	Description
label	String	Specifies the anchor text for the link. Defaults to Next Page ».
max_pages	Integer	Specifies a maximum number of pages on which the link is displayed.

Previous Posts Link

- **Tag:** `previous_post_link()`
- **Description:** Displays a link to the previous post in an archive or category, or from a single page.
- **Returns:** True or False
- **Arguments:** 4

Parameter	Value	Description
excluded_categories	Comma-separated list of IDs	Specifies a list of category IDs from which the next post should not be retrieved from.
format	String	Specifies the format for the anchor text. Use %link as a placeholder to represent the link to the next post. Defaults to « %link.

continued

549

Parameter	Value	Description
in_same_cat	Boolean	Specifies whether the link should go to the next post in the category or the next post incrementally. Defaults to false.
link	String	Specifies the anchor text to be used for the link. Use %title as a placeholder for the title of the next post. Defaults to ('%title').

Previous Posts Link

- **Tag:** `previous_posts_link()`
- **Description:** Displays a link to the earlier posts and generally used on the front page.
- **Returns:** True or False
- **Arguments:** 2

Parameter	Value	Description
label	String	Specifies the anchor text for the link. Defaults to « Next Page.
max_pages	Integer	Specifies a maximum number of pages on which the link is displayed.

Next Image Link

- **Tag:** `next_image_link()`
- **Description:** Displays a link to the next image attached to a post.
- **Returns:** True or False
- **Arguments:** 2

Parameter	Value	Description
size	String	Specifies the size of an image. Optional. Defaults to thumbnail.
text	String	Specifies the anchor text of the link. Optional.

Previous Image Link

- **Tag:** `previous_image_link()`
- **Description:** Displays a link to the previous image attached to a post.
- **Returns:** True or False
- **Arguments:** 2

Parameter	Value	Description
size	String	Specifies the size of an image. Optional. Defaults to thumbnail.
text	String	Specifies the anchor text of the link. Optional.

Sticky Post Class

- **Tag:** sticky_class()
- **Description:** Provides a special CSS class to sticky posts.
- **Returns:** True or False
- **Arguments:** None

Post Categories

- **Tag:** the_category()
- **Description:** Displays the categories associated with a post.
- **Returns:** True or False
- **Arguments:** 2

Parameter	Value	Description
parents	multiple, single	Specifies how parent/child category relationships are displayed. Default is single.
separator	String	Specifies text or HTML to display between each category link. Defaults to an unordered list.

Post Categories (RSS)

- **Tag:** the_category_rss()
- **Description:** Displays the categories associates with a post as formatted for XML.
- **Returns:** True or False
- **Arguments:** 1

Parameter	Value	Description
type	rss, rdf	Specifies the type of feed the categories will be displayed in. Defaults to rss.

Post Tags

- **Tag**: `the_tags()`
- **Description**: Displays the tags attached to a post.
- **Returns**: True or False
- **Arguments**: 3

Parameter	Value	Description
after	String	Specifies the text or HTML to be prepended to the list of tags.
before	String	Specifies the text or HTML to be prepended to the list of tags. Defaults to Tags:
separator	String	Specifies the text or HTML to be placed between each tag. Defaults to ,

Post Meta

- **Tag**: `the_meta()`
- **Description**: Displays the post meta (custom fields) associated with the post.
- **Returns**: True or False
- **Arguments**: None

Comments tags

Number of Comments

- **Tag**: `comments_number()`
- **Description**: Displays the number of comments on a post.
- **Returns**: True or False
- **Arguments**: 3

Parameter	Value	Description
more	String	Specifies the text to display when there is more than one comment. Use % as a placeholder to specify the number. Defaults to % Comments.
one	String	Specifies the text to display when there is one comment. Defaults to 1 Comment.
zero	String	Specifies the text to display when there are no comments. Defaults to No Comments.

Comments Link

- **Tag:** `comments_link()`
- **Description:** Displays a link to the comments on a post.
- **Returns:** True or False
- **Arguments:** None

Comments Popup Script

- **Tag:** `comments_popup_script()`
- **Description:** Outputs JavaScript to be used with `comments_popup_link()` to render a comments pop-up window.
- **Returns:** True or False
- **Arguments:** 2

Parameter	Value	Description
height	Integer	Specifies the height of a popup window in pixels. Defaults to 400.
width	Integer	Specifies the width of a popup window in pixels. Defaults to 400.

Comments Link (Popup)

- **Tag:** `comments_link_popup()`
- **Description:** Displays a link to comments on a post. If `comments_ppopup_script()` is in use, this renders a pop-up window.
- **Returns:** True or False
- **Arguments:** 5

Parameter	Value	Description
CSSclass	String	Specifies a CSS class for the link.
more	String	Specifies the text to display when there is more than one comment. Use % as a placeholder to specify the number. Defaults to % Comments.
none	String	Specifies text to display when comments are disabled. Defaults to Comments Off.
one	String	Specifies the text to display when there is one comment. Defaults to 1 Comment.
zero	String	Specifies the text to display when there are no comments. Defaults to No Comments.

Comment ID

- **Tag:** `comment_ID()`
- **Description:** Displays the comment ID.
- **Returns:** True or False
- **Arguments:** None

Comment ID Fields (Threaded Comments)

- **Tag:** `comment_id_fields()`
- **Description:** Displays two hidden form fields that assist in rendering threaded comments.
- **Returns:** True or False
- **Arguments:** None

Comments Author

- **Tag:** `comment_author()`
- **Description:** Displays the comment author's name.
- **Returns:** True or False
- **Arguments:** None

Comments Author with Link

- **Tag:** `comment_author_link()`
- **Description:** Displays the comment author's name linked to the URL provided.
- **Returns:** True or False
- **Arguments:** None

Comments Author Email

- **Tag:** `comment_author_email()`
- **Description:** Displays the comment author's e-mail address. Please be careful with this so as not to disclose someone else e-mail address to the general public.
- **Returns:** True or False
- **Arguments:** None

Comments Author E-mail with Link

- **Tag:** `comment_author_email_link()`
- **Description:** Displays the comment author's e-mail as a link. Please be careful with this so as not to disclose someone else e-mail address to the general public.
- **Returns:** True or False
- **Arguments:** None

Comments Author URL

- **Tag**: `comment_author_url()`
- **Description**: Displays the comment author's URL.
- **Returns**: True or False
- **Arguments**: None

Comments Author URL with Link

- **Tag**: `comment_author_url_link()`
- **Description**: Displays the comment author's URL as linked.
- **Returns**: True or False
- **Arguments**: None

Comments Author IP Address

- **Tag**: `comment_author_ip()`
- **Description**: Displays the comment author's IP Address.
- **Returns**: True or False
- **Arguments**: None

Comment Type

- **Tag**: `comments_type()`
- **Description**: Displays the type of comment is being displayed.
- **Returns**: True or False
- **Arguments**: 3

Parameter	Value	Description
comment	String	Specifies the text that is used if the comment is a normal comment. Defaults to Comment.
pingback	String	Specifies the text that is used if the comment is a pingback. Defaults to Pingback.
trackback	String	Specifies the text that is used if the comment is a trackback. Defaults to Trackback.

Comments Text

- **Tag**: `comment_text()`
- **Description**: Displays the content of the comment.
- **Returns**: True or False
- **Arguments**: None

Comments Excerpt

- **Tag:** comment_excerpt()
- **Description:** Displays up to a 20 word maximum excerpt of a comment.
- **Returns:** True or False
- **Arguments:** None

Comment Date

- **Tag:** comment_date()
- **Description:** Displays the date the comment was made.
- **Returns:** True or False
- **Arguments:** 1

Parameter	Value	Description
d	Date format	Specifies the format the date should be formatted in. Defaults to the date specified for WordPress.

Comment Time

- **Tag:** comment_time()
- **Description:** Displays the time the comment was made was made.
- **Returns:** True or False
- **Arguments:** 1

Parameter	Value	Description
d	Date format	Specifies the format the date should be formatted in. Defaults to the time specified for WordPress.

Comment Form Title

- **Tag:** comment_form_title()
- **Description:** Displays text based on the status of a comment reply.
- **Returns:** True or False
- **Arguments:** 3

Parameter	Value	Description
linktoparent	Boolean	Specifies whether to make the authors name link a link to their comment. Defaults to true.
noreplytext	String	Specifies the anchor text for the reply link when not replying to a comment. Defaults to Leave a Reply. Optional.
replytext	String	Specifies the anchor text for the reply link when replying to a comment. Defaults to Leave a Reply to %s. Optional.

Comments Author (RSS)

- **Tag:** `comment_author_rss()`
- **Description:** Displays the comment author's name encoded for XML.
- **Returns:** True or False
- **Arguments:** None

Comments Text (RSS)

- **Tag:** `comment_text_rss()`
- **Description:** Displays the comment text encoded for XML.
- **Returns:** True or False
- **Arguments:** None

Avatars

- **Tag:** `get_avatar()`
- **Description:** Based on the acquired Gravatar service, this function displays an avatar from Gravatar or plugin-supplied source.
- **Returns:** String, image tag
- **Arguments:** 4

Parameter	Value	Description
alt	String	Specifies alt text for the image tag.
default	String	Specifies a URL for a default image if no avatar exists. If omitted, uses the setting from WordPress.
id_or_email	Integer, String	Specifies the WordPress user ID or an e-mail address.
size	Integer	Specifies size in pixels for height and width of avatar. Defaults to 48.

Permalink Comments (RSS)

- **Tag:** `permalink_comments_rss()`
- **Description:** Displays a link to the permalink that the comment is associated with formatted for RSS.
- **Returns:** True or False
- **Arguments:** None

Comment Reply Link

- **Tag:** `comment_reply_link()`
- **Description:** Displays a link that enables readers to reply to a specific comment.
- **Returns:** True or False
- **Arguments:** 3

Parameter	Value	Description
args	Array	Specifies an associative array that overrides defaults. See separate table. Optional. See http://codex.wordpress.org/Template_Tags/comment_reply_link for more information.
comment	Integer	Specifies the comment ID being responded to. Optional.
post	Integer	Specifies the post ID that the comment is displayed on. Optional.

Cancel Comment Reply Link

- **Tag:** `cancel_comment_reply_link()`
- **Description:** Displays a link to cancel comment replies.
- **Returns:** True or False
- **Arguments:** 1

Parameter	Value	Description
text	String	Specifies anchor text for the Cancel reply link. Defaults to Click here to cancel reply.

Previous Comments Link

- **Tag:** `previous_comments_link()`
- **Description:** When comment pagination is turned on, this will display a link to newer comments on a post.

- **Returns:** True or False
- **Arguments:** 1

Parameter	Value	Description
label	String	Specifies anchor text for the previous comments link. Defaults to « Older Comments.

Next Comments Link

- **Tag:** next_comments_link()
- **Description:** When comment pagination is turned on, this will display a link to older comments on a post.
- **Returns:** True or False
- **Arguments:** 2

Parameter	Value	Description
label	String	Specifies anchor text for the next comments link. Defaults to Older Comments ».
max_pages	Integer	Specifies the maximum number of pages to render.

Comment Pagination Links

- **Tag:** paginate_comments_links()
- **Description:** Renders page numbers, when comment paging is enabled.
- **Returns:** True or False
- **Arguments:** 2

Parameter	Value	Description
add_fragment	String	Specifies a URL fragment to add to the end of the permalink. Defaults to #comments.
base	String	Sets the URL format for the pagination links, using %#% as a placeholder for the page number. (You could probably leave this alone as the default behavior is generally acceptable.)
current	Integer	Specifies the current page. Use to override WordPress behavior.
echo	Boolean	Specifies whether the list of pages should be printed or returned to PHP. Defaults to true.
format	String	Currently unused.
total	Integer	Specifies a maximum number of pages to render.

Category tags

Categories

See reference earlier in this appendix for `the_category()`.

Categories (RSS)

See reference earlier in this appendix for `the_category_rss()`.

Categories (Dropdown)

See reference earlier in this appendix for `wp_dropdown_categories()`.

Categories (List)

See reference earlier in this appendix for `wp_list_categories()`.

Currently Browsing Category Archive Title

- **Tag:** `single_cat_title()`
- **Description:** Displays or returns the category title for the current page. Cannot be used in the Loop.
- **Returns:** True, False, or String
- **Arguments:** 2

Parameter	Value	Description
display	Boolean	Specifies whether the result should be printed or returned to PHP. Defaults to true.
prefix	String	Specifies text to be displayed before the category name.

Category Description

- **Tag:** `category_description()`
- **Description:** Returns (does not echo) the description of a specified category.
- **Returns:** String
- **Arguments:** 1

Parameter	Value	Description
category	Integer	Specifies the ID of a category.

Tag/Taxonomy tags

Tags

See reference earlier in this appendix for `the_tags()`.

Tag Description

- **Tag:** `tag_description()`
- **Description:** Returns (does not echo) the description of a specified tag.
- **Returns:** String
- **Arguments:** 1

Parameter	Value	Description
tagID	Integer	Specifies the ID of a tag.

Currently Browsing Tag Archive Title

- **Tag:** `single_tag_title()`
- **Description:** Displays or returns the tag title for the current page.
- **Returns:** True, False, or String
- **Arguments:** 2

Parameter	Value	Description
display	Boolean	Specifies whether the result should be printed or returned to PHP. Defaults to true.
prefix	String	Specifies text to be displayed before the tag name.

Tag Cloud

- **Tag:** `wp_tag_cloud()`
- **Description:** Produces a "tag cloud" displaying frequency of tag use in font sizes.
- **Returns:** True, False, or String
- **Arguments:** Array or query string

Parameter	Value	Description
echo	Boolean	Specifies whether the cloud is echoed or returned to PHP. Defaults to true.
exclude	Comma-separated list of IDs	Specifies a list of tags to not include.
format	flat, list, array	Specifies how tags are rendered. flat indicates that tags are separated by whitespace. Designating list places tags in an unordered list. Specifying an array is useful if you are returning the tags to PHP (echo = false). Defaults to flat.
include	Comma-separated list of IDs	Specifies a list of tags to only include.
largest	Integer	Specifies the largest font size used.
link	view, edit	Specifies whether the link goes to a Tag archive or to an edit tag page. Defaults to view.
number	Integer	Specifies the maximum number of tags to display. If you specify 0, all tags will be displayed.
order	ASC, DESC, RAND	Specifies the order by which tags are sorted: ascending, descending or random. Defaults to ASC.
orderby	name, count	Specifies the means to order the tag list. Defaults to name.
smallest	Integer	Specifies the smallest font size used.
taxonomy	post_tag, category, link_category	Specifies which kind of taxonomy is used to generate the tag cloud. Defaults to post_tag.
unit	pt, px, em, %	Specifies the unit of measurement used for font size. Defaults to pt.

Author tags

The Author

- **Tag:** `the_author()`
- **Description:** Displays the author name in the Loop.
- **Returns:** True or False
- **Arguments:** None

The Author Link

- **Tag:** `the_author_link()`
- **Description:** Displays the author name as linked in the Loop.
- **Returns:** True or False
- **Arguments:** None

The Author Post Count

- **Tag:** the_author_posts()
- **Description:** Displays the number of posts an author has written in the Loop.
- **Returns:** True or False
- **Arguments:** None

The Author Post Count Link

- **Tag:** the_author_posts_link()
- **Description:** Displays the author name as linked to the author archive in the Loop.
- **Returns:** True or False
- **Arguments:** None

The Author Meta

- **Tag:** the_author_meta()
- **Description:** Displays metadata about an author.
- **Returns:** True or False
- **Arguments:** 2

Parameter	Value	Description
field	String	Specifies which meta key to display about an author. Can be user_login, user_pass, user_nicename, user_email, user_url, user_registered, user_activation_key, user_status, display_name, nickname, first_name, last_name, description, jabber, aim, yim, user_level, user_firstname, user_lastname, user_description, rich_editing, comment_shortcuts, admin_color, plugins_per_page, plugins_last_view, or ID.
userID	Integer	If specified, this identifies the user by which you wish to retrieve data.

Listing Authors

See reference earlier in this appendix for wp_list_authors().

Listing Authors (Dropdown)

See reference earlier in this appendix for wp_authors_dropdown().

Last Modified Author

- **Tag:** the_modified_author()
- **Description:** Displays the author that last modified a post.
- **Returns:** True or False
- **Arguments:** None.

Date and Time tags

Post Time

- **Tag:** the_time()
- **Description:** Displays the time the post was made.
- **Returns:** True or False
- **Arguments:** 1

Parameter	Value	Description
d	Date format	Specifies the format the time should be formatted in. Defaults to the time specified for WordPress.

Post Time (Modified)

- **Tag:** the_time_modifie()
- **Description:** Displays the time the post was last modified.
- **Returns:** True or False
- **Arguments:** 1

Parameter	Value	Description
d	Date format	Specifies the format the time should be formatted in. Defaults to the time specified for WordPress.

Post Date

- **Tag:** the_date()
- **Description:** Displays the time the post was made. Note that the date will be displayed once per grouping of posts on the same day. Use the_time() for post by post date/time rendering.
- **Returns:** True or False
- **Arguments:** 1

Parameter	Value	Description
d	Date format	Specifies the format the date should be formatted in. Defaults to the time specified for WordPress.

Post Date (Modified)

- **Tag:** the_date_modified()
- **Description:** Displays the time the post was last modified. Note that the date will be displayed once per grouping of posts on the same day. Use the_time_modified() for post by post date/time rendering.
- **Returns:** True or False
- **Arguments:** 1

Parameter	Value	Description
d	Date format	Specifies the format the date should be formatted in. Defaults to the time specified for WordPress.

Post Date (XML)

- **Tag:** the_date_xml()
- **Description:** Displays the time the post was made in XML format.
- **Returns:** True or False
- **Arguments:** None.

Current Month

- **Tag:** single_month_title()
- **Description:** Displays or returns the month title for the current page.
- **Returns:** True, False, or String
- **Arguments:** 2

Parameter	Value	Description
display	Boolean	Specifies whether the result should be printed or returned to PHP. Defaults to true.
prefix	String	Specifies text to be displayed before the title.

Edit links

Edit Post Link

- **Tag:** edit_post_link()
- **Description:** Places an admin-visible link for a post, providing quick access to edit the post.
- **Returns:** True or False
- **Arguments:** 4

Parameter	Value	Description
after	String	Specifies text or HTML to append to the link.
before	String	Specifies text or HTML to prepend to the link.
link	String	Specifies the anchor text for the edit link. Defaults to Edit This.
post	Integer	Specifies a post ID to edit. Optional.

Edit Comment Link

- **Tag:** `edit_comment_link()`
- **Description:** Places an admin-visible link for a comment, providing quick access to edit the comment.
- **Returns:** True or False
- **Arguments:** 3

Parameter	Value	Description
after	String	Specifies text or HTML to append to the link.
before	String	Specifies text or HTML to prepend to the link.
link	String	Specifies the anchor text for the edit link. Defaults to Edit This.

Edit Tag Link

- **Tag:** `edit_tag_link()`
- **Description:** Places an admin-visible link for a post, providing quick access to edit the tag.
- **Returns:** True or False
- **Arguments:** 4

Parameter	Value	Description
after	String	Specifies text or HTML to append to the link.
before	String	Specifies text or HTML to prepend to the link.
link	String	Specifies the anchor text for the edit link. Defaults to Edit This.
tag	Integer	Specifies a tag ID to edit. Optional.

Edit Bookmark Link

- **Tag:** edit_bookmark_link()
- **Description:** Places an admin-visible link for a post, providing quick access to edit the bookmark.
- **Returns:** True or False
- **Arguments:** 4

Parameter	Value	Description
after	String	Specifies text or HTML to append to the link.
before	String	Specifies text or HTML to prepend to the link.
bookmark	Integer	Specifies a tag ID to edit. Optional.
link	String	Specifies the anchor text for the edit link. Defaults to Edit This.

Permalink tags

Permalink Anchor

- **Tag:** permalink_anchor()
- **Description:** Outputs a identifier or ID link for a post.
- **Returns:** True or False
- **Arguments:** 1

Parameter	Value	Description
type	id, title	Specifies the type of anchor to use. id indicates an anchor with the post ID and title does the same, except with the post slug. Defaults to id.

Permalink for a Specified Post

- **Tag:** get_permalink()
- **Description:** Returns the permalink for a specified post.
- **Returns:** String
- **Arguments:** 1

Parameter	Value	Description
id	Integer	Specifies the post ID for a specific post. Can be used outside the Loop.

Permalink for a Post

- **Tag:** `the_permalink()`
- **Description:** Displays the permalink for a post in the Loop.
- **Returns:** True or False
- **Arguments:** None

Permalink for a Single Post (RSS)

- **Tag:** `permalink_single_rss()`
- **Description:** Displays the permalink for a single post formatted for RSS.
- **Returns:** String
- **Arguments:** 1

Parameter	Value	Description
file	String	Specifies a file to handle the post. Optional.

Links tags

Listing Bookmarks

See reference earlier in this appendix for `wp_list_bookmarks()`.

Get Bookmarks

- **Tag:** `get_bookmarks()`
- **Description:** Retrieves an array of bookmarks for use with PHP.
- **Returns:** Array
- **Arguments:** Array

Parameter	Value	Description
category	Comma-separated list of IDs	Specifies which link categories to retrieve from.
category_name	String	Specifies the name of a category to retrieve from. Overrides category.
exclude	Comma-separated list of IDs	Specifies a list of tags to not include.
hide_invisible	Boolean	Specifies whether to display bookmarks marked as private. Defaults to true.

Parameter	Value	Description
include	Comma-separated list of IDs	Specifies a list of tags to include.
limit	Integer	Specifies the maximum number of bookmarks to display. --1 will display all bookmarks. Defaults to –1.
order	ASC, DESC	Specifies which order to sort. Defaults to ASC.
orderby	String	Specifies value to sort bookmarks on. Can be id, url, name, target, description, owner, rating, updated, rel, notes, rss, length, or rand. Defaults to name.
search	String	Specifies a word or phrase to search link_url, link_name, and link_description with.
show_updated	Boolean	Specifies whether to include a timestamp indicating the last time a bookmark was updated. Defaults to false.

Get Bookmark

- **Tag:** `get_bookmark()`
- **Description:** Retrieves information about a single bookmark.
- **Returns:** Array or Object
- **Arguments:** 3

Parameter	Value	Description
bookmark	ID	Specifies a link ID to retrieve information about.
filter	String	Unused. Defaults to raw. Optional.
output	OBJECT, ARRAY_A or ARRAY_N	Specifies the format (object, associative array or numeric array) to retrieve data as. Defaults to OBJECT.

Trackback tags

Trackback URL

- **Tag:** `trackback_url()`
- **Description:** Displays or returns a trackback URL.
- **Returns:** True, False, or String
- **Arguments:** 1

Parameter	Value	Description
display	Boolean	Specifies whether to display or return the link to PHP. Defaults to true.

Trackback RDF

- **Tag:** `trackback_rdf()`
- **Description:** Displays or returns a trackback Resource Description Framework (RDF) link.
- **Returns:** True, False, or String
- **Arguments:** None

Title tags

Blog Title

- **Tag:** `wp_title()`
- **Description:** Displays or returns the title of the blog. Most often used in the `<title>` tag.
- **Returns:** True, False, or String
- **Arguments:** 3

Parameter	Value	Description
echo	Boolean	Specifies whether to display or return the result to PHP. Defaults to true.
sep	String	Specifies text to display before or after the post title.
seplocation	right, left	Specifies where the separator is placed in relation to the post title. If specified as right, the separator will be displayed to the right. If it is anything else, it will be on the left.

Single Post Titles

See reference earlier in this appendix for `single_post_title()`.

Single Category Title

See reference earlier in this appendix for `single_cat_title()`.

Single Tag Title

See reference earlier in this appendix for `single_tag_title()`.

Single Month Title

See reference earlier in this appendix for `single_month_title()`.

Search Query

- **Tag:** `the_search_query()`
- **Description:** Displays the search query if a search was made.
- **Returns:** True, False, or String
- **Arguments:** None

Summary

- Template tags are placeholders for dynamically generated content.
- Some template tags take arguments and others do not. If the tag takes an argument, it is in a query string format or an array format.
- Included is a list of all available WordPress template tags.

What About PHP 5?

T he issue of PHP version requirements in WordPress has been a point of contention in the WordPress community. The minimum PHP requirement for WordPress is currently 4.3.0, but the PHP 4 branch has already reached the end of its life, meaning it will not receive any more security updates and is not being officially maintained anymore.

In addition, PHP 5 is much more object oriented, bringing it into its own in comparison with other object-oriented languages in use. The drive to PHP 5 in WordPress has been a long battle as developers have advocated for the new tools and features available, while core developers have maintained a PHP 4 loyalty for the sake of compatibility with the majority of Web hosts. This debate is examined in this appendix.

IN THIS APPENDIX

PHP 4 versus PHP 5: understanding core differences

WordPress and PHP 5

PHP 4 versus PHP 5: Understanding Core Differences

On August 8, 2008, PHP 4 hit the end of its life, and developers began using the event as a reason to argue that PHP 5 should be a WordPress minimum requirement. The leadership in the WordPress development community refused to adopt PHP 5 requirements, however, wanting instead to ensure that WordPress would continue to work on the most number of systems. It is expected that PHP 4 support will be going away soon. As of this writing, only 12.5% of WordPress blogs are running on PHP 4.

To understand this debate in the community, it's necessary to understand the enhancements made in PHP 5 since PHP 4. Because PHP is a language that has its roots in Perl — a language often used for command-line scripting — it has always had a procedural bent to it.

Note

Procedural code is code that is executed in a linear fashion from the top of a script to the bottom. While all PHP is executed in a generically top-down manner, Object-Oriented Programming (OOP) introduced a method of code development that has long been enjoyed in other languages, such as Java, C++, and Ruby. ∎

Web Resource

Ruby has seen resurgence in popularity due to the rise of Ruby on Rails. While Rails is not exclusively Ruby, the controllers are typically Ruby. However, Ruby on Rails developers rarely actually write Ruby. The "Rails Way" uses routines that auto-generate much of the code in a standardized "Rails Way" kind of format. A good resource for understanding "The Rails Way" can be found at www.therailsway.com — a blog maintained by Michael Koziarski, a core Ruby on Rails developer. ∎

PHP 5 fully embraces object-oriented code development, or OOP, while in PHP 4 OOP seems to be more of an afterthought. Therefore, much of the code that exists currently in WordPress, despite being object oriented, would make a PHP purist cringe.

In addition, classes are used prolifically throughout WordPress. In the wp-includes/ folder, there are close to a dozen files beginning with class- that represent libraries and code that are made up of classes. Unfortunately, most other code in WordPress uses functions that, while a form of object orientation and still absolutely necessary with or without PHP 5, are still fingerprints of procedural (top-down) code.

In a true object-oriented language, each class has a *constructor* and a *destructor*. These are methods that are automatically executed when a class is instantiated as an object or when an object is explicitly removed or unset.

In PHP 4, the constructor for a class is a method that has the identical name as the class name, as shown in Listing C.1. Most of the classes in WordPress that include a constructor, use this type of constructor for compatibility reasons.

LISTING C.1

A PHP 4–style constructor name is identical to the class name

```
class MyClass {

    var $myvar;
    function MyClass()
    {
        // Use the constructor to set defaults for object properties
        // or execute other code
        $this->myvar = 'Hello World!';
        return true;
    }
}
```

Destructors in PHP 4 do not explicitly exist; however, developers can use a manually invoked method that cleans up after the object in a destructor-style way.

In PHP 5, there are two built-in constructor and destructor methods: __construct() and __destruct(). When a class is instantiated, the __construct() method is automatically called and the __destruct() method, if included, is automatically executed for trash collection and cleanup when an object is destroyed (see Listing C.2). In PHP 5, if the __construct() method doesn't exist, a PHP 4-style constructor is used.

LISTING C.2

PHP 5–style constructors use an in-built __construct() method

```php
class MyClass {
    var $myvar;
    function __construct()
    {
        // Use the construtor to set defaults for object properties
        $this->myvar = 'Hello World!';
        return true;
    }
    function __destruct()
    {
        // Perform trash collection if necessary
    }
}
```

PHP 5 also enables developers to declare object methods and properties as private, protected, or public. These visibility keywords are not required, but as best practice, should be included. WordPress does not implement these keywords in its PHP 5-style classes, and are not strictly required.

Whenever a property is declared using the var keyword, or a method is declared, the property or method can be prefaced with a visibility keyword to instruct PHP on what level of access other objects and scripts have to the method or property.

For example, a private property can only be accessed from within the class it is declared in. It cannot be accessed from even a derived class. A protected property can be accessed only from within the class it was created in or derived from.

Public properties can be accessed internally or externally at will as either static properties or as object references. Any properties or methods declared without visibility are assumed to be public.

Listing C.3 repeats the code shown in Listing C.2 but includes visibility keywords.

LISTING C.3

Strict PHP 5 classes use the public, protected or private keywords to declare method and property scope

```
class MyClass {
    private var $myvar;
    public function __construct()
    {
        // Use the construtor to set defaults for object properties
        $this->myvar = 'Hello World!';
        return true;
    }
    public function __destruct()
    {
        // Perform trash collection if necessary
    }
}
```

Similar to visibility keywords, properties and methods can be explicitly made static. Adding a static keyword to a property or method enables them to be accessed externally without having to have an object instantiated (for example, `MyClass::crazy_function()`).

WordPress and PHP 5

Fortunately, since PHP 4 came to the end of life in 2008, most Web hosts now offer PHP 5 to customers. With this in mind, there is a hint of movement toward adopting PHP 5 in WordPress. As of WordPress 2.9, more and more PHP5 features are being integrated into WordPress. Fortunately, PHP 4 code works in the PHP 5 environment, so backwards compatibility can be preserved.

Note

By the time this book goes to print, WordPress 3.0 will have just been released or will be released shortly. At the time of writing, it is unclear how much PHP 5 will be included or if a minimum requirement is necessary. It is also important to note that though PHP 4.3 is required at the time of writing, there are already PHP 5 features, such as SSH (Secure Shell)-based upgrades, oEmbed discovery, and plugin installation. Because these are not required for WordPress to operate, the inclusion of this code does not change the minimum requirements. ■

Those of you wanting to create plugins that can leverage PHP 5-compatible WordPress, should start using class structures now, if you are not already, though continuing to write PHP 4.3 code will continue to work as well. To do this, as an example, when using WordPress hooks, pass an array with the first member referencing the class and the second member referencing the method name instead of simply passing a function name as you are used to (see Listing C.4).

LISTING C.4

Plugin developers should start developing with classes instead of only functions

```php
class Attribution() {
    public function __construct()
    {
        return;
    }
    public static function doattribution( $content )
    {
        return $content . '<p>&copy; 2010 Aaron Brazell</p>';
    }
    public function __destruct()
    {
        return;
    }
}
$attr_obj = new Attribution;
add_filter('the_content', array( &$attr_obj, 'doattribution' ));
```

All in all, WordPress is moving in the right direction, albeit very slowly. Developers can take heart that PHP 4, though the WordPress requirement at the time of the writing of this book, will be going away soon. PHP 4 served the PHP community well for many years, but because it is out of life and will not receive anymore security updates, competent Web hosting companies are now supporting PHP 5.

Tip

Bloggers looking to purchase hosting for their WordPress projects should aim for a minimum of PHP 5.2 for their WordPress installs. Versions of PHP 5 prior to PHP 5.2 had significant problems, which may have accounted for the slow adoption among Web hosts. ■

As a point of geek humor, PHP 5.3, if you're inclined to use a host providing this version or greater, has the bizarre inclusion of the goto operator. This inclusion is ridiculed among most in the PHP community as a regression worthy of the old BASIC programming language, circa 1989. In an ideal world, WordPress adoption of PHP 5 will never include adoption of goto.

Summary

- The WordPress PHP 4 compatibility requirement has long been debated in the developer community. On the PHP 5 side of the argument, developers argue for access to better and more features, purer object orientation, and so on. For PHP 4 advocates, the argument has been over compatibility with the most number of Web hosts.

- PHP 5 differences from PHP 4 revolve around better implementation of object-oriented programming, visibility operators, and proper contructor and destructor methods.

- At the time this book is written, WordPress still requires PHP 4.3. However, indications are that WordPress 3.0 will begin transitioning into a PHP 5 version requirement.

WordPress Hosting

F inding a host for your WordPress blog is not hard. Because there are so many Web hosts available (it is a thoroughly saturated industry), there are a lot of options.

Many years ago, I partnered with *Blog Marketing* author Jeremy Wright to provide Web hosting at a discount. Many individuals and companies still do this, as the barrier to entry for low-end Web hosting is very low.

This is not to say that Web hosting is easy to provide reliably. Competent hosts will not try to put too many hosting accounts on a single server, for example. Competent Web hosts will also provide backups, 24-hour support, monitoring, security patching and, of course, PHP 5.

As someone who has been in the industry of providing WordPress solutions to clients, both businesses and individuals, for years, I am frequently asked for recommendations of WordPress hosting providers. Of course, there are many options depending on need.

Features and Requirements of Web Hosts

First, it is important to look at the features and requirements of each potential Web host before making the decision to host your blog with them.

The most generic requirements for WordPress at the time of writing, is PHP 4.3 and MySQL 4.1. Regardless of which operating system is used, or which Web server is provided (most hosts are of some Linux variety and use Apache), all Web hosts must provide PHP 4.3 or MySQL 4.1. The better offerings provide PHP 5.2+ and MySQL 5+.

Besides these requirements, it is also important to consider other factors that can play into your Web-hosting decision, such as:

- How much disk space your blog will need
- How much bandwidth your blog will need
- Whether you need a host that provides backup services
- Whether the host provides Secure Shell (SSH) file transfers

Disk space

Disk space is a commodity these days and, in an average world, shouldn't really affect your decision when choosing a host. However, keep in mind that if you plan on using a lot of images in your blog, you may want to err on the side of additional disk space. Images can take up a lot of room, especially if you do not do any file size optimization (resizing) before uploading them.

Many hosting providers may tell you that they provide unlimited disk space. While this might be mostly true, disk space is a finite resource and there is practically no such thing as "unlimited" disk space. Hosts offering this kind of service make the assumption that the aggregate customers on that particular server will not utilize all of the space and so, the perception of unlimited disk space becomes the reality.

Be aware, however, that most of the time, when disk space becomes an issue, a host will generally take action to remedy the situation. This can result in a temporary account suspension, which will cause heartache to your readers, you, and, if you provide advertising, your advertisers. It is a better policy, if possible, to find a host that specifies how much allotted disk space they provide and ensure that all images, video, and multimedia files you use are created in such a way as to limit the amount of disk space that is consumed.

Tip
One way to help limit the amount of disk space your multimedia files consume, especially video, is to upload video to YouTube (www.youtube.com) or another hi-definition video service provider like Vimeo (www.vimeo.com) and using the embed codes provided by those services to insert videos into your blog. In this way, you're not storing these files yourself. ■

Bandwidth provision

Another option to consider, like disk space, is bandwidth. Bandwidth, unlike disk space, is a metric of data transferred to and from the server. Generally, bandwidth is more readily available than disk space, and all but the largest blogs probably do not need to be overly concerned with this.

Like disk space, many shared hosting providers market their hosting plans with unlimited bandwidth and, as with unlimited disk space, this is a misnomer. Though these servers are generally capable of terabytes (1000GB) of data transfer, bandwidth is still a finite resource. Still, for a mid-tier site with

75,000 page loads a month and each page weighing a moderate 500K in size, the bandwidth consumption is a mere 37,500MB per month — a fraction of the available bandwidth for a server.

Backups

Backups should never be trusted exclusively to a hosting provider; however, using a host that doesn't offer backups is dangerous. At any time, a blog can be hacked. Generally, this is not because of WordPress itself, but depending on if you are using an insecure version of WordPress, it is possible that a hack attempt can render a WordPress install unusable.

This happened as recently as September of 2009, when known security holes from WordPress version prior to WordPress 2.8.2 were exploited with a self-propagating worm. In my case, I supported a number of clients who had to get "scrubbed" and didn't have backups of their blogs. In these cases, there was nothing that could be done to recover their lost data.

Though hosts should provide their own backups if you are going to use them, you should also handle your own backups on a routine basis. These routines can get as basic or complex as you need. For example, you could write a script that archives your database and files and uses `rsync` to transport the archive to an offsite server. You could take the same script and enhance it to back up all your sites.

The script shown in Listing D.1 is a simple shell script that can be used with the Unix scheduling utility, `cron`, to run daily. It simply backs up a database and files and moves them to a backup directory. If you have ample disk space, this works well, but keep an eye on how much disk space is being used over time and think about deleting older backups as needed.

LISTING D.1

This BASH script backs up your database and files and moves the archive to a backup directory

```bash
#!/bin/bash
#### DO NOT EDIT
DATE=`date +-%y-%m-%d--%T`
#### EDIT BELOW
# If CREATE_ZIP is 0, then a tarball will be used (default). If 1, then a
   zip file will be used
CREATE_ZIP=0
# Accessible/writable directory for temp storage
TMPDIR=/tmp
# Absolute path to WordPress backup storage location
WPBACKUP=/backups
# Absolute path to WordPress install.
WPDIR=/path/to/wordpress
# Enter Database connection details from your wp-config.php file
```

continued

LISTING D.1 *(continued)*

```
WP_DBUSER=user
WP_DBPASS=password
WP_DBHOST=localhost
WP_DBNAME=dbname
#### STOP EDITING
if [ ! -d $TMPDIR ]; then
        mkdir $TMPDIR/backup
fi
if [ ! -d $WPBACKUP ]; then
        mkdir $WPBACKUP
fi
# Dumps the database
mysqldump -h$WP_DBHOST -u$WP_DBUSER -p$WP_DBPASS $WP_DBNAME > $TMPDIR/
    backup/wordpress-db.sql

# Create Archive
if [[ CREATE_ZIP -eq 0 ]]; then
        # Tarballs the Database and WP files
        tar -cvf $TMPDIR/backup/backup$DATE.tar $WPDIR/.htaccess $WPDIR/
    wp-content $TMPDIR/backup/wordpress-db.sql 2>&1
        gzip $TMPDIR/backup/backup$DATE.tar
        # Move archive to backup location
        mv $TMPDIR/backup/backup$DATE.tar.gz $WPBACKUP/
else
        # Zips the database and WP files
        zip $TMPDIR/backup/backup$DATE.zip $WPDIR/.htaccess $WPDIR/*
$TMPDIR/backup/wordpress-db.sql 2>&1
        # Move archive to backup location
        mv $TMPDIR/backup/backup$DATE.zip $WPBACKUP/
fi
```

On the Web

The code in Listing D.1 is available for download at at www.wiley.com/go/wordpressbible. ∎

Secure Shell

If you've read through the portions of this book pertaining to security, you'll know how important it is for a Web host to provide Secure Shell (SSH) and Secure File Transfer Protocol (SFTP) as a method to transfer your blog files to and from the host's server.

All hosts will provide FTP, but FTP is highly insecure because it transmits usernames and passwords in plain text over the wire. That means anyone "packet sniffing" can intercept the access information to your blog. That also means that someone could insert malicious content and modify your blog or even delete it altogether.

In addition, FTP is a *stateless* protocol. That is an elegant way of saying that if the connection drops in the middle of a data transfer, it will not simply resume where it left off. In essence, using FTP could render your blog broken.

With SSH/SFTP, there is a packet delivery verification handoff that occurs ensuring that if all packets have not arrived at their destination, nothing happens. In other words, if your Internet connection drops in the middle of uploading the `wp-load.php` file (the most critically necessary file in WordPress), `wp-load.php` will not be overwritten at all and thus, your blog can't be corrupted by a dropped connection.

Types of Web Hosts

The next step in finding a Web host for your blog is to look at the various hosting options available. Many are cheap, offering full service for just a few dollars per month. Others have much more robust offerings, including dedicated servers, shared hosting, and green Web hosting, which will be discussed later in this appendix. Options are many.

Dedicated servers

In the dedicated server industry, something that hasn't been discussed all that much is the number of WordPress-friendly providers. Keep in mind that if you choose a dedicated server or virtual private server, you as the customer are responsible for maintenance, monitoring, backups, and other administrative tasks, unless otherwise specified.

ServerBeach

ServerBeach (`http://serverbeach.com`) is a dedicated service provider owned by Peer1 (who performs the same services for Canadian and United Kingdom customers; `http://peer1.com`). They provide dedicated and colocation (you provide the server and all hardware, and they host it in their data center) with data centers in San Antonio, Los Angeles, Northern Virginia (Herndon), and London. ServerBeach provides most of the servers for WordPress.com and has been supportive of WordCamps and WordPress-oriented community events.

Layered Technologies

Layered Technologies (`http://layeredtech.com`) is a dedicated hosting provider based in Dallas with eight data centers worldwide. They are a principle partner with WordPress.com and have supported community events such as WordCamp Dallas. Data centers are offered in Dallas, Amsterdam, Tokyo, Chicago, Cedar Falls (Iowa), California, and Georgia.

Media Temple

Media Temple (`http://mediatemple.com`) is one of the hippest hosting companies around; however, they have had some negative press surrounding availability and customer support. Yet, they provide very flexible options best meant for large sites with a lot of traffic. Their Grid-Service harnesses the power of multiple servers dynamically, expanding to meet peak traffic spikes without having to bring on new hardware. Their data centers are in El Segundo, California, and Ashburn, Virginia.

Media Temple sponsored WordCamp NYC 2009 in a major way, indicating their presence and willingness to participate in the greater WordPress community.

Rackspace

Rackspace (`http://rackspace.com`) claims "Fanatical Support" as part of their trademark offering and generally, their service is pretty good. They only offer managed solutions (hands-on support and an insurance policy), though, so if you're a do-it-yourselfer, this might not be the offering for you. A fairly new offering, besides standard dedicate servers, is their cloud computing. This is in direct competition with Amazon's EC2 cloud-based server offering. Within a minute, a virtual server can be instantiated to host sites. Because the server is cloud-based, they can be scaled up virtually whenever needed.

Shared hosting

Most blog owners in the world opt for shared hosting. It's cheaper than a dedicated host and generally has a smaller, but more fitting, amount of features. However, be very careful when shopping for shared hosting and always try to go with a trusted provider.

Shared hosting comes with risks and limitations. A common problem with shared hosts is that the hosting provider puts too many accounts on one server. This ends up causing a problem when most accounts take up very few resources and a sudden demand for resources not only drowns the affected site, but also all other sites on the same server.

Additionally, sharing the same resources with unknown people opens up the opportunity for security problems. Though it is unlikely that having a shared hosting account will cause unnecessary problems such as these, the opportunity does exist, so be aware. The shared providers I have listed here have demonstrated good track records in the past.

DreamHost

DreamHost (`http://dreamhost.com`) is the ultimate shared hosting service for developers. It is created for developers by developers. Outside of their casual approach that borders on aloof, they tend to be pretty good about uptime. Their customer service leaves something to be desired and they sometimes suffer from annoyances that only developers can appreciate (for example, slow SSH). However, they are by and large a good option for folks looking for advance hosting controls.

BlueHost

Many WordPress users speak highly of BlueHost (`http://bluehost.com`). Besides being WordPress friendly, BlueHost also provides a platform for Ruby on Rails development if you're inclined, and SSH.

Green Web hosting

Green computing has become a major selling point in a world that's become more eco-conscious. *Green hosting*, also known as *carbon neutral hosting*, generally involves using "green" power sources, such as geothermal, solar, or wind power, for servers, utilization of energy efficient servers, or better, the use of virtualization and "cloud" computing for hosting servers.

Green hosting deals primarily with power sources. The reality is physical hardware is needed for hosting, even if virtualization is used, and physical hardware needs a lot of power and a lot of cooling. These two things are critical, but also leave a large eco-footprint.

For this reason, many data centers are providing power derived solely from geo-thermal, solar and wind power sources. The electrical grid providers who are harnessing this "natural" energy are able to sell it directly to data centers that can, in turn, provide it to their customers.

The reality is that green computing does not reduce the need for energy or cooling; however, it encourages the use of energy sources that are considered safer for the environment.

Hosts that provide green hosting options for WordPress continue to pop up every day and include:

- Dreamhost: http://dreamhost.com
- Rackspace: http://rackspace.com
- PlanetMind: http://planetmind.net
- ecoSky: http://ecosky.com
- AISO.net: http://aiso.net
- HostGator: http://hostgator.com
- A2 Hosting: http://a2hosting.com

Three Things You Can Do to Green Your Data Center

By Chris Bachmann

Data Centers pose a problem when it comes to being energy efficient. Servers are on all day, every day, and are expected to perform with a speed and reliability that we rarely expect from any other service. As a result, they generate tremendous amounts of heat and consume tremendous amounts of power. However, there are solutions that have come out within the past few years that make it possible to use less power while still meeting everyone's expectations.

continued

continued

Virtualization

Windows NT 4.0 had a problem. It was difficult, if not impossible, to run multiple applications on the same server. Since this was the dominant platform for corporations, this lead to a mindset among IT professionals that the more servers you have is proportional to how important you are. When the Enron debacle happened with the rolling blackouts in California, IT Managers began to change their perspective. With the introduction of various virtualization engines such as VMware (`http://vmware.com`), Hyper-V (`http://www.microsoft.com/windowsserver2008/en/us/virtualization-consolidation.aspx`), Xen (`http://xen.org`) and OpenVZ (`http://openvz.org`), it's now possible run multiple servers on a single computer or even a small computer cluster. This means that Virtual Machines can be dynamically allocated resources, as they need it and scaled back when they don't. VMware is particularly good at this since they will also power down CPUs when they are not needed.

To run a robust virtualization environment, the disk space should be separated from the CPU cluster. Disks use a finite amount of power. By consolidating the disk space to a single cluster, it is possible to only use the amount of disk space that is actually needed rather than the amount of disk space that is desired. Nearly all virtualization engines will dynamically grow VMs to only use the amount of disk space that is needed. There are also SAN systems such as EMC and Copan Systems that will dynamically power down disks as needed to further reduce the overall power consumption.

Solar Power

Many data centers are dedicated buildings. This means that there is an unused piece of real estate that goes to waste: the roof. Since solar panels are getting more efficient year by year, it's now possible for data centers to get a significant portion of their power from solar panels that are competitive to the costs of getting power from the local utility companies. While it will still take a long time for the efficiency of solar panels to equal the needs of the entire facility, it will still take a significant portion of power off the grid. During the summer months, power companies are typically struggling to keep up with the overall demands of residential and commercial AC systems. As a result, the local utilities are pressuring the data centers to reduce their power consumption. Solar is now a cheap way to do just that.

Geothermal Heat Pumps

Data centers need a tremendous amount of cooling. The more power that is consumed, the more adequate cooling is needed to keep them from overheating. Traditionally, air based cooling towers have been used to cool the rooms. Now there is a newer technology that is gaining traction: Geothermal heat pumps.

Geothermal heat pumps are a technology that uses the temperature of the ground to heat and cool spaces above ground. The Tennessee Valley Authority has already done a large study on this technology and has shown significant savings in not only power consumption, but overall costs as well. Traditional chilling towers require a lot of maintenance, are prone to failure, and require a routine chemical treatment to prevent corrosion and freezing during the winter months. Geothermal heat pumps require fewer moving parts and produce consistent results regardless of the time of year. Furthermore, geothermal heat transfers are more efficient than air-cooling resulting in lower energy costs.

Data centers certainly have distinct disadvantages when it comes to being green. With proper planning, those problems are not insurmountable. For large enterprises that maintain their own facility, it will provide savings well into the future. For the small and medium sized businesses, consider hosting your applications and services with a company that uses these techniques to reduce their consumption. Not only will it make your operation a little more green, but less prone to failure as well.

This article was previously published on my blog, Technosailor.com, on August 5, 2008 (`http://technosailor.com/2008/08/05/3-things-you-can-to-green-your-data-center/`). Reprinted with permission.

Summary

- WordPress hosting requirements is minimal — all a host needs to provide is PHP 4.3+ and MySQL 4.1+. Better system configurations for hosting include PHP 5.2+ and MySQL 5+.

- Disk space and bandwidth are commodities that, while readily available, could cause problems for some types of blogs that include lots of images or other media files.

- Backups should never be left exclusively to the responsibility of a Web host, but are useful to have when shopping for Web hosting.

- Finding a Web host that offers SSH ensures that, when transferring files to and from your Web host, you are doing so securely.

- Dedicated server providers such as ServerBeach, Layered Technologies, and Media Temple offer reliable hosting, and also are major supporters of the greater WordPress community.

- Shared hosting providers, while cheaper, offer inherent risks. However, some shared providers, like DreamHost or BlueHost, offer reliable offerings that are WordPress-friendly.

- Many hosting providers, shared and dedicated, offer "green" hosting options that focus on eco-friendly power sources such as geothermal, solar, or wind.

WordPress Vendors and Professional Services

The beauty of free open source is that it creates an entire ecosystem of jobs and business around it. In a typical open source community, the software is free, but the services often are not. WordPress is no different. There are literally hundreds of providers that perform professional services around WordPress. Many of these services are highly specialized.

Most of the time, WordPress professional services involve things like writing or modifying a plugin, creating a theme, or migrating a blog onto WordPress. It's the everyday things in life that people need the most help with. Other times, professional services might include building out a WordPress MU (Multi-User WordPress)/BuddyPress social network or tying WordPress into enterprise systems.

For all of these jobs and more, individuals and businesses have recognized WordPress as a quality platform and want to use it for projects. However, sometimes the expertise or time is lacking and paying professionals to get the job done is more effective.

Note

As a point of full disclosure, I make my living providing WordPress-based services. These services are mainly geared toward small businesses and my specialty is migrating large blogs onto the WordPress platform, and creating specialized WordPress plugins (intellectual property) for clients. ∎

In this appendix, I recommend professional service providers but will refrain from recommending myself. It is a touchy situation as many of these providers are my direct competitors; however, I can vouch for the services they provide and would not discourage anyone from employing their services.

Top Consultants in the WordPress Community

It's important to note at this time, as a reiterative measure, that there is not enough room to list the hundreds of developers around the world. There are likely consultants that deserve to be in this book who are not listed. Developers that are listed are developers that I have had dealings with and trust.

Additionally, in the world of WordPress consulting, you will likely find consultants who are very good developers but might not be great designers. For this reason, I have attempted to identify the consultants that do design and those who do development.

Sometimes, these two worlds overlaps and great consultants hire or outsource what they do not have the expertise to handle in-house. If you have a theme that needs to be designed, don't hesitate to reach out to a developer. That developer probably is working with trusted professionals and can still handle your project.

Covered Web Services

Covered Web Services is the consulting arm of Mark Jaquith (who is also the technical editor of this book). Mark is one of the five lead WordPress core developers, and the only one doing full-time, independent WordPress consulting. He has consulted for a lot of major clients and is also the author of popular plugins, including Subscribe to Comments (`http://wordpress.org/extend/plugins/subscribe-to-comments/`) and Page Links To (`http://wordpress.org/extend/plugins/page-links-to`).

Covered Web Services does not do theme design work, but instead specializes in scaling, security, custom functionality, and strategic consulting.

For more information, go to: `http://coveredwebservices.com`.

Crowd Favorite

Alex King is the proprietor of Denver-based Crowd Favorite. Alex is no stranger to the WordPress community and has been building on WordPress for years. Alex and his Senior Developer, Dougal Campbell, are original core developers for WordPress.

Popular plugins that have been created and released by Crowd Favorite include Twitter Tools (`http://wordpress.org/extend/plugins/twitter-tools/`), Popularity Contest (`http://wordpress.org/extend/plugins/popularity-contest/`), and ShareThis (`http://wordpress.org/extend/plugins/share-this/`).

Crowd Favorite is a full service shop that can offer design services as well as coding services.

For more information, go to: `http://crowdfavorite.net`.

E.Webscapes

Lisa Sabin-Wilson, founder of E.Webscapes, is a designer who creates great custom WordPress themes. She is also the author of *WordPress for Dummies* (Wiley, 2009) and the new *BuddyPress for Dummies* (Wiley, 2010). Her team is proficient in creating front-to-back services surrounding WordPress, WordPress MU (Multi-User WordPress), and BuddyPress.

For more information, go to: `http://ewebscapes.com`.

Yoast

Dutch WordPress developer and marketer, Joost de Valk, has been involved in WordPress for a very long time. His company, Yoast, has produced dozens of WordPress plugins, including the very popular Sociable (`http://wordpress.org/extend/plugins/sociable/`) and Tweetbacks (`http://wordpress.org/extend/plugins/tweetbacks/`). His work is both WordPress-specific and online marketing-specific, and he is a rare breed of a consultant, assisting in all aspects of a project, from strategy to delivery.

For more information, go to: `http://yoast.com`.

cnp_studio

Another full service plugin, design, and development shop is cnp_studio. This company has spent a lot of time in the WordPress community managing large projects in the health care, tourism, public relations, and education industries. They have worked with clients such as Symantec, Yahoo!, and eBay to provide high value solutions.

For more information, go to: `http://cnpstudio.com`.

Directory of Automattic-Recommended Consultants

The number of people who do work with WordPress professionally grows every day. Automattic, the main proprietor of WordPress, has implicitly endorsed the consultants listed in Table E.1.

Note

These listings are provided by CodePoet.com, a global directory of WordPress consultants. Please see the most current version of the directory at `www.codepoet.com`. ■

TABLE E.1

Automattic-Recommended WordPress Consultants

Consultant	Description	URL
North America		
Automattic	Enterprise support for WordPress and WordPress MU.	http://automattic.com/services/support-network/
cnp_studio	Enterprise-level WordPress development.	http://cnpstudio.com
Covered Web Services	WordPress plugin development, content migration, security analysis, and performance tuning.	http://coveredwebservices.com
Crowd Favorite	Alex King's WordPress development shop. We build great things for and with WordPress.	http://crowdfavorite.net/development
Jessica Perilla Design	We create high quality WordPress blogs and Web sites that are fully customized and easily maintained.	http://jessicaperilla.com
Slipfire	New York-based WordPress development studio.	http://slipfire.com
Sandbox Development & Consulting	Web development firm specializing in WordPress blog and CMS (content management system) solutions.	http://sandboxdev.com/blog-and-cms-development
Watershed Studios	Offering WordPress consulting related to blogging, CMS, podcasting, plugins, and themes.	http://watershedstudios.com/services/web-design/wordpress
45royale	Web design studio that loves building dynamic sites and blogs with WordPress.	http://45royale.com/services
Andres "Dre" Armeda	WordPress theme and Web site and theme development, brand creation, social media, and startup consulting.	http://armeda.com/services
Barrett Creative	Barrett Creative designs custom sites in Minnesota using WordPress as a CMS.	http://barrettcreative.net/about
Bill Erickson	WordPress consulting, search engine optimization, and content management systems.	http://billerickson.net/index.php/wordpress-consulting
BlackBox	BlackBox is a fun, experienced, and highly professional provider specializing in WordPress.	http://blackbox-tech.com/services/wordpress-services/

Appendix E: WordPress Vendors and Professional Services

Consultant	Description	URL
Blogging Expertise	Soup-to-nuts WordPress development with a focus on quality design.	http://www.bloggingexpertise.com/blog-services/
Blogging Squared (Canada)	We specialize in delivering custom blog services for small businesses.	http://www.bloggingsquared.com/what-we-do/
Blue Print Design Studio	An innovative design studio specializing in professional WordPress design/development and marketing.	http://blueprintds.com/
BNOTIONS	A full-service interactive agency specializing in creative content management solutions.	http://bnotions.ca/WordPress
Bradley Spencer	WordPress design, consulting, and search engine optimization.	http://www.bradleyspencer.com/wordpress-consulting
BraveNewCode	Unique, clean designs and code, specializing in custom WordPress, WordPress MU, and BuddyPress Web sites.	http://www.bravenewcode.com/
Brian Oberkirch Consulting	Social media strategies, content- and community-based on the WordPress platform.	http://www.brianoberkirch.com/?page_id=104
Category 4	A full service Web design firm in Charlottesville, VA.	http://www.category4.com/portfolio
ContentRobot	Highly-customized WordPress blogs, blog-powered Web sites, and plugins for companies of all sizes.	http://www.contentrobot.com/wordpress-experts
Design Disease	Cost-effective blog design services focused on usability, accessibility, and Web standards.	http://designdisease.com/
Dizzy Fusion	Award winning WordPress Web design for low prices.	http://www.dizzyfusion.com/wordpress-web-design/
E.Webscapes	WordPress site design and blog hosting.	http://ewebscapes.com/about/
Emmense Technologies	Specializing in migrations, custom plugins, thesis theme work, and other specialized WordPress services. This is my company.	http://emmense.com/
Fireside Media	Making WordPress work for you, not against you.	http://www.firesidemedia.net/services/

continued

TABLE E.1 (continued)		
Consultant	**Description**	**URL**
Full Throttle Development	Custom WordPress Web sites, plugin development, SEO (search engine optimization), social networking, security audits, and more.	http://fullthrottledevelopment.com/services/
Gossamer Threads	Enterprise-level WordPress customization, development, theme design, and hosting.	http://www.gossamer-threads.com/services/wordpress/
InfoTrust	Expertise in WordPress as a Content Management System and advanced customization.	http://www.infotrustllc.com/wordpress-consulting/
Jay Tillery	Template integration, plugin development, widget development, SEO for WordPress, blog migrations.	http://jaytillery.com/
Michael Martine	For individuals or companies; offers design, ghostwriting, coaching, policy, and SEO.	http://www.michaelmartine.com/blog-consulting/
Mule Design	A design studio that can help you create a great WordPress-based site.	http://muledesign.com/
Nathan Swartz	Web design consultant specializing in using WordPress as a CMS for customer Web sites.	http://www.clicknathan.com/clicknathan-handmade-web-design/wordpress/
NetClarity/Mike Schinkel	Custom WordPress Plugin development including Web site integrations.	http://mikeschinkel.com/custom-wordpress-plugins/
Nicasio	Provides optimum WordPress design and development services.	http://nicasiodesign.com/wordpress.php
No Diamonds Web Services	Using WordPress as a CMS and for marketing (SEO); from Palo Alto.	http://www.nodiamonds.com/content/wordpress-consulting.php
Nolan Interactive	WordPress theme, site design, and implementation, serving the New York and Tri-State area.	http://www.nolaninteractive.com/services/wordpress-themes/
Patel Strategy	Customized and advanced WordPress designing and marketing.	http://patelstrategy.com/web/wordpress/
Pixelita	We design personal and small commercial WordPress sites.	http://pixelita.com/design/
Plaintxt.org	Scott Wallick's WordPress development and design blog; consultation, editorial, and need-to-idea services available.	http://www.plaintxt.org/

Consultant	Description	URL
Ponticlaro	We specialize in WordPress-based Web sites, custom plugins, and business-class hosting.	http://ponticlaro.com/services/
Raincoaster Media	WordPress.com and social media training for individuals and organizations.	http://raincoastermedia.com/about/
ReflexDigital	We design and develop bespoke blogs, plugins, and CMS sites based on WordPress.	http://www.reflex.net/services/overview/
Shane & Peter	Listen, design, develop, launch, and celebrate. Providing solutions for SAP, Ask.com, NBC, Boeing.	http://www.shaneandpeter.com/
Six15 Solutions	WordPress installation, customization, and training.	http://www.six15.com/
sixty4media	WordPress theme creation, customization, tutorials, and all-in-one social media consulting for personal or business use.	http://sixty4media.com/
Solostream Web Studio	Blog design and consulting for small business; specializing in WordPress design.	http://www.solostream.com/category/wordpress-wizardry/
Sozos Design	Freelance Web site design and identity development.	http://sozosdesign.com/services/
Spyre Studios	Blog design (design and CSS/XHTML), setup, optimization, and maintenance.	http://spyrestudios.com/services/
studionashvegas	Fresh design combined with compliant XHTML/CSS and great SEO — that's studionashvegas.	http://www.studionashvegas.com/wordpress-services/
StudioPress	Brian Gardner's Web design and internet consulting.	http://www.studiopress.com/
Tammy Hart	Custom WordPress themes and site design.	http://www.tammyhartdesigns.com/about/wordpress-blogs-and-cms-solutions/
The Blog Studio	Custom blogs and Web sites for small and large businesses that require high-end design.	http://www.theblogstudio.com/index.php/services/
The Design Canopy	A Web design studio deploying fresh, user-centered designs; enjoys good coffee.	http://thedesigncanopy.com/services/

continued

TABLE E.1 (continued)

Consultant	Description	URL
THINK	THINK Graphics specializes in high-end, visually appealing WordPress Web site designs.	http://www.thinkpro.net/website-design/custom-blogs/
Tinker Priest	WordPress site, plug-in and theme development throughout Canada/U.S. in English, French, Spanish.	http://tinkerpriestmedia.com/services/wordpress/
TP1 Internet 360 web agency (Canada)	TP1 provides Web services, including custom WordPress, WordPress MU, and BuddyPress Web sites.	http://www.tp1.ca/en/about-tp1/content-management/wordpress
TwoThirty	We design Web sites, applications, and logos.	http://www.twothirty.com/
Viewstream	Full WordPress consulting and development services for high-tech companies.	http://www.viewstream.com/wordpress-consulting.html
Visudo	Development experience with migration, plugin and theme development, and WordPress MU.	http://www.visudo.com/category/wordpress/
W3 EDGE	Custom WordPress theme and plugin development; marketing and server optimization solutions.	http://www.w3-edge.com/wordpress-services-consulting/
W3Lift	WordPress customization, setup, and integration for any site.	http://www.w3lift.com/
WebDesign.com	Offering affordable, attractive, and effective Web design for small businesses.	http://webdesign.com/wordpress-consulting/
WebDevStudios	Web site development company specializing in custom WordPress development and design.	http://webdevstudios.com/solutions/wordpress-and-wordpress-mu/
Wright PC Consulting	Technology consultation services for small businesses, nonprofit organizations, and individuals.	http://www.wrightpcconsulting.com/wpservices.php
Xavisys	Control your Internet with our custom WordPress creations and search engine finesse.	http://xavisys.com/web-development-for-you/control/wordpress-solutions/
Your Custom Blog	Oakland-based WordPress Consultant: CSS, XHTML. setup, customization, troubleshooting, and training services.	http://yourcustomblog.com/
Zen Dreams	We specialize in WordPress theme development and custom plugins, simple to very complex.	http://www.zen-dreams.com/services/wp/

Consultant	Description	URL
Europe		
Alex Mihaileanu (Romania)	Creative and professional WordPress solutions for personal, business, and publishing projects.	http://subiectiv.ro/work/
Altha Webdesign (The Netherlands)	Het ontwerpen van WordPress themes, plugin-ontwikkeling, installatie diensten en SEO.	http://www.altha.nl/wordpress/
Altha Webdesign (UK)	WordPress theme design, installation services, plugin development, and SEO.	http://www.altha.co.uk/wordpress/
Amine Soussi (France)	Beautiful designs, WordPress Web sites, and fresh technical support from Aix-en-Provence, Southern France.	http://www.amine-soussi.com/
Arkimedia (Finland)	We specialize in delivering highly customized WordPress-powered Web sites and blogs.	http://www.arkimedia.fi/wordpress-julkaisujarjestelma/
Blogestudio (Spain)	WordPress consultants for global business solutions (design, development, and hosting).	http://blogestudio.com/servicios/
Bloggkonsult (Sweden)	WordPress consulting company based in Sweden.	http://www.bloggkonsult.se/wordpress/
Dave Ligthart (The Netherlands)	Hire me! I'm available as a WordPress consultant, programmer, Web developer, and designer.	http://www.daveligthart.com/home/hire-me/
Edge Designs (UK)	Everything WordPress! Including Web sites and blogs, with care, from the UK.	http://www.edgedesigns.org/services/wordpress/
Ed Merritt (UK)	Creative Web design and accessible WordPress theme development.	http://www.edmerritt.com/
Electric Mill (Ireland)	Web consultancy specializing in WordPress-based applications, social media, online strategy.	http://www.electricmill.com/services/web-development/content-management-systems/wordpress-development-ireland/
Equal Design (UK)	Custom WordPress theme design, including themes from Photoshop designs and more.	http://www.equaldesign.co.uk/services/wordpress/
FreeCharity (UK)	Web and blog publishing made easy for charities and nonprofits.	http://www.freecharity.org.uk/webhosting/wordpress-consultancy/

continued

TABLE E.1 *(continued)*

Consultant	Description	URL
GNV & Partners (Italy)	Web design studio dedicated to creating beautiful and highly customized WordPress-powered Web sites and blogs.	http://www.gnvpartners.com/web/international/
iDenta Labs (Sweden)	Creating highly customized WordPress-powered Web sites and blogs, theme design, and modifications.	http://identa.se/tjanster/
Interconnect IT (UK)	Web design and development consultancy specializing in blogs, CMS, and WordPress.	http://www.interconnectit.com/category/aa-products/worpress-design-consultancy/
Kipubli (France/ Switzerland)	Professional blog hosting, white label communities, and custom services for WordPress/ WordPress MU.	http://www.kipubli.com/
Media People (Sweden)	Simple, straightforward Web sites, blogs, and online services crafted with WordPress and passion.	http://mediapeople.se/wordpress
oXfoZ Technologies (France)	Experienced Web design agency, focused on delivering open-source CMS solutions to companies.	http://www.oxfoz.com/en/wordpress/
Realitus (UK)	Making good ideas happen online: creative design of WordPress Web sites for marketing.	http://www.realitus.com/
Vision22 (Bulgaria)	Professional WordPress plugin development and customizations at low prices.	http://www.vision22.net/services_en/en/
Vladimir Prelovac (Serbia)	WordPress expert providing services for high-traffic sites and custom WordPress modification.	http://www.prelovac.com/vladimir/services
Wangstedt Nova (Sweden)	Graphic and Web design company that creates sites to fit your needs.	http://www.wangstedt.net/
WordPress France	Can help you find WordPress consultants in France.	http://www.wordpress-fr.net/services
WP Box (France)	Professional services for WordPress and WordPress MU. Specialist recognized by French WordPress community.	http://wp-box.fr/prestations

Consultant	Description	URL
WP Dude (UK)	The WordPress technical support dude for all your blogging problems.	http://wpdude.com/wordpress-coaching
Zirona (Germany)	WordPress plug-in and template development, database tuning, and blog migration.	http://www.zirona.com/
Australia and New Zealand		
Andy Howard	Online strategy, Web production, and building communities with WordPress.	http://andyhoward.id.au/services/
Finding Simple	Professional WordPress services made simple. Small to medium business specialists.	http://findingsimple.com/services/wordpress-consultant-canberra/
Instinct	WordPress plugin developers and consultants.	http://www.instinct.co.nz/projects/
Incsub	WordPress MU installation, support, and customization from the makers of Edublogs.org.	http://incsub.com/
Asia		
Digital Cube (Japan)	WordPress consulting, theme design and development, customization, SEO tuning, and technical support.	http://www.digitalcube.jp/
PointStar (Singapore)	Professional, full-service, experienced Web Team able to deliver complex WordPress customizations.	http://www.point-star.net/our-products/wordpress-based-website/
Prime Strategy (Japan)	WordPress Web sites for companies, plugin development, SEO, and Web consulting.	http://www.web-strategy.jp/service/
South America		
Creixems Web Studio (Venezuela)	We provide everything you need for a maximized, successful WordPress experience.	http://creixems.com/eng/webdev/modelweb2.0.php
Africa		
The Yellow Llama (South Africa)	Customized WordPress Content Management Systems tweaked, tailored, and hybridized to suit your exact needs.	http://www.yellow-llama.com/skills/wordpress-consultants/

Summary

- Despite being open source and free, there is a vibrant community of consultants providing professional services around WordPress.

- Covered Web Services, Crowd Favorite, eWebscapes, cnp_studio, and Yoast are some of the top consulting firms in the WordPress world. (Naturally, I did not include my own company in that mix.)

- Automattic maintains a list of recognized WordPress consultants at `http://codepoet.com`. That list is reproduced in this appendix.

WordPress in Government

O pen source software has had a difficult time making inroads in government over the years. With corporate giants like Microsoft owning the market share in IT infrastructure, deploying Microsoft solutions on desktops and servers, and implementing SharePoint instead of open source solutions, the adoption of WordPress has been an uphill battle.

In government, the concept of security by obscurity reigns supreme and hinders open source products from gaining traction. In addition, long-term licensing agreements make it difficult for a government entity to depart from long-term "white label" solutions provided by contractors who are implementing and supporting those solutions.

Fortunately, WordPress has begun to see much more adoption inside the halls of government in recent years, as government has taken the same tack as most other industries and has realized the necessity to be online and have blogs.

Though most of this appendix focuses on WordPress usage inside the United States (U.S.) federal government, WordPress is being used at the state and local levels and in other governments around the world. Notably, the availability of open source solutions, including WordPress, has special significance to governments in developing countries being hit hard by recession.

IN THIS APPENDIX

WordPress use in the federal government

WordPress use outside the United States

WordPress Use in the Federal Government

WordPress adoption in the federal government has begun to take hold. Much of this has to do with President Barack Obama, who has embraced social media and the Web as a means to communicate with, and engage, American citizens. The Obama administration seems to have a certain fondness of WordPress, which has enabled the software to make headway into various government agencies.

At WordCamp San Francisco in 2008, a list of agencies and branches of the military using WordPress was made available to the public. The number of government-owned Web sites that use WordPress has only grown since then. Federal agencies using WordPress include:

- U.S. Army
- U.S. Air Force
- U.S. Navy
- U.S. Marine Corps
- U.S. Coast Guard
- Central Intelligence Agency (CIA)
- Defense Intelligence Agency
- National Geospatial-Intelligence Agency
- National Reconnaissance Office
- National Security Agency (NSA)
- Federal Bureau of Investigation
- Drug Enforcement Administration
- Department of the Treasury
- Department of State
- Department of Homeland Security

Since WordCamp San Francisco in 2008, additional federal agencies have joined that list, including:

- U.S. Census Bureau
- National Aeronautics and Space Administration (NASA)
- Department of Health and Human Services
- Library of Congress
- Environmental Protection Agency

Government case studies

Each federal agency that has made use of WordPress has done so for its own reason. From the outside it's easy to lump the federal government into a single entity and treat all agencies as the same agency. However, each agency exists for a specific mission and each mission has different business requirements.

Outsiders have no way to know the extent of WordPress usage inside firewalls. For example, the Intelligence Community, referred to often as the *IC*, is known for using a variety of open source tools internally, though details of how or why cannot be shared.

The business reason for a government agency to choose a particular piece of software is not always known. It could be that someone in charge is more familiar with one product than another. It could be a cost-point consideration. Some notable information can be gleaned from the public usage of some tools, though. The following case studies and examples illustrate this point.

Department of State

The United States State Department uses a variety of platforms for their blogs. Their main blog, Dipnote (`http://blogs.state.gov/`), uses Expression Engine, another blog platform/content management system to produce content. However, the America.gov blogs (`http://blogs.america.gov`), shown in Figure F.1, is a WordPress MU- (Multi-User WordPress) based collection of sites.

The America.gov blogs are an elegant single-theme collection of blogs that have been standardized across multiple blogs (for example, Obama Today, By the People, and Talking Faith) and seeks to converse with Americans living or travelling abroad about cultural and societal issues relating to U.S. foreign policy.

FIGURE F.1

The State Department maintains America.gov, a conversational resource centered on cultural and societal issues with American foreign affairs. The blog portion of the site is powered by WordPress MU.

Coast Guard

The Coast Guard Compass (see Figure F.2) is the official blog of the United States Coast Guard and can be found at `http://coastguard.dodlive.mil`. It is a WordPress site that is clean and uses categories as infrastructure well.

In the case of the Coast Guard, they have implemented Featured posts — posts that have been assigned to the "Featured" category. These posts are displayed in a special area of the Web site. In addition, they have implemented a feature commonly referred to as "Asides." Asides are typically mini-posts that are not displayed in the normal format that a full post is. They are minimally rendered so as not to detract from primary content, and the subject matter is often only marginally related to the focus of the blog itself.

This category-based infrastructure is a common technique used in WordPress development because the alternative — multiple blogs containing different types of content — is not supported in standard WordPress. The Coast Guard blog does an excellent job with content separation.

FIGURE F.2

The official Coast Guard blog (`http://coastguard.dodlive.mil/`) is a single WordPress install that uses category-style infrastructure for its layout.

Office of the Director of National Intelligence

The Intelligence Community has been a powerful advocate for the use of open source in government. Besides WordPress, they have engineered a product called A-Space, which is a top-secret social network, for lack of a better word, and keeps the 20+ intelligence agencies communicating effectively. Intellipedia is a product built on Wikimedia, the same open source wiki software that powers Wikipedia.

The Office of the Director of National Intelligence (ODNI) maintains an internal, classified WordPress MU network that powers more than 7,000 blogs. They make their single install of WPMU available to 16 agencies in the IC, including NSA and CIA.

All members of the IC have access to this system and can register blogs, some of which I'm told get a tremendous amount of internal traffic.

In classified environments, such as those naturally associated with the IC, WordPress adoption speaks volumes for its ability to meet enterprise high-security needs.

Library of Congress

The Library of Congress is one of those unusual agencies that doesn't perform a massive mission (unlike the Department of Defense or the IC). While their job doesn't appear huge, the Library of Congress plays a huge supporting role. The Library of Congress is charged with preserving America's literature, arts, and documents, and, by nature, has a cultural mission.

The Library of Congress blog (`www.loc.gov/blog/`), shown in Figure F.3, is a WordPress-powered blog that provides a standardized blog layout. Its social tools enable readers to share content found throughout the blog and discuss American culture, history, and business related to the Library.

FIGURE F.3

The Library of Congress blog is WordPress-powered and uses a standard blog layout. It includes a social tools plugin, which encourages readers to share the nation's cultural and historical treasures with their friends.

WordPress Use Outside the United States

WordPress has not been without its controversy, of course. In 2007, WordPress.com was banned in Turkey after complaints of defamation by a powerful litigant in that country. The courts in Turkey sided with the plaintiff and ordered all WordPress.com traffic to and from Turkey to cease.

In addition, China has also blocked the use of WordPress.com as part of an Internet control sweep that has become known as the *Great Firewall of China*. To this day, WordPress.com is unavailable in China, though fortunately, it is possible for bloggers to download and install WordPress on their own servers without being blocked.

The sensitivity of dealing with a global phenomenon that enables free speech in nations that might be averse to such rights is a problem that any wide-scale organization faces.

Despite negative accounts, there are positives as well. In many nations around the world, WordPress is being adopted as fast as it is in the United States. For developing countries, a primary impetus for this adoption is the cost savings between free open source software and costly licenses for proprietary products. Still other countries in places such as Eastern Europe use it to reach their citizens and to find tremendous talent pools to support their open source initiatives in their own countries.

As the Open Government movement, often termed Government 2.0, evolves and becomes more mature, blogging will continue to become more main stream in government. Right now, all industries are scrambling to adopt blogging as a form of communication — especially in government.

WordPress has the advantage that it's both a cost-saving tool for developing countries around the world and a security-tested tool, approved and used by top intelligence community agencies. As the software evolves into the next decade, innovative folks inside the walls of government will continue to test its bounds and capabilities.

United Kingdom: 10 Downing Street

10 Downing Street is the British equivalent of the White House. It is the residence and seat of government for the British Prime Minister. The site www.number10.gov.uk is entirely built on WordPress, making it the only official Web site for a major head of state built on the software (see Figure F.4).

FIGURE F.4

The official Web site of the British Prime Minister, `http://www.number10.gov.uk`, is built entirely on WordPress, making it the only official major head of state Web site with that distinction.

South Africa: Province of the Eastern Cape

As the world prepares for the World Cup soccer tournament in South Africa in 2010, the Province of Eastern Cape in South Africa and its transportation department has elected to use WordPress to power their entire site. This is particularly interesting in light of the World Cup, where hundreds of thousands of fans will descend on South Africa and refer to the site for assistance in getting around using mass transportation.

Being able to use WordPress to power a site that will provide necessary transit information for this many fans is huge. Conceivably, the transportation department can use the inbuilt localization API to provide different experiences for different travelers from around the world. The site of the Eastern Coast Transport Department is `www.ectransport.gov.za/` and is shown in Figure F.5.

FIGURE F.5

The South African province of Eastern Cape is tasked with providing reliable transportation for hundreds of thousands of fans travelling to watch the World Cup in 2010. This small local government department in South Africa has selected WordPress to do it.

Summary

- WordPress, as a free and open source product, has appeal to governments trying to save money, especially in developing countries being hit hard by recession or weak economies.

- The adoption of WordPress inside the U.S. Federal government has been widespread. It is being used by most of the branches of the military, the State Department, and the Intelligence Community.

- The U.S. Department of State uses WordPress MU to power a network of blogs designed to communicate with American citizens living abroad.

- The U.S. Coast Guard powers their official blog on WordPress.

- The Intelligence Community, composed of over 16 agencies, runs a large internal blog network that is powered by WordPress MU in their efforts to foster a culture of sharing of information and collaboration. Anyone in the IC can have a blog in this network.

- The Library of Congress uses WordPress to share historical and archived information with the public.

- 10 Downing Street, the office of the British Prime Minister, powers its official Web site on WordPress, making it the only official Web site of a Western head of state to do so.

- In advance of the 2010 World Cup that will be hosted in South Africa, the Province of the Eastern Cape is leveraging WordPress with their Department of Transportation to provide the general public with travel and transportation assistance.

WordPress in Major Media

WordPress has enjoyed wide-scale adoption in every industry. Even the media industry, which has reluctantly embraced new media as an alternate format to the traditional ones, has begun to use WordPress in a large-scale fashion.

In fact, major media sources embracing WordPress has been very instrumental in pushing not only blogging as a medium forward, but also WordPress as a platform.

Newsroom Challenges for WordPress

By and large, the major media industry has been less than enthusiastic about blogging. However, in recent years, most major media organizations have jumped into the blogging pool, though the philosophical question every newsroom must address remains, "How important is blogging to what we do as a new organization?"

More and more newsrooms are considering blogging complementary to reporting the news. News organizations such as the *New York Times* and CNN have not only embraced blogging but have also begun to make it a primary point of contact with their audience, rather than an afterthought.

Media organizations such as the *Wall Street Journal* have embraced blogging (http://blogs.wsj.com) but have retained a proverbial firewall between what they do from a news business and what they do from a blogging perspective. And the *Wall Street Journal* owns one of the most elite technology blogs in existence: All Things Digital (`http://allthingsd.com`), which is anchored by superstars Kara Swisher and Walt Mossberg and powered by WordPress.

In 2008, the *Philadelphia Inquirer* made headlines after a memo was leaked in which managing editor Mike Leary told his staff that online content would take a backseat to print content. His message was that "signature investigative reporting, enterprise, trend stories, news features, and reviews of all sorts" would first be published in print and that the only content that would go online first was breaking news alerts.

This created a backlash in the online community, which has beaten the death drum of traditional media for years. One such blogger, Jeff Jarvis (who incidentally also uses WordPress), wrote the entry "A stake through the heart of the has-been Inquirer" on his BuzzMachine blog. It can be read in full at `www.buzzmachine.com/2008/08/07/a-stake-through-the-heart-of-the-has-been-inquirer/`:

> You are killing the paper. You might as well just burn the place down. You're setting a match to it. This is insane. Even the slowest, most curmudgeonly, most backward in your dying, suffering industry would not be this stupid anymore. They know that the Internet is the present and the future and the paper is the past. Protecting the past is no strategy for the future. It is suicide. It is murder. You should be ashamed of yourselves.

Earlier in the same year, a transcript of a newsroom conversation was leaked from the *Tampa Bay Tribune*, which was taking an opposite approach. In this meeting, *Tampa Bay Tribune* Editor in Chief Janet Coats announced layoffs for the newspaper and directed the staff to start looking at the Tribune's online presence at Tampa Bay Online (TBO.com) as their primary model of doing business and journalism. This was astounding for many of the staffers, who were witnessing many newspapers hunker down. However, the *Tampa Bay Tribune* recognized that a reduction in staff made a print effort much more difficult to execute on.

The entire conversation was recorded and transcribed by TBO staffer Jessica DaSilva. Her account can be read at `www.jessicadasilva.com/2008/07/02/its-worth-fighting-for/`.

Interestingly, both of these moves occurred just before the economy tanked in 2008. I don't have any empirical evidence to show how the recession has affected these two organizations with different business models.

What I can say, as an interested observer of this war between old and new, is that newspapers in some form will never go away. Newspapers will always have a place in our society, whether it is because some readers enjoy having a physical newspaper to read or the romantic nature of old style print. There will always be the newspaper. The same holds true for television and radio.

Despite the migration of viewers from television to online sites like Hulu.com, television is here to stay. It may evolve. It may not. Regardless, new shows and news programs will continue to emerge, and there will always be a need for the television.

Radio, though far less likely to grow at a rapid rate, will always exist in our society, if for no other reason than it is a lowest common denominator for communication in the case of an emergency.

What is also clear is that blogging is not going away. It is here to say. It has transformed the information sharing, news reporting, and communications landscape. That said, it is not a perfect medium. A common argument among some in the traditional journalism camp revolves around journalistic integrity and training. There are certainly flaws with bloggers dominating the news scene, and it poses an interesting challenge for newsrooms and traditional outlets who have operated without being monitored for decades.

As the recession of that began in the fall of 2008 continues to affect the bottom line of media organizations and stalwart newspaper businesses like the Tribune Company (owner of the *Baltimore Sun*, *Chicago Tribune*, *Los Angeles Times*, and more) face bankruptcy or the *New York Times* takes out operational loans against the mortgage of their New York headquarters, more news organizations are looking at blogging as a means to do more with less.

Two Big News Organizations Tackle the Online Medium

The New York Times

The *New York Times* is a WordPress advocate and user, but it is also an investor in Automattic, participating in their $29.5 million Series B round of venture capital funding. In addition to the *Times*, CNN, the BBC, many more major media outlets have adopted the platform; traditional journalists are now on the Internet with a blog medium.

The *Times* motto "All the News That's Fit to Print," should change to "All the News That's Fit to Produce" given their extensive use of Internet technologies.

At this time, the *Times* uses individual WordPress installations to power all of their blogs — all 69 of them at present count. As someone who has managed a large number of WordPress blogs, I can attest to WordPress' capability to scale in a non-WordPress MU (Multi-User WordPress) environment, and the *Times* is using WordPress to do just that.

CNN.com

CNN adopted social media and blogging in a large way leading up to the 2008 presidential election and continues to use it today. Several years ago, CNN.com became a WordPress.com VIP. Their flagship blogs, Political Ticker and Anderson Cooper's AC360, are two of the most active WordPress.com blogs around.

CNN's most popular WordPress blogs — Political Ticker (http://politicalticker.blogs.cnn.com/), AC360 (http://ac360.blogs.cnn.com/), and Jack Cafferty's Cafferty Files (http://caffertyfile.blogs.cnn.com/) — represent significant CNN efforts to participate in the blogging world using WordPress.com (and thus WordPress MU) as their platform.

The following is an excerpt from an article that I published in 2008, shortly after the Tribune Company announced they would be filing for Chapter 11 Bankruptcy Protection. The article can be read online at `http://technosailor.com/2008/12/09/the-roadmap-for-building-a-21st-century-newspaper/`:

> Yesterday, I weighed in on the Tribune Company bankruptcy filing, noting that where voids might be created by the disappearance of established newspaper brands, there was opportunity for those nimble enough and digitally savvy enough to adjust. In my mind, as I wrote that, I was thinking primarily of alternate newspapers, but had a dream somewhere in the recesses of my head that there would, or could, be an answer from the blog world. That there were blogs with enough presence and notoriety that could fill the void left by a major daily. Of course, power players exist but are generally single vertical sites (i.e., Engadget.com operates in the tech gadgets space) that don't have the wide-ranging appeal that a daily newspaper does.

However, since I wrote that piece, I've carried on a number of private conversations with folks inside the *Chicago Tribune* and the *Los Angeles Times*. The questions seem to be, "Aaron, what do you think we can do better?"

Interesting question.

I think the *New York Times*, as mentioned, has road-mapped a lot of where the newspaper business needs to be in the digital age. All of their content is robustly tagged in a machine-readable way; for example, you can find all content from Author D between the months of June and October in even-numbered years having to do with the auto industry.

The fine level of *metadata* (data describing the stories) has been applied in such a way that the *Times*, in its entirety, is opened up; ambitious people can use their data and mash it up, reapply it, and, by nature, extend the *New York Times* readership.

The road map is there.

Interestingly, with a *New York Times* approach to metadata and the variety of Tribune Company properties (not just the *Baltimore Sun*, *Chicago Tribune*, and *Los Angeles Times*, but also the *Hartford Courant*, WGN news organization, *Orlando Sentinel*, and more), it should be possible for users to create their own newspapers, and the newspaper to suggest content based on user behavior. Facebook, for example, is allover behavioral advertising and might be a willing partner.

If you provide a common sense approach to content discovery, such as across all Tribune properties, and allow readers to assemble and find content that is not only localized, but also relevant to their interests and concerns, with the understanding that the twenty-first century American is transient and not likely loyal to a metro area or metro newspaper, you have the basis for breaking the newspaper out of the early 1950s model.

It is not simply good enough to provide a way to have external content (a la "Add an RSS feed"). That does not help the greater company be coherent in the digital age. You must provide a way for content from all sources (for example, Tribune Company content) to be searched and discovered via meta-data analysis (the *New York Times* approach), and for user behavior feedback and offerings (a la Facebook).

The journalism industry as a whole certainly has a long way to go, but the roadblocks are being cleared. Bloggers and journalists are not mutually exclusive and that perception is being changed. In my mind, much of this has to do with the openness to new media since the 2008 election, but the process was already well under way before that.

Bloggers and journalists complement each other and the idea of a zero-sum game where traditional media dies at the hands of new media is a far cry from reality. Each type of media has something to offer the other one and it is my hope, and I have reason to be hopeful, that the two will continue to grow together and make each other stronger.

Roadmapping WordPress in Major Media

The conversation around the roles of major media and bloggers can be carried on ad nauseam. There is much to discuss and much ground to cover. But this book is about WordPress. Fortunately, we've seen widespread adoption of WordPress as a blogging platform and much of that has to do with the popularity, security, and extensibility of the software.

Many traditional organizations use other platforms for their blogs. Movable Type still exists as a major choice because of the well-earned perception of being able to manage large amounts of traffic. One of Movable Type's major features, for better or for worse, is the publication of static HTML, which carries a significantly smaller overhead, a benefit in high-traffic situations.

However, by using platform and plugins wisely, many of the concerns around WordPress' capability to scale can be put to bed.

In a multiple blog environment, it is surprising to see an organization like the *New York Times* choose to use individual WordPress installs for their blogs. It is certainly doable but a better solution is WordPress MU. (When I was the director of technology at b5media, we did this before WordPress MU was a worthy alternative.)

Cross-Reference
WordPress MU installation and configuration is discussed in Chapter 22. ■

Many newsrooms want accountability from commenters and require an account for people to leave comments. Using WordPress' capability to require commenters to register is an essential feature for the news organization.

Of course, major media organizations are also going to have a bigger problem with spam than the rest of us (though spam is certainly a problem for all bloggers these days). Using a service like Akismet is as surefire a way of minimizing spam as anything else. Of course, Akismet can be used on almost any platform, including Movable Type.

Cross-Reference

Akismet is discussed in Chapter 27. ■

Caching becomes a huge issue with WordPress out of the box. Of course, WordPress comes with its own in-built "query cache," but ensuring a server is configured with memcache, a PHP opcode cache like APC or eAccelerator, and using WP Super Cache (`http://wordpress.org/extend/plugins/wp-super-cache/`) is important to keep things running smoothly. Just be sure your caching doesn't interfere when you need to get breaking news alerts out!

Cross-Reference

Caching is an important part of any large site, not just major media blogs. For more information on caching options, see Chapter 18. ■

These solutions should keep WordPress MU ticking along nicely, but what about user experience? Consider the following plugins for enhancing the user experience.

WordPress MU Sitewide Tags

Whenever you have multiple blogs, you need a way to drive traffic among them all. The use of WordPress MU inherently means that no blog stands alone and the good of one is good for all. One plugin that will handle this duty by sharing tags among all of them is the WordPress MU Sitewide Tags plugin (`http://wordpress.org/extend/plugins/wordpress-mu-sitewide-tags/`).

This plugin creates a new WordPress MU blog that serves as a clearinghouse for tags used on all your blogs. It also has features that prevent search engines from indexing the blog (though I can't think of a reasonable case why you would want to do this). Figure G.1 shows the administrative panel for the WordPress MU Sitewide Tags plugin.

FIGURE G.1

The administrative panel for the WordPress MU Sitewide Tags plugin

Global Tags

Tags Blog	tags
	Blogname of the blog your global tags and posts will live in. Blog will be created.
Max Posts	5000
	The maximum number of posts stored in the tags blog.
Privacy	⦿ Tags pages can be indexed by search engines.
	○ Tags pages will not be indexed by search engines.
	Will your tags pages be visible to Google and other search engines?

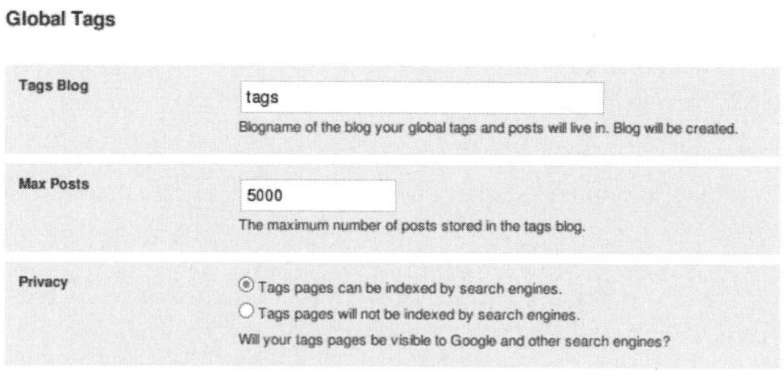

BuddyPress

Give your readers a community. Let them rally around your content and share their own experiences. You can certainly do this with just commenting, but having rabid football fans in one place is a great opportunity to enhance your local presence.

Cross-Reference
To find out more of how to install and configure BuddyPress, see Chapter 23. ■

RSSCloud

RSSCloud is a brand new plugin for WordPress that allows real-time updates via "the cloud." An alternative form of this was engineered over at FriendFeed, lightly named PubSubHubBub, and allows for instantaneous delivery of content updates.

RSSCloud is a plugin that enables WordPress to send real-time updates to the cloud that are then delivered instantaneously to subscribers. There is no better way of making sure that you are the first to deliver a story.

Download the RSSCloud plugin at `http://wordpress.org/extend/plugins/rsscloud/`.

Summary

- Blogging, by and large, has been something that newsrooms have historically balked about. The challenges of performing journalism in such a way that are relevant and accurate, and a dwindling amount of financial and human resources, have made it impossible, however, for the news industry to avoid.

- Organizations like the *New York Times* have opened up much of their news via metadata in a sign of openness to Internet technologies and development.

- By using caching, instant notification services like RSSCloud and WordPress-based community tools like BuddyPress, major media organizations can leverage the open source tools provided by the WordPress community.

APPENDIX

The General Public License

GNU GENERAL PUBLIC LICENSE

Version 2, June 1991

Copyright © 1989, 1991 Free Software Foundation, Inc.

51 Franklin St, Fifth Floor, Boston, MA 02110, USA

Everyone is permitted to copy and distribute verbatim copies of this license document, but changing it is not allowed.

Preamble

The licenses for most software are designed to take away your freedom to share and change it. By contrast, the GNU General Public License is intended to guarantee your freedom to share and change free software — to make sure the software is free for all its users. This General Public License applies to most of the Free Software Foundation's software and to any other program whose authors commit to using it. (Some other Free Software Foundation software is covered by the GNU Library General Public License instead.) You can apply it to your programs, too.

When we speak of free software, we are referring to freedom, not price. Our General Public Licenses are designed to make sure that you have the freedom to distribute copies of free software (and charge for this service if you wish), that you receive source code or can get it if you want it, that you can change the software or use pieces of it in new free programs; and that you know you can do these things.

To protect your rights, we need to make restrictions that forbid anyone to deny you these rights or to ask you to surrender the rights. These restrictions translate to certain responsibilities for you if you distribute copies of the software, or if you modify it.

For example, if you distribute copies of such a program, whether gratis or for a fee, you must give the recipients all the rights that you have. You must make sure that they, too, receive or can get the source code. And you must show them these terms so they know their rights.

We protect your rights with two steps: (1) copyright the software, and (2) offer you this license which gives you legal permission to copy, distribute, and/or modify the software.

Also, for each author's protection and ours, we want to make certain that everyone understands that there is no warranty for this free software. If the software is modified by someone else and passed on, we want its recipients to know that what they have is not the original, so that any problems introduced by others will not reflect on the original authors' reputations.

Finally, any free program is threatened constantly by software patents. We wish to avoid the danger that redistributors of a free program will individually obtain patent licenses, in effect making the program proprietary. To prevent this, we have made it clear that any patent must be licensed for everyone's free use or not licensed at all.

The precise terms and conditions for copying, distribution and modification follow.

GNU GENERAL PUBLIC LICENSE

TERMS AND CONDITIONS FOR COPYING, DISTRIBUTION AND MODIFICATION

This License applies to any program or other work which contains a notice placed by the copyright holder saying it may be distributed under the terms of this General Public License. The "Program," below, refers to any such program or work, and a "work based on the Program" means either the Program or any derivative work under copyright law: that is to say, a work containing the Program or a portion of it, either verbatim or with modifications and/or translated into another language. (Hereinafter, translation is included without limitation in the term "modification.") Each licensee is addressed as "you."

Activities other than copying, distribution and modification are not covered by this License; they are outside its scope. The act of running the Program is not restricted, and the output from the Program is covered only if its contents constitute a work based on the Program (independent of having been made by running the Program). Whether that is true depends on what the Program does.

1. You may copy and distribute verbatim copies of the Program's source code as you receive it, in any medium, provided that you conspicuously and appropriately publish on each copy an appropriate copyright notice and disclaimer of warranty; keep intact all the notices that refer to this

License and to the absence of any warranty; and give any other recipients of the Program a copy of this License along with the Program.

You may charge a fee for the physical act of transferring a copy, and you may at your option offer warranty protection in exchange for a fee.

2. You may modify your copy or copies of the Program or any portion of it, thus forming a work based on the Program, and copy and distribute such modifications or work under the terms of Section 1 above, provided that you also meet all of these conditions:

a) You must cause the modified files to carry prominent notices stating that you changed the files and the date of any change.

b) You must cause any work that you distribute or publish, that in whole or in part contains or is derived from the Program or any part thereof, to be licensed as a whole at no charge to all third parties under the terms of this License.

c) If the modified program normally reads commands interactively when run, you must cause it, when started running for such interactive use in the most ordinary way, to print or display an announcement including an appropriate copyright notice and a notice that there is no warranty (or else, saying that you provide a warranty) and that users may redistribute the program under these conditions, and telling the user how to view a copy of this License. (Exception: if the Program itself is interactive but does not normally print such an announcement, your work based on the Program is not required to print an announcement.)

These requirements apply to the modified work as a whole. If identifiable sections of that work are not derived from the Program and can be reasonably considered independent and separate works in themselves, then this License, and its terms, do not apply to those sections when you distribute them as separate works. But when you distribute the same sections as part of a whole which is a work based on the Program, the distribution of the whole must be on the terms of this License, whose permissions for other licensees extend to the entire whole, and thus to each and every part regardless of who wrote it. Thus, it is not the intent of this section to claim rights or contest your rights to work written entirely by you; rather, the intent is to exercise the right to control the distribution of derivative or collective works based on the Program.

In addition, mere aggregation of another work not based on the Program with the Program (or with a work based on the Program) on a volume of a storage or distribution medium does not bring the other work under the scope of this License.

3. You may copy and distribute the Program (or a work based on it under Section 2) in object code or executable form under the terms of Sections 1 and 2 above provided that you also do one of the following:

a) Accompany it with the complete corresponding machine-readable source code, which must be distributed under the terms of Sections 1 and 2 above on a medium customarily used for software interchange; or,

b) Accompany it with a written offer, valid for at least three years, to give any third party, for a charge no more than your cost of physically performing source distribution, a complete machine-readable copy of the corresponding source code, to be distributed under the terms of Sections 1 and 2 above on a medium customarily used for software interchange; or,

c) Accompany it with the information you received as to the offer to distribute corresponding source code. (This alternative is allowed only for noncommercial distribution and only if you received the program in object code or executable form with such an offer, in accord with Subsection b above.)

The source code for a work means the preferred form of the work for making modifications to it. For an executable work, complete source code means all the source code for all modules it contains, plus any associated interface definition files, plus the scripts used to control compilation and installation of the executable. However, as a special exception, the source code distributed need not include anything that is normally distributed (in either source or binary form) with the major components (compiler, kernel, and so on) of the operating system on which the executable runs, unless that component itself accompanies the executable.

If distribution of executable or object code is made by offering access to copy from a designated place, then offering equivalent access to copy the source code from the same place counts as distribution of the source code, even though third parties are not compelled to copy the source along with the object code.

4. You may not copy, modify, sublicense, or distribute the Program except as expressly provided under this License. Any attempt otherwise to copy, modify, sublicense or distribute the Program is void, and will automatically terminate your rights under this License. However, parties who have received copies, or rights, from you under this License will not have their licenses terminated so long as such parties remain in full compliance.

5. You are not required to accept this License, since you have not signed it. However, nothing else grants you permission to modify or distribute the Program or its derivative works. These actions are prohibited by law if you do not accept this License. Therefore, by modifying or distributing the Program (or any work based on the Program), you indicate your acceptance of this License to do so, and all its terms and conditions for copying, distributing or modifying the Program or works based on it.

6. Each time you redistribute the Program (or any work based on the Program), the recipient automatically receives a license from the original licensor to copy, distribute or modify the Program subject to these terms and conditions. You may not impose any further restrictions on the recipients' exercise of the rights granted herein. You are not responsible for enforcing compliance by third parties to this License.

7. If, as a consequence of a court judgment or allegation of patent infringement or for any other reason (not limited to patent issues), conditions are imposed on you (whether by court order, agreement or otherwise) that contradict the conditions of this License, they do not excuse you from the conditions of this License. If you cannot distribute so as to satisfy simultaneously your

obligations under this License and any other pertinent obligations, then as a consequence you may not distribute the Program at all. For example, if a patent license would not permit royalty-free redistribution of the Program by all those who receive copies directly or indirectly through you, then the only way you could satisfy both it and this License would be to refrain entirely from distribution of the Program.

If any portion of this section is held invalid or unenforceable under any particular circumstance, the balance of the section is intended to apply and the section as a whole is intended to apply in other circumstances.

It is not the purpose of this section to induce you to infringe any patents or other property right claims or to contest validity of any such claims; this section has the sole purpose of protecting the integrity of the free software distribution system, which is implemented by public license practices. Many people have made generous contributions to the wide range of software distributed through that system in reliance on consistent application of that system; it is up to the author/donor to decide if he or she is willing to distribute software through any other system and a licensee cannot impose that choice.

This section is intended to make thoroughly clear what is believed to be a consequence of the rest of this License.

8. If the distribution and/or use of the Program is restricted in certain countries either by patents or by copyrighted interfaces, the original copyright holder who places the Program under this License may add an explicit geographical distribution limitation excluding those countries, so that distribution is permitted only in or among countries not thus excluded. In such case, this License incorporates the limitation as if written in the body of this License.

9. The Free Software Foundation may publish revised and/or new versions of the General Public License from time to time. Such new versions will be similar in spirit to the present version, but may differ in detail to address new problems or concerns.

Each version is given a distinguishing version number. If the Program specifies a version number of this License which applies to it and "any later version," you have the option of following the terms and conditions either of that version or of any later version published by the Free Software Foundation. If the Program does not specify a version number of this License, you may choose any version ever published by the Free Software Foundation.

10. If you wish to incorporate parts of the Program into other free programs whose distribution conditions are different, write to the author to ask for permission. For software which is copyrighted by the Free Software Foundation, write to the Free Software Foundation; we sometimes make exceptions for this. Our decision will be guided by the two goals of preserving the free status of all derivatives of our free software and of promoting the sharing and reuse of software generally.

NO WARRANTY

11. BECAUSE THE PROGRAM IS LICENSED FREE OF CHARGE, THERE IS NO WARRANTY FOR THE PROGRAM, TO THE EXTENT PERMITTED BY APPLICABLE LAW. EXCEPT WHEN OTHERWISE STATED IN WRITING THE COPYRIGHT HOLDERS AND/OR OTHER PARTIES PROVIDE THE PROGRAM "AS IS" WITHOUT WARRANTY OF ANY KIND, EITHER EXPRESSED OR IMPLIED, INCLUDING, BUT NOT LIMITED TO, THE IMPLIED WARRANTIES OF MERCHANTABILITY AND FITNESS FOR A PARTICULAR PURPOSE. THE ENTIRE RISK AS TO THE QUALITY AND PERFORMANCE OF THE PROGRAM IS WITH YOU. SHOULD THE PROGRAM PROVE DEFECTIVE, YOU ASSUME THE COST OF ALL NECESSARY SERVICING, REPAIR OR CORRECTION.

12. IN NO EVENT UNLESS REQUIRED BY APPLICABLE LAW OR AGREED TO IN WRITING WILL ANY COPYRIGHT HOLDER, OR ANY OTHER PARTY WHO MAY MODIFY AND/OR REDISTRIBUTE THE PROGRAM AS PERMITTED ABOVE, BE LIABLE TO YOU FOR DAMAGES, INCLUDING ANY GENERAL, SPECIAL, INCIDENTAL OR CONSEQUENTIAL DAMAGES ARISING OUT OF THE USE OR INABILITY TO USE THE PROGRAM (INCLUDING BUT NOT LIMITED TO LOSS OF DATA OR DATA BEING RENDERED INACCURATE OR LOSSES SUSTAINED BY YOU OR THIRD PARTIES OR A FAILURE OF THE PROGRAM TO OPERATE WITH ANY OTHER PROGRAMS), EVEN IF SUCH HOLDER OR OTHER PARTY HAS BEEN ADVISED OF THE POSSIBILITY OF SUCH DAMAGES.

END OF TERMS AND CONDITIONS

Index

Symbols and Numerics

Index

Index

Index

D

d parameter, 564–566
Dashboard Blog option, WordPress MU, 402
Dashboard User Default Role option, WordPress MU, 402
data sanitization, 318–321
database abstraction layer, 115
database class. *See* ezSQL database class
database-intensive site, 329
databases, 33–35, 79
date_format parameter, 536
date_registered field, Registration Log table, 406
date.php template file, 182
day string variable, 145
day.php template file, 182
db_version field, Blog Versions table, 406
de Valk, Joost, 591
Debian Linux, 5
debugging, 311–313
dedicated servers, 583–584
Default Avatar option, 429
Default Language option, WordPress MU, 403
default parameter, 557
default permalink style, 231
default theme, BuddyPress, 432
Default User Profile Picture option, BuddyPress, 429
default widget classes, 107
delete_page capability, 343
deleted field, Blogs table, 405
Delicious.com, 244
Department of State, 603
deprecated properties, 125
deprecated tables, 125
depth parameter, 534, 536, 541
deregistering styles, 200
description field, 124
description parameter, 529–530, 532–533
descriptive text, 233
Design and Layout section, WordPress Codex, 59
Design Canopy, The, 595
Design Disease, 593
destructor method, 574
Developer Documentation section, WordPress Codex, 59
Digital Cube, 599
Digital Video Recorder (DVR) system, 20
Dipnote, 603
Disable BuddyPress to WordPress profile syncing option, BuddyPress, 428
Disable global forum directory option, BuddyPress, 429

Disable profile picture uploads option, BuddyPress, 428
Disable the visual text editor option, 243
Disable user account deletion option, BuddyPress, 428
disabling "nag" message, 270–275
disk space, 458–459, 580
display parameter, 545–546, 560–561, 565, 569
display_copyright( ) function, 83
display_exif( ) template tag, 370
display_name field, 120
distribution, terms and conditions for, 618–621
DIYThemes provider, 160
Dizzy Fusion, 593
DNS (Domain Name System), 395, 459
do_action( ) function, 86
do_shortcode( ) function, 456
document root (DOCROOT), 308–309, 321–322
domain field, 405–406, 408
domain mapping, 459–460
Domain Mapping plugin, 410
Domain Name System (DNS), 395, 459
domain part of URLs, 40
DotClear, 287–288
Dougherty, Mike, 382
draft status post, 240
"drag and drop" capability, Dashboard, 81
drag-and-drop widgets interface, jQuery, 197
DreamHost, 584
Drivel editor, 263–264
"drop zone", sidebar, 109
Drupal, 377
DVR (Digital Video Recorder) system, 20
dynamic content, 4, 12, 330
dynamic_sidebar( ) function, 113
Dynamically Generate Keywords for Posts Page option, All in One SEO plugin, 49

E

_e( ) function, 87
eAccelerator, 29–31, 333–336
echo parameter
  paginate_comments_links( ) tag, 559
  the_title_attribute( ) tag, 546
  wp_dropdown_pages( ) tag, 541
  wp_link_pages( ) tag, 548
  wp_list_archives( ) tag, 539
  wp_list_authors( ) tag, 534
  wp_list_bookmarks( ) tag, 537
  wp_list_categories( ) tag, 535

Index

Index

Index

Index

Index

Index

Index

wp.getComment method, 251
wp.getCommentCount method, 251
wp.getComments method, 251
wp.getCommentStatusList method, 251
wp.getOptions method, 251
wp.getPage method, 251
wp.getPageList method, 251
wp.getPages method, 251
wp.getPageStatusList method, 251
wp.getPageTemplates method, 251
wp.getPostStatusList method, 251
wp.getTags method, 251
wp.getUsersBlogs method, 251
wp-hackers mailing list, 8, 60
wp-includes/class-IXR.php file, 252
wp-includes/pluggable.php file, 379
wp.newCategory method, 251
wp.newComment method, 251
wp.newPage method, 251
wp-polyglots mailing list, 62
wp-pro mailing list, 61
wp.suggestCategories method, 251
wp-svn mailing list, 62
wp-testers mailing list, 8, 60
WPTouch iPhone Theme plugin, 198–199
wp-trac mailing list, 62
wp.uploadFile method, 251
wpurl parameter, 530–533
wp-xmlrpc mailing list, 61
:wq command, 29
Wright, Jeremy, 579
Wright PC Consulting, 596
writable cache folder, 331
Write Page screen, 183
Write Post screen, 228–229
Writing Options section, WordPress, 13

WS_FTP Professional, 314
www domain, 40–42
WXR (WordPress export format), 281, 293–298
WYSIWYG format, 186, 255

X

Xavisys, 596
XML, sanitizing HTML entities for, 318–319
XML Remote Procedure Call (XML-RPC)
    AtomPub, 252
    bundled XML-RPC library, 252
    overview, 247–248
    protocols, 248–251
    security risks, 252–254
XML-RPC editors. *See* offline editors
XSS (cross-site scripting) attack, 319

Y

YAML Ain't Markup Language (YAML), 438
year string variable, 145
year.php template file, 182
Yellow Llama, The, 599
Yoast, 591
Your Custom Blog, 596
Your WordPress forum, 64
YouTube, 457, 580
yum package manager, 29, 263

Z

Zen Dreams, 596
Zend Framework, 437
zero parameter, 552–553
Zirona, 599